From Left to Right

FROM LEFT
TO RIGHT

Lucy S. Dawidowicz,
the New York Intellectuals,
and the Politics of Jewish History

NANCY SINKOFF

WAYNE STATE UNIVERSITY PRESS

Detroit

ISBN 978-0-8143-4510-8 (hardback); ISBN (ebook) 978-0-8143-4511-5

Library of Congress Control Number: 2019945846

Published with support from the Goldman Scholarly Publication Fund.

Wayne State University Press
Leonard N. Simons Building
4809 Woodward Avenue
Detroit, Michigan 48201-1309

Visit us online at wsupress.wayne.edu

For Ezra, Miriam, and Reuben

and in memory of

Yosef Hayim Yerushalmi (1932–2009)

CONTENTS

ILLUSTRATIONS

ACKNOWLEDGMENTS

In the summer of 1989 I summited Cascade Mountain, the easiest of the Adirondacks' High Peaks, with my eldest son on my back. Little did I know then that the climb would lead to a two-and-a-half-decade pursuit of joining the Adirondack 46ers, a somewhat exclusive club of hikers who have reached the top of—and successfully descended—all forty-six highest mountains in the Adirondack park. In the summer of 2015, I finished my quest on Hough Mountain in the Dix range with my husband and a hiking partner, earning badge #9079. I read Lucy S. Dawidowicz's memoir the same year as that first High Peak step. Little did I know then that I would embark on her biography years later, after winding my way through the eighteenth-century Polish-Lithuanian Commonwealth and the salons of Frederick the Great's Berlin. Like hiking the Adirondacks, this journey has been full of extraordinary pleasures: expansive intellectual vistas, uncharted horizons, inspired collegiality, and unexpected scholarly discoveries. It has also been full of metaphorical spruce traps, weather inversions, blisters, sore muscles, exhaustion, and a few false summits. It gives me enormous pleasure now to thank the institutional, intellectual, and intimate companions who sustained me during this adventure.

Rutgers University–New Brunswick and the Departments of Jewish Studies and History have been my academic homes for over twenty years. This book has been enriched by conversations with my colleagues, including Leslie Fishbein, Ziva Galili, Paul Hanebrink, Gary Rendsburg, Paola Tartakoff, Jeffrey Shandler, Azzan Yadin-Israel, and Yael Zerubavel, with particular thanks to David Greenberg and David Fogelsong, who read the manuscript in one of its earlier iterations, and to Rudy Bell, Carolyn Brown, Barbara Cooper, Seth Koven, Phyllis Mack, Bonnie Smith, and Camilla Townsend, who offered support along the way. Early on in the process, I was the recipient of the Workmen's Circle/Dr. Emanuel Patt Visiting Professorship in Eastern European

Jewish Studies at the YIVO Institute for Jewish Research, which allowed me to dig into the YIVO's extraordinary archives. I also received support from the Hadassah-Brandeis Institute. Holding the Donald C. Gallup Fellowship in American Literature at the Beinecke Rare Book and Manuscript Library at Yale University gave me the opportunity to plumb John Hersey's papers in that wonderful place. In 2012, a semester at the Frankel Institute at the University of Michigan in the working group "Jewish Politics" allowed me to engage with colleagues equally obsessed with the questions that have preoccupied me for much of my scholarly life. Deborah Dash Moore's generosity then and later in the process of completing the book was always graciously offered. Mia Sarah Bruch and Michael Schlie gave me important critiques of my work, and Andrew Sloin continues to be one of my favorite interlocutors on modern East European Jewish social and political history. A short-term fellowship at the American Jewish Archives in Cincinnati as the Lowenstein-Wiener fellow in 2014–15 was indispensable to my being able to comb through the collections of the American Jewish Committee. A year at the Institute for Advanced Study (IAS) in 2016–17 as the Elizabeth and J. Richardson Dilworth Fellow in Historical Studies was a dream come true, giving me the space, time, and scholarly resources to complete the book's first long draft. I am grateful to Jonathan Haslam for shepherding our small group engaged with transnational politics; to Marian Zelazny for all of her administrative skills; to Marcia Tucker, Kirstie Venanzi, Cecilia Kornish, and Karen Downing for their generous assistance in the IAS library; and to Alexis May, my capable research assistant. To Robert Goulding, Rebecca Maloy, Susanne Hakenbeck, and Despina Stratigakos, I raise a glass to your friendship and scholarship.

My thanks to and admiration for the stewards of the past, the many librarians and archivists who work tirelessly to preserve documents, photographs, and artifacts that make books like this one possible, are simply boundless. Susan Malbin, Melanie Meyers, and Elizabeth R. Hyman of the American Jewish Historical Society, where Lucy S. Dawidowicz's papers are held, provided invaluable assistance over many years. So, too, did Gunther Berg, Fruma Mohrer, Stephanie Halperin, and Marek Web of the YIVO Archives; Zachary Loeb and Ilya Slavutskiy at the Center for Jewish History; Charlotte Bonelli of the American Jewish Committee Library and Archives; Rebecca Altermatt of the Hunter College Archives; Dana Herman, Kevin Profitt, Joe Weber, and Gary Zola of the American Jewish Archives; Reut Golani at the Yad Vashem Archives; Misha Mitsel of the American Jewish Joint Distribution Committee Archives; Susan Malsbury and Andrea Felder at the New York Public

Library, with special thanks to Carolyn Vega and Mary Catherine Kinniburgh of the Berg Collection; Shulamith Z. Berger, curator of Special Collections and Hebraica-Judaica at the Yeshiva University Library; Bonnie Fong, Kevin Mulcahy, and James Niessen of the Rutgers University Libraries; Dafna Itzkovich, Anat Bratman-Elhalel, Zvika Oren, and Noam Rachmilevitch of the Ghetto Fighters' House; Vincent Slatt and Jeffrey Carter of the United States Holocaust Memorial Museum; Naomi Steinberger of the Jewish Theological Seminary of America Library; and Zachary Baker, emeritus, Reinhard Family Curator of Judaica and Hebraica Collections of Stanford University.

Over the years I have had the good fortune to have had several research assistants, many of whom came to work with me through the Rutgers Aresty Undergraduate Research Program. They include David Brien, Samantha Cutler, Jessica Rabkin, Jennifer Samad, and the incomparable Nicole Kofman. I also wish to thank Ethan Schwartz—now launched on his own academic career—for his excellent work. Yet no one has been more important than Amy Weiss, PhD, whose meticulous research and organization skills, intelligence, and professionalism were essential to the book's completion. I eagerly await the publication of her own book.

Many colleagues, near and far, were incredibly generous with their time, engaging with me in email conversations, tracking down buried correspondence with Lucy S. Dawidowicz, vetting citations at what seemed like all hours of the day, and discussing different sections of the book. I am delighted to thank Natalia Aleksiun, Edward Alexander, Leyzer Burko, Boaz Cohen, Lois Dubin, Arie Dubnow, Gabriel Finder, David Fishman, Robert Franciosi, Kevin Gaines, Elisabeth Gallas, Semyon Goldin, Malachi Hacohen, Dana Herman, Brad Sabin Hill, Laura Jockusch, Edward Kaplan, Joshua Karlip, Samuel Kassow, Michael Kimmage, Rebekah Klein-Pejšová, Arthur Kurzweil, Cecile Kuznitz, Lisa Leff, Marjorie Lehman, Michael Marissen, Scott Miller, Yehuda Mirsky, Marina Mogilner, Avinoam Patt, Kathy Piess, Eddy Portnoy, Bilha Shilo, Gerald Sorin, Daniel Unowsky, Penny von Eschen, Michael Weitzman, and Laurence Zuckerman. Marsha Rozenblit merits a special thank you for her support.

Lawrence Douglas, my oldest friend and a gifted scholar and writer, introduced me to Rand R. Cooper, who took the book at its most unwieldy and helped shape it into a manageable manuscript. I am deeply grateful for his professionalism and support, which came at a critical time in the process. But it was Jacqueline Gutwirth, with her unmatched editorial eye and keen sense of literary style and with a historian's training, who walked the last miles of the book with me. My gratitude and respect for her careful reading know no bounds. The book was keyboarded with Nota Bene, the terrific academic software program that I have used since its launch in 1982. I thank Steven Siebert of Nota Bene, who responded to every query—even eleventh-hour ones—with his characteristic calm and professionalism. Seth Lipsky's marvelous portrait of Lucy S. Dawidowicz does her and the book honor, and I thank him for sharing it with me. I am also grateful to all of Lucy S. Dawidowicz's friends and colleagues who spoke with me in the course of writing the book. My greatest debt is to Laurie Sapakoff, Lucy's niece, who entrusted me with her late aunt's personal effects many years ago and has graciously allowed me to use them here and in earlier publications. Don Fehr of Trident Media Group found the perfect publisher, Wayne State University Press, for the book. I feel extraordinarily lucky to have worked with Kathy Wildfong before her retirement, and the whole team at Wayne State, including Ceylan Akturk, Kristin Harpster, Jamie Jones, Andrew Katz, Kate Mertes, Emily Nowak, Rachel Ross, Kristina Stonehill, and Anne Taylor, has been fantastic.

I thank Rachael Rosner for an unforgettable trip to western Ukraine in the summer of 2017, where I could feel the deep roots of the Jewish past in the southeastern Polish borderlands. Sato Moughalian and I met at a two-day workshop at the Leon Levy Biography Center at the CUNY Graduate Center in 2015 and have trekked the final legs of our respective biography journeys together. I have enjoyed every step of the way. Barbara Mann has always believed in the project and in me, and I am so grateful for our friendship and shared intellectual interests. Stephen Longmire, a wonderful writer and friend, has helped me think through, on more than one long walk, the meanings of displacement. Susan Oppenheimer tracked down various elusive copyright holders, an essential but small component of our deep friendship, which has nurtured me for so many years.

Rivka Schiller's linguistic excellence in Yiddish protected me from errors of translation. I acknowledge, too, the intensive study of Polish with Czesław Karkowski that continues to enrich my understanding of Polish history and culture. Martha Sullivan proofed the book with an eagle-eye attention to detail. My brother Richard did not hesitate for a minute to review my German translations even amid the pressures of his demanding job, a sign of his innate generosity and love and his wide-ranging linguistic talents. My brother Martin was always passionately interested in all matters "Lucy"; in fact, folded within the pages of my hard copy of *From That Place and Time: A Memoir, 1938–1947* is a yellowed review of the book from the *New York Times* that he sent to me in 1989. I cherish it.

This book is dedicated to the late Yosef Hayim Yerushalmi, who opened the door to the study of Jewish history for me at Columbia University in the late 1980s, insisting that the depth of the lived experience of the Jews required rigorous training in all periods of their past. Although he did not live to see this book, it is indelibly shaped by his historical and intellectual commitments. Last, I am thrilled to dedicate this book to my grown-up children, who have been my companions on many an Adirondack hike and, far more importantly, have created the loving family—with their father, my husband, Gary—that is the bedrock of my life.

A WORD ABOUT PERSONAL
AND PLACE NAMES

Lucy S. Dawidowicz's transnationality was linguistic as well as intellectual and geographic. Therefore, I have used various names throughout the book to illustrate the different languages she used and the ways by which she was known in her life as well as how she thought about herself and her names. When citing her writings, I use Lucy Schildkret for her maiden name, Libe Shildkret when she wrote in or was addressed in Yiddish, and Lucy S. Dawidowicz after her marriage. So, too, with her correspondents in Yiddish. Max Weinreich is rendered as Maks Vaynraykh, Leibush Lehrer as Leybush Lehrer, and Jacob Shatzky as Yankev Shatski when they wrote in Yiddish. In writing about Lucy S. Dawidowicz in the third person before her marriage, I refer to her as Lucy, not as Schildkret, with no intention of gendered disrespect, and as Dawidowicz after January 1948, to be consistent with how she was known. Dawidowicz's memos for the American Jewish Committee were most often signed with her initials, LSD or lsd. I have not retained those abbreviations in the footnotes but rather indicated her authorship as "Lucy S. Dawidowicz."

Place names in Eastern Europe varied depending upon political rule and language of the region's inhabitants. For example, Jews called the city of Opatów "Aft" and Wilno "Vilna." Throughout this book, I use the Yiddish appellation used by Jews, noting the Polish or Lithuanian spelling in parentheses.

The terms "antisemitism" and "anti-Semitism" have a long and vexed history. When I describe modern Jewish hatred, I use the term "antisemitism," which denotes a concept in its entirety. If the sources I cite use the form "anti-Semitism," I keep their form.

INTRODUCTION

In 1987, Lucy S. Dawidowicz, author of the best-selling history of the Holocaust, *The War Against the Jews, 1933–1945* (1975), received a plea from her good friend, the author Cynthia Ozick, entreating her not to "destroy any more papers."

> Think: you are not a "private" person. You have done landmark work, again and again. You don't have the right (any more than James did, or Ted Hughes) to put mystery in place of knowledge and clarity. Willa Cather did what you're doing; it was *wrong*. Kafka told Max Brod to burn his papers; Brod disobeyed, thank God. You yourself said you "bitterly resent" James's bonfire.
>
> Please, please stop now. Lucy, it's ruthless; it's unfair. Particularly in the case of Shimon's letters, which are "safe"—as safe as if written in code! because they're in Yiddish. . . . He would admonish you. He would beg you to stop. Lucy! Imagine Shimon's thoughts concerning what you are doing! Imagine the thought of future scholars, of your biographers! . . .
>
> Just this once, don't be autonomous. Don't go on doing this awful thing. Give your papers to a library. Please! !האב רחמנות [Have mercy!]¹

In her seventies, a widow for eight years, and blocked in writing her memoir, Dawidowicz was in despair, although the precise trigger for her despondency is not known.² In the 1980s, her public stature had diminished considerably. Her fame and recognition as an "authentic" voice of murdered European Jewry, earned with the publication of two books, *The Golden Tradition: Jewish Life and Thought in Eastern Europe* (1967) and *The War Against the Jews*, seemed to have worn off. New Left historians played down the significance of both antisemitism and the particularism of Jewish suffering during the Holocaust— hallmarks of her life's work—and their views held center stage in Holocaust scholarship, in public consciousness, and in American politics.

American political culture, too, had changed fundamentally. The fabric of democratic liberal America that Dawidowicz, like so many East European Jewish immigrant children, had taken for granted and that had been so hospitable to Jewish integration seemed irrevocably torn by the culture wars that followed the political and social upheavals of the late 1960s. The quality of city life, so fundamental to the American Jewish experience until the postwar suburban exodus, had been decaying since the mid-1960s. The fabled harmonious relations between African Americans and Jewish liberals had broken down, challenged by the New York City teachers' strike; by urban riots in New York, Detroit, and Los Angeles, among other cities; and by affirmative action. New Left students and other activists had demonstrated across the nation's college campuses, rejecting the universities' claims of meritocracy and political neutrality. The almost universal euphoria that had greeted the establishment of the State of Israel in 1948 had been replaced by a steadily mounting opprobrium that reached an ugly denouement in the 1975 "Zionism is racism" resolution at the United Nations. The wars with Lebanon (1977 and 1982) and the "cold peace" with Sadat's Egypt had put American Jewish liberals on the defensive as anti-Zionism became part of the left-liberal political agenda. And the bedrock Yiddish world and immigrant Jewish neighborhoods from which Dawidowicz had come had largely disappeared. Without a language and densely settled immigrant neighborhoods to bolster Jewish culture, little was left to sustain Jews who defined themselves in cultural, ethnic terms.

As a graduate student in Vilna, Poland, in 1938, Dawidowicz had barely gotten out before the German invasion in September 1939; she would go on to devote the rest of her life to chronicling the destruction of East European Jewish civilization. Though classical European Zionism, which rejected the possibility of a Jewish future in the diaspora, had little hold on her, by the 1980s, she feared the demonization of the Jewish state by critics on the Left. In her view, their censure of Israeli politics smacked of an antisemitic double standard and denied the political and cultural self-determination essential to the Jews' collective survival. Though she had signed a public letter criticizing the Israeli government in 1978, Dawidowicz now regretted her actions. Writing to her friend Irving Howe, the literary critic, Yiddish translator, and democratic socialist, in the aftermath of Israeli military action in Lebanon in 1982, she made clear that her commitment to Israel went beyond its temporal politics. "Israel is surrounded by enemies who wish to destroy her," she wrote. "American Jews who care about Israel—and I don't mean the political character of the government, *but Israel as the embodiment of Jewish civilization and the Jewish will to survive*—have an obligation to support it as it fights for its existence."[3]

All of these developments left Dawidowicz feeling intellectually abandoned, unrecognized, and alone.

Dawidowicz's life was both remarkable and emblematic of her place and time. Reared in a Yiddish-speaking socialist home, she dallied with communism as a college student, became a staunch FDR Democrat in the 1930s, and then was a committed liberal until the mid-1960s. But by the end of her life, Dawidowicz identified as a neoconservative. This book explores her political journey.

A myriad of books have been written about the "New York intellectuals," whose members included Irving Howe, Lionel Trilling, Daniel Bell, Sidney Hook, Irving Kristol, Norman Podhoretz, and Nathan Glazer—politically left East European Jewish immigrant sons who were socialist anti-Stalinists in the 1930s, became liberal Cold Warriors in the 1950s, and some of whom fostered the rise of neoconservatism in the 1970s.[4] But no one has paid attention to Dawidowicz's parallel political evolution from left to right.[5] Like the immigrant Jewish men of her generation who came of age in the politically intense 1930s, Dawidowicz relished a political argument, was verbally adroit, and did not shy away from a strongly worded rebuff.[6] Yet few have noted her influence on that circle of New York intellectuals or drawn connections between her European experiences, her writing on the Holocaust, and American Jewish politics. With her reputation secured through *The Golden Tradition* and *The War Against the Jews*, Dawidowicz became a central member of the New York intellectuals who associated with *Commentary* and the *Wall Street Journal* in the 1970s and 1980s.[7]

Despite comparable elements in their biographies, Dawidowicz differed from the New York intellectuals by her choice to become deeply rooted in the culture and history of East European Jewry and to defend tirelessly its particularism. In their encounter with America, most of the male New York intellectuals engaged publicly with general high culture and ideas. "Cosmopolitanism" and "universalism" were the watchwords of their youthful interwar heyday. Alienation from America and discomfort with Jewish identity were cultural prerequisites for the New York intellectuals writing for *Partisan Review*, a magazine devoted to a radical critique of politics and aesthetics in the 1930s and 1940s.[8] Though some of Dawidowicz's peers had passive knowledge of Jewish languages and culture, they minimized, both consciously and not, the significance of their Jewish backgrounds as they strove to become American. Their Jewishness provided a context to their identity, but not a positive agency.

Dawidowicz was different. She encountered America from solid Jewish cultural and linguistic ground, with a strong sense of belonging to the Jewish people. Educated at diaspora nationalist institutions, such as the Sholem Aleichem Folk Institute (SAFI) and the Yiddish Scientific Institute (known as the YIVO, its Yiddish acronym), which represented a vast transnational Jewish diasporic Yiddish-speaking world, Dawidowicz regularly wrote in Yiddish, the vernacular Jewish language of East European Jews.[9] Her later scholarly and popular writings—written in English—had a distinctly Jewish audience in mind even as they spoke to a broader, general American audience.

Where the New York intellectuals saw their political commitments, migrations, and transformations in American terms, Dawidowicz framed hers in relationship to East European Jewish history and politics. Responding to the political and cultural challenges of the postwar years in terms of the *longue durée* of the Jewish past, she interpreted American Jewish communal needs within the parameters of diasporic Jewish politics. She made two fateful trips to Europe in her early adulthood, the first to Poland in 1938 and the second to postwar occupied Germany. Her direct contact with antisemitism in interwar Poland, her work with Jewish refugees in postwar Germany, and her personal ties to individuals who had experienced the Soviet encroachment upon Eastern Europe permanently informed her critique of the New York intellectuals' liberal cosmopolitanism, which she ultimately came to regard as assimilationist and hostile to Jewish particularism and continuity.

These journeys deepened her multifaceted identity as an American Jew, an East European immigrant daughter, a Polish Jew by choice, and a Jew singed but not consumed by the fires of the Holocaust, which destroyed East European Jewish civilization.[10] While recent scholarship has shed light on the complex transnationality of immigrants to the United States, Dawidowicz's life illustrates that transnationality could originate among the native born. She created a Jewish subjectivity infused by her image of East European Jewish civilization that was as "dynamic, durable, overlapping, porous, and unpredictable" as Jewish immigrant identities.[11] Her place of birth notwithstanding, Dawidowicz's intellectual and cultural commitments to Eastern Europe meant that her life implicitly raised the question that many East European Jewish immigrants faced: "What did it mean to be an East European Jew when one lived beyond the confines of Eastern Europe?"[12] The answers she uncovered indelibly shaped her politics.

Dawidowicz's conservatism, already evident in the late 1950s, prefigured the rightward trajectory of the New York intellectuals' political turn in the late

1960s. Residing in New York City, the largest Jewish city in the world, Dawidowicz grappled directly with issues that preoccupied postwar Jewish intellectuals globally. Early on, her Europeanness informed her perspective on the major questions she sought to put before the public eye: the causes of the Final Solution, the tensions between the singularity and universality of the Holocaust, and the relationship of Jews to modern political liberalism. These issues took on a heightened urgency in the mid-twentieth century when the central challenge became how the Jews could be secure in the diaspora and still remain Jews. She also wrote extensively on other key issues informing Jewish identity in the postwar years, such as the viability of secular Yiddish culture; the "sanctity" of liberal American Jews' defense of the absolute separation of church and state; the role of Jews in political and social movements, such as civil rights, feminism, and Jewish religious renewal; and the legitimacy of American Jewish dissent on Israeli politics.

Dawidowicz's life was bookended by World War I and the fall of Soviet communism and buffeted by Nazism and the murder of the Jews of Europe. Amid such epochal historical events, it was East European Jewish history, language, and culture that played a foundational role in her emergent American neoconservatism.[13] When Dawidowicz rejected the liberal tilt of American Jewish politics in the 1970s, she did so from within a tradition of Jewish political conservatism deeply informed by her experiences in Europe, her lifelong involvement with Yiddish culture, and her commitment to Jewish cultural autonomy. Her life and work challenge the myth of the Jewish liberal "tradition," whose adherents believe that political liberalism is synonymous with Jewishness and rejection of it a kind of heresy.[14] When, in the late 1960s, the symbiosis between Jewishness and American liberalism began to show signs of wear, Dawidowicz had little compunction about defecting from a liberalism that she believed had failed to protect European Jewry from murderous antisemitism.[15]

Dawidowicz made the phrase "the war against the Jews" central to what is now called Holocaust consciousness. Her work is emblematic of what has become known as the "intentionalist" school of Holocaust historiography. Its underlying argument rests on the role of antisemitic ideology and on the systematic and consistent implementation of Hitler's blueprint, already evident in *Mein Kampf*, published in 1925, in executing the Final Solution. The "intentionalist" school was opposed to the "functionalist" position, which argues that the decision to murder the Jews was not part of Hitler's original plan but rather was arrived at slowly, the product of competing Nazi bureaucracies and personalities and the exigencies of war with the Soviet Union.[16] Dawidowicz's books became classics, and, with survivor-author Elie Wiesel, she became one of the most sought-after lecturers on the Holocaust in the postwar years. Dawidowicz would always remain ambivalent about the "Americanization of the Holocaust," which, in the late 1970s, cast the European events in universalistic and optimistic terms. While other interpreters of the Holocaust used it to champion international human rights, civil rights in America, or Jewish nationalism in its Zionist form, Dawidowicz responded to it by writing the history and commemorating the civilization of East European Jewry. Historical memory, she hoped, would give American Jews the connection they now lacked to the peoplehood of the Jews.

—

From Left to Right is an intellectual biography of Lucy S. Dawidowicz. It is also an interpretation of the historical interconnection between twentieth-century American Jewish political behavior and the European Jewish past. I am interested in the continuities and discontinuities in Jewish political thought in the diaspora, of which the American Jewish community is the largest and most important, and one whose history has often been written with only a faint nod to its European roots. Through Lucy S. Dawidowicz's life, I trace the history of the intellectual arc that characterized an important group of Jewish public intellectuals from leftist radicals to neoconservatives.[17] While neoconservatism was not an exclusively Jewish phenomenon, the influence of prominent Jewish men of letters and opinion in the movement is undeniable.[18] This book addresses the degree to which neoconservatism was "Jewish" and situates it and the individuals who professed its values into the history of diasporic Jewish politics, with particular attention to East European Jewish politics and their transformation on American soil. Dawidowicz's life, I argue, helps us connect postwar American Jewish political conservatism to the long history of Jewish politics.

Haunted by Nazism and the Holocaust, Dawidowicz's life and work intersected with the central issues and personalities that shaped Jewish life in the twentieth century. She wrote seven books, coedited two, and contributed over fifty articles to *Commentary* magazine—arguably the most important American Jewish monthly in the postwar years—at the height of its influence. Dawidowicz was an indispensable part of the research team at the American Jewish Committee (AJC, or the Committee), the foremost Jewish defense agency in the United States, as it built the Jewish liberal anti-communist consensus in the postwar period.[19] An outspoken figure in American Jewish communal life until her death in 1990, Dawidowicz became an intellectual touchstone for many of the New York intellectuals by the late 1960s, when she began to publish books, participate in public forums, and lecture throughout the country. Her correspondents included Alfred Einstein, Gershom Scholem, Irving Howe, Alfred Kazin, Isaiah Trunk, Solomon Birnbaum, Chaim Grade, Max Weinreich, Jacob Katz, Marie Syrkin, Ruth Wisse, Martin Peretz, Cynthia Ozick, and Raul Hilberg, among other intellectuals, writers, and activists whose lives were intertwined with the era's major questions of Jewish identity and politics.[20]

By the early 1970s, Dawidowicz was a member of the emergent neoconservative group that coalesced around *Commentary* magazine's editor, Norman Podhoretz.[21] This group, which included Milton Himmelfarb, Irving Kristol, Gertrude Himmelfarb, Midge Decter, and Nathan Perlmutter, had begun to question the blessings of acculturation.[22] Not only did they not take the survival of the Jews in the United States for granted, but they also questioned the assumption that intellectual Jewishness and liberal political values were synonymous. Dawidowicz shared these concerns, and later that decade, due to the recognition earned with her books on the Holocaust and East European Jewish history, she became known as a Jewish public intellectual. Her writings informed both the general American discourse about Jews and the Jewish discourse about Jewishness and modernity.

Given Dawidowicz's public stature and in keeping with my claim that American Jewish politics bear a connection to broader themes in diasporic Jewish politics, I argue that Dawidowicz's life should be situated not only among the New York intellectuals but also in a typological continuum with the European Jewish intelligentsia known as *maskilim* (enlightened Jews), who emerged at the end of the eighteenth century.[23] As Paula E. Hyman insisted, American Jewish history is part of *modern* Jewish history, and "Jewish history is contingent on local forces but not on the local alone. . . . It is useful [for Americanists] to pay attention to the transnational elements that have characterized Jewish history for centuries."[24] This book views the New York intellectuals, and particularly Lucy S. Dawidowicz, as an American variant of the East European Jewish intelligentsia who articulated a variety of ideological responses to their encounter with modernity. A social group simultaneously distinct from the communal and rabbinic leadership that had traditionally guided the Jewish community yet desirous of playing an active role in its transformation, the New York intellectuals believed the wider public would absorb their worldviews if their writings were widely disseminated.[25] Irving Howe, who coined the moniker "the New York intellectuals" in 1968, noticed the typological similarity between them and the Russian intelligentsia: "They thought of themselves as the embodied 'intelligence' . . . or 'consciousness' of the nation," he wrote. "They clearly felt an exceptional sense of apartness from the society in which they lived."[26] Both the New York intellectuals and the Jewish neoconservatives functioned as a secular intelligentsia, even if some among the latter appealed publicly to religious themes and values and upheld religious injunctions in their personal lives.[27]

The term *maskil* is grammatically and historically gendered male, so including Dawidowicz within its parameters requires some explanation. In traditional European Jewish society, only men had the requisite learning to criticize traditional Jewish culture from within. Until the last third of the nineteenth century, Jewish women were denied access to formal Hebrew education, the signal vehicle, the enlightened Jewish intelligentsia believed, for the transformation of Ashkenazic Jewish culture and of the Jews themselves.[28] Moreover, gender equality was largely absent from the agenda of the *maskilim* on the Continent.[29] Yet the connotative meaning of the term *maskil* suits Dawidowicz. A self-conscious anti-feminist with regard both to American politics and to Jewish ritual practice, she would have rejected the linguistically female-gendered term *isha maskilah* (enlightened Jewish woman). She believed that male pronouns connoted the universal and balked when feminists claimed otherwise.[30]

A married Jewish woman in a postwar America where intellectual power resided among male editors, writers, public intellectuals, and university professors, Dawidowicz wanted to be accepted on public, male terms. Her mentors and muses, including Jacob Shatzky, Leibush Lehrer, Max Weinreich, Zelig Kalmanovitch, Salo W. Baron, Alfred Kazin, Irving Howe, Georges Borchardt, Rabbi David Mirsky, Neal Kozodoy, Samuel Klagsbrun, and Szymon Dawidowicz, were all male. Throughout her writings, both public and private, Dawidowicz dismissed "sentiment," a quality she associated with intellectual flabbiness and emotionalism, which she may have marked as specifically female. She viewed second-wave feminism much the way she did other social movements of the late 1960s and early 1970s, as a kind of special group pleading that was antithetical to an American liberalism based on individual, not collective, rights. Third-wave feminism's insistence on thrusting subjectivity into the public sphere also put her off. Yet, professionally—at the New York YIVO during the war, with the American Jewish Joint Distribution Committee (JDC, or the Joint)[31] in postwar Europe, at the American Jewish Committee after the war, and as a professor at Stern College—she was often the only woman in the room.[32] An intellectual tomboy, Dawidowicz wanted to be treated as an individual, not as a woman. But she could not escape her sex. Pitching her proposal for *The War Against the Jews* to Aaron Asher, she noted that she was negotiating with her dean for release time and commented, "He assures me that the appropriate arrangements will come through, even though I am a woman."[33]

Dawidowicz's dismissive attitude toward feminism notwithstanding, gender and sexism are critical to an exploration of her life. However influential she may have been in postwar American Jewish public life, she is largely absent from the scholarship on the New York intellectuals and the rise of the Jewish neoconservatives, which has focused almost exclusively on a small group of highly articulate Jewish men—with the notable exception of Hannah Arendt.[34] She is also hard to find in historical studies of modern Jewish women because the field has primarily focused on the historical agency of Jewish women as secular (and usually left or liberal) political activists and trade unionists.[35] Only recently have feminist historians taken seriously religious women, who are often—but not always—politically conservative.[36] Among feminist Jewish scholars, the enfranchisement of women in modern Judaism has pivoted attention to female religious reformers and spiritual activists.[37] Yet, all of this scholarship has neglected politically conservative Jewish women, mirroring an unease that feminist scholars have generally had about women situated on the right side of the political spectrum.[38]

Beyond investigating Dawidowicz's political migration from left to right, I am also interested in her struggles to be recognized as a public intellectual. Certainly her sex determined some of her self-perceptions, aspirations, and life choices, as well as the ways in which she was both ignored and accepted by the New York intellectuals in their time. Mary McCarthy and Hannah Arendt were included in the circle of the New York intellectuals in their prime, but Dawidowicz's later status as a public intellectual rested on different grounds: her fierce commitment to defending the legitimacy of Jewish life and history. Despite that Dawidowicz was a Jewish woman who only late in life held a university post and who was never an editor of a national magazine, she became the éminence grise for those intellectuals who "discovered" their Jewish roots in the 1970s as part of a general postwar ethnic awakening and in response to the Holocaust.[39]

Though other conservative Jewish women, among them Gertrude Himmelfarb, Midge Decter, and, later, Ruth Wisse—the "matriarchs" of neoconservatism in Jacob Heilbrunn's phrase[40]—were part of the group of postwar American Jewish intellectuals, it was Dawidowicz who, through her books' wide acclaim, came to exert the most influence on American Jewish and American public life. The Golden Tradition (1967), an anthology of primary sources from Jewish Eastern Europe, was widely reviewed in the major English-language press and launched her public career as a historian of East European Jewry. *The War Against the Jews* became the definitive one-volume popular history of the Holocaust.[41] Originally published in 1975, it went through twenty-seven printings by 1984 and was reissued as a tenth-anniversary edition in 1986. *A Holocaust Reader* (1976), a documentary reader of primary sources related to antisemitism, Nazism, and the Holocaust, filled the need for educational materials on the Holocaust for a general English-reading public. *The Holocaust and the Historians* (1981), a study of the treatment of the Holocaust in modern historiography, set the stage for debates about the uniqueness of the Holocaust and its significance for history writing and teaching. These works not only positioned Dawidowicz as an authority on matters related to the life, culture, and destruction of East European Jewry but also contributed to heightened public consciousness of the Holocaust. Her expertise on East European Jewry led her to a university teaching position where she developed some of the first seminars on Holocaust history ever taught in the United States and later researched *The War Against the Jews.* Though an "amateur" Holocaust historian by today's standards because she lacked a PhD, Dawidowicz helped set the agenda for many of the historiographic issues still vigorously contested in the study of the Holocaust.[42] Yet historians of the Holocaust have tended to disregard Dawidowicz, uncomfortable with her strong "intentionalist" and particularist points of view. Even when they acknowledge her contribution, they fail to recognize her background in secular Yiddish culture and her vocal involvement with American and Jewish politics. Only recently has the interest in the immediate postwar years in Europe given Dawidowicz some voice, illuminating her role in the displaced persons (DP) camps' historical commissions and in the salvage of the YIVO's archive and library, with other materials from Vilna.[43]

Another reason for contemporary neglect of Dawidowicz's significance to postwar American public life and modern Jewish politics is methodological. Most books on American Jewish liberalism and neoconservatism have relied on published materials. Yet, almost every pamphlet published by the Domestic Affairs Committee of the American Jewish Committee or every speech given by one of its directors between 1949 and 1969 reflects research done by Dawidowicz. The archives of the AJC, the American Jewish Historical Society, the YIVO, the JDC, the Office of Military Government, United States (OMGUS), and the American Jewish Committee's voluminous print and digital materials—or the cognate archives of her scores of correspondents—reveal Dawidowicz's Rosetta stone–like role in articulating a postwar American Jewish understanding of the Holocaust and a response to the "crisis" of liberalism.

And there is the matter of temperament.

Dawidowicz was a woman full of contradictions. She was a youthful Communist turned Cold Warrior who then became deeply suspicious of the New Left; a professional woman who distrusted feminism; a lover of the Yiddish language who came to reject Yiddishism; and a patriotic cheerleader of American pluralism who, chastened by the postwar assimilationist environment, came to distrust an ideology that appeared to diminish the validity of a Jewish culture propelled by its own distinctive ethos and history. A lover of high culture—opera, the New York Philharmonic, and the classics of English and Yiddish literature—Dawidowicz was also a fanatic New York Mets fan, who was left starstruck by a chance meeting with legendary Mets power hitter Keith Hernandez in an airport.[44] She prided herself on her talents in the kitchen and yet was an addictive smoker. "Widely known as a non-pushover," in the words of Aaron Asher,[45] Dawidowicz was a tough bird. She was smart, funny, and brave but also stubborn, bitter, judgmental, and unforgiving.

While this book emphasizes the European influence of Dawidowicz's political turn in the 1970s and 1980s, From Left to Right is also very much an American story. Born Lucy Schildkret in the Bronx, Dawidowicz chose to become, in her own words, the "last witness" to the culture and history of East European Jewish civilization.[46] She did so at a particular historical moment, when the interwar generation of East European immigrant children had come of age and when Americans were particularly open to sympathizing with Jewish suffering during World War II—a war from which the United States emerged as a world power but that dealt a cataclysmic blow to European Jewry. It was a moment when Jews mattered to the American experience, their immigrant sons achieving preeminence in the white-collar "talking professions" of the professoriate, publishing, journalism, criticism, and film.

This book is structured in four parts that move back and forth between New York City and Europe. The movement echoes Dawidowicz's transnational identity as an American Jewish immigrant daughter committed to an East European diaspora nationalist vision of Jewish peoplehood. Part I ("In New York City in the Interwar Years") tells the story of Lucy Schildkret's childhood, adolescence, and college years, illustrating that she inhabited two worlds simultaneously: that of interwar New York's urban landscape and East European Jewish immigrant society. Part II ("In Poland, Refugee New York City, and Germany") narrates Dawidowicz's formative "European" years, in Vilna, Poland, from 1938 to 1939; in New York from 1940 to 1946, when she was enclosed in the European-like world of the New York YIVO with its immigrant and refugee scholars; and from 1946 to 1947, when she worked with displaced persons in the American and British Zones of Occupation in postwar Germany. Part III ("Becoming an American") traces how Lucy Schildkret—who returned to New York in December 1947 and married Szymon Dawidowicz three weeks later—became thoroughly identified as an American liberal even as Polish Jewish civilization remained inscribed in her heart. It also explores her emergence as the voice of East European Jewry as she began to publish on its history, culture, and destruction. Part IV ("Eastern Europe in America") exposes the fissure between Dawidowicz's European-inflected diaspora nationalist modern Jewish identity and the shifting definition of American liberalism, which, from the late 1960s forward, created a breach that with the escalation of the culture wars contributed to her support for neoconservatism. The epilogue examines the legacy of Dawidowicz's contribution to Holocaust historiography and the complexities of her selective view of historical agency. The appendix includes correspondence between Dawidowicz and a wide range of intellectuals and friends that illustrates the broad and important reach of her work and person.

⸺

Whatever the state of Dawidowicz's spirits in October 1987, in the end she heeded Ozick's advice and plea. Although her right-wing politics, gender, and unapologetic commitment to Jewish particularism in an East European Jewish key have resulted in scholarly neglect, this book argues that Dawidowicz's life makes visible the relationship of postwar American Jewish political conservatism to the Jews' long history.

Lucy S. Dawidowicz died in the fall of 1990, a year before the formal disintegration of the Soviet Union, the defining issue—along with the Holocaust—of her generation. By then, new challenges and threats, both real and imagined, to Jewish security in the diaspora were emerging. In the post–Cold War world, the next generation of Jewish neoconservatives no longer needed the prefix "neo" as a signifier of their conservative political commitments. They had become part of the American mainstream.[47] Dawidowicz anticipated them.

1

IN NEW YORK
CITY IN THE
INTERWAR YEARS

1

AMERICAN
IMMIGRANT
DAUGHTER

Born on June 16, 1915, Lucy Schildkret came of age in the 1930s, the eldest
daughter of East European Jewish immigrants. Her father, Max Schildkret,
hailed from Warsaw, her mother, Dora Ofnaem, from Siedlce, east of Warsaw.
Arriving in the United States after the revolutionary year 1905, they met, married, and settled in the Bronx, where they raised Lucy and her sister, Eleanor
(b. 1920).[1] Their economic status for most of Lucy's life was insecure, as they
labored—mostly without success—as small business owners or in menial sales
and factory jobs. In 1927 they had managed to buy a multifamily home in a
new development in the West Bronx, the more affluent side of the Grand Con-
course; but by 1937, they could not pay the mortgage and were forced to move to
what Dawidowicz would describe, in her 1989 memoir, as "a dismal apartment
in a dilapidated East Bronx neighborhood."[2] Lucy attended a New York City
public elementary school, as did most Jewish immigrant children in the interwar years. Encouraged by her mother to excel academically, she continued from
there to the prestigious Hunter College High School for girls and then to the
all-female Hunter College.[3] She also regularly attended a Yiddish supplementary school, known as a *shule*. These two environments—the American one of
the interwar New York City public school system and the immigrant one of the
secular Yiddish afternoon school—shaped Lucy S. Dawidowicz's hyphenated
identity from her earliest years.

Dora and Max Schildkret. (Courtesy Laurie Sapakoff)

IN THE ALCOVES OF HUNTER COLLEGE

During the difficult years of the Depression, New York's Jewish immigrants reared their children to view education as an important ticket to successful acculturation. Those children were twice as likely to complete high school and college compared to other immigrant groups, and by the mid-1930s, when Lucy Schildkret was a college student, Jews made up 80 to 90 percent of the student body at the free city colleges. While economic constraints could hamper a daughter's education more severely than a son's, Jewish women still went to college more frequently than their gentile peers. Indeed, by 1934 Jewish women constituted half of the enrollment in New York City's public colleges and three-quarters of the graduates of Hunter and Brooklyn Colleges, effectively

Lucy Schildkret as a young child. (Courtesy Laurie Sapakoff)

rendering the cultural and social milieu of higher education an extension of the Jewish immigrant neighborhood.[4]

Lucy's entry into Hunter College was eased by a highly academic high school education. At Hunter College High School, she devoted herself to English literature, becoming the editor of *Argus*, the school's literary magazine, which gave her freedom to pursue her love of poetry and writing. She later recalled: "Through *Argus*, I was introduced to the excitement of printing, the clutter of the printing shop and the clatter of the Linotype machines and presses. I felt very important as I read and corrected galley proofs, my fingers smudged with printer's ink."[5] Tellingly for someone who would later dedicate her life to chronicling the history of East European Jewry and memorializing its destruction, she wrote, "Nothing bigger can come to a being than to love a great cause and work for it," to accompany her senior yearbook picture.[6]

Lucy continued to pursue her passions for literature and poetry when she matriculated at Hunter College in 1932, becoming an English major in a department known for its demanding standards; Kate Simon, who went on to become a successful author, recalled her alma mater's rigors: "[Hunter provided] a quality education, requiring a great deal more of its students than is asked there now and in many other colleges."[7] Being a Hunter girl in those years meant being part of a lifelong club of Jewish intellectual women, exactly parallel to the experience of Jewish immigrant boys who went to City College. The novelist Elizabeth Klein Shapiro, like Lucy, had been the editor of *Argus* at Hunter College High School, and though twenty years her junior, Shapiro immediately bonded with Dawidowicz over their shared educational experience when they met in the 1980s.[8] Cynthia Ozick was another Hunter College High School graduate and took the occasion of Dawidowicz's acceptance of an honorary doctorate from Hunter College in 1987 to remind her of the archaic translation of the *Odyssey* they were required to read.[9] If City College was often invoked as the Harvard of East European Jewish working-class immigrant sons in the interwar years, Hunter College was the Radcliffe of their sisters, and they flourished there—even though many would recall Hunter's imperious teachers reminding them that they were called "girls," while students at Radcliffe and Bryn Mawr were called "women."[10]

At Hunter as an English major, Lucy wrote short stories, book reviews, and poetry. She was active on the college newspaper, the *Hunter Bulletin*, and on *Echo*, the student literary magazine. Her first contribution to *Echo* was a short story, "Romance: A Story."[11] Other original poetic contributions included "Summa cum Laude," "The Mauve," "Sing, O Barren," "Humble People" (which paid homage to T. S. Eliot's "The Waste Land"), "Lynching," and "In Memoriam: 1917." She reviewed poetry collections by Auden and Spencer in the spring 1935 issue and, combining her two worlds, translated a poem by the Yiddish writer Yehoash, "Yang-Se-Fu," in *Echo*'s winter 1935 issue;[12] she also contributed to *Silver Falcon*, the journal of the college's Shakespeare Society. It was a busy start to a life in which literature—both English and Yiddish—would remain a permanent personal touchstone.[13]

The turbulent political milieu of the urban Jewish immigrant neighborhood in 1930s New York informed Lucy Schildkret's childhood, adolescence, and college years. Through the interwar years, socialism dominated the zeitgeist of Jewish immigrant neighborhoods in America.[14] Politics was everywhere, from the formal political clubs to street demonstrations, from meat boycotts to rent strikes.[15] Not all Jewish immigrants were politically left, but the trade unionism and socialism that characterized the Jewish immigrant work experience made an enduring mark on the community's culture.[16] New York City's urban college campuses became incubators for the radical politics of Jewish immigrant youth. As Irving Howe vividly recalled, the New York intellectuals began their "perfervid" engagement with the world and political discourse in the alcoves of the City College lunchroom.[17]

Much the same held for the female students of Hunter and Brooklyn Colleges. Hunter students were engaged in all manner of international organizations, ranging from the Labor Zionist Organization to the Pan-American Student League to the Model League of Nations. It was peace activism, however, that captured the broadest section of the student body. In April 1934, during Lucy's sophomore year, Hunter students participated in the first of what became annual antiwar student strikes.[18] The college's "Liberal Club" boasted that its growing enrollment reflected "the increasing politicization of Hunter students," noting that meetings had been devoted to discussions on trade unions, fascism in Germany, and antisemitism and racism in the United States.[19] That same year, Hunter's Peace Council pledged to make "the students of Hunter College aware of the need to oppose the growing war danger, and . . . to provide organizations for student anti-war sentiment."[20] Hunter students also challenged tuition increases, protested the incarceration of the Scottsboro Boys,[21] and resisted the Nunan Loyalty Oath bill, which mandated oaths of loyalty to federal and state constitutions at all public institutions of higher education and had been slimly passed by the New York State Legislature. A banner headline under the *Hunter Bulletin* of March 1, 1935, proclaimed: "Students Protest Nunan Bill!" and a letter to the editor from the Young Communist League noted acidly that the loyalty oath bill had been presented at a time when funds for free textbooks at the city colleges were being capped and the US government was ramping up military spending. "We communists, consequently, call upon all students to act together immediately against the Nunan Bill," the letter urged, "and for academic freedom against imperialist war and fascism."[22]

In 1934, Lucy became editor in chief of *Echo* and moved the magazine's editorial policy leftward. The cover of the November 1935 issue blared bright red, signaling the editorial staff's sympathy for communism. A member of both the Young Communist League and the National Student League,[23] Lucy used the magazine's foreword to broadcast the Communist Party's "Socialist Realist" line on the relationship between art and society, literature and radical politics.[24] "*Echo* has set for itself a critical standard parallel to the high scholastic rating of the college," the young editor announced. "The foundation for our critical approach is determined by our understanding of the artist's position and function in society." She continued:

> The artist exists and is a living part of the society around him. . . . Art, in order to flourish, must focus on and reveal the flux and flow of the lives of the masses of people. And the fingers pointed against these people are also pointed against the very foundations of art. Now we are threatened by war and the imminence of fascism. The artist . . . must act against the obvious destruction and reaction that is bred by war and fascism. He must take sides not only for his own self-preservation, but for the enlightenment and redemption of all of society. . . . [Students] must unite with the broad masses of humanity, who, like us, want peace, freedom, and progress.[25]

Letters from her Young Communist League years to her childhood friend Evelyn Konoff quipped about bearing "the burden of the revolution on [her] shoulders,"[26] and confided that "there's nothing like a magazine and the approaching revolution to keep one busy."[27] The Hunter College administration, particularly its president, Dr. Eugene Colligan, and Dean of Students Hannah Egan, was known for its intolerance of student activism and suspicion of communism. They did not hesitate to suspend students, withhold recommendations for jobs, or threaten expulsion.[28] The prevailing attitude was expressed by an English professor, Eleanor Grace Clark, who took her grievances with Lucy's pink-shaded *Echo* editorial to the "Open Forum" pages of the *Hunter Bulletin*, charging that "[t]here is much in Miss Schildkret's blurb for the November ECHO that is inflated and untrue." She continued, suggesting that "sheer ignorance could account for much, for her distressingly unidiomatic English, or for her complete lack of literary background or critical capacity; but only egoism could have inspired the ludicrous generalities and the pompous cliches which 'sully' her statement of editorial policy." Professor Clark concluded by blasting the politics of Lucy's editorial:

> Such utterances form the stock-in-trade of typical proletarian propaganda. The artist who "creates culture," who boasts of cherishing "the living pulse of the masses," who "takes sides" for the enlightenment of society is the all too easily recognized leader of "the cultural vanguard" of the uneducated. These

so-called artists are gods to the "masses." . . . BUT, the question is: What is such a one doing in the vanguard of Hunter College?[29]

Lucy responded in the Bulletin's next issue with a combination of defensiveness and combativeness that would characterize her future public persona: "An editorial comment is always a statement of opinion, and any statement of opinion is labeled propaganda by those who disagree with it." Addressing Clark's comments, she added that they "were derogatory toward me personally and only indirectly aimed at the foreword. Her language was not critical, but vituperative."[30]

Apparently confident to take on a member of the Hunter faculty, Lucy, however, was beginning to feel that the demands of the editorship and of her political commitments were exacting too great a toll on other aspects of her life. To Evelyn, she confided that politics was getting in the way of her schoolwork, describing her life as "one meeting after another with a hot dog (or hamburger) thrown in for supper." She was getting too little sleep, had written only one poem, and "Furthermore, I have been getting hell from the Dean for cutting as much as I have. . . . To add to all my troubles, I haven't thought one single thought in all this time, or communed with my sacred inner self. Any one of these days I shall go into retreat, peace, and meditation and talk to my soul. It's really quite uncomfortable not to know what my standing is with my own self."[31] Lucy soon resigned from the editorship of Echo as well as from the Young Communist League.[32] Relaying the news of her resignation to Evelyn in February 1936, she signed her letter, "Yours, A citizen of the world, an unaffiliated student, and a free agent."[33]

World events, meanwhile, loomed ever larger. While peace activism dominated the school's corridors, the Jewish immigrant girls of Hunter were also acutely aware of the Nazi threat in Europe, and in 1935 student activists held an anti-fascism conference to denounce the treatment of Jews. Domestic anti-semitism also shadowed their lives. In September 1935, Lucy wrote to Evelyn, expressing a hodgepodge of political views based in opposition to demagoguery and larded with characteristic snark: "Fortunately for you I'm in a very good mood, because Huey Long died, and I hope in great agony. All I now ask of the Almighty is that I read the same of Hitler and [William Randolph] Hearst. Mussolini and [Father Charles] Coughlin thrown in wouldn't distress me unduly."[34]

But the most pressing concern for working-class Hunter College graduates in the insecure 1930s was getting a job. Economic vulnerability afflicted the great majority of them. All of the Jewish immigrant girls who contributed to Ruth Markowitz's study *My Daughter, The Teacher* spoke about their families' poverty. Five decades later, Lucy's classmate Sylvia Cole recalled the deprivations of the Depression in a 1982 letter to her college friend, describing nights when she had to sleep in Central Park because she was homeless.[35] Lucy herself recalled that "Keats and Wordsworth and lyric Yiddish poetry provided me with a refuge into which I could escape from my parents' quarrels, the hot-water boiler, and the constricted world of the East Bronx in which we lived."[36] College students were expected to assist with the family economy by working in offices, libraries, lunchrooms, and movie theaters. So many Hunter College graduates found employment as part-time workers in the department store giant Macy's on Saturday and Thursday evenings that the school yearbook referred to the store as "'the Saturday branch' of Hunter College."[37] Lucy, too, worked at Macy's after graduation.[38] Aspiring to gain a foothold in the middle class, Hunter girls, more than students from any other institution, applied en masse for teaching licenses in 1932.[39] Kate Simon remembered her mother's advice: "Study. Learn. Go to college. Be a schoolteacher and don't get married until you have a profession."[40] Many Jewish applicants experienced subtle and not so subtle forms of social antisemitism, particularly on the oral exam, which tripped up immigrants with Yiddish-inflected speech. Lucy apparently was one of those casualties.[41] But, in the fall of 1935, during her senior year at Hunter, Lucy informed her friend Evelyn that she had landed a part-time job: "I'm so damn excited I can't breathe. Of course, it's this silly National Youth Administration business, but I, for one, can't afford to be snippy about it."[42]

Despite the tanglings with deans, the endless political meetings, and the boy trouble (or lack thereof),[43] Lucy's Hunter years formed a significant component of her later self, nurturing her intellect and shaping her goals and dreams. Four decades later, when the Alumni Association of Hunter College honored her with its award for distinguished achievement, she confessed in a letter to the chair that the award "has given me an immoderate and immodest amount of pleasure,"[44] and at the event itself, she noted wryly the irony of her receipt of the award, given her history at Hunter: "In 1936 it would have seemed wildly improbable that I should ever be standing here, a judgment which I'm sure the late Dean Hannah Egan would have most emphatically shared."[45]

Those warm reflections glossed over the insecurities created by the economic fragility of post–Depression era New York City and the increasingly harrowing European political climate of the late 1930s. Unemployed after her graduation from Hunter, Lucy had a lot of free time on her hands but little disposable

Lucy Schildkret's Hunter College graduation. (Courtesy Laurie Sapakoff)

income for leisure and no clear professional direction. She threw herself into the activities of the Sholem Aleichem Youth Organization and immersed herself in Yiddish literature, finding refuge and community in the Yiddishist world that had nurtured her through childhood and adolescence.

STARTING OUT IN YIDDISH IN THE 1930S

Heady with youthful enthusiasm for leftist politics, Lucy wrote a self-possessed and self-mocking Yiddish letter to Evelyn Konoff on a newly acquired Yiddish typewriter in the mid-1930s when they were students at the Sholem Aleichem Folk Institute *mitlshul* (high school): "This [the typewriter] is new to me," she wrote, "and I hope you will be astounded. First I got the typewriter and then I took it upon myself to learn [how to use it]. I will straight away strike out into the world. God only knows how long it took me to write these few sentences, but it will all work out." She continued: "Do you see that the typewriter is given out by the Communist Party?" Switching over to a red ribbon, she typed, "Down with the Capitalist System! Long Live the Soviet Union!" and signed the let-ter, "With love, Libe."[46] Her enthusiasm for the Yiddish typewriter marks the way in which Lucy's commitment to Yiddish culture was so very different from that of many other East European Jewish immigrant children in the 1930s. Her formal education in the supplementary Yiddish school system of the Sholem Aleichem Folk Institute and her involvement with its Yiddish summer camp stamped her for life. Her personal connections to Leibush Lehrer, a diaspora nationalist theoretician who was head of the Psychology and Education Sec-tion of the YIVO, and to historian Jacob Shatzky, both Polish Jewish intellec-tuals living in New York City, deepened her intellectual sympathies with East European Jewish culture.[47] While Lucy's immigrant roots were similar to those of the New York intellectuals, her nonpartisan Yiddishist background distin-guished her encounter with interwar American culture and with the Jewish politics of the period. Her perspective on American Jewish politics was always informed by her knowledge of and attachment to the East European Jewish historical experience.

Jewish educational institutions founded by immigrants reflected the intense political ferment of the period. In New York City, as in other centers of East European Jewish immigrant life, Yiddish-speaking Jews established afternoon and weekend schools. Their aim was to support linguistic continuity between the generations and to foster in their children a secular national-cultural iden-tity based on the ideology of diaspora nationalism.[48] As in the creation of the Yiddish press, theater, literary societies, and workers education, the movement to establish secular Yiddish schools for the children of East European Jews who rejected traditional Judaism was transnational, a product of the proletarian-ization, secularization, and migration of East European Jewry.[49] The Yiddish modernist writer Isaac Leibush Peretz encapsulated the sentiment behind the creation of institutions to foster secular Yiddish culture at the famous 1908 Czernowitz Yiddish conference: "We are a Jewish people and Yiddish is our language and in that language we will create our cultural treasures, arouse our spirit, and unite ourselves culturally across lands and generations."[50]

To that end, Yiddishists created schools in Russia, Poland, Argentina, Can-ada, and Mexico, as well as in New York City, anywhere East European Jewish immigrant communities existed. Many of the schools were politically radical, associated formally and informally with socialists, left-wing Zionists, Bundists, Territorialists, and, after the Bolshevik revolution of 1917, Communists.[51] In Soviet Russia, where Yiddish was considered an official language of the Jewish ethnic minority, the state funded Yiddish schools as a means of inculcating loyalty to the Soviet Union and to its communist ideology.[52] In 1910, activists from the Socialist-Territorialists and Labor Zionists (Farband) and from the Workmen's Circle (Der Arbeter Ring) founded the first Jewish secular schools in North America. Since many activists feared that explicit Jewish education would deviate into what Marxists called "nationalist chauvinism," contravening the values of international socialism, the earliest schools did not necessarily instruct the children in Yiddish.[53] Even among Yiddishists, a spectrum of ideological commitments to leftist values created tensions between those who defined secular Yiddishism as a complete break with traditional Judaism and those who believed that it represented the apotheosis of modern Jewish culture, a distinction that David Fishman calls the "radical" and the "national-romantic" trends of secular Yiddishism.[54] Already in 1916, Yiddishists uncomfortable with subordinating their secular Jewish cultural agenda to the Socialist Party formed the nonpartisan Sholem Aleichem Folk Institute. The SAFI created its own network of institutions, including elementary schools, a high school, the Jewish Teachers' Seminary, a publishing house (Matones), a summer camp (Boiberik), and a children's periodical (*Kinder zhurnal*).[55] In 1918, the Workmen's Circle levied a modest school tax on its members to support supplementary Yiddish schools. Subsequently, it opened a weekend high school, a teachers training course, and its own summer camp, Kinderring. When the Socialist Party split apart due to the Bolshevik revolution, the institutions of the Yiddish-speaking immigrant world followed suit. Known as the *linke* (the Left), pro-Bolshevik Jewish immigrants broke with the Jewish Socialist Federation. Adopting the name "the Communist Federation," they set out to create a separate network of parallel institutions to the socialist Workmen's Circle, the *Forverts* (Forward) newspaper, trade unions, and schools. They created a newspaper, *Frayhayt* (Freedom), a radical Yiddish theater (Artef), housing cooperatives, a fraternal order (the International Workers Order—IWO), and a children's supplementary Yiddish school system, complete with children's literature and another summer camp, Kinderland.[56] The peak year for the Yiddish schools was 1934, with 10 percent of American Jewish children receiving some form of Jewish education sponsored by either the Farband, the Workmen's Circle, the IWO, or the Sholem Aleichem Folk Institute. A typical schedule for a child attending a supplementary Yiddish school meant going three days a week after elementary school; all four movements ultimately taught Yiddish language and literature and used Yiddish in their instruction.[57]

Lucy's parents leaned left like so many East European immigrant Jews, but they were not political ideologues. Nor were they observant of Jewish law. Yet the mature Dawidowicz insisted that the distinction between Jew and non-Jew was nurtured in her from infancy. Sending Lucy and her sister to a Sholem Aleichem Folk Institute *shule*, they disavowed any formal affiliation with politics in their children's education. The SAFI's founding principles emphasized a commitment to the Yiddish language and Jewish secular culture on a non-political basis.[58] Her parents had high literary aspirations and read the Yiddish daily *Der tog* (The Day), not the socialist *Forverts*, the religious *Morgn Zhurnal* (Morning Journal), or the communist *Frayhayt*. In sending her to the Sholem Aleichem *shule* and to Boiberik, her parents hoped to foster in her a commitment to the Yiddish language, "the cementing force that united the Jewish people and would ensure its continued existence."[59]

The Schildkrets had no doubt about who they were. "Ours," Lucy wrote in her memoir, "was a distinctly Jewish household, even though we never attended a synagogue, even though my sister and I were never taught the rudiments of the Jewish religion."

> On Jewish festivals my parents closed the store, not only in deference to what the neighbors might say but also out of a sense of Jewish solidarity. . . . My mother fasted on Yom Kippur, the Day of Atonement, on the ground that it was healthy to fast once in a while, but she never appreciated the solemnity of the day.[60]

Diaspora nationalism and Yiddishism undergirded the ethos of the Sholem Aleichem Folk Institute as they did the YIVO in Vilna, Poland, where Lucy would later spend a crucial year after college. Established in 1925, the YIVO constituted the institutional embodiment of a modern, secular Jewish "university" dedicated to the academic study of East European Jewish culture, language, and society. It wedded its academic mission to diaspora nationalism. The ideological activists in the SAFI, including Yiddish writer Chaim Zhitlovsky,[61] Yiddish critic Shmuel Niger, and, most importantly, Leibush Lehrer (who was also the YIVO's chairman in New York), were all associated with the YIVO and affirmed its commitment to diaspora nationalism. Lehrer played a formative role in Lucy's adolescence and became her epistolary sounding board during her year in Vilna. His Yiddishism belonged to the "national-romantic" trend. Decades later, Dawidowicz reflected on his worldview:

> Unlike the radical Yiddish secularists who rejected Judaism as superstition and unlike the Marxists who believed that religion was the opium of the people, Lehrer saw Judaism as the product of a folk culture. He reinterpreted its religious traditions and beliefs in ethnic-national terms. Aware of the profound emotional power which long-lasting traditions and their symbols played in shaping and strengthening Jewish identity, he tried to retain as many as were compatible with the pervasive anti-religious temper of the time.[62]

LOST IN MIGRATION: LEIBUSH LEHRER'S AMBIVALENT SECULARISM

Born in Warsaw in 1887, Leibush (Mordecai) Lehrer received a traditional Jewish education in Maków and Novominsk. He began to work at an early age but also continued his studies and attended the Université Nouvelle in Brussels in 1906. In 1909, he immigrated to New York City, worked in the garment district, and pursued the necessary requirements to matriculate at an American university. Lehrer received his BA and MA from Clark University in social psychology, a discipline that made an enduring imprint on his analysis of Jewish communal life. By 1918, he had begun to teach in the schools associated with the Sholem Aleichem Folk Institute.[63]

Of all the institutions of American Jewish life, none represented the aspiration for the future like the Yiddish school movement. From the very beginning, *shule* activists and educators designed curricula to transmit the values of secular Yiddish culture in order to create a new generation of secular Jews committed to the perpetuity of the Jewish people and to the Yiddish language. They also worried about linguistic assimilation, the effects of outmigration from densely populated urban centers, and the generational conflict between immigrant parents and their Americanizing children.[64]

In his role as one of the foremost secular Yiddish educators of the interwar years, Lehrer struggled philosophically and pedagogically to foster a secular Yiddish culture that would ensure the survival of the Jews in the modern world. A trained psychologist, he was no mere Yiddishist ideologue but rather a communal activist who sought to understand the human—and Jewish—soul and its need for ritual expression. Despite this commitment, in all of his work one can detect ambivalence about the success of his efforts to foster Jewish secularism in the open, liberal environment of the United States. In a 1936 essay, "The Jewish Secular School," Lehrer addressed the problem posed by the term "secularism," which he considered infelicitous and unsuited to the modern Jewish condition. He argued that secularism emerged in Europe in response to the scientific revolution, the centralization of political authority, and the rise of democracy. Describing secularism as the result of a long struggle between church and state, he argued that it "aims to emphasize values over which state jurisdiction is more in the interest of the people than ecclesiastical control." This, he asserted, "is either wholly inapplicable to events in Jewish life, or is only very remotely related to it," since there is no "church" or "state" in diasporic Jewish life. In Lehrer's view, for secularism to have any meaning for modern Jews, it had to be redefined. He repeated this call for redefinition throughout his life, preoccupied with creating meaningful rituals for secular Jews that would draw on Jewish tradition and folkways (shtayger).[65]

Influenced by the American progressive educators John Dewey and William Heard Kilpatrick, Lehrer insisted on the need to transform educational ideas into concrete praxis. A practical yidishkayt that would prove cohesive would have to rely upon "tradition, historical connectedness, sanctified symbols, and conscious additions that guide in the same direction."[66] The Yiddish language would be beneficial but not essential. What would be essential was the creation of some kind of center or kehile, a secular "beis-keneses [synagogue], a physical center, around which all of the public work of manifest forms of yidishkayt and the kehile centers." Lehrer allowed that while it was not clear what would constitute these "forms," he was certain of the need for ceremonies related to Jewish tradition, including rituals to mark the Sabbath, festivals, holidays, mourning days, bar mitzvahs, weddings, funerals, and other ceremonial communal moments. The task of the kehile was to work out the forms of secular ceremonial life that would "penetrate the private life of its members" and appeal to young people, creating a center for Jewish learning.[67]

Throughout his life, Lehrer strove to create a coherent structure of nontheistic ritual behaviors that would convey to his youthful charges both a Jewish national identity and a link to traditional Jewish culture. Camp Boiberik, a name selected by the children from the Yiddish writer Sholem Aleichem's stories, was his laboratory. The summer months away from the city allowed for the creation of an intense Jewish secular environment articulated in Yiddish, a kind of holistic Jewish space shielded from the non-Jewish world. It would be easy to underestimate Boiberik's importance. The camp was much more than a bucolic setting for summer fun. It created an East European environment in the United States where Jewishness, the Yiddish language, and the concept of a Jewish people were harmoniously interwoven. In his many years overseeing Camp Boiberik, Lehrer endeavored to institutionalize his belief that Jewish national commitments informed and bolstered universalist values. Opening as a day camp in 1918 with ten campers, Boiberik was able to purchase land for an overnight camp in 1931. It boasted a registration of between three hundred and four hundred campers each summer until it closed in 1984. Throughout the 1930s and 1940s, the camp's heyday, campers spoke, sang, cheered at sporting events, complained, and got homesick, all in Yiddish.[68]

Leibush Lehrer wrote that the camp's motto, *Di mentshlekheste dertsiyung far a yidish kind iz a yidishe* (The most humane education for a Jewish child is a Jewish education)—a motto in which universalist goals preceded Jewish ones—was a concession to the sizeable group of parents and lay leaders in the Sholem Aleichem Folk Institute who were uncomfortable with his explicit commitment to Jewish tradition. But his "national-romantic" brand of Yiddishism informed the camp's programming. Its rituals included *oyneg shabes*, the festive Friday night dinner for which campers marched in formations to the dining room, where white tablecloths covered the tables and Jewish music was piped in. Campers enjoyed *kinder tog*, a kind of upside-down Purim-like day devoted to silliness; Lehrer himself would often don a Superman costume. *Mid-sezon*, begun in 1923 as a masquerade day, became a day to dramatize Jewish history; campers were introduced to the heroic Jewish past, such as the Exodus narrative, the Bar Kokhba revolt, and the founding of Mordecai Manual Noah's utopian colony, as well as to important Jewish historical personages. Lehrer also innovated a secular, collective rite-of-passage bar mitzvah celebration for children with summer birthdays.[69] *Felker yomtov* (Holiday of Nations), a noncompetitive color war inspired by the ideals of prophetic Judaism and the League of Nations, capped the summer. Preparation for the event took three weeks, with campers divided into national groups, dressing in that nation's colors and singing Yiddish songs attributed to "their" nation, and it concluded with the Yiddishist anthem expressing hope for world peace, *Ale mentshn zaynen brider* (All Men Are Brothers).[70] After World War II, Lehrer introduced a camp ritual devoted to commemorating the victims of the Holocaust by enacting a secular T'isha B'Av.[71] In time, compelled both by his own commitments to Jewish survival and by a camper population that increasingly came from homes with a far less immediate connection to Yiddish or to Eastern Europe, Lehrer strove to make the "ideas, ritual forms, or activities conveying Jewish information, more conspicuous and emphatic."[72]

Lucy attended the Sholem Aleichem Folk Institute's elementary schools and its high school. She traveled to the SAFI's *mitlshul* near Union Square on Saturdays and Sundays to attend class, becoming active in its youth organization, the Sholem Aleichem Yugnt Gezelshaft (SAYG). She edited the student journal, *Shrift* (which she sometimes referred to as "short shrift"), whose mission was to cultivate Yiddishism among the next generation of American Jews in order to counter assimilation. Lucy often contributed to *Shrift*'s English section, seeking to reach "that large section of Jewish youth that has not our particular orientation toward Yiddish."[73] The editorial "The Way to America" asserted that "we, who are interested in the development of the Sholem Aleichem Yugnt Gezelshaft as a force in the lives of American Jewish youth, cannot accept the doctrine [of assimilation]. Our organization is built on an almost axiomatic principle: that Jews can be Americans, and *are*, as well as Jews, that they can contribute richly to the life of America, which, of necessity, is the life of the Jews."[74] Like others in the Yiddishist world, Lucy was deeply aware of the impending crisis in Europe in the 1930s, writing in 1937 the editorial "You Will Not Drive Them Out," which rejected the antisemitic demand that Jews—considered non-Poles by many of their countrymen—emigrate from Poland.[75]

Marginally employed after college, disengaged from leftist politics, and professionally adrift, Lucy threw herself into the Sholem Aleichem Folk Institute's youth society. She turned her literary skills to reading Yiddish and writing Yiddish essays and poetry, reporting about the effort—as always—to Evelyn Konoff: "I am staying at home all during the day, and so far have written one rotten sonnet, but it's something, and I'm painfully trying to get out of my despicable state of not thinking or doing any work." Her future plans, she disclosed, included continuing to translate Yehoash, reading "a hell of a lot of Yiddish," and "reading [Leon] Kobrin's novel . . . and Chaim Zhitlowsky's Memoirs—aloud with my father. And what a job. But I'm learning a lot."[76]

The SAYG's nonpartisanship did not mean a rejection of leftist values; the platform adopted at its second conference, in February 1937, stressed the compatibility of "modern and progressive Yiddish culture" with the "incessant struggle against fascism" and applauded the establishment of Birobidzhan, the autonomous Soviet-Jewish republic founded in 1934.[77] On May Day in 1937, the SAYG marched with New York City's workers, affirming their hope for the "foundation of a just, human life and the revival and renaissance of the 'cultural-national collective,' which calls itself the Jewish people and whose language is Yiddish."[78] Later that summer, Lucy and others met with Paul (Peysekh) Novick, editor of the *Frayhayt*, regarding the upcoming communist-sponsored World Jewish Culture Congress in Paris. Lucy later recalled that "the Yiddish literary luminaries were utterly swept away by the basic idea that attention was being paid to them and their creative work. Hardly anyone could resist the temptation to take part."[79] But many Jewish socialists argued that the congress was a front for Soviet ends. In the summer of 1937, a declaration opposing the congress appeared in the *Forverts* and *Der tog*, signed by twenty-six prominent Yiddish writers, including I. J. Singer, David Pinski, Aaron Glantz-Leyeles, Jacob Glatshteyn, and S. Margoshes, among others.[80] The New York Yiddish world was torn apart, including the SAYG. Efforts to broaden the congress's criteria to include Mendele Moykher Sforim and I. L. Peretz failed. Dawidowicz remembered that the Communist Party rejected Peretz's "romanticism of religion and hasidism," admitting only the proletarian writers into its Yiddishist canon.[81]

By 1938, Lucy expressed her final break with communism and the Soviet Union. Writing to Evelyn, she commented acerbically that "the Soviet trials have worked wonders" in leading her to the conclusion "that dictatorship, no matter who is the dictator, even Lenin or Trotsky, despite their excellent theories and understanding of matters like the class-struggle, is undesirable." Calling the trials a "farce," she continued:

I've been wondering what our local communists have to believe if they accept as true the accusations and the confessions. In that case, it seems to me that they must come to the conclusion that the revolution was [a] trick pulled by a gang of crooks, thugs, and murderers. That the Soviet Union is a hoax in itself. The situation becomes more and more appalling, and smells worse than anything the Czars ever pulled strings on.[82]

Amid these swirling currents of ideas, politics, and world events, there remained the question of what to do. All of Lucy's Yiddishist activism affirmed her sense of belonging to a secular Yiddishist community but did little to advance her bleak employment possibilities. In September 1936, after graduating from Hunter, she enrolled in Columbia University's Graduate School to study English literature but left after two weeks, writing in her memoir decades later, "Keats and Wordsworth no longer interested me."[83] Adrift, she credited Jacob Shatzky, her teacher in *mitlshul*, with steering her toward the study of history in general and of Jewish history in particular. Shatzky, who eagerly had supported the creation of the YIVO as an independent center devoted to Yiddish scholarship, urged Lucy to return to graduate school in the field of history. Following his advice, she transferred to the Columbia University History Department and began work on her MA thesis, a study of the Yiddish press in nineteenth-century England.[84] Yet her family's steadily declining economic status soon ruled out the possibility of her being a full-time student. Determined to prove her mettle, Lucy continued to research her thesis in the Jewish Division of the New York Public Library. She wrote to Evelyn, "My address from now on is: Jewish Room, 42nd Street Library."[85] As Lucy's research expanded beyond the holdings of the New York Public Library to archives in Europe, Shatzky urged her to consider applying to the YIVO's graduate program, called the Aspirantur, in Vilna, Poland. In February 1938, she contacted the administration of the Vilna YIVO, explaining to them that she had thought about requesting several Anglo-Yiddish newspapers for the YIVO branch in New York but that she no longer needed them, as "it is possible that I will be an *aspirant* [graduate fellow] in Vilna, so I will be able to use the brochures and newspapers there."[86]

In May, Lucy received her acceptance letter from the YIVO's director, the linguist Max Weinreich. He stipulated that before coming to Vilna she had to do cognate research on the nineteenth-century English press and improve her Yiddish. Lucy responded with delight: "It's superfluous to say that my heart is filled with pride that you are giving me the opportunity to fulfill my wish."[87] The American Yiddishist community took note of the young woman setting off to Jewish Eastern Europe. The YIVO's American division, Amopteyl (*Amerikaner opteyl*), prepared a press release in English and Yiddish, and the Yiddish press covered the story of her fellowship and departure. On August 10, 1938, *Der tog* headlined, "American Jewish Girl Goes to Study at Vilna YIVO," and the *Forverts* of August 28 featured her Hunter graduation picture along with a photograph of a "new generation of Yiddish writers" in Poland, which included the current cohort of fellows and their teachers, Max Weinreich, Zelig Kalmanovitch, and Zalman Reisen.[88] And once Lucy finally arrived in Vilna, her celebrity status was assured. "Oi, oi, the compliments I got that day," she wrote to her parents.[89]

When she left New York City on August 10, 1938, Lucy Schildkret traveled against the patterns of modern Jewish migration; she went from west to east, from the New World to Jewish Eastern Europe, from New York City to Vilna. To be sure, there was a long tradition of Americans traveling to Europe, particularly to Paris, to discover themselves.[90] In the postwar years, Susan Sontag described her frequent sojourns in Paris as part of a process of becoming a "self-Europeanized American."[91] Poland, however, was not France. It beckoned not as a modernist haven but as the center of the European *Jewish* heartland.

Going "in reverse," as Dawidowicz herself noted many years later, the young Libe Shildkret in fact went forward, to a new identity.[92] Living in Vilna from September 1938 until August 1939 and later marrying a Polish Jewish immigrant helped transform Lucy's personal sense of self from a New York immigrant daughter into a transnational American Jew with a Polish Jewish soul. Many decades later she would reflect on these experiences: "I look back upon this episode in my life as a search for wholeness."[93]

II

IN POLAND,
REFUGEE
NEW YORK CITY,
AND GERMANY

2

AN AMERICAN
IN VILNA

When Lucy Schildkret stepped onto the deck of the MS *Batory* and set out for Vilna, Poland, in the summer of 1938, she faced a deeply ominous European political climate, one particularly threatening to Jews. Her Vilna year and the traumatic flight from Poland through Nazi Germany in late August 1939 became seminal experiences in her personal transformation into a European Jew. As Libe Shildkret, an American immigrant daughter, she was spurred to go to Vilna because of her passionate commitment to secular Yiddish language, literature, and culture. Ironically, however, her year in Poland led her to the conclusion that the worldview of secular Yiddishism could not sustain Jewish life in the modern period. As she wrote in 1989 in her memoir:

> I would never have predicted that in Vilna, the citadel of Yiddish, I would come to realize that Yiddish was an insufficient basis on which to maintain one's Jewish identity, that it could not ensure Jewish continuity. Reluctantly and unwelcomingly I accepted that conclusion. It didn't mean that I wanted things to be that way. It didn't mean that I loved Yiddish any the less. Sometimes I felt I was watching the end of a world I had come to love.[1]

Though her secularism was challenged, living in Yiddish, being in Poland, and working so intensely at the YIVO immersed Lucy in the totalizing world of modern East European Jewish culture. Indirectly victimized by European antisemitism, she would return to the United States motivated to chronicle the history and vitality of East European Jewry and to support Jewish life in the United States, the largest East European Jewish diaspora community in the world.

THE MEN AND WOMEN OF THE YIVO

Once she arrived in Vilna, Max Weinreich and Zelig Kalmanovitch became Lucy's intellectual, psychological, and personal mentors, taking over the roles played by Leibush Lehrer and Jacob Shatzky in New York. To her friend Evelyn, she wrote that Weinreich "really is a remarkable man. But Kalmanovitch more so."[2] These men, together with Zalman Reisen, a Yiddish journalist who was the editor of the daily *Undzer tog* and a member of the YIVO's executive committee, were the center of the transnational diaspora nationalist and secular Yiddishist circle—along with the YIVO itself—to which Lucy was now bound as an *aspirant*.[3]

Max Weinreich, born in Courland, a German cultural region of Latvia, was drawn to Yiddish at a young age. By all accounts, he was a workaholic, and

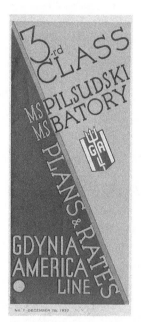

Third-class ticket to Poland on the MS *Batory*. (Courtesy the American Jewish Historical Society)

Yiddish secular culture, the Yiddish language, and the YIVO were the objects of his obsessive intellectual drive. At the University of St. Petersburg from 1913 to 1917 he became interested in Yiddish journalism, later writing for the Yiddish press in the United States under various pseudonyms, and pursued a doctorate at the University of Marburg in 1919–23 in Yiddish linguistics. He came to Vilna in 1923, marrying into one of the city's most illustrious Jewish families, the Szabads, and taught at the Yiddish Teachers' Seminary. When the idea of the YIVO circulated in 1925, Weinreich was immediately enthusiastic and threw himself into its activities. A room in his apartment was the YIVO's first Vilna address.

The founders of the YIVO conceived of the institution's mission in clear contrast to that of Wissenschaft des Judentums, the German-Jewish historiographic school born of West European Jewry's nineteenth-century encounter with political emancipation. The fathers of Wissenschaft, though trained at German universities, were forbidden from teaching in Prussian universities because they were barred from civil positions in the state bureaucracy. Their training emphasized the high culture of the Jews, focusing on postbiblical rabbinic literature and the "rational" streams in Jewish thought.[4] They were particularly enamored with Sephardic Jewish culture of the High Middle Ages, which they viewed as a model for the fusion between Jewish culture and European society that mirrored their own quest for integration. The YIVO, the brainchild of East European Jews, many of whom were self-educated, owed its intellectual debt to the Russian-Jewish historiographic school initiated by Simon Dubnow in the late nineteenth century. Born into a traditionally observant Russian Jewish home, Dubnow embraced secularism and nationalism, as had many East European Jewish intellectuals of his place and time, while cultivating a deep commitment to Jewish life and identity through the study of history.[5] Settling in Odessa in the 1890s among a circle of modern Russian-Jewish intellectuals, which included Mendele Moykher-Sforim (Sholem Yankev Abramovitsh), Ahad Ha-Am (Asher Zvi Ginzberg), and Hayim Nahman Bialik, Dubnow began to write popular history, to advocate for the establishment of a Russian-Jewish historical society, and to write textbooks. In 1891, in the aftermath of the expulsion of the Jews from Moscow, he penned a manifesto, "Let Us Search and Research: A Call to the Wise of Our People Who Volunteer to Collect Material on the Jews in Poland and Russia," in which he exhorted East European Jews to make historical research their national ethos:

> I will call all of you, come and join the camp of the builders of history! Not everyone who can read and write can be a brilliant writer or chronicler of events, but every one of you can be a collector of material, an aid to the building of the edifice of Jewish history. . . . Let us work together, let us collect all the remote sources from the scattered places, and let us arrange them and make them known to the public and use them for the building of the edifice of history. Let us search and research![6]

Writing at a juncture of modern Russian Jewish history when intellectuals fiercely debated the locale of the Jewish future, Dubnow articulated his faith in diaspora nationalism's ideological stance that remained committed to a Jewish collective future in Eastern Europe. In 1897, he began to write "Letters on Old and New Judaism," articulating his philosophy of history and its relationship to Jewish politics.[7] In this series of epistolary essays, he expressed his credo that historiography had to be purposeful, directed toward nation building.[8]

Dubnow's commitment to Jewish nationhood was diaspora based and independent of political or territorial sovereignty. Four components defined his historiographic agenda. First, he focused on Eastern Europe as the center of modern Jewish history, in contrast to Wissenschaft's Iberian exemplar.[9] Second, he redirected Jewish historical writing away from the elite and their ideas to the masses and their daily lives. Third, he advocated popular source collection and history writing as tools in the development of Jewish nationalism. Finally, he argued that history was the inheritance of every stratum of Jewish society, not only that of intellectuals. In sum, he held that Jewish historiography and the nationalist ethos that its study produced would provide a substitute belief system for Jews who had broken with the narrative of sacred Jewish history, in which God was the central agent in historical change and the Jewish people were His subjects. As Robert Seltzer wrote, "More than any other Jewish thinker, Dubnov saw Jewish history as conveying the meaning of Jewish survival for secular Jews of his generation. . . . The intensive study of the Jewish past had a deep moral, almost mystical (albeit anti-religious) significance for him."[10]

While Dubnow, who had been involved with the YIVO's founding, was the institute's spiritual guide, Max Weinreich was its on-the-ground leader, and he worked to keep the research agenda of the Vilna YIVO focused on contemporary Jewish life as well as on the Jewish past.[11] Weinreich was acutely aware of the challenges facing East European Jewish youth. In 1932, he went to Yale University as a Rockefeller Foundation Fellow to study the effect of culture on child and adolescent development and then to Vienna in 1934 to study with Siegfried Bernfeld, one of Freud's students, which propelled him to create the YIVO's Youth Division and to design and conduct several youth autobiography projects.[12] In 1935, he published in Vilna a pathbreaking volume, *Der veg tsu undzer yugnt: yesodes, metodn, problemen fun yidisher yugnt-forshung* (The Way to Our Youth: Elements, Methods, and Problems of Jewish Youth Research), combining his interest in youth culture, Yiddish, and social psychology.[13]

Four research sections had been established with the YIVO's founding: historical, philological, economical-statistical, and psychological-pedagogical. Under Weinreich's guidance and influence, the research agenda of the Vilna YIVO focused on Jewish folklore, Yiddish language, ethnography, and the sociological study of contemporary Jewish life. The Warsaw YIVO, in contrast, focused on history.[14] In 1935, the Vilna YIVO's research agenda included studies on the social relations between Jews and non-Jews, diet and hygiene, name changes, household budgets, religious observance—or lack thereof—among Vilna's Jews, and changes in the Yiddish press.[15]

THE ASPIRANTUR

September 1938 marked the beginning of the fourth year of the Aspirantur. Established in 1935 on the occasion of the YIVO's tenth anniversary, the fellowship was created to train a new generation of modern Yiddishist scholars who would find in Vilna the scholarly mentors, library and archival resources, and linguistic-cultural environment to further the creation of a modern Jewish secular culture. Dubnow gave the keynote address at the Aspirantur's inauguration, urging students to continue their work documenting the East European Jewish past despite the mounting anxieties of the present. Weinreich personally directed the Aspirantur: he set the framework for the research projects, conducted the seminars, and invited the guest lecturers. His agenda found expression in the topics pursued by the research fellows. In Lucy's year, these included "Jewish Small Industry in Vilna," "The Publication of A. Landau's Dictionary," "Teaching Singing in Elementary Schools," "A Lexicon of Jewish Clothing in the First Half of the 19th Century," "Jewish Jokes," "Children's Play," and "Budgets of Jewish Families in Vilna," among others.[16] Their research methods, which included questionnaires, individual biographies, and reports, were informed by Weinreich's belief that direct observation should be a guiding research tool and that the Jewish individual was as important as the Jewish collective.[17] During the year, the *aspirantn* heard such lectures as "Principles of Modern Psychology," "Chief Principles of Psychoanalysis," "Jewish Economy after WWI," "Yiddish Phonetics," "Jewish Economic History in 19th Century Poland," and "Yiddish Grammar."

During their year's fellowship, the *aspirantn* also strengthened their Yiddish language skills and worked for the YIVO archives and library.[18] Lucy coyly asked Leibush Lehrer in one of her first letters, "Has my Yiddish improved a little bit?"[19] At twenty-three, she was the youngest of the fellows in the fourth cohort, all of whom, except for her, were born in Eastern Europe.[20] Most had some university training, and several had already been at the YIVO for a year or more. The qualifications for admission had been a source of tension from its beginning. Weinreich struggled between his commitments to academic excellence and to the interwar Jewish social and economic reality, accepting some *aspirantn* who had only completed gymnasium.

In her memoir, Lucy described her compatriots bluntly. Of Nechama Epstein, she wrote, "The first thing I notice . . . was that she was an unattractive woman." Esther Schindelman was "not attractive as a woman or as a person, chattering incessantly about boyfriends of whom we never had any evidence and who—so we agreed when we gossiped about her—were probably figments of her overheated sexual fantasies." The historians among the fellows lacked "historical imagination," she wrote to Leibush Lehrer, admitting that "my first enthusiasm about the Aspirantur is turning to questioning and doubt" and dismissing the other fellows as "unlicensed lawyers, unemployed teachers, university graduates, people without a particular goal"—people, she said, "who can't find a place for themselves and who use the Aspirantur to delay, year by year, their making some decision about their future."[21] Her memoir's research notes reveal some perspective on her own shortcomings, commenting dispassionately on her own appearance ("short, bobbed brown hair, nice eyes, moderately attractive") and her demeanor ("on the one hand, very serious, almost with a sense of mission, comitteed [sic]; hard-working, energetic, responsible; also cheerful, funny, gay; also snotty and superior, with a lot of self-confidence . . . also changeable about people, easily bored").[22]

The only American in the Aspirantur, Lucy possessed a national status that was both a personal novelty and an asset among her peers, and, later, a form of salvation. Years later Dina Abramowicz, the Vilna-born librarian at the YIVO in New York, recalled the impression Lucy made in Vilna as a young woman, remembering her reputation as "an unusual guest from America . . . a very gifted lady, the pride of the Yivo aspirantur."[23] Lucy herself knew that her Americanness was immediately apparent. Interwar Poland's Jewish poverty was of a completely different degree than that of interwar New York Jewry.[24] And her political innocence distinguished her even further from her peers. Growing up in the United States, as she would write in her memoir, she had "never experienced the terrors of war," while many of her fellow *aspirantn* has suffered dislocation, flight, exile, and pervasive hardships during World War I. "Besides that difference in our experiences," she observed, "my American passport constituted an ever-present difference between me and them. Whenever I chose to do so, I could run away to the safety of the United States, finding refuge in my American home far from the war that we all felt would surely come."[25]

The *aspirantn* faced a challenging yet rewarding routine. Weinreich was known as an uncompromising perfectionist who sought to maintain the highest level of intellectual work in all of the YIVO's academic ventures. The *aspirantn* were in awe of him. To Lehrer, Lucy wrote that "Every opportunity to speak with him [Weinreich] is a divine-thing and I'm not the only one who feels this way. He is beloved by everyone but he doesn't seem to know how others feel about him."[26] To her parents and sister, Eleanor, she wrote: "Besides being one of the most outstanding linguistic and psychological research experts, he's a marvellous person." Weinreich was "not just a bookworm," she added, recounting his pleasure in the beautiful Polish countryside or in a game of croquet.[27] Describing his astonishing discipline, academic erudition, charisma, and drive, she attributed it to his passionate commitment to Jewish secularism and to Yiddish, which she believed was "the center of his Jewishness."[28]

The YIVO's engagement with the Jewish folk masses meant a constant negotiation with the politically charged environment of Poland in the 1930s. Though Weinreich was a Bundist, he endeavored to make the YIVO a meeting place for all modern secular Jews, regardless of political affiliation: "The Institute as an institution must stay outside of political struggle," he wrote.[29] Like Lehrer, Schiper, and Kalmanovitch, he saw the YIVO's research into the problems facing Jewish society as nonpartisan. When the youth movement *Bin* (I Am), which Weinreich founded in 1927, became too politicized, he dissolved it. When Jacob Berman, a member of the Warsaw Historical Commission, joined the Polish Communist Party in 1929, the commission and the YIVO activists objected to his membership. Weinreich insisted that the *aspirantn* refrain from party politics.[30]

Weinreich's commitment to scholarship in the service of the Jewish community also meant walking the line between "objective" academic scholarship and "subjective" communal concerns. In his 1937 article on the Aspirantur, Weinreich stated that the word "objectivity" should be struck from the dictionary. Acknowledging the epistemological fact that no researcher chooses a particular problem by happenstance and adducing an observation by Charles Beard—"Problems are not inferred from facts, problems are tensions that emerge in the person's mind at the time he observes facts"—Weinreich urged his students to be rigorously self-conscious about their subjective engagement in their subjects. They must be critical, methodological, and systematic; otherwise, "one would not be able to distinguish between alchemy and chemistry."[31] In these comments, we can see his debt to the positivism that had informed his German university training. Yet his belief in pursuing rigorous academic research that addressed the contemporary problems of the Jews informed his whole career. So, too, Kalmanovitch's. On September 9, 1938, members of the cohort met and introduced themselves to one another, reviewed their responsibilities, and heard Kalmanovitch reiterate the communal mission of

The fourth cohort of the Aspirantur and teachers. First row: Lucy Schildkret, Yirmiyahu Shapira, Esther Schindelman, Chaim Munitz, Nechama Epstein; second row: Shlomo Berezin, Rachel Golinkin, Shmuel-Zeinvel Pipe, [?] Hofenshtand, Chana Smoshkovitch, Max Weinreich, Ber Schlossberg; third row: Shmuel Friedland, Jacob Rivkin, Pinhas Tikoczinski, David Arnstein, Zalman Reisen, Elihu Teitelbaum (missing: Chana Piszczacer Mann and Zelig Kalmanovitch). (Courtesy the American Jewish Historical Society)

the YIVO, emphasizing that the political and ideological disagreements that had discomfited Zionists and wealthier, more Germanized Jews were no longer apposite. He stressed to the *aspirantn* that the YIVO's academic goals and their individual research projects should aid in addressing a fundamental, existential question: "Who are we?"[32] Weinreich's and Kalmanovitch's communal commitments—informed by the Dubnowian historiographic ethos—in turn shaped the young Lucy Schildkret.

For her part, Lucy filled her days with research on the Yiddish press, work for the YIVO, and participation in the required seminars. Being an American also meant doing a lot of translation—formally for Weinreich and informally for her pesky fellow students. She worked on a Yiddish translation of anthropologist Franz Boas's *The Mind of Primitive Man* (1911), helped Weinreich with his book on Jewish youth autobiographies, and translated an extensive table of contents for the third volume of *Historishe shriftn* into English for

Kalmanovitch. Her notes about the autobiography project mention translating communications to newspapers, organizations, and individuals, an arduous chore. "Such things take time and seem a waste of it, but are really not. I feel drawn into the very essence and heart of YIVO's work."[33] These tasks also deepened her relationship with Weinreich and Kalmanovitch as mentors and father figures.

Lucy's project on the history of the Yiddish press in England occupied but did not captivate her, yet her experience as a research fellow under Weinreich's wing shaped her future work as a historian of the Jews. In that year, she learned how to conceptualize a viable research project, do the research, and present

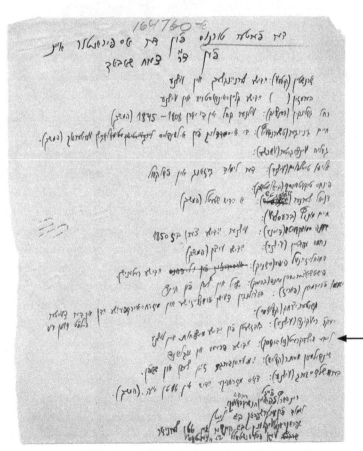

List of research topics of the fourth cohort of the Aspirantur. "Libe Shildkret (New York): Yiddish Press in England" is third from the bottom. (Courtesy the YIVO Archives)

Lucy Schildkret at the YIVO library, 1938. (Courtesy the American Jewish Historical Society)

findings in a systematic and engaging manner. Hardworking and anxious, Lucy was in many ways a typical graduate student. After giving Weinreich some of her preliminary written work in Yiddish and English, she wrote to Lehrer of his response: "He said my work was pretty good and that I should expand the introduction about Jewish working-class life, with more details and better sources."[34] She found three issues of the periodical *Hashofar*, a Yiddish newspaper first published in 1874, in the Strashun Library.[35] She also read contemporaneous Yiddish newspapers, such as *Kol mevaser* (published in Russia) and the Lemberg *Israelit* (published in Austrian Galicia), plumbed the available secondary literature, and incorporated her findings from the New York Public Library. Honing her research skills, she wrote to the *Jewish Chronicle*, the British Museum, and the Jewish Historical Society of England with queries about her topic.[36]

Oscillating between confidence and insecurity, Lucy confided to Jacob Shatzky in New York, "I have accomplished very little, this means, in terms of the Aspirantur, but it seems to me I have one thing for certain—and this is already a little step—a method. I have certainly learned how to work—however, I have not yet learned how to work *intensively* for a *lengthier* time.... Let's hope that I will have more to show in my second year."[37] Nervous about the level of her spoken Yiddish and about her findings, she first presented her conclusions to Nechama Epstein, a fellow *aspirant*. Weinreich, meanwhile, seeking to dispel her anxiety—and taking advantage of her English—engaged her in typing letters for him. Lucy, enthralled by her mentor, wrote, "He's a true psychologist," and added, "I love him."[38]

The notes to her preliminary report, detailing her topic's justification, methodology, and preliminary conclusions, illustrate how dutifully Lucy had imbibed the YIVO's commitment to "history from below." When she presented her findings in December 1938, her comments repeatedly emphasized her desire to understand how the Yiddish press informed the lives of the Jewish working masses of England. Her seminar report also anticipated her later preoccupations with the unreliability of memory, noting the gap that existed between the memoirs of journalists and their actual newspaper work.[39] She gave the final version of the report on May 4, 1939. Noting that she had worked like a slave, she nonetheless commented, "Weinreich was pleased and said that I had made remarkable progress in methodology and language in the time I've been here." After the obligatory question-and-answer period, it was "Weinreich in his extraordinarily clear, near-genius manner [who] summarized everything."[40]

Though Weinreich continued to play a major role in Lucy's life before, during, and after the war, in reflecting on her year in prewar Vilna, she would come to regard Zelig Kalmanovitch as the greatest influence on unsettling her ideological assumptions, including her most basic belief in secular Yiddish culture and her lingering leftist orientation. Kalmanovitch, a second-generation diaspora nationalist, had received a traditional Jewish elementary education in a boys *kheyder* (elementary school) and more advanced study in a *beysmedresh* (study house) in his native Latvia. He continued his education in a state gymnasium, attending university in Berlin and Königsburg, where he received his doctorate in Semitic philology. Following the failed Russian Revolution of 1905, Kalmanovitch became a member of the Jewish Socialist Workers Party, which advocated Jewish cultural autonomy within the future socialist Russian state, and wrote for its journal, *Di folksshtime* (The People's Voice). Eking out a living as a translator, he also wrote for a highbrow Yiddish periodical, *Literarishe monatsshriftn* (Literary Monthlies), where one of his first pieces, "Di yudishe shprakh-lehre" (1914), argued for the centrality of Hebrew to the development of Yiddish as a distinct language from German. Yiddish, for Kalmanovitch, was ontologically Jewish; its philological development could only be understood in relationship to its roots in Jewish communal and religious life.[41]

After World War I, Kalmanovitch ended up in the Soviet Union, where he remained active in diaspora nationalist and Yiddishist politics. But, as his 1914 essay attested, he had already begun to fight against the subordination of Yiddishism to politics. Writing to the Yiddish literary critic Shmuel Niger in May 1920, he expressed hatred for what would become official Soviet Yiddish culture. Bemoaning what he saw as the corrupt essence of the Yevsektsiya, the Jewish Section of the Communist Party, he asserted that a "culture which has these people as its supporters is impure at its root." Of the Bolsheviks, his assessment was bitter and implacable:

> Everything Jewish which is not on their side, just like every other aspect of culture, is buried. They destroyed the Jewish soul more than all the pogroms here. For me personally, there is only one salvation, if it is not too late, and that is to get out of here.[42]

Kalmanovitch fled the Soviet Union in 1921. In his 1931 essay, "Perspectives for Yiddish Culture in the Soviet Union," he affirmed his rejection of the orthographic revolution to rid Yiddish of Hebrew-component words, a position that reflected the Soviet Union's campaign against religion (and was embraced by some non-Soviet Yiddishists who supported the reform on the grounds of phoneticization). By 1934, Kalmanovitch had settled in Vilna, where he devoted the rest of his life to fostering a nonpolitical Yiddishism through the YIVO. His alienation from socialism, autonomism, and secularism became acute after the German invasion of Poland and the Soviet occupation of Vilna in 1939. With his colleagues Elias Tcherikower and Israel Efroikin, Kalmanovitch issued a journal, *Oyfn sheydveg* (At the Crossroads), that articulated their criticism of modern secularism. They advocated for a "return" to the wholeness of premodern Jewish civilization in which the national collective and the religious tradition were seamlessly joined. Only that bond—not the Yiddish language—they concluded, answered the existential question of Jewish existence. In the April 1939 issue of *Oyfn sheydveg*, Tcherikower queried, "Why specifically Yiddish? If there is no national, historical or, dare we say, religious feeling of connection with the collective then why be a Jew in a country where you can freely partake of the general rich culture?"[43]

The Kalmanovitches, both Zelig and his wife, Riva (née Rebecca Luria), whom everyone called Rivele, took Lucy Schildkret under their wing as soon as she arrived in Poland, welcoming her generously and warmly and putting her up initially in their home. Though she went on to room with a young couple, the Rudenskys, Lucy saw the Kalmanovitches every day. Writing to Lehrer shortly after her arrival, she told him that there were "no words" to describe Rivele—"she is not a person, but an angel."[44] In her memoir, Lucy recalled that

"At their home, I felt enveloped in a warmth and protectiveness that I had seldom experienced before."[45] The feeling contrasted sharply with her feelings about her childhood and parents. *From That Place and Time* is almost completely silent about her personal relationship with her parents—in fact, it does not even include their names, an omission that speaks volumes about her lifelong search for mentors and parental surrogates.[46]

Untangling her emotional attachments to the Kalmanovitches from her doubts about the viability of Jewish secular culture is impossible. While Dawidowicz's love and respect for Zelig Kalmanovitch informed her later unalloyed condemnation of the Jewish Left and all universalist ideologies, her own earlier turn away from her student communism may have been the impetus that led her to him in the first place. Though Kalmanovitch had long abandoned traditional observance when she met him, his secularism was informed by a profound respect for Jewish tradition. Lucy wrote regularly to Lehrer about Kalmanovitch, echoing his view that modern secularists were misguided if they wished to sever Yiddish from Hebrew and modern Jewish culture from its premodern Jewish religious past: "Every day it's clearer to me that you can't build an organization on the basis of Yiddish culture, that literature is no way to generate a spark of Jewishness among our young people in America, YKUF [Yidish kultur farband, or Yiddish Culture Union] and CYCO [*sic*; TYSHO, tsentral yidishe shul organizatsye, or Central Yiddish School Organization], notwithstanding. . . . I'm more and more convinced by the bankruptcy of Yiddishism, perhaps because I've come under Kalmanovitch's influence."[47] In the research notes for her memoir, she recalled that "for Kalmanovitch my kind of Jewishness has absolutely no value."

> He doesn't need Jewish holidays and festivals, in fact, he works on Yom Kippur, but not in the same spirit as the Bundists. He thinks there's something unnatural in my search for a Jewish festival, perhaps even insincere. And yet he's the most dedicated and most loyal Jew and Yiddishist I've ever known. I understand why he doesn't need the festivals, because he still remembers with enormous love "the real festivals" of his home. He would think our [Sholem Aleichem *mitlshul*] Pesach a mockery.[48]

She also shared with Lehrer Kalmanovitch's conclusion that modern Jewish culture was not dependent on a democratic or liberal society to flourish. Since Jewish culture had been resilient under oppressive political circumstances, he argued, "the struggle against fascism or for a new society has nothing to do with the survival of the Jewish people."[49] At this point, in 1939, Kalmanovitch had yet to argue for a post-emancipatory return to the "ghetto" as a means of preserving Jewish culture from the corrosive effects of modernity, as he would do later when incarcerated in the Vilna ghetto.[50] His critique of Dubnow's faith in emancipation and the possibility of true Jewish acceptance into the modern liberal state put him at odds with other YIVO activists, as well as with secular Yiddishists and Jewish intellectuals beyond Eastern Europe.

In an essay in *Oyfn sheydveg's* April 1939 issue, "Under the Hammer of History," Kalmanovitch concluded that capitalism, emancipation, and the Jewish Enlightenment (Haskalah) had undermined the premodern wholeness of Jewish civilization. Lucy, writing again to Lehrer, asked if he had read the essay[51] and also related Kalmanovitch's response to Salo W. Baron's three-volume work, *A Social and Religious History of the Jews* (1937). Baron was a Galician-born, Viennese-trained, and New York–based historian of the Jews, whose vast erudition decisively shaped the study of Jewish history in the twentieth century, particularly in the United States, to which he immigrated in 1926. His work boldly marked a reaction against the methodological assumptions of his nineteenth-century predecessors, the practitioners of Wissenschaft des Judentums who focused on intellectual and spiritual history, and also against Dubnow's secular nationalist approach to the Jewish past. His *History* categorically rejected Wissenschaft's de-emphasis on the social and national factors of Jewish history and dismissed the secularist ethos of Dubnow's work and the premise that the Jewish nation preceded Judaism. For Baron, social and religious components were inextricably bound to one another in Jewish history, a point made explicit in his book's title. His introduction emphasized the essential interdependence of Jewish nationality and Judaism, a view that Kalmanovitch affirmed and internalized in his theorizing about Jewish continuity and survival. Jewish civilization's positive content came from the mutually reinforcing relationship between its social component—the formal Jewish community with its autonomous structure of self-rule—and its religious component, the tradition guided by Jewish law.[52]

Lucy summed up Kalmanovitch's views to Lehrer, reporting that "according to him Baron was quite right in saying that until Emancipation Jews survived because of their national religion. Not that there was first a people and then a religion, but that both were forged together."[53] His comment, and, indeed, Baron's perspective on Jewish modernity, betrayed a pessimism—or at least a qualification—about the cohesion of the Jewish collectivity in modern Europe.

In this pessimistic view, the liberal emancipatory state, which affirmed individual rights over the group, could not be hospitable to Jewish national claims.[54] Baron also expressed severe reservations about the fate of the Jews in the context of the modern nation-state's drive toward ethnic homogeneity, concluding that "the status of the Jews was most favorable in pure states of nationalities (i.e., states in which several ethnic groups were included, none having the position of a dominant majority); least favorable in national states (i.e., where state and nationality, in the ethnic sense, were more or less identical); and varying between the two extremes in states which included only part of a nationality."[55] This insight was not lost on Kalmanovitch and other Jewish intellectuals in interwar Poland, where supporters of Polish nationalism increasingly viewed the Jews as a foreign element alien to Polish society. Kalmanovitch concluded that the best option was a territorialist solution that allowed for the flourishing of an autonomous Jewish collectivity. Accordingly, by the mid-1930s he had become an activist in the Freeland League. Founded in 1935 in London, the league and its Freelanders hoped to obtain a tract of land for the collective settlement of East European Jews on their own social, political, and linguistic terms.

Like Zionists who articulated a similar rejection of emancipatory assimilation, the Freelanders nonetheless had reservations about Jewish settlement in Palestine.[56] Lucy attended a Freeland meeting with the Kalmanovitches in January 1939, at which Australia was discussed as a possible territory for settlement, and was impressed by Kalmanovitch's reasoning. She reported to Lehrer that "Kalmanovitch spoke wonderfully, in his way, and demonstrated the bankruptcy of Yiddishism as a movement, because it's satisfied with a program of reading a Yiddish book and newspaper and going to a Yiddish theater once in while." That could only be a movement, in Kalmanovitch's view, "for people with a literary bent." Lucy went on to gloss his insistence that "Jews need a broader program and need to be like other peoples, to have their own territory where they can live normally" and—to his audience's perplexity—that "the struggle against fascism has nothing to do with the struggle for the survival of Yiddish." She conveyed her admiration for Kalmanovitch:

> It's hard to put a label on him. He's a territorialist and one of the most profound people I've ever met. Because he's constantly occupied with great doubts about Yiddish and Jews, he thinks that the YIVO's greatest accomplishment would be to clarify just what a Jew is. People don't understand him and think he's an enemy of Yiddish. But I tell you that his doubts arise from

his enormously great love for Jews and for Yiddish. Kalmanovitch realizes that a people can't survive just for its language, not even for its culture. . . . Everyday Jews can't be satisfied with culture. They need to buy bread and repair their shoes and work—all in another language, the language of the country they live in. So long as they don't have a normal Jewish life, they won't be able to survive as a people and surely not maintain their language. The only solution is for Jews to have their own territory.[57]

In her letter Lucy revealed that most of the audience was noticeably cool toward Kalmanovitch's attempt to show that Jews and Yiddish did not need a free political society to survive—an argument that seemed to disconnect the struggle for Yiddish continuity and Jewish survival from the battle against fascism. It wasn't that Kalmanovitch welcomed fascism, she reported. But he had come to the conclusion that liberalism and political openness led to Jewish assimilation in all forms: linguistic, political, and cultural. She reported that "He stopped here, perhaps because the logical development would lead to dangerous conclusions. As it was, people didn't understand him and began to protest: Kalmanovitch is a fascist."[58]

These intellectual discussions took place as the specter of war loomed ever larger. Immersed in the YIVO's Yiddishist protective bubble within the escalating political terror of the interwar years, and as an American national, Lucy remained relatively insulated from most of the existential concerns of her mentors. Weinreich and Kalmanovitch continued to work at the YIVO, trying to maintain a semblance of normalcy, but they were both acutely aware of the fragility of the Yiddishist enterprise generally and of the even more perilous situation of impoverished and politically vulnerable Polish Jewry. They did their best to shield her from their concerns. For Lucy, however, one element of danger in interwar Polish Jewish urban life that plagued Vilna's Jews—and that she experienced directly—not only penetrated her sense of well-being but would also become embedded in her later analysis of the Holocaust and of Jewish-Gentile relations in Eastern Europe: hooliganism or spontaneous group violence against Jews.[59] Indeed, her interpretation of the antisemitic attitudes that saturated the interwar period in Poland would shape her views of urban anti-Jewish violence in the United States in the 1970s. Having experienced the positive, intuitive collectivity of prewar Polish Jewry, Lucy also felt its obverse: the negative "otherness" or "apartness" of the Jews in Poland and the threat that mob violence posed to their daily lives.

CHRISTIAN AND JEWISH POLES

In chapter 8, "Them and Us," of her memoir, *From That Place and Time*, Dawidowicz focused on Polish-Jewish relations and Polish antisemitism in interwar Vilna. The chapter's title revealed her perspective on Polish-Jewish relations, which had been shaped both by the peculiarities of Vilna's political and demographic past and by the complex political, social, and economic issues of the new Polish state. Regarding the latter, a paradox characterized the vexing question of how to incorporate the Jewish community into the modern European state. Conceptions of modern Polish nationalism—born in the late eighteenth century—varied. Some Poles, such as those affiliated with General Marshal Józef Piłsudski's Polish Socialist Party (Polska Partia Socjalistyczna), defined their national aspirations in liberal, ethnically heterogeneous, and politically inclusive terms. Others, like Roman Dmowski, who represented the National Democrats (Narodowa Demokracja), articulated the slogan "Poland for Poles," explicitly excluding Jewish Poles.[60]

Such sentiment was widespread. The Minority Treaties, a legacy of the 1919 Versailles Treaty, were largely viewed by Poles as continuous with the long history of oppressive imperial meddling in Polish affairs and were amplified by the political and economic instability that plagued the young republic.[61] Polish Jewry generally was overjoyed at the reassertion of Polish independence after 123 years of partition, and even the General Zionists under the leadership of Yitzhak Grynbaum enthusiastically participated in the new Polish parliamentary politics. But the fragility of the structural, economic, and political fabric of the new republic was apparent at its origins and created a palpable sense of tenuousness. With six currencies, five separate provincial administrations, three legal codes, and two different railway gauges, the new Polish state had major problems in structural integration. Its already neglected economy was badly damaged by World War I and the subsequent economy of scarcity. The government responded by supporting certain key industries (i.e., liquor, salt, coal, mining, and steel), support that largely bypassed the Jewish economy. Ethnic cooperatives for Poles excluded Jews, who experienced new competition in the middle-class, urban commercial sectors of the economy that had historically been their niche. The worldwide Depression of 1929 exacerbated the already strained Jewish economic position in independent Poland, leading to wide-scale poverty. Economic antisemitism accused the Jews of siphoning off Poland's limited resources.[62]

During the interwar period, every major Polish city—Kraków, Vilna, Łódź, Lwów, and Warsaw—was home to a Jewish population of between 20 and 30 percent, but each urban environment had its own distinctive ethnic cast, developed over the long history of partition.[63] Before World War I, Vilna had been under Russian Imperial rule and had always been a Polish and Jewish—not a Lithuanian—city in terms of population. Linguistically and culturally, its Polish residents identified as Poles, hating the obligatory Russification imposed after 1871, while its Jews identified with the Russians. Many Jews, however, maintained Yiddish as a spoken language even if they were at home linguistically in Russian culture. During the Second Polish Republic, Vilna (Wilno in Polish) was extracted from the larger Vilna region, which became part of independent Lithuania. Lithuanian nationalists rued the excising of Vilnius (in Lithuanian), the city they viewed as their historic capital, from the new state. But in the interwar years, Vilna was hardly populated by Lithuanians. Rather, it was home to a population that was 45 percent Polish, 35 percent Jewish, 10 percent Lithuanian, 5 percent Belorussian, and 2 percent Russian. Independent Lithuania, in contrast, was practically ethnically and linguistically homogeneous, home to a population that was 81.7 percent Lithuanian, with only 6.7 percent Jews, 4.1 percent Germans, 3 percent Poles, and 2.3 percent Belorussians.[64]

Though the new Polish republic was modeled as a liberal, democratic state with a constitution, issued in 1921, deeming "all citizens equal before the law," its democratic promise was not actualized in the interwar period. The legacy of the partitioning powers' anti-Jewish legislation—including bans on public use of Hebrew and Yiddish in former Austrian lands, the exclusion of Jewish rabbinical students from the military exemptions granted to Roman Catholic seminarians, and the prohibition of Jews from mining and other industries— remained in place. On January 1922, a draft of legislation that would have removed all inherited government restrictions on Jews was introduced into the Parliament (Sejm), but the legislation was postponed, indicating the persistence of a double standard against Polish Jewish citizens. It took until April 10, 1931, for all restrictive legacy of the partitions to be rescinded, but this de jure equality coexisted with de facto discrimination.[65]

More pernicious, however, was the introduction of new anti-Jewish legislation. A particularly grievous form of discrimination was the preoccupation with Jewish enrollments in higher education, characterized as a "flood." Already in 1923, the All-Polish Youth Organization called for limiting Jewish enrollments to their percentage (roughly 10 percent) in the population. This call and others were largely kept at bay during the early 1920s, despite the ever-recurring collapse of the government. In 1926, Piłsudski staged a coup d'état, creating a "moderate" dictatorship with an empowered executive branch. Ignacy Mościcki, the president of Poland, was at the nominal helm of the state while Piłsudski, who was sympathetic to the integration of the Jews into modern Poland, held the political reins. Piłsudski prevented the most virulent forms of anti-Jewish laws from being promulgated, but his death in 1935 allowed the Mościcki government to become increasingly dominated by the nationalist right-wing parties, the National Democrats and the Party of National Unity, neither of which hid their crypto-fascism, militarism, or antisemitism. From 1936 forward, several Sejm bills were introduced excluding Jews from certain industries, prohibiting kosher slaughter and the manufacture of ritual objects, and ordering boycotts of Jewish stores.[66] The de facto antisemitic climate pressured shopkeepers to post signs in their stores' windows and doors to indicate the owners' ethnic background.[67] Other attacks included limiting or outright prohibiting the hiring of Jewish legal apprentices and establishing "ghetto benches"—separate seating for Jews in classrooms—in an effort to augment the discrimination of the numerus clausus (educational quotas) for Jews. Ghetto benches were first introduced on December 8, 1935, at the Lwów Polytechnic and then spread to other institutions. The enrollment statistics illustrate the success of this campaign: Jewish enrollments in higher education plummeted from 20.4 percent in 1928 to 7.5 percent ten years later.[68]

The heightened calls in the 1930s for the emigration of the Jews illustrated how deeply and broadly antisemitism was rooted in the new republic. The Camp of National Unity (Obóz Zjednoczenia Narodowego, or OZN) and the National Radical Camp (Obóz Narodowo-Radykalny, or ONR), a splinter group from the more mainstream right-wing National Democrats, were particularly vocal in their demand that Jews leave Poland. At the same time, as Piotr S. Wandycz has emphasized, the right-wing, antisemitic atmosphere of the post-Piłsudski period was not comparable to German and Italian fascism. And, as Szymon Rudnicki wrote, though the stark legal disenfranchisement of Jews in Germany beginning in 1935 was not introduced in Poland,[69] a climate of anathematizing 10 percent of Poland's population continued in the last years of the Second Republic. This environment—in which equality coexisted with social and economic discrimination—was the one that Lucy Schildkret entered when she arrived in Vilna.

As an American woman, Lucy mostly experienced antisemitic threats indirectly. In general, hooligans refrained from harassing women, targeting only male Jews.[70] Yet her relative security could not shield her altogether. Lucy recalled walking home one evening from an event with Chaim Grade, when he swiftly guided them away from a threatening street.[71] In research notes referring to articles from Yiddish newspapers reporting attacks against Jews, she wrote, "a pretense is made of arresting the hooligan, if he's caught and idenitfied [sic]. He's brought to the police, but usually freed. On the other hand, if a Jew should make any attempt to hit back, he's arrested and fined or imprisoned for disturbing the peace, no matter if he's badly wounded."[72] Weinreich himself was blind in one eye, injured by a stone-throwing student mob in 1931.[73] Yet according to Dina Abramowicz, who studied at the University of Vilna before the ghetto benches, the virulence of Polish antisemitism took the generally liberal YIVO activists, Weinreich included, by surprise. "The story of intensified anti-Semitism in the last year of independent Poland is relentless," she wrote decades later to Dawidowicz, describing that "it is like a delirium of somebody who is in agony and is trying to find an outlet for its rage." Abramowicz recalled that Weinreich himself—though a victim of antisemitism—never viewed Jewish life in Poland as impossible. He was known to say: "A little anti-Semitism, a pogrom, is in the Vilna tradition, as is the Vilna tradition to overcome it."[74]

Antisemitism was the ever-present shadow enshrouding Lucy's Vilna year. The antisemitism she observed was not limited to disgruntled lower social classes but also permeated the most educated and elite strata of society.[75] Writing about Polish antisemitism in *From That Place and Time*, she linked hooliganism with the university, uncoupling the liberal Enlightenment assumption that aspiration for broadened intellectual horizons meant an equally expansive conception of ethnic and civic toleration. The numerus clausus and the ghetto benches encouraged the view—even among the country's "enlightened" professoriate and youth—that Jews were not Poles. Indeed, Lucy noted, "The most zealous practitioners of hooliganism and the most reliable source of supply for hooligans were the students at the University of Vilna."[76] In 1979 she recalled the part that the university elite played in demonizing the Jews in interwar Poland.

> I remember the shock of my first encounter with that Polish nationalist anti-Semitism. It was just then the beginning of the school year and Polish university students were picketing a stationery store—a Jewish stationery store—which sold school supplies. The store was on one of Vilna's main streets. School children as well as adults who wanted to buy there were assaulted and even pedestrians walking by who looked Jewish were insulted and abused.... *For me it was the first lesson in what would become a system of*

continuing political education: the university was no bulwark against prejudice
and neither the study of philosophy nor the pursuit of literature would prove to be
a defense against the sickness of bigotry and anti-Semitism.[77]

The predations against the Jews of Vilna became deeply embedded in Lucy's psyche, leaving her acutely attuned to the ways in which hooliganism undermined her YIVO friends' belief that toleration was born of the free exchange of ideas and that the rootedness of the Jews in Poland assured their future there. In the spring of 1939 this belief in *doikeyt* (Yid., "hereness," or belonging) was proved illusory when the exhibit "Jews in Poland" was canceled by a state educational commission. Prepared by Jewish schoolchildren attending the schools of the Central Yiddish School Organization of Poland and already shipped from Vilna to Warsaw in the spring for its opening in April, the exhibit documented Jewish life in Poland from its origins until the present day.

In late August 1939, only a few days before her hasty flight from Vilna, Lucy went to Warsaw, where she was granted permission to view the now cordoned-off exhibition, one of the few people ever to have seen it. The exhibit, displaying the children's maps, drawings, models, and dioramas of factories, workshops, schools, and entire towns, asserted the Polishness and rootedness of Polish Jews. A huge black map dotted with electric lights greeted would-be visitors at the top of a staircase, illuminating Jewish settlement throughout Poland from the thirteenth century to the present. Other exhibits focused on Jewish engagement with Polish politics—including the struggle for Polish independence—literature, the economy, and the press.

She later reflected that it was not hard to see why the Polish authorities had closed the exhibit. At a time when "the government and the anti-Semitic parties at its helm were clamoring to drive the Jews out of Poland, charging that they were alien to the country," the exhibition "graphically documented just the opposite. It showed the deep roots that Jews had struck in Poland and how abundantly they had contributed to Poland's industrial development and cultural endeavors. It was a message that Poland did not wish to have delivered."[78]

DAYS OF DECISION

The constant news of an ascendant Nazism from the West, the palpable encounters with antisemitism in Vilna, and a general malaise and homesickness rattled Lucy in the summer of 1939. Since she had no clear employment prospects in New York, Weinreich worked to persuade her that the YIVO needed

Lucy Schildkret in Vilna, August 1939. (Courtesy Laurie Sapakoff)

her skills for another year. Already in March, she wrote to Lehrer about Weinreich's efforts to sway her to stay. "I'm puzzled by his eagerness. He utterly confused me and has this devilish smile, he can even prove that my staying will be good for my mother. I can't decide what to do."[79] A *siyem*, a graduation ceremony, on June 20, 1939, marked the official end of her *aspirant* year.[80] Weinreich convinced her to stay through September to help him translate the lectures of John Dollard, a Yale psychoanalytic sociologist slated to come to Vilna.

Though Lucy had been productive that spring—writing several reviews for *YIVO bleter* of English-language books on topics close to her interests: a survey of research done by the federal Works Progress Administration, a history of the *Times* of London from 1841 to 1884, and a booklet on juvenile literature[81]—the pull to return to the States prevailed. She booked a ticket home from the

Polish port of Gydnia for September 4 and from Copenhagen to New York on September 5, a departure date that would allow her to fulfill her promise to Weinreich. These plans blew up on August 22, when the American embassy sent a letter to all US nationals in Poland urging them to leave. The next day, German foreign minister Ribbentrop and Soviet foreign minister Molotov signed the German-Soviet Non-Aggression Pact, which offered up Poland for invasion, partition, and occupation. Despite Lucy's protests, Rivele Kalmanovitch insisted that she leave Poland immediately.[82]

AMERICAN EMBASSY

Aleja Ujazdowska 29

Warsaw, Poland, August 22, 1939.

1. In view of the recent developments in the international situation, of which you are undoubtedly acquainted through the press and otherwise, it is suggested that you give immediately serious consideration as to whether in case an emergency arises, you would remain in Poland or depart. In case you should have the intention to depart from Poland in such circumstances, it is further suggested that as transportation and other facilities might be interrupted or made difficult, arrangements for a planned departure should not be delayed too long.

2. American citizens in Poland are expected at all times to comply fully with Polish law and regulations, including the measures promulgated recently for the defence of the country, such as anti-air, gas defense, and similar measures.

3. American citizens should study carefully all requirements of this nature with a view to being thoroughly familiar with them in case any emergency arises.

American embassy warning to US nationals, August 22, 1939. (Courtesy the American Jewish Historical Society)

Lucy Schildkret with Rivele Kalmanovitch, 1939. (Courtesy the
American Jewish Historical Society)

The outbreak of the war on September 1 wreaked havoc on Lucy's journey.
Since it was now impossible to sail from Poland, she traveled by train from
Vilna to Warsaw, through Germany via Berlin, and then north to Copen-
hagen, where she could board her ship home. In Berlin, she arrived at the
Schlesischer Bahnhof and encountered, as she would write decades later in
Commentary, "an endless sea of soldiers and Nazi flags, with the equipage of
war—cavalry, tanks, cannons—rising like heavy swells above the human tide."
Though in the Nazi capital "barely two hours" and possessing "my American
passport and bravado of youth," she was "frightened by the massive German
military presence."

The atmosphere was thick with swagger, bluster, and bullying. Despair tempered my rage against the Germans. One did not need to be a political expert to know that war was inevitable, or a military expert to know that Poland was no match for Germany.[83]

Lucy's trip home was fraught with foreboding. From the train's window, she could see people digging up the municipal parks in Warsaw in anticipation of mass funerals.[84] She shared her compartment with a German, an English-speaking gentleman sporting a swastika pin on his lapel; he was courteous and calm, even as he described Poland's alleged belligerence toward Germany. Lucy chose not to disclose her Jewish identity. Seeking refuge in her American legal nationality, she observed the disjunction between his civility and his triumphal sense of historical destiny. She later wrote that "It was like listening to a very polite lunatic."[85]

In Copenhagen, she reunited with Max Weinreich and his youngest son, Uriel, and made the acquaintance of the Davidsons, linguist colleagues of Weinreich who were YIVO activists, and the Jakobsons, Czech refugees. There they learned of the German invasion of Poland. Weinreich, on his way to the Fifth

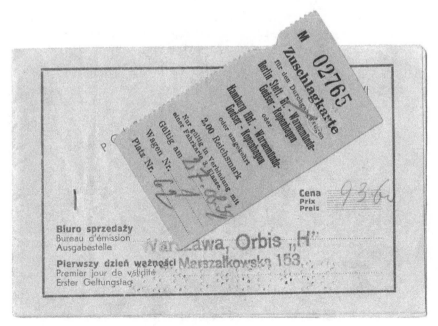

Train ticket from Vilna to Warsaw to Berlin and to Copenhagen, August 1939. (Courtesy the American Jewish Historical Society)

International Conference on Linguistics in Brussels, now could not return to Vilna. Everything was uncertain. In a letter to her parents, Lucy reported that her boat, the Pilsudski, was "stuck someplace in England. . . . God knows what will happen. Just expect a wire from me when I find out something."[86] Her letter expressed her fear of the Germans but also of the Soviets, who would "get there [to Vilna] instead of the Germans. And they're just as bad."[87] Several other letters followed, both to her parents and to the Konoffs, Evelyn's parents, who were helping to cover the costs of the passage home. They oscillate between newsy dispatches about spending time sightseeing in Copenhagen with Uriel Weinreich and concern for her friends in Vilna, for the YIVO, and specifically for Weinreich. "He can't get home, and I don't see what good he would do if he did. I'm trying to convince him to see what he can do about going to America. He may be able to do more for the Institute from there than here or in Wilno."[88] On September 6, Lucy wrote to her parents that she had received a postcard from Kalmanovitch, dated three days before the invasion of Poland, saying "that everyone was well and that they were hoping for peace. I cried like a baby when I read that."[89]

Lucy finally got a ticket on the SS *Donald McKay* for September 16, due to arrive in Boston two weeks later.[90] Three days into her cross-Atlantic journey,

Svatava Pirkova (Mrs. Roman Jakobson), Uriel (Elia) Weinreich, and Lucy Schildkret in Copenhagen, September 1939. (Courtesy the American Jewish Historical Society)

Luggage ticket for the SS *Donald McKay* from Copenhagen to New York, September 1939. (Courtesy the American Jewish Historical Society)

on September 19, her worst fears were realized: Vilna fell to the Red Army.[91] This event set into motion not only the end of autonomous Jewish life there but also the complex and combustible relationship between East European—in this case, Lithuanian—nationalism, Soviet domination, and the concomitant relationship of Jews to Marxism, both real and imagined. Soviet communism, shaped by an appeal to universalist Marxist theory, had no room—at least theoretically—for independent national cultures.[92] Polish Jews under Soviet rule would be caught between these two warring factions, sometimes creating alliances based on shared ideology but mostly forming ties to the ruling authorities for practical purposes. To be sure, in 1939, Soviet and Lithuanian rule was preferable to that of Nazi Germany.

Lucy's year in Vilna, begun with delightful curiosity, ended with the world she had grown to love perched at the precipice of catastrophe. In time she would find her role as the voice of Ashkenazic Jewish civilization and culture, from its medieval origins in German lands to its extermination in the mid-twentieth century in Eastern Europe. As she wrote in 1989 about the summer of 1943, when the horrifying news of the destruction of the Jews of Eastern Europe had become known to the YIVO community: "We were then still too close to the terrible events, too shocked by the immediate deaths and daily disasters, to realize *that we were mourning the destruction of the 1,000-year East European Jewish civilization.*"[93]

3

THE NEW YORK YIVO IN WARTIME

BACK IN THE UNITED STATES

In August 1940, having spent an unremarkable year living in New York City and in Albany, where she had landed a civil service job upon her return to the United States, Lucy Schildkret received a call that proved as fateful as her decision to go to Poland two years earlier. Weinreich had been able to make his way to New York from Copenhagen. Planning to transfer the YIVO's main activities to the Amopteyl, the American branch of the institution, he needed a secretary and wanted someone who offered continuity with the Vilna YIVO.[1] For the next six years, Weinreich and Lucy worked directly together on all of the YIVO's work, effecting a personal transnational tie with prewar Vilna. This role placed Lucy directly at the center of some of the earliest scholarly efforts on US soil to analyze the fate of the Jews under German occupation, inform the world of what had befallen them, and begin the process of historicizing what would later be called the *khurbn* by Yiddish-speaking Jews and the Holocaust by English speakers.[2] It also allowed her to continue working at the "Ministry of Yiddish" with its intense commitment to the Yiddish language, and with Weinreich, "the Master of Vilna."[3]

The Amopteyl leased the YIVO's first New York headquarters on Lafayette Street in Lower Manhattan in a building that was a far cry from the imposing modern edifice on Wiwulski Street in Vilna. The architecture and setting highlighted the precarious state in which the institute found itself. In the critical period of Lithuanian rule between October 1939 and June 1940, the YIVO's temporary administration in Vilna, composed of Kalmanovitch, with Weinreich contributing what he could from Copenhagen, remained ambivalent about formally transferring the institution to New York. For Weinreich, giving up Vilna as the YIVO's headquarters meant acknowledging that Eastern Europe could no longer be viewed as the center of the Ashkenazic diaspora. The YIVO activists in New York, however, asserted their scholarly agenda. In January 1940, they held a conference, sponsoring papers on American Jewry and its social history. Soon thereafter *YIVO bleter* (January–February 1940) appeared for the first time under the Amopteyl's auspices.[4] The institute also launched the bilingual newsletter *Yedies fun YIVO* (YIVO News, later renamed *News of the YIVO*) to document its growing activity in both Yiddish and English.

Weinreich came to New York with his son Uriel in mid-March 1940 on a fund-raising mission. Far from reconciled about being transplanted to New York and bolstered by Kalmanovitch's uncharacteristic optimism about the vibrancy of the YIVO under the Lithuanians, Weinreich planned to return to Vilna in the fall. World events intervened. In mid-June 1940, the Red Army reentered Vilna, and by the summer Lithuania had been annexed by the Soviet Union. Vilna—and the rest of Lithuania—experienced rapid Sovietization, and any vestige of the YIVO's autonomy was quickly annulled. Kalmanovitch's hatred for the Soviet regime was no secret, and the YIVO's leadership was quickly transferred to Marxists, including Moshe Lerer and Noah Pryłucki.[5] The staff at the Amopteyl was able to secure a visa to the United States for Kalmanovitch and his wife, Rivele, but, holding out to immigrate to Palestine to join their only child, Shalom, who had left Europe in the fall of 1938, they were caught in the maelstrom of the Nazi invasion. Kalmanovitch later perished in a labor camp in Estonia and Rivele in the pits of Ponar.[6]

In New York, Weinreich got to work with his customary tirelessness. One of his most important projects was completing an authoritative bibliography of the YIVO's publications from its beginnings in 1925 until 1941. The project, begun in 1939 to commemorate the YIVO's fifteenth anniversary by *aspirantn* in Lucy's cohort under the stewardship of Ber Schlossberg and Chana Piszczacer, remained incomplete.[7] Working again with Weinreich, Lucy continued the effort of her Vilna peers. Appearing in 1943, the *YIVO bibliografye* cataloged more than thirty thousand pages of academic material published in books, journals, and pamphlets. Weinreich's understated introduction to the volume underscored the transnational significance of the bond between the Vilna YIVO and the New York YIVO and Lucy's role in the endeavor:

> In New York, we started this project anew. Libe Shildkret from New York was also among the *aspirantn* in Vilna who participated in the work [and] . . . has been working in the New York Aspirantur since we renewed it here in 1940. Miss Shildkret recataloged the entire material according to the princi-ples that had been elaborated earlier and added the publications from 1940 and 1941; she also finished the complicated technical work of preparing the manuscript for offset. The fact that a young colleague from the YIVO pre-pared this work here and there (*do un dortn*) underscores for me the conti-nuity in the YIVO's entire enterprise.[8]

During the war years the YIVO became a site of continuity with secular East European Jewish scholarship in the United States. As Lucy noted in her memoir, the influx of Polish Jewish immigrants enriched Jewish scholar-ship in the United States with a distinctive European perspective for several decades.[9] The YIVO now boasted a significant cadre of scholars, including Jacob Shatzky, Raphael Mahler, Yudl Mark, Judah Joffee, Shmuel Niger, Israel Knox, Roman Jakobson, Jacob Lestchinsky, Abraham G. Duker, Nathan Reich, Rachel Wischnitzer-Bernstein, and Joseph Opatoshu, among numerous others working in New York City. Elias Tcherikower, the head of the YIVO's His-torical Section, and his wife, Riva, came from Paris in the summer of 1940. A year later, the Tcherikowers helped Szajke Frydman (later Zosa Szajkowski), a Polish Jew who worked as a journalist in the Parisian Yiddish press in the 1920s, come to New York. He quickly joined the Aspirantur under Weinreich's stewardship.[10] The YIVO also became a haven for a group of "political" Euro-pean Jews, Mensheviks and Bundists in danger from both the Nazi and Soviet regimes. Another stream of refugees, lucky recipients of emergency political visas secured through the efforts of Varian Fry, a volunteer for the Emergency Rescue Committee, and the intervention of the Jewish Labor Committee with Secretary of State Cordell Hull, arrived soon thereafter.[11] An estimated two thousand refugees entered the United States between 1940 and 1941, some with the aid of Chiune "Sempo" Sugihara, who helped ten thousand Jews leave Lithuania. These refugees, along with the Yiddish-speaking American staff of the Amopteyl, were acutely aware of the steady strangulation of Jewish life in Europe. They read the Yiddish press, filled with terrifying reports of the massacres of Jews gleaned from the underground press and from the Polish government-in-exile in London.[12] In 1939–41, America was still gripped by isolationism and a sense of distance from the European stage. At the New York YIVO the war was anything but far away.

Lucy was particularly worried by the situation facing her friends and loved ones in Poland, now occupied by the Germans and the Soviets. Daily contact with the recent refugees allowed her to experience both a sense of continuity with her prewar year and a feeling of doom about the future. The vulnerability of the YIVO's library and archive, of Vilna's Jews—especially the Kalmanovitches—and of Warsaw under the Nazis were the focus of her worry. Warsaw's Jews were the first to be ghettoized behind a prisonlike wall. The *YIVO bleter* of November–December 1940 featured an article on Warsaw, and Lucy was charged with drawing the ghetto's outline onto the city's map.[13]

She also honed her writing in *YIVO bleter*, contributing several articles in 1941, including "Anti-Nazi Literature" in its May–June issue.[14] At the YIVO's sixteenth conference on January 11, 1942, Shlomo Mendelsohn, a Bundist, journalist, and Jewish educator, read a paper on the horrifying condition of Warsaw's Jews under the Nazis.[15] He had become a main source of information about Warsaw's Jews through his contacts with the Bund and the Polish underground. By June 1942, definitive news of the systematic murder of Polish Jewry reached the West via reports by Shmuel A. Zygielbaum, a Polish-Jewish socialist who had arrived in New York that year on an emergency visa, and by Ignacy Schwartzbart, a Polish Zionist. Both men were members of the Polish government-in-exile in London.

Lucy would be increasingly obsessed with the dire condition faced by Warsaw Jewry as the war marched on. Sometime in 1942, she met Szymon Dawidowicz, a Bundist political refugee who had immigrated to the United States in 1940 on an emergency visa from Moscow and had come to work at the YIVO as a copy editor.[16] His wife and two children, Zarek and Tobtsche, remained behind in Warsaw, incarcerated and starving in the ghetto.[17]

As news poured in of European Jews caught in the path of the Wehrmacht and the Einsatzgruppen, protests were organized in New York, often held at Madison Square Garden. Lucy later described the atmosphere at the YIVO in late 1942 as a "protracted Yom Kippur, a time of fasting and mourning" for the Jews of Europe.[18] In the spring of the next year, the institute was on edge, having received news that the remaining Jews in Warsaw—roughly 55,000 out of a ghettoized population of 450,000—had readied themselves for armed

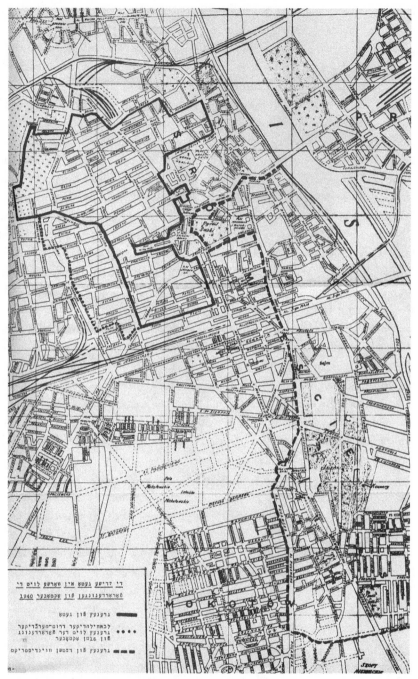

Map of the outline of the Warsaw Ghetto, drawn by Lucy Schildkret. *YIVO bleter* 16, no. 2 (1940): after p. 200. (Courtesy the YIVO Archives)

Szymon and Tobtsche Dawidowicz in Warsaw. (Courtesy Laurie Sapakoff)

resistance. By late April 1943, news of the Ghetto Uprising and of the Nazis' burning of the ghetto as retribution became public. The events had direly personal implications for the YIVO community. "The people I knew had lost children, wives, parents, their dearest friends," Lucy would write.[19] Szymon could only assume that his family had perished. He later learned that his daughter, Tobtsche, caught in the burning sewers of the ghetto, could not escape because of a twisted ankle.[20] In her memoir, Lucy would movingly—yet discreetly—describe her future husband's grief: "One friend mourned his daughter, a member of the resistance organization, who had died during the fighting. I went to pay a condolence call. . . . Other visitors were there. But he didn't speak to

Tobstche Dawidowicz and her mother, Rojzla (née Szczep-
kowska) Dawidowicz, in the Warsaw Ghetto. (Courtesy Laurie
Sapakoff)

anyone. He lay on his bed, his face turned to the wall. For three days, he didn't
eat, drink, or speak."[21]

In addition to her other YIVO duties, Lucy took on the role of managing editor of *Yedies*, becoming deeply involved with the effort to commemorate
the East European Jewish dead while researching their culture, language, and
history. *Yedies*'s February 1944 issue announced an exhibit of photographs of
interwar Warsaw Jewry by Roman Vishniac. The photographs, taken under
the auspices of the American Jewish Joint Distribution Committee from 1935
to 1938, depicted Polish Jewry as a community wracked with poverty and living on the edge of destruction.[22] That issue also reported that Shlomo Mendelsohn read a paper titled "Resistance in the Polish Ghettos," which "evoked

intense emotion among the listeners" and "upon the spontaneous request of someone in the audience, Kaddish [the Jewish prayer for the dead] was recited by Rabbi Leo Reichel."[23]

Though the term *khurbn forshung* (research on destruction) would not be coined until after the war, the New York YIVO had of necessity turned toward it to begin the process of documenting, analyzing, and publicizing the destruction of the European Jews. *Khurbn forshung's* historiographic mission included several goals: meeting a moral obligation to bear witness, amassing evidence that could be used in future trials, and writing history as an act of commemoration.[24] Yet, as Laura Jockusch notes, many of the survivors also saw themselves as "part of a distinct eastern European Jewish tradition of history writing as a response to catastrophe according to which documenting anti-Jewish violence and persecution equaled armed resistance in its significance and honorability."[25] *Khurbn forshung* aspired to the highest levels of academic rigor and objectivity even as it became enlisted in the efforts to secure justice for the murdered after the war.

The YIVO played a central role in presenting the Holocaust to the New York public in the war's bitter final year and immediate aftermath. Its many ties to Poland influenced the institution's core mission.[26] The September 1944 *Yedies* announced plans to publish Jacob Shatzky's history of the Jews of Warsaw "in connection with the tragic fate of Polish Jews in the present war."[27] It also gave the first inkling that some of the YIVO's rich repository of Yiddish and Jewish culture might have survived, reporting that Avrom Sutzkever, a poet, a YIVO activist, and a partisan who had survived in the Soviet Union with a group of the YIVO's personnel, had smuggled precious documents in and out of the ghetto.[28]

TROUBLE ON THE YIVO'S HOME FRONT

By 1943, Lucy's relationship with the YIVO had begun to sour. The reasons are not completely clear. In a letter to her sister, Eleanor, that March, she complained that she had gotten "fed up with them" and was seeking a position that would pay at least thirty-five dollars per week.[29] Yet letters from Zosa Szajkowski to Elias and Riva Tcherikower confirm that she remained at the YIVO through October 1945, though not very happily. In Szajke's view, the problem was that she had been turned into "a mere clerk." He commented further that "if she had spent any time on her doctoral thesis, she might have become an academic herself and wouldn't be leaving YIVO."[30] Szajke and Lucy were twins of a sort. Both had been *aspirantn*, Lucy in Vilna in 1938, Szajke in New York in 1941. Both were deeply enmeshed in the YIVO yet fiercely independent. Inducted into the US Army in January 1943, Szajke helped recover missing documents from the YIVO archive as well as records of the Nazi Propaganda Ministry, which he donated to the YIVO. Both he and Lucy were practicing historians who, because they never earned PhDs, were viewed by many as amateurs. They appear to have had a close if occasionally contentious friendship at the YIVO during the war. In his letters to the Tcherikowers and to Riva after Elias's premature death in 1943, Szajke mentions "Libe" numerous times, commenting on her moodiness, joking about her affection for hats and shoes, asking Riva to request that Libe send him pens, copies of articles, and other YIVO materials, and telling Riva to inform Libe that he saved some silk parachute material for both of them to make into scarves.[31] Hoping to complete a bibliography of Elias Tcherikower's work, he wrote to Riva that he wanted Lucy to be on the project. "I can't see another person who could do it."[32] Letters to Max Weinreich in July and October 1943 from Saul Reisen, Zalman's son—who with his father was arrested by the Soviets in 1940 but survived imprisonment and received amnesty granted to Polish citizens after the Nazis abrogated the Hitler-Stalin pact—also inquired after Libe and expressed regret that a letter she sent never arrived.[33] These letters attest to the impression the young Lucy made at the skeletal YIVO during the war years.

A major rupture occurred between Lucy and the YIVO, and specifically between Lucy and Weinreich, in the late spring of 1946, one that propelled her to consider working for the JDC in occupied Germany. There does not appear to have been one precipitating event.[34] In the summer of 1946, Leibush Lehrer wrote to Weinreich to tell him that Lucy had come up to Camp Boiberik specifically "to explain her behavior." He also chastised Weinreich for not giving him a full account of what had caused her to leave.[35] Weinreich wrote back a four-page explanatory letter, enumerating in sixteen bullet points his surprise that Lucy had gone to see Lehrer at Boiberik, his skepticism that she herself fully understood why she had left, and then his more specific appraisal of her work, detailing her shortcomings. Citing staff squabbles and clashes of ego, he noted that "she was an element of friction among the employees." "Libe has a tendency to be bossy," he commented, adding, "There isn't enough effort [on her part] to assess that the interests of the Institute demand that she control herself as much as possible." Ultimately, he told Lehrer that a combination of factors led him to decide that "Libe does not suit us" now but that

She has too many brilliant qualities [to disqualify her returning to the YIVO]. I have a feeling that after her sojourn in Europe, she may once again want to come to us, and we will be very interested in having her. If Libe had remained, we would have had to settle the problem. . . . But if she is away, it is as though a bridge had been washed out. One would rebuild the old bridge, [but] the new one [can be built] from scratch.[36]

In her memoir, Lucy claimed that Weinreich viewed her decision to leave the YIVO as a kind of apostasy, one that irrevocably changed their relationship.[37] Whatever the precise cause of the fissure, the impact they had on each other's lives—and on the transfer of Yiddish scholarship and the YIVO's institutional body to New York—was incalculable. Both remained bound by the profound awareness that the world of East European Jewry in which the YIVO had been born was utterly destroyed.[38] Many years later, Dina Abramowicz remarked to Dawidowicz, "Your collaboration with Weinreich proved to be extremely important to both of you—no wonder that your separation was rather painful to him. But you give him his due in your book—who better than you could see his genius and accomplishments!"[39] Dawidowicz would honor Weinreich in several of her future publications, including serving as an organizing member of the editorial board for his *Festschrift*.[40]

Having left the YIVO in the late spring of 1946, Lucy was without work and once again adrift. She had returned to Columbia University to take courses in history toward a master's degree, building on the research she had done on the Anglo-Yiddish press in Vilna in 1938–39. When she decided to return to Europe as an educational worker for the JDC, she approached Salo W. Baron, her Columbia adviser, for a letter of recommendation. Citing her qualifications, she noted, "What I think should be most emphasized is [my] knowledge of Jewish life, history, and literature, and of Yiddish and the ability to apply this knowledge to practical purposes: planning of courses, subjects to study, assistance in obtaining sources for cultural programs (theatricals, musicals, readings, etc.), and, of course, journalistic work."[41] Baron did not hesitate to recommend her.[42] She thanked him, and in a subsequent letter she expressed the hope that her departure did not mean the end of her formal studies. She also articulated her desire to switch her field from European to American Jewish history.[43]

Appointed as an educational officer of the JDC in July, Lucy sailed to Europe in September 1946, bound for France on the SS *Marine Perch*.[44] *Yedies* announced Lucy's new position in its September issue, reporting that "Miss Lucy Schildkret, secretary to the Research Director of the Yivo, is now

Lucy Schildkret's American Jewish Joint Distribution Committee employment letter, July 16, 1946. (Courtesy the American Jewish Historical Society)

in Europe as a member of the JDC staff in charge of cultural work among Jewish Displaced Persons in the United States occupied zones of Germany and Austria."[45] In anticipation of her arrival, Koppel Pinson, a historian from Queens College and a YIVO activist who was working for the JDC as the director of education and culture for the Jewish displaced persons, cabled Lucy with a last-minute request: "MOST PRESSING NEED NOW FOR TEXTS SECULAR SUBJECTS FOR LARGE NUMBER CHILDREN FROM POLAND STOP BRING THESE AND TOYS AND WRITING MATERIALS IN EXCESS BAGGAGE."[46]

Left: Lucy Schildkret, New York City, August 1946. (Courtesy Laurie Sapakoff)

Below: Lucy Schildkret's UNRRA passport. (Courtesy the American Jewish Historical Society)

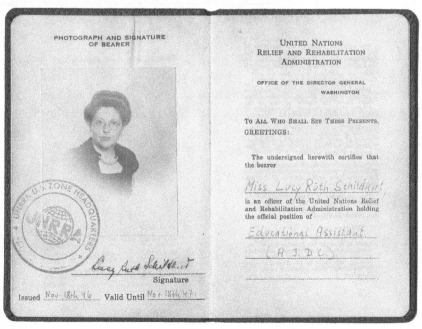

Lucy Schildkret and Szymon Dawidowicz, New York City, 1946. (Courtesy Laurie Sapakoff)

In her memoir, Dawidowicz telescoped the years 1943–46, emphasizing her struggle to reckon with the catastrophic nature of what had befallen European Jewry as a whole, East European Jewry in particular, and her beloved friends in Vilna individually. Restrained grief and expressed rage shaped chapter 12, "New York, 1944–1945: The Reckoning": "I couldn't stand to read about it [the Nazi campaign of mass murder], but I did. We all read the newspaper reports, but we never spoke about them. I was deafened by the silent screaming inside my head."[47] Returning to Europe in 1946, she would be confronted directly by the results of the war: the deafening silence of the complete absence of Polish Jewish civilization.

4

IN THE AMERICAN AND BRITISH ZONES OF OCCUPIED POSTWAR GERMANY

Arriving in Paris in September 1946, Lucy traveled first to Heidelberg, then to Frankfurt, where she met Dr. Joseph Schwartz, head of the JDC's European operations, and finally to Munich, the JDC's headquarters for the American zone. She was now on Hitler's home turf—"the land of Amalek," as she called it in her memoir.[1] Employed for fifteen months in postwar Germany—first in the American zone and then in the British—she worked with an international group of Jewish colleagues from the United States, Germany, Britain, and South Africa on behalf of Jewish DPs from all over Europe. Though she herself was still unknown, her position placed her among the major figures of the transnational, postwar Jewish intelligentsia, including Hannah Arendt, Salo Baron, Hugo Bergmann, Philip Friedman, Judah Magnes, Koppel Pinson, Cecil Roth, Gershom Scholem, Marie Syrkin, and Max Weinreich, all of whom were grappling with the fate of postwar European Jewry and its cultural legacy.[2] Working with the JDC also introduced Lucy to some of the first efforts to document the Holocaust. Her postwar European sojourn intensified her identification with Europe's vanished Jewish communities, while also revealing her distinctiveness as an American Jew of East European origin.

In the summer of 1945, the DPs created the Central Committee of the Liberated Jews of the American Zone in Germany. Under its auspices, a group of survivor historians—including Moshe J. Feigenbaum, Philip Friedman, Shmuel Glube, Israel Kaplan, and Levi Shalitan—established the Central Historical Commission (Centralna Żydowska Komisja Historyczna, or CŻKH) in November of that year.[3] They began collecting materials, including some of the first survivor testimonies documenting the destruction of European Jewry, as early as the summer of 1944.[4] Increasing political pressure by the Soviets on Poland compelled Friedman, hired by the JDC to head the Education Department, to move the CŻKH from Łódź to the American zone in 1946. In Munich, he became Lucy's supervisor, and the two worked closely together, if not always entirely amicably.

Friedman's responsibilities included designing educational programs for the DPs. Initially, Lucy's job was to procure supplies, including textbooks, paper, theater props, writing utensils, and curriculum materials, for the educational institutions in the American zone.[5] She was also charged with obtaining licenses for the Yiddish camp newspapers—a task that suited her linguistic background and research interests. Obstacles to publication were compounded by the paucity of printing facilities, chronic paper shortages, and bureaucratic snags. Moreover, there was only one set of Yiddish matrices (font sets) in Munich. Obtaining the Yiddish matrices gave Lucy direct contact with the first efforts on the part of survivors to publish documentary evidence of the tragedy that had befallen European Jewry.

In February 1946, Kaplan, Friedman, and Feigenbaum began preparation for a Yiddish-language historical journal, *Fun letstn khurbn: tsaytshrift far geshikhte fun yidishn lebn beysn natsi-rezhim* (From the Recent Destruction: Journal of Jewish History during the Nazi Regime). Viewing their newspapers as a communal repository of the experience of the Jewish masses during the Nazi era, Kaplan and Feigenbaum focused on the words and testimonies of the DPs, making them available to the transnational Yiddish-reading public now dispersed in Palestine, western Europe, the Americas, and the DP camps themselves. They produced ten issues, with a circulation eventually reaching eight thousand.[6] Getting the project off the ground proved challenging because of the lack of Hebrew font sets in Germany. In January 1947, the Central Historical Commission bought 150 kilograms of Hebrew characters, setting them in a German print shop. But it was not until Lucy succeeded in securing a Linotype machine from *Die Neue Zeitung*—the former publisher of the *Völkischer Beobachter*, the official Nazi Party paper—that the printing of *Fun letstn khurbn*

Lucy Schildkret in the uniform of the American Jewish Joint Distribution Committee in Munich in front of a poster of Der Dybuk, Teater Amcho, November–December 1946. (Courtesy the American Jewish Historical Society)

could proceed. Lucy recounted that the idea for getting the Linotype machine from *Die Neue Zeitung* came from Feigenbaum, but in pursuing it she had to work with (and to "work on," she wrote) Levi Shalitan,[7] Chaplain Abraham Klausner,[8] and Major Hans Wallenberg, a German Jew who edited the newspaper. Through wrangling and pressure, she succeeded in getting the mats for the Hebrew fonts and in training German linotypists to set the type.[9] In July 1947, she was able to obtain four more sets of Yiddish matrices for Linotype machines,[10] "the first sets of Yiddish Linotype matrices manufactured in Germany since before the deluge," she noted, giving most of the credit for the coup to Feigenbaum.[11]

Lucy remained impressed with Feigenbaum and *Fun letstn khurbn* and was eager to publish a small English book of excerpts from the journal's first four issues.[12] She discussed a similar publication with Weinreich, but the YIVO declined.[13] She noted to Henrietta K. Buchman, the executive assistant of the New York JDC, that she would "do the translations in her spare time and then scrounge for paper. Feigenbaum will get it printed."[14] Though the project never saw the light of day, her efforts eventually appeared in Leo W. Schwarz's *The Root and the Bough* (1949), one of the first English-language collections of survivor testimonies.[15] Other tasks that fell to Lucy included assisting in the selection of student scholarships for refugees funded through the B'nai Brith Hillel Foundation and the National Council of Jewish Women, a task she approached avidly, commenting that "each kid out is so much won."[16] The program, however, had mixed success, since it had a surfeit of applicants and lacked sufficient funds.[17]

As vital as these undertakings were, Lucy's most enduring role as an educational worker for the JDC would be the restitution of the remnants of the YIVO's library and archives—and other materials from Vilna—from the Offenbach Archival Depot (OAD) and their shipment to New York in June 1947.[18] Much more was at stake than merely ascertaining ownership of valuable books, religious objects, and art. Underlying the salvaging of the YIVO's library—like the restitution of all the plundered property of European Jewry— was the fundamental question of who should be the authoritative voice of "the Jewish people" in the aftermath of the catastrophe.[19] The care and settlement of postwar Jewish refugees and the restitution of Jewish cultural property raised pressing issues of postwar Jewish survival and communal reconstruction, issues that directly touched upon the essential question of modern Jewish existence that the Nazi assault had laid bare: If Jews were no longer secure in the European diaspora, where should the Jewish community look to its future—the United States or Palestine—and who should speak on their behalf? There had been no consensus on such questions among European, Palestinian, and American Jews before and during the war.[20] In the war's aftermath, intellectuals among these groups, some of them Holocaust survivors, debated these questions again, with renewed urgency.

The Nazis' plan to exterminate the Jewish community in Europe included a carefully orchestrated campaign to destroy Jewish culture. The Nazi theoretician and propagandist Alfred Rosenberg, a virulent antisemite, had been authorized by Hitler to study the so-called enemies of Nazism. In 1940, he established the Einsatzstab Reichsleiter Rosenberg (Reich Leader Rosenberg task force) to pillage European Judaica collections. By 1942, he had set up offices throughout Europe and proceeded to loot its cultural treasures. He spread his net to include 375 archives, 957 libraries, 531 research and educational institutes, and 402 museums in Eastern Europe alone.[21] Aiding Rosenberg was Dr. Johannes Pohl, an expert in Hebrew literature whose thievery benefited from his studies at the Hebrew University from 1934 to 1936. Pohl, who was dedicated to the concept of *Judenforschung ohne Juden*, "Jewish studies without Jews," oversaw the collection and shipment of Vilna's valuable Judaica to Rosenberg's Institut zur Erforschung der Judenfrage (Institute for Research on the Jewish Question) in Frankfurt.

Max Weinreich, who remained in close touch with the YIVO activists in Vilna for as long as possible, was acutely concerned about protecting the YIVO's property during the Soviet and Lithuanian occupations of the city in 1939 and 1940 and the subsequent German occupation in 1941.[22] In June 1942, Weinreich wrote to Green H. Hackworth, a legal adviser in the US State Department's Division of Cultural Relations, notifying the US government that the German occupying forces had "carried away everything from the building of the Yiddish Scientific Institute at 18 Wiwulski, Vilna," in anticipation of a future restitution at war's end.[23]

As Weinreich's secretary, Lucy had typed many of the memos and letters related to the efforts to secure those materials during the war, and she was privy to most of Weinreich's official efforts to restore the remnants of the YIVO's library to New York.[24] The first evidence that parts of the YIVO's library might still exist came on June 20, 1945, in a cable from Captain Abraham Aaroni, a YIVO activist, to his wife, Celia, reporting the discovery of part of the library. He noted excitedly that the find was more extensive than expected:

> It is not 200 boxes of books, from all over the world that I found, but about 1,000, which means a store of about 100,000 volumes, including, 1) איווא (YIVO) 2) Ecole Rabbinique in France 3) Rabbinical Seminary of Amsterdam 4) Jewish Student Organization of Königsberg University. 5) A number of modest private libraries. It would take a staff of about 20 men to assort all this, for besides books, I've found *sifrei torah* [Torah scrolls]. My primary job today is to try to convince Military Government authorities the importance of removing all this priceless treasure to a more appropriate place.[25]

A month later, General Lucius D. Clay, commander of US forces in Germany, informed the US War Department of the discovery of books with the YIVO's ex libris stamp. George W. Baker, an assistant chief in the State Department's Division of Economic Security Controls, responding to letters from Weinreich from June 28 and July 6, 1945, confirmed that two repositories of the YIVO's materials had been found, one in Frankfurt, the other in Hungen. He assured Weinreich that "Steps have been taken to insure [*sic*] the preservation and security of these collections and their eventual consolidation at one point where they can be sorted, arranged and made accessible for examination at a later date."[26] At roughly the same time, the acclaimed Yiddish poet Avrom Sutzkever had given manuscripts to Ella Winter, the writer and activist Lincoln Steffen's widow, in Moscow. Weinreich sent Lucy to the home of a Moscow correspondent of the *Herald Tribune* to retrieve the package. Unpacking it was an emotional experience; the book was a copy of volume 2 of the YIVO's *Studies in Psychology and Education,* edited by Leibush Lehrer in 1938 and sent to the Vilna YIVO. Only forty copies had been printed.[27]

As soon as Weinreich received news that the YIVO's library might be recoverable, he set out to assert the institute's claims. His letter to Green Hackworth at the State Department reflected his single-minded drive to get to the bottom of the issue of the YIVO's property. With formidable restraint, he asked: "Is the building of the Yiddish Scientific Institute in Vilna, at 18 Wiwulski Street, still intact, or has it been destroyed?" and "What has become of the tremendous library, archive and museum collections? Were they destroyed, or were they carried away by the Germans prior to their evacuation of the city?"[28]

Weinreich knew that the question of the restoration of Jewish cultural property would be a thorny one, compounded not only by the complex structure of the postwar German occupation and international law but also by competition among Jewish institutions in Europe, the United States, and Palestine to speak for the murdered Jews of Europe and to control what remained of their literary culture.[29] The issue was particularly fraught because not only did postwar Jewry have no legal standing in an international law founded on claims made by nation-states,[30] but also Polish Jewry, with 90 percent of its prewar population murdered, had almost no one to lay claim to its cultural heritage. The YIVO's claims to its books rested on identifying them as the institute's prewar property. It also needed to convince the American government that the Amopteyl was now the organization's only address.

Weinreich relentlessly pursued these two tactics from 1945 to 1947, enlisting everyone he knew in his effort to salvage the YIVO's library and archive and to bring it to New York. He approached, among others, John Walker, a special adviser to the Roberts Commission; Albert E. Clattenburg Jr., assistant chief of the State Department's Special War Problems Division; Archibald MacLeish, assistant secretary of state for public and cultural affairs; John Slawson, executive vice president of the American Jewish Committee; and Raymund L. Zwemer, acting chief of the State Department's Division of Cultural Cooperation. To Rabbi (Major) Judah Nadich, adviser on Jewish affairs to General

Dwight Eisenhower at Supreme Headquarters Allied Expeditionary Force, Weinreich expressed his worry that many of the YIVO's holdings—including works from his personal library—would be mistaken as "heirless," because the war had interrupted the cataloging process and many of the books lacked the YIVO's stamp: "I trust that you will be able to help us in this matter with true military speed."[31]

THE OFFENBACH ARCHIVAL DEPOT

Plundered Judaica fell directly under military jurisdiction and was brought to the Offenbach Archival Depot, a repository for printed materials—as opposed to works of art—pillaged by the Nazis.[32] Three million items in its storerooms were inventoried and identified between its opening in 1946 and its closing three years later. In mid-December 1945, Judge Simon Rifkind, American adviser to Jewish affairs for the US military, had approached General Clay to request loans from Offenbach to serve Jewish educational needs in the DP camps. Clay, concerned about books leaving the depot, insisted that accurate records be kept. Rifkind appointed Koppel Pinson to head a three-person commission to oversee the Judaica in Offenbach. In a cable to Leibush Lehrer that closed with "very urgent," Pinson contacted the YIVO in New York to serve as a liaison between the YIVO's books at the OAD and the loans to the DP camps.[33] Pinson worked with Rabbi Alexander Rosenberg, director of the Religious Section of the JDC, and Samuel Sar, dean of Yeshiva College and a representative of the Central Orthodox Committee in the DP camps. From January 1946, Pinson also worked with Seymour Pomrenze, the OAD's director from March to May 1946, sorting and cataloging the books.[34]

In March 1946, Weinreich authorized Pinson to be the YIVO's official representative at the OAD. On the question of which books Pinson could borrow for the DP camps, Weinreich reluctantly agreed to the loan of twenty thousand volumes. He was worried about the safety of the collection, observing that "Important as our library was even in prewar days, whatever has been salvaged has now become one of the great cultural monuments of the Jewish people."[35] Having been told by Pinson that Russian and Polish officers had removed materials during the absorption of Lithuania into the USSR in the summer of 1946, Weinreich also worried about Soviet designs on the collection.[36] Evidence that the YIVO's press archive had been found in Czechoslovakia added to the urgency.[37] In a July letter to Marcus Cohn, Washington representative of the AJC, Weinreich sought advice and made a claim on the "libraries [that] rightfully belong to this Institute [YIVO]." These included the collections of the Jewish Teachers Institute of Vilna, the S. Ansky Jewish Historical-Ethnographic Society of Vilna, and the Strashun Library. Also mentioned were the library and archives of Simon Dubnow and the personal papers of YIVO associates, among them Zalman Reisen, Shlomo Bastomski, Judah Leib Cahan, Moshe Lerer, Zelig Kalmanovitch, Alfred Landau, Pinchas Kon, and Weinreich himself.[38]

Lucy arrived at the OAD in February 1947 as the official representative of the JDC, exclusively authorized to draw books for distribution to the DPs.[39] Her first task was to identify "unidentifiable" or "heirless" books to be used in the DP schools to fulfill an original agreement signed between the Office of the Military Government of the United States and the JDC in January 1946 for the loan of twenty-five thousand books. Five thousand books still needed to be selected. She set to work, cataloging both stamped and unstamped books that she recognized as belonging to the YIVO, thus ensuring that they would not be considered "unidentified" or "heirless." The task was arduous but personally meaningful, often poignantly so; the books she pored through included ones she had used years before, as an *aspirant*. She wrote to Weinreich that she had found books with "inscriptions in Yiddish or Hebrew, a great many inscribed to Zalman Reisen and I assume that he gave them to Yivo."[40] She also found books with Weinreich's name and handwriting, including a second edition of his *Der veg tsu undzer yugnt* (The Way of Our Youth, 1940).

Despite her strained departure from the YIVO the preceding summer, she and Weinreich were now working in cahoots. On February 14, she cabled him: "AIRMAIL RUSH COPIES ALL PAPERS RELIBRARY [SIC] BETTER MORE THAN LESS STOP CHANCES FAIRLY GOOD TO GET ALSO STRASHUN WILL WRITE DETAILS LUCY SCHILDKRET."[41] He cabled back: "MANY THANKS FOR TELEGRAM DURING RECENT WEEKS WE HAVE BEEN VERY ACTIVE IN ASCERTAINING YIVO RIGHTS AND ARE HOPEFUL OF SUCCESS DETAILED LETTER FOLLOWS BEST REGARDS."[42] That same day, Weinreich wrote to Seymour Pomrenze, then employed at the Library of Congress and actively involved with the fate of the YIVO's library, maintaining that the YIVO should be regarded as the proper owner of the Strashun collection.[43]

Weinreich's letter on February 15, 1947, to Lucy emphasized the urgency of their task and informed her that the Commission for Cultural Reconstruction of European Jewry, Baron's organization, was getting in the way.[44] Weinreich had become increasingly frustrated that assurances made to the YIVO about treating its claims separately from Baron's commission and the general claims of cultural restitution were being ignored. He decided to press forward on his own.[45] He and Mark Uveeler, the YIVO's executive director, negotiated with the State Department to assert the YIVO's ownership and appealed to Pomrenze for help. Weinreich awaited more details from Lucy regarding the most efficient and cost-effective way to ensure the cataloging and transport of the books to New York. Lucy, meanwhile, had to negotiate with her superiors at the JDC to give her leave time or to consider her work at the OAD as part of her JDC responsibilities.[46] Weinreich cautioned her about assuming too quickly that she could undertake the cataloging and transporting of the YIVO's books on her own, yet he assured her that "the real thank you will come when our complete Vilna library will, with God's help, stand on the shelves in New York."[47]

Timing and personnel were not the only obstacles. Lucy had to win the confidence of Theodore Feder, deputy director of the JDC in the American zone, and Joseph Horne, the OAD's director in 1947–48, that accurate cataloging would ensure that books did not disappear and that books claimed by the YIVO actually belonged to the original Vilna collection.[48] An earlier loan of twenty thousand books to the JDC—under Koppel Pinson's watch—had been a disaster for the relationship among the JDC, the OAD, and OMGUS. On February 16, 1947, Lucy wrote a long and "highly confidential" memo to Weinreich, in which she detailed one of the primary obstacles to their work.[49] The main difficulty was that what "are considered the most important Hebrew and Yiddish manuscripts have disappeared from Offenbach." She named various suspects, including Chaplain Herbert Friedman, "in collusion with Professor Scholem from Palestine for the Hebrew University."[50] Apart from this missing material, she asserted with certainty—"there is no question in my mind"—that many of the twenty thousand books designated for the camps never got there. "There is a lot of talk about Pinson's having collected a private library for himself."[51] Horne affirmed Lucy's frustrations with the thefts that now obstructed her work at the OAD: "It is clear that she is distressed by the mess which her predecessor [Koppel Pinson] made of the whole affair, and it is believed that she sincerely desires to clear up whatever irregularities can be cleared up."[52]

Gershom Scholem, Koppel Pinson, and Chaplain Herbert Friedman were all implicated in the disappearance of five boxes—including eleven hundred manuscripts—from the OAD in December 1946, material that ultimately ended up at the Hebrew University in Jerusalem. Scholem had earlier been to Prague and carted off cultural property that he did not want sent to the American zone, where, in all probability, it would have been shipped to the Jewish Theological Seminary in New York City. He spent July 1946 working in the OAD, identifying which manuscripts were valuable. Chaplain Friedman went to the OAD in December 1946 and signed a receipt with Pinson's name for the five boxes of materials. They were trucked out by the JDC, brought to the Jewish Agency for Palestine in Paris, where they were falsely designated as Chaim Weizmann's personal library, and smuggled to Palestine.[53] A military investigation was conducted, and in May 1947 the American consulate in Jerusalem received a directive to return the manuscripts and to dismiss Bencowitz and Friedman. However, the stolen materials, amounting to 366 manuscripts, remained in Jerusalem. Scholem and Friedman later expressed pride in what they had accomplished.

The episode risked the Joint's reputation with the US government and the leadership of the OAD, and Lucy came to the depot under a cloud of suspicion. Richard Howard, chief for cultural restitution of the Monuments, Fine Arts, and Archives (MFA&A) Section of the Reparations and Restitution Branch of the Office of the Military Government in Germany, acknowledged that Lucy worked hard to clear the JDC's name.[54] She told him that it was common knowledge that Friedman, Rabbi Philip Bernstein, and Pinson had colluded in the heist and that Pinson was known to have between four thousand and five thousand books in his New York library that came from the OAD.[55]

Weinreich was particularly focused on the many "unidentifiable" books at the OAD that came from Vilna.[56] Because of the thefts, Horne and his superior, Major Lester Born, were reluctant to let any books leave the depot whose provenance had not been established, though they were aware that they lacked the expertise to assign ownership. Lucy assured Weinreich that she had convinced Horne of the latter's indispensability. Horne, she wrote, "thinks that he needs you more than you need him." She also informed Weinreich that no one from the Soviet Union had made a claim on the materials and that she had "helped" Horne see "that there is no hope for renewed Jewish cultural life in Poland. There may be a Jewish community there, but he feels that no one will ever make use of the material."[57]

Preoccupied with assuring that the Strashun Library's holdings—and those collections he considered part of the "Associated Libraries" category—be included in the YIVO's claim, Weinreich wrote to Pomrenze on February 17, 1947, and copied Lucy.[58] Detailing the history of the Strashun, he described its origins as a Talmudic library and its transformation into an institution devoted to all Jewish religious literary production. The Strashun and the YIVO, he asserted, were two realms of the same civilization—its religious and secular components—and for the fifteen years before the war had established an interlibrary exchange system. With the war's outbreak, he explained, a plan emerged to centralize all the Jewish libraries and books in Vilna, including the research section of the Society for the Spread of Enlightenment (Mefitsei haskoleh) and Weinreich's own collection of six thousand volumes. "No one had any doubt that the central place was to be Yivo." The Germans themselves considered the Strashun part of the YIVO, "and our own staff, headed by Z. Kalmanovitch, like a slave brigade, sorted and packed all these books for the Germans."[59] On February 26, after receiving a letter from Lucy urging him to come to Europe, Weinreich informed her that Pomrenze's intervention—along with her own work—would be sufficient. He felt assured that they had made clear the YIVO's claim on the Strashun materials. He informed her that the Strashun Library's books had already been in the YIVO building when the Germans removed them, calling the YIVO "the natural center" for a larger Jewish library to which the Strashun would belong.[60] The State Department ultimately agreed.[61]

On March 17, 1947, Lucy drafted a secret memo to Theodore Feder, stressing the importance of identifying the YIVO's books, completing the cataloging and distribution of the five thousand remaining volumes, and negotiating leave from her JDC responsibilities to work at the OAD.[62] She drafted another memo, this one non-secretive, in which she described herself as "the authorized agent to act for the AJDC at the Depot" and pledged to "protect myself and the AJDC from possible misuse of these books" by personally overseeing their allocation and distribution.[63] Lucy informed Feder that when she came upon the YIVO's books while sorting educational materials for the JDC, she had put them aside, fully cognizant of the improprieties of former colleagues. And— without naming names—she urged Feder to allow her to work on the YIVO's books to safeguard their integrity: "We are faced with a situation where the identification of a further part of the Yivo library is possible only if the AJDC assigns me to this work. If not, it means the loss to Yivo of possibly several thousand volumes."[64] Feder apparently did her a personal favor by allowing her to work on the YIVO's materials while still on the Joint's payroll. According to a letter she wrote to a JDC official in a semiofficial capacity, with "a large glass of good Offenbacher beer" on her desk, it wasn't a simple task to convince the JDC to allow her to work at the OAD or to convince the OAD people, under the jurisdiction of the United Nations Relief and Rehabilitation Administration (UNRRA), to allow the loan of five thousand additional books to the DP camps because of "some very serious discrepancies between the inventory and the actual property at hand."[65] It was critical to Lucy that her work for the

YIVO not be seen in personal terms. The recovery of the YIVO's library was historically significant, regardless of her own history with the institute:

I'm very stubborn when I think that something important is concerned. I don't think many things important, but this I do, as you can see by my readiness to stick to it even if I have to live on cigarettes. Of one thing at least you can be assured: that my presence in the Depot will not cast one iota of suspicion on [the] Joint or Jews for dishonesty or thievery or irresponsibility. My relations with the MFA&A are excellent and I intend that they remain that way.[66]

The work was tedious, as she related in a memo-like letter home. "I have the goddamnedest job. Sometimes I think I'm crazy to have undertaken it, but I guess it was the chance of a lifetime—for Yivo and not for me."[67] She described the drudgery of going through hundreds of cases filled with books, Talmuds, brochures, pamphlets, and other printed materials. Lucy quipped that she expected "to develop a permanent squint when I see a stamp (book stamp) or a signature" and "no doubt will get asthma, TB, and any number of respiratory diseases from the dust," but boasted that "I can now toss a hefty Talmud volume in the air and watch it somersault before I catch it again." She also made it clear that she did not like working with German personnel.[68] At the same time, she made good use of her connections to the black market—as well as of the solicitousness of some of the German staff—to buy handbags, suitcases, art prints, or anything else she and her Munich friends wanted.[69]

In May, Lucy drafted another memo to Feder, detailing her accomplishments and the obstacles she faced. The report's subhead, "Difficulties Encountered," revealed the distrust that OMGUS had for the Joint's work in the Offenbach Archival Depot.[70] OMGUS, she wrote, would not release the five thousand books "unless certain guarantees and reports were presented." Furthermore, it requested an exact accounting of the distribution of the books lent previously, expressing "dissatisfaction that some of the books had been sent into the British and French Zones and indicat[ing] a desire for the return of these books to the U.S. Zone."[71] Lucy had drawn up a catalog in March and April and copied the list, and the OAD staff had alphabetized it. German workers in the depot packed up the books. As she had requested, OMGUS granted her the authority to distribute the books directly. Dr. Philip Friedman, she wrote, had agreed to the distribution plan.[72] Her memo also affirmed OMGUS's agreement that she would sort out the YIVO books and be empowered to prepare them for restitution. Her original estimate of six to eight weeks to complete the work was too optimistic, and she informed Feder that completing the work would likely take three months. Indeed, in three months, Lucy cataloged 162,683 Yiddish and Hebrew volumes, identifying 32,894 of them. Of these, 75 percent belonged to the Strashun and to the YIVO.[73]

Though she had urged Weinreich to come to Europe, Seymour Pomrenze came instead. Weinreich understood that without the muscle, manpower, and money of the US government, the YIVO would likely not be able to afford to transport the collections to New York. Pomrenze, he reminded Lucy in a February letter, could get the trucks necessary to transport the YIVO's books from Offenbach to the port in Bremen.

And then there's the question of the costs to ship the books overseas. Pomrenze understands very well that he has to sit in Bremen until the ship with YIVO's property sets sail, but he thinks it will go easily. Do you think that you or I would be able to pull this off as quickly and easily?[74]

In May, Weinreich again wrote to Lucy, summarizing why Pomrenze was the right person to be on the ground in Offenbach.[75] At the same time, he confirmed with Pomrenze that his passport would be ready, explaining he was eager to inform Libe Shildkret, "who is now working on fishing out our property," of his arrival. He also assured Pomrenze that "Libe Shildkret wrote the letter in English because she didn't have a Yiddish typewriter, but know that she speaks and writes Yiddish just as I do." Last, he queried Pomrenze about the State Department's and the Library of Congress's mission in Prague.[76] Once it was clear that Pomrenze would oversee the transfer of the YIVO's property from Offenbach, and perhaps from Prague, he turned to Lucy about other issues, including German books, literature about Yiddish in other languages, and dictionaries from his own personal library, which were to be included in the catalog of the YIVO's possessions.[77]

On May 24, 1947, Lucy composed a draft memo to Horne—which she never sent—expressing her views on the relationship of the books at the OAD and the future of European Jewry. She wrote with characteristic bluntness. For Lucy, any effort to continue trying to locate the original owners of books now held at the OAD was, at best, a waste of time and resources and, at worst, a willful denial of the Nazis' successful destruction of European Jewry, its leadership, its institutions, and its communities. The view that European Jewry could not recover was shared by many other intellectuals and activists in the immediate postwar years. In May 1946, Jerome Michael, who headed the Jewish Restitution Commission's legal group and who would later work with Salo W. Baron and Jewish Cultural Reconstruction, Inc., had articulated the same opinion to Dr. Luther H. Evans, the Librarian of Congress. The books and other cultural items should be removed from Europe, he wrote, because, with the "annihilation of millions of European Jews, including most of their religious leaders, scholars and teachers, and [with] the dispersion of the survivors, Europe is no longer, and it is very unlikely that it can again become, a center of Jewish spiritual and cultural activity."[78]

Lucy held that the OAD should be closed because it lacked a staff knowledgeable in Jewish languages and the history of the Jews during the war. She illustrated this latter point by drawing attention to books belonging to various *Judenräte*, the Jewish councils established by the Nazis to control Jewish life in the ghettoes. The books, she explained, had belonged to persecuted Jews who, together with the ghetto leaders, were in all likelihood dead. Endeavoring to find their original owners was futile. Of the possibility of Jewish life being revived in the Soviet Union or Communist Poland, she was equally dismissive. In "both countries," she wrote, "the Jewish population was largely decimated and ... the revival of Jewish cultural institutions and the flourishing of Jewish culture are problematic."[79] Throughout her life, Lucy would remain unwavering in her negative assessment of the possibility of any form of independent or autonomous Jewish existence under communism.[80]

Similarly, postwar Germany was no place for Jewish books. She expressed her opinion in moral terms: "It is the conviction of the undersigned that no German institution as, for example, the Stadt- und Universitätsbibliotek at Frankfurt has any moral or practical right to any Judaica, even though such books may bear the stamp of German institutions."[81] The day before, she had made the same point to Dr. Werner Peiser in the JDC's Restitution Department, arguing that German institutions had disqualified themselves because "they have forfeited the moral right to their ownership and [that] they cannot show either competent personnel to care for these books or readers and/or scholars to make use of the books."[82] Though she acknowledged that there were Jews living in German lands, she essentially rejected any possibility of the renewal in the near future of Jewish communal life.[83] Lucy knew that when she departed, the OAD would lack staff members literate in Hebrew or Yiddish, and she therefore recommended that the cataloging work cease and that the remaining "heirless" books be restored to one central place, where they could be used by what she regarded as a viable Jewish community. To Weinreich, she wrote that "*once the Yivo library is out of the Depot* the problem is not who will identify what and what categories to make and what catalogues to make etc. etc., but to get all the books shipped out on the basis of a principle to be established by the State Department together with competent Jewish representation."[84]

Having cataloged the books known to have been part of the YIVO's prewar collection—and overseen the inclusion of many other of libraries from Vilna in the shipment—Lucy felt that her work was done. Relating to Weinreich that she planned to leave the OAD once the YIVO's affairs were discharged, she wrote: "I am sick and tired of the work. It is deadly boring and physically tiring. I would like to get back to some dynamic work."[85] But she was at the OAD on June 15, 1947, when Seymour Pomrenze returned to oversee the shipment of the YIVO's library. Two days later, the books were loaded onto the freight trains destined first for Bremen and then for New York City, and writing to Weinreich, she noted excitedly that "the big day has come." Informing him that 420 cases were loaded, she commented, "Everything worked out beautifully," adding that "The Depot iz gegangen oif redlekh"[86] (going like gangbusters).[87]

On June 21, 1947, Pomrenze wrote to Weinreich and Uveeler, informing them of his successful mission at Offenbach: the books had been loaded on the SS *Pioneer Cove* and were set to arrive in New York on July 1, 1947.[88] When the books landed safely in New York, Weinreich wrote to Lucy, acknowledging her efforts and urging discretion in publicizing the transfer of the property. He still harbored hope that Pomrenze would be able to secure restitution of the YIVO's press archives that had been found in Czechoslovakia, and he also wanted to conduct a fund-raising event using the restitution of the books as part of its appeal.[89] "Thank you very much for your collaboration with the whole matter," he wrote:

> If you wish, and with good reason, to grab a drink in honor of the occasion, you can imagine that we would like to be able to shout about this from every rooftop. Regrettably, we must restrain ourselves in the meantime. . . . We need to be quiet and see to it that as few people as possible know about this fact,[90] which in fact [is not merely a] YIVO affair, but a great general Jewish symbol. Anyway, sooner or later, the world will be made aware of this. You should be satisfied that you had a part (earlier here and afterwards there) in creating that symbol.[91]

Weinreich added a personal request: the recovery of a copy of his dissertation, completed at the University of Marburg in 1923, "Studien zur Geschichte

Opening crates at the YIVO with salvaged treasures from Vilna from the Offenbach Archival Depot, July 1947. Koppel Pinson, Mendel Elkin, Seymour Pomrenze, Mark J. Uveeler, Mark Zborowski, Max Weinreich, H. Abramson, and a YIVO assistant. Photograph by Alexander Archer. (Courtesy the YIVO Archives)

und dialektischen Gliederung der jiddischen Sprache" (Studies in the History and Dialect Distribution of the Yiddish Language).[92] His own copy had been lost.[93] He closed the letter with an acknowledgment of Lucy's role in the recovery of the YIVO's library: "Let us once more devote a mazel tov to the great thing that we have achieved. In connection with it we have mentioned your name many times."[94]

Weinreich's hesitation to publicize the transfer of the YIVO's library was also because materials from Vilna not originally part of the YIVO's original holdings were included in the cargo shipped to New York. A year earlier, he had written to Pomrenze about the uncataloged, unstamped materials from European Judaica collections that he felt should be included in the YIVO's claim.[95] It is clear that both Lucy and Weinreich shared the conviction that valuable European Judaica—particularly Polish-Jewish materials—belonged in the American Jewish diaspora, whether or not its provenance could be strictly linked to the YIVO. Acting on this conviction, however, required tactical discretion, and on her last day at the OAD, Lucy urged Weinreich:

REMEMBER you can have only such people whom you trust implicitly to look the stuff over. This is extremely important for everyone concerned. Another thing: something in the receipt stipulates that Yivo might have to submit a list of all materials [so] if you start unpacking anything before Pom.[renze] gets back, know what your'e [sic] doing. Also get a couple of stamps made and start stamping. Enclosed copies of Yivo ex libris which Bencowitz had made up during his time.[96]

With time, Weinreich did tell the story of the salvaging of the YIVO's property from the OAD—known colloquially as "Operation Offenbach"—but he, and others, downplayed Lucy's role in the transfer of the YIVO's cultural treasures. In August 1947 Weinreich wrote personal letters to all who had helped to recover "part of YIVO's library" but made no reference to Lucy's efforts.[97] Pomrenze made no mention of Lucy in his Yiddish article, "'Operation Offenbach': Saving Jewish Cultural Treasures in Germany," nor did Leslie I. Poste, an American MFA&A librarian who worked for fifty months in the American zone. In 1951 Lucy was briefly noted in a column on the library in *Yedies*.[98] In Philip Friedman's 1957 article, "The Fate of the Jewish Book during the Nazi Era," he failed to mention Lucy's role in cataloging and salvaging the YIVO's collection, though he showcased the work of Jewish Cultural Reconstruction, Inc., which took over after 1949.[99] Likewise, when on April 24, 1960, *The Eternal Light*, the radio broadcast produced by the Jewish Theological Seminary of America, aired "The Golden Chain," a program about the recovery of the YIVO's archive, Lucy Schildkret's role remained unmentioned. Weinreich had overseen the script's accuracy and insisted that Seymour Pomrenze's name be inserted in the drama.[100]

And so for several years no one at the YIVO recognized Lucy's indispensable role in cataloging the Vilna materials, leaving her work—with all its fastidiousness and tedium—as a thankless task. Her strong personality, evidenced in the conflicts with Pinson and Friedman, and gender—combined with Weinreich and key figures in the US government deeming it unwise to publicize the role that the American authorities had played in transferring the YIVO's material—rendered her contributions almost invisible. Dawidowicz's full role only came to light when she published her memoir in 1989.

In this slighting, she wasn't alone. There were many other female employees of the JDC, among them Rae Blitstein, Lillian Cantor, Edna Goldman, Anna Kalmanowitz, Vida Kaufman, Rose Shepatin, Ruth Stein, and Celia Weinberg, whose work in the postwar years has been little noticed. As Laura Jockusch has

Lucy Schildkret, Gaby Sklarz, Dr. Hudie Goldstein, and the local staff of the Frankfurt office of the American Jewish Joint Distribution Committee. (Courtesy Laurie Sapakoff)

noted, the efforts of dozens of women active in the postwar historical commissions have also gone largely unrecorded.[101] Only recently has Hannah Arendt's work with Jewish Cultural Reconstruction, Inc., in the postwar years been recognized.[102] Similarly overlooked is the indispensable role played by women, including Ardelia Ripley Hall, Rose Valland, Anne Olivier Popham Bell, and Edith Standen, in salvaging European art during and after the war.[103]

Lucy's own sense of the importance of her work is evidenced in her memoir, written over forty years later. She ended *From That Place and Time* with the efforts to salvage the books in the depot. Their restitution, she wrote, was a form of expiation for her guilt at abandoning her Vilna friends in 1939.[104] Despite the boredom of the cataloging, Lucy's work in the OAD had empowered her, both personally and professionally. In a long letter written from her next JDC post in the British Zone of Occupation to Leo W. Schwarz, former director of the JDC in the American zone, Lucy added a postscript that affirmed her view that the books' "home"—where they belonged in the postwar years—was in New York City. She expressed pride in her role in having made that a reality: "A wonderful operation," she wrote, "and much more satisfying than anything else

I have done here."[105] It was an operation of lasting consequences. Lucy's efforts helped to establish the YIVO as a distinguished American Jewish research institution and the New York City YIVO as a critical institutional link to the East European Jewish past.

IN THE BRITISH ZONE

After leaving the Offenbach Archival Depot in June, Lucy had half a year outstanding on her American Jewish Joint Distribution Committee contract.[106] Though the staff at the OAD would have been eager for her to continue cataloging the depot's other holdings, she wanted to move on.[107] Letters home expressed dissatisfaction with her work for the Joint, and in Munich she had what she described as "stiff fights," making it clear that she planned to resign after finishing her work at the OAD. But during a trip to Paris in June when transporting a group of refugees, Lucy was offered a transfer to the Belsen DP camp in the British zone, where she had paid a professional visit already on April 29–May 4, 1947.[108] She accepted the transfer, even though leaving her friends from Munich and Frankfurt left her feeling, as she wrote to Jacob Joslow, "exiled."[109] Joslow responded sympathetically. He was "sorry to read that you consider your assignment in Belsen as a 'transfer to Siberia.' I am sure that the work in Belsen is just as vital as anywhere else and I know that once you sink your teeth into the problems you will feel a lot better."[110]

Because Lucy constructed *From That Place and Time*'s narrative on her relationship to Vilna, to Yiddish secular culture, and to the YIVO, the British zone phase of her work in occupied Germany barely appeared in the book.[111] But, in fact, the time spent with DPs under British rule proved as momentous as the year before and deeply shaped her future. In Belsen, she encountered the Zionist activism of Jewish DPs; the British obstruction of Jewish emigration to Palestine, highlighted by the international debacle over the *Exodus 1947* refugee ship; and the United Nations' announcement of the vote to partition Palestine. During this time she formed a lifelong friendship with Pearl Ketcher, a British doctor working for the JDC, who later immigrated to Israel. Pearl's apartment in Jerusalem became Dawidowicz's symbolic home in the Jewish state.[112] Many other friends from the Belsen period, including DPs themselves, would write to Lucy years later, after she had become a well-known historian, and express warm recollections and gratitude for her work. Israel Kaplan, a member of the Central Historical Commission, wrote to her on February 27, 1966, gushing in

Yiddish, "Dear and Important Libe-Lucy," thanking her for the attention she bestowed upon him during a recent visit to New York, and sending her regards from Moshe Feigenbaum.[113]

The Belsen DP camp—the largest in the British zone—was officially named Hohne, but all of the survivors, camp administrators, and Jewish communal activists called it Belsen. It was situated next to the notorious Bergen-Belsen concentration camp, which had been liberated on April 15, 1945. At liberation, there were sixty thousand inmates, many of whom were dying from chronic illnesses and starvation. The camp was burned to the ground shortly after the Allies entered to prevent the further spread of an already epidemic typhus, and by May 21, 1945, there were only twenty-seven thousand surviving souls. Very quickly, Jewish survivors, notably Joseph Rosensaft (referred to by most as "Yosele"), who had been interned in Auschwitz, organized a committee to be the representative voice of the Jews in the camp. It later developed into the forceful Central Committee of Liberated Jews in the British zone. Almost immediately, tensions erupted between the committee and British authorities. The main issue of contention was the British policy that refused to recognize the Jews as a distinct nationality. Effectively, this meant that the original population in Belsen, which included Jews and other national groups such as Poles and Ukrainians—some of whom had participated actively in the Final Solution—was forced to live together in close proximity.

The British position was shaped primarily by the fraught political reality of Palestine, with its tinderbox of Jewish and Arab claims. Yet, British attitudes also reflected a lurking antisemitism, one that was often expressed disingenuously—as when British officials argued that all-Jewish camps would amount to a continuation of Nazi racial policy.[114] International Jewish welfare organizations such as the JDC, the Hebrew Immigrant Aid Society, and ORT (Obschestvo Remeslenova i Zemledelcheskovo Truda, or the Society for Trades and Agricultural Labor) had to work around the British authorities, and tensions remained a constant feature. Food rations supplied by the British for the DPs were inadequate, forcing the Joint to augment them.[115] Lucy herself noted that the "Joint sends in more rations because of the low supply from the British, and doctors its figures so people get more food and amenities."[116] Her coworker Sadie Sender wrote to Joslow in the JDC's New York office: "None of the Jewish people here in Germany, as you know, can live on the Unrra [UNRRA] or German rations, and the Joint supplementary supplies do not add many calories to the daily diet of these people."[117] As late as the spring of 1948, complaints from Belsen to the Munich office of the JDC registered that educational supplies, including books, had still not arrived.[118]

The British Jewish Relief Unit (JRU) ended up shouldering more of the welfare, health, and educational burden than the American Jewish organizations.[119] Still, in Belsen the JDC provided textbooks and supplies for schools and equipment for vocational training courses conducted by ORT, including dressmaking, automobile repair, and maritime training. It also provided moral and emotional support to the Jewish DPs. It maintained an orphanage in Blankenese on the site of the former estate of Max Warburg. The JDC actively supported Yiddish culture, including the Belsen publication *Undzer shtime* (Our Voice), and in 1947 subsidized the tour of Yiddish actor Herman Yablakoff. It established a library, imported religious items, and provided health care. Dr. Fritz Spanier, a Dutch-born physician interned during the war in the camp at Westerbork, where he worked as the chief medical officer, later headed up the JDC medical operations in Belsen. With the help of the JRU, DP physicians and nurses, and German personnel, Spanier—with Pearl Ketcher as his assistant medical director—oversaw work at the Glyn Hughes Hospital, in the dental clinics, and at Blankenese.[120] The JDC also supported the convalescent home at Bad Harzburg.[121]

Lucy arrived in Belsen on July 21, 1947, the start date of the second congress of the Central Committee of Liberated Jews.[122] Held in Bad Reichenhall, the congress called for an immediate loosening of emigration policies. Unmoved at this point in her life by the Zionist cause, Lucy commented little on the proceedings. She found them "boring" but reported to Szymon that she had met some interesting people among the welfare workers and journalists in attendance, as well as many stateless Jews and DPs. Her letters focused on her daily tasks and on the vexing issues of the black market and the "infiltrees." The "infiltrees" were refugees—predominantly Jewish—from Eastern Europe, many of whom had survived the war on Soviet soil or had fled postwar Poland in the aftermath of anti-Jewish violence, notably the notorious Kielce pogrom of 1946.[123] The influx strained both the American and British Zones of Occupation but was especially galling to the British, who knew that some of these individuals' movement into Germany was aided by the Brichah movement, which was abetting illegal immigration to Palestine. The British and UNRRA did not consider the "infiltrees" official DPs, since they were not direct victims of Nazi brutality, and their presence swelled the population of the DP camps and taxed resources, particularly rations, which were already lower in the British zone. Belsen's population increased to eleven thousand by August 1946, and the Central Committee simply divided up the existing rations to accommodate the larger numbers, knowing that the Jewish welfare agencies would spirit more food into the camp.[124]

Lucy's work in Belsen continued her educational efforts in the American zone. She secured educational materials, created recreational and cultural programs, and improved the reporting system for supplies.[125] In a chatty letter to Szymon she expressed optimism about the work and the personalities in the British zone and noted the importance of the Joint's efforts given the tensions between the British and the Central Committee. Many of the books that arrived in Belsen from Munich had been printed under Lucy's earlier watch. She also secured "ink, crayons, drawing pads, paint sets, etc. all of which are greeted with shrieks when delivered to [the] Central Committee."[126] Her letter also mentioned delivering religious items, culling through unwanted materials that could be converted into paper for a literary magazine, and referring "welfare cases," such as an illegitimate baby or a sixteen-year-old stutterer who needed care, to the JRU.

Her work also meant visiting and working in Celle and Lübeck and other DP camps in the British zone. She took responsibility for wresting 230 kilograms of flour impounded by the Germans and buying toys and sports equipment for the DPs, as well as overseeing the completion of a paint job in a school. In her letters, she made light of the work she was doing, at one point claiming that "people around here get the idea that I work hard, but I really don't."[127] In her typical nonplussed fashion, she also described the visit of the United Nations Special Committee on Palestine to the British zone in early August, the day designated for official emigration. Impatient with the proceedings, she wrote, "Finally, Yosel[e Rosensaft] made a speech, everyone sang Hatikvah; the correspondents had a field day and everyone was satisfied." As an aside, she noted that she had tried to "get someone in the Cultural Committee to collect the life-histories of concentration-camp experiences," but conceded that it would be impossible to do without more supplies and personnel.[128] Her letters also shed light on the underbelly of DP daily life: fraternization between Jews and Germans, incidences of rape, and retributive justice.[129]

While serving the day-to-day educational needs of the DPs had its share of drama and pathos, nothing compared with the epochal events surrounding the debarkation of the refugees from the *Exodus 1947*. In the summer of 1947, the *Exodus 1947*, formerly the *President Garfield*, an old American warship refurbished by the Haganah, sailed from France to Palestine with forty-five hundred

The Dramatic Club in Belsen, August 1947. (Courtesy Laurie Sapakoff)

Jewish refugees, all of whom were DPs or Holocaust survivors. The British authorities, determined not to allow the ship to disembark its passengers in Tel Aviv, sent ships to trail the *Exodus 1947* and discourage its entry into Palestinian waters. A terrific battle ensued, with three passengers killed and ten injured, and the refugees were ultimately forced onto three British navy cargo ships near the port of Haifa and sent back to France. However, in Port de Bouc, they refused to disembark, and the French rejected the use of force to make them do so. After a stalemate in which the passengers engaged in a hunger strike, the ships set sail for Germany, where they found port in Hamburg, under British rule. The bitter irony of sending survivors back to Germany enraged international opinion and captivated the press. Lucy's letters home describe these events as they unfolded and affected her life as a JDC worker; they also illustrate how little moved she was at this point in her life by the Zionist cause.

The Jewish welfare agencies in the British Zone of Occupation were well aware of the events surrounding the *Exodus 1947* and were quickly pressed into service, caught amid the general human drama and the particular tensions among the British authorities, the Central Committee, and the DPs themselves. Lucy found herself right in the middle of the turmoil. On September 7, she was dispatched with other JDC workers to Hamburg to deal with the refugees. She related to Szymon that the three ships presented "quite a problem" and that "we expected a lot of trouble at the port."[130] She considered all of the Zionist drama a pain, complaining that "all leave has been cancelled and my sumptuous plans for Brussels and Amsterdam during the holidays have been shot to hell." On September 8, at 1:00 a.m., she wrote a cryptic note to Szymon:

> Rode to Hamburg in an open jeep with Pearl and Egon Fink, supply director. Exodus, arrived in Hamburg at around 10; the whole evening was quite fantastic; dozens of reporters descending on us and asking for information (saw the AJDC flashes) and we're not talking. Moishe [Maurice] Pearlman[131] and [Marc] Jarblum[132] sitting in the bar, Phoning Bremen, phoning Belsen, drinking Cognac. The ships are outside Hamburg. One ship is to be debarked at 6 a.m. No reporters until after 7 a.m.... The atmosphere is hysterical... tense.... I don't know exactly what I'll do but will try to drop you a line.

Continuing the next day, at 12:30 a.m., she referred once again to the hectic nature of the scene, calling it "difficult to describe"—"the changing reports, the phone calls, the press reports, the meetings—someday when we have all the time we want I'll tell you everything—of chasing back and forth, of typing 50 copies of a clandestine leaflet, of spies and provocateurs."[133]

Lucy's letter to Szymon confirmed the JDC's support for the *Exodus* refugees, nicknamed "Operation Cultural Oasis," playing on the British name "Operation Oasis" for the operation to prevent the ship from docking in Haifa. The Joint had already provided food to the refugees when the boats were anchored off the coast of France and docked in Hamburg. Finally, on September 13, after negotiating with the British, the passengers left the ships—some putting up a struggle—and entered two DP camps, Am Stau and Poppendorf. Provisions, religious items, toiletries, and Hebrew and Yiddish books were all supplied by the Joint. A Jewish medical team with doctors from both the JDC and the JRU and nurses from the Jewish Agency for Palestine treated the infirm. The JDC also sent clothing to the *Exodus* passengers, emptying its warehouses and asking for supplies from the American zone.[134] On September 12, 1947, Lucy wrote to Szymon: "Just completed Operation Cultural Oasis, to spite the British.... I had to get notebooks, pencils (for letter-writing—a big problem, as you can understand), newspapers, books, machzorim [High Holiday prayer books] and siddurim [prayer books] for the holidays, etc." She described filling up an ambulance with stuff that she had sorted in Poppendorf and Am Stau, working "like a horse," and complained about the lack of cigarettes. Despite the constant demands on her time, she noted to Szymon how beautiful the German

Top: Dr. Kuzlowski, Dr. Pearl Ketcher, and the medical staff in the Poppendorf DP camp, the British Zone of Occupation. (Courtesy the Ghetto Fighters' House Museum, Israel / Photo Archive)
Bottom: Dr. Pearl Ketcher and Lucy Schildkret, 1947. (Courtesy Laurie Sapakoff)

countryside was and her hope that she would be able to enjoy a few days of vacation with Pearl Ketcher in Bad Harzburg.[135]

Between September and early December 1947, few letters are extant, but the ones that are reveal that Lucy was ready to come home. Intimacies expressed to Szymon speak of her impatience to see him again. On September 12, she wrote, "You have no idea how I loved your letter. I read it so far about three or four times and when I read your letters I can see you so well and hear you talk. . . . Szymon, I'm so sure that we'll be happy. I want so much to do things for you and to have you worry about me; I want you to give me money and tell me what to do, but I want to buy ties for you and pick your suits and see that you eat what is good for you."[136] She then asked him about a book he was working on with Avrom Sutzkever but then shifted her tone: "Don't write too much about it; I would rather you tell me that you love me and that you know how much I love you. Darling Szymele, I don't think there is a living minute that passes that I don't think about you."[137] By the early winter of 1947, with her contract almost up, Lucy was ready to return to New York. On December 8, aboard the SS *Matchless*, sailing from Bremen to Boston, she wrote to Szymon, taking stock of the friendships she had made and describing the big goodbye party her coworkers, including Pearl, Fritz Spanier, and Yosele Rosensaft, had thrown for her ("Dinner was very good. Liquor before, liquor afterwards.").[138] On December 17, the ship docked in Norfolk, Virginia. Three weeks later, Szymon and Lucy were wed, and Lucy Schildkret became Lucy S. Dawidowicz, a married American woman with a refugee husband and a Polish last name.

The fifteen months in postwar Europe had affected her deeply. Along with her heroic labors in salvaging the YIVO's library and archive, her work in the DP camps and personal relationships in those years also shaped her postwar commitments. While her prewar year in Vilna had affirmed the glory of East European Jewish civilization, Lucy's postwar sojourn strengthened her commitment to the Jewish people as a whole, beyond Europe, beyond Ashkenaz, and now to include the United States, the Soviet Union, and Palestine/Israel. Decades later, in 1984, addressing the second International Conference on Children of Holocaust Survivors held in New York City, Lucy gave a talk, "American Jews and the Sheerith ha-Pleta" about the work of Jewish welfare agencies among survivors in the DP camps and the impressions it made on her.[139] Though her letters home at the time had mostly spoken of the quantity of cigarettes in the army PX, the inanity of her coworkers, and the ineptitude of the various bureaucracies with which she worked, forty years later Dawidowicz expressed the enduring influence of the period. "In 1946, before most of you were born," she told her audience, "I quit my job with a Jewish research organization and went to work for the JDC in occupied Germany."

> I was one of the thousands of American Jews who were there, working for the Army, for UNRRA, or for the JDC. Let me tell you something about us. Many among us didn't know any Yiddish and couldn't readily communicate with the *Sheerith ha-Pleta*. Even fewer were familiar with the liturgy of Judaism, the facts of Jewish history, or the politics of Zionism. In such respects, many of us were a sorry lot. The *Sheerith ha-Pleta* made fun of us, when

they didn't resent us. Why were we there? Even if there were those among us [who] didn't know the letters of the Hebrew alphabet, nonetheless all of us wanted to play a role, no matter how small, in this great drama of Jewish history of our lifetime. Being there in Germany among the *Sheerith ha-Pleta* was our way of claiming a stake in those great events of our people. It was our way of bearing witness to the terrible past. It was our way of expressing our solidarity with *klal yisroel* and demonstrating our fraternal love for Jews everywhere in the world.[140]

Her retrospective assessment of her work for the JDC notwithstanding, at the time of her departure from Europe, Lucy was still unsure of her professional path. In August 1947, when she was still in Belsen, Max Weinreich wrote a "direct" letter to her, engaging the subject of her returning to work for the YIVO once she was back in New York. Informing Lucy that he would like very much for her to return to the YIVO, Weinreich professed concern over her relationships with coworkers. Money, of course, was also a concern. The letter hedged on making her an offer.[141] Meanwhile, Weinreich discussed the possibility of Lucy's return to the YIVO with Leibush Lehrer, who cautioned against it, warning that Lucy's strong personality would be an obstacle to cordial and productive relationships with her coworkers, particularly with Mark Uveeler but also with Hene Bercovich, the assistant to the director. Lehrer bluntly put it to Weinreich that despite her changed personal status, Lucy's return to the YIVO would lead to internal difficulties: "That Libe has become a Dawidowicz does not interest me at all. I believe that the difficulty lies in Libe and not in Mrs. Dawidowicz."[142]

Back in New York City, Lucy had to get a job quickly. Szymon's position as a copy editor at the YIVO was not sufficient to support them. Hanging over her head, too, was her incomplete master's degree at Columbia and her ambivalent feelings toward Weinreich. By April 1948, she was on her feet, at least temporarily, working for the American journalist and novelist John Hersey, aiding him with research for *The Wall*, a fictional account of the Warsaw Ghetto Uprising.[143] Hersey had been stationed in Moscow during the war and traveled with the Red Army at the war's end into Poland, observing the total destruction of Warsaw as well as the evidence of the Final Solution in visits to Klooga, a concentration camp and forced labor subcamp in German-occupied Estonia.[144] He decided to write *The Wall* in documentary fiction form and needed Lucy's expertise in translating Yiddish documents.[145] Hersey most probably was introduced to Dawidowicz through Edward M. M. Warburg,

Hersey's childhood friend and the head of the JDC board. The JDC not only lent Hersey and Dawidowicz books for their research but also paid her salary and that of Mark Nowogrodzki, Hersey's Polish translator.[146]

Working with Hersey opened up another pathway for Dawidowicz, helping to further her training as a historian of East European Jewry generally and of Jewish political behavior specifically. Immersed in research for *The Wall* for Hersey, Dawidowicz encountered the thorny issues of Holocaust representation, including the differences between universal and particularist interpretations and in Jewish and non-Jewish approaches to the catastrophe.[147] Her fact-checking, transcriptions, translations, and recordings of Yiddish documentary sources represented another stage in her apprenticeship in the as-yet-unnamed field later called Holocaust Studies. Translating for Hersey, reading the Yiddish sources from ghetto survivors, such as the Bundist Bernard Goldstein's *Finf yor in varshever geto* (Five Years in the Warsaw Ghetto),[148] checking copyrights on Yiddish songs sung in the ghetto, and proofing galleys, Dawidowicz was doing professional history. Working on *The Wall* honed her historical instincts, correcting Hersey on errors and questioning certain of his interpretations.[149] But she had yet to become herself a historian of East European Jewry and of the Holocaust. Female, untrained, without academic pedigree, and unconnected socially and financially, it took Dawidowicz almost twenty years to write *The Golden Tradition: Jewish Life and Thought in Eastern Europe*, a book that put her name and the world of East European Jewry into the American public's eye.

While working for Hersey, she applied for a full-time position at the American Jewish Committee as a secretary, a position that offered her a segue into a two-decade association with the oldest and most important American Jewish advocacy organization.[150] Her postwar experiences working for the JDC, and subsequent work with the AJC, further distanced her from her youthful leftist politics, "mainstreaming" her understanding of diasporic Jewish political behavior. Not unlike the immigrant sons who became less alienated from American culture after being inducted into the US Army, fighting against Hitler, and benefiting from the host of federally sponsored programs to integrate returning GIs into postwar American culture, Lucy, in her JDC work, became more of an American.[151] Wearing the chevrons of the JDC, she would note in her memoir, was not unlike being conscripted into the US Army.[152] She had earlier experienced the clout of an American passport when she fled Vilna in 1939. After the war, she witnessed and participated in the power of the American occupying force, battling for the causes associated with her

Americanism and her diaspora nationalism. Her postwar work in occupied Germany positioned her to become an active participant in the struggle to construct an American Cold War liberalism to protect those values. There was no better place to do this than at the American Jewish Committee in the 1950s and 1960s.

III

BECOMING AN AMERICAN

5

INSIDER POLITICS
AT THE AMERICAN
JEWISH COMMITTEE

In January 1949, Dawidowicz began her work in the Information and Research Services Department of the American Jewish Committee (AJC), the oldest Jewish advocacy organization in the United States. She would work there for almost twenty years. The position gave her an important institutional home from which to develop and express her research interests and politics. She researched and wrote about a range of topics: communism, Soviet antisemitism, the influence of the Soviet Union in the Middle East, the role of religion in American life and politics, and Negro-Jewish (in the parlance of the day) relations. In time, she came to publish regularly in the *American Jewish Year Book* and began to write actively in *Commentary* magazine, becoming an influential book reviewer and commentator on Jewish issues.[1]

The AJC played a central role in the construction of a postwar Cold War liberalism that championed American political pluralism, capitalism, and religious faith as a bulwark against Soviet communism's totalitarian and godless society.[2] In the postwar years, Judaism became accepted as a key vertex in the American monotheistic religious triangle, making Jews and Jewish organizations allies of Catholicism and Protestantism in the Cold War.[3] Dawidowicz was instrumental in the AJC's efforts to create policies for the liberal anti-communist Cold War. The 1950s' embrace of religion as a core American value likewise informed her growing doubts about the viability of Jewish secularism for sustaining

Jewish life, doubts that had begun in Vilna. Associating with the mainstream American Jewish communal leadership gave her an insider's perspective on Jewish communal politics, which, in turn, shaped her political evolution from left to right. Critical to Dawidowicz's political evolution was its internal Jewish dimensions born of her European experiences. Fear of anti-Jewish hatred and a commitment to Jewish survival on autonomous cultural and religious terms were the constants in her worldview.

Though raised in the socialist zeitgeist of modern, leftist secular Yiddish culture, Dawidowicz had become a Roosevelt Democrat, and the Allied victory over the Nazis only confirmed her loyalty. Her attachment to Roosevelt, a sentiment shared by many American Jews, boosted her patriotism and anti-communism. Her gratitude to the United States also derived from the fact that American citizenship had been the lifeline that enabled her to leave Europe on the eve of the war and that the United States had accepted Polish-Jewish political refugees—most notably her future husband—in 1940. The US government had also expedited the transfer of the YIVO's library and other East European Jewish cultural treasures from Germany to New York City—books that "went through my hands," Dawidowicz wrote, "under the protection of the American Army."[4]

From its origins the AJC was an intensely American and Americanizing organization, so Dawidowicz may have experienced some initial culture shock. Founded in 1906 in the aftermath of anti-Jewish violence during the failed Russian Revolution of 1905, the American Jewish Committee was guided in its early years by acculturated Jews of Central European origin (often referred to as "German Jews," even though the origin of many was Prussian Poland). They believed that the Jews were a group only by virtue of a shared religious tradition and not by any particular ethnic or national attachment, the kind of attachment that had shaped Dawidowicz's life. The AJC's leaders vigorously embraced American nationality, rejecting claims of dual national allegiance. Louis Marshall, one of the Committee's founders and later its president, wrote explicitly about *not* creating an organization that would be seen as "indicative of a purpose on the part of the Jews to recognize that they have interests different from those of other American citizens." Marshall asserted that "there can be but two tenable theories on which the Jews have the right to organize: firstly, as a religious body, and secondly, as persons interested in the same philanthropic purposes."[5] To that end, the AJC believed that Jewish security was best served by expanding the civil rights of all Americans as individuals.[6] It developed its liberal public policy ethos through mainstream channels of political power, in contrast to the confrontational, class-oriented politics of much of the East European Jewish immigrant community in the United States. The AJC's watchwords were *dialogue, compromise, rationality,* and *research.*

In her early years at the Committee, Dawidowicz worked in three main areas under the auspices of the Domestic Affairs Committee (DAC): anticommunism, intergroup relations associated with urban problems—specifically Negro-Jewish interactions—and church-state relations. She was now close to the seat of diasporic Jewish political influence and power.[7] The AJC also provided her with two new male mentors: Milton Himmelfarb, a senior researcher and editor of the *American Jewish Year Book,* and Norman Podhoretz, editor of *Commentary.* Himmelfarb was a thoroughly erudite thinker and expert researcher on Jewish life and also an observant Jew. A tough and tireless defender of Jewish interests, whom Charles Liebman characterized as carrying "his Judaism like a chip on his shoulder,"[8] Himmelfarb pugnaciously wore the word "parochial" as a badge of honor[9] in the face of leftist Jewish universalists. Cut from similar cloth, he and Dawidowicz became close personal friends.[10] Podhoretz, for his part, gave her a writing platform. Over the years she wrote dozens of articles for *Commentary* under his watch, and the pair became, in his words, "real political allies." From the 1970s on, they were both unrelenting anti-communists and fierce supporters of Israel—"no small accomplishment," Podhoretz quipped, given Dawidowicz's Bundist associations.[11] They also shared a love of opera.[12]

At the beginning, however, Dawidowicz was largely invisible outside the AJC. Working behind the scenes in a predominantly male environment and making significant contributions to the policy of a major American Jewish organization, she was often the only woman in attendance at meetings. Dawidowicz did the research and drafted the reports for the materials circulated at board meetings, incorporated into press releases, and edited for keynote lectures at annual meetings. Sometimes, but not always, her name—or merely her initials—appeared on these materials.

While working at the AJC, Dawidowicz also completed a master's degree in history at Columbia University. Fittingly, she wrote her thesis on Louis Marshall, AJC president from 1912 to 1929 and one of the most important Jewish political actors—in both domestic and international affairs—in the first quarter of the twentieth century.[13] Dawidowicz focused her research on Marshall's support of a Yiddish newspaper, *Di yidishe velt* (The Jewish World) in the early twentieth century.[14] Her topic was an extension of her long-standing interest in Jewish journalism and in the power of the written word. Dawidowicz took language and rhetoric very seriously, honing her writing style to be as precise as possible, a quality mentioned by all of her friends, colleagues, and reviewers—even those who disagreed with her views. Long before postmodernism, she believed language was power and understood that ideas—and the ways in which they were expressed—had political import. Dawidowicz's master's thesis also conjoined her deep interests in Yiddish culture and Jewish politics and allowed her to think through these issues in the American environment of the Committee.

In 1943, John Slawson, a European-born psychologist, replaced Morris D. Waldman as the AJC's executive vice president. Slawson brought a commitment to social science research based on rational empiricism as a means to combat antisemitism and foster American Jewish integration. Under his stewardship, enlightenment optimism and faith in education as tools to reduce prejudice within the existing social and economic structures of capitalist society—in contrast to a Marxist interpretation of intolerance deriving from social class conflict—became the bedrock of the Committee's operating principles.[15] In 1944, Slawson helped found the AJC's Department of Scientific Research, which sponsored the publication of the well-regarded *Studies in Prejudice* series with the Institute of Social Research at Columbia University. Their most famous publication was *The Authoritarian Personality* (1950), which assessed prejudice as a social pathology.[16] In the 1940s and 1950s, the leadership of the AJC did not view antisemitism as a distinctive form of prejudice. Rather, they saw it as an irrational, psychologically derived group hatred. They believed the surest way of combating this hatred was by supporting intergroup relations, serving Jewish interests through inclusive, universalist efforts to create a more pluralistic and egalitarian society. The other major American Jewish defense organizations, the Anti-Defamation League of B'nai B'rith (ADL) and the American Jewish Congress, also embraced intergroup relations, working with Christian groups, the unions, the American Civil Liberties Union (ACLU), the National Association for the Advancement of Colored People (NAACP), the Urban League, and other organizations devoted to reducing discrimination. In 1947, the National Association of Intergroup Relations Organizations was founded to promote racial, ethnic, and national harmony among groups in a society of equal opportunity.[17] Dawidowicz later commented that the field of intergroup relations "was practically invented" by Jews.[18]

The mandate of the AJC's Information and Research Services Department (also called the Library of Jewish Information, or LJI) was to gather information, conduct and coordinate studies, and write reports, primarily for internal institutional use. It also published the *American Jewish Year Book*. Directors and AJC chapter heads used these reports for speeches, press releases, and other public-directed material. The research unit became indispensable to the Committee's construction of Cold War liberalism. Almost immediately after she was hired, Dawidowicz was enlisted in the AJC's anti-communist efforts. The AJC believed that dissociating Jews from the taint of communist affiliation or support was necessary to reduce the antisemitic suspicion that Jews were potential conspirators against the American government.

SEEING RED

In the postwar United States, political conformity was the watchword of the increasingly suburban and middle-class Jewish community that was eager to assert the loyalty of American Jews to the US government during the Cold War.[19] The three major Jewish defense organizations cooperated, to varying degrees, with McCarthyist demands to expel Communists and their sympathizers from their ranks. The tense conformity of the 1950s led the liberal Jewish defense organizations to define their missions as working against all authoritarianism, whether it originated on the left or the right.[20] Indeed, when the American Jewish Committee's research wing published *The Authoritarian Personality*, it elided the distinction between Nazi and Soviet authoritarianism. Still, the leaders of the Jewish liberal defense organizations were acutely aware of the danger McCarthyism presented in its potential to foment antisemitism, and they struggled to balance their staunch historic civil rights stance with the battle against communism. Stuart Svonkin concluded that the battle against communism compromised the civil liberties' commitments of the AJC and of the Anti-Defamation League and tellingly even of the American Jewish Congress, whose origins reflected the democratic socialist roots of East European Jewish immigrants.[21]

Of particular concern to the Jewish defense agencies during the Cold War was the fear of revitalizing the close association between East European immigrant Jews and radicalism that had been a legacy of the Red Scare in the 1920s. They feared that the old transnational myth of the Jew as communist (Żydokomuna) would find new roots in American soil. To squelch any perception among the American public that Jews were particularly disposed toward radicalism, the LJI generated research to support the Committee's liberal campaign against communism in the late 1940s and early 1950s. Dawidowicz's role as a researcher for studies exposing communist activities was central to the Committee's mission and the LJI's work.[22] Writing to "All Staff Members Participating in the Program on Communism," S. Andhil Fineberg noted that "*Morris Fine* has designated Lucy Dawidowicz as the person who is to receive all memoranda, clippings, letters, etc. or copies thereof and will serve as the central source for information in regard to local developments in reference to Communism that are of interest to the AJC."[23]

Dawidowicz's memos against communism, begun in 1950, were later supplemented by published articles and book reviews in which she stated her anti-Soviet position. By 1952, she also contributed regular articles on American foreign policy on Israel and the Middle East, depicting the United States as jockeying with the Soviet Union over strategic interests in the region. On the question of civil liberties for Communists, Dawidowicz argued that the authoritarian illiberalism of communism and Soviet antisemitism trumped the threat to civil liberties and the fear of stimulating antisemitism on American shores.[24]

In December 1950, Dawidowicz became secretary of the Staff Committee on Communism and later became a full-fledged member of the committee. Her knowledge of Yiddish, expertise on the Yiddish left, and interest in the press proved to be assets for the committee. She quickly became the point person for research into the Jewish People's Fraternal Order (JPFO), the fifty-thousand-member-strong Jewish branch of the International Workers Order, the Jewish Fraternalists (the Jewish youth association of the JPFO), the Yiddish communist newspaper *Frayhayt*, and its English-language magazine, *Jewish Life*.[25] By this time, Dawidowicz viewed Stalinist and Nazi totalitarianism as twin antisemitic evils, even if the former subordinated its anti-Jewish aims to broader political goals while the latter had singled out the Jews for destruction. The DAC and the AJC leadership used LJI research to justify expelling Communists from mainstream American Jewish communal life. On June 27, 1950, the DAC adopted a policy toward communist-affiliated and communist-led organizations, calling their ideology "so inimical to the welfare of the American community and to Jewish needs and problems as to make impossible any collaboration." The memo described the Communist Party as prone to a totalitarianism analogous to that of the "Fascist Right" and utterly incompatible with "the security and free development of Jewish life no less than the survival of democratic civilization." It concluded that membership in Jewish communal institutions should be denied to any organization that could be proven to be

Communist affiliated or led.[26] This meant supporting the ousting of the JPFO from the Social Services Employees Union, a pro-communist union that the Congress of Industrial Organizations had expelled in 1950.[27]

In October 1950, Dawidowicz authored the research memo "The National Jewish Youth Conference (NJYC): Example of Communist United-Front Policy in Action," which examined the efforts of the Jewish Fraternalists to circumvent the expulsion of the JPFO from the major Jewish organizations by working from within the NJYC, an umbrella organization of Jewish youth movements under the auspices of the mainstream Jewish Welfare Board. Relying on an article in *Political Affairs*, a communist journal, that called for communist involvement in the NJYC, Dawidowicz's memo drew a line between the politics of the Jewish Fraternalists and other left-oriented Jewish youth movements. For Dawidowicz, the Fraternalists' views, in particular their opposition to the Marshall Plan, their support for Soviet-directed Yiddish culture, and their criticism of Zionism and Judaism in the Soviet bloc, derived not from an autonomous evaluation of the political issues but from rigid subservience to the Soviet line. Cowed by Soviet discipline, the Fraternalists had forfeited their legitimacy.[28]

The LJI also worked to unmask the antisemitism of the Soviet Union. Its aim was twofold: to end any attraction that American Jews might have to communism and to erase from the American public's mind any connection between the Jewish community and communist politics.[29] Dawidowicz's memos focused on exposing communist tactics to win the allegiance of left-wing Jews. Her "Communist Approach to Jews: A Study of Communist Periodicals of July to October, 1950, Relating to Jews" sought to debunk the ways in which the communists shaped their rhetoric to appeal to the Jewish community.[30] A November 1950 memo, "The National Committee of the Communist Party of the U.S.A. on Work Among the Jews," emphasized that the Communist Party, recognizing the decline of official Yiddish communism in the United States, had turned to *Jewish Life*, its English-language Communist Jewish magazine, to attract Jews. Edited by Morris Schappes who had recently been dismissed from his teaching position at City College as a communist, *Jewish Life* became the party's semiofficial Jewish organ.[31] And in "Communist Propaganda on Germany," she acknowledged the problem of the West's leniency with regard to war criminals reentering West German society, while showing that perpetrators of war crimes had also made their home in East Germany. She warned that "pacifists and others who for legitimate reasons are opposed to some of the activities of the American government in reference to Germany, Korea, etc., must be careful to avoid exploitation by those whose purpose is to further Communist ambitions."[32]

Dawidowicz found the communist tactic of depicting its opponents as Nazis particularly galling. She stressed this point in her October 20, 1950, memo, where she cited a July 24, 1950, editorial from the *Frayhayt* that depicted the Stockholm Peace Conference as the bulwark against "the terror of the Maidaneks, Buchenwalds, and Oswiecims" and characterized the West as *pogromchiks*, perpetrators of violence against Jews in Poland and Russia, which the article rhymed with *atomchiks*, supporters of atomic war. She also cited an October 10, 1950, *Frayhayt* editorial that exhorted: "Jews must be the first to fight against the war-mongers, against the crusaders for a war against the Soviet Union. They have paid with six million sacrifices in the second world war, and the lives of all remaining Jews are in jeopardy in case of a third world war."[33] In the black-and-white world of Jewish Cold War polemics, both the communist and anti-communist sides used the Holocaust to anathematize their opponents.[34]

The trial, conviction, and death sentence of Julius and Ethel Rosenberg, perhaps more than any other event in the immediate postwar years, unsettled American Jews of all political persuasions. The case was deeply associated with American Jewish politics because all the parties involved—the defendants, the prosecution, and the defense—were Jews. It opened the specter of what could be perceived as government-sponsored anti-Jewish violence, antisemitic appropriation of the Żydokomuna myth, and the exploitation of the Holocaust on American soil. Convicted of espionage on March 29, 1951, the Rosenbergs were sentenced to death a week later. They denied the espionage charges even as they faced execution, and while their case was appealed, the American Jewish public watched anxiously. Deborah Dash Moore has called the Rosenberg case "a definitional ceremony in which opposing versions of American Jewish identity competed for ascendancy," emphasizing the socioeconomic class distinctions between the different sides in the case.[35] Yet those opposing versions more accurately had less to do with class than with the relationship of Jews to mainstream American political power, with supporters of the Rosenbergs vested in the oppositional politics of the immigrant left and their opponents committed to upholding American law. The case revolved around the central question of American Jews' political loyalty in a period in which loyalty to the United States was being legislated. At stake was American Jewry's *political* identity. There was a perilous lose-lose cast to the choices facing American Jews: if they identified with the Rosenbergs, they might be perceived as harboring treasonous beliefs toward the United States and affirming the affinity between Jews and communism; if they condemned the Rosenbergs, they could be viewed as being disloyal to other Jews, abandoning their democratic commitment to due process while turning a blind eye to McCarthyist demagoguery, and ignoring the possibility of a state-sponsored antisemitic attack. Finding a middle ground that affirmed American patriotism, Jewish loyalty, and a commitment to civil rights and legal due process was extraordinarily difficult. The Rosenbergs died in the electric chair on June 19, 1953. Their execution was broadcast on the airwaves, and their deaths took on martyrological meaning. Even today the case continues to permeate American Jewish culture, politics, and interpretations of Jewish political history.[36]

In two articles for the *New Leader*, a socialist anti-communist paper sponsored by the Tamiment Institute, and one for *Commentary*, Dawidowicz condemned the Rosenbergs' actions and the tactics of the Committee to Secure Justice for the Rosenbergs, founded by the communist journalist William A. Reuben in 1952. Her positions were clear. The US government was not antisemitic; the guilty conviction of the Rosenbergs was deserved; and their punishment befitted the crime. They were unrepentant, she believed, not because they were innocent but because they desired to be communist martyrs. Had the Rosenbergs cherished their lives—and their children's—they could have pleaded guilty and plea-bargained, as did Morton Sobell.[37] In "'Anti-Semitism' and the Rosenberg Case: The Latest Communist Propaganda Trap," Dawidowicz traced what she saw as the bald manipulation of American Jewish fears of antisemitism by communists, particularly by Jewish communists writing in both Yiddish and English.[38] In her view, the claim that the Rosenbergs' "Jewishness" informed their arrest and sentence had no foundation. She considered the rhetoric deployed by communist propagandists as overblown. She cited William L. Patterson, executive secretary of the Civil Rights Congress, the Communist Party's legal arm, who equated the Rosenbergs' sentence with American racism and Nazi genocide, warning that "The lynching of these two American Jews, unless stopped by the American people, will serve as a signal for a wave of Hitler-like genocidal attacks against the Jewish people throughout the United States."[39] The Committee to Secure Justice for the Rosenbergs, preying on Jewish anxiety, regularly compared the mainstream Jewish anti-communist organizations to the *Judenräte*, the Jewish municipal councils in the Nazi ghettoes, implying that they, too, were traitors to their people.[40] Another oft-cited communist analogy compared the trial against the Rosenbergs to the late nineteenth-century Dreyfus trial, in which a French Jewish officer was falsely convicted of treason against the French state.[41] In "'Anti-Semitism' and the Rosenberg Case," Dawidowicz condemned these tactics. She directly accused the communist defenders of the Rosenbergs of fomenting antisemitism, rather than combating it, by their assignment of Jewish collective guilt for the crimes of the couple: "It is well to be on guard.... We have seen how similar campaigns of identification and accusation have strengthened the hands of anti-Semitic forces elsewhere."[42]

In exposing communist exploitation of antisemitism, Dawidowicz also broached the most problematic aspect of the Rosenberg case: the death sentence. In "The Communists and the Rosenberg Case," she conceded the sentence's severity but accused the Committee to Secure Justice for the Rosenbergs of caring less about the accused's lives than about their serving as an example of communist fidelity: "Past experience has taught that the Communists are least of all concerned with the lives of those who serve them," adding darkly her suspicion that "the Communist party would prefer to have two dead martyrs rather than two live potential witnesses against it."[43] In "The Rosenberg Case: Hate-American Weapon," Dawidowicz defended the sentence, arguing that with the exception of someone who "is a principled opponent of capital punishment (for Goering *and* Slansky *and* Rosenberg)," the only reason to commute the sentence was to hope that military or foreign-policy intelligence could be wrested from the defendants.[44]

In juxtaposing Rudolf Slansky's name with Goering's and Julius Rosenberg's, Dawidowicz sought to expose the hypocrisy of communist support for the Rosenbergs as *Jews* but the failure to support Slansky and other Czechoslovak communists when they were driven from their positions because of their Jewish origins. In November 1951, Slansky, the general secretary of the Communist Party, was arrested and accused of supporting Yugoslavia's leader, Josip Tito, who had distanced himself from Stalin. Moscow orchestrated a purge of fourteen Czechoslovak comrades and held show trials to "prove" their sedition.[45] The Slansky Trial was particularly notorious for its blatant use of antisemitic tropes; Slansky and thirteen officials were charged with high treason, "Trotskyite-Titoism," and Zionist activities in the service of American imperialism. Of the fourteen, all of whom confessed, eleven were Jewish. On April 30, 1953, Dawidowicz prepared the memo "The Reaction of American Communists to Soviet Anti-Semitism" on the Slansky case, detailing the ready acceptance of their guilt in the pages of the *Daily Worker*, *Frayhayt*, and *Jewish*

Life and the party's later admission of the trial's anti-Jewish tenor, evidence of its political zigzagging.[46]

For Dawidowicz, Soviet communism was analogous to National Socialism in its hatred of the Jews. Dedicated to exposing communism's danger to Jews, she argued that atheistic authoritarianism could not tolerate any kind of ethnic or religious distinctiveness. At its very root, communist universalism was inimical to Jewish particularism. Though communist strategy had occasionally allowed for expressions of Jewish culture (i.e., during the Popular Front and after June 1941), the utilitarian use of Jewishness should not be confused with real freedom for Jewish expression. While other Cold Warriors saw Soviet communism and German National Socialism as analogous totalitarian systems, Dawidowicz—always alert to the question of Jewish autonomy—focused on the two systems' different ways of discriminating against Jews. Writing again on the Slansky case in "The Crime of Being a Jew," Dawidowicz charged that "a whole generation of Jews was on trial . . . doomed by their origin and early training to be 'enemies of the working class.'" Slansky and his Jewish codefendants, she continued,

had no vestige of all Jewishness, either secular or religious, nationalist or internationalist. Yet, the fact that they were born Jews was the most serious charge against them. . . . Hitler believed in the *racial* impurity of some people because they were born Jews. The result was that six million Jews were murdered by the Germans. For some years now Stalin has been trying to establish the *political* impurity of some people because they were born Jews. The result is that Jews in the Soviet Union have been removed from positions of leadership in the Communist Party, in the government, in the arts. The "homeless cosmopolitans," against whom a ruthless campaign continues to be waged, are merely Jews under a transparent disguise.[47]

In "False Friends and Dangerous Defenders," Dawidowicz continued her argument that Moscow's expressed concern with antisemitism in the United States was nothing but a bald manipulation undertaken to win adherents. Acknowledging the existence of antisemitism in the United States, she nonetheless noted that "its manifestations here are, happily, a far cry from traditional anti-Semitism in Europe, particularly in Eastern Europe."[48] The communist press was determined to read antisemitism into the fabric of American society and government policy. Citing the case of a group of teenagers who assaulted a

rabbi, an assault that the police determined had nothing to do with bias, Dawidowicz scoffed at the notion that "a couple of juvenile delinquents [who] . . .
pushed a rabbi when he wouldn't let them pass on the sidewalk" constituted
antisemitism. "But it does not really matter to the readers of *Jewish Life*," she
wrote acerbically. "Sprinkle the article with a few mentions of Buchenwald and
Auschwitz and every charge is thereby proved."[49] In keeping with the American Jewish Committee's efforts to dissociate Jews and communism, Dawidowicz reiterated the danger of Soviet rhetorical and propagandistic use of
American antisemitic incidents, particularly those that stemmed from populist
anti-communists. The fact that some anti-Semites equate Jews with Communists "serves to give some twisted validity to what is otherwise a specious bit
of reasoning. The Communist proposition is that all anti-Communists are
anti-Semites or must become such. The proposition could be summarized as
follows: 'The only way the Jews in America can avoid the gas chambers is to
defend the Communists.'"[50]

The American public needed to be reminded that the Soviets were not actually interested in combating antisemitism; the Slansky show trial provided the
clearest of evidence. "We must understand that the Communists are not fire-
men playing hoses of water on anti-Semitic fires; they are arsonists, and their
hoses are filled with oil," Dawidowicz warned.[51] She remained skittish about
the Jewish attraction to the Left throughout her life. In 1961 she wrote to John
Slawson, noting that Nathan Glazer's *The Social Basis of American Communism*
was perceptive about the party's appeal to Jews, but concluded that she was "not
at all sure that its publication is particularly good for Jews."[52]

Dawidowicz's research and perspective were becoming increasingly central
to the AJC's mission. In a July 1, 1953, memo, S. Andhil Fineberg urged that
reprints of her article in *The Reconstructionist* be disseminated among American Jewish organizations in order to expose the Communist Party's tactics.[53]
John Slawson praised Dawidowicz for her *New Leader* article, "Trojan Horse
Returns," in which she detailed the plans of American Communist Party
members to infiltrate unions and liberal organizations such as the Americans
for Democratic Action, the NAACP, and the ACLU, noting that it had created "quite a stir." Senator Hubert Humphrey had entered the article into the
Congressional Record, Congressman Dick Bolling requested it for the Democratic leaders in Kansas City, and "numerous leaders of liberal organizations
phoned or wrote for extra copies."[54] In 1956, the AJC also widely distributed
the pamphlet *Now They Admit It . . . Communist Confessions of Crimes Against
Jews*, which Dawidowicz had drafted. It synthesized all her research on the

communist exploitation of American Jewish fears of antisemitism while illustrating the Soviet discrimination against Jewish culture.[55] The FBI, too, took note of the AJC's anti-communist stance and efforts and of Dawidowicz's work on its campaign, and in 1956 she received a letter from J. Edgar Hoover, thanking her personally for "Now They Admit It."[56]

In July 1959, the AJC's leadership dissolved the Staff Committee on Communism, finding it unnecessary in the post-Stalin political climate.[57] Fineberg resurrected the committee in 1961 as the Special Projects Committee—and included Dawidowicz and Himmelfarb as committee members—with the task of continuing the work to "disassociate Jews from Communism in the public mind."[58] But the weakness of the Communist Party in the United States after 1956 made such a goal superfluous, and the committee began to focus on Jewish life in the Soviet Union, advocating for those Soviet Jews who sought connections with other Jews worldwide and greater freedom for religious practice. Publicizing the plight of Soviet Jews served the committee's original goal of dissociating Jews and communism: "The fact that the Communist regime cannot tolerate manifestations of Jewish culture and religion has brought greater sympathy for Jews throughout the free world. The persecution of the Jews in the Soviet Union has helped to destroy the Jewish-Communist myth."[59] For Dawidowicz, being a member of the Special Project Committee connected her anti-communism with a newly stirring interest in Jewish religious expression.

INTERGROUP RELATIONS IN BLACK, WHITE, AND JEWISH

If communism posed a threat to Jews' security in America because domestic antisemites could implicate them as pro-Soviet revolutionaries, urban tensions in the postwar years presented their own challenges. While many Jews joined the migration of white Americans to the suburbs in the 1950s and 1960s,[60] many chose to stay in their urban neighborhoods and for the first time found themselves in direct contact with African Americans, who, beginning in 1916 and continuing until 1970, had begun to move to cities in the north and northeast during the legendary Great Migration. Between 1950 and 1960, the African American population in New York City increased 46 percent, in Chicago 65 percent, and in Philadelphia 41 percent.[61]

The new, close contact between urban Jews and African Americans would challenge the much mythologized alliance between the two groups in the postwar years. Already in 1946, the African American psychologist Kenneth B.

Clark had written a forthright article in *Commentary* outlining the key differences between the Jewish and black experiences of discrimination in the
United States and exposed mutual misconceptions that threatened the part-
nership between the two groups.[62] The AJC leadership, concerned about the
mounting challenges to intergroup relations in the changing urban environment, convened a meeting of the DAC in November 1958. The confidential
memo "Negro-Jewish Tensions" that Dawidowicz had written a month earlier
served as the basis for discussion.[63]

The forty-nine-page memo anticipated by a decade the issues that led to
the painful rift between African Americans and Jews in the late 1960s. Basing
her research on "standard books on Negroes," including *An American Dilemma:
The Negro Problem* by Gunnar Myrdal,[64] and on her own six-month survey
of representative newspapers, Dawidowicz highlighted the persistence of discrimination and the varied African American responses to it, ranging from
the work of the NAACP to black nationalism. Her memo briefly mentioned
the activism of Black Muslims Elijah Muhammad and Malcolm X and fore-
saw the identification of African Americans "with the colored peoples of Asia
and Africa." Noting that successful postcolonial rebellions had "enhanced the
self-esteem of the American Negroes," she observed that Third World identification of Israel as a colonial power often translated to anti-Zionism. Her
analysis continued by describing the triad of economic relationships between
urban blacks and Jews that had historically created conflict: (a) Jewish employ-
ers and black domestic workers, (b) Jewish landlords and black tenants, and
(c) Jewish small businessmen-employers with black customers and employees.
These relationships, she argued, were one-sided, with African Americans in a
position of inferiority. The postwar migration and social mobility of blacks created expectations of more equal relationships, but those expectations had not
been met. Dashed hopes fueled anger and resentment. Finally, "white flight" had
exacerbated relations between Jews and blacks left behind. Housing, education,
communal services, employment, and political representation all became areas
of bitter contention.

Though eschewing the term "racism," Dawidowicz did not shy away from
what she called "anti-Negro feeling among Jews." Many Jews were guilty of
grouping African Americans into one indistinguishable mass. Moreover, pride
in rapid postwar Jewish social and economic mobility had created a sense of
superiority that led some Jews to criticize blacks for their economic shortcomings. Now securely in the middle class, these Jews recoiled at what they
perceived to be a lack of shared values with African Americans regarding

"family, education, sobriety, material success." Fear of social unrest, quite simply, spooked Jews, leading some to impugn all African Americans for the acts of a few. "Any middle-class group dislikes violence," Dawidowicz wrote, "but it is not unreasonable to believe that because of their historical traditions, most Jews have a special horror of it."[65]

Supporting equal rights for African Americans as a *group* posed a fundamental challenge to the American Jewish Committee's long-standing view that civil rights were best expanded by tearing down the barriers to *individual* mobility, not by asserting the needs of an ethnic, racial, or religious community. Minutes from a DAC meeting in February 1963 stated this position: "Jews place the greatest stress on individual rights and equality of opportunity for the individual whereas Negroes stress group rights."[66] In part motivated by the fear of charges of dual loyalty, the AJC constructed its conception of modern Jewish existence on the renunciation of group rights, defining Jews as a religious group with no hegemonic political structure in American society.[67] Indeed, the AJC's battle to make the United States more inclusive to Jews was predicated on combating antisemitic forces that sought to define and anathematize the Jews as a national group.

The wide-ranging discussion at the 1958 meeting on "Negro-Jewish Tensions" reveals the complexities of defending the Jewish path to integration by downplaying Jewish group identity while supporting African American integrationist efforts that highlighted group discrimination. Arguing that the AJC's programming related to African Americans had to shift, S. Andhil Fineberg pointed out that segregation involving massive group discrimination had been largely unknown to Jews in their American experience. David Danzig, the mover and shaker behind the AJC's intergroup relations efforts, warned that as African American politics evolved, the traditional, paternalistic efforts of Jewish philanthropies to improve the lot of African Americans might "no longer earn good will" and that growing political power and political emancipation among African Americans might lead to their adopting "an 'ethnic' foreign policy." Several committee members raised concerns about changing urban demographics, citing the Jewish flight from New Rochelle, New York, as an example, and the need for the AJC to work with Jewish builders and landlords to support voluntary compliance with the Fair Housing Practices Law. No specific plans were formulated, but the attendees agreed "that it was likely that the subject would become increasingly important in the near future."[68]

Dawidowicz became progressively more involved with these issues. In a September 1959 memo for David Danzig, "Intergroup Tensions in Northern

Metropolises," she detailed the effects of the Great Migration of southern blacks in the postwar period, which had led to white flight, the deterioration of city centers, and rising frustrations among blacks at the slow pace of upward mobility and social acceptance.[69] While historically the North had been the "conscience" of the nation when it came to race, it was now challenged "to make good on its principles" in its cities. Housing, school and employment tensions, increased crime, expressions of prejudice, demand for proportional representation: all these issues desperately needed attention. Dawidowicz, always acutely aware of the transnational dimension of Jewish existence, noted in this memo that domestic tensions were never far from international concerns. Race problems were global:

> The rise of the colored peoples of Asia and Africa from colonial status to independence has heightened Negro racial pride and strengthened Negro self-esteem. The competition between the East and West for the friendship and support of the new nations of Asia and Africa has made the racial issue worldwide. The race and color issues have been exploited by the Communists in the Bandung Conference[70] and other international arenas. The aspiration of the United States for world leadership has been significantly hampered by the record of prejudice and discrimination inside its borders and the situation of the Negroes in the United States has become a factor in the international struggle.[71]

Dawidowicz then turned directly to the sensitive point of Negro-Jewish relations, the driving force behind the AJC's concern with urban decay. Treating it as a subproblem of Negro-white relations, she noted that both Negroes and Jews had absorbed negative stereotypes about the other from whites and Christians. Given the historic role that Jews had played in supporting African American rights, expectations ran high among them regarding Jewish behavior. For their part, many Jews who had risen up into the middle class and were now fearful of the collapsing center city had chosen to move to the suburbs. Those Jews who stayed behind experienced heightened tensions in an urban space that was increasingly home to people of color, while socioeconomic and political power often remained in the hands of whites and Jews. It all added up, Dawidowicz wrote, to a prescription for abiding tension: "Negroes are growing more self-reliant and less dependent upon the good-will of 'tolerant' whites. This changing attitude held the potential of affecting Negro relations with Jews, personally and institutionally."[72]

On October 22, 1959, the AJC's Institute for Human Relations' Domestic Affairs Committee Sub-Committee on Big City Tensions met.[73] Chaired by Philip E. Hoffman, it focused on several major areas affecting the quality of life in American cities that bore directly on intergroup relations: housing, education, crime, economic opportunity, and political representation. Dawidowicz, as a staff member and researcher, participated in all of the subcommittee's meetings and often recorded the minutes. Her memo "The Crisis of the American Metropolis," written for the AJC's executive board, became the basis for Hoffman's address. It began with a clear-eyed assessment of the urban crisis:

> Probably the greatest domestic problem besetting America today is the crisis of the metropolis, from New York to California. Strangled traffic, neighborhood decay, juvenile delinquency, overcrowded schools, the near-collapse of commuter railroads, the cold war between city and suburb—all these are but particular aspects of the larger crisis. And intimately involved in it, as well as in most of its particular aspects, is the problem of intergroup tensions. For, as we shall shortly see, the proportion of non-whites to whites in our big cities has been rising steeply, and so have overt and potential conflict.[74]

Consistent with the AJC's default liberal optimism regarding conflicts between varying ethnic and religious minorities in the United States, the memo made clear that "the rising proportion of non-whites in our big cities—Negroes, Puerto Ricans, Mexicans (i.e., Mexican Indians, for the most part)—is not responsible for the woes of the metropolis." The crisis in cities began with poor planning that did not accommodate the rapid growth of the urban population, many of whom were poor, and that targeted nonwhite areas for urban redevelopment. The memo highlighted social class, race, and geography as a combustible trio leading up to the current urban malaise affecting, most prominently, Newark, New York City, Chicago, Los Angeles, and Washington, DC. Segregated housing undermined educational opportunity for poor, inner-city nonwhites: "Bad neighborhoods had bad schools—antiquated, hazardous and inadequate for the swelling school population." Yet civil rights solutions, such as voluntary school desegregation, had aroused public protests. So too had the strategy, urged by some black civil rights activists, for blacks to "buy black" and boycott white establishments. The close contact and unequal social status between middle-class whites and lower-class nonwhites had unleashed acts of violence that, in turn, "have intensified white hate, fear and prejudice." The memo recognized the special plight of nonwhites whose racial difference was a "double burden" compared to the discrimination faced by earlier urban immigrants. Still it warned that "Negro Militancy" nurtured by profound economic inequity held "explosive potential" for conflict.

The memo also underscored the problem of "scapegoating." Scapegoating persisted because most Americans viewed African Americans and Puerto Ricans—a minority group sometimes grouped with African Americans in the AJC's literature—as a group, not as individuals, treating the sins of one as the sins of all. "It is a simple step from the stereotype of *group behavior*—the notion that delinquency is characteristic of a group, whether for reasons of environment or of culture—to the idea of *collective guilt*," which had to be avoided at all costs. Discrimination in housing, education, and employment; the use of negative imagery and stereotyping; and poor media coverage of intergroup relations were all characteristic parts of the Committee's work, but the memo urged the AJC and its chapters to push further to rectify these social ills.

In March 1960, in response to the AJC's recognition that African Americans were increasingly frustrated with the pace of civil rights, Dawidowicz drafted two memos: "Big City Tensions: Housing" and "Big City Tensions: Schools."[75] She shaped her housing memo as a series of questions followed by action resolutions. Noting that the AJC had worked with the National Committee Against Discrimination in Housing, the memo acknowledged that the housing crisis for nonwhites had not abated and asked whether the AJC should support federal aid for low-cost housing, encourage brokers to sell to nonwhites, and foster easier mortgage financing for minorities. On issues related to discrimination and prejudice in housing, the memo queried whether the AJC should support benign quotas and encourage neighborhood activism. It resolved that the AJC should support litigation against discrimination and participate in community organizations involved in neighborhood change. On the issue of slum clearance, urban renewal, and highway construction, which in 1956 "was estimated to have displaced 90,000 families" without providing acceptable relocation plans, the memo suggested surveying those who had been affected by relocation. The final question asked whether the AJC should encourage city planners of both renewal projects and new developments to plan in terms of racial and socioeconomic groups and resolved that it should consult and cooperate with housing, zoning, planning, and relocation authorities, both public and private, "to make them sensitive and receptive to problems of racial and ethnic minorities."[76] The memo's action items reveal the AJC's nonconfrontational, mainstream approach to civic and social problems.

The Sub-Committee on Big City Tensions, in a meeting on March 23, 1960, agreed in principle that the AJC should support federally aided low-cost housing but suggested that implementation be community specific. Its urban chapters could be helpful in studying housing, surveying local needs, calling attention to inadequacies, and providing assistance for the passage of remedial legislation. Yet quotas, even "benign" ones intended to achieve racial integration or balance, were a red flag, requiring what the subcommittee called "a serious deviation from the principle for which we have long fought—namely, complete equality of treatment based on individual merit."[77] While some subcommittee members argued that "a deliberate process of selection did not necessarily mean abandoning or compromising the principle of non-discrimination," others dis-agreed, arguing that "deliberate selection, with percentages by racial or religious composition agreed upon in advance, must necessarily result in the exclusion of someone because of his race or religion. Such exclusion was directly contrary to the principle which this agency is seeking to have accepted."[78] (AJC officers were certainly aware of the history of the numerus clausus that had been used against Jews.) The debate in many ways anticipated the full-fledged opposition of the Jewish defense agencies, not only the AJC, to "hard affirmative action" methods, such as racially based quotas of the 1970s, when affirmative action would become a major strategy of civil rights activists.[79]

Education posed another set of serious challenges to the relations between African Americans and American Jews. Ever since the years of the early repub-lic, the Jews arriving on America's shores had viewed public education both as a right and as a means of integration. Public education had been the con-duit for the integration of the huge urban population of Jewish children in the years of mass emigration of Jews from Eastern Europe. Between 1920 and 1960, Jews constituted the city's largest "ethnic-religious" element in New York City schools. At their highest numbers, 33 percent of all students and 45 percent of all teachers were Jews.[80] The demographic weight of Jewish immigrant children in interwar New York City neighborhoods made the public school—along with the Democratic political club—an anchor of the Jewish public civic sphere.[81] As Dawidowicz's own career path illustrated, the public school had been a cen-tral rung on the American Jewish ladder of social and economic success. It is likely that all of the members of the AJC's Domestic Affairs Committee were products of public schools. The AJC's engagement with school integration highlighted the public school as the urban space in which Jews and nonwhites were most likely to meet—and to suffer conflict.[82]

In February 1960, Dawidowicz prepared a memo for David Danzig, "Interracial Problems in Berkeley Public Schools," summarizing a report issued by the Berkeley Board of Education. Though small compared with New York City or Chicago, Berkeley had experienced "big-city" demographic and racial changes,[83] and its experience bore directly on the ways in which school dysfunction informed intergroup relations. The report affirmed that the racial composition of the schools reflected segregated housing patterns, which exacerbated the relations between whites and African Americans when the two populations met in high school. In 1958, the NAACP requested systemic changes in the schools in which African Americans predominated "to help raise the cultural and educational level" in those environments. The report "Committee to Study Certain Interracial Problems in the Berkeley Schools and Their Effect on Education," issued on October 19, 1959, made a series of recommendations, while stopping short of supporting compulsory integration. True to the social-psychological orientation of the AJC, the report stressed the importance of emotional factors on school success. It urged educators, however, to maintain "recognition according to ability and merit" while being sensitive to the psychological effects on their students. Other advice included sponsoring intergroup relations training for teachers, encouraging home visits, supporting job training and preparation workshops, reinvigorating parent-teacher associations, and encouraging better attendance among nonwhite parents.

Dawidowicz's memo "Big-City Tensions: Schools" formed the basis of the May 23, 1960, meeting of the Sub-Committee on Big City Tensions, which featured position papers on school integration and federal aid to school construction.[84] Her memo recognized the intertwined problems of class and race that created obstacles to African American academic achievement, noting that "Tensions affecting public schools exist, to state it in bare terms, between middle-class white and lower-class nonwhites. . . . Their [lower-class nonwhites'] poorer showing [on tests] is generally conceded to be a matter not of race but of class." Both the history of slavery and the discriminatory practices currently in effect, Dawidowicz wrote, worked to deny African American children equal educational opportunities. The segregated schools that were the norm in black neighborhoods all but assured "feelings of inferiority, hypersensitivity, submissiveness, lowered expectations and retarded academic achievement." And while African American civil rights activists favored the integration of schools as a means to redress the inequities, the white middle classes feared integration, believing it would weaken the schools' function as a "steppingstone to social mobility." What was good for one group was not necessarily good for another, and so intergroup tension was seen as inevitable.

Given the AJC's concern about integration's potential to increase tensions between urban Jews and blacks, it is not surprising that Dawidowicz stopped short of advocating for school integration. Her memo concluded with urging more federal aid to support inner-city schools, suggesting special bond issues to finance the programs that could aid minority children. Palliative efforts, such as increasing the visits of dedicated volunteers to "raise the educational and cultural horizons of deprived children," should be encouraged. She emphasized, however, that the African American community needed to help its own by stressing the value of achievement through merit and cited a comment in Eli Ginzberg's *The Negro Potential* (1956) urging the leaders of the African American community to "convince their fellow Negroes that equality cannot be bestowed; it must be earned."[85]

Did other members of the AJC's Sub-Committee on Big City Tensions similarly qualify their optimism about the disinterested meritocracy of the public school system with African American interests in redressing systemic biases? A range of opinions existed within the organization, as they did among African American civil rights activists at that time. Sharp divisions emerged at the "Staff Meeting to Review AJC Policy on Desegregation in Northern Schools" in July 1961, which Dawidowicz attended. One viewpoint stressed the responsibility of public education to foster integration; the other proposed that educational leaders concentrate their energies on improving education for *all* children through better facilities, programs, materials, and teachers, with special attention to the disadvantages facing many minority children. David Danzig—whose frustration can be sensed even in the dispassionate language of meeting minutes—urged the group to define the AJC's position.[86]

Dawidowicz, never one to show ambivalence, voiced her caveats in a long memo to John Slawson, copying Danzig, on July 25, 1960.[87] Barely concealing her own paternalistic views, Dawidowicz maintained that African Americans themselves needed to take a more assertive role to raise the educational level of their children; she pointed to the example of Jewish institutions, such as the Educational Alliance, which had provided educational programs for Jewish immigrant parents to aid in their children's acculturation. So, too, might postwar Japanese immigrant mobility serve as a model. "Young Negroes," she wrote, "must raise their occupational sights." She conceded the "extraordinary pressures" besetting the African American community: "low expectations and aspirations as a result of a long history of discrimination, continuing discrimination in various occupations, and inadequate training."[88] She also pointed her finger at the media. Rather than projecting middle-class success, "The mass media have generally tended to popularize the extremes in the Negro community: . . . the top baseball players and entrepreneurs at one pole, and the delinquents, dope addicts and criminals at the other."[89] Her toughness notwithstanding, Dawidowicz's memo the following year to Danzig urged the AJC to do more than rely on the inherited faith of the liberal welfare state to redress inequality, commenting that the organization "ought to have something [more than philosophy] to offer."[90]

Dawidowicz hoped that Negro-Jewish relations could improve with steady socioeconomic mobility on the part of African Americans. Yet she took the opportunity to voice concerns about Jewish identity as it related to intergroup relations work, concerns that would later become central to her worldview, writing, and politics. In a section of the memo headed "Jews and Jewish Group Individuality," she warned that "By emphasizing intergroup relations and intergroup tensions, we have tended to minimize and sometimes overlook the specific Jewish aspect." The concept of intergroup relations, she continued,

> has popularized the idea that Jews (or Negroes) are just one among many religious, racial or ethnic groups whose relations with others need improvement. This concept equates antisemitism with general bigotry and prejudice. It was probably intended also to lower the visibility of Jews. It may be said to have disguised the Jewish particularity. . . . To some extent we have been victimized by our own propaganda. We sometimes fail to see the specifically Jewish—or anti-Jewish—aspect.[91]

What prompted this memo? It appears that already in 1960 Dawidowicz sensed that the cohesive, implicitly ethnic, Jewish identity of the immigrant generation was eroding. She urged Slawson to consider the role the AJC could play in fostering adult Jewish education as a means of ensuring group survival. American Jews were becoming steadily more American, distant from the European past, and culturally remote from the autonomous Jewish culture produced in the modern state of Israel: "It seems that American Jews are increasingly becoming associational Jews only," Dawidowicz wrote. "Knowledge of Judaism, Jewish tradition and Jewish history is scant. There is no longer any reservoir of a flourishing Jewish life in Eastern Europe to draw from. Nor can we count very much upon Israel in this respect. An indigenous Israeli culture will scarcely be suitable for transplanting to America." A forthright view of the AJC's future meant recognizing that its work in non-Jewish areas would decline as minorities stepped in to act on their own behalf. If only for "institutional interests," she wrote, "we ought to be prepared to stress Jewish needs."[92]

FIRST CRACKS IN INTERGROUP RELATIONS

The year 1963 was momentous for the civil rights struggle. In August, the massive March on Washington for Jobs and Freedom brought over 250,000 citizens to the nation's capital to protest continued discrimination against African Americans and the Kennedy administration's slow pace in legislating civil rights. Though the march was peaceful, violence against African Americans continued in the South—including the June 12 murder of Medger Evers, a civil rights activist—with incidents of white violence against African American protesters in Maryland, Arkansas, North Carolina, Tennessee, Florida, and Mississippi. The March on Washington also revealed deep fissures within the civil rights community between activists who continued to support nonviolent tactics, such as the NAACP, the Urban League, and the Southern Christian Leadership Conference, and those, like the Committee on Racial Equality (CORE), the Student Nonviolent Coordinating Committee, and Malcolm X, who embraced "direct action" strategies for redressing African American grievances.

The AJC's Domestic Affairs Committee noted the rising temperature of domestic race relations. On October 29, 1963, Dawidowicz provided Danzig with "supplementary data" for the executive board's meeting.[93] Her memo exposed the mounting pressure to transform American society more quickly and expressed concern that urban violence could target Jews. Dawidowicz also noted that 1963 had raised the stakes on preferential hiring when the US Labor Department issued new regulations on discriminatory hiring practices in federal apprenticeship programs. The memo cited a Gallup poll from September that concluded that 50 percent of white Americans felt the pace of civil rights was too quick. Another Gallup poll showed parental opposition to integrated school settings in the North. Dawidowicz cited Dr. Buell G. Gallagher, the president of City College, who charged in October 1963 that "special admissions" in the city colleges to bring in Negroes and Puerto Ricans were "proposals of despair." The memo's section titled "Jewish Attitudes Toward Negroes" highlighted the contradictions between Jewish liberal thought and behavior in relation to intergroup relations, citing data showing that "While most Jews approve of equality for Negroes, 52 per cent would object to having Negroes move into their neighborhoods."[94] Just as Jews were found guilty of harboring antiblack attitudes, a study released in 1962 by two members of the Psychiatric Institute of the University of Maryland showed that blacks "regarded Jews as clannish, strange, and unpredictable." James Farmer, the national director of CORE, was also reported to have said that he often heard antisemitic comments among blacks. Yet the memo affirmed that Jewish social welfare agencies were still committed to civil rights as they evolved "policies in harmony with their own needs."[95]

The cracks in northern Jewish support for civil rights grew from 1964 forward as American society imploded.[96] In June 1964, during the "Freedom Summer," James Earl Chaney, Andrew Goodman, and Michael Schwerner, three young civil rights workers trying to increase black voter registration, were murdered by Klansmen in Mississippi. On July 2, the historic Civil Rights Act of 1964 became law, after eight months of legislative wrangling. But only two weeks later, on July 16, violence erupted in Harlem after the fatal shooting of an African American teenager. Six days of rioting followed, spreading to other neighborhoods in New York City. In August, more violence, provoked by police brutality, broke out in Rochester, New York; Philadelphia; Chicago; and Jersey City, Paterson, and Elizabeth, New Jersey. These incidents of social disorder pulled the veil off northern complacency. Discrimination was not just a southern problem. Neither was civil unrest.

Within the AJC and in the pages of *Commentary* and other journals, diverse views existed regarding the pace of the civil rights movement, the threats to Jewish security, and the role of the Committee in furthering liberal goals and intergroup relations. In 1963, Murray Friedman published "The White Liberal's Retreat," tracing the worries of northern white liberals confronted with African American political demands on their own doorstep. "Northern migration has shifted the center of the race problem to the metropolitan areas of the North and West," Friedman wrote. "The Negro is no longer an abstraction to the white liberal but a concrete reality—in many instances, a potential or actual next-door neighbor, a classmate of his child's, a coworker at office or workbench."[97] The "retreat" of white liberals from the radicalizing civil rights movement, he concluded, was not simply a display of hypocrisy but reflected actual changed priorities on the part of middle-class liberal whites who had moved to the suburbs, chosen private over public education, and advocated for grouping or tracking students in classes based on performance. These decisions reflected the desire for upward mobility, societal security, and maintenance of educational standards, values that, while deeply ingrained in American society, served to reinforce color lines and further systemic racism. Friedman sought to put the tension into a larger sociopolitical perspective. In the South, reactionaries actively created obstacles to social change. In the North, white liberals favored gradualist change that they believed would better prepare African Americans for a more successful experience of the American system. Yet African Americans demanded immediate tangible social results, not just aspirations, from the legislative process. Finding common ground among these groups in American society was daunting.[98]

A year later, David Danzig responded to the changing tactics within the civil rights movement by reasserting the AJC's support for the movement. In "The Meaning of Negro Strategy," he criticized the liberal assertion that social integration and upward mobility had always been predicated on the individual, not the group. Negroes had made it very clear that "the rights and privileges of an individual rest upon the status attained by the group to which he belongs ... [that is,] by the power it controls and can use." The solidarity among African Americans and the demand for more concrete signs of social change reflected a "feeling of collective self-awareness, of peoplehood." Danzig cast "maintaining standards" as an "ethnocentric reaction" to any serious threat from outsiders and challenged his liberal compatriots to create job training and other programs to address the core problem of income and class inequality underlying the civil rights movement. His essay emphasized white violence against civil rights activists, evincing less concern with African American tactical radicalization, though he conceded that "the potential [exists] for unprecedented violence."[99]

As domestic tensions continued to escalate, Dawidowicz provided research for the Committee's chief executives on Negro-Jewish relations, writing four memos on the topic to Danzig over the course of 1964. The memos—"The Use of the Referendum Against Civil-Rights Legislation," "White Resistance in the North to School Integration," "Differences between Leaders and Masses," and "Recent Jewish Voting on Civil-Rights Issues"—confirmed that the opposition to civil rights came from traditionally conservative elements in American society.[100] In "Recent Jewish Voting on Civil-Rights Issues," she concluded that the "liberal political tradition which has long been characteristic of Jews and repeatedly recorded in the way they vote is still strong—though Jews are not immune to prejudice, fears of declining property values, and resistance to neighborhood change." Even in Baltimore and Detroit, where African American urban settlement had replaced inner-city Jewish residency, "Jews have voted overwhelmingly for equal rights."[101]

Dawidowicz's long essay in the 1965 *American Jewish Year Book*, "Civil Rights and Intergroup Tensions," summarized the dramatic events of 1964, underscoring those issues that directly informed the AJC's work on intergroup relations.[102] Her article devoted space not only to the support for civil rights among Christian denominations and Jews but also to the rising risks of civil rights activism and to tensions within the civil rights community over strategy. She began by detailing the contested road to President Johnson's signing of the Civil Rights Act of 1964, focusing on the opposition tactics of the segregationist South, including Senator Strom Thurmond's historic seventy-five-day filibuster and the use of referenda by white opponents of the bill to prevent its implementation. She noted, too, Senator George Wallace's successful appeal to racism in three primaries, which won him support from a range of southern whites. Turning to the 1964 presidential election, Dawidowicz focused on Barry Goldwater's candidacy and his effort to capitalize on the sentiment of "small-town and rural white Protestant America, nostalgic for bygone days." Gauging the degree to which his distant Jewish origins played among Jewish voters, she judged that the candidate had not made any inroads into the Jewish liberal tradition. Though Johnson had won in a landslide nationally, Dawidowicz noted that Goldwater had run strong in the South, showing that the country was divided in its attitude toward civil rights and that white resistance to expanding American's promise to people of color "was enormous."

The essay laid bare the internal struggle liberal Jews were confronting in the face of a radicalizing civil rights community. Holding fast to their liberal ethos, Jews in the North found themselves increasingly disquieted by the violence and social disorder that accompanied the civil rights movement. Educational change remained a sticking point between the two communities, reflecting their different investments in the social structures that had allowed Jews, but not African Americans, mobility and integration. The New York City Board of Education had been "continuously embroiled in community controversy about school desegregation." The American Jewish Committee's New York chapter had opposed the February 3, 1964, boycott of the city's schools, an action supported by all the major African American civil rights organizations—along with a few Jewish groups. The Jewish Education Committee of New York and the New York Board of Rabbis opposed busing on the grounds that it would undermine the after-school religious education of over fifty thousand Jewish children.

Antisemitism, her summary concluded, remained a pressing concern, in both the South and, more troubling, the North. The handbills and pamphlets opposing efforts to register African Americans in the South had warned that "Jew-Communists [Are] Behind Race Mixing." Dawidowicz noted that

Michael Schwerner, who wore a beard, was identifiable as a Jew and that the Ku Klux Klan had targeted him "for 'extermination' as much as six weeks before the actual murder." The riots of the long hot summer of 1964, which targeted white-owned businesses, pointed to the gap between the leadership of the civil rights movement and the African American masses. While Martin Luther King Jr. condemned the looting of Jewish property in the *Southern Israelite*, pledging to uphold "the fair name of the Jews," the Jewish Telegraphic Agency estimated that 80 percent of the wrecked and looted businesses were owned by Jews. It was difficult to assess how much of the violence had been directed at Jews as Jews or as whites.

Dawidowicz's comments about conflict in Bedford-Stuyvesant and Crown Heights, adjacent Brooklyn neighborhoods that were home, respectively, to African Americans and Jews, illustrate her projection of the European Jewish experience onto America. Describing the civilian radio car patrol organization organized by a Lubavitch Hasidic activist, she wrote that it was "patterned after the self-defense groups which Jews in Tsarist Russia had formed to protect themselves against pogromists."[103] She also expressed concern with the radicalization of the civil rights movement as it partnered with other leftist movements potentially hostile to Jews. Dawidowicz concluded that Black Muslim activism and the appeal of pan-Africanism were real threats to continued white and Jewish engagement with the civil rights movement. She closed by asserting that the "responsible leadership" of the civil rights movement faced a juncture. If, like Bayard Rustin, the prime mover behind the 1963 march, the civil rights movement wanted to move its agenda forward, it ought to embrace "intensified political action, involving voter registration and political education *in an alliance with labor and liberal professional elements in American society.*"[104] Separatism, nationalism, and radicalism would only undermine white, middle-class, and Jewish support for the movement.

The phrase "responsible leadership" resonated deep in Dawidowicz's political consciousness. Her thesis on Louis Marshall, an icon of the "uptown" acculturated, German-Jewish community of New York City, had focused on his efforts to encourage the integration of the "downtown" East European Jewish community through the vehicle of a Yiddish newspaper. Marshall and a cohort of wealthy peers, including Jacob Schiff, Felix Warburg, and Isidore Straus, funded the establishment of *Di yidishe velt* in 1902 in order to redirect the huge voting bloc on the Lower East Side away from Tammany Hall's Democratic machine, to de-radicalize the immigrants, and to steer its editorial policy toward Americanization.[105] Marshall resented the opinion pieces run by

Zvi Hirsch Masliansky, the paper's editor, which advocated Zionism and other nationalist causes. Masliansky had chastised Theodore Roosevelt for not intervening more directly in the plight of Russian Jewry after the infamous Kishinev Pogrom of 1903. Marshall, in turn, rebuked Masliansky in December 1903 for encouraging dissent and withdrew his financial support from the paper, which spelled its end.

Dawidowicz's thesis sympathized with Marshall's leadership, which balanced his universalist and particularist commitments. He favored behind-the-scenes diplomacy over demonstrative protest politics, and his access to political power and money made him an effective advocate for the less-established and economically more marginal East European Jewish community.[106] In time, she concluded, the appeal of America and the social-economic mobility of the immigrants, what she termed "more natural or persuasive forms of acculturation," triumphed over radicalism. "Marshall's world prevailed."[107] Dawidowicz's memos, taken together with the *Year Book* summary, illustrate that by the early 1960s she was well aware of the emerging differences between the once historic allies, liberal Jews and African Americans. Though she still supported their alliance in the cause of civil rights, Dawidowicz increasingly saw the value in incremental social change and in the role that mainstream Jewish leadership and communal institutions could play in fostering Jewish national and cultural interests. Marshall's "responsible leadership" was now her model of effective political behavior.

6

WHITHER
SECULARISM?

Just as Dawidowicz had played a central role in the American Jewish Committee's anti-communist campaign, and in its efforts to understand the implications for American Jews of the civil rights movement, so too did she help
inform and guide the AJC leadership's shifting position on the place of religion
in the American public sphere. The Cold War's depiction of the Soviet Union
as both totalitarian and godless shaped the ways in which postwar American
culture positioned religious practice as the linchpin of a healthy democracy.
Defining the Jews as a religious group, not a national one, the AJC's leadership believed that the Jews' best interests were served not by special Jewish
pleading but by making the civic sphere religiously pluralistic, a process that
both abetted the secularization of postwar American public life and allowed for
Jewish religious distinctiveness. The AJC's religious definition of Jewishness
married harmoniously with Cold War liberalism's affirmation of religion as a
bulwark against the compulsory atheism of communism. Liberal Catholics and
Protestants welcomed Jews as an equal partner in the postwar construction of
the Judeo-Christian tradition, viewing it as a fundamental component of the
American democratic ethos.[1]

But defending Judaism as a religious foot soldier in the battle against atheistic totalitarianism was different from asserting that it belonged in the public sphere. Earlier than most of her AJC peers, Dawidowicz challenged the
liberal organization's assumption that the Jewish community's best interests
were served by an iron wall of separation between church and state. Already

in the late 1950s, she had begun to voice skepticism about the uncompromising position of the AJC on four major issues that informed the debate over
church-state relations among liberal Jewish organizations. Those issues were
(a) federal aid to education (private and parochial); (b) release time programs
(for religious education); (c) school prayer; and (d) joint holiday celebration.[2]
In adopting a stance that deviated from the AJC's avid confessionalism and
strict separationism, Dawidowicz was influenced by her Yiddishist background
and experiences in Europe. Her commitment to an autonomous and vital Jewish culture had led her to question secularism during her year in Vilna. Now, at
the Committee, she again began to ask if the future of modern Jewry, whether
in Europe or in the United States, could be assured without Judaism. Her
research memos and summaries in the *American Jewish Year Book* from this
period illustrate her evolutionary rapprochement with religion generally and
Jewish tradition specifically.

HOW HIGH THE WALL?

American Catholics had historically been the most vociferous religious group
in the struggle to allocate state funds for religiously based education. Their
argument rested on taxation. While they were taxed like other Americans,
their children who attended private parochial schools did not benefit from
those monies. Sectarian advocates for state funding first argued that the cost of
textbooks, regardless of the school in which they were used, should be borne
by taxation. In 1930, the Louisiana state court upheld the ruling in *Cochran v.
Louisiana State Board of Education* that textbooks purchased with federal funds
could go to parochial schools, and the Supreme Court affirmed the decision.
Opponents argued that the decision opened the door for federal money to
purchase athletic equipment, renovate buildings, and hire teachers in religious
schools, thus dissolving the wall of separation between church and state. In
1941, after the Catholic Church had supported an amendment that permitted
the transportation of parochial school pupils using public funds, a suit was
brought by a New Jersey taxpayer who claimed that reimbursement to parents
of parochial school students violated the First Amendment. The case, *Everson
v. Board of Education*, went to the Supreme Court.

Everson grappled with the First Amendment's two clauses, that is, preventing the establishment of religion, or prohibiting the free exercise thereof, and
with the Fourteenth Amendment's due-process clause and whether it could be
applied in the case. The Court handed down its decision in February 1947. By a

five-to-four decision, it ruled that transportation was a social good, not a religious one, and that federal funds could be used to transport children to parochial and private schools without violating the constitutionality of the First Amendment. Insisting that the wall of separation between church and state was inviolable, Justice Hugo Black argued: "The First Amendment has erected a wall between church and state. That wall must be kept high and impregnable. We could not approve the slightest breach. New Jersey has not breached it here." In a dissenting opinion, Justice Robert H. Jackson called the rhetoric of Black's decision "utterly discordant with its conclusion."[3] The AJC, in its publication "A Fact Sheet on Religion and the Public Schools," expressed its concern that the wall separating church and state was eroding.[4]

Another challenge to the "inviolable wall" emerged over the issue brought to court by American Catholics of "release time" for public school students to attend religious services. The practice of release time was initiated in 1913 in Gary, Indiana. By 1946, it was reported that two thousand communities, with the approval of local school boards, provided religious education in cooperation with the public schools for more than 1.5 million pupils.[5] In 1947, James Terry McCollum sued the Illinois Board of Education for the harassment he suffered when he chose not to participate in his school's release time program. Many Jewish organizations, the AJC among them, issued amicus briefs to support strict separation. Fearing the encroachment of religion into the public schools while still championing the centrality of religion to American democracy was difficult terrain to negotiate, as the AJC's position illustrates:

> The Jewish community of America is deeply concerned with secularistic tendencies in contemporary American life, which, if permitted to grow unchecked, may work great harm to the moral and spiritual basis of American democracy. . . . [But] we believe that the maintenance and furtherance of religion are the responsibility of the synagogue, the church and the home, and not of the public school system.[6]

At the same time, the AJC leadership recommended that Jewish organizations not initiate opposition to release time where such programs already existed, cautioning that it would be unsound for local Jewish groups to take an official position.[7] In 1948, the Supreme Court in *McCollum v. Board of Education* ruled that release time violated the First Amendment; but four years later, reversing that ruling, *Zorach v. Clauson* upheld New York State's release time programs. Justice William O. Douglas insisted that the Bill of Rights did not encode "a philosophy of hostility to religion" and characterized Americans as "a religious people whose institutions presuppose a Supreme Being."[8]

As the 1950s advanced, pressure escalated to include some kind of religious component within public school curricula. The American Jewish Committee files give evidence of extensive debate within the organization over how to attend to American children's spiritual development while protecting the public schools from sectarian demands. A March 5, 1953, memo to the Subcommittee on Teaching About Religion in the Public Schools illustrated the pressure to add religious instruction to the public school curriculum, noting that "In recent years there have been charges from reputable sources that the public schools are Godless," resulting in "insistent demands" that religion receive some treatment in curricula.[9] The following year, a revised draft of the AJC's "The Factual Study of Religion" affirmed that it was "essential that children become familiar with the major religions of mankind; that they acquire insights into the pluralistic sources of American life . . . [and] should be taught an understanding of difference, including religious difference, and be given a clear conception of the diversified American cultural pattern, to help fortify them against prejudice and bigotry."[10] The liberal Jewish organizations also opposed school prayer. As the AJC put it, prayer "constitutes an act of worship, and therefore has no place in the public schools. Since Jews regard the Lord's Prayer as sectarian rather than universal, we cannot accept it as permissible practice for the schools."[11] Recognizing that there were schools in which passages of the Bible would continue to be read, the AJC urged that selections come from "the Old Testament only," taking the implicit pluralistic position that because Catholics, Protestants, and Jews all held the Old Testament in reverence, its recitation bolstered American democracy.[12]

The issue of joint holiday observance around the Christmas season highlighted the disjunction between the leadership of the American Jewish liberal organizations and their constituents, as well as within the organizations themselves. Joint holiday observances illuminated a fundamental tension for the AJC's leadership: it wanted to keep the public sphere—particularly the schools—free from sectarian religiosity in order to prevent any missionizing toward Jews. At the same time, it wanted to ease the acculturation of Jews into American society. In general terms, the American Jewish Congress and the American Jewish Committee opposed joint holiday celebration, while the ADL opposed only those celebrations that were considered "religious."[13] Civic ecumenical holiday celebrations, which might include songs with a religious caste, were given a green light by certain Jewish leaders, especially if they included Jewish songs or the lighting of a Hanukkah menorah. Many Jewish parents had no objections to their children participating in these pluralistic celebrations of American ecumenicism.[14] Moreover, the AJC was well aware of the public relations dangers that could arise should American Jews campaign publicly against Christmas celebrations woven into the fabric of American culture, warning in one memo that "any action, no matter how well intentioned or how soundly based in principle, carries with it the possibility of grave damage to the entire Jewish community."[15] While the AJC opposed joint holiday observances (Christmas-Chanukah, Easter-Passover), it recognized that their conjoined celebration had entered the public sphere in a non-sectarian manner. Internal memos of meetings with other organizations in the Jewish community revealed there was no consensus on how to contend with sectarian holiday celebrations in the public schools.

Church-state issues continued to challenge the liberal Jewish organizations. At an April 1956 meeting, the AJC's Domestic Affairs Committee, with Dawidowicz in attendance, grappled with the issue of federal loans to private colleges, which appeared to violate church-state separation.[16] In 1961, when the Senate considered a bill that would allow the federal government to grant aid directly to private and parochial educational institutions, Reform Rabbi Stephen S. Wise testified in a Senate subcommittee against the bill, supported by other members of the Reform, Conservative, and modern Orthodox leadership. Agudath Israel, however, a traditional Orthodox group led by many East European-born Hasidic rabbis, dissented and urged Congress to include money for parochial education in its aid-to-education bill.[17] The divide between liberal Jewish organizations and Orthodox ones, already present in the early 1960s, would only widen.

In her memo to John Slawson on July 25, 1960, Dawidowicz expressed concerns with the absolute separation of church and state, challenging a cardinal position of the AJC. "We speak always of the Jews as one of the three great religious groups in America," she wrote. "We stress the religious rather than the ethnic or cultural character of the Jewish group. Yet we consistently—inconsistently, to be correct—take secularist positions on matters affecting church-state relations."[18] In support of her claims, Dawidowicz referred to her earlier December 1959 paper, "The Jewish Position on Released Time and Bible Reading." The twenty-eight-page memo surveyed the history of the American Jewish communal opposition to any forms of religious education in the public schools. It noted that only the Hasidim consistently supported measures that would allow Jewish parents to educate their children in Judaism on public time and in public space. She qualified the opinion that strict separationism was ultimately in the Jewish interest and provided evidence of successful release time programs that benefited the Jewish community by providing religious instruction to highly assimilated Jewish youth with no or little Jewish educational background. She cautioned that Jewish opposition to Bible reading could backfire. Arguing that most Americans felt completely comfortable with some short reading of scriptural passages in the schools, she noted that "Jews seem[ing] to be the only important religious group contesting Bible reading may create an undesirable impression."

Needing a liberal Jewish interlocutor to express her growing hesitancy about strict separationism, Dawidowicz cited Louis Marshall, who in 1925, noting a severe decline in religious education among Jews, stated: "Personally I believe that it would not do our Jewish children a bit of harm to become familiar with the Bible even though it be read in the public schools."[19] Refined in August 1960 to a report, its last section, "Value of Reconsideration," challenged the AJC's assumptions that Jewish support of release time programs would damage interreligious relations. Dawidowicz suggested instead that Jewish participation would increase goodwill among Jews and other religious groups toward a common affirmation of metaphysical values. Echoing Marshall's assessment of the dire state of Jewish education, Dawidowicz suggested that Jewish religious, educational, and communal leaders might "do well to make the most of any opportunities, however limited, to reach more Jewish children."[20]

In the spring of 1963, Dawidowicz sent a memo to Milton Himmelfarb, "List of Examples Where Church and State Are Not Firmly Established." The list included "1. personal status, such as marriage ceremonies and baptismal records; 2. the Federal hiring and salarying of chaplains; 3. the participation of clergy in public ceremonies, such as inaugurations, as well as the use of a Bible for official ceremonies; and 4. Federal aid for a whole host of religious purposes." She noted that religious institutions were exempt from federal taxes. Federal money through the National School Lunch Act supported school lunch programs for the poor, whether in public, private, or parochial schools. Hospitals and other welfare agencies run under religious auspices regularly received federal grants-in-aid. The G.I. Bill, providing veterans with low-cost educational loans, did not distinguish between religious and nonreligious institutions. From her personal experience working with the JDC after the war, she noted that sectarian agencies had played a major role in postwar reconstruction, providing direct and indirect support: "Surplus commodities, free transportation, cooperation with American military forces are the most important instances."[21] Her list made her position clear: the AJCs's dogmatic view of the inviolable wall separating church from state had to be rethought in light of the glaring inconsistencies in the way the First Amendment had been interpreted and applied in actual federal and state programs. Furthermore, in her view, the complete divorce of issues of "church" and "state" was impossible for the Jews, whose ethnic and cultural bonds inherently blurred the distinction between the two spheres.

The AJC wrestled with church-state issues throughout the 1960s, as did Dawidowicz, who was often called upon to provide research to the organization's various committees. Her May 1963 memo "Changing Public Opinion on Church-State Questions" argued that the relationship between church and state was shifting in America.[22] While historically only conservative thinkers would have objected to the Court's decision (in *Engel v. Vitale*) forbidding school prayer, Dawidowicz noted that concerns had been voiced by liberal Protestants. Reinhold Niebuhr, professor of theology at Union Theological Seminary, viewed the ecumenical prayer as a "model of accommodation to the pluralistic nature of our society." Bishop James A. Pike of the Episcopal Church of California charged the state with establishing a religion—secularism—on the American public. Dawidowicz cited evidence that resistance to federal aid to denominational schools had shifted noticeably, with more and more Americans supporting some limited contribution on the part of the state. Withholding federal aid from the millions of American children who attended parochial schools not only was, in the view of Robert M. Hutchins, president of the Fund for the Republic, "arbitrary and unreasonable" in its interpretation of the First Amendment but would lead to the creation of a second- and third-tier educational system. Public opinion on federal aid to church-related colleges and universities was also shifting. In June 1963 the American Association of University Professors proposed a resolution in support of federal aid to sectarian institutions of higher learning. Though narrowly defeated, that such a proposal existed indicated changing views on the inviolability of the church-state divide.[23]

Recognizing the "variety among Americans about the role of religion in society and a desire to take account of these differences in some suitable civic arrangement," Dawidowicz urged a less separationist interpretation of the First Amendment. She suggested "Shared Time" programs and the exemption of Saturday Sabbath observers from the Sunday closing law as possible solutions to the current stalemate between Americans who wanted more religion in the public sphere and those who feared its influence. Dawidowicz emphasized that new conceptions of civic pluralism required increased tolerance of religious difference and observed that even stalwart Jewish separationists were changing their views: "The once seemingly monolithic Jewish position advocating the complete separation of church from state and of religion from society seems to show signs of breaking down." As proof, she adduced the fact that the entire rabbinate, not merely the Orthodox, had begun to seek federal aid for Jewish schools.[24]

Dawidowicz's article synthesizing the status of church-state relations in the 1965 *American Jewish Year Book* noted that the Supreme Court had struck down state-prescribed prayer and Bible readings to a "storm of protest." She pointed out that "the critical response to the Court's decisions did not come entirely from the Court's unreconstructed Southern opponents or from troglodytic rightists, but also from forward-looking civic and religious leaders and distinguished legal experts, many of whom were reluctant to draw the far-reaching conclusion that the juridical separation of church and state meant an actual separation of religion from society."[25] Americans of every religious stripe were concerned that religious values were being relegated to an "obscure corner of human life." Protestant theologians, long suspicious of Catholic aspirations to shape civil society, had begun to speak about the need for both "separation and interaction," the title of the National Council of Churches' February 1964 statement. Participants at the meeting unanimously agreed that government "may appropriately recognize in its public practice and in its publicly supported educational programs the role of religion in American history and life." Even among Jews, who still favored "the strictest separation of church from state because states in which the church was dominant in the pre-Hitlerian and pre-Soviet European past were more hostile to Jewish existence than secular states . . . some stirrings of a changing attitude have been apparent."[26]

In a memo to AJC staffer Anne Wolfe in March 1965, Dawidowicz summed up the work she had done on church-state matters, wryly noting that the Jewish position on federal aid was simple: only Orthodox Jews are in favor. "All other Jewish organizations, except the AJC (and I still don't understand that one), appear not to be interested either in Jewish education or any education for that matter. They just want to make sure the Catholics do not get a penny."[27] Later that year, Dawidowicz wrote "Religious Liberty and Separation of Church and State," in which she articulated her shifting position on the wall between church and state and its relationship to religious liberty and to liberalism. Noting that "One of the more frequently repeated pieties of American liberalism is the notion that 'religious freedom is most secure where church and state are separated and least secure where they are united,'" she added that "a corollary proposition has been that Jews have prospered where church and state are sep-arated and suffered when united."

> But the argument is logically and historically unsound. The security of Jews and the exercise of religious freedom depend, not on the separation of church from state, but on how much political liberty a state tolerates and how much religious and social nonconformity its society permits.[28]

England, she argued, despite having an established church, supported reli-gious freedom and tolerance while the Soviet Union, whose constitution artic-ulated the protection of individual conscience, brooked no free expression of religious beliefs: "Every schoolchild knows that the Orthodox Church in Russia is barely tolerated today (an improvement over past treatment), while minority religions—particularly Judaism, Roman Catholicism, and Protestant sects (especially Jehovah's Witnesses)—are actively persecuted."[29] She argued that the free expression of religious beliefs and practices depended upon the "politi-cal and social conditions in a given country," and not on an absolute separation of church and state. Enumerating the variety of constellations of church-state relationships in western European states, she noted that "the practice in one country can seldom serve as a model for the practice in another." Her broader position was clear: absolute separatism might not necessarily guarantee the fullest expression of religious conscience for Americans—and particularly for Jews practicing Judaism—when the voluntaristic structure of American society militated against strong, financially secure Jewish educational opportunities.[30]

Dawidowicz wrote a follow-up survey on church-state issues for the *American Jewish Year Book* in 1966. Here she noted a further rise in the "legal, legal-istic, and philosophic controversy over the meaning of the First Amendment's no-establishment and free-exercise clause." Religion's advocates now came from a new source: social activists, including rabbis, ministers, and priests, in the civil rights movement. Energized to expand the social welfare net to combat poverty and ignorance, they advocated for federal aid to help poor children, regardless of their school setting. Strict separationism stood to further harm the most vulnerable Americans. For the most part, she reported, Jewish groups remained skeptical:

> Most Jews were less willing than Protestants to reexamine their views on the separation of church and state in the interest of ecumenism. Jewish

community-relations agencies as well as national Reform and Conservative bodies continued to adhere to their strict separationist views. Orthodox organizations, however, held sharply divergent opinions: they believed religion should not be legislated out of public life and, maintaining a considerable educational establishment, they welcomed the benefits of federal aid. These groups began to challenge the non-Orthodox hegemony in Jewish communal life and to lobby independently for their interests. Thus, they became a new political influence in the Jewish and general community, and are to be reckoned with.[31]

Jewish social service agencies continued to accept federal monies and tax breaks—as did all sectarian social welfare groups.[32] Opposition to federal funding of these programs was led by Americans United for the Separation of Church and State, the ACLU, and the American Jewish Congress. Regional differences persisted, and social conservatives in southern states used the First Amendment's separationism to contest federal money to aid the African American poor. President Johnson's expansion of aid through the Elementary and Secondary Education Act (April 11, 1964) and the Higher Education Act of 1965 (November 8, 1965) aroused opposition from strict separationists, even from such liberal organizations as the American Jewish Congress, who supported the president's anti-poverty program. The AJC, representing the liberal, civic spectrum of Jewish communal organizations, remained decidedly "cool" on the issue.

If the mainstream Jewish communal organizations were unwilling to re-examine their strict separationism, Dawidowicz was not. Her surveys of church-state issues supported her own growing openness to religious values in addressing civic problems.

THE PERSONAL IS POLITICAL

Dawidowicz's questioning of the AJC institution's traditional advocacy of strict separationism was a product, in part, of her growing doubts about the wisdom of the liberal Jewish community's support for secularization. Not only did strict separationism seem out of step with American society as a whole, but secular Jewishness as a program for Jewish survival increasingly struck her as a dubious enterprise. These doubts had already surfaced in her prewar Vilna year when, influenced by the YIVO activist Zelig Kalmanovitch, she began to question her secularist assumptions. The 1950s Cold War culture celebrating American religiosity contributed to her new thinking about the role of religion in society, a thinking further affirmed by her close association with Milton Himmelfarb, who harbored deep skepticism about First Amendment absolutism.[33]

Her analysis of contested church-state issues also held deep personal meaning for Dawidowicz. In November 1964, she wrote a letter to her younger sister, Eleanor, who was in the middle of a painful separation from her husband. In their conversation, Eleanor mentioned a John Updike short story to Dawidowicz because it had been helpful to her during this difficult period in her life. In response, Dawidowicz—ever the literary critic—first criticized Updike's work ("There is a precious quality in his writing that irritates the hell out of me.") but then went on to share with Eleanor her thoughts about personal morality and individual responsibility. Joking that "in my old age"—she was forty-nine—"I am becoming increasingly concerned with individual morality, at least my own," she confessed to her sister that her attempts to live by "my own standards for goodness and decency," and to live charitably with the people around her, were "bringing me closer and closer to a religious outlook." "Be prepared," she warned playfully, "someday I may even become a really observant Jew."[34]

Dawidowicz's reconsideration of the role of religion took place not only in the context of the global Cold War, and of her private life, but also in the postwar New York world in which East European Jewish refugee scholars and poets—and the Yiddish language—were still a critically important part.[35] She and other Yiddishists were coping with the trauma of the Holocaust, its effect on Jewish life, and the devastation that Hitler's policies had perpetrated on Yiddish speakers, their language, and their secularist worldview. More than half of the prewar 11 million Yiddish-speaking Jews had been murdered, and the question remained whether their numbers could ever be recoverable. In reviewing the creation of *The Great Dictionary of the Yiddish Language*, a project begun by the Viennese philologist Alfred Landau and continued by Yudl Mark after the war when Landau's library was restituted with the YIVO's, Dawidowicz discussed the origins of the Yiddish language, concluding that "in the final analysis the religious culture created the Yiddish language."

> The religion and the way of life it imposed on its believers separated the Jews from their neighbors in medieval Germany. It determined the vocabulary and from the very inception made Yiddish different from German. Later on, other factors came into play, strengthening and supplementing the role of Judaism in shaping Yiddish: residential separation and occupational differentiation; governmental and popular antisemitism and the persecution

of Yiddish itself, which, in fact, only reinforced the language; restriction of educational opportunities and discrimination in employment; and finally, national consciousness—most nearly a substitute for Judaism—and the will to maintain Yiddish. Today, it appears that only the most old-fashioned kind of Judaism, national consciousness, and national will remain as effective agents to perpetuate Yiddish.[36]

In her view of the interrelationship between Yiddish and Judaism, Dawidowicz was greatly indebted to Max Weinreich. Already in the late 1920s, in two little-known essays—"Pictures from Jewish History in the 17th Century" (Vilna, 1927) and "Pictures from the Yiddish Literary History from the Beginning until Mendele" (Vilna, 1928), which appeared in the American Yiddish periodicals *Forverts* and (in parts) *Di tsukunft*—Weinreich insisted on the connection between the Yiddish language and the "religious" civilization of Ashkenazic Jewry.[37] In response to the destruction of the world of East European Jewry, Weinreich promoted his view of the religious-national-linguistic "ghetto" of Ashkenaz that afforded Jews an organic, holistic existence. His 1953 essay "*Yidishkayt* and Yiddish: On the Impact of Religion on Language in Ashkenazic Jewry," published as part of a volume celebrating the seventieth birthday of Mordecai M. Kaplan, the founder of Reconstructionist Judaism, leaned on the latter's conception of "Judaism as a civilization."[38] (Dawidowicz was one of the editors of the English section of the volume.) In Ashkenaz, Weinreich concluded, religion, culture, and language were inseparable. Indeed, the word "religion," he insisted," was "an inadequate term to describe traditional Ashkenazic Jewry."

> It was a way of life and, even more important, an outlook on life. I know of no word that would convey this idea of inclusiveness as cogently as the Yiddish term for Jewishness, *yidishkayt*. . . . Yiddish came into being as the linguistic vehicle of a community set apart from the outside world by its religion. Be it stressed again that we refer to a period in which religion was supreme; even cultural patterns that our age would tend to explain in economic or social categories at that time were conceived of as manifestations of religion and their exposition was couched in religious terms.[39]

The essay also insisted that secularism—understood as the absence of religious values—was nonexistent in the culture of traditional Ashkenazic Jewry; "every nook and corner of life was permeated with *yidishkayt* and it has been shown how deeply this has affected the language as well." Ashkenazic bilingualism, the intimate relationship between Hebrew-Aramaic and Yiddish, was a dichotomy not of sacred and profane but of written and oral expression.[40] Weinreich's article made a strong impression on his community of readers. On June 14, 1953, the Yiddish writer Isaac Bashevis Singer wrote to the YIVO's director, affirming the piece's conclusion that "*yidishkayt* created Yiddish." He shared Weinreich's perspective on the inseparability of Yiddish and *yidishkayt*: "My thesis was that Yiddish, to a great degree, must remain that which it was right in the beginning, and that the Yiddish language cannot become an instrument of absolute secularism."[41]

For her part, Dawidowicz by the mid-1960s had already begun to disassociate herself from the secularist assumptions of most of the Yiddishist world. In 1965, reconciled after their postwar rupture, Weinreich had asked her to comment on a proposal he had drafted for a sociological study of Polish Jewry in the two decades before the war. Dawidowicz insisted that even the material life of the Jews had to be studied in the context of their cultural life, and it had to include religion. Implicitly reminding Weinreich of his own definition of Jewish culture, she commented, "No sociology of Jews in Poland can afford to partition the religious culture off from Jewish communal life."[42] Weinreich defended his proposal's use of the term "sociology" but thanked her for the "emphasis on traditional Jewish life and its continuity in the quasi-antagonistic secularism [in modern life]."[43]

Further evidence of Dawidowicz's discomfort with a strict secularist approach emerged in a project she undertook with the Yiddish poet Arn Tseytlin to honor Leibush Lehrer, who had died in September 1964.[44] That spring, she and Tseytlin collaborated on the translation and bilingual publication of Lehrer's pamphlet *Simbol un tokh* (Symbol and Substance), which they hoped to reissue for a memorial to be held at Camp Boiberik in the summer.[45] *Simbol un tokh* articulated Lehrer's atypical "secularist" perspective. The essay affirmed the centrality of symbols for a healthy, full human life, asserting that "symbols prevail because they do something for us, because they have the ability to satisfy inner needs."[46] Lehrer claimed that the most powerful symbolic expression was effected through group rituals. Citing Émile Durkheim, he concluded that Jewish society "sanctioned" common rituals that conveyed deep symbolic meaning to its members and created a web of human bonds. "Social approval elevates custom to the rank of national symbol," he wrote, "and for the individual who is associated with the community of Israel, it becomes a sort of spiritual passport which testifies to his personal Jewish identification."[47] As in his 1941 essay

"Yidishkayt—vos darf men ton?" (*Yidishkayt*—What Should We Do?)[48] Lehrer emphasized the role of the Jewish home as the most important site of the ritualized behavior crucial to the continuation of Jewish life in the diaspora.

Lehrer well understood the challenges American society posed to his conception of *yidishkayt*. In *Simbol un tokh*, he noted that the theoreticians of Jewish secularism had come from "that very unsecular Eastern Europe." They proclaimed their theories about Jews and *yidishkayt* "without the least recognition that the whole theory originated in Eastern Europe and could perhaps be applied only within its boundaries." The secularism that was born in Eastern Europe became "an expression of complete deJudaization" in the United States. "In the end, all secularists are left with is a publishing house . . . surely too little to preserve a coming generation."[49]

To assess the legitimacy of his concerns, Lehrer conducted a series of surveys in 1959 with sociologist Nathan Goldberg to measure the success of the Yiddish school movements in generating Jewish commitment among their graduates. The surveys' results illustrated that Jews who had attended Yiddish schools and camps in the interwar years and who later identified themselves with the secular Jewish community did so according to religious criteria, yet the graduates were unconscious of their shift in identification. Postwar American Jews saw their identities in ambivalent, conditional terms composed of a "medley of identities," in which they could dismiss religious belief while at the same time claiming that they celebrated the Jewish holidays of Passover and Rosh Hashanah. Lehrer concluded that "the desire for Jewish survival found no adequate verbal or symbolic forms of expression." He poignantly noted that the ideologically inconsistent American form of Jewish secularism would have "bewildered" an East European Jew.[50]

Correspondence between Dawidowicz, Peretz Kaminsky, a Yiddish poet and editor, Tseytlin, and Salka Lehrer—Lehrer's wife—began in early 1964 and continued through the summer of 1965, with back-and-forth discussions over Tseytlin's Yiddish introduction and Dawidowicz's English translations.[51] Remaining faithful to Lehrer's worldview in English translation proved challenging. Dawidowicz struggled with translating Tseytlin's neologism *yidishkaytizm* to describe Lehrer's ideology; she rendered it as "traditionism," not "traditionalism," in order to preserve its meaning and innovative coinage.[52] Her difficulty in translating the words *yidishkaytizm* and *yidishkayt* into English highlighted her belief in the essential disjunction between East European and American conceptions of Jewish secularism. East European secular Yiddishism had emerged in the context of traditional Jewish society and folkways with their implicit ethnicity and a commitment to the Yiddish language.

In 1968, Dawidowicz delivered a talk, "The Relevance of an Education in Sholem Aleichem Schools: Some Personal Remarks," at a Sholem Aleichem Folk Institute school conference in Lehrer's memory.[53] In those remarks she paid homage to the East European Jews who, in founding the SAFI, "wanted to transmit what was viable of East European Yiddish culture to their children, namely its ambience—the mood, the spirit, the values of the internal Jewish society from which they had come and which they cherished." At the SAFI, she recalled warmly, "We were taught *ahavas-yisroel* [Love of the Jews][54] and love of knowledge; to love Jews and Jewishness and to relish Jewish experience and to cherish Jewish creativity." Yiddish language and its literature were the vehicles that transmitted the school's values. In those pre-Holocaust years, Dawidowicz remarked, literature seemed to embody an "ethical code"; morality "was determined by Mendele, Sholem Aleichem, and Peretz." And language, too, was much more than a means of communicating. Like literature, it served as a vehicle for what she valued most: "Jewish continuity and identity."

In contrast, she told her audience, the meaning of "tradition" for secularists was ill defined and, perhaps, undefinable. While Lehrer knew this, he insisted that the concept, however amorphous, had to inform the curriculum of the SAFI's schools. Dawidowicz recalled that her mentor struggled with the spiritual meaning of life and how to impart its mysteries and challenges to young, Yiddishist Jews in America. Unanchored from traditionalist prescriptions, he understood that they would have to be bound in some manner to Jewish tradition if they were to remain Jews. She invoked Lehrer's conviction that "if Jews are to survive, tradition must outlast revolution," noting that he "became the traditionalist among the secularists, with brilliant insight into men's emotional needs and the changing patterns of our Jewish and American society." Though Lehrer did not live to see the spiritual revival among young Americans, including Jews, in the late 1960s, it "would have confirmed his wise and profound knowledge that men need something to believe in beyond themselves, that there are no glib easy answers for the mysteries of existence."[55] And this knowledge both informed and affirmed the truth that she herself had come to embrace: "We are all of us part of East European Jewry and bearers of its heritage."

At the same time that Dawidowicz was reflecting on Leibush Lehrer's influence and legacy, she was hard at work on *The Golden Tradition: The Jewish Experience in Eastern Europe*, a book that represented a seminal effort in translating—in the broadest sense of the term—the culture of East European Jewry to an English-speaking audience. In many ways, her difficulty with translating and explaining Lehrer's *Simbol un tokh* for a postwar American Jewish audience forced her to confront the limits of transmitting East European Jewish culture to American Jews, even those with some knowledge of the Yiddish language. The difficulty of translating the Yiddish word *yidishkayt* into English embodied the problem. She would return to this linguistic-cultural-ideological conundrum explicitly in the next decade.

Historians have generally attributed the American Jewish communal elites' "inward" turn to the years after 1967, spurred by the rise of Black Power, the threat to Israel's existence evidenced by the Six-Day War, and the rise in Holocaust consciousness.[56] Yet Dawidowicz's internalist turn began much earlier. Even before 1967, she had already begun to pull back from the liberal Jewish consensus that characterized so many of her peers in New York City and at the American Jewish Committee. In many ways, the men who would later become prominent neoconservatives were just catching up with her. Her coworkers at the AJC, such as Milton Himmelfarb, Nathan Perlmutter, and Norman Podhoretz, were already well aware of Dawidowicz's reassessment of Jewish liberalism as well as of her capacious knowledge of and commitment to Jewish life. But it would take the publication of her first major book, *The Golden Tradition: Jewish Life and Thought in Eastern Europe*, written in the last years of her AJC tenure, to bring her personality, worldview, and erudition to the general public's eye.

7

REPRESENTING
POLISH JEWRY

The Golden Tradition

In 1967, Lucy S. Dawidowicz published *The Golden Tradition: The Jewish Experience in Eastern Europe*. An anthology of autobiographical primary sources translated from Russian, Polish, Yiddish, German, and Hebrew, it represented the diversity of Jewish life in Eastern Europe. The work earned her instant acclaim among the New York intellectuals and the New York literary public writ large.[1] Widely reviewed, the book launched her public career even as it served as dress rehearsal for her major work on the Holocaust, *The War Against the Jews, 1933–1945* (1975), and the books that followed, *A Holocaust Reader* (1976) and *The Holocaust and the Historians* (1981), which together helped cast Dawidowicz as the "authentic" historical voice of murdered European Jewry and a sought-after lecturer in both academic and public venues.

Dawidowicz wrote *The Golden Tradition* as a scholarly book for a general audience and was thus instrumental in placing the life and destruction of the European Jews into the American cultural landscape. It emerged from Dawidowicz's personal experiences in Europe, her study of Jewish history and antisemitism, and her engagement with contemporary American and American Jewish politics in the postwar period. The book's appearance in 1967 was perfectly tied to cultural and political shifts in American and Jewish culture, including the emergence of the New Left, the growth of the Black Power movement, and the

victory of the Israeli army in the Six-Day War, which helped give rise to ethnic politics. In this fraught climate, the East European past and the Holocaust
came increasingly to be seen as critical to Jewish identity. *The Golden Tradition*
was pivotal to its construction. The book illuminated the historical agency of
East European Jewry by emphasizing its cultural, political, religious, and ideological diversity, all of which informed the American Jewish public's changing
view of its past.

When Dawidowicz set out to collect, translate, and edit the materials included in *The Golden Tradition*, she drew upon the relatively young tradition of
East European Jewish historiography inspired by the Russian Jewish historian
Simon Dubnow. Dawidowicz's debt to Dubnow stemmed from the monumental role his writing and life played in the emergence of modern historical writing
in Eastern Europe and also from his long involvement with the YIVO—which
lasted from its inception in 1925 until his brutal murder in the ghetto of Riga in
1941. Though prominent Polish-Jewish historians, including Philip Friedman,
Jacob Shatzky, Raphael Mahler, Isaiah Trunk, and Elias Tcherikower, among
others—some of whom had experienced the Nazi assault—made their way to
the United States and devoted their energies to continuing the Dubnowian legacy in their new home, it was Dawidowicz, the native-born and native English
speaker and writer who became the key American link in this tradition.[2] Her
history writing sought to document the life and murder of European Jews, to
commemorate the dead, and to imbue her American Jewish readers with a
usable past through which they might create a Jewish future in a diaspora far
removed from its East European Jewish heartland.

WRITING JEWISH COMMUNAL LIFE IN THE DIASPORA

Simon Dubnow saw Jewish communal autonomy as the key to his diaspora
nationalism, to his historiography, and centrally to the survival of the Jewish
people.[3] Dubnow argued that the communal institutions of an exilic people
embodied its political life. Writing in the multiethnic, multiconfessional, and
multireligious context of Imperial Russia, he never lived to apply his optimistic
theories of diaspora nationalism to the political conditions of a liberal, tolerant, integrationist democracy such as the United States.[4] Dawidowicz picked
up that challenge. Her earliest work at the AJC and in *Commentary* magazine,
which predated *The Golden Tradition*, already reflected her Dubnowian perspective. Dawidowicz set out to plumb the questions of Jewish communal life
and politics in an environment of "autonomy and freedom" in postwar America,

focusing on the ways in which Jews in the diaspora actively shaped their communal, cultural, and political lives.

In "Middle-Class Judaism: A Case Study," published in 1960, Dawidowicz surveyed the patterns of Jewish communal life and religious institutions in the second-generation Jewish neighborhood of Jackson Heights, New York, which she called "Garfield Hills."[5] Wary of the Americanization of Judaism, she critically assessed the religious lives of Reform, Conservative, and Orthodox Jews in Garfield Hills and concluded that these three groups within American Judaism, despite their assertions of difference, represented variations on the same suburban American middle-class theme. None of them embodied the naturalness and authenticity of East European Jewish life. "As for religion itself, Orthodoxy, Conservatism, and Reform as practiced in this country have come to resemble each other more closely than any of them do the Halachic Judaism from which they all ultimately derive," she wrote, adding that their middle-class values created a "pattern of nearly uniform observance."[6] While this seemingly diluted Judaism held little appeal for Dawidowicz, she nonetheless believed that these communal institutions maintained Jewish life in the diaspora. Even without a formal *kahal* (the Jewish municipality or institution of self-government in Europe) to compel Jewish group identity, postwar American Jews felt a sense of community, and their electoral choices both reflected and maintained those communal bonds. Dawidowicz's research affirmed her belief that Jewish communal life was a source of Jewish national, political, and spiritual vitality.

The AJC, however, had to walk a tightrope between affirming Jewish communal life and its values and preventing the perception that those values created a "group" political stance, which could lead to anti-Jewish discrimination. In fact, at a Domestic Affairs Committee meeting in September 1960, concern was voiced about the upcoming presidential election and the prospect of anti-Catholicism harming Kennedy's candidacy[7] and about an article in the *New York Times* that alluded to the existence of a Jewish voting "bloc."[8] The meeting's minutes called the article "deplorable," criticizing "the kind of loose talk about an alleged Jewish vote that has been a part of every election campaign since 1940." They also noted that only in the case of a "demonstrably anti-Semitic" candidate would the AJC counsel "legitimate Jewish partisanship," stressing that the Committee's public mission disavowed any specific Jewish group "interest" except combating anti-Jewish discrimination.

The AJC's discomfort with publicly recognizing the existence of group voting patterns did not prevent the DAC from supporting research on the voting behavior of Jews and other ethnic groups in the 1960 presidential campaign. In

1963, Dawidowicz and Leon J. Goldstein, a professor of philosophy at SUNY–Binghamton, published *Politics in a Pluralist Democracy: Studies in Voting in the 1960 Election*, a result of a study done on behalf of the DAC because of the anti-Catholicism that had emerged during the presidential race.[9] The study was designed "to disabuse the claim that a 'bloc vote' is something sinister, manipulatable, or 'deliverable'" when "practiced by Jews or Catholics or Negroes." Even as the study discredited this fear, it illustrated that a typical voter was influenced by the "historical and cultural features of the group to which he belongs." Dawidowicz and Goldstein studied a number of cities and rural areas with different religious and ethnic groups, using interviews, poll data, and "restrained speculation."[10] They concluded that religion and ethnicity were significant factors in voting but that their respective influence varied according to socioeconomic and political cross-pressures. Daniel Patrick Moynihan, coauthor of the influential *Beyond the Melting Pot: The Negroes, Puerto Ricans, Jews, Italians, and Irish of New York City* (1963),[11] favorably reviewed Dawidowicz and Goldstein's book in *Commentary*, noting the challenge of ethnicity's persistence to American civil society. Calling group rights a "perplexing problem," he observed that "Groups do not *have* rights in America; only individuals do. But groups have interests, have problems, have identities, and ought to have responsibilities."[12]

Despite the AJC's discomfort with singling out its community's political predilections, Dawidowicz and Goldstein devoted a substantial section of their book to Jewish voting behavior, finding that the "Democratic vote among middle-class and upper-middle-class Jews still is much higher than among others of equal status."[13] In chapter 11, "The Jewish Liberal Tradition," Dawidowicz and Goldstein concluded that the American Jewish attachment to liberalism derived from the European past. American Jews were heirs to the knowledge that the conservative clergy, the nobility, and other traditional elites had opposed the political emancipation of the Jews in the nineteenth century, which encouraged Jews to support liberal political parties. Liberalism, embodied by Roosevelt's inclusive social welfare politics, knitted Jewish loyalty to the Democratic Party by advocating a society in which individual merit, not family, race, or religious confession, mattered. Dawidowicz and Goldstein speculated that further integration of the Jews into American society, and increased distance from a Europe that linked the Right with anti-Jewish attitudes, would lead to a more decisive role of social class in diversifying Jewish voting patterns.[14] *Politics in a Pluralist Democracy* gave Dawidowicz the opportunity to publish her analysis of the relationship among religion, communal life, and politics in the

United States. In *The Golden Tradition* she turned back to the history of those relationships in the European Jewish heartland: Eastern Europe.

KHURBN FORSHUNG FOR THE AMERICAN PUBLIC

Dawidowicz credited the Polish Jewish rabbi and philosopher Abraham Joshua Heschel with suggesting she write a book on East European Jewry. On the occasion of *The Golden Tradition*'s reprinting in 1988, she recalled that already in the 1950s Heschel had said to her, "You should write a book about the Jews of Eastern Europe. You're one of the last people to have been there, to have lived in that world."[15] Heschel, the scion of a prominent Polish Hasidic family, was an intellectual polymath known for his openness to all aspects of Jewish traditional life as well as to secular studies. In the interwar years, he pursued a doctorate at the University of Berlin while simultaneously writing Yiddish poetry and studying for liberal rabbinic ordination at the Hochschule für die Wissenschaft des Judentums. In October 1938, he was deported back to Poland, where he lectured on Jewish themes at the Warsaw Institute for Jewish Studies. Six weeks before the Nazi invasion, Heschel made his way to London and then to New York, where he began an illustrious career as a Torah scholar, public intellectual, and civil rights activist. At the New York YIVO conference in 1945, Heschel delivered "Di mizrekh-eyropeishe tkufe in der yidisher geshikhte" (The East European Era in Jewish History), a lecture-cum-eulogy for the murdered Jews of Eastern Europe. It was published in 1950 in English with a new title, *The Earth Is the Lord's*.[16] (Max Weinreich also spoke at the conference, and his address, "The YIVO Faces the Post-War World," made a sharp turn away from his prewar emphasis on the rupture between West and East European Jewries, stressing instead the seamlessness of Ashkenazic civilization.[17])

Though Dawidowicz was not a literal survivor of the Holocaust, she was haunted by her eleventh-hour flight from Vilna, by the annihilation of her Lithuanian Jewish friends, and by the photograph of her husband's murdered daughter, Tobtsche, that hung—with her posthumously awarded Silver Medal of Merit from the Polish government—above Szymon's desk, shrine-like, in their bedroom.[18]

Dawidowicz considered herself "a survivor only in imagination, in guilt," telling the novelist Henia Karmel-Wolfe, author of *The Baders of Jacob Street*, that "People like me live in a shadowy in-between world of pseudo-survivordom," adding that "Driven by memories not rightfully mine, I now inhabited a shadow world of murdered European Jews."[19] In 1966, she wrote

```
CONSULATE GENERAL
OF THE REPUBLIC OF POLAND
149-151 EAST 67TH STREET                    September 17, 1948.
NEW YORK 21, N.Y.




              Honoring a hero of the Warsaw Ghetto Uprising.
              --------------------------------------------- --

                   In a simple but moving ceremony at the Polish
              Consulate General, 151 East 67 St., New York,
              Consul Roman Kwiecień, in the presence of Attaché
              Alexander Lenowicz-Gordin, handed over today to
              Mr. Szymon Dawidowicz, now resident of New York,
              315 West 76 Street, the Silver Medal of Merit
              bestowed posthumously upon his daughter, TOBA
              DAWIDOWICZ, by decree of the President of Poland.
                   Toba Dawidowicz was killed by the Germans in
              the tragic battle of the Warsaw Ghetto, in April
              1943, at the age of 19. She was one of its outstand-
              ing heroes.
```

Polish consulate press release, "Honoring a Hero of the Warsaw Ghetto Uprising," September 17, 1948. (Courtesy Laurie Sapakoff)

about her fantasies of rescue to the poet Irving Feldman after reading his collection "The Pripet Marshes." The title poem began: "Often I think of my Jewish friends and seize them as they are and transport them in my mind to the
shtetlach and ghettos."[20] Apologizing for "thrusting my confession upon you,"
Dawidowicz revealed that the poems "uncovered my secret game."

> I was not there (nor were you), yet what happened there has been central in
> my life. I am forever putting myself and the people I know in the Warsaw
> ghetto, testing myself, testing them, pushing myself and them beyond the
> edge of experience.... Sometimes I think we here are not real at all, but we
> are all merely rehearsing for that time. So you see it was as if you had written
> my name on "The Pripet Marshes."[21]

The Golden Tradition's original title had been "A Vanished World: Jewish
Life and Culture in Eastern Europe, 1860–1939." The term "vanished" reinforced
both the distance between American Jews and the East European Jewish past

and the method of salvage anthropology that shaped the works by Chagall, Herzog and Zborowski, Heschel, and Samuel.[22] But when Dawidowicz submitted the first draft to her editor, Arthur A. Cohen, it had a new name, *The Golden Tradition*. The title no longer directly invoked the destruction of East European Jewish civilization but instead offered the American Jewish public a metaphor of shining continuity.[23] The response to the reader's report—an unsigned memo but likely written by Dawidowicz herself—explicitly spoke to the question of audience, noting that the book "would speak meaningfully to the American reader, Jewish and gentile, and ... would demonstrate the richness of Jewish religious and intellectual life and the multiplicity of ways to express Jewish identity."[24] The book's pragmatic—and elusive—goal was to foster American Jewish consciousness and identity in the present by a skillful deployment of the Ashkenazic past. The material showed how people had "searched for ways to harmonize tradition and modernity, to preserve their Jewish identity and retain their community."[25] Dawidowicz informed her readers that her book was about "East European Jews in crisis, challenge, and creativity ... until their

Szymon Dawidowicz (center), with Aleksander Lenowicz-Gordin and Roman Kwiecień, receiving a Medal of Honor for Tobtsche Dawidowicz at the Polish consulate, September 17, 1948. (Courtesy the American Jewish Historical Society)

cataclysmic destruction in the Second World War."[26] Like Dubnow and the practitioners of *khurbn forshung*, her anthologizing of the experiences of East European Jewry was meant to serve a national-cultural purpose: "[Though] East European Jewry was cruelly cut down ... vital elements of its culture survive. Perhaps we, heirs of that culture, can continue its tradition of conserving Jewish identity by fusing the old and the new."[27]

Published in January 1967, *The Golden Tradition* contained a lengthy historical introduction, maps, and an anthology of sixty primary texts in translation, each prefaced by a short biographical and interpretive description.[28] Dust-jacket blurbs from four Jewish intellectuals represented a targeted range of American Jewish readers: Norman Podhoretz, editor of *Commentary* magazine, for the literate nonprofessional Jewish reader; Salo W. Baron, the foremost Jewish historian in the United States, for professional Jewish scholars; Maurice Samuel, Sholem Aleichem's first English-language interpreter, for the secular Yiddishist intelligentsia; and Heschel for postwar American Jews who defined their identities in religious terms.

The Golden Tradition's effort to honor the memory of the vital culture of the East European Jews among whom Dawidowicz lived in prewar Vilna was not lost on reviewers. Irving Howe anointed Dawidowicz and her interpretation of East European Jewish life with a glowing evaluation in *Book Week* on February 12, 1967. Praising her "enormous and splendid anthology" as a "necessary corrective to *shtetl* romanticism," and contrasting it favorably with more sanitized descriptions of the old country, he concluded:

> Having now read, enjoyed, and suffered with *The Golden Tradition* over the past few months, I find myself unable to praise it too highly. It is quite as if a whole culture had been rescued from the dust, and all of its inner qualities, its half-forgotten voices and passions, have been brought to vivid life. ... For here is the world of our fathers,[29] or at least *some* of our fathers, drawn not in the delicate line of idyll or the charcoal softness of nostalgia, but with the heavily textured complications and even harshness of reality.[30]

Curt Leviant, a scholar, novelist, and translator of Hebrew and Yiddish literature, praised the book in the *New York Times Book Review*, also underscoring its lack of sentimentality:

> The volume is perhaps as important for what it is not as for what it is. It is not belles-lettres, or an exercise in sentimentality, or a study of *shtetl* life.

"The Golden Tradition" is an anthology that epitomizes the various spiritual crosscurrents that affected East European Jews from the end of the 18th century up to World War II. . . . [The book is] an ideological sampler, a stethoscope to the heartbeat of the Jews, reaction to their encounter with modern Europe, a record of the Jews' prismatic intellectual experience.[31]

In her introduction, Dawidowicz herself claimed the mantle of revisionism, stating that "I was guided also by the desire to show the diversity of Jews and their culture, the centripetal and centrifugal forces that moved them, and the variety they brought to Jewish thought and life. *East European Jewry was not, as the sentimentalists see it, forever frozen in utter piety and utter poverty.*"[32] Distancing her book from the folkloristic approaches that conflated *shtetl* Jewry with all of East European Jewry, she included variegated sources that would add breadth to the static view of the Jewish past. These included selections from the writing of Hasidic masters, traditional rabbis, *maskilim*, publicists, poets, and even converts (the latter a category of Jewish liminality accepted today but farsighted in her time). Correcting *shtetl* romanticization meant offering excerpts from urbanized modern Jews, among them visual artists, revolutionaries, and, notably, women writers.[33] In the first draft of the introduction, she described the attempt "to make our selection sufficiently varied in time and place, in class and education, in degree of religion and national commitment, to reflect the variety of the era."[34]

Dawidowicz chose autobiographical source material for her anthology because, citing the German historian Wilhelm Dilthey, she believed it to be "the highest and most instructive form in which the understanding of life confronts us."[35] Reflecting years later on her method, Dawidowicz would write that she wanted to be able to narrate history "from the perspective of the participant or the participant-observer," a perspective, she observed, that "conveys an immediacy and immanence that cannot always be captured in history which is written on the basis of documents alone from a remote past."[36] The first-person narratives allowed the reader to enter the contemporary world of the writers and anchored Dawidowicz's narration of Jewish history in Jewish sources. Her focus on autobiographical materials may have also owed a debt to her JDC colleague Leo W. Schwarz, who had published several English anthologies of memoir and other first-person material before 1967, including *The Root and the Bough: The Epic of an Enduring People* (1949), for which Dawidowicz contributed a translation of "Life in a Bunker" by M. J. Feigenbaum, an activist in the Central Historical Commission.[37]

Despite Dawidowicz's claim that autobiography made history intimate, her translation strategy created an invisible layer of distance from the past. The original languages of the selections included Yiddish, German, Hebrew, and Russian, but Dawidowicz's English translations generally came from secondary Yiddish translations of the originals, resulting in a kind of Yiddishist projection onto the diverse linguistic landscape of modern East European Jewry. The anthology also reflected the credulity of her period regarding autobiographical source material, a perspective that would not hold up now among professional historians.[38] Likewise, Dawidowicz included hagiographic accounts of Hasidic rebbes by their disciples that lacked the critical perspective scholars today would require.[39]

The egalitarian impulse of a "participant-observer" ethos that drew from all segments of East European Jewry notwithstanding, Dawidowicz favored writings by the Jewish intellectual elite, and *The Golden Tradition* was unrepresentative of Jewish society's nonliterate groups. As a historian Dawidowicz—in sync with the American historiographic tradition of the postwar period—was interested in "event-making men," those "whose genius was so adapted to the receptivities of the moment . . . that they became ferments, initiators of movement, setters of precedent or fashion."[40] Dawidowicz viewed ideas and ideology as the most significant forces in history, in contrast to social class or political structure, a perspective she would further develop in all of her later historical writing. In 1975, she wrote to George Mosse: "I am very grateful to you, for you are among that small company of scholars that take ideas seriously."[41]

DUBNOW'S OTHER DAUGHTER

Dawidowicz's fealty to Dubnow's historiographic ethos is nowhere more explicit than in *The Golden Tradition*'s eighty-page introduction, "The World of East European Jewry," which was a virtual catechism of Dubnowian principles. Originally titled "Tradition and Modernity: The Response of East European Jews to the Modern World"[42]—arguably a more accurate title for the book— it chronicled Jewish modernity in Eastern Europe from the mid-eighteenth century until the Nazi invasion of Poland and focused on the experiences of modernizing Russian and Polish Jews. Dawidowicz presented readers a historical overview of the culture of premodern Polish Jewry. The introduction described a community historically governed by a *kahal*, which, in encountering the modern world, gave rise to a natural efflorescence of ideological, political, and linguistic creativity that reflected that community's national-cultural autonomy. Dawidowicz directly cited Dubnow's view of the Council of the Four Lands, early modern Polish Jewry's highest administrative body, as "a surrogate for national political activity, [which] thereby sustained its awareness of its autonomy, [and] safeguarded and developed its own individual culture."[43] Assuming a static binary between the modernization of West and East European Jewries, Dawidowicz concluded that Western Jews were largely incapable of maintaining their communal cohesion in the face of Enlightenment and emancipation. But "Eastern Europe was different," and her anthology aimed to introduce American Jews to the personal experiences of East European Jews who had successfully negotiated the challenges of modernity by preserving their identity and retaining their community.[44] Dawidowicz, intellectually and emotionally bound to the Jews of interwar Poland, viewed the history of Polish Jewry as a metonym for the whole East European Jewish past. No other Jewry in the world enjoyed the political, cultural, and social autonomy experienced by Polish Jews in their long sojourn in Europe.[45]

Dawidowicz's affirmation of an enduring Jewish historical agency was picked up again in the penultimate section of *The Golden Tradition*'s introduction, "Jewish Politics: Under Despotism and Dictatorship," where she assessed the effect of political enfranchisement on the life of Jews in interwar Poland. Agency was a subject she was to engage again in *The War Against the Jews*, but already here she took it upon herself to defend East European Jewry against charges of political passivity and political collaboration. She argued that despite official Polish political pressure to denationalize the Jewish community by recognizing it as a religious union, Polish Jewry retained its identity as a national-religious community. She characterized the internecine multiplication of Jewish parties that many saw as irresponsible given the extent of antisemitism in Polish society "as an instrumentality for strengthening Jewish identity and increasing Jewish self-reliance."[46] Indebted to Dubnow, she found strength in the Jews' political powerlessness, which, she concluded, gave them moral authority, "a unique Jewish quality that no other politically powerless minority in Poland exercised."[47] It was the deep diasporic communal identity of Polish Jewry—rooted in its *kehillot*, in adherence to Yiddish, and in its vibrant national-political life of the interwar years—that shaped its response "under despotism and dictatorship" and preserved its collective solidarity.

Dawidowicz also affirmed Dubnow's positive view of the role of religion in shaping Jewish culture. By 1967, Dawidowicz had become increasingly dubious about the ability of secularism to ensure Jewish survival in the modern world. In *The Golden Tradition*, Dawidowicz adduced Dubnow to support her own evolutionary rapprochement with Judaism. Though she knew he was an avowed agnostic, Dawidowicz nonetheless claimed that he was "too much a Jew" to excise Judaism from Jewishness and quoted his own words from "The Doctrine of Jewish Nationalism" (1897) to advance her interpretation. "If we wish to preserve Judaism as a cultural-historical type of nation," Dubnow had written,

> we must realize that the religion of Judaism is one of the integral foundations of national culture and that anyone who seeks to destroy it undermines the very basis of national existence. Between us and the orthodox Jews there is only this difference: they recognize a traditional Judaism the forms of which were set from the beginning for all eternity, while we believe in an evolutionary Judaism in which new and old forms are always being assumed or discarded and which adjusts itself unceasingly to new cultural conditions.[48]

The inclusion of Dubnow's comments on Judaism points to a basic paradox in her thinking about the larger project she had undertaken. Dawidowicz hoped *The Golden Tradition* would show American Jews that in Eastern Europe, nonreligious or even anti-religious Jews were part of the Jewish "world" even if they personally rejected all religious demands. Of course, that they remained an integral part of the Jewish world was *only* because they inhabited a civilization in which the religious tradition was deeply embedded. She hoped that the increasingly nonreligious American Jewish reader would come to see the necessity of Judaism for the construction of an American Jewishness that, like the integral Jewishness of Eastern Europe, went well beyond the merely religious.

Dawidowicz's postwar liberalism, discussed earlier, can be seen in her dismissal of utopian, universalist political movements. In her introduction's section titled "New Religions: Science, Progress, Humanity," she described their impact: "These ascendant scientific theories and philosophical currents [i.e., nationalism, positivism, socialism, and secularism] had an explosive effect on the emerging educated classes in Eastern Europe. They had a convulsive effect on Jewish traditional society."[49] Three figures in this section emerged as her intellectual heroes: the cultural Zionist Ahad Ha-am, Dubnow, and the Yiddishist-turned-Orthodox Jew Nathan Birnbaum. Despite their differences, they shared a belief in the interdependence of Jewish identity and Jewish national existence; in Dawidowicz's view, they "rejected secular messianism, choosing instead the continuity of Jewish culture and traditions."[50] Without this unified foundation, modernizing Jews in the diaspora could not have sustained themselves when buffeted by modernity's individualistic and secular assault.

If Dawidowicz owed a clear debt to Dubnow, her introduction also bore the stamp of Max Weinreich's influence. The Eastern Europe of her book's title was not a geographic entity, but a mentalité. The term in her usage actually meant "Ashkenaz," whose roots lie in medieval German lands, but had come to encompass, in Weinreich's postwar formulation, the ethos of a civilization.[51] In her 1969 eulogy for Weinreich, "The Scholarship of Yiddish," she summarized his definition of Ashkenaz:

> [It] was the Jewish community, with its language, literature, culture ... born some 1,100 years ago in the Middle Rhine-Moselle territory and, in the course of the centuries, slowly moved eastward. Until 1500 its metropolises were in Central Europe: Mayence, Worms, Ratisbon, Prague. Thereafter Ashkenaz shifted to Eastern Europe: Cracow, Lublin, Mezbizh, Vilna, and Warsaw. Consequently ... Ashkenaz became "freed of its territorial connotations; geography, as it were, has been transformed into history."[52]

She cited his 1951 YIVO conference paper, "Ashkenaz: The Era of Yiddish in Jewish History," in which he concluded that "wonderful transcendental values from both a Jewish and universal viewpoint" were contained in the "culture and language of Ashkenaz" and warned that "it would be a cultural catastrophe" for the future if those values vanished.[53] Like Dubnow, whose nationalist historiography was suffused with the Jews' survival through history,[54] and like Weinreich, who in 1941 insisted on the crucial role of the YIVO's *visnshaft* (scholarship) in creating a national community,[55] Dawidowicz sought existential meaning in the writing of Jewish history.

Grappling with her own existential dilemmas, Dawidowicz found herself drawn to an unlikely source: an autobiographical reflection on religious transformation, *Vom Freigeist zum Gläubigen* (From a Freethinker to a Believer), written by Nathan Birnbaum in 1919. Birnbaum, a Viennese Jew of East European origins, traveled through the most powerful ideological streams of modern Ashkenazic Jewish life—materialism, secularism, Zionism, diaspora nationalism, and Yiddishism—before landing on the shores of "Tradition."[56] Credited with coining the phrase "Zionism" before Theodor Herzl, Birnbaum was an activist at the Czernowitz conference on Yiddish language in 1908 and a spokesman for Yiddishist autonomism, as well as the editor of *Jewish War Archives* (the World Zionist Organization's newspaper documenting the refugee crisis during and after World War I) and an activist in the ultra-Orthodox political party Agudas Yisroel in interwar Poland.

In his *Freethinker* essay, Birnbaum struggled with the challenges of Jewish modernity and expressed the existential ruminations that had resulted in his personal transformation.[57] Disillusioned by the instability of secularist nationalism, he revealed that once he had "discarded" it and began "putting greater stress on peoplehood as a living reality," he realized that "the innermost nature of the Jewish people ought to be expressed in its religion and that it therefore deserved serious attention and the utmost respect."[58] Modernity's materialism was bankrupt, and rational philosophy was limited: "Little by little, I realized . . . that there was a higher state of thinking than logic, of which the senses are aware, and a higher level of emotion than pure psychophysical sensitivity, and that, in essence, we cannot interpret the great and elevated revelations of spirit in history as the inevitable effects of senseless dead matter."[59] His former worldview broken, Birnbaum turned to religious observance. Change proved difficult: "I had to surmount strong inner opposition, besides outer obstacles. A man who for decades valued and served individualism in its subservience to matter cannot simply divest himself of the effects of his education, of all Western habits and traits which contravene the meaning and the rigorous will of Judaism, as he would take off clothes he had put on a few hours before."[60]

Dawidowicz worked from the Yiddish translation of Birnbaum's original German pamphlet, and an excerpt of her translation caught the eye of his son Solomon when it was published in *The Jewish Observer*, an organ of Agudas Yisroel, in the spring of 1967.[61] That year, Dawidowicz wrote revealingly to Solomon about the profound impression his father's pamphlet had made on her:

> The essay which I translated had a deep personal influence on me, and on the changes, perhaps small by some standards, in my life. As I worked on it (and I devoted myself painstakingly to that translation), I felt that Nathan Birnbaum was challenging me personally. I had to decide, once and for all, in what direction I was to go. For me this is all quite intimate and precious, and I am rather embarrassed to write about it. But I thought that perhaps you would like to know that translating your father's essay was not merely a literary or intellectual exercise for me.[62]

The Birnbaum correspondence is especially poignant because it confirms Dawidowicz's inner struggle with her Yiddishist-secularist past, a struggle dating back to her year in Vilna before the war.

It bears noting that Dawidowicz's selections for *The Golden Tradition* were a reflection of the liberal climate of the time. Made in the early to mid-1960s, they were politically ecumenical. Section 10, "In the Revolutionary Movements," gave voice to the radical Yiddishism of Chaim Zhitlovsky but also to Leon Trotsky's aversion to Jewish nationalism and to Sholem Schwartzbard's violent anarchism. Had Dawidowicz compiled *The Golden Tradition* in the 1970s, it is almost certain that her rightward political shift in reaction to the rise of the New Left and the counterculture would have led her to exclude left-wing ideologues and activists.[63] In the period of the book's making, however, her only bias in the selections was a "pro-Jewish point of view."[64] She even devoted section 8 to "Marginals" and included Daniel Chwolson, Abraham Uri Kovner, Jan Bloch, Henri Bergson, and Leopold Infeld. In spite of these authors' formal conversion from Judaism or total distance from normative forms of Jewish life,[65] their inclusion underscored her diaspora nationalist sensibilities: regardless of religious affiliation—or lack of it—these men could not erase their Jewishness.

In this regard, *The Golden Tradition*, in offering a more complex portrait of East European Jewish society than the static and romanticized image of the early postwar works, also presented it as a holistic model for American Jews. In Dawidowicz's imagination, within East European Jewish society's diversity lay the integrated unity of Ashkenazic civilization, which bequeathed to East European Jews the ability to fuse "the old and the new." She positioned her assemblage of Jewish personalities on a spectrum of existential "return" to an identification with the Jewish people. "East European Jews, too, turned and returned," she wrote. "Their return was toward a more intense form of Jewish identity and a passionate reaffirmation of their ties with the Jewish community and its fate. Every Jewish movement, no matter how secular, offered the possibility of such return."[66] Hearing the diverse Jewish voices contained in *The Golden Tradition* might stimulate American Jews to reconfigure their Jewishness, to stay their desire to assimilate, and to choose to "return." She affirmed this hope by citing Heschel's *The Earth Is the Lord's* as evidence of the holistic nature of East European Jewish society: "The Jews had always known piety and Sabbath holiness. . . . The new thing in Eastern Europe was that somewhat of the Sabbath infused into every day. One could relish the taste of life eternal in the fleeting moment."[67] There was, too, the implicit message that postwar American Jews, heirs to the civilization of Ashkenaz, were charged with historic responsibility: the affirmation of positive Jewish identity because their East European Jewish forebears had been "cut down forever."[68] *The Golden Tradition* could be their guide.

Dawidowicz hoped that by providing postwar American Jews insight into the grandeur of Ashkenazic Jewish civilization, *The Golden Tradition* would help foster American Jewish historical consciousness and its complement, identification with the Jewish people. In a letter written to Salo W. Baron on the occasion of his seventieth birthday, Dawidowicz revealed her great debt to his example of combining historical scholarship with national commitments. "Permit me, then," she mused,

> to write what I would blush to tell. The encounter with your vast erudition and your exacting scholarship has been an enriching intellectual adventure; your generous humanism and *ahaves-yisroyel* (love of the Jews)[69] an inspiration, and your optimism about the Jewish future, so firmly grounded in your creative understanding of the Jewish past, a comfort. And if this were not enough, you have combined scholarship and study with service to the Jewish community and provided a model for all of us to follow.[70]

Twenty years later, Dawidowicz would again write a letter brimming with gratitude to Baron, informing him of "how large your presence has been in my life." Calling him her "teacher *par excellence*, who unfolded the panorama of Jewish history as no one else has ever done," she summed up his influence on her work:

> Two things you taught me. One was that history is the great drama of Jewish existence and that the scholar participates in that drama by reconstructing it. *The other was that the scholar should not isolate himself from his community. Being a Jewish historian, that is, a historian of the Jews, means having a commitment to the Jewish people.* For teaching me these things and for being what you are, I thank you.[71]

If Baron was Dawidowicz's teacher par excellence, Dubnow was her spiritual and intellectual father.[72] The latter's belief that collecting and preserving Jewish historical sources could fuel the development of Jewish national consciousness found a passionate disciple in Dawidowicz. She shared his belief that historical research could further historical consciousness, which, in turn, would foster national belonging and cohesion, particularly for modern Jews who had rejected both religion and assimilation.[73] Dubnow's ideology had informed the work of several generations of Jewish historians in Eastern Europe,[74] but it was Lucy S. Dawidowicz who became the critical American link to the East European national-cultural historiographic chain. Dubnow's influence on her historiography, which resonated throughout *The Golden Tradition*, became the centerpiece of the book that made her famous, *The War Against the Jews, 1933–1945*.

8

DEFENDING POLISH JEWRY

The War Against the Jews

The Golden Tradition gave Dawidowicz authority and stature. In the fall of 1969, she left the American Jewish Committee and began to teach at Stern College and the Wurzweiler School of Social Work of Yeshiva University. Initially slated to teach the courses "The Jew in American Society" and "Jewish Communal Organization,"[1] she soon found herself drawing on her expertise to conceive what became one of the first university courses in the United States on the history of the Holocaust.[2]

She quickly faced a problem: an almost complete lack of a bibliography in English suitable for teaching undergraduates and an educated lay public about the Holocaust from the victims' perspective.[3] In December 1969, Dawidowicz approached Aaron Asher to propose a book that would be a synthetic history of the Holocaust, bringing together the "German Final Solution with the Jewish responses." "The Jewish material," she explained, "will be based largely on first-hand Yiddish and Hebrew documents, of which relatively little has appeared in English."[4] In 1970, her highly critical review of Nora Levin's *The Holocaust: The Destruction of European Jewry, 1933–1945* pointed out "the scarcity of solid scholarship on many aspects of the Holocaust" and illustrated her sense of what the field needed—namely, "a good, popular narrative history that

Stern College for Women
Yeshiva University

History 95

THE HOLOCAUST. A seminar.   Limited to 20 students.

German antisemitism and its political, legal, bureaucratic, and intellectual substructure; preparations for
the "Final Solution," the destruction of European Jewry;
the stages of its execution in the countries of Europe;
how European Jews lived and died under German rule;
moral and ethical aspects. Emphasis will be on reading and discussion. A term paper will be required.

Prerequisites: European history, modern Jewish history.

Course Outline

1. Antecedents and substructure: From Mein Kampf to the Wannsee
conference
Background of German antisemitism and racism; Nazi
legislation; the enlistment of the professors and intellectuals; organization of the bureaucracy for the
destruction of the Jews.
(Four sessions)

2. Carrying out the "Final Solution"
Stages: Expropriation, evacuation and concentration,
ghettos; deportations and mobile killings; slave labor
and death camps.

By countries: Central and Eastern Europe (Poland,
Russia, the Baltic countries; Rumania, Hungary,
the Balkans, the Reich Protektorat); Western

Above and facing page: "The Holocaust: A Seminar,"
syllabus, Stern College, Yeshiva University, March 1969.
(Courtesy Yeshiva University Archives)

is intelligibly set in a conceptual framework and is written with more literary
and intellectual discipline than Miss Levin musters."[5]

When, in 1970, Yeshiva University received funds to support research and
teaching on the Holocaust, Dawidowicz was appointed the university's Leah
and Paul Lewis Professor of Holocaust Studies[6]—the first chair in an American university devoted to the study of the catastrophe.[7] She held the position
for five years, giving her space, time, and income to research *The War Against
the Jews*. Published in 1975, the book was a popular, synthetic history both of
Nazi antisemitism, with its culmination in the Final Solution, and the Jewish
response to it. Christopher Lehmann-Haupt's review in the *New York Times*
praised it as a book that "blends in an ideal fashion narrative and conclusion."
He aptly boiled down its argument "to a single syllogism: Hitler set out to annihilate European Jewry; this had never happened before; therefore European
Jewry could not possibly have known how to respond effectively."[8]

Still in print four decades later, *The War Against the Jews* earned Dawidowicz

Europe ~~the "civilized" countries~~ (France, Holland,
Belgium, Italy); the exceptional countries (Denmark,
Bulgaria).

Discussion will deal with background of antisemitism
and relations between Jews and gentiles in each country;
factors of national character and cultural traditions;
the role of social and political institutions (churches,
labor, intellectuals, political parties, undergrounds).

(Ten sessions)

3. Life and death of the European Jews

In the ghettos: social, economic, and political aspects
(social welfare and self-help, education, religious life,
cultural activities).

Judenraete: their origins, purposes and functions,
composition, activities; leaders (Warsaw, Vilna, Lodz);
moral dilemmas.

Martyrdom and resistance: the varieties of Jewish responses; underground organizations and political parties,
armed revolts (Warsaw ghetto), partisans, kiddush ha-Shem.

(Ten sessions)

4. "While Six Million Died"

Responses of the Allies, the neutral nations, and the
Jews in the United States and Palestine.

(Two sessions)

5. War crimes

The concept of genocide; the Nuremberg trials; the
Eichmann trial; collective guilt and collective
responsibility.

(Two sessions)

6. Summing up

Jewish losses; faith after Auschwitz; Israel and
Jewish existence in the light of the Holocaust.

(Two sessions)

Lucy S. Davidowicz
March 1969

pride of place in the "intentionalist school" of Holocaust historiography. The book responded directly to the interpretations of Raul Hilberg's *The Destruction of the European Jews* (1961) and Hannah Arendt's *Eichmann in Jerusalem: On the Banality of Evil* (1963), the two most influential examples of "functionalist" and perpetrator analyses of the Nazi onslaught in the postwar period.[9]

THE CENTRALITY OF ANTISEMITISM TO HITLER'S INTENTIONALISM

In *The War Against the Jews*, Dawidowicz set out to address three fundamental problems: How was it possible for a modern state to carry out the systematic murder of a whole people for no reason other than that they were Jews? How was it possible for a whole people to allow itself to be destroyed? And how was it possible for the world to stand by without halting this destruction?[10] In "Part I: The Final Solution," she presented her "intentionalist" reading of German antisemitism, which addressed her first question. "Part II: The Holocaust," in which her defense of the culture and history of East European Jews rebutted the regnant Germanocentric views of Jewish history presented by Hilberg and Arendt, addressed the second. The book never fully treated the third question.[11] Only in the 1980s would Dawidowicz take on the question of the degree to which the US government, the formal American Jewish community, and the general American Jewish public were guilty of standing by during the Holocaust. Her position exculpated all three groups.[12]

Dawidowicz focused her interpretation of the Holocaust and the Final Solution on East European Jewry, which, until 1942, was the largest Jewish community in the world. East European Jewry and its almost total destruction had become, as noted earlier, a metonym for European Jewry as a whole.[13] In her introduction to *The War Against the Jews*, Dawidowicz, echoing Max Weinreich's view of Ashkenazic civilization, wrote: "The destruction of East European Jewry brought to an end the thousand-year-old culture of Ashkenazic Jewry that had originated in the Rhine Basin and that by 1939 was concentrated in Eastern Europe. . . . It was a culture unique in all Jewish history, and East European Ashkenazic Jewry, which fashioned that culture, was the wellspring of Jewish creativity for Jewish communities throughout the world."[14] Following Dubnow, Dawidowicz stressed the tenacity of Jewish communal life, both in freedom and "in crisis and extremity."[15]

It bears emphasizing that from 1945 to the mid-1960s, the Holocaust was not yet a proper noun in the United States. To be sure, in the immediate postwar years, the American public, both Jewish and gentile, was aware of the destruction of European Jewry, but it had not yet become central to the construction of Jewish identity. As Kirsten Fermaglich has shown, American academics and social scientists in the war's aftermath analogized the Holocaust in universalist terms. Writers Stanley Elkins, Betty Friedan, and Robert Jay Lifton compared the brutalization of European Jewry, respectively, to African American slavery, the plight of suburban American housewives, and the victims of Hiroshima. Psychologist Stanley Milgram designed his 1963 obedience experiment to mimic the authority structure in the concentration camps.[16] Lawrence Baron has argued that Gerald Reitlinger's *The Final Solution* (1953), Leon Poliakov's *Harvest of Hate* (1954), and Joseph Tenenbaum's *Race and Reich: The Story of an Epoch* (1956) created an American memory culture that could be called "holocaust" and not "Holocaust" consciousness; the Jewish specificity of the destruction was downplayed.[17] In his study of American television, Jeffrey Shandler showed the destruction of European Jewry played often in American households in the 1950s and 1960s.[18] But most Americans linked the destruction of European Jewry to bigotry in general, and the Holocaust was cited to promote civil rights. Michael Staub showed that in the postwar years, American Jews across the political spectrum deployed the Holocaust for political purposes: "There was never any agreement on what the lessons for the American context were, but all agreed that there were lessons."[19] While it is true that the American public commemorations, ceremonies, and memorials acknowledged the ruination of European Jewry, most of them remained within the confines of local Jewish communities.[20] They did not cross over into the American mainstream, nor were they central to the Jewish community's educational or social policy agendas.

The publication of *The War Against the Jews* indicated a signal shift in interpretation, changing both the terms of memory and the interpretation of history. If *The Golden Tradition* was Dawidowicz's first salvo in rebutting the view that East European Jewry lacked agency, *The War Against the Jews* went further, claiming that Hitler's assault on Europe was singularly focused on the destruction of the Jews, who responded as best they were able to the virulent antisemitism that aimed at their complete extermination. The book's very title declared her perspective.

The New York intellectuals took serious note of *The War Against the Jews*. At least thirty reviews of the book appeared in a wide variety of American and American Jewish academic and popular periodicals, ranging from the *New York Times* to *Hadassah Magazine*. Praise for the work also came in private form.[21]

Irving Howe's review appeared on the first page of the Sunday *New York Times Book Review*:

> Books about Nazism are endless, and so too about anti-Semitism, but Mrs. Dawidowicz's "The War Against the Jews" comes to us as a major work of synthesis, providing for the first time a full account of the holocaust not merely as it completed the Nazi vision but as it affected the Jews of eastern Europe. Drawing upon materials in half a dozen languages and writing with a restraint that seems almost beyond credence, Mrs. Dawidowicz, a professor of history at Yeshiva University, has produced a work of high scholarship and profound moral import.[22]

The War Against the Jews, divided into three sections, is best known for its first part, "The Final Solution." Here Dawidowicz presented her intentionalist view of the causes of the Holocaust. This historiographic approach argued that Adolf Hitler's murderous antisemitism was not only the driving force of Nazi policy but also the reason for the invasions of Poland in 1939 and the Soviet Union in 1941.[23] Intentionalists emphasized Hitler's singular role in orchestrating the Final Solution, which could not have occurred were it not for the power of ideas and ideology in history generally and of antisemitism in Germany in particular.[24] Dawidowicz's intentionalism dated the origins of the Final Solution to 1918, to Hitler's manipulative interpretation of the causes of Germany's defeat in World War I; she wrote that "Through the maze of time Hitler's decision of November 1918 led to Operation Barbarossa. There never had been any ideological deviation or wavering determination."[25] For Dawidowicz, the war and the annihilation of the Jews were part of a coherent, consistent, and orderly sequence of intentional events that were present from the very beginning of Hitler's rise to power. She presented this thesis on the book's opening page: "The mass murder of the Jews was the consummation of his [Hitler's] fundamental beliefs and ideological convictions."[26] A decade later, in the tenth anniversary edition of *The War Against the Jews*, she would reiterate her view that "hatred of the Jews was Hitler's central and most compelling belief and that it dominated his thoughts and actions all his life." She argued that all the documents

> Amply justify my conclusion that Hitler planned to murder the Jews in coordination with his plans to go to war for *Lebensraum* (living space) and to establish the Thousand Year Reich. The conventional war of conquest was to

be waged parallel to, and was able to camouflage, the ideological war against the Jews. In the end, as the war hurtled to its disastrous finale, Hitler's relentless fanaticism in the racial/ideological war ultimately cost him victory in the conventional war.[27]

Antisemitism as a powerful, unrelenting, and protean force in European society, with origins in Christian anti-Judaism, formed the crux of Dawidowicz's interpretation of Hitler,[28] Nazism, and the Final Solution. With this interpretation, she played several historiographic hands. First, she believed that ideas and ideology were motor forces in history, a belief strengthened by the Cold War.[29] Second, she argued that individuals were the most important components of historical change—an argument that rejected structuralist or Marxist approaches to the past that emphasized socioeconomic conflict, bureaucratic formation, or the alienating framework of modernity. She believed that individuals were agents of their lives and made moral or immoral choices. Her focus on Hitler's actions and on ideology as historical forces was both a historical and a political judgment. Ideas were not merely theoretical constructs; they had consequences in the world. She acknowledged that other factors, including Germany's defeat in World War I, economic depression, and fear of Soviet imperialism, affected the course of modern German history and modern Jewish history, but they were secondary causes and paled in comparison with Hitler's monomaniacal antisemitism and its roots in the broader German demonization of the Jews. "Without Hitler, the charismatic political leader, who believed he had a mission to annihilate the Jews, the 'Final Solution' would not have occurred."[30] She argued further that

> Without that assertive and enduring tradition of anti-Semitism by which the Germans sought self-definition, Hitler would not have had the fecund soil in which to grow his organization and spread its propaganda. Without the paranoid delusion of the Dolchstoss that masses of Germans shared in the wake of Germany's defeat, political upheavals, economic distress, and humiliations of the Versailles Treaty, Hitler could not have transformed the German brand of conventional anti-Semitism into a radical doctrine of mass murder.[31]

Dawidowicz's interpretation of Hitler's antisemitism emphasized its chiliastic elements. Hitler "believed himself to be the savior who would bring redemption to the German people through the annihilation of the Jews, that people who embodied, in his eyes, the Satanic hosts."[32] In his speeches, he used words associated with millenarian prophecy, such as "consecration," "salvation," "redemption," "resurrection," and "God's will." *Mein Kampf*, Dawidowicz argued, should be regarded not as a fantastical text of a raving lunatic but as a concrete blueprint of Hitler's murderous plans. "*Mein Kampf* is a vision of the apocalyptic conflict between the Aryans and the Jews, of the two world systems struggling for domination. It was his own Manichean version of the conflict between good and evil, between God and the Devil, Christ and the Antichrist."[33] Dawidowicz directly linked Hitler's antisemitism to Nazi foreign policy. The Jews were not only Germany's internal enemy but also the diabolical force behind the Communist Soviet Union. War against the Soviet Union was therefore inevitable and necessary. A Nazi victory would at once crush the international Jewish conspiracy behind Bolshevism and give the German *Volk* the *Lebensraum* it needed and deserved. In this millennial vision, the vast territories of Soviet-occupied Poland and the USSR, cleansed of Jews, would restore Germany's virility and purity.

Dawidowicz positioned her interpretation against the historians known as "functionalists." Broadly speaking, their view, as evidenced in the work of the German historians Uwe Adam, Hans Mommsen, Götz Aly, and Martin Broszat, was that the Final Solution was not a product of one man's ideological fervor but rather the evolutionary product of competing Nazi bureaucracies during the expansion of the Nazi war effort into Russian territory.[34] The functionalists viewed totalitarianism, not antisemitism, as Nazi Germany's fundamental problem. In this reading, the victimization of the Jews was a by-product of National Socialism's push toward the creation of a homogeneous ethnic state. Ideology, for the functionalists, was at best merely instrumental.

The interpretations against which Dawidowicz found herself most in contention were those of Raul Hilberg and Hannah Arendt. In fact, she conceptualized *The War Against the Jews* as an argument against Hilberg's pathbreaking study of the Nazi bureaucratic machine, *The Destruction of the European Jews*, and Arendt's *Eichmann in Jerusalem*, works she viewed as the first texts of the functionalist school in the United States.[35]

DAWIDOWICZ AND HILBERG, PART I

Raul Hilberg, an Austrian-Jewish refugee from an acculturated Jewish family, arrived in the United States on September 1, 1939. He attended Brooklyn College, but the draft interrupted his studies, which he did not complete until 1948.

He continued his graduate work in history and political science at Columbia University, pursuing his massive research project on the German state's systematic murder of the Jews. Hilberg's interest and accomplishment as a historian lay in describing the precise manner in which the modern German state and its bureaucracy perpetrated the Final Solution.[36] Though he attended Salo W. Baron's lectures on Jewish history, Hilberg chose to write his dissertation in German under the guidance of Franz Neumann. His book is a masterful example of what has come to be known as "perpetrator history," a study of the way in which a modern state systematically turned on and destroyed a civilian community living within its borders.

Though Philip Friedman, then at Columbia University, supported the dissertation and sent it to Yad Vashem, the Israeli center for Holocaust research and commemoration, Hilberg encountered numerous obstacles in getting his work published.[37] Despite the book's formidable evidentiary focus on the German perpetrators, its brief excursus on the Jewish responses to the Nazi assault undermined its reception. The offending paragraphs appeared in the "Precedents" and "Reflections" sections that bookended his meticulous study of the murderous Nazi bureaucracy. In "Precedents," Hilberg laid out his theories of Jewish responses to the Nazi assault, which he placed on a visual grid with five categories: resistance, alleviation, evasion, paralysis, and compliance. He argued that over the long span of Jewish history in the diaspora, Jews faced with persecution had resorted almost exclusively to alleviation and compliance. Alleviation meant resorting to "petitions, protection payments, ransom arrangements, anticipatory compliance, relief, rescue, salvage, [and] reconstruction."[38] Compliance meant simply obeying the ruling authorities, even in the case of anti-Jewish legislation or support of anti-Jewish actions. These millennial-old strategies had persisted because they were successful. At first misunderstanding the barbaric nature of Nazism and then willfully repressing the truth of the Final Solution, European Jews resorted to their old reaction patterns. "But this time the results were catastrophic."[39] At the book's close, in "Reflections," Hilberg reiterated his views of Jewish responses to antisemitism, writing the sentences that would bedevil his historiographic contribution forever: "It is the *interaction* of perpetrators and victims that is 'fate.' . . . *We must therefore discuss the reactions of the Jewish community and analyze the role of the Jews in their own destruction.*"[40]

Dawidowicz did not review Hilberg's book when it was first published. But correspondence between them, as well as a later review of his reissued work, illustrates that she initially respected his contribution to the historiography on the perpetrators.[41] They also agreed on the limitations of Yad Vashem's approach to the Holocaust. Yad Vashem was established in 1953 by a law of the Israeli Knesset that founded the Martyrs' and Heroes' Remembrance Authority. It was charged with two contradictory missions: the commemoration of the victims of the Holocaust through the lenses of martyrdom and heroism and a scholarly investigation of the events that had engulfed Europe and destroyed European Jewry. Dawidowicz and Hilberg commiserated over Yad Vashem's 1968 conference on Jewish resistance, held on the twenty-fifth anniversary of the Warsaw Ghetto Uprising, which failed in their view to assess the question of Jewish behavior with sufficient rigor.[42] Finding skilled researchers grounded in European history, Jewish history, and all the requisite languages in the early 1960s was difficult, so much of the early work was done by survivors, not professional historians.[43] The institution strongly promoted those books that portrayed the Jewish victims in a favorable light.[44] Yad Vashem's rejection of Hilberg's dissertation for publication left him with a lifelong bitterness. Years later, reflecting on his life and career, Hilberg wrote that he had always refused to engage in the "campaign of exaltation" of the victims, which by magnifying their resistance had "obscured the reality of Jewish life in the ghettos and camps."[45]

Dawidowicz shared Hilberg's reluctance to participate in the cult of the ghetto fighter. In "Toward a History of the Holocaust," published in *Commentary* in 1969, Dawidowicz gave an overview of the 1968 conference and outlined her fundamental positions on the nascent field.[46] She pointed out that Yad Vashem's dual mandates were mutually exclusive. Conference participants from the Ghetto Fighters kibbutz (*Kibuz Loḥamei Hageta'ot*) who were survivors were too close to the subject, lacked the proper training, and engaged too intimately with the politicization of Holocaust memory to write good history. She wrote scathingly of the conference's preoccupation with resistance, calling it "a subject well suited to commemoration, for it is likely to evoke reverent tributes to heroism, courage, and self-sacrifice, and to stimulate a flow of rhetoric that soothes as it stirs."[47] Her critique was twofold. The focus on the relatively few Jews who actively resisted the Nazis through armed rebellion condemned the behavior of the majority of the murdered Jews who did not take up arms. And the efforts of scholars to include the quotidian acts of everyday life as resistance efforts, in an attempt to make "resistance" the norm of Jewish responses to Nazi persecution, "strained" the word's meaning. While she understood the impulse, Dawidowicz wrote, "This elevation of resistance to a preciousness equal to or above other ultimate virtues—truth, respect for human life—strikes me, however, as alien to Jewish tradition and history."[48] In her view, scholarship aimed at imparting values or prescriptions for behavior, such as the emphasis on resistance, was destined to be flawed. Study of the Holocaust, she wrote, "can expand our [human beings'] self-knowledge, show us what we are capable of being and doing, for good or evil, under stress, in shock or trauma." For Jewish historians, it could become—and here her debt to Dubnow is manifest—"a secular act of bearing witness to Auschwitz and to the mystery of Jewish survival."[49]

In 1970, Hilberg wrote to Dawidowicz asking for her opinion on an article he had written about the 1968 conference at the request of Shlomo Katz, the editor of *Midstream*, a monthly journal of Jewish affairs, who ultimately rejected it. Hilberg admitted to Dawidowicz that his article was "impressionistic in style and approach."[50] In her reply, she respectfully agreed with Katz's decision (though siding with Hilberg that he should have been given a kill fee). Her comments are revealing. She warned Hilberg against letting his emotions—in this case, his pain at the enormity of the destruction of the Jews—get in the way of his scholarship, cautioning him that "you are not necessarily being objective and you are certainly not being dispassionate." She continued:

> Hannah Arendt protected herself against the passion and hatred for the Germans by wrapping herself in a heavy cloak of irony. You, on the other hand, are all ice when you write of the Germans and aquiver when you come to the Jews. You protect yourself from the hurt with rage and aggressiveness. . . . Let me say that I have enormous respect for your book. I use it as a basic text in my course, but I don't like what I call the *obiter dicta*, the remarks about the Jews. I think they mar what is otherwise a superlative work of scholarship—hard and tough-minded. One should be tough-minded about Jews too, but rage and anguish are no substitute.[51]

The correspondence between Hilberg and Dawidowicz in the early 1970s contained no shade of the animus between them that broke out later in the decade. Her reaction to Hannah Arendt's work was a different matter entirely.

DAWIDOWICZ AND HILBERG—AND ARENDT, PART 2

The War Against the Jews took direct aim at the arguments in Arendt's *Eichmann in Jerusalem*. Part II, "The Holocaust," responded to Arendt's assessment of Eichmann's behavior as a product of modern society's bureaucratic structures

and its implication that totalitarian societies with highly bureaucratized structures made individuals morally impotent. In Arendt's view, Eichmann was an
Everyman, a citizen following orders; representing the norm under the conditions of the Third Reich, he harbored no personal hatred against Jews and,
she claimed, had joined the SS out of boredom.[52] The murder of the Jews was
the outcome of a modern totalitarian state in its normal, inexorable functioning and could have happened anywhere. This interpretation deemphasized
the role of ideology as a force in history generally and downplayed Hitler's
antisemitism—as well as his personal leadership—in orchestrating the Final
Solution specifically.[53]

Dawidowicz never stepped back from her assertion in *The War Against
the Jews* that the Final Solution was an intentional aspect of Nazism from its
beginnings. If part I of *The War Against the Jews* demanded that readers take
personality, ideology, and antisemitism as the incontestable causes of the Final
Solution, in part II, "The Holocaust," she took on the issue of Jewish agency.[54]
Examining the perpetrator component of some functionalist historians, Dawidowicz argued that their focus on the motivations and behaviors of the Nazis
implicitly denied the Jewish victims' historical agency.[55] Insisting that the long
tradition of Jewish communal autonomy shaped the behavior of Jews even in
extremis, she detailed the coping strategies of the Jewish councils in the ghettos
of Eastern Europe.

Her attention to Jewish communal life under duress also served two additional purposes. First, it gave a historical voice to Jews facing imminent extinction. Second, it moved Holocaust historiography away from a reliance on
German documents to one that utilized Jewish sources and centered on the
Jewish response. Dawidowicz took particular aim at Hilberg's and Arendt's
condemnation of the Jewish political "tradition," and specifically at the latter's
denunciation of the behavior of the Jewish councils. Their analyses, in Dawidowicz's view, had encouraged two unfortunate trends in Holocaust historiography: "the diabolization of the *Judenrat*" and the accompanying "apotheosis
of resistance."[56]

For Dawidowicz, no understanding of Jewish behavior during the period
1933–45 could afford to ignore the centrality of the collective in Jewish life
and history. *The War Against the Jews*'s attention to both components of
Ashkenazic society—west (in German lands) and east (in Polish and Russian lands)—illustrated her debt to Weinreich's postwar view of the internal coherence of that civilization. Her book put forth her wistful view of
Ashkenazic civilization:

It was a culture whose language was Yiddish ... [a language that was] a vehicle for a great religious and secular culture, and it generated a rich literature. ... East European Jewry created a culture that venerated the *sefer*, the book of religious learning, but whose people laughed at themselves. It was a culture that put its people, familiar with poverty and hardship, on speaking terms with God. It was a culture unique in all Jewish history, and East European Ashkenazic Jewry, which fashioned that culture, was the wellspring of Jewish creativity for Jewish communities throughout the world.[57]

Dawidowicz devoted "The Holocaust" section of her book, comprising eight chapters, to Jewish communal life, beginning with the organizations of German Jewry, the Centralverein deutscher Staatsbürger jüdischen Glaubens (Central Association of German Citizens of Jewish Faith, founded in 1983), the Zionistische Vereinigung für Deutschland (Zionist Federation of Germany, founded in the 1920s), and the Reichsvertretung der deutschen Juden (Reich Representation of Jews, founded in 1933).[58] Moving eastward, the book's chapters focused on Jewish communal life, leadership, and methods of survival, emphasizing the concept of "community": "Death and Life in the East European Ghettos," "The Official Community: From *Kehillah* to *Judenrat*," "The Alternative Community," "The Countercommunity: The Political Underground," and, in pointed rebuttal to Hilberg and Arendt, "Jewish Behavior in Crisis and Extremity."

Her focus on Jewish communal life contained a twofold historiographic and political agenda. First, it reflected her Dubnowian belief that the *kahal*, the Jewish municipality, embodied the collective historical agency of the Jewish people. Second, its concern with the leadership of the Jewish community both in Nazi Germany and later in Nazi-occupied Poland in what were no longer autonomous *kehillot* but Nazi-appointed *Judenräte* (Jewish councils)[59] underscored her identification with normative institutions of Jewish communal life. Both components informed her historical argument with Hilberg and Arendt regarding the putative "passivity" of European Jewry when confronted by the Nazis. This argument, in turn, informed Dawidowicz's position as a Jewish public intellectual, providing the historical evidence for her defense of mainstream Jewish communal leadership and policies in the embattled social and political climate of the 1970s and 1980s in the United States.

"The Holocaust" section begins with German Jewry, the western component of Ashkenazic civilization. Dawidowicz first treated the Jewish communal agencies in pre-1938 Nazi Germany, arguing that while these organizations never had the ability to change the course of Nazism, they served to strengthen

Jewish communal and cultural life, endeavoring to hold "on to the achievements of the Emancipation."[60] She viewed the Jewish community's response to oppression as one of limited historical agency with regard to the implacable denationalization and de-emancipation of the Jews of Germany prior to Kristallnacht. Yet, with regard to inner Jewish life, Dawidowicz interpreted these organizations' actions as expressing the spirit of internal Jewish historical autonomy and agency: "The National Socialist victory in 1933 had shaken the Jewish community," she observed, "but within a few short months it had rallied, summoning an energy and will for organizational unity and fraternal solidarity and stimulating a powerful resurgence of Jewish identity. The wellsprings of this energy were the hope, faith, and belief that the German dictatorship would be short-lived or, at the very least, that a tolerable *modus vivendi* would be established."[61]

For Dawidowicz, when the Gestapo turned the Reichsvertretung der deutschen Juden into the Reichsvereinigung der Juden in Deutschland (Reich Association of Jews in Germany) in early 1939, ending all vestige of an autonomous Jewish community, the external fate of the Jews was then entirely out of the community's hands. Dawidowicz's unwillingness to condemn those Jewish communal leaders who continued to serve in the newly established Reichsvereinigung, despite its absorption into the Nazi bureaucracy, characterized her general view of Jewish communal organizations in the Nazi period. The Nazis held all the cards. For Dawidowicz, the parameters of any decisions made by Jews serving in Jewish organizations were dictated from without. Her view of the limited agency of the *Judenräte* allowed her to defend the behavior of the Jewish communal leadership in its darkest hour. It bears emphasizing that Dawidowicz, no doubt due to Dubnow's historiographic influence, anticipated much of the current literature distinguishing between "resistance" defined as military action and as *amidah*, a Hebrew word whose meaning registers somewhere among nonviolent resistance, durability, and steadfastness.[62] She believed that the Jews tried to survive as best they could, with what little resources they had. As she had stated in her critique of the 1968 Yad Vashem conference, she held that historians and others evaluating their behavior should resist elevating that behavior into "resistance" in order to valorize Jewish heroism.[63]

Dawidowicz was yet well aware of the exceptional heroism of the youthful rebels, many of them identified with the left-wing political parties, who staged military actions against the Nazis, either when ghettoized or as partisans.[64] But she devoted her attention to the unexceptional Jews, the victims of Nazi hatred who did not rebel militarily and still perished. She demurred on writing an introduction to a book of survivor testimonies because, as she explained to John Thornton, its editor, "The perspective out of which I write about the Holocaust is not that of the survivors, but of the six million."[65] She dedicated her work to the Jews who were murdered, emphasizing that rebellion and the politics of agitation were no more successful guarantors of survival than any other, less "heroic" strategy. She thus rejected the historiographic attention given to armed resistance, repudiating even the term "passive resistance" to describe the ordinary daily efforts to survive.[66] Fellow historian George Mosse affirmed Dawidowicz's views on what he called "this continuous debate about resistance." "Mere survival and keeping as much of one's dignity as possible was certainly a form of resistance, perhaps the only one possible."[67]

The War Against the Jews described the partisans and other advocates of rebellion and violent resistance—many implacably opposed to the *Judenräte*—in communal terms. They were an "alternative community" (chapter 12) and a "countercommunity: the political underground" (chapter 13). Dawidowicz posited the communal will to live as the decisive rebuttal to accusations of Jewish passivity; the Jews' powerlessness, she reminded her readers, was not an epithet or political judgment but a fact, one that informed her assessment of their response. "To facilitate their survival in powerlessness," she wrote, "and to lessen the impact of humiliation and suffering, the Jews made virtues of self-discipline, prudence, moderation, foregoing present gratification for eventual benefit. They learned to practice nonviolent means of resistance and to find ways of circumventing discrimination and deflecting persecution."[68]

Dawidowicz's defense of all Jews extended, significantly, to the functionaries of the *Judenräte*, who bore the brunt of Arendt's contempt.[69] In *Eichmann in Jerusalem*, Arendt had excoriated the Jewish leadership's behavior in stark terms, charging that "To a Jew this role of the Jewish leaders in the destruction of their own people is undoubtedly the darkest chapter of the whole dark story," and noting that "it had been known about before, but it has now been exposed for the first time in all its pathetic and sordid detail by Raul Hilberg," in *The Destruction of the European Jews*. Conceding that the Jews, "in the hour of their greatest need," had "possessed no territory, no government, and no army," Arendt nonetheless insisted on the complicity of their leaders:

The whole truth was there existed Jewish community organizations and Jewish party and welfare organizations on both the local and international level. Wherever Jews lived, there were recognized Jewish leaders, and this leadership, almost without exception, cooperated in one way or another, for one reason or another, with the Nazis.[70]

Dawidowicz disagreed, passionately. Her defense of the *Judenräte* derived from personal, historiographic, and political considerations. In *The War Against the Jews*, she described their members as "men of decency and integrity, imbued with the tradition of service to the community."[71] While emphasizing the discontinuity of Nazi persecution with the forms of premodern anti-Jewish hatred, she stressed that the behavior of the communal leadership during the Holocaust was continuous with earlier patterns. The communal functionaries in the *Judenräte* employed intercession and bribery—age-old methods of Jewish-Gentile interaction—to cope with Nazi demands. They tried to buy time by emphasizing the community's economic productivity, hoping that a productive ghetto would offset plans for its liquidation. They continued to practice the symbolic politics of *dina d'malkhuta dina* ("the law of the land is the law"),[72] upholding gentile law, not realizing that the murderous nature of Nazi rule—unlike that of most gentile states of the premodern Jewish past that protected "their" Jews—was completely new.[73] Dawidowicz described an evolutionary development in the relationship of the ghetto population to the *Judenräte*. At first, the Jews viewed the *Judenräte* "as a legitimate successor to the kehilla"; but with the escalation of Nazi terror and the inexorable weakening of the *Judenräte*, the community no longer validated these functionaries. "Naked coercive power" increasingly defined the relationship between the Nazi state and the Jews. Though Dawidowicz noted the particular cruelty of *Judenräte* leaders such as Chaim Rumkowski (Łódź), Moses Merin (Sosnowiec), Jacob Gens (Vilna), and Ephraim Barash (Bialystok), she defended them to the very end.[74]

Conversely, she attacked Arendt to the bitter end. In *Eichmann*, Arendt accused the Jewish police of aiding the Nazis, rounding up the Jews of Berlin, and maintaining that the roundups would have been impossible "without Jewish help in administration and police work." She implied that these Jews were equivalent to the collaborationist governments in occupied territories or worse, since "the members of the Jewish Councils were as a rule the locally recognized Jewish leaders, to whom the Nazis gave enormous powers."[75] The *Judenräte* betrayed their own. In rebuttal, Dawidowicz insisted that "For all their weaknesses, failings, and wrongdoings, these men—Rumkowski, Merin, Gens—were not traitors." Once again, the key differentiating reality was temporal political powerlessness:

The accusation that some Jewish leaders "cooperated" or "collaborated" with the Germans arises out of distortions of the historical record. Cooperation and collaboration with the Germans were policies voluntarily undertaken by leaders of nations that retained all or part of their independence and autonomy. In the ghettoes of Poland, where German rule was total, where Hans Frank reigned as king, where Himmler's SS kept order, and where the German army operated the economy, Germany did not ask for or get either cooperation or collaboration. SS force and terror extracted compliance from the Jews and aimed to bring them to a state of unresisting submissiveness. Unlike Quisling, Laval, and Vlasov, no Jew—not even an underworld black-guard who sold information to the Gestapo—ever awaited German victory. No Jew ever hoped for a New Order in Europe. The officials of the Juden-räte were coerced by German terror to submit and comply. To say that they "cooperated" or "collaborated" with the Germans is semantic confusion and historical misrepresentation.[76]

Dawidowicz only named Arendt explicitly in a footnote, one written with unveiled sarcasm and contempt: "Miss Arendt's penchant for grand philo-sophic schemata flourishes on her disdain for historical evidence. One would have expected, nevertheless, that the expert on totalitarian terror in its philo-sophic aspect would have recognized the phenomenon of totalitarian terror in its historical reality."[77]

The alleged treachery of the *Judenräte* would continue to touch a nerve and put Dawidowicz on high alert. In 1978, she was asked to write a blurb for Leslie Epstein's *King of the Jews*, a comic novel whose protagonist was based on Chaim Rumkowski, the head of the *Judenrat* in the Łódź ghetto. Dawidowicz categori-cally refused, writing to Epstein's editor, Joseph Kanon:

> As if it were not enough that the Germans and their helpers murdered six million European Jews, we now have Leslie Epstein to turn that murder into grotesquerie, black humor, and even slapstick. And if it were not enough to mock the slaughtered Jews, Leslie Epstein must also accuse them of complic-ity in their own murder.[78]

"No words can convey my anger and anguish over this novel," admitted Dawid-owicz, an anguish heightened by the fact that "Leslie Epstein, having thor-oughly exploited the substance of my book [*A Holocaust Reader*], should have also derided its perspective and conclusions."

It was not simply Epstein's fictional approach to the destruction of European Jewry that enraged Dawidowicz, though there were very few works of literature about the Holocaust that she would recommend unequivocally. It was that Epstein had played loose with the facts about a critical issue: the date on which the *Judenräte* in European ghettos actually understood the diabolical nature of the Final Solution. When Chaim Rumkowski fully grasped that the Jews of Łódź were to be murdered in the notorious gas vans en route to Chełmno, the first extermination camp, is still debated. What is clear is that he did *not* know in December 1941. The first "resettlements" of Jews from the Łódź ghetto began in January 1942. Epstein's fictive protagonist, however, knows the fate of "his" Jews and does not resist Nazi orders to round them up to be killed. Even more egregious, from Dawidowicz's perspective, was that the novel's survivor narrator, a young boy named Nisel Lipiczany, cites directly from an overheard conversation of two SS officers that the Jews inside the van were said to have wept "just like in a synagogue." Epstein's dialogue was not fiction. It came directly from historical testimony published in Dawidowicz's *A Holocaust Reader*, the documentary companion volume to *The War Against the Jews*.[79]

In Dawidowicz's view, Epstein's novel had betrayed East European Jewry. He failed to do what John Hersey had done in *The Wall* and what critics like Irving Howe and Lionel Trilling had counseled artists to do—namely, to "regulate his imagination in accordance with artistic integrity [and] a commitment to reality." *The King of the Jews* was "neither true to life nor to history." Worse, Epstein had given fodder to Arendt's merciless interpretation of the Jewish leadership.[80]

DAWIDOWICZ AND HILBERG, PART 3

By the late 1970s, Dawidowicz's relationship with Hilberg had become acrimonious. The long-term fallout of the *Eichmann* controversy, the radicalization of the civil rights and peace movements with the simultaneous valorization of resistance and agitation as societal ideals, and the disagreements that beset the 1978 President's Commission on the Holocaust, on which they both initially served, widened the gap between the two scholars. The question of how the Jews had responded to the Nazi assault had grown more heated and—in the current political climate—the stakes were higher. For Dawidowicz, prioritizing resistance and anathematizing the leadership of the Jewish community not only besmirched the memory of the European Jews but also appeared to justify the radicalization of political culture in the United States. As student radicals in general sought to defy the authority of mainstream political leadership, Jewish student radicals looked to Jewish ghetto fighters as models of a usable past.[81]

In 1979, Dawidowicz was asked to review Hilberg's publication of the diary of Adam Czerniaków, the head of the Warsaw *Judenrat*, who had committed suicide in 1942 after being ordered to begin the mass liquidation of the ghetto. She dismissed the historical value of Hilberg's edition. Though she herself had included excerpts of Czerniaków in *A Holocaust Reader*,[82] she criticized Hilberg's choice to publish a diary that was "neither history nor literature, but only a rich source of raw material from which history can be constructed" without a critical apparatus to guide the reader. Both the Hebrew and Polish versions had scholarly apparatuses, and Dawidowicz professed to be "at a loss to understand why the American editors did not make more copious use of the substantively richer notes in the Hebrew and Polish editions, particularly because they themselves appear to be unfamiliar with Polish Jewish history and culture."[83] Czerniaków's laconic diary concealed as much as it revealed, and an untutored audience influenced by Arendt's view of the *Judenrat* and by the American political climate that distrusted authority could hardly be expected to understand Czerniaków's predicament.[84]

Tensions increased in 1985, when Hilberg reissued *The Destruction of the European Jews*. In her review for the *Washington Times Magazine*, Dawidowicz assailed him for heedless and errant views of Jewish leaders under extreme Nazi pressure.[85]

> In dealing with the complex problems of Jewish leadership in times of extreme persecution, of men who had to perform their duties under duress, Mr. Hilberg again failed to make the necessary discriminations. He did not differentiate between genuine communal leaders and those who derived their authority from the Germans. He furthermore failed to chart the changes in the functions of Jewish communal institutions as they were adapted from prewar times to the German occupation. Finally, he made blanket accusations against Jewish communal leaders, charging them with having "appeased" and "collaborated" with the Germans.[86]

Dawidowicz described the way in which Hilberg's book, originally published before the capture and trial of Eichmann, had become the source for Arendt: "Miss Arendt, with a near-parasitical dependence on Mr. Hilberg, adopted his thesis about the 'collaboration' of the Jewish leaders with the Germans."[87] The gap between the initial publication of *The Destruction of the European Jews* in

1951 and its reissue in 1985 gave Hilberg the opportunity to reconsider some of his conclusions, particularly those related to Jewish history and to the responses of the Jews caught in Hitler's murderous schemes. But he had squandered his chance. Though he had revised parts of his work on the role of the Jewish councils and softened his accusations of Jewish "collaboration,"

> Mr. Hilberg still holds fast to his notions of Jewish passivity, retaining every wrong-headed pronouncement he originally made about that mythical 2,000-year-old-tradition. None of the criticisms leveled against his work in this regard for the last 24 years has led him to reconsider his ideas and correct his misreadings of Jewish history.[88]

Dawidowicz affirmed that *The Destruction of the European Jews* had been a major achievement, but Hilberg's methodological orientation as a political scientist and his focus on the perpetrators meant that he had not solved the problem of causality. He had failed, she concluded, as a historian; and in the end,

> only history can instruct us about the causative role of nationalism, anti-Semitism and racism, in Germany and all Europe; about the politics of crisis in Weimar Germany and the rise of Adolf Hitler to power; about Hitler's commanding role as ideologue, planner and architect of the murder of the Jews; and about the goals, motives, decisions and accomplishments of all the actors—Germans, Jews, Europeans, even Americans—in the terrible drama of the murder of 6 million European Jews.[89]

Dawidowicz's interpretation of the catastrophe that befell European Jewry, which played a central role in the creation of Holocaust consciousness in the postwar years, is best understood as part of a historiographic continuum initiated by Dubnow and fostered by the community of scholars associated with the YIVO. Her impact also reflects the evolution of the New York intellectuals' reception of Hannah Arendt. The group had been besotted with Arendt, but the love affair had ended abruptly in 1963 with the publication of *Eichmann in Jerusalem*. In Israel, the response to *Eichmann* was particularly ferocious. Arendt's friendships with German-Jewish compatriots Gershom Scholem and Leni Yahil were sorely strained, even broken, by her book.[90] The transnational Jewish intellectual community, scorched by the Holocaust and endeavoring to understand its impact on Jewish life, was now primed for an embrace of Dawidowicz and her perspective in *The War Against the Jews*.

9

UNIVERSALISM AND
PARTICULARISM
AMONG THE
NEW YORK
INTELLECTUALS

The deteriorating relationship between Hilberg and Dawidowicz can be traced in their personal correspondence, book reviews, and memoirs.[1] The two died, respectively, in 2007 and 1990, and today their defining books, *The Destruction of the European Jews* and *The War Against the Jews*, are read primarily as exemplars of "old school" Holocaust historiography, with Hilberg seen as the quintessential functionalist and master of perpetrator history and Dawidowicz as the foremost proponent of intentionalism. While Hannah Arendt continues to spark intellectual inquiry—as evidenced by monographs, conferences, and symposia devoted to her oeuvre; a 2012 biopic, *Hannah Arendt*; a 2015 documentary, *Vita Activa*; and an opera, *The Hat*, about her first meeting with Martin Heidegger[2]—Lucy S. Dawidowicz's persona and work have largely fallen by the intellectual and public wayside.

The relative status of Dawidowicz's and Arendt's public reception today presents a reversal of the 1960s and 1970s, when Arendt's star dimmed and Dawidowicz's rose. Their oscillating reputations, along with their conflicting perspectives on the destruction of European Jewry and on the Jewish response to Nazism, have mirrored long-standing debates among Jewish intellectuals grappling with the security and vulnerability of the Jews in the modern world.[3] At stake were questions about whether Jews should maintain principal loyalties to fellow Jews or embrace the universalist perspective of the Enlightenment; whether they should assimilate and pursue individual freedom or maintain a distinctive collective and national identity; and whether they had genuine allies within gentile society or needed to rely exclusively on Jewish modes of political life. Though these questions had been posed already in the late eighteenth century, they resonated acutely among the New York intellectuals, who struggled to find a balance between their commitments to universalist and particularist values as they integrated into American culture.[4]

The New York intellectuals' enthusiastic reception, and then rejection, of Arendt's person and thought and their subsequent turn to Dawidowicz can be read not merely as a response to their internalization of the horror of the Holocaust but also as a marker of their faith—or lack thereof—in total assimilation. Playing a critical role in the complicated process through which the New York intellectuals publicly worked out their relationship to Jewish culture and Jewish particularism, Arendt's and Dawidowicz's biographies, geographies, and cultures made them mirror images of one another. When Dawidowicz voluntarily went "backward" to Europe, she internalized the culture of Eastern Europe at the same time that Arendt, a German-Jewish refugee from Nazism, was distancing herself from it.

Historians of modern European Jewry have long recognized that at the end of the eighteenth century, when Enlightenment values affirming universalism met the birth of the modern nation-state, western Ashkenazic Jews (i.e., from German lands and the Prussian Empire) were better positioned socially, politically, economically, and culturally to enter into the modern world than were eastern Ashkenazic Jews (i.e., from Austrian and Russian Poland).[5] The slower pace of modernization and the demographic strength of East European Jewry allowed traditional Jewish life to flourish in Poland, Russia, and Austrian Galicia well into the twentieth century—even as it transplanted itself to East European immigrant settlements throughout the West. The vast migration of 1.5–2 million Jews from Central and Eastern Europe to New York between 1881 and 1924 reshaped American Jewry. This largely eastern Ashkenazic diaspora re-created many aspects of East European Jewish society in New York City. They established an ethnic Jewish communal structure through hometown societies (*landsmanshaftn*), credit associations, schools, political parties, synagogues, newspapers, and theaters, most of which were voiced in Yiddish.[6]

Coming of age in the interwar years, Jewish immigrant children encountered America as ethnic outsiders. As East European Jews strove to acculturate into the norms of gentile society, they did so—as in Europe from the eighteenth century forward—in a curious process of both mirroring and distancing themselves from their more Westernized brethren.[7] Many eastern Ashkenazic Jews strove to wrest themselves from their own culture, which—adjudged by Western mores—they viewed as parochial and backward.[8]

The journey from insular parochialism to cosmopolitan humanism was a feature of the narrative construction of the self among the New York intellectuals. Aspiring to become an intellectual and political vanguard that would make a signal mark on mid-twentieth-century American life and culture, the New York intellectuals constructed a worldview whose goals of "cosmopolitanism" assumed a certain basic alienation from their own ethnic heritage.[9] Their marginality, they believed, gave them intellectual bona fides. In David Riesman's view, "The intellect is at its best, and its ethical insights are at their best, when one is in a marginal position that is not too overpowering."[10] Alfred Kazin recalled that "The *Partisan Review* group . . . believed in alienation, and would forever try to outdo conventional opinion even when they agreed with it."[11] They strove to embrace the spirit of Enlightenment toleration; to reject ethnic and religious parochialism; to transcend boundaries of nationality, race, and religion; and to emphasize the complexity and diversity of the modern world. Flight from their East European Jewish immigrant milieu was necessary, as Irving Howe observed: "In the 30's . . . it was precisely the idea of discarding the past, breaking away from families, traditions, and memories which excited intellectuals. They meant to declare themselves citizens of the world and, that succeeding, perhaps consider becoming writers of this country."[12]

The first line of Norman Podhoretz's 1967 memoir, *Making It*, encapsulated the distance between their self-perceived parochialism and the cosmopolitan world: "One of the longest journeys in the world is the journey from Brooklyn to Manhattan—or at least from certain neighborhoods in Brooklyn to certain parts of Manhattan."[13] And the leitmotif in Alfred Kazin's memoir trilogy was, in critic Robert Alter's view, "the story of the particular self that had crossed the distance, so small in space, so immense in the realm of values, between Brooklyn and the heights of Manhattan."[14] Brooklyn connoted the immigrant milieu with its poverty, its Yiddish, its old-world religion, its suffocating and cramped apartments, all shaping the particularistic (read: parochial) bonds of a distinct ethnic group. Manhattan meant upward mobility, America, the glories of the English language, secularism, humanism, and intellectual openness. The immigrant sons left Brooklyn, the Lower East Side of Manhattan, and the Bronx, metaphorically and in reality, as an act of rebellion against their parental homes and in search of the broad, cosmopolitan world of non-Jewish ideas and letters. A similar symbolic and geographic journey had been made by East European Jews in the late eighteenth century to seek enlightenment in cosmopolitan Berlin.[15] There they sought to acquire *Bildung*, the enlightened educational ethos of moral, aesthetic, and humanistic self-cultivation and self-transformation that promised a society in which ethnic and religious differences were utterly irrelevant.[16]

Before the war, the New York intellectuals viewed their Jewishness as an obstacle to full participation in American culture and helped to create a neutral society in which their ethnic backgrounds would blend without a trace into American culture. Many were students of the Left, and until Pearl Harbor held pacifist and isolationist views.[17] The fate of European Jewry did not weigh heavily on their minds. Saul Bellow remarked to Cynthia Ozick in the 1980s, "'Jewish writers in America' (a repulsive category!) missed what should have been for them the central event of their time, the destruction of European Jewry."[18] Reflecting on those years, Milton Himmelfarb recalled, "We were far less concerned than our elders and the Jewish Establishment about Jewish woes."

> Many agreed that fascism was only capitalism *in extremis*. Our own ambitions and opportunities were blocked or diverted by antisemitic discriminations, but we took it for granted that to concern ourselves directly with antisemitism, as our parents and the official Jews did, was to worry about a mere symptom.[19]

Even in the immediate aftermath of the war, the news of the destruction of the Jews of Europe hardly factored into the New York intellectuals' trajectory of acculturation.[20] Universalist values continued to shape their hearts and minds in the 1940s and 1950s. In 1946, *Jewish Frontier*, a labor Zionist journal, published an exchange between Daniel Bell and Ben Halpern, the magazine's managing editor, regarding the role of Jewish intellectuals in postwar America. Bell saw no purpose in an ethnic-religious worldview. Jewishness, to have meaning, had to be linked to a secular universalist, this-worldly *Weltanschauung*. Halpern, the Zionist activist, challenged Bell's alienation from Jewish communal life, asserting the value in Jewish national fellowship.[21]

ARENDT'S ALLURE

Given their rush to acculturate, it is no wonder that the New York intellectuals were enthralled with Hannah Arendt. Arriving in New York during their cosmopolitan peak, she perfectly represented their aspirations and values in numerous ways. Born in 1906 in Hanover, Germany, Arendt studied at the Universities of Marburg, Freiburg, and Heidelberg, writing a dissertation on the concept of love in St. Augustine's thought. Fleeing Germany after Hitler came to power, she went to Paris, where she did social work for Youth Aliyah, and in 1941 escaped to the United States, where she was granted entry through a limited visa program for German intellectuals. She quickly mastered English and within two years was writing for a host of English-language journals, both Jewish and general, including *Jewish Social Studies, Partisan Review,* and *The Nation.*[22] Working as research director of the Conference on Jewish Relations and as chief editor of Schocken Books from 1945 to 1951, she was also associated in varying capacities with Salo W. Baron's Jewish Cultural Reconstruction, Inc. But Arendt's passion was for the intellectual life of reading, writing, and teaching.[23] Writing for *Partisan Review* was the union card necessary to being considered a New York intellectual, and Arendt, though a late arrival and female, was soon welcomed into what Norman Podhoretz called "The Family."[24] Her pathbreaking book, *The Origins of Totalitarianism,* published in 1951, founded a whole school of thinking that viewed Nazism and Soviet communism as analogous forms of state terror and secured her place among the New York intellectuals. The book touched a particular chord, outlining the threat to individual freedom posed by these two monstrous twentieth-century state systems whose bureaucracies institutionalized state terror in the form of the Nazi death camp or the Gulag. Arendt became a fixture in the academy, teaching at Princeton University, the University of Chicago, Wesleyan University, and the New School for Social Research.

Literate, engaged with politics and high culture, and herself a product of the modern German culture so coveted by the New York intellectuals, Arendt personified the cosmopolitan ideal in which Jewishness and universal culture were a seamless whole. Richard Wolin, assessing Arendt's protean German-Jewish identity, has remarked that the ferocity of attachments and attacks on Arendt illustrates the "profound intellectual magnetism she must have exuded."[25] Steven Aschheim has explained that her appeal reflected "her capacity to integrate Jewish matters into the eye of the storm of world history, to make them explanatory factors in the great catastrophes of twentieth-century history"—and in so doing, to provide "a kind of dignity and importance to a previously marginalized, even derided, existence."[26]

As a German-Jewish cosmopolitan intellectual, Arendt commanded intellectual and cultural "capital" for the East European Jewish New York intellectuals. Yet these factors alone do not explain the ease with which she was accepted by them. Arendt also possessed a kind of sexual agency or power that captivated many of these male intellectuals; she had "feminine" or "sexual" capital.[27] In New York Jew, Alfred Kazin wrote evocatively of his friendship with Hannah and her husband, Heinrich Blücher, recalling his first meeting with them at a Commentary dinner in the fall of 1947, where he had been "enthralled [by Hannah], by no means unerotically."[28] Richard Cook, Kazin's biographer, remarked that "Kazin was crazy about her, even in an erotic sense," and that he described how "he blushed with pleasure holding her arm on the subway."[29] Kazin told his young fiancée, Ann Birstein, whom he once abandoned in the balcony of a lecture hall so he could sit in the orchestra with the object of his infatuation, that he could not love her if she did not love Arendt.[30] Diana Trilling recalled that Arendt was attracted to her husband, Lionel Trilling, and "made believe that I did not exist even when we were a few feet apart, staring into each other's faces."[31] Irving Howe, looking back in his autobiography, recalled that "While far from 'good-looking' in any commonplace way, Hannah Arendt was a remarkably attractive person, with her razored gestures, imperial eye, dangling cigarette." He noted, too, that Arendt "made an especially strong impression on intellectuals—those who, as mere Americans, were dazzled by the immensities of German philosophy."

> But I always suspected that she impressed people less through her thought than the style of her thinking. She bristled with intellectual charm, as if to reduce everyone in sight to an alert discipleship. Her voice would shift register abruptly, now stern and admonitory, now slyly tender in gossip. Whatever room she was in Hannah filled through the largeness of her will; indeed, she always seemed larger than her setting. Rarely have I met a writer with so acute an awareness of the power to overwhelm.[32]

Her allure resulted in two marriages and what we now know was a lifelong love affair with her philosophy professor at Heidelburg, Martin Heidegger.[33] Arendt's sexual confidence could be felt by men and women in her circle.[34]

Then came Eichmann in Jerusalem. The book's publication in 1963 and the controversy it enflamed were part of the process by which the cosmopolitan

New York intellectuals began a reassessment of Jewish concerns and, in some cases, a renewed commitment to them. To many of the New York intellectuals of Jewish origin, *Eichmann in Jerusalem* constituted a perverse moral inversion: the absolution of an arch-Nazi and a crude blaming of his victims. Arendt's accusation that the Jewish communal leadership had aided the Nazis—when coupled with her German-Jewish dismissal of the East European Jewish background of the defense attorneys and her damning side comments about the irritations of modern Hebrew and the foreign quality of Israeli society— seemed to give the lie to Arendt's claim that her book was merely a trial report. Clearly it was much more: a referendum on Jewish history and identity.[35] For the New York intellectuals, the book challenged their universalist assumptions and punctured their long-held fantasies of the superiority of German culture.

Arendt and Dawidowicz represented the two streams of the same historical-cultural process by which Ashkenazic Jewry—western and eastern, respectively—had negotiated its entry into the modern world. Symbolizing opposing positions on the relationship between universalism and Jewish particularism, they triggered different receptions among the New York intellectuals as they grappled with the major existential and political questions facing western Jewry in the twentieth century. Dan Diner has categorized Arendt's perspective on the destruction of European Jewry as part of a "Western Jewish narrative," which took the individual and her break with community and tradition as a starting point.[36] The "Eastern Jewish narrative," in contrast, was constructed upon a basis of collective, national experience that assumed the existence of and ties to a people. Gershon Hundert described the worldview that shaped this narrative as a mentalité. Polish Jewry was secure in itself and experienced "elemental continuities that persist[ed] from the early modern period almost to the present."[37]

DAWIDOWICZ'S AUTHENTICITY

Enter Lucy S. Dawidowicz as the personification of this "Eastern Jewish narrative." With their turn toward Jewish particularist concerns, the New York intellectuals discovered Dawidowicz and the world of *their* fathers: not the world of Berlin but rather that of Warsaw, Łódź, Minsk, and Vilna or of one of the hundreds of market towns, *shtetlakh*, that defined the Jewish landscape of Eastern Europe. In the voluminous literature on the *Eichmann* controversy, Dawidowicz's *The War Against the Jews, 1933–1945*, published twelve years after Arendt's book, generally falls out of the historiography on the New York intellectuals. Yet it was a signal text in their reconceptualization of the balance between universalism and particularism.

Dawidowicz was unknown to the New York intellectuals in their cosmopolitan peak in part because of her age. Born in 1915, she was only fifteen years old when *Partisan Review* first appeared.[38] Moreover, she only briefly shared their fervor for universalism. And she was not considered an object of sexual desire. The immigrant sons distanced themselves not only from the cultural world of their fathers but also from the domestic world of their mothers.[39]

Whereas Arendt represented the unattainable German-Jewish ideal, intellectually and sexually, Dawidowicz initially represented the attainable, but unattractive, East European archetype. Maleness and male sexuality were the tickets of admission to the New York intellectuals' group.[40] Only the comeliest women gained entry into the group—Arendt, Mary McCarthy, Elizabeth Hardwick, Diana Trilling, and, much later, Susan Sontag—and then only one woman at a time. As Norman Podhoretz commented in *Making It*, there could be only one "Dark Lady" of American letters, and she had to be "clean, learned, good-looking, capable of writing family-type criticism as well as fiction with a strong trace of naughtiness."[41] Dawidowicz lacked the academic pedigree, the universalist bona fides, and the requisite "feminine capital" to be accepted into the inner circle.[42] She herself felt insecure about her physical attractiveness. Her private papers reveal her disparaging comments about her own looks, height, and general lack of sexual appeal.[43] Dawidowicz married at thirty-three, late by the standards of the time. Her husband, Szymon, was twenty years her senior, and while she adored him, and the few letters between them express ardor, Dawidowicz kept a strong wall between her personal life and her scholarship. With no public sexual allure, she could not captivate the attention of the male New York intellectuals.

That said, Dawidowicz eventually became an éminence grise for many of the New York intellectuals, but only later, when they "discovered" their Jewish roots. By the late 1970s, partly in reaction to their frustrating encounter with the New Left and the growing power of Holocaust consciousness in the American public, a clear shift in their worldview as liberal Americans and cosmopolitan Jews can be seen. "We were living directly after the Holocaust of the European Jews," Irving Howe wrote.

> We might scorn our origins; we might crush America with discoveries of ardor; we might change our names. But we knew that but for an accident of geography we might also now be bars of soap.[44] At least some of us could not

help feeling that in our earlier claims to have shaken off all ethnic distinctiveness there had been something false, something shaming. Our Jewishness might have no clear religious or national content, it might be helpless before the criticism of believers; but Jews we were, like it or not, and liked or not.[45]

This primal recognition, part of the "ethnic turn" many of the New York intellectuals made in the late 1970s, allowed them to embrace Dawidowicz's particularistic perspective on Nazism's campaign against the Jews. Her entry into the circle of New York intellectuals served to certify her perspective on Jewish history and politics. It also meant that they, in turn, gave her views more prominence than they might have as an unknown female historian working at a Jewish college.

After the publication of *The War Against the Jews*, Dawidowicz went on to publish two other book-length studies related to the Holocaust (*A Holocaust Reader*, 1976; *The Holocaust and the Historians*, 1981) and articles on the topic in an array of scholarly and popular journals. True to her core beliefs about the Jewish past, she remained hopeful about diasporic Jewish life despite the heinous crimes perpetrated against the East European Jewish community. Dubnow's insistence that the Jews had always created dynamic centers of Jewish life outside the land of Israel continued to inform her conception of Jewish history. The American diaspora, already an important center in Jewish life, awaited its narrators and interpreters. Dawidowicz hoped to make a major contribution to this effort, but it never came to fruition. Her archives house a vast repository of her notes for a history of the Jews of America that she never completed.

She did, however, continue to write about American Jewish communal life and politics and held up the banner of Dubnow's optimism regarding the liberal rule of law. In the 1970s and 1980s, she argued that the leadership of the Jews in the American diaspora was best advised to follow the political lead established by the law of the gentile hosts among whom they lived. This posture informed her writings on the Jewish Left, particularly on the renewed attraction to communism and radicalism in the 1970s, as well as her defense of the United States and FDR against accusations of having abandoned Europe's Jews during the war. Dawidowicz maintained her strong ties to *Commentary* magazine as it moved rightward politically, a turn that paralleled her own.

IV

EASTERN EUROPE
IN AMERICA

10

THE EUROPEANNESS OF THE JEWISH "NEOCONSERVATIVE TURN"

In 1970 Dawidowicz sent back her contract for *The War Against the Jews* to her agent, Georges Borchardt, with the note, "Enclosed my initials, wholesale, like pigeon droppings, all over both copies of a very nice contract, indeed. Thank you. I used to think my initials stood for £sd but they're more sinister."[1] Spooked by the tremendous social and political upheavals of the 1960s, Dawidowicz and other middle-class Jewish liberals who had entered the decade as Democrats exited it as Republicans-in-the-making. The ongoing quagmire of Vietnam, the radicalization of the civil rights movement, the rise of the counterculture, of feminism, and of new kinds of ethnic consciousness, including new forms of Jewish identity as well as Soviet antisemitism and anti-Zionism, all challenged the liberal integrationist ethos that allowed Jews to feel "at home" in the United States. By the end of the 1960s, urban riots, violent student protest, and revolutions in China, Cuba, and South America captivated young radicals sympathetic to the Third World's revolt against American imperialism. The fateful year 1968 brought protests and police violence to the Democratic National Convention, the institutional symbol of liberal democracy. The bullets that felled Martin Luther King Jr. and Robert F. Kennedy struck at the core of liberal hopes for racial harmony. Confrontations at Columbia, Harvard, and other major American universities and attacks on the meritocracy of the public school system evidenced by the New York City teachers' strike in Ocean Hill–Brownsville defied liberal faith in education as a palliative for social ills. Civil society appeared to be unraveling.[2]

If the 1960s blasted the postwar consensus apart, the 1970s realigned American politics. Political insecurity characterized foreign policy and domestic politics alike. Political violence seemed to emerge everywhere: in Ireland, Japan, Germany, Italy, Vietnam, Cambodia, and Chile. In 1979 the Ayatollah Khomeni overthrew the Shah in Iran, destabilizing further a region buffeted by Arab nationalism, socialism, and Islamism.[3] In the United States, the decade marked the beginning of a retreat from the grand 1960s liberal policies to redress racial discrimination and economic inequality. Northeastern cultural and political hegemony began to lose ground to the South and the West as the population moved to the Sunbelt. Faith in the marketplace replaced confidence in the welfare state and the federal government, which had been delegitimized by the Watergate scandals and Nixon's resignation. Religion reawakened, though not necessarily through established institutions. New Age movements empowered individual forms of spiritual expression, ranging from est to Baptist revivals and women's and men's retreats. The 1960s rallying cry, "Down with Authority," had stimulated the erosion of postwar formality and decorum in the 1970s. Americans were letting it "all hang out." Cultural nationalism—the insistence on cultural difference—replaced the universalist, integrationist ethos that had supported intergroup relations. The private sphere became a refuge from the disappointments and disillusionments created by the political and social upheavals of the 1960s. In Bruce J. Schulman's words, the 1970s decade allowed American citizens to create "congeries of separate private refuges."[4]

Jewish Americans were, of course, influenced by these social, cultural, and political currents. Many prominent New York intellectuals began to make what would later be called the "neoconservative turn." What made the neoconservatives "neo" was that they had all been socialists, Democrats, and liberals, who, viewing their own leftist past as benighted, renounced it. The liberalism they contended with contained two broad and politically contestable elements: first, a defense of individual civil liberties and laissez-faire economic policy, and second, support of the welfare state initiated by Roosevelt and expanded during President Johnson's Great Society. The first focused on individual freedom, a free market, civil liberties, the separation of church and state, religious toleration, and pluralism. The second focused on social justice to be achieved through programs funded by the welfare state. The latter required revenue generated by taxes, which led to the creation of what some critics began calling "big government."[5] The neoconservatives embraced a critique that pitted these two facets against one another, arguing that the social justice agenda of the Great Society and later of the New Left imperiled protection of individual rights.[6]

Neoconservatism in the 1970s and 1980s was neither a political party nor a coherent movement. Irving Kristol famously considered it a "persuasion," not a movement.[7] Yet some generalizations about the worldview of its central actors can be made. In the 1970s and 1980s, neoconservatives rejected utopian ideological solutions to society's problems, reflecting disillusionment with their own youthful socialism. They criticized the policies of the Great Society, such as government poverty programs and redistributive tax policies, which endeavored to redress economic inequality, and educational programs, such as affirmative action, busing, and community control, which sought to level the playing field of racial discrimination. The neoconservatives held these policies to be misguided, arguing that unabated socioeconomic disparities proved their failure. Politically, the counterculture, the New Left, and the militant Black Power movement—avatars of what Lionel Trilling called the "adversary culture"—became a focus of neoconservative animus.[8] Though critical of the Vietnam War early in the 1960s, the neoconservatives affirmed the basic goodness of American society. Reflecting the anti-communism forged in the interwar years and sharpened in the two decades after the war, they continued to view the Soviet Union as the greatest threat to American society and values and distrusted the anti-Americanism of the postcolonial revolutionary upheavals. Jewish neoconservatives were particularly alarmed by the New Left's association of Zionism with racism and imperialism and by the growing power of antidemocratic societies in the United Nations.[9] Domestically, in response to feminism and the sexual revolution, the neoconservatives waged a no-holds-barred defense of the nuclear family and heterosexuality, with some appealing to traditional religious practice.[10]

From the long perspective of Jewish history, the retreat of the Jewish New York neoconservatives from the Democratic Party can be understood as part of a tradition of Jewish negotiation with the competing claims of individual and group rights within the host states in which they lived, a negotiation inaugurated explicitly in Europe during the French Revolution (and implicitly in the United States at its revolutionary moment). The late eighteenth century set modern Jewish politics in motion, a politics that took many forms— liberalism, socialism, nationalism, residual forms of premodern politics, and hair-splitting varieties and admixtures of them all.[11] Liberalism in the form of political emancipation based on individual rights emerged during the contentious debates in the French National Assembly. Culminating in the famous saying by Count Clermont-Tonnerre that Jews living in France should be granted "everything as individuals, nothing as a nation,"[12] the emancipation contract had been set, at least theoretically: liberal republics would admit Jews as individuals provided that Jewish national claims were understood to be inadmissible in the modern state's legal structure.[13]

The New York intellectuals had negotiated their place in postwar American society by making no claim for group recognition; indeed, they had distanced themselves from precisely such claims as they successfully acculturated. Though economic, political, and social struggle—and socialism as a political response to those struggles—was deeply embedded in the fabric of their childhoods, the postwar years allowed them to benefit from the G.I. Bill, gain access to higher education and inexpensive suburban housing, and become middle-class. These opportunities allowed several New York intellectuals to earn positions at major American universities after the war. Thus, by the postwar period, the New York intellectuals were well integrated into mainstream liberal politics and generally comfortable with support of the American state. Partisan Review announced the New York intellectuals' reassessment of their former alienation in a three-issue symposium in 1952, under the patriotic-sounding title "Our Country, Our Culture."[14] The success of Jewish social and economic mobility illustrated that Jews, while a religious minority, had a stake in the universalist and meritocratic claims of legal equality that worked for white Americans.[15]

When the group of Jewish New York intellectuals turned rightward in the 1970s, they disavowed the government's role in the creation of the Great Society, in large measure because President Johnson's expansion of FDR's social welfare bureaucracy—coupled with an energized and radicalized civil rights movement—strove to redress economic inequality and racial discrimination by recognizing "group rights." At stake was their conception of civil society and what constituted the glue of the social contract.[16] Gertrude Himmelfarb articulated this tension in a 1980 Commentary magazine symposium on liberalism: "We may begin to suspect that the liberalism that brought us into modernity, that gave us our freedom as individuals and tolerated us as Jews, has been replaced by a new liberalism that is inhospitable to us both as individuals and as Jews." The "beleaguered" proponents of old-school liberalism "have lost the battle."[17] That old-school liberalism had insisted that a healthy civil society could weather the coexistence of antagonistic components without fear of collapse. The New York intellectuals who moved rightward worried that the radical movements of the late 1960s threatened the basic health—the *civility*— of the public sphere. This preoccupation with civility reveals a Jewish intelligentsia in postwar New York engaged in a modern encounter that echoed the experience of their European forebears: the quest to integrate into the middle class, acquire its culture, and abet the creation of a secular civic sphere that would safeguard their rights as Jews.

And so while neoconservatism was not "Jewish," those neoconservatives who were Jewish were animated by specific Jewish concerns anchored in a specifically Jewish response to the new turbulence of American society.[18] "The Family" and its intra-Jewish communal fights were an American manifestation of modernizing European Jewry's culture wars, which can also be traced back to the late eighteenth century. *Maskilim*, first in Prussia and later among their East European brethren in Galicia, Russia, and Poland, embraced the rationalism and optimism of the European Enlightenment and exhorted their fellow Jews—whom they viewed as parochial and insular—to do likewise. The tenacity of American exceptionalism in the writing of American Jewish history has obscured the typological similarity, mutatis mutandis, between East European *maskilim* and American Jewish public intellectuals of East European origin. Both were rooted in East European Jewish culture and sought to integrate into non-Jewish general society; both aspired to be the new intellectual leadership of a modern Jewish community independent from rabbinical authority because both believed they knew what was in the best interest of their fellow Jews; and both considered the written word in the form of didactic popular journals to be the optimal vehicle through which to spread their views.[19] In 1965, Irving Kristol quipped that he, Daniel Bell, and Nathan Glazer had not run for political office to counter the "fantasies" of the 1960s; rather, they "started a magazine [*The Public Interest*]—on a shoestring."[20]

No better an illustration of the Jewishness of the culture wars is the anecdote recorded by Irving Howe in his postwar collection of essays, *Steady Work*. Recalling a confrontation with student activists at Stanford University in a faculty cafeteria in the mid-1960s, Howe describes offering a retort that signaled the internal Jewishness of the political divide between the Old and New Lefts:

One day a group of SDS [Students for a Democratic Society] students led by a fellow named *Cohen* forms a semi-circle behind us, chanting hostile slogans. They mean to carry the battle against decadent liberalism to the heart of the enemy. This continues day after day. Go elsewhere for lunch? My pride won't allow it. One noon, [I spin around] to the group . . . and shout at *Cohen*,

"You're going to end up a *dentist!*" *Cohen* blanches—the insult is simply too dreadful—and I march off in miniature triumph.[21]

Cultural warriors like nothing better than to characterize their opponents as traitors and heretics,[22] and in this regard postwar American Jewish liberals and neoconservatives were no different from their European forebears. Different groups within the variegated American Jewish community had radically different interpretations of what political behavior in the American diaspora was actually "good for the Jews," and not infrequently they charged their opponents with betraying the Jews' true interests.[23] Much of the postwar Jewish public, and most of the intellectuals among them, viewed liberalism as "applied Judaism"[24] and therefore regarded neoconservatism as anathema to Judaism and Jewish culture. In 1973, Irving Howe voiced his disappointment at *Commentary's* view that the United States, by not being more aggressive in its response to the OPEC oil embargo, had lost its backbone. "I find it troubling," he wrote, "that the most influential and respected Jewish journal in the United States should in the last few years have veered so sharply to the Right in its politics."[25] In *Commentary's* 1980 symposium on Jews and liberalism, *Village Voice* writer Jack Newfield expressed that the prospect of "Jews betraying liberalism" caused him "great pain."[26] Later, Jewish neoconservatives returned the favor. In 1992 Ruth Wisse wrote *If I Am Not For Myself . . .* and subtitled it *The Liberal Betrayal of the Jews,*[27] and in 1999 Podhoretz's memoir-like account of his falling out with the Trillings and Hannah Arendt, among others, was titled *Ex-Friends.*[28]

Signaling the Jewishness of the "neoconservative turn" among certain New York Jewish intellectuals, and the ways in which the culture wars of the late 1960s and 1970s in the United States shared features with earlier periods of Jewish history, is by no means a dismissal or diminishment of the local, contextual forces informing that history. As Moshe Rosman has written, "Jewishness is defined by a constellation of factors, all of which are never present simultaneously, but a significant number of which, in various permutations, are always in evidence."[29] Rosman's claim derived from his insistence that Jewish agency as *Jews* throughout history be accorded its due, without apologetics. Likewise, this book claims that the *longue durée* of the Jewish past, not only the realities of contemporary America, significantly informed the development and evolution of the Jewish neoconservatives' worldview and politics.[30] They were intellectual Jews engaged with Jewish ideas. Some of them had significant Jewish educations and spoke or read Jewish languages. Some practiced Judaism and were familiar with the liturgy and Jewish calendar. Most had been reared in Jewish neighborhoods, surrounded by East European immigrants and their communal associations and institutions. All of those components—ideas, language, religion, and community—contributed to a collective sensibility that informed the rightward turn of certain American Jewish intellectuals in the 1980s.

In many ways, Lucy S. Dawidowicz was out of the gate before them.

JEWISH NEOCONSERVATIVE *AVANT LA LETTRE*

For her part, Dawidowicz was acutely aware of the influence of the Jews' long history in the European diaspora on the contemporary reality of American Jews. She rejected the enshrinement of liberalism as an essential characteristic of being Jewish much earlier than the New York intellectuals did. Already in 1963, she (with Leon Goldstein) had concluded in *In Politics in a Pluralist Democracy: Studies in Voting in the 1960 Election* that the American Jewish attachment to liberalism derived from the European past.[31] American Jewish liberalism was not a genetic trait, in her understanding, but a politics born of history.

Dawidowicz also always insisted on the Jews' distinctive historical path and wanted her fellow Jewish intellectuals to recognize and utilize the political tactics that had served them so well in the past. Where other Jewish neoconservatives unconsciously invoked political patterns from premodern European Jewish experience as they reframed their conception of American Jewish politics in the late 1960s, Dawidowicz did so consciously. Her conviction was shaped by Salo W. Baron's interpretation of the relative security enjoyed by Jews in medieval times compared with Jewish vulnerability in the modern period.[32] Historically, European Jewish leaders had wisely negotiated alliances between the formal Jewish community and their host societies' highest authorities. Faith in temporal protection had given vulnerable Jewish communities hope in their long diasporic history.[33] These were historical models that were still apposite in the contemporary political moment. Amid the upheavals and violence of the late 1960s and through the 1970s and 1980s, Dawidowicz reasoned that American Jews and their leaders would be wise to take not only a page but a chapter out of the European Jewish historical-political playbook by aligning with the ruling political party, even if that party was Republican. Dawidowicz's unabashed articulation of how these concerns animated her rightward shift makes visible the relationship of postwar American Jewish political conservatism to the long history of diasporic Jewish politics.

THE PROBLEM OF VIOLENCE AND BLACK POWER

The tactical gap between the Old and New Lefts widened as political move-ments turned violent. With the escalation of the Vietnam War, the young rad-icals of the 1960s refused to toe the line of the Old Left's Cold War liberalism. Enchanted by the revolutions in China, Cuba, and South America, certain groups within the New Left justified the use of violence to upend the Amer-ican political status quo.[34] Infamously, the *New York Review of Books*, a leftist intellectual monthly, ran a cover illustration in 1967 of how to make a Molotov cocktail.[35] Impatient with the slow pace of civil rights progress, frustrated by the continued glaring economic deprivation of so many African Americans, and embittered by ongoing violence against black people perpetrated by the police and by white racists, African American activists like Stokely Carmichael and Malcolm X challenged the integrationist approach of Martin Luther King Jr., Roy Wilkins, and Bayard Rustin, founding a Black Power movement that threatened to resort to violence to redress systemic racism.[36]

Carmichael, the charismatic leader of the Student Nonviolent Coordinat-ing Committee (SNCC), is widely credited for including violence as a polit-ical strategy in the Black Power movement. In the aftermath of a June 1966 nonviolent march at the University of Mississippi that went awry, he refused to condemn violence. "It is not for us to tell black communities whether they can or cannot use any particular form of action to resolve their problems," Carmichael told a *New York Times* reporter. "Responsibility for the use of vio-lence by black men lies with the white community."[37] Such sentiments both challenged the tradition of nonviolence within the civil rights movement and heightened the distrust between whites and nonwhites in the movement, spur-ring white backlash.

For self-conscious Jewish intellectuals, the violence of the mid-1960s rep-resented not only the dangers of mass culture (of which the New York intel-lectuals had long been disdainful)[38] but a resurgence of populist antisemitism in American culture.[39] The insecurities felt by now middle-class, integrated American Jewish intellectuals were heightened when the New Left attacked the university as an incarnation of imperialism, privilege, and racism. In Neil Jumonville's words, the Old Left felt as if "their fortress was being stormed."[40] Left-wing intellectuals had put their hopes in the masses; but what happens, Daniel Bell asked in the aftermath of the 1968 Columbia strike—sparked by anti–Vietnam War activism and the revelation that the university planned to build a new gymnasium in neighboring Morningside Park with separate entrances for the largely African American community and the predominantly white student body—when "a mass gets out of hand and becomes a mob?"[41] A student representative of SDS who participated in the strike expressed her contempt for the Old Left professors who believed that social change came through restrained use of a typewriter and a petition. They were, she said, "terrified of the mob."[42]

Deep-seated Jewish fears of mob violence alienated some of the New York intellectuals, propelling them away from their former alignment with disenfranchised social groups and toward support for the American state's right to enforce domestic security. Only one generation removed from the immigrants with memories of pogrom violence, the Jewish intellectuals were threatened by what seemed to be a familiar historical script that had all too often culminated in populist antisemitism. Kristol, Bell, Glazer, Podhoretz, and Dawidowicz, among others, recoiled at the urban violence that pitted poor, disenfranchised African Americans against lower-middle-class Jewish shopkeepers.[43]

Not surprisingly, Dawidowicz's identification with the Jewish victims of East European pogroms and her experience with interwar Polish hooliganism led her to project the experience of Europe onto her interpretation of American unrest. Her notes for a 1964 research project, "Extremism in American Social and Political History: A Proposed Study," concluded that in "The present racial upheaval in the United States, Negroes—or more precisely, some Negroes— are introducing a variety of antisemitism, anti-Jewish hostility that is new in America and very old in Europe, particularly Eastern Europe."[44]

In March 1966, Dawidowicz proposed a research project, "Negro Antisemitism: Outline for an Analysis," to help the Committee understand what seemed to be a new phenomenon of black antisemitism.[45] In the memo she emphasized three areas of concern: economic, intellectual, and socioreligious. Economic tensions between urban Jews and African Americans emerged from power relationships in housing, retail, and education. Among upwardly mobile middle-class blacks, Jews were increasingly perceived as being "obstacles to Negro advancement." Most discomfiting for liberal Jewish intellectuals, who prided themselves on their universalism, tolerance, and commitment to civil rights, was the perception that the black intelligentsia harbored anti-Jewish feelings. Dawidowicz was alarmed by the emergence of anti-Jewish sentiment among "otherwise responsible activists and leaders in the civil rights movements, among Negro artists and intellectuals, in the Negro middle class and among Negro professionals." In her memo, Dawidowicz blamed James Baldwin, who had fallen out with Norman Podhoretz,[46] for exhorting African

American writers to vent their rage indiscriminately at white society. Asserting that "Negro writers have been given free (so it seems) rein to their feelings, sexual and social," she described their basic message as one of "profound hurt and profound hate. . . . this new writing has encouraged Negro authors to vie with each other in the expression of implacable hatred against white people, not infrequently Jews." She also took seriously the impact of Christian anti-Jewish teachings among black churchgoers and urged the AJC "to learn as much as possible about specific anti-Jewish elements of Muslim anti-white hatred."[47]

Dawidowicz suggested that the research study focus on an analysis of the specific ideologies of antisemitism in order to discern such "so-called objective factors" as the economic relationship between middle-class white Jews and lower-class African Americans. Raising uncomfortable questions, she asked, "Were African American leaders using antisemitism to establish their *bona fides*? Is antisemitism being used to leverage political power?" Proposing that the AJC research team examine the role of Jewish intellectuals and activists in abetting the African American and leftist hostility to the urban middle class, she singled out "the problem arising from the prominence of Jews—compared to other 'white' ethnics—in the civil rights movement, many of them radicals and most, alienated Jews."

> They share the Marxist-cum-populist distrust of the merchant and the middleman. Most, escaping from the bourgeois comforts of home, shout their contempt for the Jewish community, which for them is merely momma and poppa. They have disdain for Judaism and its institutions. To what extent have these Jews influenced Negroes, reinforcing Negro feelings of hostility and providing Negroes with ideological rationalization and psychological justifications of antisemitism?[48]

Having herself ascended the socioeconomic ladder from the immigrant working class to the American middle class and now a resident of Elmhurst, Queens—a predominantly white, Jewish neighborhood in metropolitan New York—Dawidowicz was particularly sensitive to charges of middle-class economic predation. In the early 1950s, her friend Pearl Ketcher had teased her about their former socialist disdain of middle-class aspirations and acquisitions: "I'm glad you've got your own apartment and even as you say it's bourgeois to like and enjoy a home of your own I am all for it."[49] Dawidowicz looked with dismay and alarm at the Jewish-owned businesses that had been wrecked during the riots, concerned with the predicament of the Jewish "bourgeoisie" in

America's tumultuous cities. Writing to Max Weinreich in 1965, Dawidowicz professed interest in "a history of the idea of 'productivization,'" a hallmark of the worldview of the *maskilim* and later of some Zionists that argued that the concentration of Jews in trade and commercial professions was responsible for their alleged cultural backwardness, economic ineffectiveness, physical weakness, and general unfitness for integration into European society. She explained her suspicion that "productivization" may have "originated as an anti-Jewish concept" and may have been "later widely disseminated by the radical Jewish and non-Jewish movements."[50] Implicit in her comment is the accusation that those elements within Jewish society that criticized the concentration of Jews in trade and middle-class professions for their own internal ideological reasons had contributed to later antisemitic assaults on the Jews from the Left. Voicing her growing distance from her fellow Jews to her political left, Dawidowicz viewed their critique of the predominance of Jews in the middle class as alienated self-hatred. This assessment, and her reconciliation with capitalism generally, was shared by other Jewish neoconservatives.

In July 1966, Dawidowicz wrote a seven-page memo in which she elaborated on the economic elements of Negro-Jewish tensions and articulated her wariness concerning African American charges of exploitation by Jewish merchants.[51] Emphasizing the need to distinguish between "simply doing business" and conscious exploitation, she proposed to examine "the social and economic conditions of doing business in Negro ghettos, analyzing profits and profitability, together with the attendant costs and risks." Price gouging should be investigated, she conceded, but the thrust of her memo was that the economic critique of Jewish shopkeepers in predominantly African American slums was based on older, symbolic fictions of Jewish middle-class exploitation, not on an objective reality. American blacks had absorbed anti-Jewish middle-class animus, displaying a traditional "peasant distrust of merchants and middlemen" whose historical roots went back to Europe. Her deep-rooted anxiety about the vulnerability of Jews could not have been more clearly expressed: "Populist and socialist notions about business and trade became part of the ideological baggage of national socialism, and the boycott of small Jewish retail stores was a hallmark of antisemitic movements throughout Europe. At first they wanted to drive Jews out of business, later they wanted to drive them out of the country. (Then came the Final Solution.)"[52] In a follow-up memo, "Proposal for a Study of Negro-White Customer-Merchant Relations," Dawidowicz noted that the "pejorative" usage of the word "exploitation" was "becoming increasingly common . . . when used to describe Negro-white customer-merchant relations," suggesting that "the merchant is basely, illegitimately, and unethically taking advantage of his customer." The most basic question, she suggested, was "At what point does legitimate business and and [*sic*] 'exploitation' begin?"[53]

Dawidowicz's memos reveal a kind of analogical binary that cast African Americans as antisemitic East European peasants goaded on by an antisemitic Russian intelligentsia or by alienated Jewish intellectuals in the socialist movements of mid-nineteenth-century Europe. This mode of presentation became central to her rhetorical strategy and, indeed, to her worldview. She made similar historical analogies in a symposium sponsored by *Midstream* magazine in December 1966. Shlomo Katz invited twenty-seven influential Jewish and African American thinkers to discuss the emergence of a separatist, culturally nationalist Black Power element within the civil rights movement and its effect on relations between urban Jews and blacks.[54] Katz asked his Jewish respondents about the relationship between Jewish ethics and a commitment to civil rights. He included a question about what today would be called the Jews' "whiteness," asking whether an increasing identification with white American society had caused Jews to distance themselves from African Americans.[55] In his introduction, Katz compared the American Jewish community's historic trust in the state and its liberal institutions with African Americans' justified distrust of those very institutions. He saw civil rights activists and even Black Power advocates as proponents of national self-determination, the latter not dissimilar to radical Zionist activists.[56] In the symposium, he urged Jews to understand the rage of African Americans, citing the passage in the Passover Haggadah, "Pour out thy wrath upon the nations," which asks God to exact vengeance upon those who do not acknowledge Him.[57] Privately, however, Katz condemned violence as a political tactic and expressed concern over antisemitic rhetoric used in African American protest discourse.[58]

In her *Midstream* response, Dawidowicz reached back into European Jewish historical typologies to explain the crisis in the American city, commenting that Negro-Jewish relations filled her with "a sense of *déjà vu*." It was "like watching an old Russian movie about the 1870's, in black and white, with English subtitles."[59] That old movie put forth what she viewed as age-old rationalizations for antisemitism, the same ones that civil rights leaders were cynically repurposing:

A prominent psychologist (Negro) recently redefined antisemitism on a national-network television program. To hate Jews because you think they killed Christ is the rankest prejudice, he said, but to hate them because you believe they exploit Negroes is the sheerest objectivity. Alexander III,

Emperor and Tsar of all Russia, also found such objective reasons to justify the pogroms of 1881: "The exploitation of the peasants by the Jews."[60]

As in her AJC memos, Dawidowicz sought to refute what she called "the crescendo of charges about 'exploitation' by 'Jewish merchants' and 'Jew-landlords,'" noting that "without trade the economy would perish." Returning to her analogizing of European history, she referred to African Americans as "America's serfs," "a landless peasantry forced to seek work in the cities"—whose vulnerabilities had been exploited and sentiments manipulated by "revolutionaries" and their "anti-business, anti-capitalist ideologies . . . arousing the peasants against the exploitation of merchants and innkeepers." Again, she pointed her finger at the role of intellectuals in fomenting the discontent of the masses. "[A]ctivists, militants, nationalists in the Civil Rights Movement," she charged, "are America's populists, articulating and escalating the latent and patent prejudices of their masses, hoping to stir them out of apathy into revolution." Russian history again served as a model for the contemporary political climate:

In 1881, Narodnaya Volya, [Russian] agrarian populists who embraced violence, applauded the pogroms in Russia as an unexpected revelation of the peasants' use of "revolutionary methods of struggle." Stokely Carmichael and LeRoi Jones[61] are America's Narodnaya Volya, preaching revolution, violence, and a species of economic antisemitism.[62]

Dawidowicz's assumption of the lack of African American agency is quite striking. It reflected not only her preoccupation with the role of ideas and intellectuals' dissemination of them in the creation of social movements but also her paternalistic view of African American culture and experience.

Not all of Dawidowicz's peers disregarded the political agency of the African American community. The respondents to the *Midstream* symposium did not speak in one voice, though several writers (Howard Fast, Leslie Fiedler, Jacob Glatshteyn, and Arthur Hertzberg) invoked the European Jewish past and others (Joel Carmichael, Arthur A. Cohen, and Ben Halpern) adduced the Christianity of American blacks as the primary cause for the latter's animus toward Jews. Other commentators, however, rejected the idea that antisemitism lay at the core of urban rioting that had targeted the middle class. Jacob Cohen, a former CORE activist, roundly rejected the European analogy and the influence of antisemitism—except among a few exhibitionist figures like Jones—writing that "The Negro is not a peasant as of old; he is an indifferent nativist, all efforts to incorporate him into a populist majority, including recent efforts, having failed. As the real anti-Semites in this country best know, the Negro has been and will be America's Jew."[63] Other voices worried about Jews joining the white backlash against the civil rights movement.[64] And Conservative rabbi Arthur Hertzberg noted that both African Americans and Jews were being pulled toward white supremacist norms as they acculturated, observing that there is "a kind of ambivalence among Jews: on the one hand, both religious tradition and historic memories impel us to side with the Negro; on the other hand, there is the unworthy impulse to become part of the majority, as white men. In sum, if the Negroes can 'join' society through antisemitism, Jews can 'join' it as whites."[65]

Dawidowicz was ever haunted by Europe. The specter of anti-Jewish violence shadowed all her writings on civil rights, even those that evidenced a more dispassionate tone, such as her 1967 summary "Intergroup Relations and Tensions in the U.S.," written for the *American Jewish Year Book*.[66] She began by contrasting Jewish feelings of security with African American feelings of insecurity and prejudice that drove the "accelerated drive for civil rights."[67] But the threat of social unrest and lawlessness, and their potential for unleashing violence against Jews, disquieted Dawidowicz, whatever the source. Even in the face of evidence that radicalism did not represent the majority opinion among African Americans, she remained concerned that riots, violence, and looting among African Americans had been "received in some quarters with permissiveness and unexpected tolerance . . . even praised . . . by some segments of the civil-rights movement as liberating expressions of selfhood."[68] Her summary mentioned that many "responsible Negro leaders," among others, Dorothy Height, A. Philip Randolph, and Bayard Rustin, had publicly repudiated the militancy of the Black Power slogan and reaffirmed support for the democratic process.[69] Her report also acknowledged the continued violence against African Americans on the part of the police and gentile white ethnics. Yet at the same time that her report illustrated the ever-widening gap between African American aspirations and the reality of their daily oppression, it also revealed the degree to which many American Jews felt committed to the stability of American society and disenchanted with the radicalizing civil rights movement.[70]

THE LANGUAGE AND LITERATURE OF POWER— AND ANTISEMITISM

Dawidowicz's acute sensitivity to words, and her belief that language and rhetoric used in the public sphere could easily be harnessed to destructive political movements, made her especially suspicious of the speeches of the Black Power movement, which, to her mind, gave license to "racism, black separatism, and, above all, a mystique of violence."[71] In her experience, general verbal appeals to political violence could quickly redound to antisemitic rhetoric and thus to physical attacks on Jews. Events at a February 1966 CORE meeting, in which Clifford A. Brown, the educational director of the Mt. Vernon chapter, shouted that Hitler should have killed more Jews, affirmed her fears. Even though James Farmer distanced himself from the comments, he went on to equate the crimes of Auschwitz with contemporary discrimination against African Americans.[72] Jewish financial support for CORE plummeted after the events, illustrating that Dawidowicz was not alone among American Jewish liberals who grasped how political speech, though protected by the First Amendment, could advance into hateful behavior.[73]

In November 1967, Dawidowicz helped Bertram Gold, the newly appointed executive vice president of the AJC, prepare his board address. In "Cultural Antisemitism," she warned against a threatening linkage of gentile resentment of Jewish cultural preeminence with African American rage. "The writers, intellectuals, and academicians who are not Jewish feel excluded from the hot center, from the Establishment, from wherever great and lively things are going on." Those outsiders "feel left out of what they presume to be the close-knit friendship/kinship circles of Jewish intellectuals, where careers and reputations are made or broken," and as a result, the Jews end up being seen "as a coherent group, tactless, crude, snobbish, and smug." The "New York City intelligentsia" are seen, she wrote, as "'rootless,' the most characteristic of anti-semitic expletives."[74] More subtle, but as pernicious, were the comments of Carl Bridenbaugh, president of the American Historical Association, who had coded his distaste for Jewish immigrant historians in an address, decrying that the "younger practitioners of our craft . . . [are] products of lower middle-class or foreign origins, [whose] emotions not infrequently get in the way of historical reconstructions."[75] Cultural antisemitism, Dawidowicz noted, also took the form of expressions bemoaning the dechristianization of the United States,[76] citing a 1962 survey claiming that 51 percent of public school administrators thought the Supreme Court was wrong in ruling against prayer in the public schools. Critics of the decision, including attorney Erwin N. Griswold, a recipient of the AJC's American Liberties Medallion, insisted that the United States had been founded as a Christian nation.

Even more disturbing to Dawidowicz was the perceptible antisemitism among the black nationalist literary elite. She highlighted Harold Cruse's *The Crisis of the Negro Intellectual* (1967) and LeRoi Jones's 1965 poem "Black Art" as "crude and vicious antisemitism."[77] The Black Arts movement rejected the earlier integrationist ethos of the civil rights movement.[78] Dawidowicz voiced concern that the celebration of black nationalist writing by the literary establishment would "provide an opening and a channel to make anti-semitism acceptable, even fashionable, among white liberal and leftist intellectuals."[79] When Bertram Gold addressed the AJC's National Executive Board in December 1967, he thanked Dawidowicz for her "invaluable help," incorporating whole sections of her memo into his speech. Though he emphasized the socioeconomic component in African American attitudes toward Jews, noting that in general "the greater the income, the less anti-Jewish hostility and vice versa," he warned against the great danger of increased antisemitism among black nationalists—including intellectuals—and white radicals. The AJC should, therefore, "support and work with responsible Negro leadership" and "insist, if necessary, that these leaders make their stand on reverse racism and Negro anti-Semitism crystal clear and unequivocal."[80]

Nearing the end of her tenure at the AJC, Dawidowicz continued to raise the thorny issues of African American literary antisemitism and the dangers of inflammatory rhetoric. In the spring of 1968, the explosive events in the predominantly African American neighborhoods of Ocean Hill and Brownsville justified her prescience.[81] In May, a new school board empowered by a decentralization plan, known as "community control," fired thirteen tenured teachers—all, save one, Jewish. The teachers' union, led by Albert Shanker, demanded reinstatement of the staff, while the school board insisted on community control with authority to hire new teachers. This led to a walkout by sympathetic teachers and a total shutdown of the public schools for thirty-six days. A war of words ensued. Teachers' mailboxes were stuffed with antisemitic literature, including a lurid leaflet blaming "The Middle East Murderers of Colored People" for "Years of Brainwashing And Self-Hatred That Has Been Taught To Our Black Children By Those Bloodsucking Exploiters and Murderers."[82] Shanker publicized the leaflets, and matters worsened when Julius Lester, a radio host, asked Leslie Campbell, an African American teacher, to read an antisemitic poem written by one of his students. Titled "Anti-Semitism" and dedicated to Shanker, it began: "Hey, Jew Boy, with that yarmulka on your head / You, pale-faced Jew boy—I wish you were dead."[83]

In June 1968, Dawidowicz drafted a memo to Milton Himmelfarb on the subject of an Ocean Hill–Brownsville study. She emphasized the use of anti-semitism as a political tool, the relationship between the African American elite and the black lower classes, and the gap between the Jewish elite and the Jewish community. In her view, the strike of predominantly middle-class white Jewish teachers illustrated the growing distance between their lived experience of integration and the theoretical commitments of Jewish elites, many of whom had not set foot in a New York City public school since their youth. Officials in the mainstream liberal Jewish communal organizations may have been unaware of the intimidation that Jewish teachers had faced. She described Shanker's tactics as a way "to inform, in a dramatic fashion, the Jewish community of the dangers which they perceived to be immediate and threatening, yet which were not widely known or even acknowledged to exist."[84] In an earlier memo to Bertram Gold, she had wondered about the gap between affluent suburban Jewish leadership and the less well-to-do urban rank and file, many of whom were feeling abandoned. "Jewish leaders were making public-policy declarations about what they thought was right for other people to do." In their zeal to promote intergroup relations, these leaders "have forgotten that their real constituency is the Jewish community."[85]

True to its core values, the AJC remained committed to civil rights and to good relations between African Americans and Jews, even as Dawidowicz continued to promote research into literary antisemitism and hate speech against Jews.[86] This interest remained a constant concern, and after she left the Committee, her research informed her later public writings. Her 1970 *Commentary* essay "Can Anti-Semitism Be Measured?" criticized Claude Brown, author of *Manchild in the Promised Land* (1965), for spreading "the stereotype of the Jew as swindler and exploiter, as ancient a stereotype as that of the Jew as Christ-killer." Her critique shows her again transposing the political economy of European Jews onto the American street:

The new articulateness of today's American blacks—many of whom form an uprooted peasantry becoming urbanized—simply gives fresh currency in the United States to one of Europe's oldest myths. It is indeed only in terms of the myth that one can understand the psychological process that makes this urban peasantry blame the Jews, rather than other ethnic groups whose occupational roles afflict Negroes far more severely than do Jewish merchants and landlords. . . . And it is the myth, more than the experience, which makes it possible for young blacks today to parrot the pseudo-scientific mouthings of anti-Semites in Germany and Austria one hundred years ago.[87]

Herein lay the paradox of Dawidowicz's identity and that of many American Jews with strong immigrant ties and memories: they embraced and celebrated an America that posed few obstacles to their acculturation, socioeconomic mobility, and religious acceptance. But they could not shake the fears inculcated over years of European "otherness."

POSTCOLONIALISM AND THE EXTERNAL CRITIQUE OF JEWISH "POWER"

The combative antisemitic rhetoric on the domestic scene was paralleled and heightened by global politics. In the late 1960s, Dawidowicz and other Jewish neoconservatives reacted to the emergence of militant postcolonialism— what they called "Third World" politics—posed by the North Vietnamese, the Sandinistas in Nicaragua, and the African National Congress, viewing it as a form of violent, international utopianism. To be sure, their fierce Cold War anti-communism shaped their rhetorical hostility to these social movements. Yet, added to this was something new: the emergence of Palestinian nationalism in the ongoing conflict between Israel and its Arab neighbors. Israel's triumph in the Six-Day War in June 1967 and its pyrrhic victory in the Yom Kippur War of 1973 set in motion two related issues that would test the politics of American Jewish liberal intellectuals: Israel's occupation of land on the West Bank of the Jordan River and the emergence of messianic forms of Zionism. Israel's victories widened the cracks within the American Jewish community about what politics best served Jews, many of whose identities were informed by a commitment to Jewish peoplehood in both Israel and the diaspora.[88]

From 1967 onward, radicalized black nationalists, informed by their own transnational and political identities, joined the chorus of criticism against Israel. Breaking with the integrationist mainstream civil rights movement that had supported Zionism as a legitimate form of Jewish self-determination after the Holocaust, SNCC announced its support for the Arabs in a newsletter that asked its readers: "Did you know . . . that the Zionists conquered Arab homes through terror, force, and massacres? Did you know . . . that the U.S. government has worked along with Zionist groups to support Israel so that America may have a toehold in that strategic Middle East location, thereby helping white America to control and exploit the rich Arab nations?"[89] While SNCC defended its anti-Zionism as a just component of its anti-colonialism and anti-imperialism, Jewish readers of the newsletter found it difficult to separate its critique from old-fashioned antisemitism. Cartoons that traded on stereotypes of Jews as economic predators, as well as an article that referenced the Rothschilds and their wealth, did not help. Stokely Carmichael was particularly vocal regarding "Zionist aggression," linking the cause of African Americans fighting US imperialism to the struggle of Egypt—which he depicted as the black motherland—against Israel, the West's proxy.[90] The rhetoric of the *Black Panther*, the party's organ, was notoriously vicious, telling its readers that the "Zionist fascist state of Israel is a puppet and lackey of the imperialist and must be smashed."[91]

Synergy between a radicalized civil rights movement and a radicalized student movement strengthened the anti-colonialist components of both. William Sales, one of the students involved in the Columbia University protests, proclaimed: "If you strike a blow at the gym, you strike a blow for the Vietnamese people. [If] you strike a blow at Low Library, you strike a blow for the freedom fighters in Angola, Mozambique, Portuguese Guinea, Zimbabwe, [and] South Africa."[92] Zionism had become linked with colonial expansion and oppression. Earlier in the academic year, the National Conference for New Politics met in Chicago and demanded that participants accept a thirteen-point platform, including one point that categorized the Six-Day War as an "imperialist Zionist war."[93] Both sides published competing ads. One on June 28, 1970, signed by sixty mainstream African American activists, supported Israel and called for peace. Another, on September 1, 1970, signed by socialist and black nationalist organizations, criticized the US government's support of the Zionist state. The growing fissure between mainstream integrationist civil rights leaders and radical African American nationalists continued to be expressed in attitudes toward Israel throughout the decade.

Though not a Zionist, Dawidowicz paid careful attention to Israel's fate and to the relationship of American Jews to the Zionist cause.[94] For over a decade she wrote about the Middle East and American foreign policy in the pages of the *American Jewish Year Book*, beginning in 1954 and ending in 1968 with a thirty-page chapter on American public opinion after the Six-Day War.[95] Her reports emphasized the persistent unresolved issues in the Middle East, such as border tensions between Israel and its Arab neighbors; the relocation or compensation of Arab refugees from the 1948 war; maritime conflicts at the Suez Canal and the port of Aqaba; political divisions among and within the Arab states; the development of nuclear capacity in Israel; and the steady encroachment of Soviet influence—with the concomitant arms race—in the region. Dawidowicz's articles frequently cited editorials and surveys reflecting American public opinion about Israel, particularly among the mainstream Christian churches. She also covered tensions between Israel's Zionist leadership and Zionist organizations in the United States. In 1962, her account revealed that David Ben-Gurion, despite assurances dating from his conflict with AJC president Jacob Blaustein in 1950, continued to insinuate that American Jews and American Jewish Zionists were living "incomplete" lives outside Israel.[96] Toward the middle of the decade, her analyses began to mention the effect of the radicalization of the civil rights movement and the growth of black nationalism as well as the implications of both in the erosion of support for Israel among African Americans and the New Left.

In her long essay "The Arab-Israel War of 1967: American Public Opinion," Dawidowicz stressed the surprising intensity of American Jewish identification with the beleaguered Jewish state in the month before and during the war. The Holocaust loomed in her interpretation of why American Jews—even those disaffiliated with Jewish life—felt as they did:

> As the Arabs began to close in on Israel in the second half of May, American Jews, so frequently accused of indifference and passivity, turned into a passionate, turbulent, clamorous multitude, affirming in unprecedented fashion that they were part of the Jewish people and that Israel's survival was their survival. The Arabs had pledged Israel's destruction. . . . *For the second time in a quarter of a century the Jewish people was facing annihilation.*[97]

In the aftermath of the Six-Day War, the American Jewish Committee abandoned its previous concerns with dual loyalty and embraced the Zionist cause.[98] Dawidowicz's essay did not focus on the AJC's new stance toward Zionism but looked instead on how the war affected American Jewish youth and the liberal professoriate. Both groups, she noted, experienced a clash of commitments. Accustomed to pacifist positions, left-wing students and professors found themselves profoundly rattled by fears of Israel's near extinction and equally buoyed by its victory. Dawidowicz cited the myriad volunteer efforts of high school and college students to support Israel, which included signing petitions, attending teach-ins, conducting prayer vigils, organizing marches, and donating blood. Academics, too, even those formerly alienated from Jewish communal life, came to Israel's aid and support. July saw the founding of

American Professors for Peace in the Middle East, with over eight thousand scholars signing on. Yet, for both leftist students and professors, reconciling anti-imperialist positions forged in opposition to the Vietnam War with their newfound pride in Israel's triumph was not easy. If war itself was unjust, oppressive, and a symbol of the crisis of capitalism, how could Israel's preemptive strike be considered just?[99] The Six-Day War exposed the challenges of harmonizing a Jewish identity based on a commonality of feeling with other Jews—a form of particularism—with the claims of an absolutist conception of universalism that admitted no national, ethic, religious, or gender-based bonds. It also exposed the fault lines of leftist identity based on victimhood and on contradictory visions of who the *real* victim was—Israel or the Arab states and their populations—before, during, and after the war. For many Jews in the United States, the threats to Israel's existence in 1967 awakened a historic sense of vulnerability.

Pride in Israel, and in being Jewish, coalesced after the Six-Day War at the very same time that militant civil rights organizations began to construe Israel's military prowess as a colonial force, victimizing Arabs and casting its Jewish supporters as right-wing racist nationalists. Dawidowicz concluded that the war exposed the Left's true posture, one that was inhospitable to Jews.[100] She feared that the "Third World idea" now provided a unifying theme—attractive to black nationalists as well—against Israel and its Jewish supporters.[101] Though some colleagues urged caution and the need to resist the withdrawal of support for civil rights ("there should be no hysterical reactions to this," urged Hyman Bookbinder, AJC's Washington representative, in a confidential memo),[102] Dawidowicz held firm in her suspicion. Six months after the war, she drafted a memo for Bertram Gold, "New Dimensions in Anti-Semitism," providing an overview of recent signs of antisemitism. She highlighted her fears of the fusion of black nationalism with anti-Zionism in left-wing movements that "seem to be united," she wrote, "in their increasing hostile attitude towards Jews."

> The reaction of the left to the Six Day War; the SNCC attack; the New Left Convention and its anti-Zionist pronouncements, are well known to all of us. What is most disturbing is the open alliance of these groups with Black Nationalist extremists and the notion that the non-whites throughout the world will constitute a third force in world politics. This adds a new ingredient to extremist anti-Semitism. It adds a philosophical base which permits anti-Semitism to be used as an open political weapon.[103]

Dawidowicz observed that the Six-Day War pushed Israel and its Jewish supporters in the diaspora out of the embracing arms of the Left, an exile that continues until today. And together with the universities and the civil rights movement, the United Nations became the site of a growing chasm between Jewish particularism in the form of support for Israel and liberalism in the mid-1970s.

THAT "INFAMOUS" RESOLUTION

Born in the aftermath of World War II, the United Nations embodied the hopes of liberal democratic idealism, with the protection of human rights at the core of its agenda.[104] Yet Cold War jockeying unsettled the institution almost from its founding. Having supported the partition of Palestine in 1947 as well as the establishment of the Jewish state in 1948, with the notable support of the Soviet Union, the United Nations swiftly became embroiled in issues related to Israel's legitimacy, issues that reflected both Cold War rivalries and its own internal politics. Tensions between the United States and the Soviet Union intensified with the Korean War, and as more member states joined the United Nations—many from decolonizing Africa—the Cold War expressed itself in eroding relations between the Soviet bloc and the West. The increase in the number of member nations aligned against the West included nineteen Arab nations, sixteen communist countries, and forty-seven in the Organization of African Unity (OAU), stacking the political deck against Israel. Between 1962 and 1965, negotiations within the United Nations' Committee on the Elimination of Racial Discrimination (CERD) fractured over the definition of antisemitism, opening the door to the first articulation of Zionism as a racial form of discrimination. The 1964 founding of the Palestine Liberation Organization (PLO), whose charter called Zionism "racist and fanatic in its nature, aggressive, expansionist and colonial in its aims, and fascist in its methods," helped to fuse the lexical connection between Zionism and racism.[105]

The United States had hoped to include antisemitism in the CERD's resolutions as a way to pressure the Soviet Union on its treatment of religious minorities, a viewpoint shared by American Jewish organizations and Israeli representatives mobilizing around the oppression of Soviet Jews. African, Asian, and Arab countries wanted the CERD's focus to remain on racial discrimination, as did the Soviets, whose pointed critique of the shameful treatment of African Americans in the United States was a strategic element in its Cold War position. When the twentieth session of the United Nations began on October 20, 1965, the Soviets quickly opposed the inclusion of anti-semitism in the CERD's resolutions and sought to include three new catego-ries—Nazism, genocide, and neo-Nazism—the latter as a jab against the West Germans. Upping the ante, they added Zionism as a form of racial discrimina-tion to embarrass the West, to take the spotlight off the issue of Soviet Jewry, and to curry favor with the Arab nations. To salvage the CERD, a quid pro quo proposal absent any mention of any "isms" (i.e., antisemitism, Nazism, neo-Nazism, and Zionism) passed with eighty-three votes in favor, twelve against, and ten abstentions. The contested rhetorical air, however, could not be cleared so quickly. Indeed, it became more fetid in the aftermath of the 1973 Yom Kip-pur War and the Arab oil embargo of 1973–74, the latter as retaliation for the United States' support of Israel that year.

The first International Women's Year (IWY) conference, held in Mexico City from June 19 to July 2, 1975, was also rocked by debate over Zionism. Initiated by the United Nations, the IWY's mandate was to focus global attention on discrimination against women. Supported by 133 governments, the conference adopted the "Declaration on the Equality of Women and Their Contribution to Peace, 1975." It also adopted thirty-four resolutions, which included Pales-tinian rights. The declaration, reflecting Cold War and anti-colonialist political posturing, called for "the elimination of colonialism and neo-colonialism, for-eign occupation, Zionism, apartheid and racial discrimination of all forms."[106] Though the United States protested, the UN General Assembly approved the declaration. That same summer, the OAU compared Palestine to Zimbabwe and South Africa, countries that share a "common imperialist origin, forming a whole and having the same racist structure," a view repeated by the Non-Aligned Movement in August.[107]

By the mid-1970s, the United States was beleaguered domestically and its international security also felt precarious.[108] In 1974, the PLO—widely con-sidered, particularly among Jews, to be a terrorist organization—had been awarded observer status at the United Nations. Excluded from the Non-Aligned Movement, Israel was now fully in the United States' geopolitical orbit. Zionism, once considered to be the legitimate expression of the collective right of the Jews for self-determination—a right burned into the world's conscience because of the Holocaust—now found itself on the defensive. A showdown in the United Nations was only a matter of time. Daniel Patrick Moynihan, the United States' ambassador to the intergovernmental organization, stepped directly into the fray.

Moynihan, a scrappy, iconoclastic scholar-politician, was a Catholic public servant and an old-fashioned liberal who felt deeply chastened by the tenor of the times.[109] He started his political career working for W. Averell Harriman, New York's governor, and then served in President Kennedy's Labor Department as well as under President Nixon in urban affairs. Focusing on welfare reform, Moynihan became well known, and in some circles notorious, for his 1965 report *The Negro Family: The Case of National Action*, which stressed the socioeconomic implications of single motherhood in black families.[110] Moynihan was an outlying member of the *Commentary* crowd,[111] having coauthored *Beyond the Melting Pot* (with Nathan Glazer), two chapters of which had appeared in the magazine's pages, as well as through his association with the MIT/Harvard Joint Center for Urban Studies, the research institute supervising the study of the 1966 Civilian Review Board sponsored by the AJC.[112] In 1967, Dawidowicz wrote to Moynihan, asking for a copy of a lecture he had given for the Americans for Democratic Action in which he urged liberals to "see more clearly that their essential interest is in the stability of the social order," a sentiment Dawidowicz thoroughly shared.[113] "I'm a great admirer of yours," she confessed to Moynihan. "Modesty alone stopped me from writing you a fan letter on your *Commentary* piece last February—and indeed on most things of yours that I read."[114]

In 1973 Moynihan accepted Nixon's appointment as the US ambassador to India, giving him a firsthand view of the world order from the vantage point of a postcolonial state. His 1975 *Commentary* article "The United States in Opposition" depicted a cloud-shadowed political horizon for the United States and Israel.[115] Moynihan perceived the legacy of British socialist thought behind the ideology of the postcolonial movements, which demanded economic and political reparations from the "privileged" West. Rather than recoil weak-kneed from the assault on liberal, humanistic cosmopolitanism or withdraw from the General Assembly, the United States should, Moynihan insisted, recognize that it was now in the minority and become a forceful, consistent voice of opposition to Third World bullying by states cozying up to Soviet patronage: "It is past time we ceased to apologize for an imperfect democracy."[116]

Moynihan's impatience with the anti-Americanism in the postcolonial camp turned to disgust in his reaction to the "Zionism is racism" Resolution 3379, which the General Assembly supported on November 10, 1975. Now serving as US ambassador to the United Nations, Moynihan waged a blistering attack on the resolution. His speech opened with a condemnation by the United States of "this infamous act," continued with a semantic excursus about the imprecision of the term "racism" and a historical explanation of the birth of Zionism as a form of Jewish national liberation, and moved on to connect the "obscenity" of the resolution to the degradation of the international commitment to human rights that undergirded the United Nations' mandate. He concluded: "The damage we now do to the idea of human rights and the language of human rights could well be irreversible."[117] Similar condemnation of the resolution resounded throughout American public opinion, from the press, the American Bar Association, federal and local branches of government, the League of Women Voters, the labor movement, and, notably, the African American community, voiced by such groups as BASIC (Black Americans in Support of Israel Committee) and NEGRO (National Economic Growth and Reconstruction Organization).[118]

The passage of Resolution 3379 augmented the sense that anti-Americanism and anti-Zionism had permanently infected the United Nations. It also fueled the fissure between Jewish and African American aspirations for cultural recognition and dignity. Four years later, in August 1979, Andrew Young, a civil rights activist and former aide to Martin Luther King Jr. who had been appointed US ambassador to the United Nations by President Carter, resigned from his post after revelations that he had met with representatives of the PLO. The US Department of State forbade negotiations with the PLO because of its refusal to recognize Israel's right to exist. Young initially claimed that he had discussed nothing of substance with Zehdi Labib Terzi, the United Nations' PLO observer, but popular opinion among Jews concluded that Young's identification with the United Nations' postcolonial ethos had clouded his judgment. He had been quoted as calling Israel "stubborn and intransigent" in its dealings with the Arab problem and was forced to resign.[119] There was no evidence that Jewish lobbying was behind Young's ouster, but some African Americans, including James Baldwin, H. Carl McCall, and Jesse Jackson, viewed him as a sacrifice to Jewish interests, his resignation another example of the paternalism that had shaped the early civil rights movement.[120]

The blowback from the Young resignation reflected a greater issue among the Jewish neoconservatives: their distrust of President Carter, whom they viewed as feckless in the face of accusations that Jewish pressure had forced Young's resignation.[121] Carter made them uncomfortable for other reasons. He refused to toe a hawkish Cold War line, stating in May 1977 that the United States should overcome "its inordinate fear of Communism."[122] Establishing a new office of human rights within the State Department to press his international human rights agenda, Carter spoke out against violations throughout the world, including those of such American allies as South Africa and Nicaragua. Rejecting an East-West binary view, Carter instead focused on North-South divisions, economic underdevelopment, global poverty, and racial discrimination.[123]

The Jewish neoconservatives' distrust of Carter was itself a symptom of their almost decade-long disillusionment with the Democratic Party, which had begun with the chaos at the Democratic Convention in 1968 and was exacerbated by McGovern's dismal campaign and electoral rout in 1972. To be sure, Jewish neoconservatives also took issue with Nixon's diplomacy with the Soviet Union; as fierce anti-communists, they feared that détente had allowed the Soviets to overtake the United States in the arms race. In the 1976 presidential campaign, they favored the hard-line anti-Soviet position of "Scoop" Jackson, a Cold War liberal who competed unsuccessfully against McGovern for the 1972 nomination. Jackson and Charles Vanik (D-Ohio) sponsored an amendment to the Trade Act of 1974 that restricted most-favored-nation status to the Soviet Union in retaliation for a tax levied on potential Russian Jewish emigrants. Neoconservative support for Jackson also rested on his opposition to the Strategic Arms Limitation Treaty (SALT II), as well as his conservative views on affirmative action and busing—despite a record of support for civil rights—and Vietnam.[124] As the 1976 election approached, the neoconservatives, who had pinned their hopes on Jackson's presidential bid, were severely disappointed when Jimmy Carter became the Democratic candidate and won the presidency.[125] He evidently returned their feelings of suspicion. Neglecting to appoint any of them to his cabinet, the door leading to their complete disaffection from the Democratic Party was wide open.[126]

Though Dawidowicz had left the policy world of the American Jewish Committee to pursue her scholarship on the Holocaust, she remained in touch with the close-knit circle of neoconservatives at Commentary, all of whom had their eye on Carter's 1980 reelection bid.[127] Cynthia Ozick, not generally one to seek the political limelight, contributed a long spread to the New Leader, "Carter and the Jews: An American Political Dilemma," expressing Jewish neoconservative disquiet about the political choices in the 1980 election.[128] Most American Jews of Ozick's political persuasion (disheartened liberals, newly christened neoconservatives, even Republicans) shared an anxious sense that the "U.N.'s cynical obsession with Israel-hatred"—its brazen selectivity in condemning Israeli human rights transgressions while turning a blind eye to those of other member states in the United Nations—had gone unrecognized by Carter. In her "gotcha" style, Ozick averred that the problem was not Jewish acceptance of Carter, a pious Protestant southerner, but their sense that "*he* would have trouble recognizing *them*."[129] She noted that Jews were wary of how Carter had allowed the fracas about Andrew Young's resignation to boil over into accusations about Jewish influence. They were anxious, too, about the behavior of Carter's brother, Billy, who fraternized with Muamar Qaddafi, a notorious antisemite. And they deplored the ways in which liberalism, so much a part of the Democratic Party's mandate, had changed. Differentiating between "idealistic Jews" and "Jewish-agenda Jews"—a different way of phrasing the universalist and particularist claims that pulled at Jewish Americans—Ozick asserted that the "Jewish-agenda Jews," among whom she now counted herself, no longer mourned the loss of the old African American–Jewish alliance.

> For them, the old liberal standards ... still obtain: that a man or woman ought to be judged as an individual; that the condition of one's birth should not be disabling; that opportunity should be open to everyone without favoritism or bigotry or barrier; that justice is most benevolent when most blind to color and origin; that without what is today called "human rights" (yesterday it was simply "freedom") no other qualities or quantities matter. These Jews have on the whole stayed the same, steadfast with a liberalism defined in this way; but all around them others who call themselves liberals have altered.[130]

Regarding the PLO, Ozick criticized Carter's blindness to the organization's antidemocratic, intolerant ethos, expressing outrage at the Orwellian turn by which "The surviving victims of the century's most barbarous racist atrocities ... are now 'fascist racists.'"[131] She lamented that it was not clear where President Carter stood regarding giving the PLO a seat at the diplomatic table. "One wants to trust," but Carter did not make it easy for Jews to do so. She then asked, alluding to older strategies of Jewish political behavior, "Doubt says: Put not thy trust in this prince. ... *But if not Carter, who?*"[132] Milton Himmelfarb had ended an earlier *Commentary* essay on Carter on a similar ambivalent note: "Carter need not worry very much about his Jewish vote. I hope Jewish voters need not worry very much about him."[133]

As things turned out, Carter did, in fact, have to worry; in the 1980 presidential election—and with *Commentary*'s blessing—fully 39 percent of American Jews pulled the lever for Ronald Reagan (who, with the Jewish neoconservatives, had migrated from left to right[134]), more than for any other Republican presidential candidate since Warren G. Harding in 1920. The Jewish neoconservatives believed the election results illustrated that their fellow

American Jews had come to their senses and were now voting according to "Jewish interests." Of course, the definition of those "interests" was theirs. But other American Jewish intellectuals as well as some young activists—equally as vocal and equally as self-righteous—had absorbed the values of the Left, the student movement, and the experiential revival of the 1970s. They drew completely different conclusions about Jewish politics, about the American Jewish community's obligation to support Israel regardless of its policies on the West Bank, and about the promise or disappointments of America. The pitch of the Jewish internal Kulturkampf was continuing to rise, and Dawidowicz, taking note, laced up her rhetorical gloves.

11

DINA D'MALKHUTA DINA ("THE LAW OF THE LAND IS THE LAW")

UTOPIAN ANXIETY

By the late 1960s, the New York intellectuals, who had devoted so much of their youthful energy to combating left-wing totalitarianism, believed that the young radicals of the New Left were both ignorant of the past and naive about the threat posed by the Soviet Union and its satellites to American liberal democracy. The divide between the Old and New Lefts grew in the 1970s, focused on political tactics, particularly the efficacy and justification of the use of violence. The New York intellectuals warned against the dangers of militancy and advocated for political quietism as an alternative political posture. They often voiced their concern in eschatological terminology, some of which was borrowed from Cold War liberalism's critique of utopianism. Assailing the New Left for being unschooled, politically naive, and flamboyant utopians, neoconservatives collapsed utopianism with a variety of other terms, including messianism, cosmopolitanism, universalism, enthusiasm, romanticism, paganism, violence, emotionalism, sensationalism, sexual license, and spontaneity.[1]

Utopian anxiety was a transnational phenomenon; on both sides of the Atlantic, Jewish intellectuals watched as the activism of 1968 exploded into what they saw as an anarchic, messianic fervor full of dangerous potential and inevitable disappointment. As Malachi Hacohen has shown, their critique was of a piece with that of European Cold War liberals, including Raymond Aron, Isaiah Berlin, and Jacob Talmon, who also regarded revolutionary politics as a worrisome form of "political religion," secular messianism by any other name.[2] Lucy S. Dawidowicz was firmly among them.

In 1968, Daniel Bell, then a professor of sociology at Columbia University, watched as the student takeover of Hamilton Hall escalated into a bloody showdown with the New York City police.[3] *The Public Interest* (*PI*) ran a series of pieces in the fall 1968 edition on the Columbia strike in which Bell, along with Nathan Glazer, Irving Kristol, and Daniel Patrick Moynihan, expressed a commitment to societal stability and inveighed against the utopianism of the radicals. In his introduction to the anthology, Bell charged that the student radicals' temperament was "more moral than political."[4] Enraged by the Vietnam War, they had turned to the "ready-made formulas of a stilted and primitive Marxism," embracing an "anti-institutional and even antinomian" politics of "symbolic gesture" and "expressive action" that masked "a desire to disestablish and render illegitimate all existing authority."[5] Beneath this welter of expressive formulations, Bell claimed, the students had no real political goals. Supporting their criticism of US involvement in Vietnam, he denounced their assertion that the university as an institution was complicit in the war effort. For Bell, the university constituted a haven for liberalism and academic freedom. The students' turn to radical tactics, which they called "participatory democracy," was nothing but a simplistic—and ultimately dangerous—approach to the social problems facing the country, he averred.[6] For the Old Left, which valorized structure, rationalism, patience, compromise, and restraint, their tactics spelled chaos. Reflecting on the unrest years later, Bell recalled, "The events of 1968 destroyed Columbia. SDS was ready to destroy the university because they thought the revolution would come. Their tactics, it seems to me, were totally nihilistic and destructive."[7]

Bell characterized the students' politics in affective, psychological, and religious terms, comparing the New Left's adoption of utopian radicalism to a religious conversion experience.[8] Bell believed that the New Left had gone through a "Romantic Spasm," full of "grandiose dreams" and "megalomaniacal visions."[9] In "The Sensibility of the 1960s," he summed up his view of the New Left zeitgeist as loud, imprecatory, obscene, and disjunctive, brimming over with violence, cruelty, the sexually perverse, noise, and an "anti-cognitive and anti-intellectual" energy.[10] Bell was not the only New York intellectual who feared the utopian politics and adversarial, performative tactics of the New

Left. A cursory survey of *Commentary*'s pages from 1964 through 1984 reveals such titles as Nathan Glazer's "On Being Deradicalized" and "The New Left and Its Limits," Andrew Hacker's "The Rebelling Young Scholars," and Tom Kahan's "The Problem of the New Left." Irving Howe concluded his memoir with the wry note that "Negotiating for social security can hardly be as exciting as storming the Winter Palace—[but] the alternative is likely to be murderous. Yielding to the hunger for apocalypse too easily slides into moral suicide."[11]

Dawidowicz shared the New York intellectuals' disenchantment with the New Left's politics and tactics, yet her critique and animus were animated from a different source: her reading of the Jewish past and concern with Jewish continuity. She always considered cultural autonomy the litmus test of a meaningful Jewishness. In her view, any form of universalist utopianism, whatever its name, was dangerous to Jewish survival. One only needed to look at the Bolshevik revolution and the subsequent murders of stalwart Jewish communists in the Soviet Union to see the consequences of utopian ideologies. A responsible Jewish communal leadership had to disabuse Jews of the attractiveness of universalist ideologies that she saw as little more than way stations between traditional Jewish life and a "future of universal brotherhood" that spelled complete communal and national assimilation:[12] "The particular appeal of the Communist Party," she wrote in her review of Daniel Aaron's *Writers on the Left: Episodes in American Literary History*, "was its promise that all differences between groups would disappear. This vision of days to come was most appealing to those second-generation Jews who wanted to escape from their unwanted Jewishness [and] . . . the Communist promise of a society without classes, nationalities, religions offered them a way out of the Jewish situation more honorable and more rational than conversion."[13] Dawidowicz had no patience for Isaac Deutscher's "non-Jewish Jews" or for his appeal to throw out a lifeline to Jewish communists proclaiming "the message of universal human emancipation," which Aaron appeared to share.[14] In these matters, she kept court with fellow anti-communists, like Milton Himmelfarb, who insisted on Jewish collective identity, and held that there was no bringing Jewish communists back into the fold.[15] In this telescoped view of history, Jewish New Leftists were destined to make the same mistakes as their forebears in Russia in the 1880s and in the United States in the 1930s.[16]

THE NEW JEWISH LEFT AND THE INTERNAL
CRITIQUE OF JEWISH "POWER"

American Jews shared in the surge of ethnic pride in the 1970s that pushed integrationist politics toward cultural nationalism and particularist identity.[17] To describe their identity, young Jews designated themselves as members of a "nation," a term at once unfamiliar and discordant to most American-born Jews (though not, as this book has argued, to East European diaspora nationalists). Zionism, a latecomer to American Jewish politics, gained currency and contributed, along with Israel's wars and the growth in Holocaust consciousness, to the upsurge in a renewed sense of Jewish commitment among young American Jews. Yet pride in Israel's victory over its Arab adversaries contended with ambivalence about the Jewish state's having become an occupying power. Though the anti-Zionism of Mexico City and UN resolutions jolted some Jewish universalists to reclaim their Jewish identities, most did not renounce their leftist political views.[18]

"The New Jewish Left" emerged in relationship to "the New Left," embracing its style and political commitments. In July 1968, the Jewish Liberation Project's working paper announced "several basic concepts common to us as committed Jews on the American Left."

> We believe, first of all, in the unity and common destiny of the Jewish people. We are committed to the survival of the Jewish people in whatever country they are living, not only physically but also culturally. . . . True commitment to the Jewish tradition necessitates participation in revolutionary struggles. . . . We are committed to a vision of a Jewish community in which genuine Jewish culture flourishes and social justice is practiced. . . . For the American Jewish community to promote social justice, it must purge from positions of power and prestige those who participate in the perpetuation of injustice. It must overthrow the present elitist, smug and incompetent establishment and create a democratically structured community.[19]

In April 1970, eighty young Jews "liberated" the Jewish Federation's offices in New York City, charging the organization with embodying a milquetoast, plastic, suburban ethos more American than Jewish. Members of the Radical Jewish Union picketed Temple Emanu-El, the well-heeled high Reform temple on Fifth Avenue, to protest the war in Vietnam. With their in-your-face outspokenness, these new Jews adopted a posture of empowerment and ethnic identification and a critical stance toward bourgeois, mainstream, "accommodationist" postwar Judaism. Jewish college students printed their protests in a range of new Jewish periodicals with outré names like *ACIID* (A Critical Insight Into Israel's Dilemmas), *Davka*, and *Chutzpah*, among others, revealing the adversarial culture of the New Left in Jewish terms.[20] *Dry Bones*, a syndicated comic strip by Jerry Kirschen, skewered both mainstream American Jews who supported the war in Vietnam and New Left Jews whose commitments to civil rights included every cause except that of Soviet Jews. Other Jewish radical groups included Jews for Urban Justice, the Brooklyn Bridge Collective, the Socialist Zionist Union, the Jewish Defense League—though it leaned heavily right, not left—and Breira: A Project of Concern in Diaspora-Israel Relations. Breira (Heb., "alternative"), founded after the 1973 Yom Kippur War, advocated direct negotiations with the PLO on the condition that it accept "the right of Israel to live in peace."[21] It quickly became a national membership organization, boasting twelve thousand supporters by the spring of 1977.[22]

Many of these young critics were Zionists and saw themselves in the same ideological trenches as their Israeli peers.[23] Indeed, the student movement, radicalism, and the counterculture expressed itself internationally; young Israelis, even soldiers, found themselves criticizing their own behavior and that of their government in the wake of the Six-Day War.[24] Breira sponsored speaking tours of Israeli military doves; published translations from the Israeli press; created a journal, *InterChange*; and took out ads in major US newspapers urging Israel to present a viable peace plan and exposing the activities of Gush Emunim (Bloc of the Faithful), the nascent settler movement of the West Bank.[25] Defining themselves as internal communal critics, who were breaking taboos within the "hierarchical and exclusive nature of Jewish organizational structures," they insisted that they were not heretics to be rejected or suppressed. However, Breira's advocacy of meeting with representatives of the PLO, the very issue that had muddied the waters between the Carter administration and the mainstream Jewish community, was seen by many as a bridge too far.[26]

Dissent about what constituted legitimate criticism of Israeli policy on the territories acquired after the Six-Day War began soon after the ceasefire, but until November 1976, Breira had a seat at the Jewish communal table. Its relations with the mainstream Jewish community went downhill when several of its activists met secretly that month with PLO supporters. When the meetings were leaked, American Jewish organizations that shared the aspirations of the settler movement in Israel began an offensive against Breira. In a carefully constructed, thirty-two-page pamphlet, *Breira: Counsel for Judaism*, Rael Jean Isaac argued that not only were Breira's members *not* trustworthy Zionists—as their passionate advocacy of the Palestinian cause made evident—but they were also trying to distance American Jews from Zionism, in effect, corroding support for Israel.[27] Joseph Shattan's April 1977 *Commentary* article, "Why Breira?" summarized Isaac's claims that Breira was fostering "enmity toward Israel" and accused four of its members, "well-meaning rabbis and liberal Jewish intellectuals," of being a front for the PLO.[28] The attacks worked; by the end of the year, Breira was dead.[29]

Breira: Counsel for Judaism revealed a vicious internal culture war waged among Jewish intellectuals. The controversy illustrated the growing conflict between American Jewish commitments to democratic liberalism and support for Israel and questions about its control over the West Bank. Debates erupted on such issues as whether dissent from official Israeli government policy helped or hindered the cause of peace and whether American Jews should pressure the United States to effect their political positions in its diplomatic relations with Israel. The culture wars in the United States and within the American Jewish community in the 1970s exacerbated those fissures. *Commentary* became a site for the mudslinging.[30]

In the late 1970s, Dawidowicz still positioned herself among American Jewish intellectuals willing to criticize the government of Israel publicly. After Menachem Begin, a Revisionist Zionist and founder of the Likud Party, roundly won election as Israel's sixth prime minister, Dawidowicz signed an open letter—along with other *Commentary* contributors, such as Robert Alter, Saul Bellow, Daniel Bell, Walter Laqueur, Irving Howe, and Seymour Martin Lipset, as well as Martin Peretz of the *New Republic*—denouncing the continued building of Jewish settlements on occupied land.[31] Given Dawidowicz's diaspora nationalism and her husband Szymon's Bundism—and her deep friendship with Pearl Ketcher and her extended family—her relationship to Israel in this period is best understood as a deeply personal one, but not one particularly informed or ideologically engaged. While Dawidowicz may have been conflicted about her standing with the American Zionist camp, which was moving rightward, when it came to those elements of New Left politics that she believed threatened Jewish security, she was crystal clear.

QUIESCENCE AS DIASPORIC POLITICAL SAVVY

By the late 1970s, Dawidowicz was consciously reaching into the reservoir of the Jewish past in her interpretation of Jewish politics. Other intellectuals had taken a similar route. Irving Kristol, reacting to concerns over social stability and Jewish security in the 1960s, drew a clear analogy from Jewish history in his provocative 1965 *Harper's* magazine essay, "A Few Kind Words for Uncle Tom."[32] This essay, deservedly criticized for its blatant paternalism, nonetheless bears consideration for Kristol's analysis of Jewish political culture and his view of its relationship to the African American civil rights movement. His essay examined two poles of political behavior—militant resistance and accommodation—as exemplified by Bar Kochba and Rabbi Akiva in the Jewish case and Nat Turner and Booker T. Washington in the African American instance. Kristol condemned the glorification of militancy: "We are all activists now, and cannot imagine any other appropriate response to oppression and injustice than militant protest. Witness the agonizing discussion among Jews of Hitler's slaughter of the innocents—so many people seem to think it less than human, rather than more, for a man to go to his death calmly praying rather than kicking and cursing."[33] Kristol claimed that reverence and romanticization of militancy had led to a distortion of the historical record, one that emphasized slave revolts while denigrating the nonmilitancy of Booker T. Washington, whose behavior in the face of white oppression might actually have been more effective in the long term than agitation. In the militant mood of the 1960s, Kristol noted, Washington had been dismissed as "a marginal and rather contemptible figure in American Negro history" or, worse, "*derided as a kind of Quisling.*"[34]

Kristol's points of reference illustrated how some postwar Jews projected their binary political terminology ("resistance" versus "accommodation")[35] onto the African American experience, all the while denying African Americans historical agency.[36] His comments also reflected the impact of Arendt's condemnation of the Jewish leaders in the Nazi period on American Jews who were sorting out their own politics, and their relationship to the Holocaust, in a time increasingly riven by societal instability and violence.[37] Kristol closed his essay with a call for a return to the politics of quiescence. "One can see what is most valuable and memorable in this [Jewish] history—Jewish piety, Jewish humanism, Jewish survival itself—derives relatively little from a series of acts of rebellion and very much from a series of acts of accommodation which transcended all daily indignities while achieving a serenity of spirit that is a permanent legacy of the human race."[38]

Dawidowicz similarly hoped that American Jews would see value in the traditional rabbinic calculation of *dina d'malkhuta dina* ("the law of the land is the law"). For Dawidowicz, the dictum meant that American Jewish political interests should remain aligned with the American state and its lead-ers, even as elements within the government moved rightward.[39] As we have seen, for Dawidowicz, neither liberalism nor socialism—and certainly not communism—was the only natural form of premodern European Jewish politics. She wrote, "Jewish participation in the Communist movement has, in my view, represented a digression from both Jewish political tradition and Jewish political behavior."[40] Dawidowicz, and other Jewish neoconservatives, now asserted that the interests of the Jewish community lay in a symbiotic, not antagonist, relationship to the gentile state and its authority to maintain social stability.

This perspective informed the valedictory speech Dawidowicz drafted in 1968 for Morris B. Abram, who was leaving the AJC to become president of Brandeis University.[41] In his four years as the AJC's president, the Georgian-born Abram had displayed a deep commitment to civil rights.[42] The speech, written shortly after the assassination of Martin Luther King Jr., focused on race and poverty as obstacles to the acquisition of the American dream by Afri-can Americans, while cautioning against the use of violence to achieve those ends. Dawidowicz, like most liberal white Americans, was alarmed by King's assassination,[43] noting in her diary, "I am so afraid for America."[44] Writing for Abram, she emphasized the "moral grandeur" of nonviolent protest and its efficacy even in the face of racist counterviolence and warned that "the vio-lence and anarchy let loose by black and white militants will not win them rights or power or meaningful victory."[45] She assessed the consequences for the Jewish community:

> These developments are dangerous. In all our history we have depended upon law and order for survival. There is an old piece of wisdom in the Say-ings of the Fathers [Pirkei Avot]. Rabbi Hanina said: "Pray for the welfare of the government, because were it not for the fear it inspires, every man would swallow his neighbor alive."[46] We cannot afford to neglect the lessons of past Jewish history which warn us to beware when masses take to the streets.[47]

Dawidowicz ended the speech by underscoring the cardinal postwar Amer-ican Jewish belief in institutional meritocracy and urged that it not be under-mined. "Negroes as a group are entitled to their share in America's affluence and power. But they should not expect us to yield the democratic principles and practices of reward by merit because we Jews have benefited more from this than they have."[48]

BESIEGED, BOTHERED, AND BEWILDERED: THE ENTHUSIASMS OF THE COUNTERCULTURE

Dawidowicz's and other Jewish neoconservatives' suspicion of "participatory democracy" intensified with the counterculture's embrace of personal transformation. In his provocative cover story in *New York* magazine in August 1976, Tom Wolfe had christened the 1970s, with its emphasis on personal growth, self-exploration, and direct religious or spiritual experience, "The 'Me' Decade and the Third Great Awakening."[49] A myriad of what came to be called "New Age" movements grabbed the American imagination throughout the decade, including est, the training at the Esalen Institute, Scientology, Daytop Village, and Primal Scream.[50] Young Americans discovered Zen, yoga, and the East. They flocked to Baba Ram Dass, Maharaj Ji, and Sun Myung Moon and read the *East West Journal*. Established religions also spawned new forms, and evangelical Christianity bred charismatic new leaders, such as Jim Bakker, Pat Robertson, Jimmy Swaggart, and Oral Roberts. All the new movements emphasized *personal* experience of the Divine, whether Christ or some vaguer transcendent spirit or personal guide.[51] They stressed, as prerequisites for personal growth, a fervor and immediacy that older forms of religion seemed incapable of providing. Irving Kristol dryly observed, "Young people, especially, are looking for religion so desperately that they are inventing new ones."[52]

The grandchildren of the Jewish immigrant generation, many raised in suburban environments that while ethnically Jewish were religiously minimalist, sought to find meaning in new forms of spirituality in the 1970s, in what Jonathan Sarna termed "The Postwar Revival" in American Judaism.[53] They drew on the do-it-yourself ethos of the counterculture, creating new religious forms, groups, and rituals; emphasizing personal engagement and education; and rejecting the staid temples of their childhoods with their decorously garbed clergy and hierarchical synagogue board leadership.[54] In 1976, taking a page out of the *Whole Earth Catalog*—the how-to manual of the new communitarianism—young activists in Havurat Shalom, a new religious collective, created *The First Jewish Catalog: A Do-It-Yourself Kit*.[55] Published in paperback and sporting a homespun aesthetic, *The First Jewish Catalog* was dedicated by its "editors" (the quotation marks indicating that the writers were distancing themselves from hierarchical forms of cultural production) "To an old rambling yellow house in Somerville, Mass. / to Krishna Kat / to those who daven and study there, / eat together / argue and love; to Havurat Shalom / In every generation, each person should search for his own Yavneh."[56]

While these young activists viewed their appropriation of Jewish tradition as a mark of personal renewal and communal reinvigoration, the older generation of American Jews instinctively spurned these new forms.[57] Just as Breira's founding led, ultimately, to fissures among American Zionists and deepened the wedge between the Left and the Right, so, too, did the new spirituality. In his 1971 article "Appropriating the Religious Tradition," which formed part of a series called "Revolutionism and the Jews," biblical critic Robert Alter went for the jugular. His piece excoriated the New Jewish Left's distorted use of historical analogy to justify its politics as misuse of the Jewish past.[58] He chided their equating members of Congress with "Pharaohs" and police brutality with Auschwitz and admonished them for clothing themselves in the mantle of the biblical prophets. Alter showed no mercy toward Arthur Waskow's *Freedom Seder* (1968), a text that collapsed New Left heroes with biblical archetypes: Allen Ginsberg became a "tzaddik," Bob Dylan a "prophet," Hannah Arendt a "rabbi," and Eldridge Cleaver a "shofet (judge)." Citing the same rabbinic text that Dawidowicz had written into Morris Abram's 1968 speech to support the claim of a conservative Jewish political tradition, Alter accused the New Jewish Leftists of being historically ignorant of the long tradition of Jewish politics that had sought stability.[59]

The general posture of "Revolutionism and the Jews" did not go unanswered. Eugene Borowitz, a Reform rabbi and liberal Jewish theologian who had founded *Sh'ma: A Journal of Jewish Responsibility* in 1970 as a forum for the ever-widening spectrum of Jewish opinion,[60] expressed his revulsion at *Commentary*'s sudden interest in Jewish affairs, which he viewed as a pretext to discredit the Jewish Left: "Are they interested in Jewish rights or are they manipulating Jewish pride so as to enfeeble what remains of Jewish liberalism? Do they really care about the Jewish people?"[61] In response, Dawidowicz, as ever fiercely loyal to the magazine and its editor, fired off a letter to Borowitz for *Sh'ma*.[62] It was another salvo in the Kulturkampf that had been steadily brewing among American Jewish intellectuals about what constituted "responsible" engagement with and criticism of the issues of concern to Jews. Calling the name of his journal "arrogantly peremptory and presumptive" and its mission contradictory, she charged that it confused responsibility with freedom and amounted to little more "than a vehicle for the expression of capricious feelings and heedless opinions of solipsists and narcissists." The New Jewish Left had learned nothing from the perils of sacrificing Jewish distinctiveness for universalism; it was oblivious to the dangers threatening Jews domestically and internationally. Drawing an analogy between the 1930s and the 1960s, Dawidowicz castigated Borowitz:

> *Sh'ma*, for its part, has been singularly obtuse in recognizing the profound changes now occurring in the Jewish situation. I think I understand why. The changes in the Jewish situation are related to the changes in the situation of the black community, to changes in the situation of the Arab states, to changes in world alignments—changes which *Sh'ma* welcomes and applauds. *Sh'ma*'s editors think these developments are more important than the Jewish ones and if they occur at the expense of the Jews, too bad for the Jews. It is the Thirties all over again. Only the parochial Jews worried about what Hitlerism meant for Jewish survival. The universalists who regarded Hitlerism as the last stage of imperialist capitalism were not as little-minded as the particularists.[63]

INTELLECTUAL TOMBOY

Dawidowicz brought her temperamental suspicion of anti-intellectualism, generational mistrust of the New Left's politics, personal investment in privacy, and steady rapprochement with the normative Jewish tradition to her views of 1970s feminism and the feminization of Jewish ritual. In her worldview, normative Judaism meant the culture drawn from the rabbinic Judaism of early modern Lithuania, colloquially called "Litvish" or "yeshivish," which came to represent a "hard-boiled rationalist" as opposed to a "tender emotionalist" associated with Polish and Galician Hasidim.[64] Despite her parents' origins in central Poland, she had earned her "Litvak" stripes through her long association with the YIVO and its deep connection to Vilna's Litvish aura. On the occasion of the publication of *From That Place and Time*, the writer Allen Hoffman wrote warmly to Dawidowicz, "you have written a Litvisher love sonnet."[65] Ruth Wisse likewise told Dawidowicz, "Dear Lucy, I've just finished reading your book and am still very much under its spell. It is a Litvak's book—and thus very very close to me in spirit. A steady flame burns at the centre with cold heat, intellectual passion."[66] In her binary political and cultural outlook—which the culture wars of the 1930s, 1950s, and 1970s only exacerbated—feminism, a movement born in the political and social upheavals of the 1960s and 1970s and predicated on opposing women's victimhood based on sex, and feminist spirituality, encouraged by the spiritual and religious revivalist climate of the 1970s, never stood a chance with her.[67]

Dawidowicz viewed feminism much the way she did other social movements of the late 1960s: as a kind of group special pleading, antithetical to an older conception of American liberalism based on individual and not collective rights. She wanted to be taken seriously as an intellectual, not as a *female* intellectual, and believed her achievements were based on merit, like those of her male peers.[68] She would have resented the claim—expressed by the Brooklyn Bridge Collective in its 1971 statement "Jewish Women: Life Force of a Culture?"—that "What the world has *always* done physically to *all* Jews, Jewish men and Jewish Women, the Jewish man does psychically to the Jewish Woman."[69] Dawidowicz dismissed the charge that she and other Jewish women were victims of systemic patriarchal discrimination in which Jewish men were implicated. She rejected the argument that women's culture was distinct and had different ends than men's and therefore deserved a sphere of its own. Much as she had done in her quarrel with African American demands, she argued that culture had to be based on creative values, not merely on resentments.

Moreover, Dawidowicz was an extremely private person and shunned the 1970s feminist credo "the personal is political." Restraint was the guiding literary and emotional principle of Dawidowicz's historical writing. When conveying appreciation to Henia Karmel-Wolfe for her novel *The Baders of Jacob Street*, Dawidowicz confessed that she had "wept when I finished, not out of sentimentality (I hope), but I think out of a sense of recognition."[70] Several years later, to her editor at Weidenfeld & Nicolson, the British publisher of *The War Against the Jews*, Dawidowicz commented, "As for the personal involvement [in her work on the Holocaust], I suppose you may be thinking of the dedication to my husband's children by his first marriage. Let's leave all personal involvement out of any promotion. It's really irrelevant."[71] When her younger friend Francine Klagsbrun, a committed Jewish feminist, eulogized her in 1990, she noted that Dawidowicz "eschewed sentiment of any kind."[72] Dawidowicz's dismissal of sentiment, while temperamental in part, also derived from her 1950s consensus-historian's positivist belief that history could be written objectively and that malleable and subjective sentiment distorted the past.

For Dawidowicz, not only did New Left and feminist politics, with their emphasis on sentiment, subjectivity, and emotion, misrepresent the past. They also posed dangers to the Jewish present and future. Many Jewish social conservatives considered feminism's critique of the nuclear family suspect, in part because female independence challenged the primacy of women's procreative function. Already in 1963, Milton Himmelfarb sounded the alarm that Jewish survival depended upon higher birthrates among Jewish women.[73] The following year *Look* magazine confirmed his fear in "The Vanishing American Jew," warning that "Jews may fade from 2.9 to 1.6 percent of the U.S. population by the year 2000," in great part due to intermarriage, itself a by-product of religious indifference.[74] Natalism, however, does not explain Dawidowicz's hostility to feminist agitation. In fact, she had confided in her friends that she and Szymon did not miss not having had children together.[75] Rather, Dawidowicz's rejection of feminism came from her hostility to utopian politics and her concern with the content of Jewish identity that she felt guaranteed her people's survival.

Dawidowicz's anti-feminism set her apart from some of her female friends. In 1985, Marie Syrkin addressed the tension between the individualism of feminism and the collectivism of Jewish national movements in her *Midstream* essay "Does Feminism Clash with Jewish National Need?" Dawidowicz's rejoinder concluded that second-wave feminism clashed with Jewish national needs because it bore all the signs of the exclusivist vanguardism of earlier revolutionary movements. Feminists were willing to run roughshod over the Jewish common good in order to realize single-minded, separatist goals. Pointedly, she wrote to Joel Carmichael, *Midstream*'s editor, "Feminism is actually intellectually tiresome, since it is utterly without ideas. It's really only a politics of resentment. I wrote this piece only to show my respect for Marie."[76] Moreover, sex for Dawidowicz was a private matter, and she rejected second-wave feminism's assumption that male and female needs were inherently antagonist. The essential binary for Dawidowicz was "Jew" and "non-Jew." Her primary loyalty was to the Jewish people, not to her sex.[77]

Dawidowicz's wariness concerning contemporary feminism was also grounded in her late-in-life admiration for traditional rabbinic culture and practice. Like other Jewish neoconservatives, she began to articulate the need for religion as the foundation of morality to anchor the anomie of modern life.[78] As noted earlier, she had long ruminated over the viability of secularism to ensure Jewish survival. Devoted to commemorating the Ashkenazic Jewish civilization that had been shaped by its strong rabbinic tradition, Dawidowicz approached Judaism from within that tradition. Turning to men who could best represent it, she found guidance from Gerson D. Cohen, David Mirsky,[79] and Milton Himmelfarb, as well as from Solomon Birnbaum and Jacob Katz. Arthur A. Cohen and Norman Podhoretz were also models of Jewish learning, even if they had mostly abandoned normative practice. Though such writers as Isaac Bashevis Singer, Elie Wiesel, and Cynthia Ozick also explicitly engaged religious themes, by the 1970s Dawidowicz no longer turned to literature for moral guidance. Instead, she sought meaning through religious observance.

Homelife complicated Dawidowicz's desire to be more observant, since her husband Szymon remained a secular Bundist until his death in 1979. Still, the couple respected each other's identities; just as she valued his East European *veltlekhkayt* (secular this-worldliness), he accommodated her interest in religious practice. Dawidowicz attended synagogue occasionally, and the two would have a modest religious Passover seder by themselves. In an interview with Carole Kessner at the end of her life, Dawidowicz touchingly recalled that Szymon had fled from a "very pious household," yet he honored her desire for more traditional ritual:

> We had one quarrel, when we moved into this apartment [in Manhattan] about fifteen years ago. I said that I wanted to put up a mezzuzah. He said he didn't want a mezzuzah, because it separated Jews from their non-Jewish neighbors. I argued that it was not a question of separation, but of identification. And I won! Seder was a problem because his friends only had a knaidlach[80] *seder* and he didn't want to go to a full religious seder. So he made a traditional seder, even wearing a yarmulke. I told him he didn't have to, but he wanted to. The only condition was that I didn't invite other people; he was doing this for me.[81]

When Dawidowicz first began to attend synagogue in her fifties, she was living in Queens and went to an Orthodox service. Writing in 1968 of her experience in "On Being a Woman in Shul," she noted, "To my astonishment—for I thought myself modern—I like the partition [separating men and women]."[82] Dawidowicz defended the separation by sex: Judaism was a male religion constructed on a symbolic theology with God as male and the Divine Presence as female. Noting that kabbalistic imagery imagined the pinnacle of religious experience to be the union of God (male) and Israel (female), with the choreography of this marriage union enacted on the holiday of Simkhat Torah (the Feast of Tabernacles),[83] she recalled her discomfort participating at a celebration of the same festival at a Reconstructionist service. Reconstructionism, founded by Mordecai Kaplan in response to the communal needs of pragmatic second-generation American Jews, turned away from theocentrism and supernaturalism and affirmed the principle of gender equality in its liturgy.[84] While she commented that the holiday was too transcendent and too supernatural for them to assimilate into their modern, "reasonable" practice, what really set her off was the feminist appropriation and transformation of rabbinic tradition that she believed bordered on antinomianism.

> I did not mind the dry-as-dust service so much as I minded the feminist spirit which informed it. Women have equal rights in this synagogue all year 'round and Simhat Torah was no exception. . . . They were also given the privilege of *Hatan Torah*, which, Reconstructionists being strict rationalists, was renamed *Kallat Torah*. Watching the women embrace the Torah, I found myself seized by wicked and perverse thoughts. Wicked: how insensible was this movement to the festival's symbolism, to its music and poetry. Perverse: Only here could transvestism appear as innocent farce.[85]

Dawidowicz concluded that, were women to gain complete equality in Jewish ritual practice, the synagogue would become either "Italianicized," like a church in which the clergy assumes all the sacerdotal functions while the congregants are passive, or "Hadassah-ized," meaning that women, with their organizational skills and drive, would take over the synagogue. In both cases, men would take flight. Affirming her preference for the separation of the sexes in Jewish ritual life and for the "ignorant piety" of Orthodoxy over the "literate brevity" of Reform, Dawidowicz elected to pray words she did not fully understand rather than use an abridged English prayer book. Nonetheless, she admitted her loneliness in the *ezrat nashim* (women's section). In her ideal world, she would be able to share the women's gallery with a group of literate women.[86] Late in life, she seemed to have found it at the Orthodox Lincoln Square Synagogue, where Rabbi Saul Berman presided. To Pearl Ketcher, Dawidowicz wrote about her pleasure in attending services, describing its unusual circular-shaped sanctuary, its "short sermon [that is] unusually intelligent[, and the fact that] most women *don't*—repeat—do *not*—talk during services, which is a blessing."[87]

Among her friends and like-minded colleagues, "On Being a Woman in Shul" was very well received.[88] Even Michael A. Meyer, an ordained Reform rabbi and professional historian of German Jewry, found himself in agreement with her conclusions and shared with Dawidowicz an essay he had written as a student at Hebrew Union College in the early 1960s.[89] Hardly part of the neo-conservative camp, Meyer was concerned with the vitality of non-Orthodox Judaism and argued that the breakdown of gender distinctiveness in liberal Judaism had resulted in passionless, feminized services. What was missing was the "release of emotion we find in the Hasidic Shul and we nostalgically long for it in our own congregations."[90] Reform Judaism had to "regain its virility," and its rabbis needed to "put back into [their] ministry the masculinity of hard logical thinking."[91]

Dawidowicz's essay, and her exchanges with Meyer and other American Jewish intellectuals over the challenges of creating a vital liberal Judaism, formed part of a continuum of Jewish intellectual debate over the competitive pull of Enlightenment values, including gender equality,[92] with the equally powerful force of Jewish survival in the modern world. Dawidowicz chose survival over liberalism. Yet in her turn to Jewish practice, she was quintessentially modern and American. Pushed by Carole Kessner to explain her partial embrace of Jewish ritual, Dawidowicz admitted that she was incapable of adopting certain practices, such as "the counting of the Omer" between Passover and Shavuot—"I don't even know what that means." She continued, "When people ask what kind of a Jew I am—Orthodox, Conservative, Reform—I joke and answer that I belong to the Selective branch of Judaism. I love the Orthodox service; nothing else will satisfy me, but I observe only what makes sense to me."[93] Moreover, despite her rejection of the feminization of Jewish ritual and of feminism itself, Dawidowicz was aware of her singularity as often being the only woman at scholarly and board meetings or on the roster for public lectures. Speaking with the alumni of Yeshiva University's rabbinic school in 1971, she thought to begin her remarks, though she later excised them, by noting her sex, warning the "gentlemen" in her audience that "you may be in trouble for talking overmuch with women."[94]

Dawidowicz shaped her Jewish consciousness in reaction to the enthusiasts and universalists of her day. These would have ranged from the New Jewish Leftists and spiritual seekers, including Jewish women determined to reshape the tradition, to the radical assimilationists who willfully distanced themselves from Jewish life. While she respected the questions that led young American Jews to reject secular assimilation in search of some form of transcendence, her own spiritual penchant never strayed far from the Litvish guidelines of her Polish mentors.[95]

Dawidowicz's discomfort with the counterculture's embrace of emotional, performative piety that threatened normative rabbinic culture fit with the views of others in the *Commentary* circle who decried the mystical stream within Judaism as Gnostic in origin. Though her own archives reveal no familiarity with the work of Eric Voegelin, whose writings on the relationship of Gnosticism to twentieth-century political terror became a kind of gospel for Cold War anti-utopian liberals, she was undoubtedly familiar with his popularizers and knew well the scholarship of Gershom Scholem, whose work on Gnosticism appeared in *Commentary*.[96] In 1979, Irving Kristol delivered a lecture to professors and students of divinity in which he argued that the contemporary divide between political radicals and conservatives—whether in Europe or in the United States—owed its origins to the ancient split between prophetic and rabbinic trends in Second Temple Judaism. In Kristol's understanding, ancient Israelite prophecy resembled Gnosticism in its assumption of a direct line of communication to the Divine that provided a road map to the world's perfection. In contrast, the classical Sages in the post-Temple period imagined a transcendent God, rejected millenarianism, emphasized the imperfectability of the human condition, and affirmed law as the blueprint for a spiritual life. Kristol used this binary to define the New Left's utopianism, spiritual enthusiasm, adversarial politics, and apocalypticism as modern Gnosticism, a movement dangerous for the country and for the Jews, who over their long history had valorized the rabbinic pathway. With its belief in the possibility of creating a perfect society, the prophetic character, Kristol concluded, led inexorably to socialism, while the rabbinic penchant was at home with capitalism and bourgeois society. It was not much of a stretch for him to assert that a capitalist society was the best guarantor of freedom and its economic system the most compatible with Jewish practice.[97] By the late 1970s, Dawidowicz had come to agree.

MAKING PEACE WITH CAPITALISM

Though best known for her work on the Holocaust, Dawidowicz desperately hoped to make her mark as a historian of American Jews. In 1976, when she was awarded a Guggenheim Fellowship, Dawidowicz embarked on a comprehensive history of the American Jewish experience. Her archives contain thirty-seven boxes of research for this much-anticipated book, including notes, photocopies, memos, transcripts, book reviews, and even credit histories. These materials covered a broad range of topics related to American Jewry: its political history, including the relationship of Jewish notables to the presidency and the political activity of Jewish mayors and members of Congress; its religious life, including communal organization, synagogue structure, the rabbinate, the cantorate, and kosher slaughter, as well as the denominational diversity among American Jews; the Jewish press in the United States in its diverse languages, Yiddish, German, and English; and relations between Jews and non-Jews, touching on missionary activity, nativism, and other forms of antisemitism from Sunday, or blue law, prohibitions to university quotas to cartoons with

Jewish stereotypes. Her research notes pay attention to the United States' regional diversity, to demographic statistics and patterns of immigration and settlement, and to the ways Jews made a living.[98]

The last topic was of particular interest to Dawidowicz.[99] She wanted to understand the unprecedented social and economic mobility that Jews had experienced in the United States. Her aim was to write a *social* history of American Jews, in which Jewish economic history would play a major role, focusing on Jewish work. In the drafts of an essay, "Building Blocks for the Economic History of American Jews," later published posthumously as "The Business of American Jews (Notes on Work in Progress),"[100] she declared, "I want to know how Jews in America made a living from 1789 until 1967, the *terminus ad quem* which I have set for my history."[101] In researching Jewish economic life, Dawidowicz turned the commitment to social history that she learned from Jacob Shatzky and her mentors at the Vilna YIVO on its head: instead of researching the Jewish working classes and the Jewish poor, who were the dominant demographic in interwar Poland, she proposed to focus on the processes by which an artisanal immigrant working class became the socially and economically mobile Jewish middle class in the United States.

The ideological underpinnings of Dawidowicz's historiographical agenda in her essay are clear. Having abandoned her youthful sympathy for socialism, she now embraced the historical role of the Jewish businessman. Entrepreneurship, she believed, had been the path to Jewish integration into American society. Economic success had brought once marginal Jews closer to political power and active engagement in American political life. Her essay trumpeted the value of Jewish mercantile and commercial activity, both to the host societies in which the Jews lived and to the Jewish community itself. Where would the Jewish community have been historically without its *ba'alei batim* (middle-class householders), its businessmen, its entrepreneurs? Why hadn't contemporary professional historians explored their contribution?

Her investigations into American Jewish economic life helped Dawidowicz formulate a series of research questions in the early 1980s that resonate with many concerns of Jewish historians today. What were the determinants that led Jews to participate in particular sectors of the economy? Was it family, community, prior familiarity, opportunity, group proclivity, or social exclusion? How could a new immigrant capitalize his business? What was the relationship of business acumen to political power? What role did Jewish entrepreneurs play in founding and supporting Jewish communal, religious, and social welfare organizations? The credit histories Dawidowicz consulted not only detailed successes but also illuminated bankruptcies and business failures, particularly the crises of 1857 and 1873.[102]

Dawidowicz's focus on Jewish economic behavior directly challenged the "new" social history—referred to as "history from below"—that since the mid-1960s studied the politically disenfranchised, the working class, and ethnic and racial minorities.[103] In her essay Dawidowicz wrote:

> I would like to restore to the merchant and businessman the recognition of their social usefulness and the moral dignity of which they were stripped first by the French Enlightenment, then by the German Marxists, and finally by the East European revolutionaries. . . . All of us are, by the force of Jewish tradition, heirs to those ideas which for generations have denigrated trade and commerce, and which have romanticized the peasant and the proletariat.[104]

Her polemical embrace of capitalism was shared by her neoconservative friends. Norman Podhoretz preceded her, vigorously championing capitalist upward mobility in *Making It*.[105] Irving Kristol followed with a series of essays on the relationship of capitalist economics to bourgeois virtue, a topic that Gertrude Himmelfarb would later explore in her scholarly work on Victorian England.[106] In 1978, *Commentary* ran a symposium titled "Capitalism, Socialism, and Democracy." The editors posited "an inescapable connection between capitalism and democracy," as well as a "totalitarian temptation . . . intrinsic to socialism," and then invited a group of prominent economists, philosophers, social scientists, historians, journalists, and other public figures to weigh in.[107] Few of the panelists affirmed the "inescapable" linkage of capitalism and democracy and socialism with totalitarianism. Some even ventured to suggest that the rhetoric of "inescapability" and "ineluctability" made the neoconservatives even more determinist than the Marxists.[108] The symposium demonstrates that by the late 1970s the neoconservatives—most of whom were not trained economists—had come to believe that democracy and socialism were inherently contradictory. Capitalism, they implied, was the only economic system that could be democratic. And capitalism rightly understood would support and bolster their own conservative values. By the early 1970s, their rejection of the New Left's flirtation with communism and its attacks on middle-class American values sealed their hostility to left-wing politics and economics.[109]

Dawidowicz never completed her major work on American Jewish history.[110] She found it impossible to distance herself from topics related to the destruction of European Jewry.[111] Yet her research proved fruitful. It resulted in an essay to commemorate the centenary of the beginning of the mass migration of East European Jews to the United States, published first in the *American Jewish Year Book* and later as *On Equal Terms: Jews in America 1881–1981.* Her 1983 review of Gerald Krefetz's book *Jews and Money: The Myths and the Reality* incorporated insights from "The Business of American Jews."[112] Her research was also prescient. Dawidowicz's focus on Jewish economic behavior anticipated the recent "economic turn" in American Jewish historiography.[113] While Dawidowicz's efforts were motivated by her sense that history writing had become politicized by the Left, at root she wrote "The Business of American Jews" because she believed that business—a metaphor for bourgeois civic society—was good for the Jews.

12

WARSAW AND VILNA ON HER MIND

Dawidowicz entered the last decade of her life in fisticuffs. She never really stopped fighting, even though toward the decade's end, she returned to her first love, literature, and especially to Yiddish literature. But the ideological collision course between her neoconservatism and the American Jewish political landscape continued through the 1980s, informed by the complexities of her transnational identity that oscillated between two poles of "Jewishness," American and East European. In the 1980s, despite her efforts to escape the Holocaust's fierce grasp on her psyche—and on her time—Dawidowicz became embroiled in several knotty issues that kept her tied to the subject.

THE HOLOCAUST ON THE MALL

The War Against the Jews had made Dawidowicz a household name and a public intellectual on matters related to the Jews of Eastern Europe and the Holocaust. Her later works, *A Holocaust Reader* and *The Holocaust and the Historians*, became central texts in shaping Holocaust consciousness among American Jews, but by the 1980s, Dawidowicz saw that she had no control over the larger narrative of the European catastrophe. Its interpreters had multiplied, and its meaning had been appropriated by a variety of expositors. Representation of the Holocaust had developed a life of its own; in the United States, this took the form of broad popularization, including via television and radio, as well as in fiction and poetry.[1]

In 1978, tired of teaching, worried about her husband's deteriorating health, and determined to wrest herself away from Holocaust scholarship in order to finish her book on American Jewish history, Dawidowicz gave notice at Stern College. To Alfred Kazin she confessed to living "in a state of constant panic [about Szymon], which is eased best by absorption in my work," and complained that teaching had come to feel "like walking on warm tar."[2] Yet she could not easily divest herself from the role as iconic interpreter of the destruction of European Jewry. Moreover, without a steady salary, she needed the money from lecturing.[3] Along with Elie Wiesel, she was one of the foremost public authorities in the United States on the Holocaust and was invited to speak throughout the country.[4] Thus, Dawidowicz became an obvious choice to participate in the commission to commemorate the Holocaust established by President Carter on November 9, 1978, and she responded affirmatively to an invitation to join.[5] Yet she soon became a thorn in the commission's side. In a memo drafted on February 15, 1979, she insisted that the Holocaust memorial emphasize the centrality of antisemitism and stress the "uniqueness" of the Nazi campaign in the murder of the Jews: "To be sure," she wrote, "since time immemorial, human beings have killed one another for spoils, land, or power, but never before had one people denied another people the fundamental right to live. This is the uniqueness of the Holocaust."[6] She went on to assert that the memorial's central mission should be to inform the public of the Nazis' successful annihilation of the Jews' "millennial culture and civilization." She also argued that New York City, "the center of the Jewish population in the United States and the cultural crossroads of the modern world," not Washington, DC, should be the site of the memorial. Finally, she maintained that the US memorial to the Holocaust should not include a museum or sponsor academic research, education and curricula, or art or music projects. These activities were duplicative of existing institutions and belonged in the purview of private civic associational life: "From the earliest days of this Republic, Americans individually and in private associations have organized themselves to do good works within their own circles and for American society at large. No Presidential mandate is required for such activities."[7]

Dawidowicz's opinions pointed to the complexities of the commission's charge: what narratives about the events that had transpired during the period 1933–45 were central to their telling and representation for the American public? The commissioners and the White House quickly found themselves divided over the Holocaust's relevance to universal genocides—the definition of which itself was hotly debated—versus the singularity of the Nazi war against the Jews. Venue was also a contested topic from the very beginning. Gerson Cohen, a member of the initial commission, spoke to both issues in correspondence to Wiesel, the commission's chair, on June 5, 1979. While neutral on the question of Washington, DC, versus New York City, Cohen argued strongly that any Holocaust memorial "should be devoted exclusively to the victims of the Nazi policy of decimation of the *Jews*" and that any attempt to include "other minorities . . . would only dilute the results" of the project.[8] Earlier in the deliberations, Hyman Bookbinder, the AJC's Washington representative, had presented the universalist position in a private letter to Wiesel. Asserting that "consciousness of the Holocaust makes us conscious too of other outrages against humanity," Bookbinder admitted to being "at a loss" to understand what he called "this apparent suspicion and resentment over what they perceive to be some effort to dilute the concept of uniqueness and singularity of *the* Holocaust."[9]

When the commission concluded its deliberations, Dawidowicz remained in the minority, the lone dissenting voice who did not sign the report. The commission proposed the establishment of a memorial in Washington, DC, which would include non-Jewish victims of Nazism and other genocidal crimes against humanity; it also urged the creation of a federally funded research institution. Rather than approve the final report, Dawidowicz wrote a firm "NO" on it, in red pencil, and resigned from the commission.[10] Wiesel wrote to her that "members of the Commission and the Advisory Board have been much influenced by your work and your thoughts," thanking her "for serving with integrity and dignity."[11] Executive Order 12169 defined the Holocaust as "systematic and State-sponsored extermination of six million Jews and some five million other peoples by the Nazis and their collaborators during World War II," enshrining the American and universalist interpretation of the European catastrophe.[12]

Dawidowicz never altered her views. Writing to *New York Times* correspondent Judith Miller in 1989, she reiterated her position and commented that "Instead of Holocaust museums, I'm in favor of museums of Jewish history, depicting Jewish creativity."[13] Allan Greenberg, a renowned architect, contacted Dawidowicz in May 1990 to express his agreement with her position and to share his design for a memorial in Battery Park in New York City to the murdered Jews of Europe. This effort, too, was thwarted. Dawidowicz was deeply moved and wrote back to profess herself "glad to find that I'm not alone in the world" in believing "that a museum or study center is not an appropriate means to remember the Dead of the Shoah." She thanked him "from the bottom of my heart for writing to me."[14]

STUNG BY STINGO

While representing the suffering of political prisoners, gay people, and members of the Roma community was a fraught issue for the commission, the question of the suffering of civilian East Europeans during the war was explosive. Wiesel had reluctantly accepted the category of "righteous Gentiles" but balked when pressured to include anti-Nazi Lithuanians as victims.[15] The Polish American Congress also lobbied the commission. Its president, Aloysius Mazewski, insisted that three million non-Jewish Poles "shared" the Holocaust with the Jewish victims.[16] With Eastern Europe still under control of the Soviet Union, there was not, as there would later be, a "dual genocide" or "dual occupation" narrative positing parallel suffering under the Nazis with oppression under the Soviets. But there were voices urging the commission to represent the story of Polish misery under German occupation.[17] Cynthia Ozick, in her *New Leader* piece, noted that the commission is "under Administration pressure to alter its character to include Poles, Ukrainians, etc.—dispiriting those who believe in the need for a memorial to the wholly vanished Jewish communities of Europe."[18]

Ozick was in complete sync with Dawidowicz's perspective. Already in 1960, Dawidowicz had expressed outrage at the depiction of the righteous Pole, as well as of a repentant Nazi, in Rod Serling's "In the Presence of Mine Enemies," a *Playhouse 90* television drama that was set in the Warsaw Ghetto.[19] Blurring distinctions between perpetrators and victims, Serling's Nazi fell in love with the Jewish daughter who had been raped by his commander. The gentile Polish friend of the Jewish family committed suicide in despair over his neighbors' fate, and the Jewish father, a rabbi, castigated his son for vengeful feelings against their oppressors.[20] Proprietary about the Holocaust generally, but especially about representations of the fate of the Jews of Warsaw and Vilna, Dawidowicz fumed in her review that there wasn't a single moment in the play "that did not offend or outrage with its falseness and fraudulence." The play's characterization of the righteous Pole drew particular wrath.

Yes, there were decent Poles who risked their lives to help Jews hide from the Nazis—a few hundred, perhaps a few thousand. But there were tens of thousands who sold Jews protection at outrageous prices, who turned them in for a half-pound of sugar, who helped the Nazis hasten them to the gas chambers. The Poles were not like the Danes, the Dutch, the French, Belgians or Italians. Only the Ukrainians outdid them in helping Germans wipe out the Jews. But Serling has created a Pole who not only helped, but who sacrificed himself for Jews.[21]

When William Styron gave literary expression to Christian Polish suffering in his best-selling novel *Sophie's Choice*, Dawidowicz, among other Jewish intellectuals, was outraged.[22] She resisted the universalization of the Holocaust with every fiber of her being and could not countenance the book's focus on gentile Polish victimhood as a representation of the catastrophe. All the dedications of her major works invoked the destruction of European Jewry.[23] Her intense identification with the Polish Jewish victims of Vilna and Warsaw meant that she never forgave the Polish Christian population for its behavior under German occupation, whether as bystanders or collaborators. Yet her negative assessment of *Sophie's Choice* owed just as much to her view that Styron's novel was making a leftist political statement, promoting a universalism that shared the New Left's bias against Jewish cultural distinctiveness. Other critics agreed.[24] Eric Sundquist concluded that for Styron "the Holocaust was an act of totalitarian terror that swept up Jews and non-Jews alike." Irony or deep insensitivity led Styron to make Sophie not only a victim of Nazism but an active antisemite.[25] In his 1979 review, Alvin Rosenfeld wrote that Styron took "the Holocaust out of Jewish and Christian history and place[d] it within a generalized history of evil, for which no one in particular need be held accountable."[26] He called Styron a "revisionist," guilty not only of universalizing the Holocaust but also of profaning the Jewish victims' memories and exonerating their executioners. Rosenfeld's review pointed out Styron's egregious identification of Hans Frank, the notorious Gauleiter of the General Government, as a Jew.[27] During the war, Frank was directly responsible for terrorizing the civilian population and overseeing the mass murder of the Jews.[28] In Styron's reading, the most notorious perpetrators of genocidal crimes against Jews were Jews, and even the figure of Nathan, the psychotic Jewish Brooklynite, Sophie's lover, tortures her.[29] *Sophie's Choice* was, wrote Rosenfeld to Dawidowicz, "a strange, strange blend."[30] For Dawidowicz, Styron's plot was a clear distortion of the past. It also reinforced the wrongheaded view—still current today—of Auschwitz and the concentration camp as the iconic experience of the Holocaust and anticipated Auschwitz's commemoration as a place of Christian martyrology.[31] *The War Against the Jews* endeavored in the 1970s to remind the public that millions of Holocaust victims never saw a concentration camp but died anonymously in the killing fields and mass graves of Eastern Europe.[32]

Dawidowicz also found herself intellectually entangled with Rabbi Richard L. Rubenstein. His book, *The Cunning of History: Mass Death and the American Future* (1975), construed Auschwitz as the end product of a long continuum of Western civilization.[33] In his view, the concentration camp, like chattel slavery, was a system of total domination. Styron, deeply impressed with Rubenstein's work, gave it a positive review in the *New York Review of Books* and quoted it in his novel. In turn, Rubenstein used Styron's review as the introduction to his book's reissue—with a new subtitle, *The Holocaust and the American Future*.[34] In the introduction, Styron affirmed Rubenstein's view of Auschwitz as the inexorable link to global slavery. He asserted the essential universalism of the Holocaust, exposing the "fatuousness" of the television personality David Susskind, who had asked his non-Jewish guests why they cared about Auschwitz. "Mr. Susskind should be enlightened as to the vast numbers of Gentiles who shared in the same perdition visited upon the Jews, those who were starved and tortured at Ravensbrück and Dachau, and the droves who perished as slaves at Auschwitz."[35] He continued by praising Rubenstein for approaching Auschwitz

> with a knowledge of the titanic and sinister forces at work in history and in modern life that threaten *all* men, not only Jews. I intend no disrespect to Jewish sensibility, and at the same time am perhaps only at last replying to Mr. Susskind, when I say how bracing it is to greet a writer who views totalitarianism as a menace to the entire human family. As an analyst of evil, Rubenstein, like Hannah Arendt, is serene and Olympian, which probably accounts for the unacceptability I have been told he has been met in some quarters.[36]

For Dawidowicz, any invocation of Hannah Arendt post-*Eichmann* doomed an argument a priori and exacerbated her general suspicion of imaginative literary representations of the Holocaust.[37] But it was the fact that Styron and Rubenstein had subsumed the particularity of Jewish suffering under the Nazis into a more generalized suffering that, as always, she could not accept. Though Nazi totalitarianism had been a "menace to the entire human family," it had been a total catastrophe for European Jewry. That distinction, Dawidowicz insisted, had to be maintained.

BABI YAR, THE WAR IN THE EAST, AND
UKRAINIAN-JEWISH RELATIONS

In September 1981, Dawidowicz published a major article in the *New York Times Magazine*, "Babi Yar's Legacy," raising provocative questions about local gentile complicity in the murder of East European Jewry during the Holocaust and also about the postwar Soviet erasure of distinctive Jewish victimization in regions once occupied by the Nazis.[38] The article drew on the research she had done for a chapter in *The Holocaust and the Historians*, titled "Palimpsest History: Erasing the Holocaust in the USSR."[39] Dawidowicz's purpose in the book was to chart the degree to which contemporary historiography in Britain, the United States, Germany, the Soviet Union, and Poland recognized her essential argument: that the Holocaust *was* the singular and intentional exterminationist war against the Jews and that antisemitism directed Hitler's course. Her perspective was still supported by some of the New York intellectuals. In fact, Irving Howe helped secure a fellowship for her from the Memorial Foundation for Jewish Culture for the book's research, informing her in a postcard dated April 21, 1978, "Dear Lucy, 'Tis done—with a clang (?) of adjectives! Irving."[40] The book, published in 1981, was judged polarizing, "tendentious," "incomplete," and also "important" and "insightful." Widely reviewed, its reception revealed the partisan passions that accompanied its subject.[41] The topic of Holocaust historiography was not a new one for Dawidowicz, but the issue would explode full force, seven years later, in the *Historikerstreit* (The Historians' Battle) in Germany.[42]

In "Babi Yar's Legacy," Dawidowicz affirmed her Cold War view of the Soviet Union as a monolithic top-down totalitarian society that shaped official Soviet treatment of the killings at Babi Yar. Paradoxically, it was the ways in which she had truly become an *American* Jew by the 1980s that made Dawidowicz's anti-communism render new forms of Soviet Jewish (and postwar Polish Jewish) identity invisible to her.[43] She viewed Soviet Jews and all postwar East European Jews and Jewish communities in the Eastern Bloc through her American cultural Cold War perspective. "In the Soviet Union the historian is not permitted freedom of historical inquiry, or the luxury of pluralist approaches, or the indulgence of reflection on the meaning of the events he is studying. The Soviet historian is at bottom in the position of a homager of the state, expected to show his allegiance by faithfully adhering in his writing to the party line."[44] That line had flip-flopped throughout the 1920s, become entangled with the signing of the Ribbentrop-Molotov Pact in 1939, and zigzagged again after 1941, when former allies became mortal enemies and former enemies became allies. Recording, depicting, interpreting, and later commemorating the victimization of Jews on Soviet-occupied Polish lands remained a murky issue for Soviet historians and journalists, some of whom were Jews. In the ideological echo chamber of the Soviet authorities, the Great Patriotic War had been fought against racist, nationalistic, and fascist Germany, the apotheosis of a capitalist state, whose victims were targeted indiscriminately, regardless of ethnicity. According to the official Soviet line, Jews could claim no special sorrows. To do so would be playing into the racialized ideology of the Nazis. This reasoning erased the specificity of Nazi targeting of Jews that drew directly from the antisemitic policies of Hitler and the Reich,[45] turning it into a "non-subject."[46] Her chapter in *The Holocaust and the Historians* used the mass killing at Babi Yar to prove her points about local collaboration during the war. "When the German armed forces and the murdering *Einsatzgruppen* swept into the Soviet Union, they found substantial numbers of Lithuanians, Latvians, Estonians, White Russians, Ukrainians, Great Russians, Tartars, Kalmyks, and others willing to collaborate with them." These groups had "many and varied" reasons for hating the Soviets, but "a common spirit binding the disaffected peoples with the Germans was their pervasive anti-Semitism."[47]

The *New York Times Magazine*'s article, which insisted on Ukrainian participation in the massacre, brought many of Dawidowicz's historiographical concerns to the general public:[48] "In the Ukraine, as in other parts of the Soviet nation occupied by the Germans, many people welcomed the invaders and some actively collaborated in the wholesale slaughter." Using the horrifying evidence by the German military itself of a three-day murder spree that included participation by the Ukrainian militia, Dawidowicz reported the execution of 33,771 Jews in cold blood in two days in September 1941:

> Babi Yar is haunted. The ghosts of its Jewish dead hover over the desolate field in a perpetual purgatory of historical denial. For the Soviet Government has ordered the memory of their murder to be erased from the records and minds of the Russian people. Yet the remembrance of Babi Yar persists.[49]

Though Dawidowicz had always insisted on the singularity of the Nazi campaign against the Jews and the deep-rootedness of antisemitism in modern German nationalism, this article emphasized the noxious power of East European nationalism in the murder of the Jews in Soviet-occupied Poland and Ukraine.[50] Prior to the article, Susan Jacoby, author of *Moscow Conversations*, sent a memo to Dawidowicz with an excerpt from a testimony given by a woman named Tanya who had escaped death at the ravine outside Kiev.[51] Her identity card had a Russian, not a Jewish, ethnic stamp, making it possible for her to convince the Ukrainian guards that she didn't belong in the group being herded to the pits. Her testimony affirmed not only Ukrainian police participation but also the unresponsiveness of the Jews' former neighbors.

> There were Ukrainians who came to help their Jewish friends, to accompany the old and the sick, though most watched the mournful procession [to Babi Yar] with indifference. And some Ukrainians even rejoiced in the misfortune of the Jews—people who had been neighbors, schoolmates, shop mates, even friends, jeered. The Jews were unprepared for abandonment and betrayal by those among whom they had lived in peace for two decades. They were unprepared for the ease and speed with which some Ukrainians slipped back into the anti-Semitism that had tainted Ukrainian history for centuries.[52]

Ukrainian nationalists—and some scholars—pushed back.[53] Lev E. Dobriansky, president of the Ukrainian Committee of America, Inc., wrote to the *Times* in December 1981: "No Ukrainians, whether in police uniform or not, took part in the Babi Yar massacre, which was committed by special Nazi liquidation units. Moreover, the Jews were not alone in that tragic massacre, because many thousands of Ukrainians were also killed by the Nazis."[54] The debates over what happened at Babi Yar, who participated in the mass killing of Jews, and how the event has been remembered—and disputed—in popular history and scholarly treatments are indicative of Dawidowicz's preternatural ability to put her finger on contested issues.[55] Was the *New York Times Magazine* article polemical, fired by her Cold War anti-communism? Surely. But were its conclusions correct about the essential facts of what happened in Babi Yar? In the main, yes. When Dawidowicz was researching her article, the Soviet erasure of Babi Yar's Jewish memory had already played a role in galvanizing many Soviet Jews' Jewish identity. As she well knew, the site became a locale of commemoration and emigration activism.[56] Given her Cold War sympathies, Dawidowicz took aim at those Soviet Jews who supported the regime that had sanctioned the distortion of the truth about what had happened in the bloody ravine near Kiev.

It would take almost twenty-five years for the full, devastating documentary evidence about what had happened outside Kiev to be recovered and published. The most horrifying account of the murder of the Jews in the regions of

Soviet-occupied Poland after 1941, including in Babi Yar, came from the extraordinary two-thousand-page anthology *The Black Book*. Compiled between 1943 and 1946 by Ilya Ehrenburg and Vasily Grossman, two veteran Soviet journalists who were members of the Jewish Anti-Fascist Committee, *The Black Book* documented atrocities committed against the Jewish communities of Soviet-occupied Poland by the Nazis and their henchmen. It contained official documents, dozens of testimonies, and other personal documents, including letters sent directly to Ehrenburg, a well-known and well-respected member of the Sovietized Jewish intelligentsia. Deputized to produce a work that would mobilize domestic and international Jewish support for the Soviet war effort, Ehrenburg and Grossman created a book that dutifully served the aims of the Soviet government.[57]

In Ehrenburg and Grossman's lifetime, a complete version of *The Black Book* was never published. Censored amid the anti-cosmopolitan campaign of the postwar period, the *Black Book* that made its way to the West was fragmentary and propagandistic.[58] When Dawidowicz wrote *The Holocaust and the Historians* and "Babi Yar's Legacy," she was working with the incomplete version. Its universalist bias became fodder for her view of Ehrenburg and Grossman's support of Soviet erasure of the Holocaust and their elision of any collaboration of local non-Jewish East Europeans with the Nazis. In 1982, Joshua Rubenstein (no relation to Richard) positively reviewed another edition of the book, this one based on a Russian-language version given to Yad Vashem in 1965. While he recognized Ehrenburg's highly controversial persona, referring to him as a "Stalinist apologist," he closed his article by acknowledging Ehrenburg's "attempt to compile and preserve a record of the greatest catastrophe to befall Soviet Jewry."[59] Dawidowicz's attitude toward Ehrenburg and Grossman vacillated, but more often than not it led to condemnation. In *The Holocaust and the Historians*, she discussed Ehrenburg's work on *The Black Book* as a product of his "own sense of Jewish identity [that] was deeply stirred by the murder of the European Jews,"[60] but in *Commentary* she excoriated him as "the foremost house Jew of the Stalinist regime." She attacked Rubenstein as well for overlooking *The Black Book*'s act of glossing over the Holocaust in Soviet lands, charging that his "hyperbolic enthusiasm" for the book ignored the "stringent external censorship" imposed upon and internalized by these writers. In her concluding salvo, she took Rubenstein to task for calling Vilna "Vilnius" (its Lithuanian name). From Dawidowicz's proprietary perspective, any discussion of the Holocaust as it affected Jews had to start with a Jewish commitment. Vilna could never be Vilnius.[61]

Rubenstein, in response, and anticipating the revisionist approach to "totalitarian" Sovietology, expressed the difference in his and Dawidowicz's approaches to the subjectivity of Jews living under the Soviets:[62]

> People preserve internal motives of their own. The history of the Jewish Anti-Fascist Committee is troubling and complex; it is unwarranted oversimplification, in my view, to ascribe everything done by [Shlomo] Mikhoels, Ehrenburg, and Itzik Fefer . . . as simply a response to NKVD [the Soviet secret police] commands. In the case of Ehrenburg, who is the most controversial figure of all, I think his internal motives with regard to *The Black Book* superseded whatever cues he was receiving from above.[63]

In 2008, when Rubenstein and Ilya Altman issued the full, unexpurgated version of *The Black Book*, the inclusion of all of Ehrenburg's and Grossman's original materials illustrated that the two editors, despite pressure from the Central Committee, had collected materials that unflinchingly showed that "the Holocaust could not have taken place without the complicity and active support of local populations."[64]

POLISH-JEWISH RELATIONS AND THE WARSAW GHETTO UPRISING

If Ukrainian-Jewish relations were thorny, the issue of prewar, wartime, and postwar Polish-Jewish relations was nothing less than a thicket of contested historical grievances.[65] In 1979, a Polish American–Jewish American task force was formed to "overcome misunderstandings and to promote mutual respect" with prominent members of both communities.[66] Several members of the task force participated in a pioneering conference held on March 6–10, 1983, at Columbia University, "Poles and Jews: Myth and Reality in the Historical Context." Harold Segel, a Columbia professor associated with the Institute for East Central Europe and one of the organizers, asked Dawidowicz to give a lecture objectively assessing "Polish-Jewish relations during the [German] occupation, especially in view of our distance in time now from the events and the literature that has appeared on the subject."[67] Knowing how heated the emotions were likely to be, Segel was looking for "sobriety" and wrote to Dawidowicz, "I can't think of anyone more able to do this than you and I do hope that we can count on your participation."[68] She declined, expressing her view of the futility of Polish-Jewish relations. Given that over the years she had received hostile mail from Poles in response to her work, she predicted that "I'd be nothing more than a sitting target for your Polish friends." She continued, "As it is, even before they see my new book, I get a substantial amount of abusive mail from Poles ("Dawidowicz's War Against the Poles" was the title of a nasty two-part article in some emigre sheet published in the U.S.)." Segel expressed regret but understood her unease, "[having] some idea of what she ha[d] already experienced."[69]

Dawidowicz also felt she had said everything in "Appropriating the Holocaust: Polish Historical Revisionism," in *The Holocaust and the Historians*.[70] That chapter surveyed Polish and Polish-Jewish writing on the Holocaust from the war years until 1970, a terminus that illustrated Dawidowicz's view that Polish Jewish life had essentially ended with Władysław Gomułka's 1968 antisemitic, anti-"Zionist" campaign, in which Polish Communists had "put the finishing touches to the Final Solution of the Jewish Question which the Germans had so efficiently accomplished for them."[71] The chapter touched on the key issues contested by Polish and Jewish historians: the causes, character, and representation of Jewish resistance; Jewish and Polish suffering under the German occupation; the effect of Sovietization on Polish lands; and Polish-Jewish relations before and during the war. Dawidowicz argued that distrust at best and active hatred of the Jews at worst formed part of the Polish national character and had been strengthened by nineteenth-century Polish romantic messianism. Modern Poland had never divorced itself completely from its religious past or from its image as the suffering Christ of Nations. In an earlier lecture, she cited evidence from a letter written by the Archdiocese of Warsaw to the Polish government-in-exile regarding the "providential blessing that the Germans . . . showed us the possibility of liberating Poland from the Jewish plague."[72] Antisemitism, she concluded in *The Holocaust and the Historians*, was "endemic" to Poland.[73]

Communist ideology had emboldened Polish nationalist historiography by refusing to recognize the Nazis' specific campaign to exterminate the Jews. Dawidowicz harbored particular animus toward Jewish communists who had remained in Poland, loyal to the regime, despite the immediate postwar violence, the crisis of 1956, and the antisemitic duplicity of 1967–68, events that to her mind had proved the Polish view of Jews as alien to their society. As with Soviet Jewish writers and intellectuals, Dawidowicz allowed for no possibility of tension between an outer semblance of loyalty and an inner doubt among Jews who stayed in Poland. That said, she gave credit to the efforts of historians at the Jewish Historical Institute (ŻIH) between 1956 and 1968, commenting that "if we discount the political claims and distortions, knowing how to read texts written under political pressure, we can conclude that the Jewish Historical Institute accumulated an impressive record in the historiography of the war, notably in publishing documents retrieved from the ashes of the Holocaust."[74] And, despite what she acknowledged as her "Jewish" perspective on the Polish Jewish past and her rage at Polish treatment of the Jews, her chapter recognized Polish suffering during the war. She acknowledged that "the Germans intended to destroy the Polish state and to reduce its population to a state of peonage" and that "the Polish language, and Polish culture were to be extirpated, a fate intended also for the Russians and other Slavic peoples." Still, a fundamental difference had to be recognized: "The Poles were not destined, in the Nazi scheme of things, to biological destruction. Instead they were to suffer restrictions on their biological growth, an unhappy fate, yet to be distinguished from destruction."[75]

Commenting on a book by Władysław Bartoszewski, a gentile Auschwitz survivor, about Poles who helped Jews during the war through the Council to Aid Jews (Rada Pomocy Żydom, or Żegota), Dawidowicz deemed it a "truthful book, documenting actual incidents of aid to Jews by the Polish Home Army, the Delegatura, and Catholic Church groups."[76] Yet Bartoszewski's book also served as an apologia for the Polish authorities, failing to include "the massive and impressive documentation of prewar and wartime anti-Semitism among the Polish population and in the Home Army."[77] In the end, despite the efforts of the Council to Aid Jews and the selfless acts of other Christian Poles, most "did nothing on behalf of the Jews, satisfied to observe how the Germans were now solving *their* 'Jewish problem.'"[78]

In the main, her chapter argued that the theme of military resistance permeated the historiography about the Holocaust, with faithful party historians overemphasizing the Communist Party's role in the Warsaw Ghetto Uprising. As we have seen, Dawidowicz had staked her reputation on broadening the view of Jewish responses to extremis in *The War Against the Jews* and had a particular axe to grind when the role of Bundists and Zionists were shuttled to the side. Her chapter exposed the problematic bias in the work of the communist loyalist Bernard Mark, director of ŻIH from 1949 until his death in 1966.[79] Her earlier review of works on the Ghetto Uprising had already sounded the theme of communist interpretive hyperbole.[80] Mark, who had testified in the 1959 Warsaw trial of Jürgen Stroop, the Nazi commander who had suppressed the Ghetto Uprising, accentuated Polish communist support for Jews in the ghetto by citing the Red Army's victory in Stalingrad as the inspiration for Warsaw's ghettoized Jews.[81] Yitzhak ("Antek") Zuckerman, one of the founders and commanders of the Jewish Fighting Organization (Żydowska Organizacja Bojowa, or ŻOB) in the Warsaw Ghetto, challenged Dawidowicz's suspicion of communist bias in their earlier correspondence.[82] Contacting him in September 1972 while working on *The War Against the Jews*, Dawidowicz included a long series of questions about the relations of the political parties in the ghetto—which included the Bund, the Polish Workers Party (Partia Polska Robotnicza, or PPR), the left-wing Zionists, and the Revisionists (Jewish Military Organization, or Żydowski Związek Wojskowy)—to the Jewish National Committee (JNC; Żydowska Komitet Narodowy).[83] Zuckerman replied with a thorough description of the variety of Jewish and Polish underground organizations operating in and outside the ghetto in the spring of 1942. He informed her that "within the framework of the JNC and JCC [Jewish Coordinating Committee] in this period, no precautions were raised, from either side—not from the general Zionists—toward the PPR (the Zionist Workers Party had also worked already with the PPR in April–May 1942 in the framework of the Anti-Fascist Bloc). The 'Bund' showed no negative position regarding working with the PPR."[84]

Dawidowicz, undoubtedly begrudgingly, included Zuckerman's fair-minded assessment of the communist role in the ghetto underground in her book.[85] But her evenhandedness in presenting the public with the complex political dynamics within the youth movements and the ŻOB could not defuse her anti-communist attitudes after the war. So, too, her work on the primary sources related to the pitifully armed Jewish underground appealing in vain to its Polish comrades, coupled with her long-simmering grievances against the Poles, corroborated her view that Jewish suffering during the Holocaust, while not caused by the Poles, had not provoked much regret among them.

The proceedings from the Columbia conference were never published—though many of the papers found homes in peer-reviewed journals afterward—yet they set the agenda for many of the subsequent international symposia. The historical papers focused on the relations of Jews and Poles in medieval and early modern times, through the long century of partition, and moved into the interwar, war, and postwar years. Literary topics comprised four other panels, from both Jewish and Polish perspectives. Participant Łukasz Hirszowicz reported that putting American Jews and American Poles into the same room to reflect on their past had not been easy and that "the political, extra-scholarly interest could be felt throughout the Conference."

In fact, latent and open controversy of a political character which appeared in the discussions reflected not only opinion on, and emotions aroused by, the issue of Polish-Jewish relations, but also touched on other subjects, e.g. Jewish political controversies in inter-war Poland and present-day Polish policies.[86]

A year later, a similar conference held at Somerville College, Oxford, hosted one hundred European, North American, and Israeli scholars.[87] Again, emotions were raw, particularly in the sessions devoted to World War II and the Holocaust. The conference concluded with a debate between two participants who had "moral credentials to speak on the subject," Israel Gutman and Władysław Bartoszewski, both Auschwitz survivors. Antony Polonsky reported that the debate, conducted in Polish, was tense and difficult but concluded that a degree of catharsis was experienced.[88]

When, in 1986, *Shielding the Flame: An Intimate Conversation with Dr. Marek Edelman, the Last Surviving Leader of the Warsaw Ghetto Uprising*—the English translation of Polish journalist Hanna Krall's 1976 book-length interview with Edelman—arrived in bookstores, public interest ran high.[89] Marek Edelman had been reared in a Bundist home whose values of anti-communist socialist internationalism, secular humanism, Polish-Jewish symbiosis, and anti-Zionism remained constants in his long, complicated, and inarguably heroic life.[90] The interview, published as a transcript interspersed with Krall's own reflections, focused on the period in the ghetto after the Great Deportation. It played down the alleged moral superiority of the ghetto comrades who took up arms, while honoring their memories and those of the hundreds of thousands of doomed Jews in Warsaw who walked to the Umschlagplatz. Krall cited Edelman's view of resistance—which pushed back against both Polish nationalist ideas of heroic doomed martyrdom and Zionist notions of heroic armed struggle—as the book's epigraph: "Those people went quietly and with dignity. It is a horrendous thing, when one is going so quietly to one's death. It is infinitely more difficult than to go out shooting."[91] Edelman's complex attitude toward armed resistance was not the only symbol of his iconoclasm. Unlike most survivors, Edelman remained in Poland until the end of his life. Working in relative obscurity in the postwar years as a cardiologist in Łódź, he eschewed publicity, but the book—and his symbolic role in Solidarność, the trade union movement that emerged in the early 1980s to advance Polish workers' rights and stimulate social change—cast him into the spotlight. As Timothy Garton Ash noted in his introduction to Krall's volume, the interview led to Edelman's "secular beatification."[92]

The publication of *Shielding the Flame* also contributed to a public controversy in the pages of the *New York Review of Books* and *Commentary* over the unresolved issues of the historical relations between Jewish and non-Jewish Poles—especially in the interwar years—their respective fate under German and Soviet occupation, and the representation of their experiences in World War II in the popular media. Krall's book appeared only a year after Claude Lanzmann's epic documentary *Shoah* (1985), the nine-and-a-half-hour-long exploration of the perpetration of the Holocaust on Polish soil, which was based on eyewitness accounts and testimonies.[93] For many Polish cinema goers, Lanzmann's film miscast the villain of the war, appearing to blame the Poles, not the Germans, for the Final Solution.[94] Dawidowicz had a different set of problems with the film.[95] Though she, too, questioned its focus on Polish collaborators and bystanders, finding it "strange that Hitler's name is not mentioned once," with the consequent implication "that the Poles were the chief culprits," her primary objection had to do with the film's historiography:

> I have a great distaste for the functionalist approach, which Lanzmann seems to have adopted, by way of [Raul] Hilberg's emphasis on how the machinery of destruction (especially the railroads) operated. It all becomes impersonal, automatic, as if no human agency was ever involved, no human will at work.[96]

Lanzmann's film released the ugly elephant in the room, the fundamental question that still dominates the interpretations of 1939–45: to what degree were Poles complicit in the crimes of the Holocaust?[97] Whether Edelman intended it or not, his interview with Krall became yet another referendum on Polish antisemitism and Polish-Jewish relations. Abraham Brumberg, a Polish Jewish historian from a Bundist background who fled Poland in 1939 and settled in the United States, became embroiled with British-Polish historian Norman Davies after the latter's glowing review of *Shielding the Flame* in the *New York Review of Books*. Brumberg had reviewed it earlier in the *New York Times*,[98] and his review emphasized Edelman's rejection of the culture of heroism that dominated both the Polish nationalist discourses regarding Poland's nineteenth-century insurrections against Russia and the 1944 Warsaw uprising against the Nazis, and the Jewish nationalist discourse, particularly as enunciated by Zionists, regarding the Warsaw Ghetto Uprising.[99] Both national narratives glorified the image of the fighter, dismissing the behavior of the majority of Poles and Jews who never shouldered a rifle. Brumberg also argued that Edelman's 1977 interview, conducted in the repressive atmosphere of Communist Poland, in which universalist camaraderie was the party line, exhibited a great degree of self-censorship regarding Polish-Jewish relations. In fact, Brumberg emphasized that in a later interview given by Edelman in the journal *Czas*, the commander had concluded "that the ghetto fighters, despite their pleas, received virtually no arms from the Polish underground; that the Polish Home Army (which, incidentally, refused to admit Jews into its ranks) was rent by anti-Semitism, so much so that when he [Edelman] left the ruins of the ghetto after its liquidation he was afraid to seek the protection of the Home Army lest he be killed by them."[100] Davies's review, in contrast, stressed the common history of Poles and Jews, described their shared fate under German and Soviet occupation, and appealed to what he believed was the prewar Polish and Jewish aspiration for a tolerant future in a pluralistic Poland. Simmering with resentment at Lanzmann, Davies viewed Edelman's rejection of Zionism and unusual decision to remain in Poland as the exemplary moral choice.[101] The dark side of Polish-Jewish relations, commented Davies, came not from the historical experience of Jewish life in Poland but from the pens of the "professors of anti-semitic studies, whose courses proliferate on American campuses."[102] For Davies, Polish antisemitism was a product of the Soviet and German occupations, which consumed non-Jewish Poles as well as their Jewish neighbors. While Davies acknowledged that over 90 percent of Polish Jewry was murdered during World War II, his review's purpose was to shine a light on Polish suffering for the American public. "Somehow, one needs to escape from narrow ethnic interests, from racist categories dictated by the Nazis, and from the coyness of our wartime allies, and to look more evenhandedly on the experiences of all concerned."[103]

Daggers came out of their scabbards. Brumberg, in a letter to the editor, pushed back at Davies's "bizarre version of Polish-Jewish relations before and during World War II," which had sanitized the past, characterized antisemitic attitudes as fringe phenomena, and posited toleration as the norm. Davies, Brumberg claimed, missed the irony in Edelman's comment that the Poles were a "tolerant people," adding that the Bund never "underestimated its [antisemitism's] virulence and magnitude." The truth was that "even though many Poles risked their lives to help Jews," most Poles were indifferent or hostile to Jews.[104] In response, Davies characterized Brumberg's letter as "desperate" and "intemperate." Showing little empathy for the impossible choice faced by Jews when Poland was divided, Davies cited Jewish "collaboration" with the Bolsheviks and Red Army as the cause of Polish suspicion and animus toward Jews.[105] While he acknowledged that the majority of Polish Jews were not pro-Bolshevik, he nonetheless reinforced the image of Żydokomuna: "Indeed, in most towns, the Jews *did* welcome the Bolsheviks with bouquets, with speeches and with declarations of allegiance and so on." Despite disclaimers that he was not suggesting a symmetry between the Jewish and Polish experiences during the war, in the end, for Davies, the numbers told the truth: Polish and Jewish suffering *were* similarly grievous. Criticizing the American and American Jewish public's ignorance of Poland's tragic past and bloody experience in World War II, Davies ended his comments with the hope that "other, related tragedies" would garner some of the "immense publicity given the Holocaust."[106]

Davies's idealization of Edelman and of Polish-Jewish history enraged Dawidowicz. In her 1987 *Commentary* review "The Curious Case of Marek Edelman," Dawidowicz explained her refusal to regard Edelman as a hero.[107] She began with the book's form, which she likened to "chatter" that diminished the "gravitas of what Edelman has lived through." She voiced her anger and incomprehension at Edelman's seeming equanimity regarding the human ability to hate, kill, and destroy other human beings. Rather than expressing rage at human beings who had abetted the genocide of the Jews, he had reserved his anger for God. Explaining why he had remained in Poland in 1968, when all of his comrades, including his wife and children, had left, he likened his decision to his role as a physician, "shielding the flame" and protecting the breath of life from its last exhalation. So, too, he remained in Poland to keep guard over all the Jewish dead. Dawidowicz distrusted the ways in which Edelman wielded his honest ideological anti-Zionism, born of his socialist Bundism, as a polemical stick to beat the modern state of Israel, which he deemed irrelevant to contemporary Jewish life and also to Jewish security. She then turned to psychology, delving into Edelman's deep ties to his mother, who had died when he was in his teens, and to her Bundist values.

Dawidowicz's foray into Edelman's psyche, her hostility to his iconization and to the valorization of armed resistance (a critique that he shared throughout his life), and her reference to the Stanford lawsuit being waged by Davies—in a tenure case that became a test of Polish-Jewish relations—set the stage for the controversy that followed.[108] After her review, letters to *Commentary* came in, including from Davies, who demanded extra space for his reply, commenting that "it takes much longer to scrape mud off the wall than to sling it."[109] *Commentary* printed ten pages of responses to Dawidowicz's article before giving her the last word.[110] In her retort, Dawidowicz defended her psychological view of Edelman's choice to remain in Poland as a form of homage to his mother's universalist values. She then moved on to what she considered Davies's bias against Jews, as evidenced by his equating the condition of the Jews under German occupation to that of the Poles. In *God's Playground: A History of Poland*, Davies had written, "To ask why the Poles did little to help the Jews is rather like asking why the Jews did nothing to help the Poles."[111] Dawidowicz erupted:

> No one with even the most superficial knowledge of World War II and the fate of the Jews could equate the situation of Poles and Jews under the German occupation. Anyone familiar with the bare facts would straightaway recognize the wrongness and—yes—the wickedness inherent in making such an equivalence. It is another example of Mr. Davies's historical malfeasance.[112]

Dawidowicz then weighed in on Davies's suit with Stanford, citing the university's *Campus Report*, which referred directly to his scholarship on interwar Polish-Jewish relations as "insufficiently analytical." The *Campus Report* also noted his reference to "Zionist cells" and his hinting at a Jewish "conspiracy" at Stanford. In a private note to Edward Alexander, Dawidowicz wrote that the vicious anonymous letters she had received "were part of an organized campaign—organized by Davies himself." She added:

> In fact, I heard that before Davies wrote his reply—which accounts for the delay in publishing, he went to Poland to try to enlist Edelman on his (Davies's) side against Abe Brumberg and me. He was unsuccessful, so score up another Brownie point for Edelman. I've been at the center of many controversies, but nothing as ugly as this. That's the Poles for you. The chapter I'm now working on in the Vilna memoir, which I'm calling "Them and Us," is about anti-Semitism as I encountered it—live and in politics—in 1938–39. It'll give THEM something to ponder, and even more to hate with a great hatred. I'll have to get an unlisted number.[113]

At root these recriminations both arose from and obscured the real cause of Dawidowicz's animus toward Davies's perspective: the inescapable fact that "the Polish people survived the war and have their country and nation, even if its political system is not to their liking. The Polish Jews, however, did not survive."[114] No matter how much the Poles had suffered, and she recognized that they had, the European catastrophe represented the end of Ashkenazic civilization. The history of Polish Jewry's destruction in the twentieth century had to be written from a Jewish perspective and with a commitment to Jewish survival. It had to admit of the irreparable loss that shrouded her soul.

At the end of her life, in an interview that accompanied the publication of her memoir, Dawidowicz reasserted, one last time, her view of interwar Polish-Jewish relations: "It's very fashionable now among some historians to say that Polish anti-Semitism has been greatly exaggerated. I hope that by spelling out, in small detail, what really happened, my book will help to set the record straight."[115]

13

RAPPROCHEMENT
WITH
REPUBLICANISM

RECRIMINATIONS ON AMERICAN SOIL

So well respected was Dawidowicz that despite her resignation from the federal Holocaust memorial and museum project, in 1981 former Supreme Court
justice Arthur J. Goldberg invited her to join the board of the American Jewish
Commission on the Holocaust. The goal of what was later called the Goldberg
Commission was "to publicize the lessons to be learned from what occurred
[so that] such a holocaust will never happen again."[1] The commission had the
academic imprimatur of the Graduate Center of CUNY but was funded by
Jack Eisner, a wealthy survivor, whose political sympathies lay with Revisionist
Zionism and its American delegation under the leadership of Peter Bergson
(né Hillel Kook).[2] The commission's initial conclusions damned both mainstream Zionism organizations and American Jewish communal institutions—
and by extension American Jews as a whole—for turning a blind eye to the
suffering of European Jewry during World War II. Though Dawidowicz never
sat on the commission (in fact, she declined Goldberg's invitation),[3] she soon
became embroiled in the issues surrounding the behavior of the American Jewish public and its leadership toward their European brethren during the war.

Dawidowicz published three major articles on these topics in the popular press: "American Jews and the Holocaust" (1982) in the *New York Times Magazine*; "Indicting American Jews" (1983) in *Commentary*; and a review of David S. Wyman's *The Abandonment of the Jews: America and the Holocaust, 1941–1945* (1985) in the little-known periodical *This World*.[4] All three pieces defended Roosevelt's war policy and efforts to save European Jewry and rejected criticism of the American Jewish leadership against the charge of indifference. The review of Wyman's book, originally solicited by the *New Republic*, was turned down when Dawidowicz refused to revise her piece as insisted by Leon Wieseltier, the magazine's literary editor.[5] By the early 1960s, Dawidowicz was already reconsidering the role of mainstream American Jewish organizations and their leaders with regard to safeguarding Jewish interests domestically and abroad. Her tenure at the American Jewish Committee had led her to embrace a politics of *dina d'malkhuta dina* ("the law of the land is the law") that affirmed the wisdom of political quiescence and obedience to authority. Dawidowicz's defense of the wartime behavior of the US government, mainstream American Jewish organizations, and American Jews as a group grew out of a political defensiveness and a patriotism chastened by the New Left's critique of American society. Given the contemporary political climate of the early 1980s, she wrote, "when it is fashionable to denigrate any establishment, it is no surprise that the conduct of the establishment Jewish organizations during the war should also come in for its share of criticism."[6]

Dawidowicz's support for Roosevelt reflected not only loyalty to the president who had declared war on Nazi Germany in the face of powerful isolationist sentiment but also her rightward move over the decades. Her belief that "men in power" could be more politically efficacious than demonstrative activists informed her defense of the Roosevelt administration and her corresponding critique of the symbolic protests of the "Bergson Boys," as the group of Revisionists were popularly known, and what she called their "extremist methods."[7] She defended the activity of American Jewish organizations, who had to contend with domestic antisemitism and charges of dual loyalty; she also recognized that in the spring of 1942, when news of mass killings became known via selective dissemination in the English-language press, many American Jews could not actually absorb the horror. Marie Syrkin, writing in 1982 about the meeting at the *Jewish Frontier* when she and Hayim Greenberg were confronted with the reports of mass deportations and murder, reported that *Frontier* staffers were "unable to assimilate the written words," and "buried the fearful report in the back page of the September issue in small type, thus indicating that we could not vouch for its accuracy." Incomprehension, not indifference, was the response, Syrkin recalled.

> Even in retrospect I think that this inability reflects more on our intelligence than on our moral obtuseness. Today when genocide, gas chamber, and mass extermination are the small coin of language, it is hard to reconstruct the innocent state of mind when American Jews, like the Jews of Europe's ghettos, could not immediately grasp that the ascending series of Nazi persecutions had reached this apex.[8]

Syrkin had already addressed what she called the distinction between "proficiency and effort" (to publicize the fate of European Jewry) to Dawidowicz privately. In a letter from January 1981, she recounted that during the fall of 1942, after she and Greenberg had become convinced that "the evidence [of Hitler's actions against the Jews] had to be believed no matter how much our spirits rebelled against it," the two took action: "We spent the month of October gathering material (I know, I did it) and the November, 1942, issue of *Jewish Frontier* appeared in black borders and wholly devoted to the Holocaust." That November issue, she wrote Dawidowicz, "has the melancholy distinction of being the first attempt in English to bring the news to the American public." Syrkin recalled that "from this point on the fate of European Jewry was *our* abiding concern."[9]

Characteristically, Dawidowicz refused to denounce Jews of the period for not fully grasping Hitler's genocidal intentions. Over two decades earlier, she had reviewed Ben Hecht's 1961 book, *Perfidy*, about Rudolf Kastner, the Hungarian-Jewish journalist who negotiated with Adolf Eichmann to save over fifteen hundred Hungarian Jews. He was later accused of collaboration because he kept the news of the Final Solution from the victims. Dawidowicz wrote that Hecht had not sufficiently considered "the limits of freedom and choice the Nazis imposed on the Jews and how those parameters informed the decisions of Kastner."[10] Analogizing Kastner's behavior to that of the *Judenrat* generally and to Adam Czerniaków of Warsaw in particular, she posed the question: "If Jews in Warsaw couldn't believe the reality of the death camps, why do Jews in New York assume they are prophets?"[11]

In the *Times*'s article, Dawidowicz now turned to defend Stephen S. Wise against the charge that he had ignored a cable, transmitted by Gerhart Riegner of the World Jewish Congress to the State Department on August 8, 1942, about the mass extermination of Jews by "Prussic Acid" in German-occupied

Poland. She pointed out that Wise never received the cable directly from the State Department. Three weeks later, upon receiving a copy from Riegner, he called an emergency meeting. Most Americans at that time were preoccupied with the flagging war effort, and Wise had to act with caution, weighing his distress against the pressure on Roosevelt, who was often accused of allowing Jews to sway US foreign policy. "Caution, as a rule, governed the actions of Jews in high places."[12] Her article nonetheless pointed out the existence of anti-semitism in the State Department and the failings of both the British and the US governments' refugee policies. Finally, she cited the internal disagreements among the Zionist and non-Zionist organizations, who battled over which effort should take priority, opening up immigration to Palestine or pushing for statehood.

In her view, both the contemporaneous and ex post facto charges of apathy or callousness were wrongheaded and politically motivated. All the attacks against Roosevelt and the Jewish mainstream leadership during the war smacked of the New Left's oppositional politics that took aim at well-established authority structures without understanding either the history involved or the consequences of their attack on these democratic institutions. (Along these lines she slammed Wyman's book, which she considered tainted by New Left anti-Americanism and Protestant moralism).[13] In fact, Dawidowicz insisted, Wise and other American Jewish leaders had tried to keep the fate of European Jewry in the public eye. Thousands of people attended protests rallies at Madison Square Garden, and thanks to Henry Morgenthau Jr.'s yeoman efforts, Roosevelt decided to create the War Refugee Board in January 1944.[14] Nonetheless, all these efforts to thwart Hitler's "unalterable determination to annihilate the European Jews" were unsuccessful. "Rescuing the European Jews was an unachievable task. Most European Jews were inaccessible, beyond the reach not only of the American Jews, but even of the Allied armed forces." "They were," she wrote, "in Hitler's vise."[15]

Dawidowicz's articles produced a cascade of rebuttals in letters to the *Times* and *Commentary*. Norman Podhoretz published over twenty pages of readers' letters. Many came from figures she had criticized, including Arthur J. Goldberg, David S. Wyman, and Seymour Maxwell Finger; others came from men of the Left, including Irving Howe[16] and Morris U. Schappes, editor of *Jewish Currents*.[17] They accused Dawidowicz of political partisanship, of shoddy research, of doing a hatchet job, and of red-baiting. Defending her views, Dawidowicz forcefully asserted her own commitment as a historian to make "implicit and explicit moral judgments" if they were arrived at through carefully adduced evidence—evidence, she claimed, that her critics lacked. She insisted on the distinction between American Jewish political powerlessness, which she deemed an objective "fact," and the charge of indifference, a moral judgment and, in her view, a mistaken one. She cited Hayim Greenberg's tragic admission of helplessness in the face of evidence of the Nazi campaign to destroy European Jewry: "If it is still objectively possible to do anything, then I do not know who should do it and how it should be done."[18]

In several respects, time has validated Dawidowicz's position. Deborah Lipstadt recently noted that the issue of American culpability with regard to the Holocaust is colored by "emotional, political, ideological, and generational factors," as well as by the subjectivity of its interpreters.[19] Reassessing the generational constraints and the "Myth of Silence," the charge that the war generation was indifferent to the fate of their European brethren and only focused on the Holocaust after 1967 in response to the Six-Day War, Lipstadt maintained, "It is a-historic, if not facile, to expect from the wartime American Jewish community a level of organization, political clout, and impact characteristic of political behavior of the Baby Boom/Vietnam-era protest generation."[20] She also acknowledged Dawidowicz's claim that Wyman's work was influenced by "a tradition of Protestant moralism" and "Christian love."[21]

Dawidowicz's defense of Roosevelt has also largely been accepted by the most recent books on the subject, even if many critics have queried the ferocity of her attacks.[22] Her rage is best understood as a reaction to her alarmed perception of political déjà vu. For Dawidowicz, the criticism against Roosevelt's administration and the Jewish mainstream leadership was a dangerous reiteration of the opportunistic politics of the 1930s, when European communists attacked socialists, social democrats, and liberals and, in weakening the center, allowed the rise of a murderous antisemitic fascism. Those who implicated the American government and American Jews in the crimes of the Nazis were ignorant of history. Ignoring the consequences of their attack on these democratic institutions, they jeopardized American freedoms.

Such views earned her considerable opprobrium among her liberal friends, and her increasingly hard line regarding the role of American Jews in public criticism of the state of Israel didn't help, nor, of course, did her support of Reagan's candidacy. Dawidowicz never stepped back. By the 1980s, her Jewish culture war was now firmly entangled both with the American culture wars and with the internal Jewish Kulturkampf over Israel's use of its military power.

OPERATION PEACE FOR GALILEE AND
ISRAEL-DIASPORA POLITICS

Ascending to power in Israel as a hawk, Menachem Begin, the head of the Likud Party, became the first Israeli prime minister to broker a lasting peace with a neighboring Arab country.[23] Egyptian president Anwar Sadat had made a momentous trip to Israel in November 1977, where he addressed the Israeli Parliament and expressed a willingness to make peace based on two key UN resolutions, 242 and 338. The first insisted on Israeli withdrawal from territories acquired in 1967 and on the termination of violent resistance by all parties in the conflict. The second affirmed the ceasefire agreement promulgated after the 1973 Yom Kippur War. Over thirteen secretive days in September 1978, Begin, Sadat, and President Jimmy Carter formulated the Camp David Accords, which recognized the "legitimate rights of the Palestinian people" and supported a five-year process to give them a measure of autonomy in the occupied territories. Yet the accords did not address several pressing issues, including the fate of Palestinian refugees and the legitimacy of Palestinian national claims; Syria's relations with Israel, including the tensions in the Golan Heights; President Assad's designs on Lebanon; and the status of Jerusalem. Moreover, the Palestinians themselves had no representative at Camp David. While the accords led to the 1979 Israel-Egypt Peace Treaty and the momentous withdrawal of Israel from the Sinai Peninsula, they did not significantly advance a resolution to the conflict between the Israelis and the Palestinians.

In fact, both the United Nations and the PLO rejected the "Framework for Peace in the Middle East" put forth in the accords. Meanwhile, Jewish settlement activity in the West Bank continued, as did Palestinian attacks on Israel and Israelis, often from southern Lebanon, which by the 1970s had become a quagmire for all of the region's major geopolitical actors—Egypt, the United States, the Soviet Union, Syria, Israel—and for the Lebanese and the Palestinians.[24] The Coastal Road Massacre in March 1978, perpetrated by the PLO, claimed the lives of thirty-eight Israelis, including thirteen children, and confirmed for most Jewish Israelis and many American Jews that the organization would never be a reliable partner in peace. In retaliation, the Israeli Defense Forces (IDF) penetrated into southern Lebanon up until the Litani River to push the PLO northward beyond striking distance and to strengthen the Southern Lebanon Army, Israel's ally.[25] Carter was dismayed by the collateral damage caused by cluster bombs purchased from the United States during Operation Litani, as well as by the unresolved, and growing, refugee crisis.[26]

The UN Interim Force in Lebanon was created to enforce a demarcation line and to ensure Israeli retreat. On March 28, 1978, the PLO leadership finally ordered a ceasefire.

Carter wanted Begin to desist from settlement activity in the occupied territories. The president's willingness to criticize Israel and to acknowledge Palestinian rights made Israelis and American Jews wary of where the United States' allegiances lay. It appeared to some that Carter demanded more concessions from the Israelis than from the Palestinians. In Israel, the Peace Now movement, formed in 1978 by left-wing, dovish Israelis in response to Gush Emunim's vigilantism on the West Bank, supported territorial compromise in exchange for peace.[27] By 1981, American Jews who hoped for an equitable solution to Palestinian political disenfranchisement and homelessness, within a framework of guaranteeing Israel's security, had organized American Friends of Peace Now (AFPN). AFPN played an even more visible role after the escalation of violence in Lebanon in the spring of 1982. By then, however, Dawidowicz was no longer signing its display ads.

On June 6, 1982, the Israeli defense forces launched Operation Peace for Galilee, a military incursion into southern Lebanon to dislodge the PLO, which had successfully rebuilt its base there to promote violent resistance against Israel's northern communities.[28] Initiated by Defense Minister Ariel Sharon and Chief of Staff Raphael (Raful) Eitan, and supported by the Likud government of Begin and Yitzhak Shamir, the "first" Lebanon War resulted in over five hundred Israeli military casualties, a nine-week siege of Beirut, thousands of civilian deaths, and ultimately the departure of the PLO, but not of all Palestinians, from southern Lebanon.

The 1982 war, which also created a new set of refugees, marked a significant political turning point in domestic Israel politics and in Israel-Diaspora relations.[29] From the outset, opinion was split on the justice of Israel's incursion: was it a defensive measure to keep northern Israel safe from PLO aggression, or did the Begin government use it as a pretext to crush not only the PLO but also broader Palestinian national aspirations? In other words, was Operation Peace for Galilee an act of justified Israel defense or one of unwarranted aggression that bordered on imperialism? The question heatedly engaged both critics and supporters of the Likud government's foreign and domestic policy.

With dear friends in Israel with sons who had been called up, Dawidowicz— like many American Jews with intimate ties to Israel—experienced the anxiety of the war vicariously. Allen Hoffman informed her that everyone in Israel was worried and also expressed ambivalence about whether the incursion into Lebanon would actually secure Israel's northern border and keep "PLO katyushas and artillery away from the Upper and Western Galilee."[30] On June 14, 1982, Arthur Goren, a friend and fellow historian, wrote to Dawidowicz about a fateful IDF clash with the PLO in which an Israeli general had fallen, an action in which his own son Amos had been involved.[31] He also informed her of the death of another friend's son, commenting that "at the moment, understandably, it doesn't seem worth it." Despite his extreme distrust of Defense Minister Sharon, whom he described as arrogant, reckless, and untruthful, Goren commented, "But who knows? In a shitty world maybe he will succeed this time. If not, it will be a broch [Yid., 'disaster']."[32]

In the eyes of many, the war was reckless and an unnecessary display of military power. After the initial routing of the PLO from southern Lebanon, Sharon commenced a second attack, with the goal of establishing a government in Lebanon to make peace with Israel.[33] The war escalated as the IDF moved into the suburbs of Beirut with the goal of forcing Arafat to remove his fighters from Lebanon entirely. The United Nations, the United States, and Israeli opponents of the Likud government protested against the expansion of the war effort. Dueling ads in the *New York Times* throughout the summer alternately condemned and supported the Israeli war effort, the intransigence of the PLO, and the role of the United States.[34] Extensive civilian casualties provoked international and domestic concern and moral outrage. The event that catalyzed the greatest condemnation was the September massacre of Palestinian refugees in two camps, Sabra and Shatila, by Lebanese Christian Phalangists. Implacable enemies of the PLO, and ostensibly retaliating for the September 14 assassination of Bashir Jemayel, the newly elected president of Lebanon, Phalangist soldiers entered the refugee camps and mercilessly slaughtered over seven hundred people, with the knowledge of the IDF.[35] Once the news hit the airwaves, Israel's actions triggered immediate censure from within Israel itself, by the international community, by Ronald Reagan, and among American Jews.[36] The question quickly emerged as to how much the defense minister and the IDF's chief of staff knew about the looming Phalangist "mop up" action in the camps.[37] The views of Ariel Sharon and Raful Eitan on the timing of the soldiers' entry into the camps were not consistent. Demands for an inquiry into Sharon's decisions were initially rejected, but after a massive demonstration on September 25 in Israel, the Kahan Commission of Inquiry into the Events at the Refugee Camps in Beirut was established.

The gruesome events, broadcast on television, covered extensively in print media, and compounded by the Israeli government's initial silence, amplified collective self-scrutiny among Israeli and American Jews. Editorials condemn-ing the IDF, Sharon, Begin, and the Likud government became commonplace in the American press, most notably the influential editorials by Anthony Lewis in the *New York Times*. For American Jewish supporters of Israel, the question of the legitimate parameters of dissent voiced in the English-language press—present throughout American Jewish history but far more vociferous since 1967—became hotly contested again. Voicing their support for Peace Now, a group of American Jewish intellectuals took out a half-page ad in the *Times* on September 24, 1982, asserting that "the Begin-Sharon government must accept a share of the responsibility for the massacre," adding that "We grieve for the victims of Beirut."[38] As Ze'ev Schiff, a military correspondent for the daily paper *Haaretz*, would write two years later, "Sabra and Shatila had become synonymous with infamy."[39]

Not all agreed with this assessment. In September 1982, Norman Podhoretz used his platform at *Commentary* to publish "J'Accuse," a blistering critique of what he saw as the liberal media's and the international community's double standard regarding Israel.[40] Evoking Emile Zola's famous salvo against the bla-tant antisemitism of the anti-Dreyfusards in nineteenth-century France, Pod-horetz sought to expose the disproportionate vilification of Israel's conduct in Lebanon. In his view, analogies that compared Israel to the Nazis and the Leb-anon War to Vietnam not only were misguided but also conspicuously held Israel to a higher geopolitical standard than other nation-states. "[I]f we are looking for analogies, a better one," wrote Podhoretz, "would be the invasion of France by allied troops in World War II. The purpose was not to conquer France but to liberate it from its German conquerors, just as the purpose of the Israelis in 1982 was to liberate Lebanon from the PLO."[41] Assessing the international opprobrium against Israel, Podhoretz concluded that the outcry against the actions in Lebanon was antisemitic because the critics condemned Israelis (Jews) for exercising the right "to do things that all other people are accorded an unchallengeable right to do." Israel, he objected, was expected to forgo its right of self-determination and self-defense while "all other peoples have the right to protect their borders."[42]

Dawidowicz, as we have seen, had once sided with Israel's Jewish diasporic critics. Yet in the aftermath of the Lebanon War, she feared the demonization of the Jewish state by leftist opponents. Moreover, she shared Podhoretz's view that censuring Israel smacked of an antisemitic double standard, one that denied the political and cultural self-determination essential to the Jewish peo-ple's existential survival. Disturbed by the casual Holocaust analogizing that

accompanied so much of the criticism of Israel's actions in Lebanon, Dawidowicz was stirred by Podhoretz's argument. After reading "J'Accuse," she wrote
to him, calling it "the most stunning article I ever read." The letter disclosed a
level of emotion unusual for Dawidowicz. "You are the true defender of the
Jews. And if this too has an ironic ring, I still mean it as seriously as when I
speak of myself. . . . God bless you forever and ever."[43]

None of Dawidowicz's letters or writings touching on the war in Lebanon
reveals any serious consideration of policies and perspectives that might have
complicated her evaluation of the war's meaning. Apparently, she never discussed the Reagan administration's pressure on Begin and Shamir to avoid
entering Beirut, the (failed) Reagan peace initiative to create a kind of Palestinian protectorate under Jordanian sovereignty,[44] or the Kahan Commission's
conclusion that Sharon was personally responsible "for not ordering appropriate measures for preventing or reducing the chances of a massacre" in the
camps.[45] Actual geopolitics were not Dawidowicz's concern. Rather, she was
a soldier in the war of words about Israel's behavior and Jewish morality. By
the 1980s, she had settled into her role as a tough and protective watchdog of
her people.

A SMALL CIRCLE OF FRIENDS

Dawidowicz's post-1982 position rejecting all public criticism of the Israeli government pitted her against many friends. Her letters from the last decade of
her life express her new opinion on the limits of American Jewish dissent on
Israel's policies and her decision to disengage from relationships with former
friends whom she now viewed as political opponents.[46] In October 1983, she
informed Leon Wieseltier that since the war in Lebanon, "I prefer the company
of like-minded people," a comment that "rankled him."[47] Lore Segal, the refugee novelist who was part of the coterie of Dawidowicz's female Jewish writer
friends, was unable to win back her favor after they disagreed about politics.[48]
Her correspondence with the two lodestars of the New York intellectuals,
Irving Howe and Alfred Kazin, illustrates the hardening of her position. She
and Howe, bound to one another through their commitment to the Yiddish
language, agreed to disagree. On the last day of 1982, he wrote to Dawidowicz,
following up on a conversation: "[T]here is little point in some of us quarreling
about Israel's policies: we all have our opinions, sincerely held, and that is a fact
of life." He continued:

But there was something you said last night that really disturbed me deeply. You asked, first, why I devoted attention to Israeli matters and, second, why if I cared so much about it I didn't go there. Now what I want to ask you is this: Would you put the same questions to someone like Norman P[od-horetz], who essentially defends the current Israeli policies, or is it only to people of my persuasion that you would ask why don't they go back to where they didn't come from?[49]

In her response, she affirmed the "necessary" justice of Operation Peace for Galilee as a defensive war. She argued that "Israel is surrounded by enemies who wish to destroy her," that its only friend among the nations of the world was the United States, and that America had a special responsibility to encourage that friendship. "American Jews who care about Israel—and I don't mean the political character of the government, but Israel as the embodiment of Jewish civilization and the Jewish will to survive—have an obligation to support it as it fights for its existence."

To condemn Israel in the middle of a war, when she is being condemned by all her enemies who indeed wish her dead, and to condemn her in the one country that supports her is—to my mind—nothing less than an act of [ugly—the word typed and then crossed out] betrayal. It's one thing to be an Israeli and criticize your own government. It's another to be an American and criticize Israel. What would you say to a Soviet Jew who acted this way? The Peace Now people in this country were motivated by narrow partisan politics and at the very height of the Lebanese war they drew out of the woodwork to *their* support a host of ex-Stalinists and present Stalinoids, as well as outright enemies of the state, now posing as "Zionists" so that they took [*sic*] could get their licks in.[50]

Dawidowicz's long friendship with Marie Syrkin, born of their time together in postwar Europe, their love of Yiddish and poetry, and their shared commitment to Jewish peoplehood, remained intact. Corresponding about the Lebanon War and the legitimacy of Jewish diasporic criticism of the Begin government, Dawidowicz must have chastised Syrkin for signing an American Friends of Peace Now's display ad in the *Times* on July 4, 1982, under the heading "A Call to Peace," which addressed "Hardliners on Both Sides," "Palestinian Spokesmen," "American Jews," and "Moderates in the Middle East." Syrkin admitted that the letter "was not strong enough in its condemnation of the PLO." Nonetheless, she agreed with its major thrust and added that an independent Lebanon that would be friendly to Israel was "beyond Israel's power to achieve." She concluded that it was "a pipe-dream" that the PLO was done for. "It will renew itself in every Arab capital. And Saudi Arabia can resupply their armament instantly. In short the brilliant military victory of the first week is turning, I fear, into a political and geo-political disaster."[51] Despite their differences, the bedrock friendship between Syrkin and Dawidowicz endured. At Syrkin's memorial service, Dawidowicz told the audience that she missed her friend of fifty years: "Marie's opinion mattered greatly to me, for from Marie I knew that I would always hear the truth."[52]

In contrast, Dawidowicz and Alfred Kazin feuded and did not reconcile. Their falling-out was precipitated by Kazin's report in the *New York Review of Books* on the February 1983 conference of the Committee for the Free World (CFW).[53] Founded by Norman Podhoretz and Midge Decter, the CFW sought to counter what it saw as the excessive anti-Americanism of the New Left and to propagate the views of former liberal intellectuals like themselves who supported the Reagan revolution.[54] Its conference's title, "Our Country, Our Culture," echoed the famous 1952 *Partisan Review* symposium as a way to assert CFW's continuity with the New York intellectual tradition of critical inquiry and patriotism. Kazin's article, "Saving My Soul at the Plaza," marked his effort to reckon once and for all with the neoconservative "revolution" and, in particular, its advocacy of the United States' use of global power. He took aim at the *Commentary* crowd, including Podhoretz, Decter, Kristol, Gertrude Himmelfarb, Hilton Kramer, Jeane Kirkpatrick, and Joseph Epstein. Kazin accused them of turning their backs on America's most vulnerable populations and on the oppressed peoples of the world and seeking out alliances with autocratic, racist, and imperialist governments that pushed back against the leftist political and social movements of the late 1960s. In their triumphalism, the neoconservatives had forgotten that being pro-American did not demand "jingoism" but rather the opposite. "Our tradition is a pluralistic, democratic America with its constitutional prescription of mixed powers, intellectual freedom, and some ineradicable awareness that this buoyant and exciting society still rides cruelly over millions." In the defiant voice of postwar liberalism, he averred, "There has been no stronger American tradition than the struggle for a just society."[55]

The friendship between Dawidowicz and Kazin had begun with mutual admiration in the 1960s, when he—newly anointed as the voice of Jewish immigrant New York with the publication of *Walker in the City*—became aware of Dawidowicz's *Commentary* columns. They corresponded regularly and warmly through the 1970s, during which time Kazin wrote an effusive blurb for *The War Against the Jews*.[56] Their letters reveal intimacies about Szymon Dawidowicz's declining health, Kazin's marital woes and joys, and anxieties about their respective books.[57] For Kazin, Dawidowicz represented Jewish authenticity. In 1977, after reading her book of essays, *The Jewish Presence*, he wrote to her, saying that "no one else combines exact knowledge of the Jewish community and of Jewish history in America with such an inner devotion to the legendary *meaning* of the Jews." He continued: "You really do believe in *Jewish* history and a Jewish spirit, and that more than anything else needs to be brought out these days in this altogether secular and too easily psychologized condition we are living through."[58] Kazin's intellectual admiration meant the world to Dawidowicz, an outsider who, despite her success, had only grudgingly been allowed membership in the exclusive club of the New York intellectuals.

Their mutual affection made the break all the more painful. In early 1981, Kazin's wife, Judith Dunford, had written a series of genial letters to Dawidowicz when she was at Stanford as a Visiting Chair in Jewish Civilization. Their correspondence lapsed but then resumed in January 1985 when Dunford sent a birthday note to Dawidowicz. The note revealed the fissure that had opened in their relationship. "What I want to say is that I miss you (*we* miss you) and have been thinking about you. It would be nice to see you again and to declare a truce in the civil war which, though serious, is certainly not personal."[59] Reluctantly rejecting Dunford's peace offering, Dawidowicz responded, "Your letter touched me and flattered me. And it hurts me that I can't respond to your friendship. After all, it's not you, and has never been you, who has been the cause of the rupture between us." The break had been caused by her husband and specifically by his article "Saving My Soul at the Plaza."

> The civil war between Alfred and me is serious *and* personal. That's been Alfred's doing. He personalized the politics. Yes, I have other friends with whom I don't share politics. But they have never smeared everything important to me as Alfred has. Nor have they, as he has, used politics to defame and vilify my friends—Ruth Wisse and Bea Kristol, to name only two. I'm sorry we can't turn the clock back. I'm sorry that Alfred, by his writing and public speaking, chose to renounce our friendship. It wasn't I who did that.[60]

Now estranged from Dawidowicz, Kazin used a 1987 column in *Dissent* to defend David Wyman and to get back at her:

> The book [by Wyman] is attacked by my old friend Lucy Dawidowicz, author of a great book on the Holocaust, who was once so absorbed in the tragedy of the Jews that she became a thrilling example of a historian *living* her subject. Now, happy as she can be with Reagan's *Macht* and *Realpolitik*, she absolves the U.S. government on the grounds that nothing could have been done for the Jews before victory over Nazism. . . . American Jews knew what Lucy Dawidowicz in her patriotic fervor is pleased to forget. Roosevelt, whether or not he personally "abandoned" the Jews, thought it politically wise to do that.[61]

A child of the 1930s, when ideological passions ran high and so much was at stake, Dawidowicz, a "quasi-survivor," in her own words, now considered the security, vitality, and autonomy of Jewish collective existence a nonnegotiable component of her identity. By the early 1980s, she had cast her lot with Jewish neoconservatism because she believed its adherents would not tolerate anti-Jewish hatred or bargain with Israel's future.[62] As she had earlier articulated to Irving Howe, Dawidowicz now believed that Israel represented "the embodiment of the Jewish people and concentration of a Jewish cultural and political center."[63] Defending it was an act of diaspora nationalist honor, necessary to protect from the left flank within the Democratic Party.

CROSSING THE AISLE

In December 1984, Dawidowicz gave "The State of World Jewry Address" at New York City's 92nd Street YW-YMHA. Established in 1980, the annual address was an influential public forum for "a discerning Jewish leader to assess the spiritual, political and social condition of the Jewish people in Israel and throughout the Diaspora."[64] Dawidowicz's predecessors in the lecture were Abba Eban, Israel's foreign minister; Stuart E. Eizenstat, chief domestic policy adviser under President Carter; Gerson Cohen, chancellor of the Jewish Theological Seminary of America; and Norman Podhoretz. Cohen, who—with his wife, the American Jewish historian Naomi—was a personal friend, introduced Dawidowicz as the author of classic works on the Holocaust and characterized her as "a person who is inspired, original in perception, fearless, brilliant, and articulate. In short, a great teacher."[65]

Taking the stage in Kaufmann Hall, before an audience of a thousand people, Dawidowicz began with a self-deprecating joke: "I am probably the shortest speaker that ever stood here at the 92nd Street Y and that includes any thirteen year-old violin prodigy."[66] The talk she delivered, however, was no laughing matter. In what amounted to a verbal manifesto against the liberal Jewish "tradition," she rebuked Jews who had not supported Reagan's second term. Publicly voicing her own rightward shift, Dawidowicz urged American Jews to rethink their fealty to the Democratic Party and to its conception of liberalism, which she believed blinded them to the antisemitism and anti-Zionism from the Left and thus threatened Jewish security. The threat to world Jewish existence came not from the church or traditional right-wing antisemites but from the Soviet Union, its political subordinates in the Third World and their anti-Zionist spokesman in the United Nations, and from student radicals.[67] "The scale of this anti-Semitic enterprise in the last two decades would have stirred envy in Adolf Hitler."[68] And so from the famous hall on whose walls are inscribed the names of iconic Jewish and American patriarchs—a symbol of the "cult of synthesis" that since the 1930s joined Americanness and Jewishness in an ethos of liberalism—Dawidowicz exhorted her audience to support Ronald Reagan.[69]

Dawidowicz saw no cause for the liberal American Jewish fear of Jerry Falwell's Moral Majority, the prominent right-wing Christian political organization. She felt secure in her feeling that Falwell's group would not erode the country's tolerance of religious pluralism. Moreover, evangelical support of Israel encouraged her. "And even if the Evangelicals supported Israel only for ulterior and ultimate religious ends," she argued, "better such support now than the hostility which distinguishes their politicized brethren in the National Council of Churches."[70] She maintained that antisemitism on the Right had declined, as seen in such developments as Vatican II and the disclaimer articulated at the historically antisemitic passion play at Oberammergau.[71] And yet, she observed, "Jews are reluctant to acknowledge that the anti-Semitism of the right and of the Christian churches . . . has dwindled to a shadow of its past."[72] The Democratic Party had been hijacked by a Soviet-dominated, New Left agenda that threatened Jewish interests by tolerating the antisemitism of black intellectuals and the anti-Zionism of the United Nations. "Most Jews who voted Democratic believed that they were voting the age-old liberal agenda, for the extension of rights to those still deprived of them." But the new Democratic Party was not the Democratic Party of old, and Jews should not let themselves be hoodwinked. "The current agenda of those who call themselves liberals is less a matter of rights and more of what the philosophers call distributive justice—that is, how to redistribute the political and economic pie, to take from those who have and give to those who haven't."[73] Reiterating her views about the dangers of universalism and utopianism to Jewish collective identity, Dawidowicz warned about the messianic impulse undergirding radical Jewish politics.

> The revolutionary Left promised a social order from which evil, injustice, and inequality would be eliminated—in short, a utopia. The terms and tactics of its politics were secular, yet the commitment which the revolutionary movement demanded of its followers [was] the equal of any religious movement. This attitude of political messianism especially characterized the Jewish radicals. They had, after all, abandoned their old religious traditions and were in need of new ones.[74]

Her lecture went on to lay out her new appreciation for religious values and their role vis-à-vis the public sphere. Insisting that religion and politics were inseparable, and that the American Founders had never intended to banish religion from public life, she urged liberal Jews to begin "staking out an independent position and resisting an automatic commitment either to the Democrats or to the Republicans."[75] Dawidowicz concluded with the hope that the religious awakening informing young American Jews' lives would, at some point, also redound to the political sphere, resulting in sympathy for a more conservative approach to the problems of Jewish life in American society.

The 92nd Street Y's audience was noticeably cool to Dawidowicz's talk, and in the days that followed, several audience members wrote to the organizers to express their discontent.[76] Two months later her lecture was published as "Politics, the Jews, and the '84 Election" in *Commentary*, and the letters to the editor flooded in.[77] Most of the responses took issue with Dawidowicz's insistence that right-wing antisemitism, the populist Christianity of the Moral Majority, and the anti-Israel views of Senator Jesse Helms posed no substantive threat to American Jews. One reader defended Jewish political liberalism as an extension of eighth-century BCE "prophetic Judaism," others as an expression of a natural inclination for Jews to side with the oppressed. Regarding Dawidowicz's preoccupation with racial quotas, a reader wrote that "Jews do not see affirmative-action quotas as a danger to themselves, their group, or their nation. They view reverse discrimination as a temporary burden, a kind of racial reparations for slavery and segregations."[78] Several letters from self-identified Orthodox Jews also enjoined American Jews to be less preoccupied with secular politics and more attentive to "Judaism," meaning, to religion. A majority supported Dawidowicz's distaste for Jesse Jackson, agreeing with her that he was incorrigibly antisemitic and seconding her condemnation of the Democratic Party for not disavowing him.[79] In her letter to *Commentary*, Marie Syrkin squirmed between loyalty to her friend and her own support of Walter Mondale, despite the Democratic Party's "shabby failure to repudiate the Jackson-Farrakhan combine." She insisted that many Jews hesitated in the voting booth, ultimately weighing "nuclear war, social justice, abortion, equitable taxation, the deficit," and support for Israel and the rise of antisemitism, before deciding against what she called "the mellifluous Social Darwinism of Reagan." American Jews continued, Syrkin argued, to show their political independence and willingness to sacrifice their socioeconomic interests in the name of "broader national and international concerns, and an instinctive reverence for a Jewish tradition older than the 'dream' of the French Revolution—that of prophetic Judaism."[80]

Dawidowicz reserved most of her two-and-a-half-page reply to the subject of the First Amendment and its relation to religion in American public life.[81] Illustrating how far she had traveled since the late 1960s, when her "Cultural Antisemitism" memo to Bertram Gold warned of the accusations made by some prominent Christian Americans against Jewish "establishment clause" absolutists for "de-Christianizing" the American public sphere, Dawidowicz cited the position of Erwin N. Griswold, dean of the Harvard Law School, that religious pluralism need not mean the absolute banishment of religion from the public sphere. She hoped that "our otherwise latitudinarian society would provide alternative possibilities which would allow religion into the public space of our culture." She urged her readers to reconsider the paradox involved in adopting a stance of permissiveness toward pornography while prohibiting the public expression of faith: "I, for one, would prefer to see a crèche on West 42nd Street than to look at what's there now." And she closed her remarks with a familiar *cri de coeur*: American Jews should resist the blandishments of "cultural" or "secular" Jewishness, which "has shown its bankruptcy as a viable Jewish tradition and conduit for Jewish continuity."

> We have witnessed the rise and fall of at least two generations of Jewish secularists. They have lived off the capital of traditional Judaism and have by now exhausted their patrimony. It may be my own idiosyncratic view, but I believe that it is no longer sufficient to be a Jew just by supporting Israel

(though that is a *sine qua non* for being a good Jew) or by being sentimental about Yiddish or by attending a bagels-and-lox UJA meeting.[82]

American Jews needed to pay closer attention to the religious revival around them. Her closing comment spoke to her transnational self-definition: American Jews would better understand themselves if they could see themselves "as Jews who are members of a religious community, citizens of the United States," and "as part of the Jewish people."[83]

Coming as it did after many decades of engagement with the complexities of Jewish identity and politics, Dawidowicz's 92nd Street Y lecture marked a public declaration of her long political journey from left to right. Interviewed widely in 1989 when her memoir was published, she responded to queries about her political shift with characteristic defiance: "I had been a lifelong Democrat, but the upheavals in the Democratic Party in the 1960s led me to move in a different direction. I am not a Republican but an independent neo-Conservative, and if that makes me Attila the Hun, so be it."[84]

REAGAN, BITBURG, AND GERMAN GUILT

Dawidowicz's view that the Democratic Party of the 1970s tolerated—even abetted—antisemitism on the Left played a critical role in her championing of Ronald Reagan, whose Cold War stance married well with her anticommunism. But her support for Reagan was challenged when the president announced in April 1985 that in a visit to Germany—which did not include what had become a de rigueur commemorative visit to a concentration camp site—he intended to lay a wreath at a German military cemetery in Bitburg. Rebuffed a year earlier at the fortieth anniversary of the Normandy landings by France and England, Chancellor Helmut Kohl of West Germany had invited Reagan to assert his role in shaping postwar Europe and to underscore the strength of the German-American alliance. When it was revealed that members of the SS were buried in the cemetery at Bitburg, a publicity firestorm ensued, made worse by Reagan's characterization of the fallen Nazi soldiers as "victims" of the war. Veterans groups protested, stunned Jewish organizations were outraged, and several congressmen publicly admonished Reagan. His administration eventually backtracked, changing the itinerary to include laying a wreath at Bergen-Belsen prior to visiting Bitburg and adding a visit to a neighboring US airbase.[85] Jewish protests persisted despite the change in the itinerary. At a ceremony at the White House where he was honored with a presidential medal, Elie Wiesel, the most famous voice of Holocaust survivors and then chairman of the United States Holocaust Memorial Council, told Reagan: "That place [Bitburg], Mr. President, is not your place."[86]

The Jewish intellectuals associated with *Commentary* were caught between their support for Reagan and their insistence that the Republican mainstream did not tolerate antisemitism. In August 1985, Midge Decter criticized Reagan but pointed out how little censure most commentators expressed regarding Helmut Kohl's decision to include Bitburg in Reagan's visit. She also warned American Jews against drawing lessons from the Holocaust to support their liberal politics, reminding them that the catastrophe that had engulfed European Jewry illustrated democracy's vulnerability to forces on the Left as well as on the Right.[87] For her part, writing in the *Wall Street Journal* in December, Dawidowicz went light on Reagan.[88] Instead, she used the Bitburg blunder to address what she considered the larger issues of Holocaust memory and German collective guilt and their effect on contemporary German politics.

In part, she trod lightly because she was still trying to come to terms with her own changing views of "the Germans." In October 1985, Dawidowicz participated in a conference in Berlin sponsored by the Leo Baeck Institute (LBI). Founded in 1955 as a direct response to the Holocaust and with branches in New York, London, and Jerusalem, the LBI sponsored archival and research projects devoted to the history of German-speaking Jewry. The institute only began to have a presence in West Germany in the late 1970s, and the 1985 conference, "Self-Assertion in Adversity: The Jews in National Socialist Germany, 1933–1939," represented a major rapprochement with the German-Jewish diaspora and the new Germany. Luminaries in the field of modern Jewish history attended, including Peter and Ruth Gay, Jacob Katz, Michael A. Meyer, Robert Wistrich, and Ismar Schorsch. The conference gave Dawidowicz, an LBI board member, the opportunity to return to "the land of Amalek" and to reckon with her prior sojourns in Germany. "This public, collective return of the Jewish exiles, refugees, and survivors of National Socialist Germany to confront the Germans with that terrible past seemed to me to be a momentous event, a mini-drama of Jewish history," she wrote, "and so I was disposed to go to Berlin, to have a part in this eventful occasion, at least as a witness."[89]

Dawidowicz's travel diary reveals her considerable anxiety about reencountering the past.[90] Writing while on the plane, she mused about the German relationship to the horrific not-so-recent past. About younger Germans, she wondered, "Do they avoid thinking about the past? Do they try to sweep its fragments under the rug of forgetting? I think I must try to free myself, so that I don't think always that they are murderers and that I'm walking on the ashes of the European Jews."[91]

To Dawidowicz's surprise, her third trip to Berlin, though containing moments of grief and terror, convinced her that the Nazi past was over. "I looked at the people and felt that forty years ago and six million Jews ago were utterly irrelevant to them. I keep juxtaposing the past and present and can't relate them."[92] She was heartened that German officials appeared to be taking their country's past seriously, evidenced by Kohl's address to the conference on its first evening, in which he publicly apologized for Nazi crimes. The speech was broadcast throughout the country.[93] Dawidowicz's August 1986 *Commentary* report, "In Berlin Again," did not ignore the persistence of antisemitism in West Germany. Nor did she forgive the Nazis. But she noted the comprehensive exhibition in the Reichstag that did not shy away from the oppression and subsequent mass murder of the Jews. Overcome with sadness when viewing the exhibit, Dawidowicz raced outside, only to be confronted by the reality of modern Berlin. So much of the city had been rebuilt, its streets crowded with attractive young people enjoying the casual pleasures of youth. "They were not the Germans I had expected to confront. They were not the ghosts of the Nazi past. These were ordinary young people, too young to be charged with the burden of Germany's terrible history."[94]

She contrasted West Germany's efforts to come to terms with its past to Soviet denial of the specificity of the Jewish tragedy, a universalizing anti-semitic posture that was compounded by the regime's anti-Zionism. Crossing into East Berlin, Dawidowicz wrote that she was not surprised to see that the Holocaust was not commemorated. The Eastern Bloc's narrative of World War II instead emphasized the victory over fascism, making Jewish suffering invisible. On the once grand avenue of Unter den Linden, where she had gone "to see whether the Jewish ghosts were keeping vigil there as well," she saw huge window displays commemorating the fortieth anniversary of the war's end:

> Enormous posters celebrated the end of "mass murder in the concentration camps," the end of "terror against Communists, Social Democrats, and all anti-fascist democratically minded people," the end of the "expulsion of humanistic writers, artists and scientists." A man from Mars coming to East Berlin would never know that National Socialist Germany had waged a war also against the Jews.[95]

Having cast her lot with the Republican Party, Dawidowicz forgave Reagan's insensitivity toward the Jewish victims of the SS as a misstep, one made in the context of the United States' strong anti-Soviet alliance with West Germany, an alliance that she as a neoconservative supported. Coupled with her visit to Berlin, it meant a certain kind of forgiveness toward young Germans, a forgiveness she could never extend to young Poles or to Polish intellectuals. To the very end of her life, Dawidowicz could not see or accept that underneath the carapace of Soviet-controlled Poland there were activists champing at the bit to free themselves from Moscow's rule. If she noticed the Polish roundtable talks of 1989, the first crack in the Eastern Bloc's wall, Dawidowicz never mentioned them. Christian and Jewish communist Poles—like Poland itself—were irrevocably consigned, in her worldview, to the last rung of hell.

ZAKHOR

Toward the end of her life, unable to complete her history of the Jews in the United States, Dawidowicz turned back to the idea and ideals of Jewish Eastern Europe. In a fitting coda to her lifelong commitment to diaspora nationalism in a Yiddish key, she wrote *From That Place and Time: A Memoir, 1938–1947* as a memento mori for East European *yidishkayt*, the Yiddish language, and Vilna's murdered Jews.[96] Published in 1989 to wide acclaim, the memoir won the National Jewish Book Award. Concerned about the vanity involved in writing a memoir, Dawidowicz shaped the book in a dispassionate voice, insisting that it was not about her but rather about the history that had shaped her life in those crucial years.[97] She described herself as merely a witness to a dramatic past. It was by sheer coincidence that her life in Vilna coincided with what became the fateful last year of independent Poland and of Jewish life there before the Nazi onslaught. She worked hard to write a memoir without sentiment, nostalgia, or subjectivity. She needed to get her portrait of interwar Vilna Jewry "right."[98] Dawidowicz recalled the experience of guarding her private pain at the destruction of her beloved Vilna, writing that both she and Max Weinreich "never talked about this story. Nor did I ever discuss these horrors with anyone. We had learned to control our physical revulsion and to stifle our grief. We endured our despair in silence."[99]

Dawidowicz's friends and colleagues frequently referred to the power of her memoir's restrained and unsentimental writing.[100] Her mistrust of sentimentality reflected her belief, as she had written in a review in 1968, "that at times a hardheaded approach and jaundiced look may bring us closer to the reality, to see it, as the historians like to say, *wie es eigentlich gewesen*."[101] Objectivity, always central to the historian's craft, was of particular urgency when it came to the monumental task of documenting the Holocaust. Only precise, thoroughly researched, and unsentimental history—not poetry, art, music, or other representational efforts—could accurately depict the destruction of Europe's Jews. On receiving the National Jewish Book Award on June 11, 1990, she stated her credo, "In trying to bridge that abyss between past and present, the memoirist is obliged to arm himself against sentimentality, to guard against nostalgia. I was constantly aware of the desire to idealize that destroyed world, but I tried to discipline myself to portray Vilna as it was, without retouching, without removing the warts and blotches of historical reality."[102] The voluminous research notes contained in her personal archives reveal the painstaking effort she made to verify her memory. Errors could not be tolerated. They desecrated the dead.

In all of her work on East European Jewry, Dawidowicz insisted on the necessity of distance and dispassion. Yet as Barry M. Katz noted in his review of *The Holocaust and the Historians*, she may have protested too much. Katz called attention to Dawidowicz's internal tension between desiring to be a *Jewish* historian devoted to her people and her commitment to the "objective" standards of professional historiography. He claimed that the book's afterword revealed her hesitant acknowledgment of the tension between these two positions, writing that the "ideological coloring of Dawidowicz's own rhetoric [with regard to Soviet and Polish historians] in these chapters clearly betrays the elusiveness of the quest for objectivity."[103] Indeed, Katz regarded her identification with her subject as the source of her works' "unique power and authority."[104]

In the late 1960s, Dawidowicz began to explore the question of the role of the Jewish historian in supporting Jewish collective existence, well before the works of Yosef H. Yerushalmi, Amos Funkenstein, Moshe Rosman, and David N. Myers had appeared.[105] After reading Gavin Langmuir's "Majority History and Post-Biblical Jews" and "Tradition, History, and Prejudice"[106] on historiography's relationship to tradition and memory, Dawidowicz wrote to him about a controversy that had raged among East European Jewish historians about "whether Jewish history ought to be written out of 'love for Israel' (*ahavat yisroel*) or—let the chips fall where they may." The subject that precipitated the argument, she wrote, was the economic role of Jews in the Ukraine in the first half of the seventeenth century: "Were the Jews indeed exploiting the peasants? Were they actually the key holders in the Orthodox churches?" One historian with socialist leanings, she recalled, had argued that "the Jews, by functioning as economic agents of the nobility and the landowners, brought upon themselves the justified wrath of the peasantry and the Chmielnitsky massacres of 1648–49."[107] The impassioned historiographical discussion that followed illustrated that much more was involved "than factuality or even objectivity." Faced with questions of truth, love, and loyalty, what, she asked, is a professional historian to do? She told Langmuir that "while this seems like a problem every historian must face, there is a special Jewish aspect. For the Jewish historian who does not write out of love for his people may—whether he likes it or not—provide fuel for those who hate his people. So we are back to apologetics, of one kind or another."[108]

Writing to Michael A. Meyer in 1978, whose *Ideas of Jewish History* represented one of the first English-language forays into the young field of Jewish historiography,[109] Dawidowicz affirmed her identification with Dubnow, informing Meyer that she had "worked up a list of four criteria by which one could combine both professionalism and *ahavas-yisroel* [love of the Jews]."[110] With the phrase "*ahavas-yisroel*," she nodded to the famous exchange between Gershom Scholem and Hannah Arendt after the publication of *Eichmann in Jerusalem*, in which Scholem accused Arendt of lacking "*ahavat yisra'el*."[111] Positioning herself in opposition to Arendt, Dawidowicz argued for the necessity of the Jewish historian's responsibility to the Jewish people. While Meyer's response agreed about *ahavas yisroel*, writing "Any Jewish historiography which lacks it will fail in its attempt to understand," he also cautioned her about the dangers of mythologizing, noting that "myths not only do violence to truth, they often create violence in history."[112]

Dawidowicz maintained that Jewish history writing had to be purposeful, taking into account the distinctive forces of Jewish history: "Whether we are believers or skeptics about providential destiny,"

> we must admit that [Isaac] Baer was right: Jewish history follows its own laws. And also Dubnow was right: Jewish history, however dark and catastrophic, has in it the potential for Jewish survival. This sense of Jewish history and destiny is what every Jew who cares about the survival of his people feels in his bones even if he does not know the dates and events.[113]

For all the stress Dawidowicz placed on dispassionate objectivity, she rejected the notion that a professional historian's personal commitments to his people, country, religion, or language undermined his professional objectivity. To the contrary, "they enrich, historical writing."[114] She told Ruth Wisse in 1979 that she wrote from a "survivalist" point of view.[115] Four years later, reviewing *Zakhor: Jewish History and Jewish Memory*, in which Yerushalmi poignantly concluded that his generation of modern secular Jewish historians had severed their ties to Jewish collective memory, Dawidowicz asserted that all great historians have been "[d]riven by a commitment to Jewish survival . . . animat[ing] their work with that commitment."[116] She consistently asserted this view of the responsibility of the Jewish historian to the Jewish people. Reviewing (negatively) Arthur Hertzberg's history of American Jews in 1990, she began with Scholem's reproach to Arendt for lacking *ahavat yisra'el*. That lack was a curious charge for a historian, Dawidowicz conceded. But she insisted that "it was indeed possible, in writing about one's own people, for a historian both to maintain critical objectivity and to hold fast to an inner perspective, an empathetic understanding of their trials and travails, their passions and ambitions."[117] Dawidowicz strove to achieve that balance in *From That Place and Time*, which pulses with the tension among her effort to recall accurately her European experience, her desire to pay homage to the destroyed civilization of Ashkenazic Jewry, and her hope that readers would internalize that civilization's values and forge a commitment to the Jewish future.[118]

Dawidowicz's memoir is also a self-conscious wrestling with experiencing the vitality of the world of modern secular Yiddish culture even as she witnessed the beginnings of its violent extinction. While writing it, Dawidowicz founded the Fund for the Translation of Jewish Literature, a nonprofit organization devoted to the English translation of classics of Jewish literature in languages inaccessible to the American public, both Jewish and gentile.[119] Its Library of Yiddish Classics expressed the commitment to diaspora nationalist self-determination and commemoration in literary form that paralleled the Dubnowian impulse behind her historical writing. Writing to a potential funder, Bernard Rapoport, Dawidowicz commented, "For me, raising the money to make this undertaking possible has become something of an obsession, a goal that I must reach before it's altogether too late—for me personally and before we run out of people who still know Yiddish well enough to translate it and transmit it properly."[120] For a brief while, Dawidowicz also translated Yiddish columns from the *Forverts* for the English-language *Forward*, conceived and edited by her friend, Seth Lipsky, but found the exercise of translating editorials from the old Yiddish *Forverts* predictable.[121]

Dawidowicz's memoir pulses with a fundamental ambiguity, even ambivalence, about her relationship to Yiddish. *From That Place and Time* celebrates the *yidishkayt* of prewar Vilna, embedded in a living Jewish culture nurtured by traditional Judaism, but implicitly criticizes the term when it was used to define Jewish culture in opposition to Jewish tradition. By the time she wrote the memoir, Dawidowicz had rejected the secular Yiddishist culture that had nurtured her, even as she recalled the ardent Yiddishism of her youth.[122] Now a vocal advocate of Jewish survival in whatever form it might best be cultivated on American soil, Dawidowicz became bold in expressing what she perceived to be the inadequacy of a Yiddishist culture divorced from Jewish religious tradition. Her journey away from secular Yiddishism had been evolutionary, beginning with doubts she expressed about its viability to sustain Jewish life in Vilna in 1938–39 and continuing into the postwar years.

One of the clearest expressions of her insistence that a procreative *yidish-kayt* had to be nurtured by Judaism came in 1974, when Dawidowicz was asked to be a reader on Irving Howe's manuscript for what would become his masterwork on the culture of the immigrant Jewish community on New York's Lower East Side, *World of Our Fathers: The Journey of the East European Jews to America and the Life They Found and Made.* Though she and Howe had parted political ways in the late 1960s, they shared an abiding love of Yiddish literature and the Yiddish language. Dawidowicz had translated regularly for Howe and Eliezer Greenberg's series of books on Yiddish prose and poetry, and they singled her out for "her remarkably generous help in regard to a number of editorial and technical problems."[123] Howe had participated in "An Evening of Yiddish Poetry" at Stern College with Dawidowicz, Jacob Glatshteyn, and Marie Syrkin in 1970,[124] and he was a member of the board of the Fund for the Translation of Jewish Literature in the 1980s.

In reviewing *World of Our Fathers*, Dawidowicz was confronted by her former self: a secular Yiddishist rooted in Yiddish language, literature, and culture as the foundational components of personal identity. But by the 1970s, she had changed, and both her response to the book and her letters to Howe illustrate how central the issues surrounding the viability of American Jewish life without Judaism had become to her. Dawidowicz's letter to William B. Goodman, Howe's editor, read in part:

It is so rich, vivid, and lively, with stunning kaleidoscopic effects, that reading creates such a strong visual impression, as if the book were a movie. A brilliant recreation of a unique subculture, one particular strength of the book—among many—is that it brings to life the people in their milieu and is not abstract or general. In addition to the individual portraits that appear throughout the book—a fantastically diverse gallery, the book transmits a sense of the reality of life, how people lived, acted, felt, and responded, without the mediation of pedantry or (horrors) sociology.[125]

That said, she criticized Howe's use of the term *yidishkayt*, which she felt conflated the term with "the world of secular Yiddish culture." For Dawidowicz, *yidishkayt* meant "the Jewishness of the religious tradition." Writers of poetry in Yiddish, such as Avrom Reisen, "whose Jewish content is nil," could not be considered "poet[s] of yiddishkeit." In her view, Howe's "imposed definition— the world of Yiddish culture—distorts the meaning of the word." To avoid such distortion and ambiguity, she thought Howe should use a "descriptive phrase like 'secular Yiddish culture' or a coinage like 'Yiddishness.'" In her notes on the book's epilogue, she reiterated her concern with his reduction of *yidishkayt* to secular, left-leaning Yiddish culture, commenting that because Howe himself only felt at home in a subculture of modern Jewish communal life, that of socialist Yiddishism, he could not take seriously other forms of Jewish

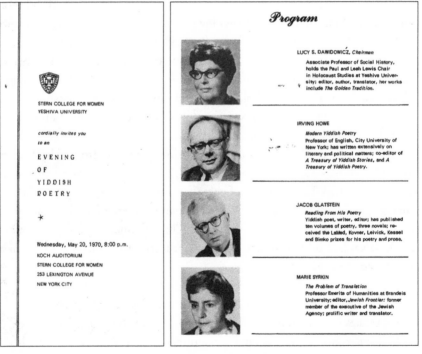

"An Evening of Yiddish Poetry," at Stern College, Yeshiva University, May 20, 1970. (Courtesy Yeshiva University Archives)

identity—which were "certainly more viable." Her handwritten notes to her typed comments included the observation directed to Howe: "not quite sure what you are mourning."[126]

Responding to her critique in a letter dated November 28, 1974, Howe acknowledged that the two did not agree on the term *yiddishkeit*,[127] which he insisted did not reflect the entirety of the immigrant experience. Rather, it represented "a cultural phase in the history of the Jews, as *a way of life* that characterized our experience for perhaps 150 or so years, one in which secular elements grew, of course, but in which the religious base was still present and strong." What interested him were the "sharp continuities *and* discontinuities between east Europe and America, [and how] that way of [life] formed the substance of the immigrant experience."[128] Though Dawidowicz's comments had compelled him to think more deeply about his use of *yiddishkeit*, he could not "dispense with the term or [his] understanding of it."[129] He also suggested, in a friendly jibe, that Dawidowicz was responding more to what she knew of him personally than to what he had written in the book and that if he were in fact guilty of a secularist bias, he detected, "gimlet-like, something of the opposite in you!"[130]

In reply, Dawidowicz professed herself "glad I was of help to you in the book, which I admire enormously, but whose premises and perspective I don't share."[131] She included a quote from an article about the efforts of "New York synagogue-based groups" to aid Soviet Jewish immigrants to be enriched by *yidishkayt*, which affirmed the "unambiguous use of the word in its authentic meaning."[132] She conceded her own "anti-secularist bias," explaining that "I came, rather late in my life, to the recognition that Yiddish secularism provided no channel for Jewish continuity." She continued:

> You are wrong when you say: "we secularists lost the battle through no special fault of our own."[133] The fault was that the secularists valued secularism and socialism over Jewishness and Jewish continuity. Furthermore, the Jewish content which Yiddish secularists wanted to transmit—or were competent—to their children was too meager to be meaningful to sustain any Jewish identity, since it lacked the original grounding in Jewish traditional life that the first generation of secularists had had. Yiddish secularism has proved to be unviable in America. That's what you regret and mourn, but without the life-sustaining force of Jewish tradition, it really was a dead end. I suspect that even had Polish Jewry been spared and had continued to live

a normal existence, Yiddish secularism there too would have withered and eventually broken off from the tree.[134]

Six years later, reviewing the English translation of Max Weinreich's magnum opus, *Geshikhte fun der yidishe shprakh*, Dawidowicz went even further in her insistence on *yidishkayt*'s inextricable debt to Judaism.[135] Praising the book itself and its comprehensive index but lamenting the translation and the lack of scholarly apparatus, Dawidowicz's review emphasized Weinreich's conclusion that Judaism—what he had called *Derekh hashas* ("the Talmudic tradition," based on a coinage of Rashi, the eleventh-century Ashkenazic exegete)—was the sine qua non for the Jewish practice of creating distinct Jewish vernaculars, no matter where Jews lived. Yiddish was born of the Jews' religious and social life in Ashkenaz. Weinreich's definition of *yidishkayt* meant the all-encompassing culture of the Jews that was circumscribed by religious tradition, Dawidowicz wrote, a definition indebted to Mordecai Kaplan's "lapidary phrase, Judaism as a civilization."[136] In her review, she further explained the term *yidishkayt* as "the sum total of the ideas and practice of traditional Judaism," a definition conceived of by Solomon Birnbaum, by then her informal adviser on matters related to Yiddish and Jewish culture's relationship to the language.[137] Dawidowicz's review underscored the inadequacy of translating *yidishkayt* as "Jewishness"—"a featureless word, which commonly suggests a watered-down quality of Jewish ethnic identity and whose secular overtones drown out the resonance of religious tradition in the original Yiddish."[138] And once again, she speculated that even if the Third Reich had not murdered secular Yiddish by destroying the majority of its speakers and readers, the language would have slowly withered, victim to the forces of modernization and integration in which it played a role: "In the remarkable success of Yiddish as a secular vehicle lay the seeds of its decline," she wrote, adding that "Once a language loses its function as a vehicle of systematic communication, it loses its voice."[139]

Unsympathetic to Yiddish's symbolic power among third- and fourth-generation American Jews,[140] Dawidowicz was reported to have scoffed at the celebration of the publication of *The History of the Yiddish Language* at the YIVO in 1980 with the outburst: "Yiddish is dead." Kenneth Libo, who co-authored *World of Our Fathers* and was then the editor of the English section of the *Forverts*, and Joseph Mlotek, educational director of the Workmen's Circle, among others, found Dawidowicz's pessimism about secular Yiddish unfair and wrote to *Commentary* to object to her review.[141] Dawidowicz responded: "Denying the bitter reality doesn't change that reality. My analysis of the rise and fall of Yiddish is, I believe, historically valid. Magical incantations ('Say it isn't so') can't and won't undo the course of events as they happened and as I described them. I had hoped that my critics who were my friends would have understood that but, as I anticipated, they didn't."[142]

From That Place and Time is a literary elegy not only for the brutally murdered Jews of Poland but also for their organic culture, one that seamlessly wove together secular and religious components and that now was shattered, the European heartland of Jewish life extinguished. Many of her readers would conclude from the book that it was the physical annihilation of East European Jewry that destroyed modern secular Yiddish culture. But Dawidowicz's doubts about the capacity of secular Yiddishism to sustain and create modern Jewish life preceded the German invasion of Poland. Her most sympathetic readers recognized the pathos with which she had written the book and her desire to narrate and commemorate, in the historiographic spirit established by Dubnow, the history of interwar Vilna Jewry in all its vitality. In his review in *Partisan Review*, Leon Edel concluded that *From That Place and Time* was both "deeply felt and soberly narrated."[143] Cynthia Ozick, overwhelmed with the power of the memoir, wrote to Dawidowicz in April 1989: "Lucy: Congratulations. You have re-created. You have fulfilled the commandment of Zakhor.[144] You have made a great and moving book."[145]

EPILOGUE

Jewish History, Jewish Politics

Dear Evelyn:
I'm using the ש when I need the א because my beloved ש is in the same place as the English "a" [on the keyboard].

—Libe Shildkret to Evelyn Konoff, 1935[1]

Europe is different now in my mind, as different from its past as if it were physically different, another continent. Europe, practically without Jews, but only Jewish monuments, monuments of past achievements and to commemorate their destruction. When I was in Paris twenty years ago, I went to Drancy on a pilgrimage and now I will go to see the Memorial to the Unknown Jewish Martyrs. Being in Paris, I should think of Warsaw and Vilna and Lodz and Minsk and Kiev.

—Lucy S. Dawidowicz, 1967[2]

Lucy S. Dawidowicz died on December 5, 1990, from complications related to cancer. After several weeks in the hospital, she refused further treatment and came home to her apartment on West Eighty-Sixth Street on Manhattan's Upper West Side to die in a hospice setting arranged by her friend, the physician Dr. Samuel Klagsbrun. As had her husband, Szymon, she died on her own terms.[3] She orchestrated her last days precisely, with visits by those closest to her, charging them with various tasks related to her effects and legacy. Ruth Wisse recalled that Dawidowicz phoned her to inform her that she was sick and wanted people to come to her home to say "goodbye." At Wisse's visit, Dawidowicz appointed her to make new stationery for the Library of Yiddish Classics and gave her a map of Vilna.[4] Norman Podhoretz received one of Dawidowicz's favorite opera recordings, *Tristan and Isolde* sung by Helen Traubel and Lawrence Melchor.[5] Rabbi Harlan Wechsler performed the religious ceremony for the funeral, which included the Yiddish recitation of excerpts from Ecclesiastes by Wisse and by Pearl Lang, a modern choreographer and a dear friend; eulogies by Podhoretz and Wechsler; the recitation of Psalms by Kozodoy, Gertrude Himmelfarb, and Naomi Cohen; and the intoning of the hymn "El Mole Rachamim" by Samuel Klagsbrun. Lucy and Szymon Dawidowicz are buried next to one another in a Workmen's Circle plot in Cedar Park Cemetery in Paramus, New Jersey. Her death left a huge hole in her small tight-knit circle of friends. In a loving tribute, Francine Klagsbrun evoked Dawidowicz's contradictory personality, one characterized by a mixture of impatience and bristly unsentimentality with deep sympathy and personal generosity to those whom she loved, writing that "even in her last breaths [Dawidowicz was worried] about hurting someone's feelings at her funeral."[6] In accordance with her wishes, Neal Kozodoy organized her papers, now at the American Jewish Historical Society, and edited a collection of her essays— *What Is the Use of Jewish History?*—with the hopes to ensure her literary and historiographic posterity.[7]

In the 1986 reissue of *The War Against the Jews*, Dawidowicz wrote that her intentionalist views were "now widely shared."[8] This belief in the universal acceptance of her historiographic claims was, as we have seen, wishful thinking. Dawidowicz's perspective on the causes of the destruction of European Jewry, on the centrality of Hitler's persona and ideology to the prosecution of World War II, on antisemitism's long history in Europe and its relation to the Final Solution, and on antisemitism's elusive, yet tenacious, transmigration onto American soil was soon viewed as amateurish and parochial.[9]

That said, public fascination with the destruction of the Jews during World War II shows no sign of abating. And while it is impossible to survey fully the state of contemporary Holocaust Studies—a field with global reach—a reassessment of Dawidowicz's key interpretations forty-five years after the publication of *The War Against the Jews* is merited here. The question, simply put, is: Of what relevance is Dawidowicz's historiographic contribution today?

Drawing a straight line between Hitler's *Mein Kampf* in 1925 and Operation Barbarossa, Dawidowicz never wavered from her intentional perspective. In one of her last published pieces, a review of two world history textbooks, *People and Our World: A Study of World History* (1981) and *History and Life* (1990), Dawidowicz credited their descriptions of "the rise of the Nazi regime, racial anti-Semitism as the underpinning of Nazi ideology, Germany's domestic and foreign policies leading to the war, and the fate of the Jews, first in Nazi Germany and then in German-ruled Europe, culminating in the premeditated and systematized murder of six million Jews." But, ultimately, she considered them flawed because both books had failed to fully explicate the link between historical European antisemitism and the Final Solution. Dawidowicz asked, "Can young people be expected to comprehend this terrible history if they do not learn about the continuous and cumulative tradition of anti-Semitism throughout the centuries that made the Holocaust possible? A couple of paragraphs about the Crusades, which some texts offer, does not suffice."[10]

Though Dawidowicz's insistence on an early dating of Hitler's intention to destroy all of European Jewry has not been accepted by many contemporary interpreters, her focus on ideology and on German antisemitism as a root cause of the Final Solution has been largely vindicated. Writing to Dawidowicz in 1975, George Mosse praised her book for having put "the whole tragedy in its proper framework . . . brilliant[ly making] clear that Hitler's declaration of war was really against the Jews." Expressing that her conclusions might be resisted, he added that he would be "interested to see whether you run into the same difficulty that I had so many years ago when in *The Crisis of German Ideology* I first put forward the idea of the primacy of the Jewish question in National Socialism. That has not even been accepted today in many quarters, in spite of all the accumulation of evidence."[11] Twenty-six years later, Yehuda Bauer affirmed that "Nazi racial antisemitic ideology was the central factor in the development toward the Holocaust" and that "The basic motivation [for the Holocaust] was purely ideological, rooted in an illusionary world of Nazi imagination."[12] In 2003, Doris Bergen confirmed the centrality of Nazi hatred of the Jews in *War and Genocide: A Concise History of the Holocaust*: "Jews were the main target of Nazi genocide; against the Jews Hitler's Germany mobilized all its resources: bureaucratic, military, legal, scientific, economic and intellectual."[13]

Dawidowicz's opening salvo in *The War Against the Jews*, in which she linked early modern Christian anti-Judaism to modern antisemitism, has also merited reassessment. Dawidowicz maintained that "a line of anti-Semitic descent from Martin Luther to Adolf Hitler is easy to draw. Both Luther and Hitler were obsessed by a demonologized universe inhabited by Jews."[14] In 1997 Saul Friedländer coined the neologism "redemptive antisemitism," linking modern, racial antisemitism with premodern anti-Judaism. Insisting that traditional religious-based fears and hatred of the Jews played a role in the Nazification of Germany society, he argued that "Christian religious anti-Semitism remained of central importance in Europe and in the Western world in general"[15] and that "German Christianity, neoromanticism, the mystical cult of sacred Aryan blood, and ultraconservative nationalism: the Bayreuth circle" all led to "redemptive anti-Semitism."[16] In his view, "redemptive antisemitism" constituted a dominant aspect of Hitler's and the Nazi worldview, pitting the Jews as the Germans' apocalyptic adversary, their annihilation necessary in the global battle for the world's redemption.[17] His view resonated with that of Dawidowicz, who had earlier written, "The Germans were in search of a mysterious wholeness that would restore them to primeval happiness, destroying the hostile milieu of urban industrial civilization that the Jewish conspiracy had foisted on them."[18]

Friedländer also argued that Hitler's renaming of the 1941 attack on the Soviet Union as Operation Barbarossa, which drew on the twelfth-century crusade of Frederick I in the East, indicated its quasi-mythical element.[19] Attacking the USSR was the necessary next step in Hitler's eschatological war against Judeo-Bolshevism and linked the Führer's ideology to his foreign policy. As Dawidowicz had done before him, Friedländer credited Deitrich Eckart and his *Der Bolschewismus von Moses bis Lenin: Ein Zwiegespräch zwischen Adolf Hitler und Mir* (1924) as a core influence on Hitler's construction of the demonic "Jew-Communist" threatening everything sacred to German society.[20] "Jewish" Bolshevik control of the Slavs, Friedländer showed, appeared already in *Mein Kampf*. For Hitler, the murder of the Soviet intelligentsia "meant the extermination of the Jewish ruling elite."[21] In *The War Against the Jews*, Dawidowicz made this linkage clear, citing a 1941 directive drafted by Wilhelm Keitel that called for "ruthless and energetic measures, above all against the Jews, the main carriers of Bolshevism."[22]

Despite Friedländer's disclaimer that "Auschwitz [was] not preordained by Hitler's ascent to power,"[23] his argument regarding the centrality of Hitler's antisemitism echoes Dawidowicz's claims.[24] While rejecting functionalist interpretations, Friedländer reemphasized Hitler's obsession with the Jews as a prerequisite for their annihilation.

> In all its major decisions the regime depended on Hitler. . . . [Though] "redemptive anti-Semitism" . . . is different, albeit derived, from other strands of anti-Jewish hatred that were common throughout Christian Europe, and different also from the ordinary brands of German and European racial anti-semitism[,] it was this redemptive dimension, this synthesis of a murderous rage and "idealistic" goal, shared by the Nazi leader and the hard core of the party, that led to Hitler's ultimate decision to exterminate the Jews.[25]

In *Rethinking the Holocaust*, Bauer, too, averred that modern German anti-semitism owed a debt to Christian antisemitism, noting that the latter originated "in the first centuries of the Christian era" and was based on "the satanization of the Jews." Yet he hedged on the link between the premodern and modern pasts: "This is not to say that there was, necessarily, a direct line of development from pre-nineteenth-century racism to the modern kind. The jury is still out on this very important issue."[26] In 2014, Alon Confino insisted that the goal of eradicating the Jews from the Third Reich was motivated by fundamentally religious values. When the Nazis burned the Bible during Kristallnacht, they "conveyed a preoccupation with ancient roots and moral authority that cannot make sense within the exclusively racial explanation." Their attack on the Bible, he concluded, illustrated the Third Reich's affirmation of "German, European, and *Christian* history."[27]

Another central argument of Dawidowicz's historiography that raised hackles was her insistence on the historical uniqueness of the intentional murder of the Jewish civilian population of Europe during World War II.[28] This insistence positioned her as a Jewish particularist. She was severely criticized for engaging in special pleading and was often characterized as unsympathetic to the sufferings of other peoples during the war and in the Holocaust. This criticism ignored her recognition of the wide and horrifying experiences of the Roma, the cognitively and physically disabled, homosexuals, political prisoners, and the civilian populations of Europe, including the Soviet Union, during the war.[29] The word "unique" has proved to be a historiographic stumbling block because of its connotation of moral superiority, itself a troubling echo of long-standing discomfort in the modern period with the concept of "chosenness" among the Jews.[30] As Geoff Eley wrote, "to insist on the uniqueness of the event is a short step to insisting on the exclusiveness of interpretation which asserts an empathetic privilege and even a Jewish proprietorship in the subject."[31] But while Dawidowicz was certainly partisan in her commitment to the Jews and their distinctive religious and ethical worldview, her view of the Holocaust's uniqueness rested not on the qualities of being a Jew but on her conviction that Hitler had waged two simultaneous wars, one for world domination and one "against the Jews," the latter impeding the prosecution of the former. The victimization of the Jews was fundamentally different from the victimization of other groups.

Despite their discomfort with the word "unique," many historians today affirm Dawidowicz's view of the singularity of Hitler's annihilation campaign against the Jews. In his later work, Bauer preferred the term "unprecedented,"[32] increasingly reluctant to use the term "unique" because it implied something unfathomable, unknowable, and unanalyzable—in short, something beyond the purview of human history and, by implication, the historian's craft.[33] He noted Dawidowicz's phrase "the war against the Jews" but qualified its use, claiming that Hitler's anti-Jewish rhetoric provided the impetus for Germany's attack on the Soviet Union with a goal of "world conquest, not necessarily the beginning of the 'Final Solution.'"[34] Yet, given that Hitler depicted the Jews, demon-like, as the masterminds of Bolshevism and that this ideology paved the way for immediate extermination on Soviet territory in 1941, Bauer would seem to be splitting academic hairs—perhaps to distance himself from the intentionalist school. His acknowledgment of the power of language, rhetoric, and ideology in the Nazi worldview muddies his own disclaimers. At what point between 1918 and 1945 does one take Hitler's antisemitism, which specifically targeted the Jews, at face value? And although Friedländer, too, did not use the term "unique," he concluded that while "all other groups targeted by the Nazi regime (the 'mentally ill,' 'asocials' and homosexuals, 'inferior' racial groups including Gypsies and Slavs) were essential passive threats (as long as the Slavs, for example, were not led by the Jews), the Jews were [according to Hitler] the only group that, since its appearance in history, relentlessly plotted and maneuvered to subdue all of humanity."[35] Friedländer's phrase "the only group" indicates that the campaign against Jewish existence was, in fact, sui generis.

Dawidowicz also anticipated the question of the number of victims as the mark of the Holocaust's "uniqueness," especially with regard to the millions of East Europeans victimized during the war by the Nazis—and later by the Soviet Union.[36] In 1980, as the Visiting Chair in Jewish Civilization at Stanford, Dawidowicz delivered a lecture, "The Holocaust and Historiography," which emphasized that focusing on the numbers of the dead during World War II distorted the meaning of the Holocaust. It was well known, she told her audience, that more Soviet citizens died than people from any other country. Yet, only the Jews as a people and civilization had been chosen for total extinction; the Holocaust's uniqueness lay in "the unique intent of the murderers and effect upon the murdered."[37]

Attention to the victimization of "ordinary" East Europeans from the period of the Bolshevik seizure of power until the fall of the Soviet Union has again led to a renewal of the comparison of the crimes of the Nazi and Soviet states, with some interpreters insisting on their parallels.[38] Most recently, Timothy Snyder's *Bloodlands: Europe Between Hitler and Stalin* (2010) highlighted the gruesome reality of day-to-day life of the civilian populations caught between the Wehrmacht/SS and the Red Army, emphasizing these lesser-known national narratives of suffering.[39] In *Bloodlands*, Snyder focused on the human cost of Soviet rule, underscoring the suffering of Soviet citizens during the great purges of the 1930s, of Poles caught in the terror of Operation Barbarossa, and of Ukrainians starved to death during the Holodomor (1932–33). But, as Omer Bartov and other historians have noted, *Bloodlands*—in its effort to present a global East European history of the terrors during the interwar years, leading up to the war, and during World War II—actually repeated an old equivalency between Nazism and Stalinism.[40] For Snyder, the ultimate proof of barbarism was death. Yet, there were many ways to die between 1939 and 1945, and it mattered if one were murdered by the Einsatzgruppen because one was a Jew or if one were shot by a Wehrmacht soldier in the Battle of Stalingrad. In Bartov's words, "By equating partisans and occupiers, Soviet and Nazi occupation, Wehrmacht and Red Army criminality, and evading interethnic violence, Snyder drains the war of much of its moral content and inadvertently adopts the apologists' argument that where everyone is a criminal no one can be blamed."[41] In the end, the central issue that Snyder's book circles around is the "uniqueness" or "unprecedented" nature (or not) of Nazi criminality in the prosecution of "the war against the Jews."

No discussion of the disjunction between Dawidowicz's stature in the late 1970s and today would be complete without facing the wide gulf between the scholarly and public reception of *The War Against the Jews*. That divide emerged again in the response to the publication of Daniel Jonah Goldhagen's *Hitler's Willing Executioners: Ordinary Germans and the Holocaust* in 1996.[42] Goldhagen focused on the *Sonderweg* of German antisemitism and, in so doing, reawakened the intentionalist/functionalist debate of Dawidowicz's period.[43] His argument was straightforward. Nineteenth-century antisemitism, an admixture of older Christian anti-Judaism and modern political, economic, and racial forms, prepared German society for what he called a distinctly "eliminationist" attitude toward the Jews, which penetrated into every social class, profession, administrative body, and cultural form in twentieth-century Germany. Employing *Alltagsgeschichte*, Goldhagen turned this historical methodology on its head. He argued that the German people as a collective whole, not merely the Nazis and their official leadership cadres, embraced the eliminationist view of the Jews that made the Final Solution a German national project. The endemic nature of German antisemitism meant that hatred of the Jews inhered in German society even during the liberal Weimar Republic. In Goldhagen's reading, German antisemitism produced Hitler—not the other way around.[44] As Dawidowicz had done, Goldhagen argued that the antisemitic rhetoric and policies of the 1930s paved the way for the "genocidal solution."[45]

Goldhagen's book garnered stellar reviews and went into numerous reprintings in the United States. It was also very well received by the German public.[46] Yet professional historians and scholars of modern German history and the Holocaust sharply critiqued his interpretation.[47] Steven Aschheim noted that the scholarly opprobrium of *Hitler's Willing Executioners* was directly correlated to its public approbation. Scholars criticized Goldhagen's book for its monocausality, its lack of nuance, and its simplistic archetype history that posited an essential divide between good and evil, German and Jew, perpetrator and victim, banality and monstrosity, and particularism and universalism,[48] charges similar to those cast against Dawidowicz.

In the mid-1970s, the American public had hailed Dawidowicz's interpretation of the centrality of Hitler's ideology in designing the Final Solution and her assertion that antisemitism was the core element in Nazi ideology. The New York intellectuals believed that *The War Against the Jews* made a compelling case for the early and deep roots in Hitler's mind and rhetoric for the Final Solution. Their support of her views helped to make her a household name. Dawidowicz's phrase "the war against the Jews" became common parlance, and while the academy has dismissed Dawidowicz's historiography, her work on Nazism and the Final Solution is still alive in the public's historical consciousness. *The War Against the Jews* is still in print, its title—and its argument— resistant to erasure.[49]

HISTORICAL AGENCY: WHO HAS IT?

The concept of "historical agency," so critical to historical inquiry, underlay much of Dawidowicz's historiography and informed her political thinking. Insisting on free will as a constitutive component of the human condition, Dawidowicz nonetheless had her biases about which historical actors had agency, a judgment linked to her ideas of what constituted "legitimate" culture. It is clear that she believed that the Jews of Eastern Europe, particularly the heirs to Polish Jewry's millennial civilization, embodied a distinct and special—even luminous—culture. Its valorization of the written word gave the Jews historical agency and a sense of collective destiny. In extremis, the Jews trapped in Nazi-occupied Europe expressed their agency by their will to live, as evidenced by the extensive cultural institutions they created even when starving in Nazi ghettos.

Yet, she was firm in her conviction that the Nazi-appointed Jewish head-ships of the Nazi ghettos (the *Judenräte*) had limited agency. The ability of the men appointed by the Nazis to act freely was circumscribed by barbaric circumstances beyond their control.[50] In *The Holocaust and the Historians*, she took Hannah Arendt to task for her accusations again the *Judenräte*:

> What was additionally perplexing was Miss Arendt's failure to give consid-eration to a subject of relevant and fundamental concern, particularly to a political philosopher: *the limits of freedom and the operation of necessity under conditions of extreme persecution*. Such a discussion might have yielded more understanding of the moral predicament in which the officials of the Juden-räte found themselves.[51]

Dawidowicz defended the actions of the men of the *Judenräte*, even though their contemporaries and, later, some of the survivors condemned them as collaborators or accomplices.[52] She took the position that "in discussing the deeds of the handful of Jewish leaders who have been charged by survivors and scholars with criminal behavior, I have been persuaded by Professor Her-bert Butterfield's view that the historian can never quite know men from the inside, because he can never carry his investigation into the interiority of their minds and hearts, where 'the final play of motive and the point of responsibility' are decided."[53]

Dawidowicz did, nonetheless, judge the interiority of Germans, writing that "in planning and executing the Final Solution, [they] played the role of the Devil and his hosts."[54] The elite leadership among the Nazis, inspired by Hitler's demonic antisemitism, had historical agency. With free will, they trespassed the universal human commandment not to murder by designing a genocide. For many years after the war, Dawidowicz grouped "ordinary Ger-mans" into her condemnation of Nazi brutality. Convinced that they had been indoctrinated with antisemitic views, she found them as guilty as their leaders in "the war against the Jews." Yet by 1986, she allowed that a new generation of (West) Germans could once again assert their free will, reentering human society with the ability to distinguish between right and wrong. The *Sonderweg* was not immutable.

This concession, however, did not extend to those subjects of the Soviet Union and its satellites. Dawidowicz's anti-communism and her view of the totalitarian nature of Soviet society left no room for "Soviet subjectivity." As we have seen from her assessment of Polish communist historiography, her book reviews, and her articles on Soviet society and culture—and on the Jews who lived within the Eastern Bloc—anyone who supported the Communist regimes relinquished historical agency. She had retorted to Reuben Ainsztein, "It is commonly known—or so I had thought—that freedom of historical inquiry was destroyed in the Soviet Union and in other Communist dictatorships."[55] In Dawidowicz's view, Soviet, Polish, and East German citizens—including Jews—constrained by totalitarianism, could not be free historical actors. History was the handmaiden of the state and party. Taking her cue from Zelig Kalmanovitch, among other anticommunist Yiddishists whom she knew in Poland and in the United States, Dawidowicz believed that Bolshevism could not a priori allow any form of autonomous Jewish historical agency.

Thus, although Dawidowicz absolved the men of the *Judenräte* of their morally problematic actions because they had limited agency to defy the Nazis' genocidal policies, she did not absolve Jewish communists of their actions, which she saw as tantamount, if not equivalent, to the Nazis' persecution of the Jews. Jewish communists, in Dawidowicz's view, aided the destruction of Jewish culture, the source of the Jewish people's survival. Nothing they did could mitigate their support of the Soviet Union and its universalist agenda.

Dawidowicz's evolving definition that Jewish culture had to include a connection to Judaism led her to project her American worldview and her American Jewishness onto the identities of the Jews behind the Iron Curtain. Despite her East European diaspora nationalist sensibilities and her commitment to the Jews as a transnational people, Dawidowicz absorbed and promoted the American view of religious liberty as a sine qua non of the definition of freedom. Without Judaism, no Soviet Jew or Polish Jew under communism could remain Jewish because, as she reasoned, no American Jew—particularly as the ties of ethnicity loosened—would be able to remain Jewish without Judaism.

As discussed earlier, by the 1980s, Dawidowicz, believing that the forces of Yiddishist secularism and ethnicity no longer could be counted on to ensure a Jewish future, moved toward a selective observance of Jewish law. The decline of legal, social, and residential antisemitism in the United States, coupled with weaker ethnic ties among Jews, illustrated that discrimination played a more muted role in Jewish identity formation than it had previously. It was this very American perspective that explains how Dawidowicz missed the fact that many Soviet Jews and Jews in the Eastern Bloc constructed their Jewish identities in distinctly secular and ethnic terms. Despite eighty years of religious suppression and the official illegality of antisemitism that nonetheless continued to influence society, some Jews in communist countries retained a strong sense of Jewishness and constructed their identities with a commitment to the Jewish people. Newer works on Soviet and East European Jewish culture under communism insist on the agency of its subjects,[56] arguing that Soviet Jews and Jews from the Eastern Bloc expressed their historical agency as Jews, albeit in ways unfamiliar to Jews in the American diaspora. And even Yiddish survived, not only in the crevices of Jewish identity but as a full expression of Soviet belonging.[57]

Dawidowicz's transnationality traveled in both directions and created cultural misunderstandings that were shaped, in part, by her politics. She viewed American Jews through her experience in and commitment to the holistic culture of East European Jewry and viewed Soviet Jews and other Jewish communities living under communism through her postwar American lens. Despite her legitimate agony at what had been lost during Hitler's "war against the Jews," the millennial foundation of premodern Polish Jewish life had not been completely erased among all the East European Jews who survived the Nazi onslaught and Soviet rule.[58] Because Dawidowicz died just as the wall between the Soviet Union and the West was falling, we cannot know how—or if—she would have revisited her opinion about historical agency under communism.

Dawidowicz's politics also informed her view of the historical agency—or lack thereof—of unlikely bedfellows: African Americans and Polish gentiles. Conflating the postwar conflicts among urban African Americans and Jews as an iteration of East European tensions between rural gentile peasants and urban Jews, Dawidowicz viewed the historical agency of African Americans who demanded group rights—in a manner that, in her assessment, compromised the liberal institutions that had safeguarded Jewish mobility—negatively. Civil rights tactics that crossed the boundary of "responsible" activism and employed violence—both imagined and real—triggered Dawidowicz's deep-seated fear of East European peasant violence and street hooliganism.[59] She never forgave the Poles for what she believed was their willing cooperation with the Nazi regime and did not trust the historical agency of nationalist African Americans. In her October 1958 memo "Negro-Jewish Tensions," written while working at the AJC, Dawidowicz concluded that Jewish and African American aspirations for separatism derived from different causes. Jews, she wrote, want "to preserve their distinctiveness of culture and group, while Negroes are not typically concerned about preserving distinctiveness." Relying on Gunnar Myrdal's work, Dawidowicz concluded that African Americans avoided white society "from a need to find shelter from bad treatment," while "deliberate Jewish separatism is likely to arise . . . from survivalist calculations."[60] In short, Jewish historical agency was proactive, while that of African Americans was reactive.

In distancing herself from Poles' and African Americans' historical agency, Dawidowicz reflected the cultural bias of her East European immigrant background and race. Paradoxically, despite—or because of—the complexity of the relationship between the modernizing aspirations of East European Jews and Western culture—as discussed in chapter 9—Dawidowicz also looked westward. Reared in a home and educated in schools that valued the classical West European canon, she came of age when East European immigrant Jews ardently participated in high culture, seeing European-inflected American letters as a ticket to belonging.[61] She had made the journey from periphery to center, from the Bronx and Queens to Manhattan's Upper West Side. In that arc of her personal transformation, she internalized the white American apprehension about African American culture and symbolically conflated it with the Jewish denigration of gentile Polish culture. If Dawidowicz's transnationality gave her a deep relationship to the Jews as a global people and to their past in

Lucy S. Dawidowicz's honorary degree from Hebrew Union College–Jewish Institute of Religion, June 4, 1978, with Alfred Gottschalk, Arthur Levitt, Dr. Jules Backman, Matthew H. Rosse, Milton Petrie, and Max Koeppel. (Courtesy the American Jewish Historical Society)

Szymon Dawidowicz, 1979.
(Courtesy Laurie Sapakoff)

Lucy S. Dawidowicz, 1988.
(Courtesy the American
Jewish Historical Society)

Headstones of Szymon and Lucy S. Dawidowicz, Cedar Park Cemetery, Paramus, New Jersey. (Courtesy Laurie Sapakoff)

Europe, it also created contradictions in her understanding of their present in the United States.

A diaspora nationalist to the end of her days, though no longer wedded to Yiddishism as an ideology, Dawidowicz tirelessly defended the legitimacy of the Jews' claims to self-definition and self-determination wherever they lived. Just as she was aware of the political shifts in the American Jewish landscape, she also sensed the growing tension for American Jews, who, reluctant to insist on Jewish group rights, nonetheless began to feel challenged by a cultural climate increasingly inhospitable to Jewish collective distinctiveness. She may have doubted that America, which had granted European Jewish immigrants such unlimited possibility, freedom, and security, was still truly hospitable to the holistic civilization of East European Jewish peoplehood. Even as Dawidowicz moved toward an embrace of Jewish religious practice, and politically from left to right, it was East European Jewish culture, written from right to left in her "beloved" Yiddish *alef-beys*, that formed the deepest wellspring of her Jewish identity. Yet *yidishkayt*, her anchor, fit uneasily into the post-ethnic, multicultural landscape of late twentieth-century America.

At the time of her death in 1990 (and still today), the majority of American Jews had not heeded Dawidowicz's call for a political realignment with the Republican Party. Yet she anticipated the deepening fissure between American Jews (as well as their Israeli Jewish compatriots) who consider liberalism to be a "Jewish" value and those who do not. The polarization—some call it a Jewish civil war—between liberal-integrationists on the Left and conservative-particularists on the Right has increased enormously in the past twenty-five years. As the ultra-Orthodox population of Jews has continued to grow, becoming a larger percentage of the American (and Israeli) Jewish demographic with greater political power, so has the tension between Jews and the liberal institutions of society.[62] If in the 1980s Dawidowicz miscalculated American Jewish political inclinations, it is well to remember her prescience. Insisting that the hallowed "American Jewish liberal tradition" was historically contingent, she anticipated many of today's political polarities and cultural challenges.

APPENDIX

Lucy S. Dawidowicz was a prolific and methodical correspondent, preserving both the letters written to her and her replies, as well as noting the date on which she did or did not respond—the latter with a clear red comment, "not replied." Her distinctive personal voice—its clarity, incisiveness, anger, and humor—emerges from her letters. I reproduce thirty-one letters here to illustrate the wide range of correspondents and issues that Dawidowicz engaged with throughout her life and to reveal a fuller sense of her inner life. I have selected these letters from hundreds to reflect their topical, linguistic, chronological, and emotional diversity. Each letter is prefaced by a short explanation of its provenance and its writer's or recipient's biography. I have reproduced them in chronological order. I have translated the German, Hebrew, and Yiddish originals, and have reproduced the German and transliterated Yiddish of distinct letters. Dawidowicz signed many of the letters in hand, so when her name does not appear in the carbon copies of the letters, I have not included it in the transcriptions.

Lucy S. Dawidowicz to Albert Einstein, March 16, 1953

(With permission of Laurie Sapakoff; Dawidowicz private papers)

My dear Professor Einstein:

In the course of reading, for professional purposes, the *Morning Freiheit*, Yiddish Communist daily, I was shocked and dismayed to see that you had lent your name to a Communist-sponsored celebration of the 10th anniversary of the Warsaw Ghetto Uprising.

I am taking the liberty of writing to you about my reactions because I hope you were unaware of the character of the group that sought your endorsement.

The group sponsoring this particular memorial of the Warsaw Ghetto consists of several Communist-directed fraternal organizations, headed by professional Communists formerly associated with the now defunct American Biro-Bidjan Committee (Ambijan). In the Jewish community, this group has spearheaded the various Communist propaganda drives; it has consistently sided with the Soviet Union and against the United States and has revealed itself to be part of the international Communist conspiracy.

Having no standing in the Jewish community, this group consistently strives to gain acceptance and broaden its circle of influence. The planned Warsaw Ghetto memorial is a means to this end, because these Communists are well aware of the honor paid by Jews throughout the world to the Warsaw Ghetto uprising. They know also that the Jewish community is planning to commemorate this tenth anniversary.

Actually, the Communist undertaking is nothing less than a desecration of the Warsaw Ghetto and all it means. In the ghetto, the Communists were anathemized by the Jews because of the Hitler-Stalin pact. Until 1941, the Communists were totally excommunicated from the Jewish community, even behind the Nazi ghetto walls. Their position changed little even after Germany attacked Russia[,] and until the very end, when the Jews of the Warsaw Ghetto rose up against the Nazis, the Communists within the ghetto were excluded from the underground community life. Furthermore, in subsequent years, after the war was over, they did not identify themselves with that tragic and glorious period of Jewish history. They did not then commemorate the Warsaw Ghetto. But as the years passed, the Communists began to rewrite this particular chapter in history, as they have rewritten and falsified many others. It is their claim now that they initiated and carried through the uprising. Nothing is further from the truth, but time obliterates much. That is why the Communists now memorialize the Warsaw Ghetto and did not do so several years ago. Thus, it is all the more painful to see the Communists usurp and degrade one of the most heroic chapters in modern Jewish history.

There is indeed another, more immediate reason why no support should be given this group. The recent exposure of official anti-Semitism in the Soviet Union and its satellites has significantly weakened the influence of Communist and pro-Communist groups among American Jews. The myth of Soviet philo-Semitism has finally collapsed. The Communist groups no longer have any prestige. Your name in support of an undertaking of theirs gives them much needed prestige. It can potentially rally new forces to them.

I am sure that you would not intend this to happen. As a scientist, you are surely aware of the suffocation, indeed the death, of free scientific inquiry in the Soviet Union. As a Jew, you are certainly not impervious to the disclosures of Soviet anti-Semitism. As a free man, you cannot be indifferent to the fate of millions in slave-labor camps and many more millions living out their lives in daily terror.

Please forgive me if this letter sounds impertinent. I had not so intended, since I have the profoundest respect and admiration for you. It was the great pain I felt, seeing your name associated with a Communist group, particularly in relation to the Warsaw Ghetto, that impelled me to write to you.

Yours most sincerely,

Albert Einstein to Lucy S. Dawidowicz, March 19, 1953

(With permission of the Albert Einstein Archives, Israel National Library; Dawidowicz private papers)

Dear Miss Dawidowicz:

Thank you for your letter of March 16th. A few days ago Dr. I[gnacy]. Schwartzbart of the World Jewish Congress[1] already informed me about the political nature of the "United Committee for the Memorial of the Warsaw Ghetto Uprising," of which I had been unaware when I consented to act as a sponsor. This was, of course, a mistake. As I have already written Dr. Schwartzbart I could not make up my mind to revoke my consent fearing that still worse misinterpretations could result from such a withdrawal.

Sincerely yours, Albert Einstein.

Born in Rzeszów, Poland, in 1929 (d. 2014), Maurice Friedberg was a scholar of Russian literature, focusing on the intersection of literature and society and publishing extensively on issues of censorship and ideology. His books included Russian Classics in Soviet Jackets, *about the legacy of prerevolutionary literature;* A Decade of Euphoria, *which examined the role of translated Western fiction, poetry, and drama in post-Stalinist Russia; and* Literary Translation in Russia, *which treated the role of translation in the overall literary process—including censorship—from the eighteenth century until the dissolution of the USSR in 1991. Friedberg was invited to the White House to brief President Ronald Reagan on problems of Soviet culture prior to the president's state visit to Moscow in 1988. He taught at the University of Illinois for most of his distinguished career.*

Maurice Friedberg to Lucy S. Dawidowicz, February 26, 1966

(With permission of Edna and Rachel Friedberg; Dawidowicz Papers, box 77, folder 9.)

P.S. PLEASE FORGIVE THE GALICIAN*LITVAK INCONSISTENCIES. I DON'T HAVE THEM IN SPEECH, BUT THEY DO COME THROUGH IN WRITING.

[Friedberg wrote the letter in transliterated Yiddish.]

Khosheve khaverte lusi,

Raishes kol, vil ikh bay aykh betn mekhile far shraybn mame-loshn oif an englisher shrayb-mashin. Azoi vi in der yidisher medine hob ikh gekent araynbrengen nur ayn shrayb-mashin, hob ikh nit gehat kayn breyre un gebrakht a mashin mit a lateinishn alef-beis. Aza ponm hobn mir, yidn, in Yerusholaim. Men tor nit forn shabes, men tor nit esen treif—mayle, vos men tor nit, volt nokh geven halbe tsores, oben men *ken nit*—un men ken nit brengen a yidishe shrayb mashin un es iz shver tsu gefunen a yidn zol redn yidish on di ale asire-babilonishe eynflusn, vi lemoshl: "der madrikh fun dem mekhes hot mir gezogt az men muz hobn savlanut, un es velt zayn beseder."

A shaynm dank far tsushikn mir di amerikn-dzhuish yirbuk, un oikh di ale tsaytungen.

Mir hobn gezen mit a por teg tsurik ayere khaverte Perl Kacher. Ze[yer] an ongeneme un kluge froi. Zi hot unz gefregt tsu ir hot bedaye tsu kumn do oif a bazukh. Oib yo, veln mir shoin gefunen a por yidn—take nit mer vu a minyen—mit velkhe ir vert kenen frabrengen [sic, should be "farbrengen"] an ovnt un redn yidish. Mit a por teg tsurik hob ikh geredt mit prezident Shazar, un azoi vi es zaynen nit genev [sic, should be "geven"] kain eydes, un tsvay politsayn hobn gehit di tirn, hobn mir, beshtike, bsod godl, geret yidish. Nur dir dertsel ikh dos, un tsvishn unz zol es blaybn.

Mayn yidine, borekh hashem, redt shoyn hebreish, abisl loshn koidesh un a sakh loshn hore. Zi hot zikh oisgelernt fun unzer dinst (ikh muz dir erklern: gevirim farmogn do vash mashinen, un oreme layt, vu lemoshel melamdim, nit far aykh gedakht, muzn zikh gebn an aytse mit a dinst velkhe vasht—ir vayst dokh vos). Di tokhter, geloibt hashem yiborekh (ir zet vi der opium fun dem folk baaynflust mayn shprakh?) vakst, shloft bay tog un shrayt bay nakht. Ikh hob a teorie: ir dakht zikh az zi iz in amerike, dos hayst az zi halt fun istern standard taym.

Ikh hob gezen reb benyomin eliav un er hot mir gezogt az ir shraybt an artikl far dem zhurnal "amerika." Oib ikh ken aikh epes helfn (tsum baishpil, in di aroikumen [sic, should be "aroiskumen"] fun shtil, kday es zol aroiskumen beser oif rusish) shraybt mir.

Efsher kent ir mir tun a toive? Tsu makht di YIVO velkhe es iz forbereitungen tsu dem fuftsiksten yortseit fun Sholem-Aleikhem? Un oib take yo, tsu kent ir mir tsushiken protim? Ikh volt aykh nit matriakh geven, ober tsu farshpraytn yidishkeit do in Yerusholaim iz a heilike zakh, un ir velt hobn a groise mitsve.

Beste grusn far aikh un reb shimenen fun mir un mayn ploineste.

Maurice (ר' מאיר משה בן יצחק פרידברג)

P.S. Zint ekh bin gevorn a tate fun a yidihsher [sic, should be "yidisher"] tokhter hob ikh nokh a daynge oifn kop: efsher vayst ir epes fun a shidekh far ir? Do in Yerusholaim iz es nit azoi poshet: men fregt aykh bald vegn nadanim un vi fil yorn kest zayt ir berayt tsu gebn dem khosen.

Esteemed friend Lucy:

First, forgive me for writing [our] mother tongue [Yiddish] on an English typewriter. Because in the Jewish state, I could only bring one typewriter, I had no choice but to bring one with the Latin alphabet. Such respectability do we Jews have in Jerusalem. One dare not travel on the Sabbath, one dare not eat unkosher meat—indeed, what one shouldn't dare do is half a problem— and one cannot bring a Yiddish typewriter, and it is difficult to find a Jew who can speak Yiddish without all of the Assyrian-Babylonian influences, such as: "The guide from customs told me that one should have patience and it will be okay."[2]

Thank you for sending the *American Jewish Year Book* as well as all the newspapers to me.

A few days ago we saw your friend Pearl Ketcher. She is a very pleasant and smart woman. She asked us if you are planning to come here for a visit. If yes, we will at once find a few Jews—indeed not more than a quorum of ten—with whom you can spend an evening and speak Yiddish. A few days ago, I spoke with President Shazar, and since there were no witnesses, and two policemen manned the doors, we, quietly, in great secrecy, spoke Yiddish. I am only telling this to you and it should remain between us.

My wife, thank God, already speaks Hebrew, a little bit of the holy language and a lot of gossip. She learned it from our maid (I have to explain: rich people here have washing machines, and poor people, for example, teachers, don't ask, have to make do with a maid who washes—you know what, after all).

Our daughter, may God be blessed (you see how the opium of the masses has influenced my speech?) is growing, she sleeps during the day and cries at night. I have a theory: she thinks she is in America, meaning, she is still on Eastern Standard Time.

I saw Mr. Benjamin Eliav and he told me that you are writing an article for the journal, *Amerika*.[3] If I can help you with something (for example, in matters of style so it comes out better in Russian), write to me.

Perhaps you can you do me a favor? Is the YIVO, whatever it is, making arrangements for the fiftieth anniversary of Sholem Aleichem's death? And if indeed, yes, can you send the details to me? I don't want to burden you but to spread *yidishkayt* here in Jerusalem is a sacred matter and you will be doing a great good deed (*mitzvah*).

Best wishes to you and Mr. Szymon from me and my Mrs.

R. Meyer Moyshe ben Yitskhok Fridberg
(Maurice)

P.S. Since I have become a father of a Jewish daughter I have another worry on my head: perhaps you know of a match for her? It is not so simple here in Jerusalem: everyone asks immediately about the dowries and how many years of parental support you are prepared to give the groom.

Lucy S. Dawidowicz to Maurice Friedberg, March 4, 1966

(With permission of Laurie Sapakoff; Dawidowicz private papers)

Dear Maurice, otherwise known as Meir moyshe reb yitskhok's:

Your letter was a jewel and I think that for a while I will take it along to parties (the few that I go to—or am invited ot [*sic*]) and thereafter will send it to the Yivo for them to preserve and cherish in their archives. It will in centuries to come be used extensively by scholars to show the conditions under which Jews managed to keep Yiddish alive in a Hebraist state.

The Yivo, nit far aykh gedakht [don't ask], is not marking Sholem Aleichem's yoyvl [anniversary] in any formal way. Dr. Weinreich told me that they had had some ideas about publishing something on same and Jewish humor but nothing came of it. I am sure, however, that the Yiddishist kultur-mentchn (like the Congress for Jewish Culture, etc.) will arrange a meeting with lectures.

If my friend Pearl is so smart, why can't she put your little girl on Israeli time instead of New York-Miami time. Israel is supposed to be a land of transformations anyway.

As for *Amerika*. I wrote the article, which I thought politically impeccable, grammatically correct, and a little dull. Apparently, the editorial board thought so too, and also too highbrow, though that's not true. Jacob Sloan, formerly an editor of the American Jewish Year Book, which the president of Israel likes, is now "lightening" it up (he is, obviously, on the staff of *Amerika*). He keeps talking about "human interest" and I'm a little worried about a Readers Digest tone, but the only thing to do is to wait and see what will emerge from his editorial surgery and stitching. I am hoping that we will be able eventually to see the Russian translation and then I would like very much for you to go over it. When I wrote the article, I thought of this problem of translation. For example, Khaverim kol yisroel ["All Jews are responsible for one another"]. Would this come out as tovarischi? Gvald. [Woe is me]. The ancient Hebrews were the original party members.

Have a happy Purim and don't get too drunk. Szymon sends his best to you and Barbara, dos zelbe fun mir tsu hern [the same from me].

Zeit mir gezunt un shtark un gedenkt az es iz do a got oif der velt, [Be healthy and strong, and remember that there is a God in the world].

———

Dr. Pearl Ketcher (1914–2003) was a British physician who worked with the JDC in postwar Germany. She and Lucy became fast friends in the British Zone of Occupation, where Ketcher was Dr. Fritz Spanier's assistant medical director in Belsen and later the chief medical officer in Poppendorf, one of the three DP camps to which the refugees from the Exodus were interned. Ketcher immigrated to Israel in 1949 and established neonatal clinics in the Negev before making her permanent home on 16 David Marcus Street in Jerusalem. She wrote this letter a week after the Six-Day War.

Pearl Ketcher to Lucy S. and Szymon Dawidowicz, June 15, 1967

(With permission of Yael Katz and Esti Berk; Dawidowicz private papers)

My dear dear Lucy & Szymon:

Today I received your letter so you can tell we are not too haywire here.

Last week—about a thousand years ago we were in the middle of a war—but since then we celebrated Shavuot yesterday—true I couldn't quite get up enough enthusiasm to make blintzes but, ברוך השם (Thank God), we weren't being shelled and the immediate war was past.

It wasn't going to be a very coherent letter, because I am still a little dazed. The two weeks before the war were very tense and unpleasant, but the[n] when the war did begin, we weren't expecting it. When the siren went I didn't really believe it and went to my normal work—but then decided to go to my emergency station at a hospital (as anesthetist). On my way there the shelling and firing began really properly and I didn't know whether to drive on or stop. I compromised and stopped for a while and then drove on and arrived all intact at hospital. There—wounded had already arrived. I have seen boys of the British and American services—but I must still take my hat off to the Israeli army—the lads are real beautiful human beings—not a murmur from the wounded lads and indeed all the civilian population behaved wonderfully. Last week Patrick O'Donovan—a British newspaperman—wrote an article for the *London Observer*, "One is Almost Ashamed *Not* to be a Jew." The whole war was so incredibly fast that we could hardly keep up with it—we had the radio over in the vicinity of the operating theater. It was all very very unpleasant. My parents and [sister] Margie were in the house and I was mostly away. My sister Leila is up in the North where fighting was very severe—but all of the family are well. However, now that the initial excitement is over, the utter weariness is here and the pain as we hear of the ones who haven't returned. Since it's such a tiny place—one knows so many of them. Moish hasn't been here since the beginning of the war—but he phones every day. Communications incidentally have been good. Incidentally—even tho' it would be nice to hear your voice— you really can cancel the phone call—now that you know we are well (memories of Sinai). I am glad I am here this time.

Lots and lots of love—I will write again soon.

Pearl

I am back at normal work again. And this minute I am off to the hairdresser to have my hair washed. P

––

Shulamith (née Schwartz) Nardi (1909–2002) was educated in New York City in a Zionist family and settled in Palestine with her husband, Noah Nardi, in 1934. She was an accomplished English editor and Hebrew-English translator and worked in both the United States and in Israel. When Zalman Shazar became president, he asked her to join his staff as an advisor on Diaspora affairs.

Shulamith Nardi, Assistant to the President of Israel, Zalman Shazar, to Lucy S. Dawidowicz, June 26, 1969

(With permission of Zvia and Eran Nardi; Dawidowicz private papers)

Dear Lucy Dawidowicz,

President Shazar, having happily read your letter, appreciatively scanned your article in Commentary,[4] and noted once more how good it is to correspond in Yiddish with an American writer, had every intention of writing you in Yiddish himself to tell you all this. He has, however, been so inundated by official duties and meetings lately that—in desperation—he asked me to write in his name (and, sadly, I'm one of those English communicators!). This, I hope, will not detract too much from the genuineness of his sentiments nor from the warmth of the greetings he sends both you and your husband (with which in my minor way I beg to associate myself).

The President trusts, too, that he will be seeing you both in Israel in the not too distant future.

Cordially,

—

Gavin Langmuir (1924–2005) was a medieval historian whose work focused on the Jews of medieval England and the history of antisemitism. His books included Toward a Definition of Antisemitism *and* History, Religion, and Antisemitism. *He spent most of his academic career at Stanford University.*

Gavin Langmuir to Lucy S. Dawidowicz, July 28, 1970

(With permission of the estate of Professor Gavin I. Langmuir; Dawidowicz private papers)

Dear Lucy:

To you about to take your holidays in the Tetons and God's country (I am a Canadian), salutations from one sunk in the distractions from the desirable caused by summer school. I write at home, impelled by your concern about official stationary to write on regular paper, and surrounded by my books and notes, which are kept far from the haunts of students. Much as I sympathize with much of the student concern, and even most of the student actions, I don't want to see eight years of work go up in the smoke of a tactical foray by the enragés. At least summer school has the advantage of a quiet political scene, unusually docile students, and no administrative work. Under those conditions a university can function well, even without a president. Come the fall and the exasperation with the political scene which I will share with the students, the picture may be very different.

Thank you for your kind words about what has happened to my marriage. Fortunately, if I can put it that way, trouble had been brewing for some time before, and it is now nearly a year from the bad news, so I am enjoying life thoroughly again. I was somewhat depressed when I finally got around to reading John Updike's Couples (I had him in a basic course at Harvard), for it seemed somewhat relevant, even if I have not experienced any of that fast marital switching. And I didn't like the picture. Since my return I seem to have heard of more marriages on the rocks than ever before. What used to be growing statistics are becoming a major concrete part of life's pattern. But I hope to find someone with whom I can put together a viable and lasting marriage. In any case, life is presently exciting and rewarding.

I am delighted that you have so enjoyed your new occupation and, I read through the lines, succeeded so well. Teaching can be most rewarding when good students are interested in what you are trying to uncover. I am not as convinced as you that teachers, even very good teachers, exercise great power over their charges—possibly because I am not teaching women in a denominational institution. My own impression is that one can provide a vehicle where through formed desires and abilities can find expression, but not much more. Very rarely there is the bright student who takes one as a model more deeply and permanently, but even then the predispositions and need for that kind of model existed before the contact. But the excitement of watching a bright, fresh mind grappling with the issues which concern one is great—and the results frequently fascinating for one's own work because of the changed perspective between the generations.

If you can teach and work efficiently on a book at the same time, you are a better man than I am Gunga Din. I can do research alright, but I find writing, with all the concentration it takes in my case, very difficult when I also have to teach and do committee work and the like. I shall wait impatiently for the outcome. My own work is proceeding slowly as usual, and if it is pretty well done in a year, I shall be happily surprised. I feel increasingly sure that I have something to say, but it is long and difficult. Your article in the July Commentary made me even surer![5]

I agree completely with your strictures on the ADL series. It is amazingly shoddy work. But on the point that you are particularly concerned with, I think the basic problem is not that of producing a standard scale but that of agreeing on what is meant by antisemitism—the problem with [which] my book is centrally concerned. If all hostility of all kinds against Jews is treated as anti-semitism, then it will be impossible to produce a meaningful standard scale, because one will be trying to measure very different things at once—which reminds me of an old joke about the peasant family which tried to get a collective urine analysis. I think I have a set of distinctions which are valuable and may even be practical.

That brings me around to the proposed conference which Milton Himmel-farb wrote to me about. (The coincidence with my writing to you, demonstrated by his knowledge of my Oxford address was so striking as to seem conclusive. Did you have nothing to do with the invitation?). If all that comes off and I am in New York in October, I shall look forward muchly to seeing you again and, hopefully, meeting your husband.

We can then discuss the wretched state of American society, which I find thoroughly disheartening. Revolutionary situations threaten things important even to those in favour of radical change. I am fearful of the defensive and increasingly active right. Nixon and his cabinet seem a proof of every criticism the radicals have been making, and the rednecks and hard hats are what one always knew, but worse in movement. The liberal center seems aimless, leaderless, and so defensive that it too does not want to look too closely at the evils which have so grown under the regime of due process. The widening Jewish swing to the right, however comprehensible, also saddens me. I find that I agree most with the intelligent radicals in regard to their analysis and critique of contemporary society, but I part company with most of their strategy for remdying [sic] the evils. While I am not opposed to illegality, (demonstrations, sit-ins, riots, etc.) so long as nothing else will make people do anything, I cannot apply Fanon or Mao to the most developed country, and I do not think the way to utopia lies through the achievement of total breakdown, starting with the universities. I know that universities were supremely blind to the black issue until the riots, BSU's [Black Student Unions], and particularly [Martin Luther] King's death, and I cannot put the sanctification of liberal procedure over a more rapid remedy of the black situation. I know that mounting pressure is needed to make universities, professors, begin to become aware of how value-oriented and indoctrinating most of the curriculum is (a knowledge of Africa may be more relevant today than Latin, which only recently ceased to be a requirement for Oxford). I know all that and sympathize, and I know that our curriculum has not given students the habit of analyzing the problems which they—and I—deem relevant. But I don't know how to get them now to back up their gut reactions with more intelligent analysis—or how to persuade the older generation that some things have to be done. That produces despair, but an atmosphere in which certain problems are being aired and there is some movement gives hope.

I found Dorothy Rabinowitz['s] picture of the radicalized professor brilliant with fascinating insights.[6] Much as I enjoyed it, however, it horrified me by its monolithic stereotypy. Imagine that brilliance applied to an equally negative stereotype of The Jew. And the thoroughly negative approach to the whole cry for change was profoundly depressing. We know the fate of the Bourbons. If students are accused of emotion without reason, what of that part of the older generation which cuts back on tax grants and donations to universities to punish their permissiveness—thereby immensely aiding the extreme radicals in their goal of bringing universities to a halt, as a very little analysis would suggest. Punish the symptoms and don't look at the causes so it will all fade away. The analysis of the brighter radicals is so far ahead of the gut reactions of Reagan and Nixon on the basic condition of American society. Polarization has deprived all sides of much of their capacity to think clearly. And if inexperience further weakens the position of many students, the play of calculated self-interest on the right narrows their vision at least equally.

Let us hope that we can discuss such matters and others face to face in October. I hope you have a wonderful holiday far from the urbanized civilization or mob.

Affectionately, Gavin

—

Yitzhak "Antek" Zuckerman (1915–81) was one of the surviving organizers of the Jewish Fighting Organization in the Warsaw Ghetto.[7] Zuckerman survived because he was outside the ghetto on the "Aryan" side when the uprising began and was later able to help his comrades escape through the sewers. Zuckerman later settled in Palestine, helping to establish the Ghetto Fighters kibbutz (Kibuz Loḥamei Hageta'ot) and the Ghetto Fighters' House, a museum on its premises. Researching The War Against the Jews, *Dawidowicz first wrote to him in September 1972: "In connection to a book I am writing about the* khurbn *(a history in English for the general reader), I am taking the opportunity to turn to you with a few questions about the specific functions of 'The Jewish National Committee' (JNC) and its relationship with the other parties that were active in organizing the uprising in Warsaw."[8] She sent Zuckerman a survey of questions and asked him to expand upon the issues related to the interactions among various Jewish political factions in the Warsaw Ghetto. He responded, after several requests, in late 1972. She turned to him again while working on* A Holocaust Reader, *in which she included several of his documents.*[9]

Libe S. Davidovitsh to Yitskhok Tsukerman, March 19, 1974

(With permission of Laurie Sapakoff; "Special" section, Archive of the Ghetto Fighters' House in memory of Yitzhak Katznelson, file 803, and copy in Dawidowicz private papers)

Esteemed Mr. Tsukerman:

Even though you didn't answer my earlier letter, I will try my luck with you again.

[I] have already finished writing my book on the Holocaust (*khurbn*) [*The War Against the Jews*] and [I] have given it to the publishing house. I'm now preparing a documentary collection about the Holocaust, a kind of supplement to my book. Among the documents that I will include in English translation is the report about the creation and development of the ŻOB [Żydowska Organizacja Bojowa / Jewish Fighting Organization], which you probaby wrote at the time. Can you authenticate your authorship for me? Were you the only author or was it a collective work? Are you prepared to write, in brief, where, when, and in which conditions the report was written?

Would you also be prepared to give me some biographical details that I can cite? I hope you will find the possiblity of meeting [with] me.

With respect, Libe S. Davidovitsh

Yitskhok Tsukerman to Libe S. Davidovitsh, March 29, 1974

(With permission of the archives of the Ghetto Fighters' House; "Special" section, Archive of the Ghetto Fighters' House in memory of Yitzhak Katznelson, file 803, and a copy in Dawidowicz private archive)

Esteemed Libe Davidovitsh:

I received your letter from March 19, 1974 and I feel a little bit guilty that I didn't respond to your earlier letter of August 8, 1973. The truth is as such: the main guilt falls upon me, [but] a little of the guilt is yours [as you wrote, "the writing is going very slowly and I have still not gotten to the chapter on the uprising," in [your] letter of August 8, 1973]. And last: the days of Yom Kippur [delayed my responding].

I have had the materials for several months, but one is always so busy and preoccupied. I am [now] sending:

1. A photostat of my letter to Bór-Komorowski,[10] November 26, 1943, made from the original copy that was kept in the archive of the Jewish National Committee and the ŻOB and was held for a long time by Dr. Adolf Berman[11]— today in our museum's archive. The original is, understandably, in London.

2. A photostat of Mordechai Tenenbaum's[12] appeal (on the second side on the right-hand corner is his postscript.[)] I enclose a typewritten copy.

3) The original Polish text from Mordechai Anielewicz's[13] letter (given by [Bernard] Mark). The signature "Kolocki" is, naturally, made up. "Malachi" is clearly written on the letter—only Berl Mark read it poorly—and in a conversation with me, confessed that he had made an error. In this case, not wanting to blame others.

I am also sending you the protocol from the meeting on March 1942 written by hand by Eliayahu Gutkowski[14] and improved by me years ago. You can compare it. The protocol from July 22 was not found.

And now to your letter of March 19, 1974:

I wrote the report for the Jewish Fighting Organization and I bear full responsibility for it. I wrote it quickly, in a few days—because I was told at the last minute (March 1944) that a shipment was going out right away to London. Four people read it: Zivia Lubetkin,[15] Marek Edelman, Joseph Sack [a member of Po'alei Zion], and Adolf Berman. Sak asked to add an unessential supplement: several sentences about the "degenerate Stehman."

On account of *sholem bayes* [Yid., "harmony"], I yielded to Berman in the excerpt on the anti-Fascist bloc, and wrote, that despite the failures in the bloc, it was the principle foundation for the Jewish Fighting Organization. Not then and not now have I appreciated its [the anti-Fascist bloc's] historical value.

In the report there is one conscious *"falsification."* In putting together the groups of the ŻOB, I wrote about the "left professional organizations" instead of the PPR [Polska Partia Robotnicza]. The reason is clear: the report went through the AK [Armia Krajowa] and the delegator to London. Throughout the time the AK accused us of being Moscow's agent. To admit that the PPR was a component of the ŻOB, I could not do, [and] erasing them from the historical record, I did not dare. Thus, the compromise: "left professional organizations."

And details about myself, in brief:

Born in Vilna ([even though] the *Encyclopedia Judaica* has determined that I was born in Warsaw), on December 13, 1915. Graduate of the Hebrew gymnasium, "Tarbut." From 1933 forward active in "Hechalutz" in Vilna, the Vilna

region, and later on in the center of "Hehalutz" and "Young Hehalutz" in Warsaw. Did (Zionist) training (*hakhshara*) on Kibbutz Lide and afterwards on the
agricultural farm, Grochów. With the unification of "Frayhayt" [Freedom] and
"Young Hehalutz" (1938), [I] was one of the two secretaries. With the outbreak
of the war, [I was in] Kovel. I was sent to Vilna, via Kovno, in order to get in touch
with the Land of Israel. I was sent back to the Soviet-occupied lands in order
to establish the secret organization ("Dror") in western Ukraine and western
Belarus. On the eve of Passover (1940), [I] was sent to Warsaw to the German
conspiracy. [I] edited the underground press [and] gave lectures in underground
seminars. [I] traveled throughout the province in its length and breadth.

To date.

And what happened afterwards has been described, more or less, in various
places.

Respectfully,
Yitskhok Tsukerman

Pearl Ketcher to Lucy S. Dawidowicz, July 16, 1975, erev ט ב'אב [Ninth of Av]

(With permission of Yael Katz and Esti Berk; Dawidowicz private papers)

Lucy, my love,

The Book arrived and Moish and I were both delighted to see it. I was also
excited to see it in print. I should think you should be pretty pleased with
yourself. It looks quite a formidable piece of work. I wonder whether Szymon
ate properly during the last year or two or three. The *N.Y. Times* is really "not
bad"—in fact, it could hardly have been better.[16]

I thought to begin to read it tonight instead of איכה [Lamentations].[17]

Lucy darling, congratulations and and and love to you both.

Pearl

Irving Howe to Lucy S. Dawidowicz, August 13, 1976

(With permission of Nina Howe; Dawidowicz Papers, box 76, folder 4)

Dear Lucy,

Once I was talking at a meeting with IB Singer. A lady was hassling him
about her nephew, who said this and said that. He got up and answered, "Lady,
you have a nephew—I have a niece." You have a paper on Jewish identity: I
return a copy of mine![18]

I won't circulate your paper, but I've read it. On the scholarship I bow, as always. But I still feel the issue itself needs to be sharpened. Two points: religion and peoplehood.

If you have religion, then there's nothing to debate about on that score. You have my respect. I don't have religion, and surely you don't want me to *will* it.

Which leaves peoplehood. But, Lucy, a deliberately vague phrase! Nationality, that's relatively precise. People living in or coming to Israel, have a nationality: they are Israelis (Does that necessarily mean Jews? Not formally). I don't have Jewish nationality, nor do you. We are, god help us, Americans. Yet we are also Jews, and I a non-religious Jew. Do I acknowledge peoplehood, and affirmatively so? Yes, in my way—I share a culture, I work actively in and for it (I don't just study it, I care about it, I participate in it); I share more—let's call it a destiny. But I have no program for continuity or survival: you've got me there. But do you? If you want to keep the synagogue alive, Halachah, etc.,; then you have a program for survival. If you want to settle in (rather than merely support) Israel. Otherwise, it seems to me, the difference between us is one of . . . temperature, or temperament.

Peoplehood is a word meant to cover a mystery, or something enormously hard to define—what it means to be a Jew if you don't join in a religious congregation, if you aren't a citizen of Israel, and—at the same time, the cultural substance of that peoplehood grows thinner and thinner, as we all know. But there are realities beyond words, or which words can't cope with.

So I see it as significant that you say on your last page peoplehood rather than nationality. And why did you do that, my dear Lucy? Because you wanted to include me in!

A sketch:

I.H.—I demand the right to my partial Jewishness, my programless Jewishness, my painful Jewishness.

L.D.—So who's stopping you? What do you want, approval, also?

I.H.—Yes, in a sense; not approval of what I say, but recognition that once "total Jewishness" came to end, as you nicely sketch it, then "partial Jewishness" is no longer an eccentricity but a form of being Jewish.

L.D.—Zoll zein mit glick! [Good luck!]

As I say, other than emotionally (unless you have indeed become a believer) I don't see that you're in a better state than I am, vis a vis Jewishness (the very word, by the way, like peoplehood, already connotes a certain ambiguity of status).

Yours, Irving[19]

Alfred Kazin to Lucy S. Dawidowicz, January 16, 1977

*(© 1977 Alfred Kazin, used by permission of the Wylie Agency, LLC; Dawido-
wicz private papers)*

Dear Lucy

It is a fine book and I have read every word of it with my usual pleasure in
your straightforward mind and your straightforward opinions. As I think I told
you moons ago, I have been a fan of yours ever since I came on your Commentary pieces—especially this one about the Belsen "banquet." You have a very
special scholarly function to perform just now, for no one else combines exact
knowledge of the Jewish community and of Jewish history in America with
such an inner devotion to the legendary *meaning* of the Jews. Howe's book[20]
was successful to the extent that he could marshal his Marxist training in sociological analysis. But you really do believe in *Jewish* history and a Jewish spirit,
and that more than anything else needs to be brought out these days in this
altogether secular and too easily psychologized condition we are living through.

The quotation from *Walker In The City*[21] was about what my parents had
impressed me as the quality and hazard of their life in the old country. It may
very well be true that *I* have not yet "chosen." But reading your book I am not
aware that you are any more devoted to the letter and ritual of orthodoxy than
I am. What you have chosen is Jewish history; I happen, in the same sense of
a scholarly choice, to have chosen literary history, modern history, etc. etc. I
am not aware that any great modern writer (speaking of literary history and
not of course of myself) has been orthodox. I even have a theory, my contribution to Jewish history, that not the "synagogue," "the collective," the *minyan*,
kept "Judaism" alive but the individuals, the mavericks, the poets and prophets,
sometimes even the rationalists within the bonds of orthodoxy, like Maimon-
ides. Odd as it may seem to think so, the great Jewish "unbelievers" who have
remained Jews, like Freud and Kafka and Chagall, even the Harry Wolfson
who called himself a non-observing orthodox Jew, have, under the conditions
of cultural cross-fertilization since the Enlightenment, been the transmitters
of our ancient heritage. Any [*sic*] in any event, as Freud knew and Marx in his
grave has found out, not choosing to be a Jew has been of no avail.

I believe in God and not in the synagogue. I believe, as Pascal said, in *Fire:
le Dieu d'Abraham, de Jacob, d'Isaac.* Can I believe alone? Not very well and not
for very long. I have not been a good, easily assured, successful "Believer." Belief
comes hard, it is an overwhelming form of love for the invisible, and sometimes
it is hard to believe in what we do not see or hear. But of course there is nothing

else *divine* to command my respect. So I go back and forth, as Hawthorne said of Melville, not happy in what he has attained and unable to be happy in anything else. God is the name of my desire. I know that is another literary quotation (this one from Tolstoy) but what does the orthodox man do in schul but read and quote and comment just as I do over my favorite writers?

No, it is not enough. But it is also a fact that you and I are the children of modernity, one that we use in the interests *of* "Judaism." My only solution must be to write it out, think it out, so that I can feel reasonably in touch with the unconscious past in me that says that anything else is meaningless.

Talking about modernism: my boss Allen Mandlebaum at the Graduate Center, who went through an old-fashioned Yeshiva education and ended up translating Vergil and Dante, was once asked what such an education was like. "Like being a lawyer who is allowed to read only Blackstone."

You could not be so fine, so peculiarly valuable a historian of people, if you weren't educated in and by "modernism." Yes, yes, Lucy says impatiently: but the "choice?" I am working on that. In some part my new book, very long and horribly personal but grounded in Jewish history of our day and of our city no less, is an effort to get myself together for the moment when the choice will be clearer than it is now.

See how you stimulate me to write letters on Sunday morning when all the world is sleeping. Thank you for the book and may nothing keep you from the important work you are pursuing.

Love and thanks always, Alfred.

Lucy S. Dawidowicz to Alfred Kazin, January 18, 1977

(With permission of Laurie Sapakoff; Alfred Kazin Papers, Henry W. and Albert A. Berg Collection of English and American Literature, New York Public Library, Astor Lenox and Tilden Foundations)

Dear Alfred:

Your letter came this morning and it has filled my whole day and I know that long, long after I will have finished this letter I will continue to talk to you. And besides, can you imagine the pride that I feel, not alone for the praise you give me—that would be enough, *dayyenu*, but for the seriousness with which you take what I write and say? I cherish your letter beyond anything you can suspect—it is after all yours.

No, I'm not devoted to the letter and ritual of Orthodoxy, because—you're absolutely right—I'm a child of modernity. And so, gradually over the last twelve years, I've undertaken to observe only those laws that have meaning for me. How can I explain what has meaning? Perhaps, most easily, whatever gives me, in my quotidian life, a sense of sacredness, a sense of holiness, of living with another dimension, beyond the needs of body and the demands of other people. It's a tired thing to say that we invented God because we need Him. You feel that too, I see from your letter. But I ["we" is crossed out] do need—and I sometimes feel that desperately—to get beyond myself and lose myself, if possible, yield to what I believe is pure and sacred. I find this often in the services in the Orthodox shul. By now I know the liturgy pretty well, though I couldn't manage all the Hebrew without the facing English text. For the most part, the language is pure—drawn from Scripture (I dislike most of the medieval liturgical poems)—how much purer can you get. The Orthodox chanting, without fancy cantorial embellishment, is very compelling. I, who am usually inhibited and restrained, find myself singing loud (if not well) and often with a passion that I wasn't aware was there. Parts of the service give me this kind of release. Other parts have come to have special meanings for me that I suppose have less to do with God and more with His people. The Shema nearly always stirs me with the sense of generations upon generations who said it in extremity. So too the Alenu. Don't think, though, that the mood for God is always with me. That's why I don't mind the repetitiveness of the service. I figure, if it doesn't reach me this time, maybe next time round. I mostly enjoy the Torah reading, because I'm always learning (though sometimes, the rabbis would say, the wrong things), and at least I try to improve my Hebrew. The worst part of any service anywhere is the sermon, during which I read, usual Pirke Avot, which I love and whose Hebrew is mostly easy enough for me to work on.

In this whole matter of belief and prayer, I've learned to make certain compromises, not to push too hard in the direction of consistency, to learn to live with all sorts of ambiguity, just as one does with husbands and friends and family.

I came to all of this as a kind of exercise in reasoning. I started with a feeling, a passion, if you will, for being Jewish. All I had was Yiddish and Jewish history. But I didn't think that either or both were viable as preservers of the Jewish people. No one died al kiddush hashem [martyrdom for God] for Yiddish or for the idea of Jewish history (unless you so transform that idea into divine history). It seemed to me only logical that one lives or dies for something of transcending significance, whose transcendence can be transmitted and communicated to the next generation. I don't have children, so I didn't have to face the problem of what to give them so they would remain Jewish, not merely by inheritance, by fate, but indeed by choice, by desire. While I was wrestling with this question, I came across the essay by Nathan Birnbaum on his conversion from skeptic to believer. (It's in *The Golden Tradition*.) Translating it became a process of getting into his head and understanding what happened to him, more than any mere reading of that rather convoluted style would have effected. That essay really influenced me to change my life. And I delight in the change.

But you're right. I'm not like my Orthodox friends. Not only are there observances I can't do, because they don't make sense to me, but there remains outside always some measure of distance, sometimes even a self-mockery at my yielding to faith and prayer and song. I've not been so much back and forth, like you and Melville, but rather neither here nor there, not entirely one, not entirely the other. I was born in New York, but I lived a year in Vilna, and that tension lives with me all the time. Somehow pulled between two poles, never quite at home in either, and above all, not wishing to be, always content at bottom for the apartness, even if I've often been lonely.

I think I've told you more than you wanted to know, more than I have told others, perhaps because I'm sure you'll see into my choice and decision even better than I have.

I'm dying to read the book you're now writing. Remember me when the time comes for reading. In the meantime, all my gratitude, admiration, and profound affection.

Lucy

p.s. Certainly, you write better than I do, but certainly I type better. L [handwritten]

—

Simon Wiesenthal (1908–2005), a Holocaust survivor who devoted his life to tracking down and gathering information on fugitive Nazi war criminals, cofounded the Jewish Historical Documentation Centre in Linz, Austria (1947), and opened the Documentation Centre of the Association of Jewish Victims of the Nazi Regime in Vienna (1961). Throughout his life, he maintained that the Holocaust referred to the systematic murder of eleven million people, of which six million were Jews and five million were non-Jews.[22] In 1977, the Simon Wiesenthal Center, a Jewish human rights organization, was founded in his honor.

Lucy S. Dawidowicz to Simon Wiesenthal, June 8, 1978

(With permission of Laurie Sapakoff and the American Jewish Historical Society; Dawidowicz Papers, box 77, folder 15; Dawidowicz's letter included a copy of Tad Szulc, "A Nazi Hunter Takes on the Russians")

Dear Mr. Wiesenthal:

Please forgive me for intruding upon your time and patience. You may know my name as the author of a book called *The War Against the Jews 1933–1945*. I am now writing a small book on the treatment of the Holocaust in contemporary history and theology. In my introduction I wish to include also some comments on the place of the Holocaust in contemporary consciousness in general. It is in this connection that I write to you.

Last December Tad Szulc published an interview with you in *New York*. In this interview, you are quoted as follows: "... we shouldn't always talk about the 6 million Jews who died in the Holocaust. I say let's talk about 11 *million* civilians...."

Could you specify for me who are the other five million? How did you, or the source you quoted, arrive at that particular figure? Where and why were they murdered by the Nazis? I would most appreciate your providing me with this information.

In addition, if you have the interest, I'd be curious to know on what grounds you justify not making distinctions between Jewish and non-Jewish victims of the Nazis. Do you really think that the problem is "reduced," that is, made less significant, if it is between the Nazis and the Jews rather than if it affects Nazis and mankind in general?

I await your reply with anticipation and interest.

Sincerely yours,

Simon Wiesenthal to Lucy S. Dawidowicz, June 14, 1978

(With permission of the estate of Simon Wiesenthal; Dawidowicz Papers, box 77, folder 15)

Dear Mrs Dawidowicz:

Thank you for your letter of June 8. As I appreciate your work very much, I am glad about the opportunity to write to you about this problem which has been weighing upon my mind for a long time now.

I realize that the question of the Holocaust victims must look different from the other side of the Atlantic. Here in Europe, we are living amidst a number of nations which are mourning their dead: The Poles, the Czechs, the Yugoslavs, the Dutch, the French, and many others—not to forget the Gypsies, whom the Nazis planned to exterminate just like the Jews. In my work, I have never attempted to separate the bodies in the mass graves; I have never made a difference regarding the nationality of the victims—or of the killers, either.

Speaking in practical terms, the Nazis and their apologists have never fought the number of eleven million victims of concentration camps and executions among the civilian population of Europe (the number does *not* include any of the "real" war victims, civilians killed by bombs, or in the course of fighting in their area; it includes only those killed by the Nazis and their helpers, in the course of events wholly unrelated to the war). The Nazis have always fought against the small number of six million murdered Jews, as this meant having a "shorter front-line," to use a technical term.

To speak of "six million victims" is not only historically wrong, it is also politically unwise, as we need the other nations for a common fight against the resurgence of Nazism. Having suffered the heaviest losses by far, it is only natural that we are stressing the number of our own dead, and the other nations understand this too—up to a certain extent.

But in Europe today, in the minds of most people, the Holocaust has been reduced to a fight of the Nazis against the Jews, something which does not concern them if they are neither.

After the war, we had the opportunity of fraternization with the families of the victims of the other nations, but we have chosen to remain apart, and have thus lost a good many friends—wittingly or unwittingly. In the question of restitution, we made the mistake of not supporting the legitimate claims of the other victims—so how can we expect them to support our legitimate claims? I have a lot of friends among the former Resistance fighters in most European countries—I am sitting on several of their committees—and I consider them our natural allies. Apart from the moral angle, I believe it makes no sense to allienate [*sic*] those friends we have.

I am sure you will understand my position, and I beg you not to forget the other victims in your work about the Holocaust; as a matter of fact, many of them died because they tried to help Jews.

With kindest personal regards,

Very truly yours,
Simon Wiesenthal

Jacob Rader Marcus (1896–1995) was a pioneering historian of American Jewry who was long associated with Hebrew Union College (HUC) in Cincinnati. Marcus received rabbinical ordination from HUC in 1920 and a PhD in Jewish history in 1925 under the guidance of Ismar Elbogen in Berlin. In 1926, he returned to Cincinnati, where he made HUC his academic home until his death. In 1947, he founded the American Jewish Archives on HUC's campus. He was the author of over fifteen books, including The Jew in the Medieval World: A Source Book: 315–1791 (1938), On Love, Marriage, Children . . . and Death, Too: Intimate Glimpses into the Lives of American Jews in a Bygone Age as Told in Their Own Words (1964), and The Colonial American Jew, 1492–1776 (1970).

Jacob Rader Marcus to Lucy S. Dawidowicz, May 9, 1979

(With permission of Gary Zola and the Jacob Rader Marcus Archives of the American Jewish Archives)

Dear Professor:

I am publishing a documentary on the American Jewess and I would like to reprint pp. 46–47 [sic] of Jewish Presence: Essays on Identity and History.[23] The selections will run about 1450 words. I would like your consent to republish the materials which I have selected.

We shall of course give you full credit.

May I have the pleasure of hearing from you.

With all good wishes to you and your family, I am
                    Most cordially, Jacob R. Marcus

p.s. I am enclosing a self-addressed stamped envelope. If you want, you can simply write your ok on this letter and send it back to me. Your initials will be adequate.

Lucy S. Dawidowicz to Jacob Rader Marcus, May 16, 1979

Dear Dr. Marcus:

Three points:

1) It's a year since I'm no longer connected with Yeshiva University. Please note my home address: Lucy S. Dawidowicz, 200 West 86th Street, Apt. 20L, NYC, NY 10024.

2) Of course, you have my permission, so long as the full bibliographical information is given (title, publisher, place, and date).

3) You'll be in BIG trouble if you use the word "Jewess." I myself hate it as a Victorian vestige and the feminists will pillory you for using it. Altogether, it

has offensive tones and overtures. "The American Jewish Woman" is the term you want.

> With all good wishes for success in your undertaking,
> Sincerely, Lucy S. Dawidowicz

Jacob R. Marcus to Lucy S. Dawidowicz, May 21, 1979

(With permission of Gary Zola and the Jacob Rader Marcus Archives of the American Jewish Archives; copy in Dawidowicz private papers)

Thank you very much for giving me permission to use your very interesting article in your book, *Jewish Presence*.

Of course we will see that all the proper credits are given. Be assured of that.

I note what you say about the use of the word Jewess.[24] You are not the first to protest. Nevertheless—I am a stubborn cuss—I am going to use that word. I think it is an honorable term. Let me point out an analogy. During the nineteenth century Jewish organizations were ashamed of the word "Jew." They meekly submitted and accepted the accusations of the Gentiles that Jew was a dirty word. Thus it was that many of the major institutions of the nineteenth century avoided that word and resorted to the use of Hebrew and Israelite. Today Jews are not ashamed of being called Jews.

The term Jewess has been rejected—as far as I know—only by Jewish women. The standard authoritative dictionaries think that it is a proper term. After I publish my large documentary I am hoping that even for Jewish women the term Jewess will no longer be a badge of shame but a patent of nobility. I have never yet met a Christian who thought the term Jewess was a dirty word. Let's see what happens.

If we can ever be of any help here at the Archives do not hesitate to call on us. As you know we now have a published five-volume catalogue of our holdings.

> With all good wishes for the coming holidays, I am
> Most cordially, Jacob R. Marcus

——

Zarek Davidson was Szymon Dawidowicz's nephew, and Senia his wife. They made their home in Melbourne, Australia, after the war but visited Europe frequently and also traveled to the United States to visit Szymon. Lucy typed this letter eight days after her husband's death. Written under extreme emotional distress, the letter is filled with uncharacteristic typographical errors.

Lucy S. Dawidowicz to Zarek and Senia Davidson, June 10, 1979

(With permission of Laurie Sapakoff)

I haven't read this—I can't. Please forgive the lapses. [handwritten]

Last Friday, after noon, got up from *shivah*, did some marketing and five loads of laundry. Yesterday, I went to shul for the first time since Yizkor on the last day of Pesach. And now I'm trying to tidy up what needs tidying up (social security, insurance, bills, bank matters, etc.—all minor and even trivial) and get back to work and see if I can still work.

Since last year I kept something of a little log on Szymon's illness in my appointment book. Just before he took to his bed, those notations (which I kept in green ink, to differentiate from other matters) took up all the space. During the last two weeks, I kept a separate sheet for each day. Mostly this was to help me see where we were at, to be able to remember accurately what happened and see if there were patterns. I could always check back when he was in hospital and what the blood count was at any time. I'll try to tell the course of the disease as best I can and I hope I'll be coherent and make sense.

Things went downhill after you left. It began with the routine admission to hospital for blood on March 2, but that night an overload brought on coronary problems and he was transferred to a coronary care unit, on a monitor, for a week. The assessment was that there was had very minor damage. After that week, he was moved to a regular unit for another week, just to be checked, came home on March 16. He continued moderately well, with the little walk daily, weather permitting. On Saturday, March 31, he felt okay and went out for a walk. He blacked out on West End Avenue; bystanders called an ambulance, but he insisted on coming home rather than to a hospital. He had not been gone long enough for me to worry. The house porter brought him to the door—he insisted on trying to open it with his key. There I confronted him, his face all bloodied, hands a bit bruised. He claimed he was now okay. I washed and dressed the face as best I could, but the chin was bad. Against his will, I called and fortunately got a doctor I know who lives a block away. He's a Sabbath observer, but he came in fifteen minutes and told me to take him to the hospital for stitched in the chin. That we did; I got in touch with our regular doctors, who advised the residents in the emergency department. They suspected it was irregular heart action, but let him go home after a couple of hours.

A week later, the appetite began to go. He managed our little seder, reading the whole Haggada and I prepared tiny portions of everything for him.

Thereafter, I noticed he was sleeping some 12–14 hours a day, with very late and slow mornings, then dozing, then the 5:30 nap. Nevertheless, with that extraordinary determination, he continued to walk, refusing to let me go with him. I, for my part, turned to thoughts of cooking. My mind was occupying with preparing food that he would find easy to swallow and also be palatable. I had this macabre idea of writing a cookbook for people with cancer of the stomach. I pureed chicken into soups, and used the food processor and the blender for more and more things.

On April 27, he went into the hospital for blood, the count down to 9.8. This time, things proceeded without incident and he came home on April 29, the CBC 12.1. But he could eat less solid food. It was agony to watch him try to chew. His will power was fantastic. He knew he had to eat and he kept trying. Friday, May 11, almost on the spur of the moment—about one–two days notive, I invited two friends of mine whom Szymon liked very much to dinner and other people came later. I was a bit apprehensive as to how he'd take it; his menu was different from ours, but the company stimulated him and he had a wonderful evening, even ate a bit better than usual. That was really that last good time.

He kept losing weight, about two pounds a week; he also had diarrhea, which he made nothing of, but which now I know was a consequence of his illness—brought on by the chemical imbalance which the tumor set off in the stomach (so I was told). May 18, he complained of nausea after dinner and May 19, after dinner, vomited. The diarrhea was worse. You had called a few hours before that and he was still dressed and walking around. On Sunday May 20, we was very weakk, took only tea, water, broth, briefly emerged from bed, but it was all too much. Everything went downhill quite fast thereafter.

The diarrhea was most debilitating; the doctors didn't want him to take Lomotil, because it would work against the urecholine. The kayopectate was hard for him to swallow and didn't work well. On May 23, the doctor suggested Imodium znd after two days it seemed to help, but we were still afraid it would inhibit the urination, which was becoming more and more painful. All the time, Szymon insisited on getting to the bathroom by himself, very loath to let him help him. He was taking maredly less food and growing dramatically weaker. The daaughter of Harriet and Carl Marcus, a public-health nurse, came to see him—as a friend rather than a profession—but we brought in a nurse's aide, for half a day, who worked under a nurse's supervision.

Nevertheless, he has no serious pain and slept a lot. People came every day to visit, but only some saw him, depending on his mood and how much he liked them.

May 30, his friend Leon Berkman visited with him for about an hour and the visit was warm and lovely. Two hours later, Mark Uveeler and his wife came (in on a visit from Israel) and Szymon really enjoyed talking to them. But May 31, he was so weak, he hardly had the energy to speak. That morning, on our doctor's advice, I order a nurse's aide for 24 hours, round the clock. When I asked Szymon if I could get him anything, he said he just wanted to expire. I had asked Dr. Glass to see him and he had agreed to come that afternoon. Szymon seemed particularly pleased by this news and all afternoon impatiently waited, kept looking at the watch every ten minutes. I couldn't imagine what he expected. Finally at 6:30 in the evening, Dr. Glass came and Szymon said: "Doctor, tell me how long this will last." Glass said he couldn't answer that, but—after examining him—said he'd make him comfortable. (That morning for the first time, we gave him tylenol with codeine.) But outside the bedroom, Glass told me that Szymon had no more than 24 to 72 hours. It turned out to be only 20.

The night was difficult, because he frequently had to urinate or move his bowels. I had a bed pain and a urinal, but he wanted to go to the bathroom. The aide helped me with him, but he was unbelieveably weak. By morning all that subsided. But he no longer had the strength to suck up tea or milk with a straw. The aid helped him a little tea and milk with a spoon, but he didn't want it and slept that dreadful sleep, with the gutteral breathing. At one p.m. the regular aide I had had all along came and he responded to me and to her, by nodding his head that he didn't want anything. At 2:00 p.m. the gutteral breathing had quieted down; I talked to him and he heard me. But fifteen minutes later, he had just expired in his sleep.

He just faded away into nothingness. He didn't really have bad pain, and by then he was exhausted by weakness and wanting to die. It was the first day of Shevuot, June 1.

It was his wish and mine for me to keep him at home and I think—as all our doctors and friends do—that was the wiser decision. At the hospital, they would have had to stick an IV into him—with his poor tiny veins—and he'd be restricted to his bed. And alone a lot. Here I was always with him, or had friends or aides to spell me. He was surrounded with a lot of love and loving care.

The funeral was on Sunday June 3. At best I could I kept it in what a I thought was a manner fitting to Szymon. A Jewish actor, David Rogow, who happened to have been Szymon's assistant in the YIVO and whom he trained to take over his work in the printing and publishing field, read Chapts. 3 and

7 from Yehoash's translation of Koheleth; Isaiah Trunk talked about Szymon very simply and movingly. (That will probably be published—in part or in whole—and I'll send it to you.) The chapel service concluded with the singing of the Bundist anthem. At the gravesite, Rogow read, in the Yiddish version, Psalms 90 and 112, my friend and our attorney Harry Silber chanted the El Mole [Rachamim], and we said kaddish. It was a driving rain at the cemetery and that was all right with me.

My friends and my few relatives have supported me beyond measure. I don't know how I would have managed without them. But now I'll have to begin to learn how to live alone.

Write soon,

Love,

—

Noam Chomsky (b. 1928) is an American linguist, philosopher, cognitive scientist, historian, political activist, and social critic. For most of his career, he taught at the Massachusetts Institute of Technology, but today he is the laureate professor at the University of Arizona. Chomsky is the author of more than one hundred books on topics ranging from linguistics to war, politics, and mass media. A noted leftist and civil libertarian, he became embroiled in the case of Robert Faurisson (1929–2018), a Holocaust denier, whose "The Debate over the 'Gas Chambers' " was published in Le Monde in 1978. Although Chomsky claimed that he disagreed with the substance of Faurisson's claims regarding the Holocaust, he signed a petition defending Faurisson's right to publish his views and wrote an essay that was used—without his permission—as a preface to Faurisson's 1980 book, Mémoire en défense contre ceux qui m'accusent de falsifier l'histoire.[25]

Lucy S. Dawidowicz to Noam Chomsky, September 10, 1980

(With permission of Laurie Sapakoff and the American Jewish Historical Society; Dawidowicz Papers, box 49, folder 3)

Dear Professor Chomsky:

Perhaps you can enlighten me on the following point. A young man who works for the Larry King radio program (a network late-night talk show) told me that you had signed a statement defending Robert Faurisson's right to speak his views, or something equally vague. This young man had called to invite me to debate Faurisson on the Larry King program.

I turned the offer down, but I'd like to know more about this defense of Faurisson's rights. Did you in fact support such a public appeal? If so, who initiated it? Who else signed it? And what reason compelled you to sign it?

I'd appreciate any information you can give me.

Sincerely yours,

Lucy S. Dawidowicz

Noam Chomsky to Lucy S. Dawidowicz, September 18, 1980

(With permission of Noam Chomsky; Dawidowicz Papers, box 49, folder 3)

Dear Ms. Dawidowicz:

In your letter of Sept. 10, you asked me three questions:

(1) Did I support a public appeal in "defense of Faurisson's rights"?

(2) Who initiated it?

(3) Who else signed it?

(4) What reason compelled me to sign it?

As for (1), yes. I signed a public appeal which made no comment whatsoever about the character or quality of Faurisson's "Holocaust research" but did protest efforts to deprive him of freedom of speech and expression and supported his right of academic freedom and the free exercise of his legal rights.

As for (2), I really don't recall. I sign dozens of such appeals every year, and don't generally keep records. It is quite possible, though I cannot say for sure, that it reached me by means of my friend Serge Thion,[26] a long-time libertarian socialist and strenuous opponent of totalitarianism of all sorts, including Nazism, Bolshevism, third-world variants of the latter, etc.—all of which I mention because of the disgraceful campaign of vilification concerning him in the French press.

As for (3), I haven't the faintest idea and could hardly care less.

As for (4), I apologize for the truisms, but I presume you want the truth. I signed the appeal because I believe that people have the right of freedom of expression whatever their views, that the importance of defending these rights is all the greater when the person expresses views that are abhorrent to virtually everyone (as in this case), and that this becomes particularly important when the person in question is thrown out of his academic position and subjected to slander, harassment, intimidation and even physical violence, which appears to be true in this case, as far as I have been able to determine—naturally one takes a certain amount on faith in these matters, as, e.g., when I sign appeals in defense of Soviet dissidents, but I am relying here on people whom I have good reason to trust because of their consistent and honorable record on such matters over many years. I thought that all of this had been settled in the 18th century, but apparently others do not agree.

I hope you will pardon what you may sense as undue acerbity in my response to your questions. I have been barraged by letters from around the world, and subjected to hysterical and lying attacks in the French "liberal" press and elsewhere because I do not share their totalitarian commitments and believe that freedom of speech should be protected, even when—crucially when—extremely unpopular views are at issue, views which may even be horrendous (since I do not know very much about Faurisson's work, and am not involved sufficiently in the issue to pursue it or evaluate it, I do not know whether this is true, in the present case; i.e., whether his views merit the adjective "horrendous").

In this context, perhaps I can ask you to enlighten me in response. I sign innumerable petitions of this sort in [sic] behalf of people with all sorts of views. I have, in fact, exerted far greater efforts than this in behalf of people whose views really are horrendous, e.g., Russian dissidents who were passionate supporters of American atrocities in Indochina and elsewhere and condemn the U.S. for not engaging in still greater savagery, and who sometimes come close to advocating measures that might well lead to nuclear holocaust. These actions have been highly public, in contrast to the present case. Yet I have never, to my recollection, received a letter from anyone asking me why I undertook to defend the rights of such people, and I—and no doubt you too—would have been shocked and indignant had this question been raised. My question, then, is why you think that a simple and elementary defense of civil liberties in the present instance arouses the response I have indicated, or at a milder level, evokes letters such as yours; and what you think this implies about the intellectual climate from which such reactions arise.

> Sincerely yours,
> Noam Chomsky

Marie Syrkin to Lucy S. Dawidowicz, January 27, 1981

(With permission of Joel Bodansky; Dawidowicz Papers, box 67, folder 14)

Dear Lucy,

Your letter came just when I was particularly exercised about a Peter Bergson film that repeats the big lie that American Jews and American Zionists were indifferent to the fate of European Jewry. I am planning to write about this—regrettably not in the New York Times.[27]

As to the "anecdote" you mention. True, the Jewish Frontier editors, Greenberg and myself, could not assimilate the terrible truth when we first heard it in August. That is why we printed a report we had then received in the back. But—and it's a large "but"—by September 1942, when we realized that the evidence had to be believed no matter how much our spirits rebelled against it, we spent the month of October gathering material (I know, I did it) and the November, 1942, issue of Jewish Frontier appeared in black borders and wholly devoted to the Holocaust. That issue has the melancholy distinction of being the first attempt in English to bring the news to the American public. I have related this story a number of times at conferences on the holocaust and it has been printed in the reports of these conferences. I think the story also appears elsewhere but I can't remember where. Anyhow, when I showed the Nov. 1942 issue of J. F. at a Holocaust conference in Seattle a couple of years ago it was seized on as a historic document. Raoul [sic] Hilberg marvelled at the accuracy of the material so early in the process. At the time (1942) we sent the issue to radio stations, the American press, etc. A few lines of notice appeared here and there in the general press. However, from this point on the fate of European Jewry was *our* abiding concern. In "The State of the Jews" you can read "Conferring in Bermuda" (written by me as an editorial) and "Free Port" to get a notion of how desperately we struggled to affect public opinion.

I have a feeling that you will probably disagree with me. I hope, Lucy, that you will not confound proficiency with effort. We tried though we failed.

I wish I could talk to you about these things.

With love, Marie

P.S. As I look back on it, a month (September) does not seem too large a stretch of time to assimilate and give credibility to so monstrous an event. Remember, that Hayim Greenberg was one of the most sensitive and dedicated of Jews— yet there was this time-lag in intellectual acceptance. [handwritten]

Israel Gutman (1923–2013) was a Warsaw-born survivor historian who fought in the Ghetto Uprising. After World War II, Gutman immigrated to Palestine, joined the kibbutz Lehavot HaBashan, and made his career at the Hebrew University of Jerusalem and at Yad Vashem, where he headed the International Institute for Holocaust Research (1993–96), served as chief historian (1996–2000), and was the academic adviser (from 2000).

Israel Gutman to Lucy S. Dawidowicz, May 9, 1981

(With permission of Dita Gutman; Dawidowicz private papers)

Dear Lucy,

Many thanks for calling and for your letter from April 13.

I was very moved by the bad news of Isaiah Trunk's passing away. He was one of the few remainders[28] who continued the tradition of the great Jewish historians in Poland, and his work was marked by deep attachment and understanding of the structure and life of the Polish Jewry. I was always impressed both by his personal modesty and profound knowledge. For quite a long time we were in permanent contact while I initiated and edited the Hebrew version of the "Judenrat."

I am glad that your work is ready and will soon be published. From my experience here I become even more convinced about the need and the importance of an analysis of the Holocaust in light of European history, or the writing of contemporary history by European and American historians.

I got a letter from Indiana Univ[ersity] Press. They prepared the manuscript toward the stage of printing, and according to their intention, the book will appear in Spring 1982.

During the spring quarter I am very busy and occupied with my current work and special obligations. My English has improved and I spend now less time in order to prepare my lectures. But, on the other hand, I have crowded classes (about 80 students) and must dedicate much time to exams and final papers. I received also many invitations to speak, from Hillel and different community circles, and this kind of presentations required a great deal of work.

The activity against the "revisionists" embraced many people, and according to the opinion of our colleagues, the University authorities ask now for a way to withdraw from their commitment to the "Institute."[29] The discussion is now focused around the interpretation of the meaning of the first amendment, and you know very well the sensitivity of the people in this country, Jews and non-Jews alike, regarding the principles embodied in the first amendment.

The time is running fast and we are already planning our return home. We appreciate very much your friendly invitation to stay with you during our visit to New-York. It could be a great pleasure, but, as you know we are four people and very concerned not to disturb your peace and order of work. In any case, we will stay in touch with you, and I thank you very much and am happy to regard you as my friend.

I hope that you considered seriously the idea of your time and staying and working partly in New-York and partly in Israel. I would like to be helpful in any possible way to carry out this plan into reality. With best wishes from me and Irit. Yours, Israel

Marie Syrkin to Lucy S. Dawidowicz, July 15, 1982

(With permission of Joel Bodansky; Dawidowicz private papers)

I decided to type in the interests of legibility but I am afraid that has not been achieved. Pardon, this is what comes of having had a secretary. [handwritten]

Dear Lucy,

Thank you very much for sending me the letter from Macarov. I would have acknowledged it sooner but I was in Washington at a meeting with what is called a small group of pro-Zionist "American Intellectuals" and a representative of Israel to discuss the disaffection of our ilk with the Begin-Sharon policies. (Result—general disagreement as to any course [handwritten]).

I admit that the letter I signed was not strong enough in its condemnation of the PLO, etc. It was read to me on the telephone and though I objected to this failure it was too late to re-circulate the letter. Since I agreed with the major thrust I signed. The names of some of my fellow-signers—when I saw the ad in thhe [*sic*] Times—did not enchant me but others are decent folk; it's a mixed bag. I wish I could believe that any good can come from the extension of the original aim of the operation—to clear Southern Lebanon of the immediate threat to Galilee. It seems to me that every day of the siege with its attendant publicity is a victory for Arafat. The alternative, an assault, inevitably bloody for Israelis and civilian Arabs, [handwritten clause] may be militarily successful but I do not think will result in an independent Lebanon, friend of Israel—this is beyond Israel's power to achieve. So Israel is stuck in a morass. My view, in which I am alone, is that the wisest course would be for Israel to declare that its aim has been achieved, and that, magnanimous in victory, it will withdraw its troops with the proviso that any move of the PLO south will bring renewed action. The notion that the PLO, whether it remains in Beirut or marches out demonstratively, is finished is a pipe-dream. It will renew itself in every Arab capital. And Saudi Arabia can resupply their armament instantly. In short the brilliant military victory of the first week is turning, I fear, into a political and geo-political disaster.

Believing all this, I nevertheless feel that now, with a pal of Saudi Arabia in the Cabinet as Secretary of State, not to mention Weinberger, opponents of Begin-Sharon must tread warily. The Iran invasion has added a new dimension, at present incalculable. What to do or say? The answer is insomnia. And dissent in Israel is growing!

By this time you get my unhappy drift. Congratulations on your computer and may your labors prosper. I wish I could talk to you. Love, Marie

Lucy S. Dawidowicz to Barry M. Katz, February 6, 1983

(With permission of Laurie Sapakoff and the American Jewish Historical Society; Dawidowicz papers, box 76, folder 7)

Dear Barry:

I've decided to use my word processor to process letters as well as books and articles. The keyboard is much easier to use and the likelihood is that the letters will be neater than if I used the typewriter and I may gain enough time to write an extra letter or two. (I'm still answering mail from last November.)

But I write this promptly to you because I was pleased for your sake and for mine to read your review.[30] Once again, what you wrote gave me great pleasure, because you're one of the very few people who understood what I was trying to do in that book and the review is not only gracious to me, but I find it interesting to read.

I think that you hit precisely on the weakness in the book, at least what I regard as its most serious weakness. In the course of writing, I soon came to realize that this book was at bottom an attack upon history as a discipline. If history is indeed subject to the personal biases of historians, their cultural warps and predispositions; if history can be and has been manipulated by governments and movements in their own interests which are not compatible with the goal of describing the past as it really was; then history is indeed a feeble undertaking whose pretension to recreate the past is little more than pretension and that perhaps the whole historical enterprise has arrogated to itself unwarranted claims. In short, history cannot ever be *scientific*.

The book to a considerable extent shows—or so I think and thought when I was writing it—that these terrible accusations are justified. Or at least justified more than one would want to acknowledge. And so in fear and trembling, I recoiled from making such conclusions. I tried to reclaim as best I could the prestige of history and establish as best I could, and this I think was my greatest weakness, some sort of objectives [sic] measures in doing history which could justify history's claim to doing honestly what it's supposed to do. I suppose if I was better grounded in the philosophy of history and also if I were more widely read in universal history, I would have been more convincing in trying to show that at bottom history is to be regarded as a serious discipline and that the practitioners of history have a wide area of common ground and common understanding on how to do history.

Anyway, I didn't mean to write a treatise here, but really to thank you for a most perceptive reading of that book.

I'm glad you had a good response from George Mosse. I confess I still haven't read your book; it's on the top of a big pile. But I'll get to it, fear not and I'm afraid I won't be an insightful critic, because I know nearly nothing about Marcuse, except what I read in the papers.

I've finally hit my stride in my work and did so in the Jewish way—I began writing from the back of the book and have just finished the first draft of an enormous appendix on Jewish rights—civic and religious—in the original thirteen states. Imagine, that no one had yet done this elementary and fundamental thing in a systematic way. Tsk, tsk, tsk.

I do hope you land something. Do keep in touch and if you come this way, let me know. I'm planning to go about for about ten days late in April, early in May, probably to Charleston and Savannah, to sit in eighteenth-century towns and ponder the ways of man.

All the best,

＝

Eberhard Jäckel (1929–2017) was a prominent German historian of the Holocaust, who shared with Dawidowicz the conviction that ideology and Hitler's antisemitic intentions to destroy European Jewry led to the Final Solution. They differed, however, on the pace of effecting Hitler's plans. The exchange below reflects their mutual esteem and also notes the influence of the Historikerstreit then raging among German academic circles on studies of the Holocaust. In his May 1986 letter, Jäckel remains firm in his criticism of "Structuralist" historians of the Holocaust but challenges Dawidowicz's view that their historiography is apologetic and politically motivated. As an aside, he dismisses David Irving (b. 1938), who began his career as a professional historian but soon became embroiled in charges of Holocaust denial, leading to the case against American historian Deborah Lipstadt in 1996, which he lost in the British High Court.[31]

Lucy S. Dawidowicz to Eberhard Jäckel, September 21, 1984

(With permission of Laurie Sapakoff and the American Jewish Historical Society; Dawidowicz Papers, box 79, folder 2)

Dear Professor Jackel:

For many years I have wanted to tell you how greatly I admire your book *Hitlers Weltanschauung*. The difference between us about the chronology of Hitler's idea about murdering the Jews in no way detracts from the enormous esteem I have for your scholarship and for your general assessment of the Nazi period.

I'm writing now because I've finally received from the bookseller my own copy of the enlarged and revised edition of *Hitlers Weltanschauung*. I feel honored that you take my reading of Hitler's ideas seriously and at the same time I respect your interpretation.

I have just completed an essay for a new edition of my book *The War Against the Jews 1933–1945*, to appear next year on the occasion of the tenth anniversary of its original publication. The essay surveys the scholarship of the past decade or so, and consists largely of a critique of the structuralist/ functionalist interpretation of the Nazi period and especially of the murder of the European Jews. I have also provided an updated supplementary bibliography, in part annotated, since my book has been widely used in the United States in college courses. I have included in this bibliography both the new edition of *Hitlers Weltanschauung* and also your most valuable edition of Hitler's early writings.

It will be my pleasure to send you a copy of that new edition when it will appear.

Most sincerely,
Lucy S. Dawidowicz

Eberhard Jäckel to Lucy S. Dawidowicz, October 15, 1984

(With permission of Lea Rosh, Dawidowicz Papers, box 79, folder 2)

Sehr geehrte Frau Dawidowicz,

es ist merkwürdig und bedauerlich, daß Autoren sich über viele Jahre hinweg nur durch Ihre Bücher kennen, ohne persönlich in Verbindung zu treten. Mir ist es in dieser Hinsicht nicht anders ergangen als Ihnen. Um so dankbarer bin ich Ihnen, daß Sie mir nun geschrieben haben. Leider komme ich, weil ich verreist war, erst heute dazu, Ihnen zu antworten.

Ich bin jetzt beschämt und finde es auch unbegreiflich, daß ich Ihnen nicht ein Exemplar der Neuasugabe von "Hitlers Weltantschauung" zusandte. Aber ich bin natürlich froh, daß Sie meine Anmerkung zu Ihrer These zur Kenntnis genommen haben und mir nicht grollen.

Ihre These hat mir wirklich sehr zu denken gegeben. Auch mein Freund Rudolph Binion neigt Ihrer Ansicht zu. Endgültig wird die Kontroverse gar nicht zu entscheiden sein, da wir ja in Hitlers wirren Kopf nicht blicken können. Aber die Dokumente scheinen mir immer noch für eine schrittweise Radikalisierung seiner Mordpläne zu sprechen. Doch am Ende ist es ein Streit von untergeordneter Bedeutung.

Im vergangenen Herbst hielt ich in Brandeis vier Vorträge, darunter einen mit dem Titel "Hitlers [*sic*] Orders the Holocaust," in dem ich von der Verwirklichung seiner Pläne sprach. Die Vorträge erscheinen demnächst in der University Press of New England als Buch "Hitler in History." Ich habe den Verlag gebeten, Ihnen ein Exemplar zu schicken. Die überarbeitete deutsche Fassung soll im nächsten Jahr als "Hitlers Herrschaft" erscheinen.

Haben Sie nochmals besten Dank für Ihren Brief und seien Sie freundlichst gegrüßt von Ihrem

Eberhard Jäckel

Dear Mrs. Dawidowicz,

I find it puzzling and unfortunate that authors often only know each other over the years through their books and not by personally getting in touch with each other. This has been our case, too. I am all the more thankful that have now written to me. Unfortunately, because I was traveling, I am only able to answer you today.

I am ashamed now and find it incomprehensible that I did not include a copy of the new edition of "Hitler's Weltanschauung." But, of course, I am glad that you have taken note of my comment on your thesis and that you do not hold a grudge.

Your thesis really made me think a lot. My friend Rudolph Binion,[32] too, is inclined toward your view. Ultimately, the controversy will not be decided, because we can not look into Hitler's confused head. But the documents still seem to me to speak for a gradual radicalization of his murder plans. But in the end, it's a minor issue.

Last fall I gave four lectures at Brandeis [University], including one entitled "Hitler Orders the Holocaust," in which I spoke of the actualization of his plans. The lectures will be published as *Hitler in History* with the University

Press of New England. I have asked the press to send a copy to you. The revised
German edition will appear next year as *Hitlers Herrschaft*.

Thank you again for your letter and kind regards from yours truly,

Eberhard Jäckel

Eberhard Jäckel to Lucy S. Dawidowicz, May 19, 1986

(With permission of Lea Rosh, Dawidowicz Papers, box 79, folder 2)

Sehr geehrte Frau Dawidowicz,

Ich danke Ihnen sehr für die Zusendung der Neuausgabe Ihres Buches *The
War Against the Jews* und für Ihre freundlichen Bemerkungen zur Neuausgabe
meines Buches *Hitlers Weltanschauung* (obwohl auf S.XXV mit falscher Wie-
dergabe meines Vornamens).

Natürlich stimmen wir in der wissenschaftlichen Beurteilung der soge-
nannten Strukturalisten ganz überein. Ich hoffe, daß Sie inzwischen auch mein
Buch *Hitler in History* erhalten haben, wenn auch zu spät für die Einleitung
zu Ihrer Neuausgabe. Seither habe ich im Mai 1984 einen Kongreß veran-
staltet, der allein der Aufklärung der Kontroverse diente. Die Referate und
Diskussionsbeiträge sind veröffentlicht in dem von mir und Jürgen Rohwer
herausgegebenen Band *Der Mord an den Juden in Zweiten Weltkrieg* (Stuttgart: Deutsche Verlags-Anstalt 1985). Leider habe ich nicht genügend Exemp-
lare, um Ihnen eines schicken zu können. Aber sicher werden Sie das Buch in
einer Bibliothek finden und dann sehen können, wie sehr ich mit Ihnen in der
Sache übereinstimme.

Die Kontroverse ist für mich auch persönlich sehr merkwürdig. Denn die
Protagonisten der Strukturalisten, Martin Broszat und Hans Mommsen, sind
zugleich meine Opponenten und meine Freunde. Sosehr ich ihre Interpreta-
tionen für falsch halte und bekämpfe, so kann ich doch mit Ihrem Urteil nicht
übereinstimmen, sie seien apologetisch (S. XXVII) und dienten politischen
Interessen (S. XXXII). Das triff gewiß auf David Irving zu, mit dem ich
keinerlei Gemeinsamkeit habe. Mit Broszat und Mommsen aber gibt es keine
Unterschiede in der politischen und moralischen Bewertung des Vorgangs,
sondern nur in der wissenschaftlichen Interpretation. Insofern hat die Kontroverse auch nichts mit nationaler Zugehörigkeit zu tun, sondern ist eine
durchaus internationale. Außer Irving, den ich nicht für einen seriösen Histo-
riker halte, ist ja auch Tim Mason, ein führender Strukturalist, Brite, und in
England hat er eine ganze Schule von Anhängern hinter sich. Bitte verstehen
Sie daher, daß ich die Struktaralisten, so scharf der Gegensatz in der Sache ist,

etwas anders sehe als Sie und sie ein wenig verteidigen möchte. Sie gehören gewiß nicht in die gleiche Kategorie wie Butz oder Rassinier und andere.

Inzwischen habe ich mein neues Buch *Hitlers Herrschaft* (mit dem Untertitel *Vollzug einer Weltanschauung*) abgeschlossen. Es ist die deutsche Fassung von *Hitler in History*, aber noch einmal völlig überarbeitet und enthält meine gründlichste Darlegung von Hitlers Weg zum Mord an den Juden. Das Buch erscheint im August in der Deutschen Verlags-Anstalt, und ich hoffe, daß ich Ihnen ein Exemplar schicken kann.

Ich empfinde es als großen Vorzug, mit Ihnen korrespondieren zu können. Bitte empfangen Sie nochmals meinen besten Dank, gute Wünsche für Ihr Wohlergehen und sehr freundliche Grüße.

Ihr Eberhard Jäckel

Dear Mrs. Dawidowicz,

Thank you very much for sending the new edition of your book *The War Against the Jews* and for your friendly comments on the new edition of my book *Hitlers Weltanschauung* (even though there is an error to my first name on page 25).

Of course, we agree completely in the academic assessment of the so-called "Structuralists." I hope that in the meantime you have also received my book *Hitler in History*, although too late for the introduction to your new edition. Since then, in May 1984, I organized a conference [lit. congress] for the sole purpose of clarifying the controversy. The lectures and round-table discussions are published in a volume edited by me and Jürgen Rohwer, *The Murder of the Jews in the Second World War* (Stuttgart: Deutsche Verlags-Anstalt 1985). Unfortunately, I do not have enough copies to be able to send one to you. But surely you will find the book in a library and then see how much I agree with you on the matter.

The controversy is also very puzzling to me personally. For the protagonists of the structuralists, Martin Broszat and Hans Mommsen, are both my opponents and my friends. As much as I deem their interpretations to be wrong and argue with them, I can hardly agree with your judgment that they might be apologetic (p. 27) and serve political interests (p. 32). This would certainly apply to David Irving, with whom I have no common ground. But with Broszat and Mommsen there is no difference in the political and moral evaluation of the process [of the murder of the Jews], but only in the academic interpretation. In this respect, the controversy has nothing to do with national affiliation, but is thoroughly international. Other than Irving, whom I do not consider a reputable historian, there is also Tim Mason, a leading structuralist, a Brit, and he has a whole school of followers behind him in England.[33] Please understand, therefore, that I see the structuralists, as sharp as the contrast in the matter is, somewhat differently from you and would like to defend them a bit. They certainly do not belong in the same category as [Arthur] Butz[34] or [Paul] Rassinier[35] and others.

Meanwhile, I have completed my new book *Hitlers Herrschaft* (with the subtitle *Vollzug einer Weltanschauung*). It is the German edition of *Hitler in History*, but once again completely revised, containing my most thorough exposition of Hitler's path to the murder of the Jews. The book will be published in the Deutsche Verlags-Anstalt in August, and I hope that I can send you a copy.

I find it a great privilege to be able to correspond with you. Please accept again my sincere thanks, good wishes for your well-being and very friendly greetings.

Yours truly, Eberhard Jäckel

Lucy S. Dawidowicz to Eberhard Jäckel, June 20, 1986

(With permission of Laurie Sapakoff and the American Jewish Historical Society; Dawidowicz Papers, box 79, folder 2)

Dear Dr. Jäckel:

I'm absolutely mortified and stricken with shame for that unforgivable error I made with your first name. Believe me that it will be corrected in the next printing. I hope that will be fairly soon, for the book has had a good track record in the number of its printings.

Yes, I did receive *Hitler in History*. I think it's a fine book, and of course I share your views on this large question. You're quite right: I received it too late to refer to it in my introduction or to include it in my supplementary bibliography. I look forward to the enlarged German edition. Have your opponents who are also your friends responded to the English version?

I've ordered a copy of *Der Mord an den Juden in Zweiten Weltkrieg*, which you coedited. Even though I'm no longer working in the field, I try to keep up with the worthwhile literature.

I'm currently writing a memoir about the years 1938–1947. I spent the year just before the invasion of Poland as a graduate student in Vilna at the Yiddish Scientific Institute. I left Poland August 27, 1939. After the war, I worked in both the American and British occupied zones of Germany with the American Joint Distribution Committee, the major Jewish relief organization.

In August I'll send you a copy of an article, to be published in *Commentary* about my trip to Berlin last November.[36] I'd be very much interested in your response.

With many apologies for my careless error
and all good wishes,

——

Shalom Luria (1920–2011) was the only son of Zelig and Rivele Kalmanovitch. A Zionist, he left Vilna in October 1938 for Palestine. When Dawidowicz published From That Place and Time *in 1990, he wrote this letter to her in Yiddish.*

Sholem Lurya to Lusi S. Davidovitsh, July 8, 1989

(With permission of Yuval Luria; Dawidowicz Papers, box 71, folder 9)

Dear Lucy Dawidowicz:

Your book, *From That Place and Time*, was really an experience for me. I swallowed it, one can say, in one breath. Bina Weinreich had earlier sent a xerox copy of pages 51–53 to me. And this was probably enough to ignite my curiosity and desire to read the whole book. I wrote to Bina, asking her to somehow send the book to me with a receipt and I would pay for it here. But here [it is], I received the book as a gift! I very much wanted to write a thank you to you immediately—but I wasn't able to obtain your address. Even worse—since [the time when] I met with you in Jerusalem at Mishkenot Sha'ananim, I have been in New York four times. The last time—a year ago [in the] summer in the boiling hot month of August—with my wife Miriam. But one can no longer get back [this missed opportunity]. But have regret, one may.

My friend Yehuda Reinharz from Boston (Brandeis University) sent your address to me. It is also possible that my cousin Mita Czarny may also meet you. I have also asked her to do this.

Your love for my parents is really limitless. I never had a sister. The only person who was close to me like a real sister was Mirke Kotler, who later married Menachem Linder. No better marital match in the world could have been possible. Regarding their fate, you know after all better than I. But your feelings for my parents naturally makes you a sister to me. I so regret that for all these years there has been no communication between us. A sin.

Several comments, which emerged as I was reading your book the first time. Your view of daily life in Vilna did not catch some substantial elements.

First of all—the political movements, [all] the Jewish varieties, which were so prominent in Vilna. For example, you did not have contact with Zionist circles. The same with certain Yiddishist circles, such as the *Freyland* people. You only mention them in connection with my father. Such prominent Vilna-ites as the lawyer, Joseph Tchernichov, and his son, Michael Astour with his "Shparber"-movement, are not mentioned at all.[37] As well, several figures were missing from the literary-journalistic world. For example, Shimson (Siomke) Kagan or Leyzer Ran, who until today lives in New York and has a colossal, enormous archive with Vilna materials.[38] But you are after all writing your own impressions and memories, and they have great value. My quibbles have no real justification. Whatever.

Aside from that, it seems to me that the date of your arrival in Vilna, August 27, 1938, is not precise. I was still in Vilna, at home, on August 27, 1938. I went to Warsaw with my mother on the 10th of September (approximately!). We were in Warsaw for about 3–4 days—with the Lindners, of course. Later, my trip to Palestine via Constantinople took about a week and I arrived in Haifa on September 24, 1938, the eve of Rosh Hashanah. If you were with my parents during your first days in Vilna—and I was already not there—then the date is not exact. Moreover, I was born in *Kiev*, in the house of Nachman Maizel (he told me this himself, here in Israel), not in Lithuania (see p. 52). We came to Vilna from Riga in the summer of 1929 and found two rooms at Mrs. Kotler's (Mirke's mother) on 6/6 Kijowska Street across from the hospital, "Mishmeres Khoylim." Sofia Markovne Gurewicz, the director of her own gymnasium on Makowa, lived with us together in one apartment.[39] I studied there for four years until it was closed.

But why should I spin you around here for so long? I only want to mention some of the people you described. Shaulke Reyzen, as you certainly know, lives in London, as does his brother Leibe. Shaulke is, unfortunately, very ill. He smoked out his lungs. It has already been 8–9 years that I have visited him yearly in London. A year ago I was there for four whole months with my wife. It was a sabbatical year. This year we are going again, at the beginning of September. I speak to him on the telephone from time to time. He is very pessimistic. This posture doesn't suit him. He used to issue flaming grievances against Israel, etc. Today, already not. We love him very much.

Aside from that, I also have contact with Avrom Sutzkever. He's a great poet and I get pleasure reading and interpreting his work.

A few words about myself: I am already retired from Haifa University. My field: Hebrew and Yiddish literature. I have been involved with the editing of a manuscript, which Abba Kovner, may his memory be for a blessing, left behind: *Megilot ha-eydut* (The Scrolls of Testimony). It's his book about the Jewish destruction in the last world war. It is very interesting and beautifully written— perhaps stronger than Lamentations. . . . Besides that I edited a book of essays by Aaron Shtaynberg *Gedanken in tsuzamenklang* (Ideas in Harmony)[40] and I'm writing a big essay about the [concept of] the hidden in his story, "King Magnus," whose protagonist is in fact my father. It is a mixture of truth and fiction, but a [singular] work of its own. I will translate it into Hebrew.

I will write another time about my family—two sons, a daughter, and five grandchildren, may they live and be well. This letter is already truly too long.

May you be well and strong, my beloved sister, and may God bless you for your dear book.

Yours, Shalom Luria (Kalmanovitch)

Allen Hoffman to Lucy S. Dawidowicz, March 19, 1990

(With permission of Allen Hoffman; Dawidowicz Papers, box 71, folder 8)

Dear Lucy,

Upon returning to Jerusalem, I immediately read your book *From That Place and Time* and found it very moving and very meaningful. Having seen some of the reviews, I was concerned that they weren't sufficiently appreciative of what you had written. It wasn't that they were wrong so much as they didn't go far enough and, thus, didn't do the work—and you—justice. I wanted to address some of these more complex issues but wasn't quite certain how I should do so. I put off writing until I had formulated what I wanted to say. Needless to say, that response never quite came together and I committed a severe injustice in not writing at all.

First of all, it is a very successful book: your story is interesting, well told, and you provide historical perspective. I am particularly appreciative for the last since the history of Eastern Europe is so woefully neglected—or it was when I was in school: in most history departments Eastern Europe is some great amorphous lump between Germany and Russia. You managed to put Vilna in a historical context, which isn't so surprising since you are a historian. All of this the reviews seemed to understand and appreciate, but, Lucy, what really amazed me about your book wasn't the European side so much as the American one. As a memoir *From That Place and Time* seems to me to be so very astonishingly American. Frankly, I was dumbfounded at its innocence and what it said about you not only as a person but also as an artist—a narrative writer as opposed to a narrative "historian." Your story of how you got to Vilna is very important and very moving and your discovery of your American identity (or your developing identity) in Vilna is even more powerful; to accept with love is more than difficult, but to reject with love—ultimately you were of New York, not of Vilna, is really very heart-rending and courageous. (To lay off the pitch because it's not quite right takes the confidence—of knowledge and identity—that only the really good hitters possess.) Then, Lucy, you returned after the war to help the surviving Jews and became involved in the discovery and recovery of the YIVO library. That's all very poetic and all very wonderful, because that's who you are—mentsch, researcher, and one very gutsy, industrious individual. (Even if eggs don't explode in your kitchen Erev Tisha B'Av you would be very special!) But after you found the library and shipped it to the United States you conclude the book, "I was ready to move ahead. I was ready to start a new life." Frankly, I was really blown away by that. What is this?—Huck Finn floating down the Wilja [Vilna] River with Chaim Grade as [slave] Jim? Lucy, are you serious? "A new life!" You only went home to write *The Golden Tradition* and *The War Against the Jews*—the "before" and "after" of your year in Vilna. Some new life! Lucy, someone else would have found the library, but you found the words! And such words—how the Jewish world of Eastern Europe had become what it was and how it had been destroyed. Yes, "in your new life" you "bestowed upon it and its Jews a posthumous life."

So what does this all have to do with Buddy Harrelson?[41] The bold innocence really shook me—for your sake. Naively, I thought that your love of baseball was basically aesthetic—Mozart in flannel pinstripes, so to speak. When I finished your memoir, I had the sad realization that historian or not, when Cleon Jones[42] or Tommy [sic] Agee[43] was racing from first to third with the tying run, the "ghosts of Vilna" were in attendance, if not in pursuit. (Given what they are dragging around those bases, isn't it amazing they don't get hernias?) I should have known, I suppose, but I didn't quite. All the knowledgeable fans are Jews—(Italians, Blacks, and Galitzianers included)—because appreciation depends upon memory. Not "instant replay" but real memory, the historical memory that believes that in the recall of a single, seemingly random event—and perhaps only there—can randomness be defeated and the universe understood. When [André] Maurois says that "memory is a great artist," he is correct as far as he goes; if he were so fortunate as to be a Mets fan who ate matzah on Pesach, he would have said that memory is the "only" artist. Through the restraint of focus, life becomes art—and life becomes knowable. It is in the mitzvah's paradoxical restraint that one understands, appreciates, and experiences life. Or in the seemingly restrictive artifice of the sonnet that Shakespeare (Galitizianers et al.) can best describe nature's beauty. (Note: we are discussing "historical memory," Cleon Jones' taking an extra base during a pennant drive; we are not discussing Jesse Orosco's relief pitching.[44] No doubt Jesse Orosco was traded for "your" sins, but he was also traded because of his own as well; your relationship with Orosco, therapeutic as it may be, is not "historical memory" so much as the simpler, more primal non-historical immediate aggressive instinct to "kill the ump." Alas, in the heart of every historian of the holocaust resides a pogromist; Freud *vais* [Yid., "knows"]. Say it ain't so, Sigmund!).

At any rate, I was somewhat saddened, I suppose, to discover that your Met base paths were clogged by more than Cub or Cardinal infielders making the pivot at second. This, I understand, is my innocence, but, after all, I come by it legitimately, having grown up a few hours down river from Hannibal.[45] As for historical memory and the Litvak, you are in very good company. Rav Soloveitchik, that is Yosha Ber, used to rhapsodize about the greatness of his ancestor, Rav Chaim Soloveitchik[46] and his contribution in introducing a very keen logic to talmudic study. A little necessary background: a "shtar" is the talmudic term for contract; a "chaspa b'olma" is literally a "shard of the world," which is to say, any old absolutely meaningless object. Well, rhapsody, as we know is better served by Hungarians and hasidim, but there was Rav Yosha Ber, practically braying praise of what his relative had done for a basic talmudic concept, "Until Zaydie [Yid., "grandfather"], it was a mere *chaspa b'olma*; Zaydie made it a *SHTAR!!!!*)" This came to mind when I first read your penultimate paragraph—"conditions of my contract" etc. and your saving "mere pieces of paper, the tatters and shards of a civilization." I grant there are differences (your delivery is much smoother, for one, especially with a runner on base), still . . . And as for America and what it can do with its thirst for heroes and all stars, on another famous occasion, Rav Soloveitchik wanted to let everyone know that no one, but no one, could carry his grandfather's, the Brisker Rav's bat, much less his Gemara,[47] and he stated very unequivocally that his grandfather was the only real Torah gadol [rabbinic "great"] in the early part of the century in someplace or other (Eretz Yisroel, perhaps) and no one else was even capable of selling peanuts while the Brisker Rav was in center field. Well, a young American born talmudist, David C., now a distinguished posek in Brooklyn, literally rose from his seat in the audience and protested at the slighting of the name of the Brisker Rav's great contemporary, the Chazon Ish.[48] Reb David C. was promptly shouted down and hustled out of the hall, a sadder, but I can assure you not a wiser talmud chacham [Torah scholar]. It wasn't David C.'s fault that he had grown up in Ebbets field with the Duke,[49] or maybe, *bayn hazmanim* [Heb., "vacation time" off from rabbinical study] had caught a glimpse of Willie Mays[50] in the Polo Grounds, but he did make a serious error—you don't go singing the Say-Hey Kid's praises in Yankee Stadium when Mickey Mantle is saying a yahrzeit shiur [lecture on the anniversary of a rabbinical teacher's death] for switch-hitters from Oklahoma!

Yes, Lucy, I know there is a fine line between the sacred and sacrilege—when they're not on the same side as they usually are. So what does all this mean?—If I could answer that question as precisely as I would like, I would have written this letter considerably earlier. Well, if I were to try to answer, I would suggest that you have written a Litvisher love sonnet whose lack of a rhyme scheme owes more to Walt Whitman than to Petrarch or Shakespeare. As for the end of the memoir, it is pure Huck Finn, of course, and like the *Adventures of Huckleberry Finn*, the greatness lies in the protagonist's moral decisions, which are simply part of himself. I suspect that such works, developmental in nature, may preclude the more "normal endings."

Lucy, all of this is not saying your memoir is not a historical memoir. On the contrary, it is suggesting that it is much more "historical" than you and Maurois might realize. And, it is that entry of the self into the memoir that creates something poetic and artistic—if not quite "normative history." So if there is in the authorial voice a love sonnet–writing Huck Finn who could carry Yosha Ber's pen, that only makes your personal dedication all the more special—Huck and Rav Yosha Ber knew something about "friendship and love." And we are appreciative. Love, Allen

P.S. We are all well and everyone sends love. My work is going well, but I shall save such things for the next letter—I owe you. [A happy and kosher Passover!]

NOTES

INTRODUCTION

1. Cynthia Ozick to Lucy S. Dawidowicz, October 27, 1987, Dawidowicz private papers. Shimon (Szymon) Dawidowicz, a Polish-born Jewish socialist and native Yiddish speaker, was Lucy's husband.

2. In fact, six months later, Dawidowicz wrote to her editors at Norton Books that though she was not in the "Slough of Despond," she was still not done with her memoir (*From That Place and Time: A Memoir, 1938–1947*), had dismantled some of its sections, but was hopeful about extricating herself. Lucy S. Dawidowicz to Amy Cherry and Donald Lamm, April 6, 1988. Lucy S. Dawidowicz Papers, American Jewish Historical Society, P-675, box 67, folder 1. Henceforth, all references to this collection will be noted as Dawidowicz Papers.

3. Emphasis is mine. Lucy S. Dawidowicz to Irving Howe, January 6, 1983, Dawidowicz Papers, box 76, folder 7.

4. Not all of the New York intellectuals were East European Jewish immigrant sons, but so many were. See Howe, "New York Intellectuals"; Cooney, *The Rise of the New York Intellectuals*; Alan M. Wald, *The New York Intellectuals*; and Jumonville, *Critical Crossings*.

5. When I started the research for this book over a decade ago, there was no critical work on Dawidowicz's life, save Adler, "Dawidowicz, Lucy S."

6. On the New York intellectuals' self-fashioning and verbal style, see Howe, "The New York Intellectuals," 41, and Daniel Bell, "The Intelligentsia in America," 38.

7. On neoconservatism, see Steinfels, *The Neoconservatives*; Dorrien, *The Neoconservative Mind*; and Vaïsse, *Neoconservatism*. On the Jewishness of prominent neoconservatives, see Ehrman, "*Commentary*, the *Public Interest*, and the Problem"; Murray Friedman, *The Neoconservative Revolution*; Heilbrunn, *They Knew They Were Right*; and Balint, *Running Commentary*.

8. Bender, *Intellect and Public Life*, and Hollinger, "Ethnic Diversity, Cosmopolitanism and the Emergence."

9. On the transnational ties among East European Jews in the twentieth century, see Green, *Jewish Workers in the Modern Diaspora*; Rosman, "Jewish History Across Borders"; Kobrin, *Jewish Bialystok and Its Diaspora*; and Kahn and Mendelsohn, *Transnational Traditions*.

10. The image of being "singed" is from a personal conversation with the writer Jonathan Rosen.

11. Kahn and Mendelsohn, *Transnational Traditions*, 5–6.

12. Kobrin, *Jewish Bialystok and Its Diaspora*, 8.

13. Her conservatism paralleled that of several prominent European émigré anti-isolationist intellectuals, including Hans Kohn, Thomas Mann, Reinhold Niebuhr, and Hermann Broch, among others. Gordon and Greenberg, "*The City of Man*, European Émigrés, and the Genesis of Postwar Conservative Thought."

14. Yet, there was always political diversity among Jews. For the American case, see Goren, "Orthodox Politics, Republican and Jewish"; Sarna, "American Jewish Political Conservatism"; and Dollinger, "Exceptionalism Revisited."

15. See, too, Wisse, *If I Am Not For Myself*.

16. See Marrus, *The Holocaust in History*; Michman, *Holocaust Historiography*; Bartov, *Germany's War and the Holocaust*, 80–81; and Kansteiner, "From Exception to Exemplum."

17. On public intellectuals, see Collini, "'Every Fruit-Juice Drinker, Nudist, Sandal-Wearer.'"

18. Eminent non-Jews, such as James Q. Wilson, Michael Novak, Francis Fukuyama, Peter Berger, Daniel Patrick Moynihan, and Fred Barnes, associated with the neoconservatives, even if they did not identify fully with them. Jeane Kirkpatrick was a notable female neoconservative.

19. Svonkin, *Jews Against Prejudice*, and Sinkoff, "The Polishness of Lucy S. Dawidowicz's Postwar Jewish Cold War."

20. This book's sources include archival holdings in libraries throughout the United States, Israel, and Germany and hundreds of never-before consulted documents that remained in the possession of Laurie Sapakoff, Dawidowicz's niece. I am grateful for her generosity in sharing Dawidowicz's private effects, which include letters, unpublished essays, artifacts, photographs, and audio recordings.

21. Norman Podhoretz was the editor in chief of *Commentary* from 1959 to 1995, when the reins were passed to Neal Kozodoy, who stewarded the magazine until January 2009.

22. The familial closeness of this group can be seen in the fact that Gertrude Himmelfarb was Milton Himmelfarb's sister and Irving Kristol's wife; Midge Decter was married to Norman Podhoretz.

23. The historiography on the Jewish Enlightenment (Haskalah in Hebrew) and its intelligentsia is vast. See Raisin, *The Haskalah Movement in Russia*; Stanislawski, *Tsar Nicholas I and the Jews*; Fishman, *Russia's First Modern Jews*; Sorkin, *The Transformation of German Jewry*; Feiner, *The Jewish Enlightenment*; Sinkoff, *Out of the Shtetl*; and Litvak, *Haskalah*.

24. Hyman, "We Are All Post-Jewish Historians Now," 57, and Kahn and Mendelsohn, *Transnational Traditions*.

25. On the claim that the *maskilim* sought to supplant traditional forms of Jewish leadership, see Lederhendler, *The Road to Modern Jewish Politics*.

26. Howe, "New York Intellectuals," 29. On the meaning of the term "intelligentsia" in the nineteenth-century Russian and Polish contexts, see Malia, "What Is the Russian Intelligentsia?"; Raeff, *Origins of the Russian Intelligentsia*; Walicki, *The Enlightenment and the Birth of Modern Nationhood*.

27. Reared in traditional rabbinic homes, the *maskilim* of late eighteenth-century Prussia and nineteenth-century Eastern Europe were a *secularizing* intelligentsia. In contrast, the New York intellectuals were already secularized. Feiner, "Toward a Historical Definition of the Haskalah."

28. For revisionist views of Jewish women's literacy, see Parush, *Reading Jewish Women*. Michael Galchinsky made a compelling case for a British Haskalah written in English by Jewish women. Galchinsky, *The Origin of the Modern Jewish Woman Writer*.

29. The great nineteenth-century Hebrew poet Y. L. Gordon, who excoriated the traditional rabbinate's treatment of women as part of his campaign against religious obscurantism, was a notable exception. See Stanislawski, *For Whom Do I Toil?*.

30. Dawidowicz dismissed the coinage of the pronoun "Ms." Maurice Friedberg revealed their shared bemusement about the term when he asked Dawidowicz for a recommendation letter to help defray the costs of typing his new "MS (כתב-יד, not Women's Lib להבדיל/[but categorically different!])." Maurice Friedberg to Lucy S. Dawidowicz, December 13, 1973, Dawidowicz private papers.

31. In many archival documents, the abbreviation for the American Jewish Joint Distribution Committee is also given as AJDC.

32. See Michael A. Meyer's recollection that Dawidowicz was the sole woman at the Association for Jewish Studies inaugural conference in 1969. https://www.jta.org/2018/12/18/united-states/jewish-studies-conference-celebrates-50-years-of-explosive-growth-in-the-field.

33. Lucy S. Dawidowicz to Aaron Asher, December 18, 1969, Georges Borchardt Inc. records, 1951–2018, box 8, Correspondence File, Rare Book and Manuscript Library, Columbia University Library.

34. Some recent treatments include Young-Bruehl, *Hannah Arendt*; Aschheim, *Hannah Arendt in Jerusalem*; Sznaider, "Hannah Arendt's Jewish Cosmopolitanism"; Benhabib and Eddon, "From Antisemitism to 'the Right to Have Rights'"; and Engel, *Historians of the Jews and the Holocaust*. Kessner, *The "Other" New York Jewish Intellectuals*, included chapters on Marie Syrkin and Trude Weiss-Rosmarin. Rosenberg and Goldstein, *Creators and Disturbers*, included Grace Paley, Justine Wise Polier, and Midge Decter.

35. Glenn, *Daughters of the Shtetl*; Orleck, *Common Sense and a Little Fire*; Rakovsky, *My Life as a Radical Jewish Woman*; and Klapper, *Ballots, Babies, and Banners of Peace*.

36. Mack, "Religion, Feminism, and the Problem of Agency."

37. Umansky and Ashton, *Four Centuries of Jewish Women's Spirituality*; Goldman, "The Public Lives of Cincinnati's Jewish Women"; Schwartz, *The Rabbi's Wife*; and Prell, *Women Remaking American Judaism*.

38. For a pioneering study of female conservatism, see Klatch, *Women of the New Right*. See, too, Collier, *Political Woman*. On October 17, 2016, the Schlesinger Library, the foremost repository of women's history in the United States, and the Radcliffe Institute held an event, "Righting the Record: Conservatism and the Archives," to address the glaring gap in the collections of major public repositories on conservative female activists. See https://www.radcliffe.harvard.edu/news/radcliffe-magazine/archiving-conservative-legacy and https://www.youtube.com/watch?v=6sJPA7Rl8OY.

39. On the New York intellectuals'"return" to Jewishness, see Levinson, *Exiles on Main Street*. On the ethnic awakening of white Americans in the 1970s, of which the Jewish "roots" explorations were a part, see Jacobson, *Roots Too*.

40. Heilbrunn, *They Knew They Were Right*, 59, 75. On Decter, see Grinberg, "Jewish Intellectuals, Masculinity, and American Conservatism," chap. 5, and Roth, "Neoconservative Backlash Against Feminism," 83–98.

41. Dawidowicz, *The War Against the Jews*. Levin's *The Holocaust* preceded Dawidowicz's book by a year but relied exclusively on secondary sources. Leni Yahil, a pioneering Dutch-Israel scholar of the Holocaust, published her major work on the Holocaust in Hebrew in 1987, yet it was only translated two decades later. Yahil, *The Holocaust*.

42. On the disregard for "amateur" female historians, see Smith, *The Gender of History*, 9.

43. Herman, "*Hashavat Avedah*"; Jockusch, *Collect and Record!*; and Gallas, "*Das Leichenhaus der Bücher*."

44. Interview with Laurie Sapakoff, December 2, 2009.

45. Aaron Asher to Lucy S. Dawidowicz, June, 22, 1983, Dawidowicz Papers, box 78, folder 6. Maurice Friedberg, a professor of Slavic Studies, was especially appreciative of Dawidowicz's enthusiastic evaluation of one of his book manuscripts because, he noted, she was "not a lenient critic, not even when it comes to personal friends." Maurice Friedberg to Lucy S. Dawidowicz, February 4, 1971, Dawidowicz private papers. Alfred Kazin commented in a postcard to Dawidowicz that he was trying to improve his typing, but he was "all a-tremble when I write to such severe no-nonsense people as L.D." Alfred Kazin to Lucy S. Dawidowicz, February 2, 1977, Dawidowicz private papers.

46. Dawidowicz, *From That Place and Time*, xlii.

47. Vaïsse, *Neoconservatism*.

1. AMERICAN IMMIGRANT DAUGHTER

1. The little we know about Dawidowicz's parents comes from her memoir, personal documents, and informal interviews with her friends and family. Dawidowicz, *From That Place and Time*. Interview with Laurie Sapakoff, December 15, 2009, and Eleanor Schildkret Sapakoff, December 16, 2011, June 22, 2012.

2. Dawidowicz, *From That Place and Time*, 6. On New York Jews in the 1920s and 1930s, see Moore, *At Home in America*, and Wenger, *New York Jews and the Great Depression*.

3. Markowitz, *My Daughter, The Teacher*. The public city colleges were segregated by sex until the 1940s. Hunter admitted men in 1946; CCNY admitted women in 1951.

4. Klapper, "'A Long and Broad Education,'" 23, and Wenger, *New York Jews and the Great Depression*, 61–63.

5. Dawidowicz, *From That Place and Time*, 9.

6. Hunter College High School *Annals*, 1932, Hunter College Publications Collection, box 7, folder 4, Archives & Special Collections, Hunter College Libraries, Hunter College of the City University of New York, New York City (henceforth, Hunter College Publications Collection, Archives & Special Collections).

7. Simon, *A Wider World*, III.

8. Interview with Elizabeth Klein Shapiro, April 26, 2012.

9. Cynthia Ozick to Lucy S. Dawidowicz, May 10, 1987, Dawidowicz private papers.

10. Simon, *A Wider World*, 113. See, too, Gorelick, *City College and the Jewish Poor*.

11. *Echo*, November 1934, 30–34, Hunter College Publications Collection, Archives & Special Collections, box 41, folder 4, and Dawidowicz Papers, box 54, folders 6 and 7.

12. Yehoash was the pen name of Solomon Blumgarten (or Bloomgarden), a Yiddish poet, scholar, and Bible translator.

13. Decades later, she wrote in her diary about a trip to London, "I paid homage to the Poet's Corner and oh-ed and ah-ed at the great names—Wordsworth, Smithey, Shakespeare, Dryden, Keats, Shelly, Handel, Jenny Lind . . . Browning, Tennyson, Darwin, Lyell." Dawidowicz travel diary, August 7, 1967, Dawidowicz private papers.

14. Howe, *World of Our Fathers*; Sorin, *The Prophetic Minority*; and Michels, *A Fire in Their Hearts*.

15. Kazin, *Starting Out in the Thirties*, 86.

16. Dawidowicz, "The Jewishness of the Jewish Labor Movement"; Liebman, "The Ties That Bind"; and Michels, "Socialism and the Writing of American Jewish History."

17. Dorman, *Arguing the World*, 44.

18. Markowitz, *My Daughter, The Teacher*, 41–42.

19. *Wistarion* 1935, 195, Hunter College Publications Collection, Archives & Special Collections, box 71, no folder.

20. Ibid., 205.

21. The Scottsboro case charged nine African American teenagers with rape. It set off a storm of protest because of the racist nature of the trial, with an all-white jury. The International Defense League, the legal arm of the Communist Party, represented the "Boys," who were posthumously pardoned only in November 2013.

22. *Hunter Bulletin*, Special Edition, March 1, 1935, Hunter College Publications Collection, Archives & Special Collections, box 36, microfiche.

23. The National Student League, founded in 1931, was a Communist student organization.

24. "Socialist Realism" had been officially promulgated at the Soviet Writer's Union Congress in 1934, demanding that the artist create "truthful, historically concrete representation[s] of reality in its revolutionary development . . . linked with the task of ideological transformation and education of workers in the spirit of socialism." Cited in Murav, *Music from a Speeding Train*, 12.

25. *Echo*, November 1935, 1–2, and Dawidowicz Papers, box 54, folder 6.

26. Lucy Schildkret to Evelyn Konoff, September 10, 1935, Dawidowicz Papers, box 54, folder 5.

27. Lucy Schildkret to Evelyn Konoff, October 13, 1935, Dawidowicz Papers, box 54, folder 5.

28. Markowitz, *My Daughter, The Teacher*, 58–62.

29. *Hunter Bulletin*, December 3, 1935, 2, Hunter College Publications Collection, Archives & Special Collections, box 36, microfiche.

30. *Hunter Bulletin*, December 9, 1935, 1, Hunter College Publications Collection, Archives & Special Collections, box 36, microfiche.

31. Lucy Schildkret to Evelyn Konoff, October 13, 1935, Dawidowicz Papers, box 54, folder 5.

32. She later claimed that her break with the party came because of her unwillingness to toe the line of the Popular Front. Dawidowicz, *From That Place and Time*, 19.
33. Lucy Schildkret to Evelyn Konoff, February 1936, Dawidowicz Papers, box 5, folder 54. *Wistarion*, the Hunter College yearbook, confirmed the resignations on its *Echo* page with asterisks next to Lucy's and Violet Smith's names. *Wistarion* 1936, 173, Hunter College Publications Collection, Archives & Special Collections, box 71, no folder.
34. Lucy Schildkret to Evelyn Konoff, September 10, 1935, Dawidowicz Papers, box 54, folder 5. Huey Long, the populist governor of Louisiana from 1928 to 1932, joined with the populist antisemitic priest Coughlin in a bid to win the presidency from Roosevelt in 1936 but was assassinated in 1935. On Long's and Coughlin's populist appeal, see Brinkley, *Voices of Protest*. Years later, Cynthia Ozick recalled Coughlin's radio broadcasts and her "cowering near the radio when that anti-Semite raved on." Cynthia Ozick to Lucy S. Dawidowicz, December 23, 1983, Dawidowicz private papers.
35. Sylvia Cole to Lucy S. Dawidowicz, October 17, 1982, Dawidowicz private papers.
36. Dawidowicz, *From That Place and Time*, 13.
37. Markowitz, *My Daughter, The Teacher*, 31.
38. Dawidowicz, *From That Place and Time*, 21.
39. Markowitz, *My Daughter, The Teacher*, 29.
40. Simon, *Bronx Primitive*, 48.
41. Interview with Eleanor Schildkret Sapakoff, December 16, 2011.
42. Lucy Schildkret to Evelyn Konoff, September 11, 1935, Dawidowicz Papers, box 54, folder 5. The National Youth Administration was a New Deal agency, operating under the auspices of the Works Progress Adminstration. It focused on providing work and education for young Americans, paying them up to forty dollars a month for "work study" projects at their schools.
43. See Lucy Schildkret to Evelyn Konoff, June 18, 1937, Dawidowicz Papers, box 54, folder 5.
44. Lucy S. Dawidowicz to Karl Leubsdorf, February 12, 1978, Dawidowicz private papers.
45. Hunter College Alumni Association, May 6, 1978, Dawidowicz Papers, box 54, folder 6.
46. Libe Shildkret to Evelyn Konoff, November 9, no year, but likely 1935, Dawidowicz private papers.
47. On Shatzky, see Lifshits, *Shatski-bukh*; Kuznitz, *YIVO and the Making of Modern Jewish Culture*, 85–88; and Aleksiun, *Conscious History*. Dawidowicz included excerpts of Shatzky's autobiography in Dawidowicz, *The Golden Tradition* (Holt, Rinehart and Winston), 263–69.
48. On diaspora nationalism, see Frankel, *Prophecy and Politics*; David H. Weinberg, *Between Tradition and Modernity*; and Simon Rabinovitch, *Jews and Diaspora Nationalism*.
49. Recent works on the Yiddish school movement, for which there is still no comprehensive, transnational study, include Sinkoff, "'Learning to Be Free'"; Shandler, *Adventures in Yiddishland*; Fishman, *The Rise of Modern Yiddish Culture*; and Freidenreich, *Passionate Pioneers*.

50. Cited in Fishman, *The Rise of Modern Yiddish Culture*, 99. On the Czernowitz conference, see Weiser and Fogel, *Czernowitz at 100*.

51. Mendelsohn, *On Modern Jewish Politics*.

52. Shneer, *Yiddish and the Creation of Soviet Jewish Culture*.

53. Freidenreich, *Passionate Pioneers*, 64.

54. Fishman, *The Rise of Modern Yiddish Culture*, chapter 7, "The Jewishness of Secular Yiddishists."

55. Leibush Lehrer, "The Jewish Secular School."

56. Buhle, "Jews and American Communism," and Michels, "Socialism with a Jewish Face."

57. Fishman, "From Yiddishism to American Judaism," 271.

58. Goodman, *Our First Fifty Years*, 136.

59. Dawidowicz, *From That Place and Time*, 7.

60. Ibid., 6.

61. Hoffman, "From *Pintele Yid* to *Racenjude*."

62. Dawidowicz, *From That Place and Time*, 10.

63. Auerbach, Charlish, and Starkman, *Leksikon fun der nayer yidisher literatur*, 5:235–37.

64. Sinkoff, "'Learning to Be Free.'"

65. Leibush Lehrer, "Camp Boiberik," 25.

66. Ibid., 8.

67. Leybush Lehrer, "Yidishkayt—vos darf men ton?" 52.

68. Leybush Lehrer, *Di tsiln fun kemp boyberik* (New York: Sholem Aleichem Folk Institute, 1962), reprinted as Leibush Lehrer, "The Objectives of Camp Boiberik."

69. Leibush Lehrer, "Camp Boiberik," 33.

70. All the nations of the world were represented in *Felker yomtov*, except Germany. Interview with Yosef Hayim Yerushalmi, October 20, 2008. Chana Mlotek confirmed Germany's exclusion from Boiberik's Yiddishist "League of Nations." Interview with Chana Mlotek, June 21, 2012.

71. Freidenreich, *Passionate Pioneers*, 382, and Leibush Lehrer, "Camp Boiberik," 34.

72. Leibush Lehrer, "Camp Boiberik," 4.

73. *Shrift*, March–April 1937, 24, Dawidowicz Papers, box 54, folder 4.

74. *Shrift*, November 1937, 48, Dawidowicz Papers, box 54, folder 4.

75. Shildkret, "Ir vet zey nit aroystraybn." See, too, Rudnicki, "Anti-Jewish Legislation in Interwar Poland."

76. Lucy Schildkret to Evelyn Konoff, Sunday morning, year undated, likely 1937, Dawidowicz Papers, box 54, folder 5.

77. *Shrift*, March–April 1937, 23–24. On Birobidzhan, see Levavi, *Hahityashvut hayehudit bebirobig'an*, and Robert Weinberg, *Stalin's Forgotten Zion*.

78. *Shrift*, March–April, 1937, 3.

79. Dawidowicz's notes for her memoir, dated Monday, August 25, 1986, Dawidowicz Papers, box 54, folder 4.

80. Hoffman, "From Czernowitz to Paris," 156.

81. At the conference itself, banners of Mendele, Sholem Aleichem, and Peretz, however, hung in the hall. Ibid., 160.

82. Lucy Schildkret to Evelyn Konoff, March 6, 1938, Dawidowicz Papers, box 54, folder 5.

83. Dawidowicz, *From That Place and Time*, 21–23.
84. Lucy Schildkret's February 1937 transcript can be found in Dawidowicz Papers, box 55, folder 4.
85. Lucy Schildkret to Evelyn Konoff, March 6, 1938, Dawidowicz Papers, box 54, folder 5.
86. Libe Shildkret to the YIVO Administration, February 17, 1938, YIVO Archives, RG 1.1, folder 437.
87. Max Weinreich to Lucy Schildkret, May 3, 1938, and Lucy Schildkret to Max Weinreich, May 14, 1938, Dawidowicz Papers, box 54, folder 4.
88. Dawidowicz Papers, box 55, folder 1. For Dawidowicz's description of Reisen, see Dawidowicz, *From That Place and Time*, 83–84.
89. Lucy Schildkret to her parents, October 10, 1938, Dawidowicz Papers, box 55, folder 1.
90. See Kaplan, *Dreaming in French*, and Blower, *Becoming Americans in Paris*.
91. Polukhina, "He Landed Among Us Like a Missile," 327.
92. Cole, "Lucy Dawidowicz—A Profile," 22. There were other Jews who went "backward" in the interwar years, such as recent immigrants, most famously the Yiddish modernist poet Jacob Glatshteyn, returning home to visit family and friends, Communists, Jewish communal activists, and religious students. See Glatstein, *The Glatstein Chronicles*; Newman, "Home Movies and the Alte Heym (Old Home)"; Soyer, "Soviet Travel and the Making of an American Jewish Communist"; and Kobrin, "American Jewish Philanthropy." Ruth Gruber, another young female Jewish free spirit, also set out to Eastern Europe in the interwar period. Gruber, *Ahead of Time*. See, too, Humphrey, *Poland, the Unexplored*, 13, 19–21. A Wellesley graduate and future travel writer and children's book author, Humphrey published five books related to her travels to Poland in the interwar period.
93. Typescript of Lucy S. Dawidowicz, "Biographical Sketch for *World Authors 1975–1980*," August, 31, 1982, Dawidowicz Papers, box 73, folder 6.

2. AN AMERICAN IN VILNA

1. Dawidowicz, *From That Place and Time*, 100.
2. Lucy Schildkret to Evelyn Konoff, March 31, 1939, Dawidowicz Papers, box 55, folder 1.
3. Dawidowicz, *From That Place and Time*, 83–85. Lucy also became close to Chaim Grade, whom she regarded as the greatest writer of Yung vilne (Young Vilna), the avant-garde Yiddish literary group. See the notes for her memoir, Dawidowicz Papers, box 53, folder 1.
4. Schorsch, *From Text to Context*; Myers, *Re-Inventing the Jewish Past*; Roemer, *Jewish Scholarship and Culture*; and Brenner, *Prophets of the Past*.
5. Seltzer, "Simon Dubnow and the Nationalist Interpretation"; and Rabinovitch, *Jewish Rights, National Rights*.
6. Cited in Jockusch, "Chroniclers of Catastrophe," 143.
7. Seltzer, "Simon Dubnow and the Nationalist Interpretation."
8. Benjamin Nathans, "On Russian-Jewish Historiography," and Jockusch, "Chroniclers of Catastrophe," 142.

9. Schorsch, "The Myth of Sephardic Supremacy," and Efron, *German Jewry and the Allure of the Sephardic.*

10. Seltzer, "[Book Review] *A Missionary for History*," 300.

11. Dawidowicz, "Max Weinreich"; reprinted in Dawidowicz, *The Jewish Presence*, 163–76.

12. Shandler, "Introduction," and Zenderland, "Social Science as a 'Weapon of the Weak.'"

13. Vaynraykh, *Der veg tsu undzer yugnt.* Lucy reviewed Weinreich's book before going to Vilna. Shildkret, "[Book Review] *Der veg tsu undzer yugnt.*"

14. Kuznitz, *YIVO and the Making of Modern Jewish Culture*, and Karlip, *The Tragedy of a Generation.* In Warsaw, Dubnow, Elias Tcherikower, Majer Bałaban, Mojżesz (Moses) Schorr, and Ignacy (Yitzhak) Schiper were the primary movers, joined by Saul Ginsberg, Israel Sosis, and Israel Zinberg from the Soviet Union, as well as by Emanuel Ringelblum and Raphael Mahler from Warsaw. On the historiographic methods of interwar Polish Jewish historians, see Eisenbach, "Jewish Historiography in Interwar Poland," and Aleksiun, *Conscious History.*

15. Fishman, *The Rise of Modern Yiddish Culture*, 135.

16. Vaynraykh, "Di untershte shure fun ershtn yor aspirantur," 101. See, too, Dawidowicz, *From That Place and Time*, 89–100.

17. Kassow, *Who Will Write Our History?*, 80.

18. For the program's regulations, detailing the time frame, stipend, academic expectations, and commitment to the YIVO's work, see Dawidowicz Papers, box 54, folder 4.

19. Libe Shildkret to Leybush Lehrer, September 19, 1938, Leibush Lehrer Papers, YIVO Archives, RG 507, box 5, folder 63 (henceforth, Leibush Lehrer Papers).

20. Aspirantur Papers, YIVO Archives, RG 1.3, folder 4053 (henceforth, Aspirantur Papers).

21. Libe Shildkret to Leybush Lehrer, December 26, 1938, Leibush Lehrer Papers, box 5, folder 63.

22. Dawidowicz Papers, box 53, folder 1.

23. Dina Abramowicz to Lucy S. Dawidowicz, May 5, 1989, Dawidowicz Papers, box 71, folder 8.

24. Dawidowicz, *From That Place and Time*, 143–45.

25. Ibid., 90, as well as 53, 75, 184, and 203, for expressions of her Americanness.

26. Libe Shildkret to Leybush Lehrer, September 19, 1938, Leibush Lehrer Papers, box 5, folder 63.

27. Lucy Schildkret to her parents and Eleanor, early September 1938, Dawidowicz Papers, box 55, folder 1.

28. Dawidowicz, *From That Place and Time*, 82–83. See, too, Dawidowicz, "Max Weinreich," and Roskies, "Maks Vaynraykh."

29. Cited in Kuznitz, *YIVO and the Making of Modern Jewish Culture*, 101, and Vaynraykh, "Undzer aspirantur un ire perspektivn," 562. The Bund was shorthand for the Jewish socialist party, the General Jewish Workers Party of Russia and Poland, founded in Vilna in 1897.

30. On Jacob and Adolf Berman, see Shore, "Children of the Revolution."

31. Vaynraykh, "Undzer aspirantur un ire perspektivn," 562.

32. Protocol from the first meeting of the cohort, September 9, 1938, Aspirantur Papers, folder 4053.

33. Notes for her memoir, based on Libe Shildkret to Leybush Lehrer, March 4, 1939, Dawidowicz Papers, box 52, folder 7, and Leibush Lehrer Papers, box 5, folder 63.

34. Ibid.

35. Shildkret, "'Hashofar.'" The Strashun Library was the creation of Matisyahu Strashun, a *maskil*, bibliographer, and historian, whose collections of over fifty-seven hundred rare Hebrew and Yiddish imprints and manuscripts in the nineteenth century constituted one of the most important Jewish libraries in Eastern Europe. Its collection included religious writings, fiction, poetry, scientific works, Jewish and Karaite historical works, and more. Strashun stipulated in his will that the collection be bequeathed to the Vilna Jewish community and ensured the funds for its upkeep. His collection became the foundation of the city's great Jewish public library. See https://www.yivo encyclopedia.org/article.aspx/Strashun_Shemuel_and_Matityahu, and Rabinowitz, *The Lost Library*.

36. Notes for her memoir, typed on March 10, 1987, based on an unidentified letter home, Dawidowicz Papers, box 52, folder 7.

37. Libe Shildkret to Yankev Shatski, May 17, 1939, Dawidowicz Papers, box 52, folder 7.

38. Notes for her memoir, typed on March 10, 1987, based on a letter home, December 6, 1938, Dawidowicz Papers, box 52, folder 7.

39. Dawidowicz, *From That Place and Time*, 94. See, too, Aspirantur Papers, folder 4048.

40. Notes for her memoir, typed on March 10, 1987, based on a letter home, December 6, 1938, Dawidowicz Papers, box 52, folder 7.

41. Joshua M. Karlip, *The Tragedy of a Generation*, 76–91.

42. Translated and cited ibid., 170.

43. Translated and cited ibid, 195.

44. Libe Shildkret to Leybush Lehrer, September 19, 1938, Leibush Lehrer Papers, box 5, folder 63.

45. Dawidowicz, *From That Place and Time*, 51–53.

46. Ibid., 4–8. To some readers, the omission glared. See Robert King to Lucy S. Dawidowicz, April 30, 1990, Dawidowicz Papers, box 71, folder 8, and Pearl Ketcher to Lucy S. Dawidowicz, January 18, 1976, where Pearl, expressing condolences to Lucy on her mother's death, noted: "I suppose you have very mixed feelings and are having a hard time." Dawidowicz private papers.

47. Dawidowicz's notes, dated March 14, 1987, from a letter to Leibush Lehrer, February 18, 1939, Dawidowicz Papers, box 51, folder 4.

48. Dawidowicz's notes, dated March 14, 1987, from a letter to Leibush Lehrer, October 25, 1938, Dawidowicz Papers, box 51, folder 4.

49. Dawidowicz's notes, dated March 14, 1987, from a letter to Leibush Lehrer, February 18, 1939, Dawidowicz Papers, box 51, folder 4.

50. Karlip, "At the Crossroads between War and Genocide."

51. Libe Shildkret to Leybush Lehrer, April 6, 1939, Leibush Lehrer Papers, box 5, folder 63.

52. Baron, *A Social and Religious History of the Jews*. On Baron, see Liberles, *Salo Wittmayer Baron*; Kirshenblatt-Gimblett, *Writing a Modern Jewish History*; and Engel,

"Crisis and Lachrymosity." See, too, Baron's history of the premodern Jewish communal structure, *The Jewish Community*.

53. Dawidowicz's notes, dated March 14, 1987, from a letter to Leibush Lehrer, February 18, 1939, Dawidowicz Papers, box 51, folder 4. Kalmanovitch may not have had either physical or linguistic access to Baron's *History*, but he would have been able to read Dubnow's review in *Di tsukunft*. Dubnow, reacting specifically to *History's* "Epilogue," which appeared in volume 3, criticized Baron's suggestion that East European Jews should learn how to accommodate to the illiberalism of Hitler's fascism and Stalin's communism. Faithful to his liberal optimism, Dubnow argued that Jewish political life needed to uphold democratic values. Dubnow, "A bukh vegen problemen in der idisher geshikhte." See, too, Liberles, *Salo Wittmayer Baron*, 151–52.

54. Baron, "Ghetto and Emancipation."

55. Cited in Engel, "Crisis and Lachrymosity," 255.

56. Alroey, *Zionism Without Zion*.

57. Dawidowicz's notes, dated March 14, 1987, from a letter to Leibush Lehrer, February 18, 1939, Dawidowicz Papers, box 51, folder 4.

58. Dawidowicz's notes, dated June 30, 1987, from a letter to Lehrer, October 25, 1938, Dawidowicz Papers, box 51, folder 4.

59. On hooliganism and pogrom violence against the Jews during World War I, the Russian Revolution, the Russian Civil War, and the Russo-Polish War, see Klier and Lambroza, *Pogroms*, and Dekel-Chen et al., *Anti-Jewish Violence*. Firsthand accounts include Babel, *1920 Diary*, and An-Sky, *1915 Diary of S. An-Sky*.

60. Brock, "Polish Nationalism," and Porter, *When Nationalism Began to Hate*.

61. Janowsky, *The Jews and Minority Rights*; Bacon, "Polish Jews and the Minorities Treaties Obligations, 1925"; and Fink, *Defending the Rights of Others*.

62. Mendelsohn, *The Jews of East Central Europe*; Mendelsohn, "Interwar Poland"; and Porter-Szűcs, *Poland in the Modern World*.

63. On Kraków, see Martin, *Jewish Life in Cracow*; on Warsaw, see Dynner and Guesnet, *Warsaw: The Jewish Metropolis*; on Łódź, see Mendelsohn, *The Jews of East Central Europe*.

64. Weiser, "The Jewel in the Yiddish Crown," 227.

65. Rudnicki, "Anti-Jewish Legislation in Interwar Poland."

66. Rudnicki, "Ritual Slaughter as a Political Issue."

67. In February 1938, Vilna city inspectors ordered shopkeepers to remove *all* Yiddish writing from their shops though there was no law against such signage. Kuznitz, "On the Jewish Street," 70.

68. Rudnicki, "Anti-Jewish Legislation in Interwar Poland," 165–66.

69. Wandycz, "Fascism in Poland: 1918–1939," and Rudnicki, "Anti-Jewish Legislation in Interwar Poland," 168.

70. Dawidowicz, *From That Place and Time*, 165–66.

71. Research notes, Dawidowicz Papers, box 54, folder 2.

72. Research notes, from *Undzer tog*, September 5, 1938, and September 27, 1938, Dawidowicz Papers, box 54, folders 1 and 2, and research notes, November 10, 1938, Dawidowicz Papers, box 54, folder 2.

73. Dawidowicz, *From That Place and Time*, 82. Majer Bałaban, a Galician-born Warsaw-trained historian of Polish Jews, also experienced physical violence at the university. In 1932, he was attacked by a group of students after his lecture, and in November 1938, he and his students were victimized again. Aleksiun, "Studenci z pałkami."

74. Dina Abramowicz to Lucy S. Dawidowicz, May 5, 1989, Dawidowicz Papers, box 71, folder 8.

75. These prewar observations informed her later perspective on the protean nature of anti-Jewish hatred. See Dawidowicz, "Can Anti-Semitism Be Measured?"

76. Dawidowicz, *From That Place and Time*, 167.

77. The emphasis is mine. Introduction to Avrom Sutzkever at B'nai B'rith, February 18, 1979, Dawidowicz Papers, box 51, folder 2.

78. Dawidowicz, *From That Place and Time*, 163. The YIVO activists Shlomo Mendelsohn and Hayim S. Kazdan urged Lucy not to write about her experience in Warsaw for fear of repercussions. She did only in 1940 and in Yiddish for an American audience. Shildkret, "Yidn in poyln."

79. Libe Shildkret to Leybush Lehrer, March 4, 1939, Leibush Lehrer Papers, box 5, folder 63, and in notes to her memoir, Dawidowicz Papers, box 52, folder 7.

80. Notes for her memoir, typed on March 10, 1987, based on an unidentified letter home, June 22, 1939, Dawidowicz Papers, box 52, folder 7. See, too, "Der siyem fun der aspirantur un pro-aspirantur."

81. With a byline only as .װ.ל, the reviews appeared in *YIVO bleter*, May 1939, 470–72.

82. Dawidowicz, *From That Place and Time*, 190.

83. Dawidowicz, "In Berlin Again," 32.

84. Lucy Schildkret to Dora and Max Schildkret, August 30, 1939, Dawidowicz Papers, box 53, folder 7, and Dawidowicz, *From That Place and Time*, 194.

85. Dawidowicz, *From That Place and Time*, 196, and Lucy Schildkret to the Konoffs, September 6, 1939, Dawidowicz Papers, box 53, folder 5. See, too, Ron Rosenbaum's interpretation of Dawidowicz's prewar encounter with this German gentleman as the key to her argument about the Nazis' deliberate rhetorical strategies to becloud their intention to murder the Jews; the polite conversation of the German office was emblematic of the glaring contradictions between "German civility and murderous deception" that marked the Nazis' verbal dissembling before and during the war. Rosenbaum, *Explaining Hitler*, 386–88.

86. Lucy Schildkret to her parents, August 30, 1939, Dawidowicz Papers, box 53, folder 7.

87. Lucy Schildkret to her parents, September 2, 1939, Dawidowicz Papers, box 55, folder 1.

88. Lucy Schildkret to her parents and Elly (Eleanor), September 5, 1939, Dawidowicz Papers, box 53, folder 5.

89. Lucy Schildkret to her parents and Elly (Eleanor), September 6, 1939, Dawidowicz Papers, box 53, folder 5.

90. Her research notes included a clipping from the *New York Times*, September 30, 1939, reporting that the SS *Donald McKay*, packed with two hundred American passengers, had taken in twelve European refugees. *Der tog* reported that Libe Shildkret arrived back in New York City on September 30, 1939, Dawidowicz Papers, box 53, folder 8.

91. The Soviets briefly ruled Vilna from September 19 to October 28, 1939, when the city was handed over to Lithuania and immediately renamed Vilnius. The process of de-Polonization and de-Russification was then set in motion. For eight months, the city became the center of Lithuanian statehood. But in June 1940, the Soviets moved in, reoccupying the capital and re-Russifying it on Soviet terms. Levin, "The Jews of Vilna under Soviet Rule," and Weiser, "The Jewel in the Yiddish Crown."

92. Newer scholarship has emphasized, however, the contradictions in Soviet nationalities policy and the persistence of pre-Soviet national identity. See Martin, *The Affirmative Action Empire*.

93. Dawidowicz, *From That Place and Time*, 245. In March 1971, Dawidowicz concluded the talk "Interfaith Relationships in Europe Prior to and after World War II" with the barest of nods to the existence of surviving Jewish communities of Europe: "But you need no one to tell you that the epoch of European Jewish history is closed. *Europe is the burial ground of the Ashkenazic era in Jewish creativity.*" Dawidowicz Papers, box 70, folder 3. In her synthetic work on American Jewish history, she wrote that the Third Reich's "only lasting accomplishment was the murder of six million European Jews and *the extinction of Ashkenazic Jewish culture on the European continent.*" Dawidowicz, *On Equal Terms*, 126. Emphases are mine.

3. THE NEW YORK YIVO IN WARTIME

1. Weinreich had already been in contact with Naftoli (Nathan) Feinerman, the head of the Amopteyl, in October 1939. Both were concerned about the YIVO's fate under the Soviets and began the transfer of institutional authority to New York, the demographic capital of the Jewish diaspora. Weiser, "Coming to America," and Shilo, "'Funem Folk, Farn Folk, Mitn Folk': Historiyah."

2. *Khurbn* (destruction) is the Yiddish word used by East European Jews for the events now generally subsumed under the term "Holocaust." The term *khurbn* comprised both the plain, secular meaning of the destruction of European Jewry in the twentieth century and the religious reference to the ancient destruction of the Jerusalem Temples.

3. Dawidowicz, *From That Place and Time*, 207.

4. The publication of *YIVO bleter*, January–February 1940, by the Amopteyl in New York remained a point of contention among Feinerman, Tcherikower, Kalmanovitch, and Weinreich. See Weiser, "Coming to America."

5. Weiser, "The Jewel in the Yiddish Crown."

6. Karlip, *The Tragedy of a Generation*, 222–23, and email correspondence of November 21, 2013.

7. On Lucy's recollections of Ber Schlossberg and Chana Piszczacer Mann, see Dawidowicz, *From That Place and Time*, 90–93.

8. Vaynraykh, *YIVO bibliografye*, 3–4.

9. Konvitz, "YIVO Comes to Morningside," and Dawidowicz, *From That Place and Time*.

10. Leff, *The Archive Thief*, 53.

11. Members of the Jewish Labor Committee—B. Charney Vladeck, a Bundist; William Green, president of the American Federation of Labor; David Dubinsky, president

of the International Ladies Garment Workers Union; and three other labor leaders, Joseph Schlossberg, Morris Feinstone, and Reuben Guskin—had been pressuring Cordell Hull since mid-1936. See https://www.jta.org/1936/04/15/archive/hull-gets-plea -for-u-s-intervention-for-polish-jews, and Isenberg, *A Hero of Our Own*.

12. Dawidowicz, *From That Place and Time*, 218, 222, 227.

13. *YIVO bleter*, November–December 1940, 200–201.

14. L[ibe] S[childkret], "Anti-natsi literatur."

15. See, too, S.[hlomo] M.[endelsohn], "Di yidishe geto in varshe."

16. Lester, "Historian of the Jews," 2.

17. Tobtsche wrote to her father in 1940: "How unjustified were people in their criticism of Peretz's story 'Bontsche Schweig'! A roll with butter is indeed a great dream." Cited in Noy, *Khurbn un oyfstand fun di yidn in varshe*, 419. Isaac Leib Peretz's story "Bontsche Schweig" (Bontsche the Silent) situated the protagonist in the world to come with the arbiters of justice, who review his modest, irreproachable quiet life. Granted whatever his heart desired, Bontsche requested only "a roll with butter." Peretz's stories were read aloud in the ghetto throughout the war. See Norich, *Discovering Exile*, chap. 4.

18. Dawidowicz, *From That Place and Time*, 231.

19. Ibid., 243–44.

20. Edelman, *Getto Walczy*, and Grupińska, Jagielski, and Szapiro, *Warsaw Ghetto*, 52.

21. Dawidowicz, *From That Place and Time*, 243.

22. Shandler, "'The Time of Vishniac.'" Scholarship has recently shown that Vishniac deliberately showcased the traditionalism and poverty of interwar Polish Jewry over its more modern, middle-class strata. Benton, *Roman Vishniac Rediscovered*.

23. "18th Annual Conference of the YIVO," *Yedies*, no. 2 (February 1944): 1–2, and Dawidowicz, *From That Place and Time*, 248. The recitation of kaddish at the meeting has had a mythical afterlife. It is most commonly reported that kaddish was recited not in 1944 but a year later on January 7, 1945, as a response to a talk, "Di mizrekh-eyropeishe tkufe in der yidisher geshikhte" (The East European Era in Jewish in Jewish History), given by Rabbi Abraham Joshua Heschel. See Moore, *East European Jews in Two Worlds*, viii, and Kaplan, *Spiritual Radical*, 397n22.

24. The term *Khurbn forshung* has been attributed to Lwów-born historian Philip Friedman. Completing a doctorate in 1925 at the University of Vienna, Friedman taught secondary school in Łódź until the outbreak of the war. Though he survived, his first wife and daughter were murdered in 1942. His academic training influenced the methodological principles for research on the Holocaust in all the postwar Polish centers and later in Israel and the United States. Friedman's work emphasized the distinction between what he called "Nazi-centric" and "Judeo-centric" sources and evidenced the tensions that would continue to inform Holocaust Studies among the commitments to "objective" historical research, the desire to commemorate the dead, and the determination to provide evidence for criminal trials. In 1947, Friedman helped organize the 1947 Paris conference, which brought together all of the groups that were collecting survivor testimonies. Most of the thirty-two delegates used the term *khurbn* to describe what had happened to European Jewry. Jockusch, *Collect and Record!* 4. On Friedman,

see Dawidowicz, "Holocaust Historian," 8, 18; Stauber, "Darko shel Filip Fridman beḥeker Hashoah"; and Aleksiun, "Philip Friedman and the Emergence of Holocaust Scholarship."

25. Jockusch, "Chroniclers of Catastrophe," 137.

26. Diner, *We Remember with Reverence and Love*, 93–95.

27. *Newsletter of the YIVO*, no. 4 (September 1944): 2. On Shatzky's history of the Jews of Warsaw, see Filip Fridman, "Yankev shatskis ort," 22–24.

28. *Newsletter of the YIVO*, no. 4 (September 1944): 7. On Sutzkever and the "Paper Brigade," see Fishman, *The Book Smugglers*, 67–89.

29. Lucy Schildkret to Eleanor Schildkret, March 21, 1943, Dawidowiz private papers.

30. Zosa Szajkowski to Moshe Kligsberg, March 10, 1943, Moshe Kligsberg Papers, YIVO Archives, RG 719, box 2, folder 60. At the time, Lucy was working on a master's degree, not a doctorate.

31. See his correspondence beginning in December 6, 1943, through October 18, 1945, Elias Tcherikower Papers, YIVO Archives, RG 81. I am grateful to Lisa Leff for sharing this correspondence with me.

32. Cited in Leff, *The Archive Thief*, 77.

33. Shaul Reyzen to Maks Vaynraykh, May 25, September 2, and October 20, 1943, Max Weinreich Papers, YIVO Archives, RG 584, box 16, folder 123 (henceforth, Max Weinreich Papers). See, too, Weiser, "The Jewel in the Yiddish Crown," 224, 240, 244.

34. Chana Mlotek suggested that the conflict arose over the planning of one of the YIVO's conferences when Weinreich had taken a leave to complete *Hitler's Professors: The Part of Scholarship in Germany's Crimes Against the Jewish People*. Dawidowicz had invited General Michael Angelo Musmanno, a naval officer and judge who had presided over the trial of the Einsatzgruppen at Nuremberg, to be the keynote at the YIVO conference. His talk was not well received, and Hayim Greenberg, a member of the YIVO's executive committee, blamed her, and Weinreich let her take the fall. Interview with Chana Mlotek, June 21, 2012.

35. Leybush Lehrer to Maks Vaynraykh, July 18, 1946, Max Weinreich Papers, box 70, folder 592.

36. Maks Vaynraykh to Leybush Lehrer, July 20, 1946, Leibush Lehrer Papers, box 3, folder 30.

37. Dawidowicz, *From That Place and Time*, 278.

38. See the YIVO's postwar mission statement published in *Yedies*, "Report on the Conference" (February 1946): 1.

39. Dina Abramowicz to Lucy S. Dawidowicz, May 5, 1989, Dawidowicz Papers, box 71, folder 8.

40. Dawidowicz et al., *For Max Weinreich on His Seventieth Birthday*. See, too, her appreciation of his work and life in Dawidowicz, "Yiddish: Past, Present, and Perfect."

41. Lucy Schildkret to Salo W. Baron, May 20, 1946, Salo W. Baron Papers, M0580, box 32, Department of Special Collections and University Archives, Stanford Libraries (henceforth, Salo W. Baron Papers).

42. Salo W. Baron to Maxwell M. Luchs, May 23, 1946, Salo W. Baron Papers, box 32.

43. Lucy Schildkret to Salo W. Baron, July 5, 1946. That same day, she also explained her departure to his wife, Jeannette. Salo W. Baron Papers, M0580, box 32.
44. *AJDC Weekly Review*, September 25, 1946, JDC NY Archives, Records of the American Jewish Joint Distribution Committee, NY AR 194554 1/1/2/2162, 1945–54 (henceforth, JDC NY Archives). These archives were digitally accessed at https://archives.jdc .org. See, too, Lucy's appointment letter from the AJDC and her United Nations Relief and Rehabilitation Administration passport, Dawidowicz Papers, box 55, folder 2.
45. *Yedies* (September 1946): 4.
46. Cable from Koppel Pinson to Lucy Schildkret, 07/19/1946, JDC NY Archives, NY AR 194554 /4/32/11/335.
47. Dawidowicz, *From That Place and Time*, 255.

4. IN THE AMERICAN AND BRITISH ZONES OF OCCUPIED POSTWAR GERMANY

1. Dawidowicz, *From That Place and Time*, 277–98. The figure of Amalek was biblical Israel's implacable enemy and became symbolically encoded throughout Jewish history as the progenitor of antisemitism.
2. Baron, "Reflections on the Future of the Jews of Europe," and Baron, "The Spiritual Reconstruction of European Jewry."
3. Jockusch, *Collect and Record!* 130, and Mankowitz, *Life Between Memory and Hope*, 40.
4. Aleksiun, "The Central Jewish Historical Commission in Poland," and Jockusch, "*Khurbn Forshung*."
5. Dawidowicz, *From That Place and Time*, 288. See the correspondence between the JDC's New York and Munich offices that mentions Lucy, including Elliot D. Sass to Maurice Egan, November 12, 1946, JDC NY Archives, NY AR 194554 /1/1/1/2126; M. Jacob Joslow to Lucy Schildkret, May 28, 1947, NY AR 194554 /4/32/10/357; and M. Jacob Joslow to Lucy Schildkret, August 15, 1947, NY AR 194554 /1/1/5/2310.
6. Jockusch, *Collect and Record!* 139.
7. Shalitan, a journalist and underground activist, had survived the Siauliai ghetto and Dachau concentration camp. Mankowitz, *Life Between Memory and Hope*, 40.
8. Even before the AJDC was permitted to enter the camps in August 1946, First Lieutenant Chaplain Abraham J. Klausner, a Reform rabbi, entered Dachau in May 1946 and visited the DP camps, personally transporting Jews to Feldafing and Landsberg. Hitchcock, *The Bitter Road to Freedom*, 314–16.
9. Lucy Schildkret to either her parents or to Szymon Dawidowicz, February 22, 1947. There is no addressee on the letter. Dawidowicz Papers, box 55, folder 3.
10. Dawidowicz, *From That Place and Time*, 295. See, too, Lucy Schildkret to Szymon Dawidowicz, July 24, 1947, Dawidowicz Papers, box 55, folder 3.
11. Lucy Schildkret to Ruth and Leo Schwarz, undated, but from the British zone. Leo W. Schwarz Papers, YIVO Archives, RG 294.1, folder 116, reel 13, frames 1391–92 (henceforth, Leo W. Schwarz Papers). See, too, Lucy Schildkret to Henrietta K. Buchman, May 12, 1947, Dawidowicz Papers, box 52, folder 4.

12. Lucy Schildkret to Ruth and Leo Schwarz, undated, but from the British zone, Leo W. Schwarz Papers, folder 116, reel 13, frames 1391–92.

13. Maks Vaynraykh to Libe Shildkret, May 29, 1947, Dawidowicz Papers, box 52, folder 1.

14. Lucy Schildkret to Henrietta K. Buchman, May 12, 1947, Dawidowicz Papers, box 52, folder 4.

15. Schwarz, *The Root and the Bough.*

16. Lucy Schildkret to her parents, February 22, 1947, Dawidowicz Papers, box 55, folder 3. The program had been initiated by Marie Syrkin. Syrkin, *The State of the Jews*, 28–29, and Kessner, *Marie Syrkin*, 374, 383.

17. Lucy Schildkret to Ruth and Leo Schwarz, Leo W. Schwarz Papers, reel 13, frames 1391–92. See, too, Lucy Schildkret to M. Jacob Joslow, June 20, 1947, JDC NY Archives, NY AR 194554 /4/32/10/357. In her memoir, she related that one young scholarship recipient had taken her own life before graduating. Dawidowicz, *From That Place and Time*, 301–2.

18. Gallas, "Preserving East European Jewish Culture," and Gallas, "Das Leichenhaus der Bücher," 40. This next section expands upon Sinkoff, "From the Archives."

19. The terms "the Jewish people" and "world Jewry" had no clear-cut definition and meant different things depending upon the ideological and political beliefs of those who used them. Defining the Jews as a "people," and not as a "nation," "religion," "ethnicity," or "race," or as a combination of these terms, was itself a product of modernization and the processes of political emancipation, linguistic and cultural assimilation, religious denominationalism, and nationalism. For a recent anthology on nineteenth- and twentieth-century writings on Jewish peoplehood, see Rabinovitch, *Jews and Diaspora Nationalism*; see, too, Pianko, *Jewish Peoplehood.*

20. Mendelsohn, *On Modern Jewish Politics.*

21. Herman, "Hashavat Avedah," 9.

22. Weinreich devoted himself during the war years to researching the connection between the German intellectual class and Nazism, issuing his study, *Hitlers profesorn: der kheylek fun der daytsher visnshaft in daytshlands farbrekhns kegn yidishn folk*, in two installments in *YIVO bleter* in 1946. His research detailed the Nazis' premeditated plan for the destruction of Jewish culture and the role that scholarship in the university played in consort with Nazism. He wrote, "This study is a report on the part of German scholarship in Germany's crimes against the Jewish people. . . . The actual murderers and those who sent them out and applauded them had accomplices. German scholarship provided the ideas and techniques which led to and justified this unparalleled slaughter." Weinreich, *Hitler's Professors*, 5–6. Lucy aided Weinreich in the book's research and asked a former Hunter professor to help him render it into readable English prose. See Dawidowicz, *From That Place and Time*, 262, and the CV she sent with her book proposal to Aaron Asher on December 18, 1969, Dawidowicz Papers, box 74, folder 8.

23. Green H. Hackworth to Max Weinreich, August 27, 1942, referencing Weinreich's June 10, 1942, letter, and Max Weinreich to Green H. Hackworth, August 3, 1944, YIVO Archives, YIVO Administrative Records, Series: Files Relating to Restitution of YIVO Property (hereafter "Records of the YIVO, Files Relating to Restitution"),

RG 100. The August 3 letter can also be found in Dawidowicz Papers, box 51, folder 7. In fact, "everything" had not been carried away from the building. The men and women of the "Paper Brigade" hid thousands of books and documents from the Germans— including those from non-Jewish libraries—*in* the YIVO building. Fishman, *The Book Smugglers*, 84–84, 87.

24. Dawidowicz, *From That Place and Time*, 268. See, too, Ben Kayfetz to Lucy S. Dawidowicz, March 30, 1990, asking if she were "the *Libe Shildkret*" who answered all of his queries to the YIVO in the 1940s. Dawidowicz Papers, box 71, folder 8.

25. Abraham Aaroni to Celia Aaroni, June 20, 1945, "Records of the YIVO, Files Relating to Restitution," with a copy in Dawidowicz Papers, box 51, folder 6, and Aaroni's follow-up letter to Weinreich of August 8, 1945, in the same box and folder. Many documents related to Dawidowicz's postwar months in Germany exist in duplicate and triplicate. These copies are held in other archives, often in the YIVO's materials, such as in the papers of Max Weinreich and in two boxes of uncataloged YIVO administrative files related to the restitution of its library from Vilna in the immediate postwar period. Lucy herself commented on the duplicative nature of her work. See Lucy Schildkret to Max Weinreich, May 25, 1947, Dawidowicz Papers, box 55, folder 4.

26. George W. Baker to Max Weinreich, July 23, 1945, "Records of the YIVO, Files Relating to Restitution," with a copy in Dawidowicz Papers, box 51, folder 6.

27. Dawidowicz, *From That Place and Time*, 269.

28. Max Weinreich to Green H. Hackworth, August 3, 1944, Dawidowicz Papers, box 51, folder 7.

29. The restitution of Jewish property was part of the international effort to restore plundered art, books, and religious artifacts to the countries formerly under the Nazis' grip. See Greenfield, *The Return of Cultural Treasures*; Kurtz, *America and the Return of Nazi Contraband*; and Intrator, *Books Across Borders*.

30. Gallas, "Preserving East European Jewish Culture," 80.

31. Max Weinreich to Judah Nadich, August 1, 1945, "Records of the YIVO, Files Relating to Restitution," and Dawidowicz Papers, box 51, folder 6.

32. Gallas, "*Das Leichenhaus der Bücher*," 40, and Herman, "*Hashavat Avedah*," 4–5.

33. Cablegram from Koppel Pinson to Leibush Lehrer, November 30, 1945, Dawidowicz Papers, box 52, folder 4.

34. Herbert Katzki to S. T. [*sic*] Pomrenze, March 12, 1946, JDC NY Archives, NY AR 194554 /3/8/1400.

35. Max Weinreich to Koppel Pinson, March 18, 1946, copy in Dawidowicz Papers, box 51, folder 9.

36. Max Weinreich to Marcus Cohn, July 24, 1946, copy in Dawidowicz Papers, box 51, folder 9.

37. Lucy Schildkret to Max Weinreich, March 29, 1947, and memos dated March 26 and April 2, 1947, Dawidowicz Papers, box 55, folder 5. See, too, Philip Friedman Papers, YIVO Archives, RG 1258, box 8, folder 394 (henceforth, Philip Friedman Papers).

38. Max Weinreich to Marcus Cohn, July 2, 1946, and Max Weinreich to Isaac Bencowitz, July 9, 1946, "Records of the YIVO, Files Relating to Restitution," with copies in

Dawidowicz Papers, box 51, folder 9. On the strained relations between the YIVO and the Ansky Historical-Ethnographic Society, see Kuznitz, "An-Sky's Legacy."

39. Theodore D. Feder to Leo W. Schwarz and to Joseph A. Horne, February 17, 1947, and Theodore A. Heinrich to Theodore D. Feder, February 24, 1947, Records of the US Occupation Headquarters, World War II, RG 260, Records Concerning the Central Collecting Points ("Ardelia Hall Collection"): Offenbach Archival Depot, 1946–51, M 1942, roll 1. See, too, Dawidowicz, *From That Place and Time*, 313.

40. Lucy Schildkret to Max Weinreich, February 16, 1947, Dawidowicz Papers, box 55, folder 3.

41. Cablegram from Lucy Schildkret to Max Weinreich, February 14, 1947, Dawidowicz Papers, box 52, folder 4. David Fishman refers to her as YIVO's "mole." Fishman, *The Book Smugglers*, 225.

42. Max Weinreich to Lucy Schildkret, February 14, 1947, Dawidowicz Papers, box 52, folder 4.

43. Maks Vaynraykh to Sholem Pomerants, February 14, 1947, Dawidowicz Papers, box 52, folder 1, and "Records of the YIVO, Files Relating to Restitution."

44. Maks Vaynraykh to Libe Shildkret, February 15, 1947, Dawidowicz Papers, box 52, folder 1. In 1949, once the YIVO's archives and books were safely in New York, Weinreich supported the creation of the JCR, Inc. as the international Jewish trustee for heirless and unidentifiable Jewish cultural property in the American zone. Herman, "Hashavat Avedah," 63, 71.

45. Shilo, "'*Funem Folk, Farn Folk, Mitn Folk*': The Restitution."

46. Lucy Schildkret to Henrietta K. Buchman, May 12, 1947, Dawidowicz Papers, box 52, folder 4.

47. Maks Vaynraykh to Libe Shildkret, February 15, 1947, Dawidowicz Papers, box 52, folder 1, and in "Records of the YIVO, Files Relating to Restitution."

48. Lucy Schildkret to Theodore D. Feder, May 13, 1947, Dawidowicz Papers, box 52, folder 6.

49. Lucy Schildkret to Max Weinreich, February 16, 1947, Dawidowicz Papers box 55, folder 3. She sent a copy of the letter to Szymon Dawidowicz, on which she had written a Yiddish endearment, evidence that their relationship had blossomed. Sinkoff, "From the Archives," 146–47.

50. Lucy Schildkret to Max Weinreich, February 16, 1947, Dawidowicz Papers box 55, folder 3. On Gershom Scholem's and Hugo Bergmann's work at the OAD, see Amit, "'The Largest Jewish Library in the World.'"

51. Lucy Schildkret to Max Weinreich, February 16, 1947, Dawidowicz Papers, box 55, folder 3.

52. Joseph Horne to MFA&A Section, March 3, 1947. Cited in Herman, "Hashavat Avedah," 169.

53. See, too, Koppel S. Pinson to Joseph Schwartz, July 29, 1946, marked as "strictly confidential," regarding the transportation of books and manuscripts from Germany to Paris, JDC Archives, American Jewish Joint Distribution Committee, Jerusalem Collection, Geneva II, Germany, box 321a, file 73, 07/29/1946. See, too, Herman, "Hashavat Avedah," 166–71.

54. Lucy Schildkret to Richard F. Howard, May 7, 1947, OMGUS, OAD roll 5, M1942, Richard F. Howard to Lucy Schildkret, June 2, 1947, and her response to him, June 20, 1947, OMGUS, OAD M1942, roll 5.

55. Herman, "*Hashavat Avedah*," 170–81.

56. Lucy Schildkret to Max Weinreich, February 16, 1947, Dawidowicz Papers, box 55, folder 3.

57. Ibid.

58. Fishman, *The Book Smugglers*, 17–18 and 196, and Shilo, "'*Funem Folk, Farn Folk, Mitn Folk*': The Restitution," 280.

59. Maks Vaynraykh to Sholem Pomerants, February 14, 1947, copy sent to Lucy Schildkret, Dawidowicz Papers, box 52, folder 1, and "Records of the YIVO, Files Relating to Restitution."

60. Maks Vaynraykh to Libe Shildkret, February 26, 1947, Dawidowicz Papers, box 52, folder 1. For a thorough discussion of Weinreich's—and Lucy's—efforts to convince the American government and the directors of the OAD, Isaac Bencowitz and Joseph Horne, that the Strashun's collection should be considered the YIVO's property, see Rabinowitz, *The Lost Library*, particularly chapters 5 and 6.

61. Max Weinreich to Joseph A. Horne, February 27, 1947, Dawidowicz Papers, box 52, folder 1.

62. Lucy Schildkret to Theodore Feder and Charles E. Israel, March 17, 1947, Dawidowicz Papers, box 55, folder 3.

63. Lucy Schildkret to Charles E. Israel, March 17, 1947, Philip Friedman Papers, folder 394. She followed up this memo on April 7 to all AJDC regional directors, requesting their cooperation in tracking down the wayward volumes.

64. Lucy Schildkret to Theodore Feder and Charles E. Israel, March 17, 1947, Dawidowicz Papers, box 55, folder 3. A copy is also in Dawidowicz Papers, box 52, folder 1.

65. Lucy Schildkret to Henrietta K. Buchman, May 12, 1947, Dawidowicz Papers, box 52, folder 4.

66. Ibid.

67. Unsigned, *Not for general circulation. Conference of the Central Historical Commission*, written in Offenbach, May 16, 1947, Dawidowicz Papers, box 55, folder 4.

68. Ibid. Dawidowicz's hatred for Germany and Germans in the postwar period was a leitmotif in her memoir. Gallas, "*Das Leichenhaus der Bücher*," 42.

69. Unsigned. *Not for general circulation. Conference of the Central Historical Commission*, written in Offenbach, May 16, 1947, Dawidowicz Papers, box 55, folder 4, and circular letter to Lucy's family, April 20, 1947, Dawidowicz Papers, box 55, folder 3.

70. Lucy Schildkret to Theodore D. Feder, May 13, 1947, Dawidowicz Papers, box 55, folder 4.

71. Ibid., and a copy in "Records of the YIVO, Files Relating to Restitution."

72. In fact, while Friedman may have agreed to the distribution plan, he deeply resented Lucy's autonomy. See Filip Fridman to Libe Shildkret, May 2, 1947, and Friedman to Samuel S. Haber, June 23 and June 26, 1947. All three letters can be found in Philip Friedman Papers, folder 394.

73. Herman, "*Hashavat Avedah*," 164. Lucy Schildkret to Theodore Feder and Charles E. Israel, March 17, 1947, Dawidowicz Papers, box 55, folder 3. See Rabinowitz, *The Lost Library*, 127 and 237n92.

74. Maks Vaynraykh to Libe Shildkret, February 26, 1947, Dawidowicz Papers, box 52, folder 1.

75. Maks Vaynraykh to Libe Shildkret, May 12, 1947, Dawidowicz Papers, box 52, folder 1.

76. Maks Vaynraykh to Sholem Pomerants, May 2, 1947, "Records of the YIVO, Files Relating to Restitution."

77. Maks Vaynraykh to Libe Shildkret, May 29, 1947, Dawidowicz Papers, box 52, folder 1.

78. Cited in Waite, "Returning the Jewish Cultural Property." Gershom Scholem, too, considered the revitalization of German Jewry's great culture impossible. See his letter to Ernest Frischer, June 13, 1946, cited in Herman, "*Hashavat Avedah*," 173n70.

79. Lucy Schildkret to Joseph A. Horne, May 24, 1947, Dawidowicz Papers, box 55, folder 4.

80. Sinkoff, "The Polishness of Lucy S. Dawidowicz's Postwar Jewish Cold War."

81. Lucy Schildkret to Joseph A. Horne, May 24, 1947, Dawidowicz Papers, box 55, folder 4.

82. Lucy Schildkret to Werner Peiser, May 23, 1947, Dawidowicz Papers, box 52, folder 1.

83. Though Weinreich consistently advocated for the removal of Jewish cultural property from postwar Germany, he admitted the possibility of the restoration of Jewish life there: "Should Jewish life in Germany be restituted at some future date to the degree of warranting the return of any part of these treasures to Germany territory, the American trusteeship established for the administration of this property would act accordingly." Max Weinreich to Archibald MacLeish, April 4, 1945, "Records of the YIVO, Files Relating to Restitution," with a copy in Dawidowicz Papers, box 51, folder 6. See, too, Brenner, *After the Holocaust*.

84. Lucy Schildkret to Max Weinreich, May 25, 1947, Dawidowicz Papers, box 55, folder 4.

85. Ibid.

86. Lucy's transliteration predates the YIVO's standard form, adopted informally by the 1940s and first fully articulated in Uriel Weinreich's dictionary in 1968. I am grateful to Alec Eliezer (Leyzer) Burko for this reference.

87. Lucy Schildkret to Max Weinreich, June 17, 1947, Dawidowicz Papers, box 55, folder 4, and Library of Congress Mission Receipt, June 17, 1947, "Records of the YIVO, Files Relating to Restitution."

88. Seymour Pomrenze to Max Weinreich and Mark Uveeler, June 21, 1947, "Records of the YIVO, Files Relating to Restitution." Fishman, *The Book Smugglers*, 226–27.

89. On July 13, 1947, Pomrenze cabled Weinreich and Uveeler, informing them that his mission to Czechoslovakia had not been successful. Seymour Pomrenze to Max Weinreich, July 13, 1947, Dawidowicz Papers, box 55, folder 5.

90. In general, all of those involved with the transfer of YIVO's property were eager to keep the mission under wraps. See Noel Hemmendinger to Max Weinreich, August 13, 1947, Dawidowicz Papers, box 52, folder 6.

91. Maks Vaynraykh to Libe Shildkret, July 3, 1947, Dawidowicz Papers, box 52, folder 6.

92. Ibid.
93. Lucy obtained a photostat of the dissertation. Lucy Schildkret to Max Weinreich, September 30, 1947, Max Weinreich Papers, box 70, folder 592. See, too, Lucy Schildkret to Dr. Rohde, Director, University Library, Marburg, September 30, 1947, Max Weinreich Papers, box 70, folder 595. Weinreich's dissertation was published as *Geschichte der Jiddischen Sprachforschung*. When the University of Marburg wanted to honor Weinreich with an honorary doctorate, he refused. Schwarz, *Survivors and Exiles*, 147.
94. Maks Vaynraykh to Libe Shildkret, July 3, 1947, Dawidowicz Papers, box 52, folder 6.
95. Max Weinreich to Seymour Pomrenze, March 19, 1946, "Records of the YIVO, Files Relating to Restitution," and Gallas, "Preserving East European Jewish Culture," 82.
96. Lucy Schildkret to Max Weinreich, June 17, 1947, Dawidowicz Papers, box 55, folder 4, and "Records of the YIVO, Files Relating to Restitution."
97. "Records of the YIVO, Files Relating to Restitution."
98. "YIVO Library Is Back Home," *News of the YIVO* 40 (March 1951): 1–2, and *Yedies fun YIVO* 40 (March 1951): 1–2.
99. Pomrenze [Pomerants], "'Operation Offenbach,'" and Poste, "Books Go Home from the Wars." See, too, Friedman, "The Fate of the Jewish Book."
100. Max Weinreich to Lois C. Schwartz, April 3, 1960, Max Weinreich Papers, folder 627. On *The Eternal Light*, see Shandler and Katz, "Broadcasting American Judaism," and Krah, "Role Models or Foils for American Jews?"
101. Jockusch, *Collect and Record!*, 92, 130, 190–91.
102. Arendt worked with Salo W. Baron as secretary to JCR, Inc., from 1947 to 1959. See Grossman, "Scholar as Political Activist," and Schidorsky, "Hannah Arendt's Dedication."
103. See Reed, "Ardelia Hall," and https://www.nytimes.com/2014/02/02/arts/design/not-all-monuments-men-were-men.html.
104. Dawidowicz, *From That Place and Time*, 318, 326, and Gallas, "Preserving East European Jewish Culture," 85.
105. Lucy Schildkret to Ruth and Leo W. Schwarz, undated, but written after June 1947, Leo W. Schwarz Papers, folder 116, reel 13, frame 1392.
106. JDC Archives. Transmigration Bureau Card Index. Digitally accessed.
107. Dawidowicz, *From That Place and Time*, 325. See, too, Lucy Schildkret to M. Jacob Joslow, June 20, 1947, relating that she needs a "new assignment," JDC NY Archives, NY AR 194554/4/32/10/357.
108. Lucy Schildkret to Szymon Dawidowicz (?), July 24, 1947, Dawidowicz Papers, box 55, folder 4.
109. Lucy Schildkret to M. Jacob Joslow, June 20, 1947, JDC NY Archives, NY AR 194554/4/32/10/357.
110. M. Jacob Joslow to Lucy Schildkret, August 15, 1947, JDC NY Archives, NY AR 194554/1/1/5/2310.
111. She only published one short article on her Belsen experience. Dawidowicz, "Belsen Remembered."
112. Lucy and Pearl corresponded for forty years, from 1950 until Lucy's death in 1990.

Concerned about Pearl's health after her stroke, Lucy charged Allen Hoffman, a mutual friend, with informing Pearl personally in the event of her death, lest her friend hear the news over the radio or in the newspapers. Interview with Allen Hoffman, June 2013. On Pearl Ketcher's medical work in Israel, see Stern, *Daughters from Afar*.

113. Israel Kaplan to Lucy S. Dawidowicz, February 27, 1966, Dawidowicz Papers, box 66, folder 9. See, too, Lucy S. Dawidowicz to Amir Feigenbaum [Moshe Feigenbaum's son], July 17, 1988, expressing regret that she had not stayed in touch with his father, Dawidowicz Papers, box 67, folder 2.

114. Grossman, *Germans, Jews, and Allies*, and Patt, *Finding Home and Homeland*.

115. Königseder and Wetzel, "DP Camps 1945–1950," 49, 62n73.

116. Lucy Schildkret to either Szymon Dawidowicz or to her parents. There is no addressee. May 6, 1947, Dawidowicz Papers, box 55, folder 4.

117. Sadie Sender to M. Jacob Joslow, April 1, 1947, JDC NY Archives, NY AR 194554/4/32/4/379.

118. Correspondence between the Central Jewish Committee (CJC) and the American Jewish Joint Distribution Committee (AJDC), Yad Vashem Archives, Collection Josef Rosensaft Bergen-Belsen DP Camp Archives, O.70/17.

119. Lavsky, "British Jewry and the Jews."

120. Königseder and Wetzel, *Waiting for Hope*, 178–81. Pearl Ketcher employment records, Transmigration Bureau Card Index, and A. A. Neuwirth to George Sugar-man, December 18, 1947, JDC Archives, Records of the Geneva Office of the American Jewish Joint Distribution Committee, 1945–1954, G 45–54/4/8/36/GER.517, 1945–54.

121. Kadosh and Nooter, "The American Jewish Joint Distribution Committee."

122. The first congress was held on September 25–27, 1945.

123. Forty-two Jews were killed and forty more wounded in Kielce. See Gross, *Fear*. Lucy noted the pressure imposed by the "infiltrees" in her letters home. Lucy Schildkret to unknown addressee, November 19, 1946, and February 22, 1947, Dawidowicz Papers, box 55, folder 3.

124. Kadosh and Nooter, "The American Jewish Joint Distribution Committee," and Königseder and Wetzel, "DP Camps 1945–1950," 49–50.

125. Reporting to Jacob Joslow that over one hundred books had been received for the camp from the *Di tsukunft* Publishing House, Lucy noted that accountability was still a problem: "I haven't heard of any arriving in Frankfurt and I think I would have been told if they had come. Maybe they are all in Munich and Pal Philip [Friedman] is sitting on them." Lucy Schildkret to M. Jacob Joslow, June 20, 1947, JDC NY Archives, NY AR 194554 /4/32/10/357.

126. Lucy Schildkret to unknown addressee—likely Szymon—August 31, 1947, Dawidowicz Papers, box 55, folder 4.

127. Ibid.

128. Ibid.

129. Lucy Schildkret to unknown addressee, December 8, 1946, Dawidowicz Papers, box 55, folder 3, and August 31, 1947, box 55, folder 4. See, too Grossman, *Germans, Jews, and Allies*.

130. Lucy Schildkret to Szymon Dawidowicz, September 7–8 and September 12, 1947, as well as notes to herself from September 20, 1947, Dawidowicz Papers, box 55, folder 4.

131. Moshe Pearlman, Pearl's brother, was a journalist who covered the *Exodus* affair for *PM* from August through October, 1947. He later founded the Israel Press Office.

132. Marc Jarblum, a Warsaw-born socialist Zionist active in Poalei Zion worked for the Jewish Agency for Palestine in Paris and chaired the Federation of Jewish Organizations in France.

133. Lucy Schildkret to Syzmon Dawidowicz, September 7–8, 1947, Dawidowicz Papers, box 55, folder 4.

134. Samuel Haber to Herbert Katzki, December 23, 1947, and Herbert Katzki to Samuel Dallob, November 3 and 17, 1947, JDC Archives, Records of the American Jewish Joint Distribution Committee, Geneva Collection, 1945–1954 4/27/3/P.I.146.

135. Lucy Schildkret to Szymon Dawidowicz, September 12, 1947, Dawidowicz Papers, box 55, folder 4.

136. Ibid.

137. Ibid.

138. Lucy Schildkret to Szymon Dawidowicz, September 7–8, 1847, and December 8, 1947, Dawidowicz Papers, box 55, folder 4.

139. The Hebrew phrase "Sheerith ha-Pleta" (the Surviving Remnant), from Ezra 9:14 and 1 Chronicles 4:43, was used by Jewish welfare agencies and by Jewish refugees who survived the Holocaust to refer to themselves and the communities they formed following their liberation in the spring of 1945.

140. Dawidowicz Papers, box 31, folder 5. On the "Second Generation," see Berger and Berger, *Second Generation Voices*, 3.

141. Maks Vaynraykh to Libe Shildkret, August 10, 1947, Max Weinreich Papers, box 30, folder 592.

142. Leybush Lehrer to Maks Vaynraykh, January 22, 1948, Max Weinreich Papers, box 30, folder 592.

143. Hersey, *The Wall*. See Sanders, *John Hersey*, and Sanders, *John Hersey Revisited*. Despite her work with Hersey, Dawidowicz still sought paid reviewing work. See Shmuel Niger, editor of *Di tsukunft*, to Lucy S. Dawidowicz, January 4, 1949, Dawidowicz private papers.

144. Hersey, "Prisoner 339, Klooga," and Hersey, "Life's Reports, Home to Warsaw."

145. Hersey, "The Novel of Contemporary History," and Hersey, *To Invent a Memory*.

146. John Hersey to Mark Nowogrodzki, October 13, 1949, personal collection of Mark Nowogrodzki. Lucy or Szymon must have introduced Mark Nowogrodzki to Hersey. Szymon and Mark Nowogrodzki's father, the Bundist secretary-general Emanuel Nowogrodzki, knew each other from Warsaw political circles. Interview with Mark Nowogrodzki, December 6, 2009. See, too, Lucy S. Dawidowicz to John Hersey, May 5–17, 1948, John Hersey Papers, Uncat ZA MS 235 box 20, Yale Collection of American Literature, Beinecke Rare Book and Manuscript Library.

147. Hersey was the son of American Protestant missionaries. His novel emphasized the universalist inhumanity of "Man against Man." Sinkoff, "Fiction's Archive."

148. Goldstein, *Finf yor in varshever geto*, later published in English as *The Stars Bear Witness*. Hersey's archives and Mark Nowogrodzki's private papers contain letters from Goldstein and Shatzkin expressing concern about the universalist cast of the novel's plot. Leonard Shatzkin to John Hersey, December 7, 1949, and John Hersey to Mark Nowogrodzki, October 13, 1949, John Hersey Papers, Uncat ZA MS 235, box 8, Yale Collection of American Literature, Beinecke Rare Book and Manuscript Library.

149. Initially ambivalent about Hersey's universalist perspective, Dawidowicz either came to appreciate his approach or was diplomatic in praising him once the book received so many accolades. Lucy S. Dawidowicz to John Hersey, February 19, 1950, John Hersey Papers, Uncat ZA MS 235, box 20.

150. Asked to provide a reference for Dawidowicz, M. Jacob Joslow wrote that "Lucy S. Dawidowicz is a person of exceptional ability, possesses a keen and analytical mind, and most loyal to the organization and to the people with whom she worked, that is, DP's. . . . Perhaps the best evaluation can be given by the fact that if Mrs. Dawidowicz would have been willing to come back to Europe, we would have renewed her contract." M. Jacob Joslow to Lillian L. Smirlock, January 12, 1949, JDC NY Archives, 1945–1964, file 2149.

151. Moore, *GI Jews*. Writing to her sister, who had volunteered for the Women's Army Corps during the war, Lucy commented, "Just goes to show, that you don't have to have boys in the family to be patriotic." Lucy Schildkret to Eleanor Schildkret, March 21, 1943, Dawidowicz private papers.

152. Dawidowicz, *From That Place and Time*, 279.

5. INSIDER POLITICS AT THE AMERICAN JEWISH COMMITTEE

1. Her first review was written in 1952, "[Book Review] Two of Stalin's Victims: *Henryk Ehrlich un Viktor Alter*," and her last, published in 1990, was "[Book Review] Hertzberg's Complaint: *The Jews in America: Four Centuries of an Uneasy Encounter*."

2. On the role of religion in America's early Cold War, see Herzog, *The Spiritual-Industrial Complex*.

3. Bruch, "The Fatherhood of God and the Brotherhood of Man," 108; Silk, "Notes on the Judeo-Christian Tradition in America"; and Schultz, *Tri-Faith America*. Will Herberg, a Marxist-turned-"believer," gave the image of the United States as a country in which Catholicism, Protestantism, and Judaism were equally accepted intellectual ballast. See Herberg, "From Marxism to Judaism," and Herberg, *Protestant, Catholic, Jew*.

4. Lucy S. Dawidowicz, draft to "Introduction to Avrom Sutzkever at B'nai B'rith," February 18, 1979, Dawidowicz Papers, box 52, folder 6.

5. Louis Marshall to Joseph Stolz, January 12, 1906, cited in Reznikoff, *Louis Marshall*, 21–22.

6. Dollinger, *Quest for Inclusion*. On the AJC, see Cohen, *Not Free to Desist*, and Sanua, *Let Us Prove Strong*.

7. Stuart Svonkin referred to the American Jewish Committee, the American Jewish Congress, and the Anti-Defamation League of B'nai B'rith as the diaspora's unofficial "department of state." Svonkin, *Jews Against Prejudice*, 2.

8. Cited in Singer, "Remembering Milton Himmelfarb," 695.

9. Milton Himmelfarb, "Is American Jewry in Crisis?" See, too, Cynthia Ozick's defense of the term "parochial" in "America: Toward Yavneh."

10. Interview with Rose Grundstein, June 30, 2010.

11. *Commentary* was editorially independent from the Committee's leadership, but it nonetheless also contributed to Cold War anti-communism. In the 1950s, it built upon the interwar anti-Stalinism of its legendary editor Elliot Cohen. Sanua, *Let Us Prove Strong*, 29.

12. Interview with Norman Podhoretz, September 21, 2009. See, too, the warm letters between them on the occasion of his twenty-fifth anniversary of editing *Commentary*. Lucy S. Dawidowicz to Norman Podhoretz, January 15, 1985, and Norman Podhoretz to Lucy S. Dawidowicz, January 17, 1985, Dawidowicz Papers, box 79, folder 1.

13. Marshall was a passionate defender of Jewish minority rights in Europe and of Jewish and non-Jewish civil rights in the United States as well as an environmental activist. Engel, "Perceptions of Power"; Matthew M. Silver, *Louis Marshall and the Rise of Jewish Ethnicity in America*; Loeffler, *Rooted Cosmopolitans*; and https://www.adirondack almanack.com/2017/08/louis-marshall-wilderness-conservationist-seeker-social -justice.html.

14. Dawidowicz, "Louis Marshall's Yiddish Newspaper" (1961). She later published "Louis Marshall's Yiddish Newspaper" (1963) and "Louis Marshall and the *Jewish Daily Forward*."

15. Not all Marxist interpretations of antisemitism reduced the causes of the phenomenon to class structure. Members of the Frankfurt School, such as Theodor Adorno and Max Horkheimer, found class conflict to be an inadequate explanation for antisemitism's tenacity in modern society. Jacobs, *The Frankfurt School*.

16. Adorno et al., *The Authoritarian Personality*.

17. Svonkin, *Jews Against Prejudice*, 27.

18. Dawidowicz, "Observations: Explaining American Jews," 86.

19. Gans, "The Origin of a Jewish Community in the Suburbs," and Goren, "A 'Golden Decade' for American Jews," 9.

20. Murray Friedman, *The Neoconservative Revolution*, 19–20.

21. Svonkin, *Jews Against Prejudice*, chap. 5.

22. Her anti-communist research can be found in three main archives: in the American Jewish Committee Records, RG 347.17.10, Gen-10, at the YIVO Institute; in the collections of the Jacob Rader Marcus Center of the American Jewish Archives; and in the AJC's digital archives (henceforth, AJC/digital).

23. The American Jewish Committee Records, YIVO Archives, RG 347.17.10, Gen-10, box 246, folder 4 (henceforth, AJC/YIVO).

24. She shared the view of Sidney Hook, a pragmatic anti-communist, whose 1953 pamphlet *Heresy Yes—Conspiracy No!* argued forcefully against toleration of Communists

as university professors because they avowed to overthrow the Constitution, which protected their civil rights.

25. Dawidowicz Papers, box 8, folder 11, contains a two-page list prepared by Helen Ritter of the AJC of all of Dawidowicz's anti-communist research memos. See, too, Lucy S. Dawidowicz, "Jewish People's Fraternal Order of the International Worker's Order," November 27, 1950, Dawidowicz Papers, box 8, folder 12.

26. American Jewish Committee memo, "Statement of Policy Toward Communist-Affiliated and Communist-Led Organizations," June 27, 1950. AJC/digital.

27. The American Jewish Committee Staff Committee on the Communist Problem, December 7, 1950, AJC/digital, and Svonkin, *Jews Against Prejudice*, 166–67. See, too, Young, "The Scorched Melting Pot."

28. Lucy S. Dawidowicz, Staff Committee on Communism, October 12, 1950, AJC/digital. Dawidowicz's authorship of this memo is affirmed by her initials on its last page.

29. Svonkin, *Jews Against Prejudice*, 116.

30. Lucy S. Dawidowicz, "Communist Approach to Jews: A Study of Communist Periodicals of July to October, 1950, Relating to Jews." October 20, 1950, AJC/digital.

31. Lucy S. Dawidowicz, "The National Committee of the Communist Party of the U.S.A. on Work Among Jews," November 16, 1950, AJC/digital.

32. Lucy S. Dawidowicz, "Communist Propaganda on Germany," April 12, 1951, AJC/digital.

33. Lucy S. Dawidowicz, "Communist Approach to Jews: A Study of Communist Periodicals of July to October, 1950, Relating to Jews," October 20, 1950, AJC/digital.

34. Staub, *Torn at the Roots*, chap. 1.

35. Moore, "Reconsidering the Rosenbergs," 21. Moore's article engendered a dispute between Dawidowicz and the board of the *Journal of the American Ethnic History*. Dawidowicz felt singled out by Moore's essay and sought a retraction by the journal. The editorial board declined, but Nathan Glazer defended Dawidowicz's interpretation of the Rosenbergs' guilt, insisting that the issue in the case was communism itself, not social class: "The Rosenberg case was ... about Communist Jews and pro-Communist Jews v. Socialist and anti-Communist Jews. There were divisions about the severity of the sentence; there was little argument over the question of guilt." Moore responded, and both letters were published in the *Journal of American Ethnic History* 8, no. 2 (1989). There is a voluminous amount of work on the historiographic culture wars of the 1980s, which provides the context for the Moore-Dawidowicz dispute. See Hamerow, *Reflections on History and Historians*, 39–75; Gertrude Himmelfarb, *The New History and the Old*; Hamerow et al., "AHR Forum." Dawidowicz remained fixated on the Rosenbergs as iconic figures of corrosive Jewish universalism until her death. See the typescript of her supportive blurb for Evanier, *Red Love*, Dawidowicz Papers, box 61, folder 5.

36. The last photographs of the couple—taken to emphasize their Jewishness—showed them lying in state, garbed in white shrouds typical of a religious Jewish burial, with Julius wearing a prayer shawl. Yet their faces were uncovered, atypical for Jewish interment. Linden, "An Introduction to the Visual and Material Culture," 240–41. Tony Kushner's 1993 Pulitzer Prize play *Angels in America: Millennium Approaches* included

a hallucinatory scene of Ethel Rosenberg's ghost visiting Roy Cohn, a member of the original prosecution team, as he lay dying in his hospital room.

37. Morton Sobell (1917–2018), a communist associate of the Rosenbergs, was found guilty and served nearly nineteen years of a thirty-year sentence. Sam Roberts, "Figure in Rosenberg Case Admits to Soviet Spying," *New York Times*, September 11, 2008.

38. Dawidowicz, "'Anti-Semitism' and the Rosenberg Case," 42.

39. Dawidowicz, "The Communists and the Rosenberg Case."

40. See Reuben, "The Rosenberg Conviction"; Reuben, "Truth About the Rosenbergs' Case"; Reuben, "What Was the Rosenbergs' Crime?"; and Dawidowicz, "'Anti-Semitism' and the Rosenberg Case," 44.

41. Lucy S. Dawidowicz, "The Defense of Ethel and Julius Rosenberg: A Communist Attempt to Inject the Jewish Issue," March 18, 1952, AJC/digital.

42. Dawidowicz, "'Anti-Semitism' and the Rosenberg Case," 45.

43. Dawidowicz, "The Communists and the Rosenberg Case."

44. Dawidowicz, "The Rosenberg Case."

45. On East European show trials in the postwar period, see Feinberg, "Die Durchsetzung einer Neuen Welt."

46. Lucy S. Dawidowicz, "The Reaction of American Communists to Soviet Anti-Semitism," April 23, 1953, AJC/digital.

47. Emphasis in the original. Dawidowicz, "The Crime of Being a Jew," 11.

48. Dawidowicz, "False Friends and Dangerous Defenders," 10.

49. Ibid., 11.

50. Ibid., 13.

51. Ibid.

52. Glazer, *The Social Basis of American Communism*. Lucy S. Dawidowicz to John Slawson, November 27, 1961, AJC/YIVO, box 249, folder 5.

53. AJC/YIVO, box 246, folder 5.

54. John Slawson to Dawidowicz, May 22, 1953, AJC/YIVO, box 246, folder 2, and Dawidowicz, "Trojan Horse Returns."

55. *Now They Admit It . . . Communist Confessions of Crimes Against Jews.* Lucy S. Dawidowicz to John Slawson, March 26, 1958, AJC/YIVO, box 247, folder 1.

56. J. Edgar Hoover to Lucy S. Dawidowicz, October 26, 1956, Dawidowicz Papers, box 77, folder 1.

57. S. Andhil Fineberg to Slawson and Danzig, July 29, 1959, AJC/YIVO, box 247, folder 7.

58. S. Andhil Fineberg to John Slawson, December 4, 1961, AJC/YIVO, box 247, folder 2.

59. S. Andhil Fineberg to David Danzig, March 20, 1962, Special Project Discussion about the problematics of total Jewish assimilation into Soviet society, AJC/YIVO, box 248, folder 2.

60. Gordon, *Jews in Suburbia*; Neusner, "Religion," 52; and Jackson, *Crabgrass Frontier*.

61. Dollinger, *Quest for Inclusion*, 195, and Wilkerson, *The Warmth of Other Suns*.

62. Clark, "Candor About Negro-Jewish Relations."

63. Lucy S. Dawidowicz, "Negro-Jewish Tensions," October 1958, for November 17, 1958,

Domestic Affairs Committee meeting, MS-780 collection, series G (Information and Research Services), box 10, folder 13, American Jewish Committee Records. From the collections of the Jacob Rader Marcus Center of the American Jewish Archives (henceforth, AJC/AJA). A year later, Philip E. Hoffman, chair of the Domestic Affairs Committee Sub-Committee on Big-City Tensions, added a note to the memo, "The subject is a rather delicate one, and it would therefore be advisable for this document to be regarded as *confidential.*" Hoffman memo, February 4, 1960, AJC/YIVO, box 164, folder 2.

64. Myrdal, *An American Dilemma.*
65. Lucy S. Dawidowicz, "Negro-Jewish Tensions," October 1958, AJC/AJA, box G10, folder 13.
66. Minutes of the Domestic Affairs Committee Meeting, Institute of Human Relations, February 19, 1963, AJC/NYC archive.
67. For a discussion of the United States' distinctive "liberal offer" of emancipation, see Katznelson, "Between Separation and Disappearance."
68. Report on Executive Board Meeting in New Orleans, October 24–26, 1958, AJC/NYC archive.
69. Lucy S. Dawidowicz to David Danzig, September 23, 1959, AJC/YIVO, box 164, folder 2.
70. Held on April 18–24, 1955, the Bandung Conference, which was the first Asian-African conference, hosted twenty-nine countries. It promoted economic and cultural cooperation and opposed colonialism.
71. Lucy S. Dawidowicz to David Danzig, September 23, 1959, AJC/YIVO, box 164, folder 2.
72. Ibid.
73. AJC/YIVO, box 164, folder 3.
74. Memo for Staff Discussion, "The Crisis of the American Metropolis," November 16, 1959, AJC/YIVO, box 163, folder 20.
75. AJC/YIVO, box 164, folder 2. The draft for this memo can be found in AJC/AJA, box G24.
76. March 10, 1960, AJC/YIVO, box 164, folder 2.
77. Domestic Affairs Committee Sub-Committee on Big City Tensions, AJC/YIVO, box 164, folder 2.
78. Ibid.
79. Deslippe, *Protesting Affirmative Action*; Kaufman, "Blacks and Jews"; and MacLean, *Freedom Is Not Enough.*
80. Lederhendler, *New York Jews,* 13.
81. Moore, *At Home in America,* 88–121.
82. Decter, "The Negro and the New York Schools."
83. Lucy S. Dawidowicz to David Danzig, "Interracial Problems in Berkeley Public Schools," February 8, 1960, AJC/AJA, box G1, folder 24.
84. Lucy S. Dawidowicz, "Big-City Tensions: Schools," May 16, 1960, AJC/YIVO, box 163, folder 21, and Philip E. Hoffman to Domestic Affairs Committee Sub-Committee on Big City Tensions, May 25, 1960, AJC/digital.

85. Lucy S. Dawidowicz, "Big-City Tensions: Schools," May 16, 1960, AJC/YIVO, box 163, folder 21.

86. Staff Meeting to Review AJC Policy on Desegregation in Northern Schools, July 20, 1961, AJC/digital.

87. Lucy S. Dawidowicz to John Slawson, July 25, 1960, AJC/AJA, box G1, folder 1.

88. Ibid. See, too, Lewis, "Parallels and Divergences."

89. Lucy S. Dawidowicz to John Slawson, July 25, 1960, AJC/AJA, box G1, folder 1.

90. Lucy S. Dawidowicz to David Danzig, October 6, 1961, AJC/AJA, box G1, folder 24. See, too, her review of a book on Israel that same year that reflected on Palestinian rage. She alluded to James Baldwin's critique of the film adaptation of *Porgy and Bess*, directed by a white man: "Baldwin was right. How can whites know what it is like to be inside a black skin in America?" Dawidowicz, "[Book Review] *Israel: A Blessing and a Curse*," 84.

91. Lucy S. Dawidowicz to John Slawson, July 25, 1960, AJC/AJA, box G1, folder 1.

92. Ibid.

93. Lucy S. Dawidowicz to David Danzig, October 29, 1963, AJC/AJA, box G1, folder 26.

94. See, too, Norman Podhoretz's comments in his (in)famous article "My Negro Problem—and Ours," in which he noted that white middle-class liberals have discovered "that their abstract commitment to the cause of Negro rights will not stand the test of a direct confrontation. . . . In practice, these whites leave the City, send their kids to private schools, resist gerrymandering, cluck their tongues over Negro militancy, and wonder if maybe there is something to biological difference." Podhoretz, "My Negro Problem—and Ours," 99.

95. Lucy S. Dawidowicz to David Danzig, October 29, 1963, AJC/AJA, box G1, folder 16.

96. American Jews were never a political monocultural. Like all Americans, their political attitudes were subject to the influences of region, social class, religious commitment, and professional achievement. See Dollinger, "Exceptionalism Revisited," and Dollinger, *Quest for Inclusion*, chaps. 7 and 8.

97. Murray Friedman, "The White Liberal's Retreat," 43.

98. In March 1964, *Commentary* published a discussion held among James Baldwin, Nathan Glazer, Sidney Hook, and Gunner Myrdal that exposed the gulf between the perspectives of white liberals and African Americans on the pace of the civil rights movement. The three white men, Glazer, Hook (both of whom were immigrant sons), and Myrdal, were cautiously optimistic that the morality of American institutions could accommodate African American aspirations for full integration and respect, yet Baldwin, the sole African American on the panel, challenged the very possibility of African Americans' finding true equality in America. Baldwin et al., "Liberalism and the Negro."

99. Danzig, "The Meaning of Negro Strategy."

100. Lucy S. Dawidowicz, "The Use of the Referendum Against Civil-Rights Legislation," March 23, 1964; Lucy S. Dawidowicz, "White Resistance in the North to School Integration," April 17, 1964; Lucy S. Dawidowicz, "Differences between Leaders and Masses," April 21, 1964, AJC/AJA, box G1, folder 27.

101. Lucy S. Dawidowicz, "Recent Jewish Voting on Civil-Rights Issues," October 19, 1964, Information Service, AJC/AJA, box G1, folder 30.

102. Dawidowicz, "Civil Rights and Intergroup Tensions."
103. Ibid., 188.
104. Ibid., 193. Emphasis is mine.
105. Dawidowicz, "Louis Marshall's Yiddish Newspaper" (1961). On the tensions between "German" and East European Jews in early twentieth-century New York, see Rischin, *The Promised City*, and Goren, *New York Jews and the Quest for Community*.
106. Mark Raider referred to Marshall's political style as that of old-world *shtadlanut* (intercession) embodied by the European "Court Jew." Raider, "Introduction, Special Issue on Louis Marshall," and Raider, "The Aristocrat and the Democrat."
107. Dawidowicz, "Louis Marshall's Yiddish Newspaper" (1963), 115.

6. WHITHER SECULARISM?

1. Bruch, "The Fatherhood of God," and Hudnut-Beumler, *Looking for God in the Suburbs.*
2. Dollinger, *Quest for Inclusion*, 148–51.
3. https://www.law.cornell.edu/supremecourt/text/330/.
4. "A Fact Sheet on Religion and the Public Schools," Religion and Schools Files 1947–49, AJC/digital.
5. Schachner, "Church, State and Education."
6. "Statement of Principles. Recommended by the Subcommittee on Religion in the Public Schools," May 26, 1949, Religion and Schools Files 1947–49, AJC/digital.
7. "The Workshop on Religion and the Public Schools," January 16, 1948, Religion and Schools Files 1947–49, AJC/digital.
8. "Before the Supreme Court: Prayers and Bible Reading in the Public Schools, A Fact Sheet," Religion and Schools Files 1947–49, AJC/digital. Dollinger, *Quest for Inclusion*, 154–55, and Bruch, "The Fatherhood of God," 111.
9. Richard H. Wels to Subcommittee on Teaching About Religion in the Public Schools, March 5, 1953. See, too, Philip Jacobson, "Dealing with Religion in the Public School Curriculum," May 4, 1953, and his 1963 pamphlet, "Religion in Public Education: A Guide for Discussion," Religion and Schools Files 1950–53, AJC/digital.
10. "Revised Draft, The Factual Study of Religion," November 22, 1954, Religion and State, Teaching Religion File, AJC/digital.
11. "AJC Statement of Views on Religion and Public Education," August 5, 1954, Religion and Schools Files, AJC/digital.
12. "Before the U.S. Supreme Court: Prayers and Bible Reading in the Public Schools: A Fact Sheet," 1963, AJC/digital.
13. "The Workshop on Religion and the Public Schools," January 16, 1948, Religion and Schools Files, 1947–49.
14. Dollinger, *Quest for Inclusion*, 156.
15. "AJC Statement of Position on Religious Holiday Observances in the Public Schools" and "Summary of AJC Position on Christmas Holiday Observances in the Public Schools," October 1, 1952, Religion and Schools File, 1950–1957.

16. Domestic Affairs Committee, minutes of April 12, 1956, American Jewish Committee Archive, Jacob Blaustein Building, New York.

17. Dollinger, *Quest for Inclusion*, 148–53.

18. Lucy S. Dawidowicz to John Slawson, July 25, 1960, AJC/AJA, box G1, folder 1.

19. Ibid. Marshall prepared the AJC brief in *Pierce v. Society of the Sisters of the Holy Names of Jesus and Mary* (1925), which argued that requiring all children to attend public schools was unconstitutional; he, fearing the creation of a godless society, believed that release time for religious study during the school day was "highly commendable." Murray Friedman, *The Neoconservative Revolution*, 19–23.

20. This is the only version of the text I found. Lucy S. Dawidowicz, "For staff discussion, the American Jewish Committee, Library of Jewish Information, The Jewish Position on Released Time and Bible Reading: A Discussion Paper," August 1960. See, too, Lucy S. Dawidowicz to David Danzig, July and August 1962, "A Well Organized and Litigious Minority: The Catholic Attitude Toward Bible Reading." Both in AJC/AJA, box G1, folder 12.

21. Lucy S. Dawidowicz to Milton Himmelfarb, May 1, 1963, AJC/AJA, box G1, folder 30.

22. Lucy S. Dawidowicz, "Changing Public Opinion on Church-State Questions," May 7, 1963, AJC/AJA, box G1, folder 30.

23. Ibid.

24. Ibid.

25. Dawidowicz, "Church and State" (1965), 208.

26. Ibid., 210–11.

27. Lucy S. Dawidowicz to Anne Wolfe, March 3, 1965, AJC/AJA, box G1, folder 30.

28. Lucy S. Dawidowicz, "Religious Liberty and Separation of Church and State," November 16, 1965, AJC/AJA, box G1, folder 30.

29. Ibid.

30. Ibid.

31. Dawidowicz, "Church and State" (1966), 128.

32. The executive committee of the umbrella organization, the National Community Relations Advisory Council, remained concerned about the acceptance of federal funds. Ibid., 130–31n3.

33. Milton Himmelfarb, "How High a Wall?"

34. Lucy S. Dawidowicz to Eleanor Schildkret Sapakoff, November 27, 1964, Dawidowicz private papers.

35. Schwarz, *Survivors and Exiles*.

36. Dawidowicz, "Yiddish," 384.

37. Roskies, "Maks Vaynraykh," 309.

38. Weinreich, "*Yidishkayt* and Yiddish." He appended a footnote to the word *yidishkayt*: "The all-embracing character of traditional *yidishkayt* is aptly rendered in the English phrase 'Judaism as a civilization' coined by Professor Mordecai Kaplan. The term *yidishe kultur*, of modern origin, has a somewhat different connotation." Ibid., 482. See, too, Weinreich, "The Reality of Jewishness Versus the Ghetto Myth."

39. Weinreich, "*Yidishkayt* and Yiddish," 482, 491.

40. Ibid., 511–12. Dawidowicz later translated another of Weinreich's classic articles on this theme. Weinreich, "Internal Bilingualism in Ashkenaz."

41. Yitskhok Bashevis Zinger to Maks Vaynraykh, June 14, 1953, Max Weinreich Papers, folder 562c.

42. Lucy S. Dawidowicz to Max Weinreich, November 29, 1965, Dawidowicz Papers, box 77, folder 6.

43. Max Weinreich to Lucy S. Dawidowicz, December 3, 1965, Dawidowicz Papers, box 77, folder 6. See, too, Dawidowicz, "Max Weinreich," 67.

44. The Warsaw-born Tseytlin came from an esteemed family of Yiddish and Hebrew writers. A poet, fiction writer, playwright, essayist, and editor in both languages, he immigrated to the United States in 1939. See Schwarz, *Survivors and Exiles*, 143–80, and https://yivoencyclopedia.org/article.aspx/Zeitlin_Family.

45. The pamphlet was originally published in *Yidishe kemfer* in 1957 and was later included in Leybush Lehrer, *Azoy zenen yidn*. Leybush Lehrer, *Simbol un tokh*.

46. Leybush Lehrer, *Simbol un tokh*, 15.

47. Ibid., 19.

48. I have not translated the Yiddish word *yidishkayt* because in many ways its untranslatability lies at the root of Lehrer's modern Yiddish secularist dilemma. Contemporary Jewish secularists, Lehrer claimed, had internalized the Western Christian definition of Judaism as a religion, which in the conditions of emancipation demanded the privatization of Jewish commitments. *Yidshkayt*, however, could never be bifurcated neatly into two opposing spheres of secular and sacred. Secular American Yiddishists were confused, he claimed, because they were trying to "fit this gentile hat onto our Jewish head, [leading] to strange distortions." Believing that if secular American Jews could come to understand the authentic meaning of *yidishkayt* as "a national-cultural system," they could remain "actively connected with the Jewish people." Leybush Lehrer, "Yidishkayt—vos darf men ton?" 47–49.

49. Leybush Lehrer, *Simbol un tokh*, 28.

50. Leibush Lehrer, *Reactions of Second Generation American Jews*. See, too, Fishman, "From Yiddishism to American Judaism," 273, and Levitt, "Impossible Assimilations, American Liberalism, and Jewish Difference."

51. Dawidowicz Papers, box 77, folder 6.

52. For a similar theoretical problem in contemporary Israel among non-Ashkenazic Jews, see Yadgar, "Tradition," and Yadgar, "Traditionism."

53. "The Relevance of an Education in the Sholem Aleichem Schools: Some Personal Remarks," May, 19, 1968, Dawidowicz Papers, box 57, later published as Dawidowicz, "The Relevance of an Education in the Sholem Aleichem Schools."

54. The term *ahavas-yisroel* (Yid., "Love for Israel" / "Love of the Jews") can be also be rendered as *ahavas-yisroyel* or *ahavat yisra'el* (Heb.), with or without a hyphen.

55. Though acknowledging the religious awakening of the late 1960s Jewish counterculture, Dawidowicz was critical of its forms: "These Jewish youngsters have not turned to our religion, not to our traditions—but to the Pied Piper attractions of inauthentic and popular Zen Buddhism, a mishmash of syncretistic Oriental religions, lured by the poetry, and imagery, by the craving for ecstasy, the awareness of mystery,

seeking a glimpse of the unseen and an echo of the unutterable. It would have hurt Leibush Lehrer to have seen this." "The Relevance of an Education in the Sholem Aleichem Schools: Some Personal Remarks," May, 19, 1968, Dawidowicz Papers, box 57, single folder, 8.

56. Sklare, "Lakeville and Israel," and Novick, *The Holocaust in American Life.*

7. REPRESENTING POLISH JEWRY

1. Reviews of *The Golden Tradition* appeared in the major American Jewish journals in both English and Yiddish and in scholarly periodicals devoted to Jewish and East European history, including the *Slavic Review,* the *Polish Review, Jewish Social Studies,* and the *American Historical Review.*

2. Her transnational identity was so seamless that Dawidowicz was often mistaken for being of Polish origin, a peer to Philip Friedman, Jacob Robinson, and Isaiah Trunk. See Michman, *Holocaust Historiography,* 369, 384n45.

3. Dubnow published the protocols of the early modern Council of the Four Lands and of the independent Lithuanian Council—the major lay institutions of Jewish communal autonomy in Polish-Lithuanian lands. Dubnow, *Pinkas hamedinah*; Ettinger, "The Council of the Four Lands"; Bartal, "The *Pinkas* of the Council of the Four Lands"; and Halperin, *Pinkas va'ad arba' arazot.*

4. Seltzer, "Affirmation of the Diaspora."

5. Dawidowicz, "Middle-Class Judaism."

6. Ibid., 493.

7. On anti-Catholicism, see Higham, *Strangers in the Land,* and Ellis, *American Catholicism.*

8. Homar Bigart, "Parties Worried by 'Jewish Vote,'" *New York Times,* September 1, 1960.

9. Dawidowicz and Goldstein, *Politics in a Pluralist Democracy.*

10. Boston, Massachusetts, for Irish Americans; Buffalo, New York, for Polish Americans; Cincinnati, Ohio, for German Americans; Providence, Rhode Island, for Italians and Yankees; Tennessee and southern Illinois for fundamentalist Protestants; Minnesota for Lutherans and Catholics; Los Angeles, Chicago, and Detroit for Jews.

11. Glazer and Moynihan, *Beyond the Melting Pot.*

12. Moynihan, "[Book Review] *Politics in a Pluralist Democracy,*" 89. See, too, Thompson, "America Demands a Single Loyalty."

13. Dawidowicz and Goldstein, *Politics in a Pluralist Democracy,* 65.

14. Ibid., 76–90.

15. Lucy S. Dawidowicz to Arthur Kurzweil, November 10, 1988, Dawidowicz Papers, box 67, folder 7. See, too, Abraham Joshua Heschel to Lucy S. Dawidowicz, June 24, 1960, Dawidowicz Papers, box 77, folder 1, and the preface to Dawidowicz, *The Golden Tradition* (Jacob Aronson).

16. Heschel, *The Earth Is the Lord's.* This slim volume—along with Maurice Samuel's *The World of Sholem Aleichem* (1943), Bella Chagall's *Burning Lights* (1946), Mark Zborowski and Elizabeth Herzog's *Life Is with People* (1952), and the staging of *Fiddler on the Roof* (1964)—became the iconic text romanticizing East European Jewry for

the postwar American public. See Shandler, "Heschel and Yiddish," 269; Kirshenblatt-Gimblett, "Imagining Europe"; and Krah, *American Jewry and Re-Invention*. Irving Kristol voiced early criticism of Heschel's rose-colored view of the East European era. Kristol, "Elegy for a Lost World."

17. "YIVO Conference Outlines Broad Program," *Newsletter of the YIVO*, no. 7 (January–February 1945): 7.

18. In 1967, Dawidowicz queried her reaction to the "Monument to the Unknown Jewish Martyr" in Paris: "The exhibition was impressive but still misses the great impact. Do I want to be assaulted? What was wrong? Was I afraid Szymon would see a picture of Tob[ts]che?" Dawidowicz travel diary, August 1, 1967, Dawidowicz private papers.

19. Lucy S. Dawidowicz to Henia Karmel-Wolfe, December 15, 1970, Dawidowicz Papers, box 77, folder 13. Karmel-Wolfe, *The Baders of Jacob Street*.

20. Feldman, *The Pripet Marshes and Other Poems*. Reviewing Abraham Lewin's ghetto diary, Dawidowicz wrote, "I was seized by an irrational wish. I wanted desperately to pluck Abraham and Ora Lewin from the consuming fire. But there was no way I could give their story a happy ending." Dawidowicz, "[Book Review] A Cup of Tears."

21. Lucy S. Dawidowicz to Irving Feldman, February 8, 1966, Dawidowicz Papers, box 77, folder 9. He responded immediately: "I can assure you that it means much to me to know that this poem has the same relation to your experience that it does to mine. This is the first time I've known of another person involved in the same game." Irving Feldman to Lucy S. Dawidowicz, February 12, 1966, Dawidowicz Papers, box 77, folder 9.

22. Kirshenblatt-Gimblett, "Introduction," xxxviii.

23. On the title change, see Lucy S. Dawidowicz to Arthur A. Cohen, April 8, 1963, and Arthur A. Cohen to Lucy S. Dawidowicz, September 14, 1964, Dawidowicz Papers, box 67, folders 6 and 7. Upon publication, Sidney Monas, editor of *Slavic Review*, praised the book in a letter to Dawidowicz but critiqued its new title: "I'm not so sure about 'Golden.' There's a tendency (not so marked in your book as in some) to sentimentalise tradition. In reading the Zborowski-Meade [*sic*] book about the shtetl, for instance . . . I was struck by the lyrical reminiscing into wondering why so many people (if the shtetl were all that warm and nourishing a place) moved so fast to get *out* of the shtetl when they had half a chance—persecution and poverty aside." Sidney Monas to Lucy S. Dawidowicz, November 22, 1968, Dawidowicz Papers, box 77, folder 7.

24. "Comments on the JPS's Reader's Report on the Historical Introduction to Lucy S. Dawidowicz, *A Vanished World: Memoirs of East European Jews, 1772–1939*," unsigned, Dawidowicz Papers, box 67, folder 6.

25. Ibid.

26. Dawidowicz, *The Golden Tradition* (Holt, Rinehart and Winston), 5.

27. Ibid., 6.

28. Hebrew texts were handled by her husband, Szymon, and a few other individual translators. He also provided the translations from Russian.

29. This might be the first time Howe used the phrase that would later become the title of his own elegy to East European Jewish culture through his study of the immigrant Lower East Side. See Howe, *World of Our Fathers*.

30. Howe, "Review of *The Golden Tradition*," 3.

31. Leviant, "The Spirit of Zion." Several other books appeared in the late 1970s that were also seen as "correctives" to the sentimental image of East European Jewish life, including Roskies and Roskies, *The Shtetl Book*; Heller, *On the Edge of Destruction*; and Dobroszycki and Kirshenblatt-Gimblett, *Image Before My Eyes*.

32. The emphasis is mine. Dawidowicz, *The Golden Tradition* (Holt, Rinehart and Winston), 6. In an interview she gave to publicize the book's reissue, she reemphasized her approach: "In reconstructing the world [East European society], I hoped to counter what I saw as the falsely sentimental image of East European Jewry." Kurzweil, "The *Jewish Book News* Interview."

33. Excerpts by Pauline Wengeroff, Puah Rakovski, and Sophie Günzburg included in *The Golden Tradition* were the first English translations of their work.

34. Lucy S. Dawidowicz, "Tradition and Modernity: The Response of East European Jews to the Modern World." April 8, 1963, Dawidowicz Papers, box 67, folder 6.

35. Dawidowicz, *The Golden Tradition* (Holt, Rinehart and Winston), 5–6.

36. Cited from a draft for *From That Place and Time* in Dawidowicz Papers, box 55, folder 7. See, too, Dawidowicz, "History as Autobiography." The term "documents" suggests that Dawidowicz distinguished between public/official records—often written in the third person—and private/personal records—written in the first person.

37. Schwarz, *The Jewish Caravan*; Schwarz, *A Golden Treasury of Jewish Literature*; Schwarz, *Memoirs of My People*; and Feigenbaum, "Life in a Bunker."

38. Miron, "Autobiography as a Source for Writing Social History"; Stanislawski, *Autobiographical Jews*; and Moseley, *Being for Myself Alone*.

39. Rosman, *Founder of Hasidism*.

40. Dawidowicz used the phrase "event-making men" in the draft for the introduction that she sent to Arthur A. Cohen on April 8, 1963. Dawidowicz Papers, box 67, folder 6. The phrase fell out of the published introduction, replaced by William James's words about "genius." Dawidowicz, *The Golden Tradition* (Holt, Rinehart and Winston), 6.

41. Lucy S. Dawidowicz to George Mosse, May 19, 1975, George Mosse Archive, Leo Baeck Institute, AR 25137/MF 671, box 34, folder 5.

42. Lucy S. Dawidowicz, "Tradition and Modernity: The Response of East European Jews to the Modern World," April 8, 1963, Dawidowicz Papers, box 67, folder 6. Dawidowicz's identification with her subject matter did not escape the Jewish Publication Society's reader's report, which criticized the book's "very conspicuous . . . biased approach. . . . [The author was clearly] a strong supporter of Diaspora existence." See "Historical Review by Lucy Davidowicz [sic] (Part I: Tradition and Modernity)," included with Solomon Grayzel to Arthur A. Cohen, October 25, 1965, Dawidowicz Papers, box 67, folder 6.

43. Dawidowicz, *The Golden Tradition* (Holt, Rinehart and Winston), 8.

44. Ibid., 5. Though Dawidowicz's stark juxtaposition between West and East European Jewry would be subject to scholarly nuance and qualification today, her conclusion that East European Jewry possessed a distinctive collective identity has recently been rearticulated in Hundert, *Jews in Poland-Lithuania*.

45. Hundert, "Some Basic Characteristics of Jewish Life in Poland."
46. Dawidowicz, *The Golden Tradition* (Holt, Rinehart and Winston), 80.
47. Ibid., 81.
48. Ibid., 86.
49. Ibid., 40.
50. Ibid., 57.
51. Weinreich, *History of the Yiddish Language* (1980).
52. Dawidowicz, "Max Weinreich," 67.
53. Ibid, 68.
54. Dubnow, "The Survival of the Jewish People."
55. Weinreich defined *visnshaft* as *visn vos shaft* (scholarship that creates). Shandler, *Shtetl*, 64.
56. Olson, *Nathan Birnbaum and Jewish Modernity*. See, too, Nathan Birnbaum, "Die jüdische Renaissance-Bewegung" and "Jüdische Autonomie" in the Berlin journal *Ost und West*, written under the name Mathias Acher, one of his pseudonyms. Translated in Rabinovitch, *Jews and Diaspora Nationalism*, 45–55.
57. Nathan Birnbaum, *Vom Freigeist zum Gläubigen*. Birnbaum's 1924 autobiographical essay "An Account" presented a linear, teleological explanation of his decision to embrace Torah observance. Olson, *Nathan Birnbaum and Jewish Modernity*, 213–21.
58. Nathan Birnbaum, "From Freethinker to Believer," 217.
59. Ibid., 218.
60. Ibid., 221.
61. Nathan Birnbaum, *Fun an apikoyres gevorn a maymin*. Solomon Birnbaum initially criticized her work and noted that he held the copyright to the pamphlet, to which she responded that it was in the public domain. When Birnbaum subsequently apologized, the two became fast friends and corresponded well into the 1980s. Solomon Birnbaum to Lucy S. Dawidowicz, May 14, 1967, and Lucy S. Dawidowicz to Solomon Birnbaum, May 19, 1967. Their last letter is dated August 1981, Nathan and Solomon Birnbaum Archives (henceforth, Birnbaum Archives).
62. Lucy S. Dawidowicz to Solomon Birnbaum, June 6, 1967, Birnbaum Archives.
63. Given her hostility to communism, Trotsky's appearance is particularly noteworthy.
64. "Comments on the JPS's Reader's Report on the Historical Introduction to Lucy S. Dawidowicz, *A Vanished World: Memoirs of East European Jews, 1772–1939*," Dawidowicz Papers, box 67, folder 6.
65. Infeld exemplifies why "marginals" mattered. A physicist deeply identified with Polishness and "oppressed by his Jewish background," Infeld left Poland in 1933 but returned in 1949. His excerpt revealed a Jewish identity informed only by antisemitism: "All my continued attempts to tear off the bonds [of the Jews] only prove that these bonds exist, and they will exist to the last day of my life." Dawidowicz, *The Golden Tradition* (Holt, Rinehart and Winston), 360–63.
66. Ibid., 88.
67. Ibid., citing Heschel, *The Earth Is the Lord's*, 97.
68. Dawidowicz, *The Golden Tradition* (Holt, Rinehart and Winston), 89.
69. Dawidowicz wrote this term in Hebrew-Yiddish characters.

70. Lucy S. Dawidowicz to Salo W. Baron, May 6, 1965, Dawidowicz Papers, box 77, folder 7.
71. Emphasis is mine. Lucy S. Dawidowicz to Salo Baron, April 1965, Dawidowicz Papers, box 78, folder 9.
72. Sophie Dubnow-Erlich, Dubnow's biological daughter, was a poet, political activist, critic, translator, and memoirist. Active in Jewish revolutionary politics as a member of the Social Democratic Labor Party and the Jewish Labor Party in Vilna, in 1911 she married Henryk Erlich, a prominent leader of the Bund in Poland. Balin, "To Reveal Our Hearts," and Dubnov-Erlich, The Life and Work of S. M. Dubnow.
73. Kassow, Who Will Write Our History?, 9.
74. Fishman, Embers Plucked from the Fire, 3.

8. DEFENDING POLISH JEWRY

1. Morton I. Teicher to Lucy S. Dawidowicz, February, 14, 1969, Dawidowicz Papers, box 77, folder 13.
2. A copy of Dawidowicz's syllabus for "The Holocaust: A Seminar," History 39 (originally coded as History 95), is included in chapter 8. Stern College—Curriculum Committee Papers, Yeshiva University Archives, YU 2007.012, box 1, folder 3. Dawidowicz also prepared an eleven-page bibliography, "A Basic Library of the Holocaust," for her students in March 1970. Isaiah Trunk Papers, YIVO Archives, RG 483, folder 270.
3. At about the same time, Yaffa Eliach (1937–2016), a survivor historian, began to teach Holocaust-related courses at Brooklyn College and founded the Center for Holocaust Studies, the first of its kind in the United States. A survey of university teaching on the Holocaust in 1998 showed that the subject entered the academy in full force only in the 1980s. Haynes, "Holocaust Education at American Colleges and Universities."
4. Lucy S. Dawidowicz to Aaron Asher, December 18, 1969; Georges Borchardt Inc. records, 1951–2018; box 8, Correspondence File; Rare Book and Manuscript Library, Columbia University Library.
5. Dawidowicz, "Review of Nora Levin, The Holocaust," 177. Dawidowicz considered the book "amateurish," an epithet that would later be used against her. Korman, "The Holocaust in American Historical Writing."
6. David Mirsky to Lucy S. Dawidowicz, November 3, 1969, Dawidowicz Papers, box 77, folder 13.
7. See the congratulatory letter from Jacob R. Marcus to Lucy S. Dawidowicz, September 2, 1970, Dawidowicz private papers.
8. Lehmann-Haupt, "A Key to the 'Final Solution.'"
9. Appearing first in a series of articles in the New Yorker magazine in 1961, Eichmann in Jerusalem: A Report on the Banality of Evil was published as a book in 1963. It set off a storm of protest among the Jewish intellectual elite that still continues. The scholarly output on the reception of Eichmann in Jerusalem is voluminous. See Podhoretz, "Hannah Arendt on Eichmann"; Cohen, "Breaking the Code"; Wolin, "The Ambivalences of German-Jewish Identity"; Wasserstein, "Blame the Victim"; Rabinbach, "Eichmann in

New York"; Aschheim, *Hannah Arendt in Jerusalem*; and Dubnov, "From Hilberg to Arendt (and Back Again?)," among many others.

10. Dawidowicz, *The War Against the Jews* (1975), xxxv.

11. Though she claimed that "A partial answer or partial answers to the third question can be found in Appendix A, 'The Fate of the Jews in Hitler's Europe,' " it did not answer the question. Dawidowicz, *The War Against the Jews* (1975), xxxv.

12. For her arguments, see chapter 13, this volume.

13. Michman, *Holocaust Historiography*, 25–26.

14. Dawidowicz, *The War Against the Jews* (1975), xvi.

15. "Jewish Behavior in Crisis and Extremity" is the title of chapter 16 in the book.

16. Fermaglich, *American Dreams and Nazi Nightmares*.

17. Baron, "The Holocaust and American Public Memory," and Garrett, *Young Lions*.

18. Shandler, *While America Watches*.

19. Staub, *Torn at the Roots*, 10.

20. Diner, *We Remember with Reverence and Love*.

21. Dawidowicz's personal archives contain letters from Zalman Shazar, then the president of Israel; Abraham Joshua Heschel; Arthur A. Cohen, the brilliant American Jewish thinker and novelist; Marshall Sklare, the well-known American Jewish sociologist; Wolfe Kelman, one of the luminaries of the postwar Conservative movement; Salo W. Baron; and Dina Abramowicz, among others. Dawidowicz Papers, box 63, folders 5 and 6.

22. Howe, "Review of *The War Against the Jews, 1933–1945*," 1.

23. On Hitler's centrality to the prosecution of the Final Solution, see Rosenbaum, *Explaining Hitler*, and Rosenbaum, "Hitler, Continued," https://lareviewofbooks.org/ article/hitler-continued-afterword-updated-edition-explaining-hitler-search-origins -evil/.

24. For discussions of intentionalism in Holocaust historiography beyond those cited in the introduction, footnote 16, see Kershaw, *The Nazi Dictatorship*; Friedländer, *Nazi Germany and the Jews: The Years of Persecution*; Engel, *The Holocaust*; Bauer, *Rethinking the Holocaust*; and Friedländer, *The Years of Extermination*.

25. Dawidowicz, *The War Against the Jews*, 163.

26. Ibid., 3.

27. Ibid., xxi.

28. Ibid., 150–66. Ismar Schorsch, who read the manuscript before its publication, praised the book but expressed reservations about the teleology of Dawidowicz's argument: "While I generally share your view, I do want to raise one caveat. The natural tendency is to write a somewhat unilinear history which moves inexorably toward a catastrophic climax. In light of the final outcome, many earlier statements and events are seen to point inevitably in that direction. . . . The most blatant instance of this mistake is in your handling of German anti-Semitism. You never fully clarified in your own mind the precise causal nexus between it and the Nazi triumph." Ismar Schorsch to Lucy S. Dawidowicz, May 16, 1973; Georges Borchardt Inc. records, 1951–2018; box 8, Correspondence File; Rare Book and Manuscript Library, Columbia University Library.

29. Hollinger, *Science, Jews, and Secular Culture*, 10.

30. Dawidowicz, *The War Against the Jews*, 163. See, too, Milton Himmelfarb, "No Hitler, No Holocaust."

31. Dawidowicz, *The War Against the Jews*, 163.

32. Ibid. See, too, the interpretations of Hugh Trevor-Roper, who described Hitler as a messianic "true believer" in his anti-Semitism. Rosenbaum, "Hitler, Continued."

33. Dawidowicz, *The War Against the Jews*, 21.

34. Kansteiner, "From Exception to Exemplum," 153–55. Uwe Dietrich Adam, *Judenpolitik im Dritten Reich* (Düsseldorf: Droste Verlag, 1972); Hans Mommsen, *Beamtentum im Dritten Reich: Mit ausgewählten Quellen zur nationalsozialistischen Beamtenpolitik* (Stuttgart: Deutsche Verlags-Anstalt, 1966); Götz Aly, *Die restlose Erfassung: Volkszählen, Identifizieren, Aussondern im Nationalsozialismus* (Berlin: Rotbuch, 1984); and Martin Broszat, *Der Nationalsozialismus; Weltanschauung, Programm und Wirklichkeit* (Stuttgart: Deutsche Verlags-Anstalt, 1960).

35. For criticism of the conflation of the interpretations of Hilberg and Arendt—and with that of Bruno Bettelheim—see Engel, *Historians of the Jews and the Holocaust*, chap. 4.

36. Hilberg, *The Destruction of the European Jews*. On Hilberg, see Michman, *Holocaust Historiography*; Stauber, "Confronting the Jewish Response During the Holocaust"; and Engel, "The Holocaust."

37. The reader's report on Hilberg's manuscript reveals that Hannah Arendt was a key figure in Princeton University Press's rejection of the book—which followed those of Yad Vashem and Columbia University Press—even though she relied on Hilberg for *Eichmann in Jerusalem* four years later, creating the distorted perception that their interpretations were the same. Dubnov, "From Hilberg to Arendt (and Back Again?)," 58–59.

38. Hilberg, *The Destruction of the European Jews*, 14, 17.

39. Ibid., 667–68.

40. The emphasis in the second sentence is mine. Hilberg, *The Destruction of the European Jews*, 662.

41. In a reader's report on a dissertation being considered for publication, Dawidowicz referred to Hilberg's "magisterial study." Lucy S. Dawidowicz to Lewis Bateman, October 25, 1976, Dawidowicz Papers, box 76, folder 4.

42. Grubsztein, *Jewish Resistance During the Holocaust*. Lucy S. Dawidowicz to Raul Hilberg, May 4, 1970, Raul Hilberg Papers, RG 074.005, University of Vermont Libraries and Special Collections. See, too, Stauber, "Confronting the Jewish Response During the Holocaust."

43. Salo W. Baron lamented the state of the field in 1950 in his keynote address, "Problems of Research in the Study of the Jewish Catastrophe, 1939–1945," at the Conference on Jewish Relations. Baron, "Opening Remarks." See, too, Philip Friedman, "Research and Literature on the Recent Jewish Tragedy."

44. Stauber, "Confronting the Jewish Response During the Holocaust," and Cohen, "Rachel Auerbach, Yad Vashem, and Israeli Holocaust Memory."

45. Hilberg, *The Politics of Memory*, 135–37.

46. She attended several sessions of the conference and was underwhelmed. See Dawidowicz travel diary, April 7–9, 1968, Dawidowicz private papers. Dawidowicz, "Toward a History of the Holocaust."

47. Dawidowicz, "Toward a History of the Holocaust," 52.

48. Ibid., 54. Though Dawidowicz mentioned both Hilberg and Arendt in the article, her tone toward Hilberg was generally respectful. Not so toward Arendt.

49. Dawidowicz, "Toward a History of the Holocaust," 56.

50. Raul Hilberg to Lucy S. Dawidowicz, April 14, 1970, Lucy S. Dawidowicz private papers.

51. Lucy S. Dawidowicz to Raul Hilberg, May 4, 1970, Raul Hilberg Papers, RG 074.005, University of Vermont Libraries and Special Collections.

52. Arendt, *Eichmann in Jerusalem*.

53. Wolin, "The Ambivalences of German-Jewish Identity."

54. Dan Michman called part 2 of *The War Against the Jews* "the Jewish section of the book." Michman, *Holocaust Historiography*, 26.

55. For a comparison of West German and American approaches to Jewish historical agency during the Holocaust, see Baader, "The Shoah, the Sacred, and Jewish Victim Identity."

56. Dawidowicz, "Toward a History of the Holocaust," 55. While positioning Hilberg and Arendt as historiographical allies, Dawidowicz distinguished between their work, i.e., ibid., 53. In her analysis, Dawidowicz was profoundly influenced by Isaiah Trunk's award-winning *Judenrat*, which she had read in the original Yiddish. It appeared in English as *Judenrat: The Jewish Councils in Eastern Europe under Nazi Occupation*. Trunk, a survivor historian, left Poland in 1950 for Israel, settling on the Ghetto Fighters Kibbutz, where he was engaged with *Khurbn forshung*. He immigrated to Canada in 1953 and soon moved to New York City, where he was affiliated with the YIVO for the rest of his career. A personal friend of both Lucy and Szymon Dawidowicz, he gave her materials when she assisted John Hersey, helped her with her book on Holocaust historiography, and delivered one of the eulogies for Szymon. See Lucy S. Dawidowicz to John Hersey, July 13, 1949, John Hersey Papers, Uncat ZA MS 235, box 20, Beinecke Library, Yale University; Dawidowicz travel diary, April 3, 8–9, and 13, 1968; and Lucy S. Dawidowicz to Senia and Zarek Dawidowicz, June 10, 1979, Dawidowicz private papers. Writing to Benton M. Arnovitz about Trunk's *Judenrat*, Dawidowicz praised the work's dispassionate examination of the councils, which "lay bare the institution's ambiguities and dilemmas." Trunk's work would ensure that "there will no longer be any excuse for glib generalizing about the *Judenrat*." Lucy S. Dawidowicz to Benton M. Arnovitz, October 22, 1972, Dawidowicz private papers. See, too, Trunk's critique of Hannah Arendt in Trunk, "The Historian of the Holocaust at YIVO," 71–72.

57. Dawidowicz, *The War Against the Jews*, xxxviii.

58. Gruenewald, "The Beginning of the 'Reichsvertretung,'" and Brodnitz, "Memories of the Reichsvertretung."

59. Dan Michman has insightfully suggested that the term "leadership" for the *Judenräte* is misleading; instead, he employs the term "headship," which connotes that its authority derived from an extra-group power (the Nazis) and not from the group (the Jewish community) over which it had power. See Michman, *Holocaust Historiography*, 161, and Michman, "Jewish Leadership in Extremis."

60. Dawidowicz, *The War Against the Jews*, 186.

61. Ibid., 195.
62. On the term, see Bauer, *Rethinking the Holocaust*, 120.
63. For a capacious view of the term *amidah*, one embracing more than "resistance," see Dworzecki, "The Day-to-Day Stand of the Jews," and Michman, *Holocaust Historiography*, 345–46. Michman noted that for Dawidowicz, the term *amidah* was apologetic, "not anchored in history... [and] used to satisfy national psychological needs." Michman, *Holocaust Historiography*, 219.
64. Dawidowicz thoroughly researched the issue of political affiliation among the ghetto fighters. See her correspondence, inclusive of telegrams and a questionnaire, with Yitzhak Zuckerman and his responses. Libe S. Davidovitsh to Yitskhok Tsukerman, September 29, 1972, January 12, 1973, August 8, 1973; Yitskhok Tsuckerman to Libe S. Davidovitsh, December 31, 1972, "Special" section, Archive of the Ghetto Fighters' House in memory of Yitzhak Katznelson, file 803. Libe S. Davidovitsh to Yitskhok Tsukerman, March 19, 1974, and May 31, 1974, Yitskhok Tsukerman to Libe S. Davidovitsh, March 29, 1974, Dawidowicz private papers. Zuckerman's account of the creation of the ŻOB can be found in Dawidowicz, *A Holocaust Reader*, 359–80.
65. Lucy S. Dawidowicz to John Thornton, March 5, 1979, Dawidowicz Papers, box 76, folder 5.
66. Dawidowicz, "Toward a History of the Holocaust."
67. George Mosse to Lucy S. Dawidowicz, April 7, 1975, Dawidowicz Papers, box 63, folder 8.
68. Dawidowicz, *The War Against the Jews*, 343.
69. Engel, *Historians of the Jews and the Holocaust*, 161–65. Alter, "Holocaust," and Syrkin, "[Book Review] Nazi Fury." Syrkin noted that Dawidowicz's book succinctly undermined Arendt's attack on the *Judenräte*.
70. Arendt, *Eichmann in Jerusalem*, 116.
71. Dawidowicz, *The War Against the Jews*, 224.
72. In its original Talmudic context (*b. Nedarim 28a, b. Baba Kamma 113ab*), *dina d'malkhuta dina* referred specifically to issues related to taxation but was later adduced to express various Jewish political postures that established a modus vivendi with gentile authority. It became a symbolic phrase that both explicitly and implicitly acknowledged the dependence of Jewish communal security on obeisance to the highest gentile ruler in exchange for protection, provided there was no contravention of Jewish law. Bildstein, "A Note on the Function of 'The Law of the Land is the Law'"; Biale, *Power and Powerlessness in Jewish History*, 56; Lederhendler, *The Road to Modern Jewish Politics*, 16; and Walzer, Lorberbaum, and Zohar, *The Jewish Political Tradition*.
73. Yerushalmi, "*Servants of Kings and Not Servants of Servants*."
74. Dawidowicz, *The War Against the Jews*, 226–27, 240.
75. Arendt, *Eichmann in Jerusalem*, 116.
76. Dawidowicz, *The War Against the Jews*, 348.
77. Ibid., 435–36n7. See, too, Dawidowicz, *The Holocaust and the Historians*, 137–38. Arendt's death in 1975 precluded a response.
78. Joseph Kanon to Lucy S. Dawidowicz, August 24, 1978, and Lucy S. Dawidowicz to Joseph Kanon, September 15, 1978, Dawidowicz Papers, box 76, folder 7. Epstein

himself appealed to Dawidowicz to reconsider. Leslie Epstein to Lucy S. Dawidowicz, September 23, 1978, Dawidowicz Papers, box 76, folder 7.

79. Kurt Gerstein's deposition was reprinted in Dawidowicz, *A Holocaust Reader*, 104–9, with the comment on 108. Alvin H. Rosenfeld, "The Holocaust as Entertainment," and his correspondence with Dawidowicz about Epstein's novel, Alvin Rosenfeld to Lucy S. Dawidowicz, June 19, 1979; Dawidowicz to Alvin Rosenfeld, June 25, 1979; Rosenfeld to Dawidowicz, July 2, 1979 and January 8, 1980, Dawidowicz Papers, box 43, folder 2, and box 76, folder 5. See, too, Sundquist, "The Historian's Anvil, the Novelist's Crucible."

80. Dawidowicz's review of Epstein's novel, "The Holocaust as Comedy," was never published. It directly linked Epstein's views to *Eichmann in Jerusalem*. Dawidowicz Papers, box 72, folder 7. Dawidowicz submitted her review to Norman Podhoretz for consideration in *Commentary*, but he rejected the piece, selecting an alternative reviewer. Norman Podhoretz to Lucy S. Dawidowicz, February 28, 1979, Dawidowicz Papers, box 72, folder 7. Wisse, "Fairy Tale," referenced Arendt's views of the *Judenräte*, criticizing the subtitle of *Eichmann in Jerusalem*.

81. Staub, *Torn at the Roots*.

82. Czerniaków, *The Warsaw Diary of Adam Czerniakow*. In 1976, however, she thought the diary of value. See Dawidowicz, *A Holocaust Reader*, 19. She also used his diary approvingly in her critique of a BBC film using SS propaganda footage from the Warsaw Ghetto that she considered "a grave distortion of historical reality." Dawidowicz, "Visualizing the Warsaw Ghetto."

83. Dawidowicz, "[Book Review] *Fragments of Isabella*."

84. For the bitter exchange of letters among Hilberg, Staron, Leitner, and Dawidowicz about the value of the diary and of Leitner's survival account, see the *New York Times Book Review*, May 12, 1979, 44. See, too, personal letters to Hilberg from Michael Berenbaum and Richard Rubenstein in support of his work, in Raul Hilberg Papers, RG 074.005, University of Vermont Libraries and Special Collections.

85. The book's reissued edition can be found in Dawidowicz's archives. Her last name is penned on the frontispiece, with notes on the following pages: "Judenrat: pp. 145–46, 315–316, 318, 666, 671," as well as on yellow-lined paper comparing the 1958 and 1985 editions. Dawidowicz Papers, box 47, single folder.

86. Dawidowicz, "Review of Raul Hilberg, *The Destruction of the European Jews*."

87. Ibid. See, too, Dawidowicz, "How They Teach the Holocaust," 30.

88. Dawidowicz, "Review of Raul Hilberg, *The Destruction of the European Jews*," 5.

89. Ibid.

90. Shavit and Michman, "Hannah Arendt and Leni Yahil."

9. UNIVERSALISM AND PARTICULARISM AMONG THE NEW YORK INTELLECTUALS

1. See Hilberg's negative appraisal of Dawidowicz, Nora Levin, and Hannah Arendt in Hilberg, *The Politics of Memory*, 142–52.

2. See the citations in introduction, footnote 33. *Hannah Arendt* (2012), a film by

Margarethe von Trotta; *Vita Activa*, a film by Ada Ushpiz (2015); and *The Hat*, an opera by Karen Siegel and Zsuzsanna Ardó, https://www.youtube.com/watch?v =jwaVbK63QAc.

3. Dan Diner concluded that *Eichmann in Jerusalem* was so controversial because it raised "all [the] relevant and existential questions of post-Emancipation Jewish life" that had been "rendered more acute because of the Holocaust." Diner, "Hannah Arendt Reconsidered," 178.

4. The tension between universalism and particularism was inherent in Enlightenment discourse, which, as Adam Sutcliffe noted, sought to "universalize and to nationalize history; to overthrow and to retrench social distinctions; and to erase and to reinvent cultural difference." In an exchange between the Sephardic Jew Isaac de Pinto and Voltaire over the question of De Pinto's acceptance as a Jew into enlightened circles of European society, Voltaire demanded that the former renounce his (particularistic) "laws, superstitions, [and] nation." Sutcliffe, "Can a Jew Be a Philosophe?"

5. Ettinger, "The Beginnings of the Change in the Attitude," and Birnbaum and Katznelson, *Paths of Emancipation*.

6. Green, *Jewish Workers in the Modern Diaspora*, and Kobrin, *Jewish Bialystok and Its Diaspora*.

7. Aschheim, *Brothers and Strangers*; Wertheimer, *Unwelcome Strangers*; and, most recently, Efron, *German Jewry and the Allure of the Sephardic*.

8. Bartal, "The Image of Germany and German Jewry."

9. Cooney, "New York Intellectuals and the Question of Jewish Identity." David Hollinger defines cosmopolitanism as the "desire to transcend the limitations of any and all particularisms in order to achieve a more complete human experience and a more complete understanding of that experience." Hollinger, "Ethnic Diversity, Cosmopolitanism and the Emergence."

10. Cited in Glenn, "The Vogue of Jewish Self-Hatred," 116.

11. Kazin, *Starting Out in the Thirties*, 157.

12. Howe, "The New York Intellectuals," 31.

13. Podhoretz, *Making It*, 3. The journalist and writer Ruth Gruber could not have agreed more: "The BMT and the Williamsburg Bridge, flung over the East River, were my escape route from Brooklyn," she would write. "Manhattan was my promised land." Gruber, *Ahead of Time*, 31.

14. Alter, "The Education of Alfred Kazin," 47.

15. Sinkoff, *Out of the Shtetl*, and Socher, *The Radical Enlightenment of Solomon Maimon*.

16. Bruford, *The German Tradition of Self-Cultivation*; Sorkin, "Wilhelm von Humboldt"; and Mendes-Flohr, "The Berlin Jew as Cosmopolitan."

17. Howe, *A Margin of Hope*, 251.

18. Cited in Atlas, *Bellow*, 546–47.

19. Milton Himmelfarb to Lucy S. Dawidowicz, September 7, 1982, Dawidowicz Papers, box 68, folder 6.

20. Alexander, "Irving Howe and the Holocaust."

21. Raider, "'Irresponsible, Undisciplined Opposition.'"

22. See the bibliography in Young-Bruehl, *Hannah Arendt*.

23. Herman, "*Hashavat Avedah*," and Baron, "Personal Notes: Hannah Arendt."

24. Podhoretz, *Making It*, 111, 117. Arendt's first article in *PR*, "Franz Kafka: A Reevaluation," appeared in the fall of 1944.

25. Wolin, "The Ambivalences of German-Jewish Identity," 1. See, too, Shklar, "Hannah Arendt as Pariah," 375.

26. Aschheim, *Hannah Arendt in Jerusalem*, 350n15. See, too, Howe, *Decline of the New*, 244–45, and Grafton, "The Public Intellectual and the Private Sphere."

27. Huppatz, "Reworking Bourdieu's 'Capital.'"

28. Kazin, *New York Jew*, 195–203, 215–18.

29. Cook, *Alfred Kazin*, 172.

30. On Arendt's power over Kazin, see Birstein's personal exposé, *What I Saw at the Fair*, 125–26, 144, 159–60, 162, 226–27.

31. Cited in Cook, *Alfred Kazin*, 175.

32. Howe, *A Margin of Hope*, 270.

33. Arendt never fully rejected the German scholarly tradition that was her intellectual inheritance and personal-psychological anchor. In her review of Max Weinreich's *Hitler's Professors*, Arendt absolved German scholars of responsibility for the Final Solution, writing that the real terror, "the ideas and techniques of the death factories . . . came from politicians who took power-politics seriously, and the techniques came from modern mob-men who were not afraid of consistency." Hannah Arendt, "[Book Review] *The Black Book* and *Hitler's Professors*," 295.

34. Jeannette Baron also remarked on Arendt's feminine capital, recalling that, interned at Gurs, Arendt's "beautiful hair" had been "hacked off"; falling victim to malnutrition, "her beautiful legs, of which she was so proud, would bear scars from untreated abscesses for the remainder of her life." Baron, "Hannah Arendt: Personal Reflections."

35. Diner, "Hannah Arendt Reconsidered." Steven Aschheim, commenting on *Eichmann's* reception among Jewish intellectuals, wrote: "Arendt, then, was not prepared to insulate or grant absolute privilege to Jewish history and suffering, despite her emphasis on the radical novelty of the exterminations." Aschheim, *Hannah Arendt in Jerusalem*, 14. Richard Cohen noted that Arendt's view of Jewish history confronted "a fundamental aspect of Jewish collective memory": the victimhood of the Jews throughout the past. Cohen, "A Generation's Response to *Eichmann in Jerusalem*," 255. Jeannette Baron remarked that she was shocked by "her [Arendt's] abysmal lack of understanding of the Jewish concept of martyrdom and the deep-rooted belief among the Orthodox that it was God's will. Passivity can be just as heroic as activism." Baron, "Hannah Arendt," 62.

36. Diner, "Hannah Arendt Reconsidered," 2–3.

37. Hundert, *Jews in Poland-Lithuania*, 4–11.

38. On the generations of New York intellectuals, see Podhoretz, *Making It*, 110–20, and Jumonville, *Critical Crossings*, xv.

39. For interpretations of the literary and linguistic rebellion of East European sons against their natal families, see Mintz, "*Banished from Their Father's Table*," and Seidman, *A Marriage Made in Heaven*. See, too, Gornick, *The Men in My Life*, for an analysis of the rage against their mothers in the works of Saul Bellow and Philip Roth, two East European Jewish immigrant sons.

40. In the 1998 film *Arguing the World*, a documentary portrait of four male New York intellectuals, Diana Trilling commented dryly—and a bit bitterly—that the women in their circle were only valued as objects of sexual desire, not as intellectual comrades. Diana Trilling, "Arguing the World," 52–53, and Cooney, *The Rise of the New York Intellectuals*, 13, 46.

41. Podhoretz, *Making It*, 154–55. Marie Syrkin, a noted beauty, was the other woman who possessed this kind of sexual power, but her fierce Jewish commitments kept her at the periphery of the New York intellectuals until the 1970s. Later in his life, when he publicly articulated his Jewish commitments, Irving Howe enfolded Syrkin into his circle. Kessner, *Marie Syrkin*, 404.

42. Likewise, Rachel Auerbach, a survivor historian from the Warsaw-based *Oyneg shabes* group, was also characterized and dismissed as an amateur historian and considered "difficult," though she was one of three people to recover the archive after the war and helped select the witnesses for the Eichmann trial. See Auerbach, *Pisma z Getta Warszawskiego*, and Cohen, "Rachel Auerbach, Yad Vashem, and Israeli Holocaust Memory."

43. Dawidowicz drolly commented at her New York Public Library lecture in 1988 that she hoped the audience could see her behind the podium, as she was standing on a "bar mitzvah *shtender*." Tape #00328, 3/24/1988, Public Education Programs of the New York Public Library. See, too, the reference to her being a "five-foot-nothing" in Dawidowicz, *From That Place and Time*, 93. Ruth Wisse noted that Dawidowicz thought her ankles were her most attractive feature, a view confirmed by Robert D. King, a professor of Yiddish at the University of Texas-Austin. Interview with Ruth R. Wisse, March 27, 2008, Interview with Carole Zabar, December 3, 2010, and Robert D. King to Lucy S. Dawidowicz, April 30, 1990, Dawidowicz Papers, box 71, folder 8. See, too, Lucy S. Dawidowicz to Dr. Warren Bargad, March 18, 1983, Dawidowicz Papers, box 65, folder 7.

44. The claim that the Nazis used fat from Jews to make soap has been thoroughly discredited. https://www.jta.org/2013/06/06/arts-entertainment/israeli-director -dismantles-nazi-jewish-soap-myth.

45. Howe, "The New York Intellectuals," 43.

10. THE EUROPEANNESS OF THE JEWISH "NEOCONSERVATIVE TURN"

1. Lucy S. Dawidowicz to Georges Borchardt, April 5, 1970. Given the association with psychedelic drugs, Borchardt suggested they dispense with her initials: "Dear Lucy (May I call you that, rather than LSD?)." Georges Borchardt to Lucy S. Dawidowicz, July 9, 1970, Georges Borchardt Inc. records, 1951–2018; box 8, Correspondence File; Rare Book and Manuscript Library, Columbia University Library.

2. Brinkley, "1968 and the Unraveling of America," and O'Neill, *Coming Apart*.

3. Borstelmann, *The 1970s*, and Schulman, *The Seventies*.

4. Schulman, *The Seventies*, xvi.

5. Gerstle, "The Protean Character of American Liberalism," and Walzer, "Why Are Jews Liberal?" The term's elasticity explains why someone like Daniel Bell, who became critical of ideological solutions to social problems and suspicious of many aspects of the Great Society, never renounced political liberalism or considered himself a neoconservative—though critics on his left flank did. See http://www.nytimes.com/2011/01/26/arts/26bell.html.

6. Vaïsse, Neoconservatism.

7. Kristol, The Neoconservative Persuasion.

8. Lionel Trilling, Beyond Culture, and Kimmage, The Conservative Turn, 9.

9. Steinfels, The Neoconservatives; Jumonville, Critical Crossings, 237n4; and Peretz, "The American Left and Israel."

10. Roth, "The Neoconservative Backlash against Feminism"; Abrams, Norman Podhoretz and Commentary Magazine; and Staub, Torn at the Roots, 243–75.

11. Birnbaum and Katznelson, Paths of Emancipation, and Mendelsohn, On Modern Jewish Politics. On the persistence of premodern politics in modern state contexts, see Bartal, Galut Ba'arez, and Bacon, The Politics of Tradition.

12. Mendes-Flohr and Reinharz, The Jew in the Modern World, 123–25.

13. Pierre Birnbaum, "Between Social and Political Assimilation."

14. Murray Friedman, The Neoconservative Revolution, 77; Balint, Running Commentary, 141–45; and Soyer, "Making Peace with Capitalism?"

15. Skin color and chattel slavery were the great exceptions to American universalist claims. It was this exception and its obdurate legacy—the persisting systemic racism against nonwhites in the United States—that created the rift between liberal Jewish integrationists and black nationalist civil rights activists in the 1960s. See Brodkin, How Jews Became White Folks; Goldstein, The Price of Whiteness; Greenberg, Troubling the Waters; Kaufman, Broken Alliance; and Murray Friedman, What Went Wrong? See, too, James Baldwin's incisive analysis of the historical reasons for the widening gulf between Jews and African Americans. However onerous and haunted the Jewish migration experience from Europe, he acknowledged, Jews, protected as a religious minority by the First Amendment and accommodated as citizens owing to their skin color, were allowed to become full Americans. This acceptance was denied the descendents of black slaves. Baldwin, "Negroes Are Anti-Semitic Because They're Anti-White."

16. Lederhendler, New York Jews, 155–59. Lederhendler's interpretation of the Jewish investment in civil society is indebted to Shils, "The Virtue of Civil Society."

17. "Liberalism and the Jews: A Symposium," 44.

18. Jacob Heilbrunn described the Jewish neoconservatives as a prophetic caste and named his chapters after biblical themes ("Exodus," "Wilderness," "Redemption"), suggesting that there is something innate about Jews—even secular ones—that leads them to embody ancient typologies. Heilbrunn, They Knew They Were Right, 77, 98, 137, 160, and more.

19. Feiner, "Toward a Historical Definition of the Haskalah," 208.

20. Dorman, Arguing the World, 157.

21. The emphases are mine. Howe, *Steady Work*, 39–40.

22. Demonizing one's opponents as heretics is not new to the modern period of Jewish history. See Scholem, *Sabbatai Sevi*; Carlebach, *The Pursuit of Heresy*; and Rustow, *Heresy and the Politics of Community*.

23. Ribak, *Gentile New York*, 188–89.

24. The term is from Kenneth D. Wald, "The Choosing People."

25. Cited in Grinberg, "Jewish Intellectuals, Masculinity, and American Conservatism," 350.

26. "Liberalism and the Jews," 57. *Commentary*'s preoccupation with this question began even earlier. See "What Is a Liberal—Who Is a Conservative? A Symposium," *Commentary*, September 1976, 31–113.

27. Wisse, *If I Am Not For Myself . . .*

28. Podhoretz, *Ex-Friends*.

29. Rosman, *How Jewish Is Jewish History?*, 184; see, too, 16–17, 45, and 45n69.

30. The literature on collective memory—Jewish memory over the *longue durée*—is voluminous, its critiques wide-ranging. See Yerushalmi, *Zakhor*; Funkenstein, *Perceptions of Jewish History*; and the journal *History and Memory*, which continues to engage the topic.

31. Dawidowicz and Goldstein, *Politics in a Pluralist Democracy*.

32. Baron, "Ghetto and Emancipation."

33. On the conceptionalization of vertical political strategies, what he termed the "royal alliance," see Yerushalmi, *The Lisbon Massacre of 1506*, and Yerushalmi, "Servants of Kings and Not Servants of Servants." See, too, Cohen, "Jews and the State," and Dubin, "Yosef Hayim Yerushalmi."

34. Brick and Phelps, *Radicals in America*.

35. Murray Friedman, *The Neoconservative Revolution*, 113, and Howe, "The New York Intellectuals," 50.

36. Murch, *Living for the City*.

37. Gene Roberts, "Black Power Idea Long in Planning," *New York Times*, August 5, 1966.

38. They railed against what they called "kitsch," "mass culture," or "popular culture." Dwight Macdonald famously dismissed popular media and art as "midcult." Jumonville, *Critical Crossings*, and Bell, "Sensibility in the 60's," 64.

39. Hofstadter, *Anti-Intellectualism in American Life*, became a foundational text linking mass culture, populism, and antisemitism. Dawidowicz illustrated her debt to Hofstadter's view of populism in the following comment: "[A]nti-intellectualism has been a recurrent theme in American social history and has been associated with violence." Lucy S. Dawidowicz, "Memo to Staff Committee on AJC Scope and Functions," AJC/AJA, box G10, folder 26.

40. Jumonville, *Critical Crossings*, 221.

41. Cited ibid., 222. Jewish political tradition had long been shaped by fears of "the mob"—an ill-defined term for a group often associated with the peasantry or other elements in society who occupied a lower socioeconomic rung than the Jews—and suspicion of political chaos and unrest. See Chazan, *European Jewry and the First Crusade*.

42. Dorman, *Arguing the World*, 148.

43. Between 1964 and 1968, 329 riots wreaked havoc on 257 American cities; in 1972, 22 Jewish businessmen were killed in Philadelphia, and 80 percent of the damaged businesses in one Philadelphia riot were owned by Jews. Dollinger, *Quest for Inclusion*, 200.

44. Lucy S. Dawidowicz, "Extremism in American Social and Political History: A Proposed Study," November 19, 1964, Dawidowicz Papers, box 38, folder 3. Other Jewish intellectuals shared her projections of the European past onto US soil. Kate Simon recalled that during a rent strike in the Bronx during her childhood, tenants ran around banging on apartment doors to warn tenants of police action, crying "Come! Out! Run! Leave everything, the cossacks [cops] are here!" Simon, *A Wider World*, 13. See, too, Norwood, "Marauding Youth and the Christian Front," and Ribak, "'They Are Slitting the Throats of Jewish Children.'" The riots that broke out on 125th Street near Jewish Theological Seminary of America in 1964 deeply frightened Gerson D. Cohen, its chancellor; four years later, after the Ocean Hill–Brownsville school board incitements, he went on a national speaking tour on pogroms. Lederhendler, *New York Jews*, 61.

45. Lucy S. Dawidowicz, "Negro Antisemitism: Outline for An Analysis," March 14, 1966, AJC/AJA, Box G1, folder 30.

46. Podhoretz wrote "My Negro Problem—And Ours" in response to a dispute he had with Baldwin over an article on Black Moslems, "Down at the Cross: Letter from a Region in My Mind," which Baldwin sold to the *New Yorker* after it had been commissioned by *Commentary*. Podhoretz charged Baldwin with duplicity, a betrayal compounded when Hannah Arendt charged that *Commentary* would not have had the courage to publish the essay. See Podhoretz, "My Negro Problem—and Ours"; Podhoretz, *Making It*, 341–43; and Podhoretz, "'My Negro Problem—and Ours' at 50." See, too, Sundquist, *Strangers in the Land*, 401–2.

47. Lucy S. Dawidowicz, "Negro Antisemitism: Outline for an Analysis," March 14, 1966. AJC/AJA, box G1, folder 30.

48. Ibid., 6.

49. Pearl Ketcher to Lucy S. Dawidowicz, October 11, 1951, Dawidowicz private papers.

50. Lucy S. Dawidowicz to Max Weinreich, November 29, 1965, Dawidowicz Papers, box 77, folder 6. On productivization, see Almog, "Productivization, Proletarianization, and 'Hebrew Labor.'"

51. Lucy S. Dawidowicz, July 21, 1966, "Negro-Jewish Tensions: Economic Aspects," AJC/AJA, box G1, folder 30.

52. Ibid., 7.

53. Lucy S. Dawidowicz, "Proposal for a Study of Negro-White Customer-Merchant Relations," January 31, 1968. AJC/AJA, box G1, folder 30 and box G10, folder 12. For a recent assessment of the role of economics in creating tensions between African Americans and Jews, see Cherry, "Middle Minority Theories."

54. Katz, "Negro-Jewish Relations in America."

55. Ibid., 4.

56. Katz, *Negro and Jew*, xiv–xv. Maurice Samuel urged Jewish thinkers to resist extrapolating the "senseless" views of a "few extremist Negro leaders" to the civil rights movement as a whole. They were no more representative of "the Negro liberation movement

as a whole than the [radical, militant] Sternists had been to the Zionist movement." Samuel cited ibid., 103.

57. Ibid., *Negro and Jew*, xv.

58. Shlomo Katz to Lucy S. Dawidowicz, December 4, 1967, Dawidowicz Papers, box 77, folder 10.

59. Dawidowicz cited in Katz, "Negro-Jewish Relations," 13.

60. Ibid.

61. LeRoi Jones (Amiri Baraka from 1967 forward) was a major cultural figure of the civil rights movement, a gifted African American writer, and a cofounder of the Black Arts movement, a cultural subsidiary of Black Power and the Nation of Islam. His poetry is, however, also known for its use of antisemitic imagery.

62. Dawidowicz in Katz, *Negro and Jew*, 16–18. She closed her essay with a Russian subhead, *Chto delat?* (What Is to Be Done?), evoking Lenin's 1902 pamphlet to suggest that "Negro Populists" were motivated by the same anti-Jewish sentiments as Russian populists.

63. Cohen cited in Katz, *Negro and Jew*, 12. See, too, the comments of Horace Kallen, ibid., 81.

64. On October 29, 1966, the AJC issued a press release stating that "the rank and file of Jews have not significantly withdrawn from their commitment to Negro equality." AJC/AJA, box G10, folder 9.

65. Hertzberg cited in Katz, *Negro and Jew*, 72.

66. Dawidowicz, "Intergroup Relations and Tensions."

67. Ibid., 63.

68. Ibid., 70. Nathan Glazer would later chastise white intellectuals—by which he meant "in large measure Jewish intellectuals"—"justifying, rationalizing, and even teaching violence." Glazer, "Blacks, Jews & The Intellectuals." See, too, Milton Himmelfarb, "Negroes, Jews and Muzhiks."

69. Dawidowicz, "Intergroup Relations and Tensions," 83n41.

70. Vacationing in Europe in 1967, Dawidowicz noted in her diary that she and friends had "chatted about London, Jews and Christians, *the revolutionary Negroes*, etc." Emphasis is mine. Dawidowicz diary entry, August 8, 1967, Dawidowicz private papers.

71. Dawidowicz, "Intergroup Relations and Tensions," 82. In contrast to Dawidowicz's belief that there was a seamless connection between written political rhetoric and political violence, see Shulamit Volkov's emphasis on the *spoken* word to explain the penetration of anti-Jewish sentiment in interwar and wartime Germany. Volkov, "The Written Matter and the Spoken Word," 52.

72. Dawidowicz, "Intergroup Relations and Tensions," 77.

73. Greenberg, *Troubling the Waters*, 217–23.

74. Lucy S. Dawidowicz to Bertram Gold, "Cultural Antisemitism," November 14, 1967, AJC/AJA, box G10, folder 11.

75. Bridenbaugh, "The Great Mutation," cited by Dawidowicz.

76. On the "dechristianization" of the American university and the public sphere in the postwar years, see Hollinger, *Science, Jews, and Secular Culture*, particularly 17–41, and Hollinger, "Christianity and Its American Fate."

77. "Black Art" enjoined activists to write "dagger poems" to stab the "slimy bellies of the ownerjews" and to crack "steel knuckles in a jewlady's mouth." McAlister, "One Black Allah," 646, and Goffman, *Imagining Each Other*, 91–110. In December 1967, Shlomo Katz alerted Dawidowicz to Jones's poem "The Black Man Is Making New Gods," which appeared in the *Evergreen Review*, an alternative literary magazine. The poem began with the stanza, "Atheist jews double crossers stole our secrets crossed / the white desert white to spill them and / turn into wops and bulgarians." Shlomo Katz to Lucy S. Dawidowicz, December 4, 1967, Dawidowicz Papers, box 77, folder 10, and Rosset, *Evergreen Review Reader*, 38.

78. Neal, "The Black Arts Movement."

79. Lucy S. Dawidowicz to Bertram H. Gold, November 14, 1967, AJC/AJA, box G10, folder 11.

80. Bertram H. Gold, "New Dimensions in Anti-Semitism," December 1, 1967, AJC/AJA, box G10, folder 11.

81. Podair, *The Strike That Changed New York*, and Weiner, *Power, Protest, and the Public Schools*.

82. Cited in Kaufman, "Blacks and Jews," 113.

83. Sundquist, *Strangers in the Land*, 342. Lester repudiated the poem in an interview conducted in 1969 but also empathized with the rage of the black community, pointing to the racism of teachers on the picket line and in the leadership ranks of the United Federation of Teachers. See Hentoff, "Blacks and Jews." Lester's later spiritual crisis and conversion to Judaism are documented in his memoir, *Lovesong: Becoming a Jew*, with pp. 46–65 devoted to the events in Ocean Hill–Brownsville.

84. Lucy S. Dawidowicz to Milton Himmelfarb, June 12, 1968, AJC/AJA, box G1, folder 30.

85. Lucy S. Dawidowicz to Bertram Gold, "Jewish Spokesmen and Jewish Constituency," October 9, 1968, AJC/AJA, box G10, folder 11.

86. "Meeting on Research," April 11, 1969, AJC/AJA, box G10, folder 12.

87. Dawidowicz, "Can Anti-Semitism Be Measured?" 42.

88. Staub, *Torn at the Roots*, 131.

89. Cited in Weisbord and Kazarian, *Israel in the Black American Experience*, 33.

90. Ibid., 37.

91. Ibid., 43.

92. Cited in Troy, *Moynihan's Moment*, 29.

93. Weisbord and Kazarian, *Israel in the Black American Experience*, 37.

94. Dawidowicz made her first trip to Israel in 1968, where she was reunited with Pearl Ketcher and her brother. See Moses Pearlman to Lucy S. Dawidowicz, August 10, 1967, Dawidowicz Papers, box 77, folder 11.

95. Dawidowicz, "The United States and the State of Israel," and Dawidowicz, "The Arab-Israel War of 1967."

96. Dawidowicz, "The United States, Israel, and the Middle East," 283–84. For the letters between David Ben-Gurion and Jacob Blaustein in 1950 debating whether American Jews were living in exile, see Mendes-Flohr and Reinharz, *The Jew in the Modern World*, 581–84.

97. Emphasis is mine. Dawidowicz, "The Arab-Israel War of 1967," 204.

98. By the early 1970s, the AJC's leadership had hired a public relations firm to defend Israel, voted to move its office to Jerusalem, started summer institutes in Israel, and allocated more of its annual budget to Israel-related expenses. Sanua, *Let Us Prove Strong*, 143–45.

99. Dawidowicz, "The Arab-Israel War of 1967," 211–17, 225–27. On the morality of Israel's preemptive strike, see Walzer, *Just and Unjust Wars*.

100. Dawidowicz, "The Arab-Israel War of 1967," 224.

101. Ibid., 227–29.

102. Hyman Bookbinder, "Inquiry into Negro-Jewish Relations," Internal Memo of Research Department, May 2, 1969, 1, 12, AJC/digital.

103. She also cataloged the growth of right-wing organizations (e.g., the Liberty Lobby, the John Birch society, the Minutemen, the Christian Crusade, the Congress of Freedom, and the Defenders of the Constitution) and expressed concern about the campaign of George Wallace, the racist governor of Alabama. Lucy S. Dawidowicz to Bertram H. Gold, December 1, 1967, AJC/AJA, box G10, folder 11.

104. Mazower, *No Enchanted Palace*, and, for earlier liberal internationalist efforts, see Pedersen, *The Guardians*.

105. Friesel, "Equating Zionism with Racism."

106. Liskofsky, "U.N. Resolution on Zionism," 115. The politicization of the conference that put Zionism on par with apartheid and racist colonialism shocked American Jewish feminists. Troy, *Moynihan's Moment*, 83; Feld, *Nations Divided*, 87–99; and Antler, *Radical Jewish Feminism*, 315–16, 319–23. For a personal account of a veteran feminist encountering anti-Zionism, see Pogrebin, "Anti-Semitism in the Women's Movement," 45–49, 62–72.

107. Wedgwood, "Zionism and Racism, Again: Durban II." Twenty-two states from Africa, Asia, Latin America, and Europe created the Conference of Heads of State or Government of Non-Aligned Countries (later, the NAM) in 1961 in an attempt to tack a midcourse between the Soviet Union and the United States. Prashad, *The Darker Nations*, 95–104.

108. Borstelmann, *The 1970s*, 56–58.

109. Ehrman, *Rise of Neoconservatism*, 46.

110. Ibid., 68–70, and Troy, *Moynihan's Moment*, 48–50.

111. In 1976, when Moynihan ran for senator of New York, Frances FitzGerald called him "the candidate from *Commentary*" in *Harper's Magazine*. Balint, *Running Commentary*, 119, 245n2. Midge Decter considered him the neoconservatives'"horse" in the race. Ehrman, *Rise of Neoconservatism*, 92.

112. Moynihan wrote the foreword to Abbott, Gold, and Rogowsky, *Police, Politics, and Race*. Dawidowicz oversaw the study's publication. See the correspondence between Dawidowicz and Moynihan in AJC/AJA, box G10, folder 16. See, too, Flamm, "'Law and Order' at Large."

113. Cited in Vaïsse, *Neoconservatism*, 56.

114. Lucy S. Dawidowicz to Daniel P. Moynihan, October 4, 1967, Series G, box 10, folder 31, AJA. She was referring to Moynihan, "The President and the Negro."

115. Moynihan, "The United States in Opposition."

116. Ibid., 43.

117. https://unwatch.org/moynihans-moment-the-historic-1975-u-n-speech-in
-response-to-zionism-is-racism/

118. Weisbord and Kazarian, *Israel in the Black American Experience*, 51–54, https://
www.jta.org/1975/04/28/archive/randolph-initiates-committee-of-black-americans
-to-support-israel, and Troy, *Moynihan's Moment*, 113–14.

119. Collier, *Political Woman*, 129.

120. Weisbord and Kazarian, *Israel in the Black American Experience*, 121–33, and Troy,
Moynihan's Moment, 224–25. In *On Equal Terms*, Dawidowicz concluded, hyper-
bolically, that Young's resignation "unleashed a rage of anti-Semitism in the black
community. Blacks everywhere blamed the Jews," 157.

121. Weisbord and Kazarian, *Israel in the Black American Experience*, 132, and Gershman,
"The Andrew Young Affair."

122. Cited in Murray Friedman, *The Neoconservative Revolution*, 145. See, too, Collier,
Political Woman, 91.

123. Borstelmann, *The 1970s*, 112–13.

124. Murray Friedman, *The Neoconservative Revolution*.

125. Heilbrunn, *They Knew They Were Right*, 143.

126. Balint, *Running Commentary*, 119; Abrams, *Norman Podhoretz and Commentary
Magazine*, 147–50; Heilbrunn, *They Knew They Were Right*, 14; and Ehrman, *Rise of
Neoconservatism*, 97–111.

127. Ehrman, *The Eighties*, 43.

128. Ozick, "Carter and the Jews."

129. Ibid., 6. See, too, Milton Himmelfarb, "Carter and the Jews."

130. Ozick, "Carter and the Jews," 10.

131. Ibid., 18.

132. Ibid., 23. Ozick here invokes *dina d'malkhuta dina* ("the law of the land is the law") in
order to subvert it.

133. Milton Himmelfarb, "Carter and the Jews," 48.

134. Oppenheimer, *Exit Right*.

11. DINA D'MALKHUTA DINA

1. See Milton Himmelfarb, "Paganism, Religion & Modernity," and Kristol, "A Foolish
Americanism—Utopianism."

2. Hacohen, "'The Strange Fact That the State of Israel Exists,'" 40.

3. Jumonville, *Critical Crossings*, 205.

4. Bell and Kristol, *Confrontation*, xii.

5. Bell and Kristol, *Confrontation*, x–xi. See, too, Bell, "The Return of the Sacred," 49.

6. "Participatory democracy," the manifesto of SDS, prioritized personal commitment as
a political strategy and advocated conflict and protest as necessary vehicles for social
change, dismissing evolutionary change and rejecting moderate, "reasonable" liberal
programs and tactics. Brick and Phelps, *Radicals in America*, 101, and Bloch, "The
Emergence of Neoconservatism in the United States," 151–53. At the 1968 Democratic

Convention, New Leftists insisted on proportional representation of women, minorities, and youth and changed the rules of nomination to reflect their commitment to full "participatory democracy." Vaïsse, *Neoconservatism*, 83–84.

7. Cited in Dorman, *Arguing the World*, 155. Howe concurred that "Tragedy, farce, brutal fantasy, delusionary pathos—all came together in the concluding phase of the New Left . . . [which imposed] a kind of [utopia] . . . in the name of an historical imperative—that [was] hell, [leading] to terror and then, terror exhausted, to cynicism and torpor." Howe, *A Margin of Hope*, 327.

8. Bell, "Columbia and the Left," 98n18.

9. Ibid., 106–7.

10. Bell, "Sensibility in the 60's," 64.

11. Howe, *A Margin of Hope*, 308–9.

12. See, too, Dawidowicz's retort to Paul (Peysakh) Novick, editor of the Communist Yiddish paper *Frayhayt*, that his paper's "use of Yiddish to proselytize for its religion [communism] does not make it a Jewish newspaper." Dawidowicz, "Letters to the Editor," *Commentary*, November 1962, 445. See similar views of Jewish radicalism as "half-way houses" in Laqueur, "Revolutionism and the Jews," 45; and Mendelsohn, *On Modern Jewish Politics*, 27–28.

13. Dawidowicz, "[Book Review] Nathan Glazer . . . and Daniel Aaron," 195.

14. Deutscher, *The Non-Jewish Jew and Other Essays*, 41.

15. Singer, "Remembering Milton Himmelfarb"; Milton Himmelfarb, "Is American Jewry in Crisis?"; and Milton Himmelfarb, "This Aquarian Age."

16. Lucy S. Dawidowicz to Daniel Aaron, February 4, 1966, and his reply back to her on February 8, 1966, Dawidowicz Papers, box 77, folder 10. See, too, Aaron, "Some Reflections on Communism and the Jewish Writer." For primary sources on the New Jewish Left, see Sleeper and Mintz, *The New Jews*, and Staub, *The Jewish 1960s*.

17. This revival of white ethnicity, born in reaction to the 1960s, did not break down simply between the Right and the Left. The celebration of white ethnic "roots" informed the student, feminist, and environmental movements and also infused conservatism. Jacobson, *Whiteness of a Different Color*; Jacobson, *Roots Too*; and Zeitz, *White Ethnic New York*.

18. Chaim I. Waxman, "The Limited Impact of the Six-Day War"; Moore, "From David to Goliath"; and Sklare, "Lakeville and Israel."

19. "Working Paper on the Orientation of the Jewish Liberation Project," 150 Fifth Avenue, Rm. 700, NY, NY, 10011, New York Public Library.

20. Jacobson, *Roots Too*, 221.

21. *Proceedings of Breira's First Annual Membership Conference*, 19.

22. Staub, *Torn at the Roots*, chap. 8, and Diner, *The Jews of the United States*, 327.

23. See, for example, Robert Loeb's letter to *Commentary* explaining the similarity between Breira's position and that of Aharon Yariv, the Israeli minister of information, and Victor Shemtov, the Israeli health minister, a position known as the Yariv/Shemtov formula for negotiating with the PLO. "Letters from Readers," *Commentary*, June 1977, 4–5.

24. See the introspective, self-critical volume, Shapira, *Si'aḥ Loḥamim: Pirkei Hakshavah Ve-Hitbonenut* (Fighters' Talk: Chapters in Listening and Introspection). An edited

collection of testimonies of the country's elite soldiers who had fought in the Six-Day War, the book exposed the divide between the soldiers' angst and the euphoria gripping many Jews in Israel and the diaspora. It became a runaway bestseller. Katriel, *Dialogic Moments*. It appeared in English in 1970 with a sacralized title, Shapira, *The Seventh Day: Soldiers' Talk about the Six-Day War*.

25. Amnon Rubinstein, "And Now in Israel, A Fluttering of Doves," *New York Times Magazine*, July 26, 1970, 8–9, 44–47.

26. *Proceedings of Breira's First Annual Membership Conference*; Arthur I. Waskow, "Talking with the P.L.O.," *New York Times*, December 16, 1976, 47; and "American Jewish Leaders Are Split over Issue of Meeting with P.L.O.," *New York Times*, December 30, 1976, 1, 6.

27. Isaac, *Breira: Counsel for Judaism*, 30.

28. Shattan, "Why Breira?" 63.

29. Staub, *Torn at the Roots*, 300–308.

30. *Commentary* had published several critical letters in response to Shattan's article, including a passionate one from Breira member Barry Rubin, who charged that Shattan and Isaac "aimed at ruining" him. Ibid., 361n8. For Rubin's letter and many others, see *Commentary*, June 1977, 6–31.

31. Linda Charlton, "37 Jews in U.S. Applaud Israelis." Three decades earlier, while working in the American Zone of Occupation, Lucy wrote that she had turned down an invitation "on a matter of principle" to a Revisionist Zionist dance, commenting that "the boy isn't particular where he dances, but I am." Lucy Schildkret, letter home, addressee unknown, November 17, 1946, Dawidowicz Papers, box 55, folder 3.

32. Kristol, "A Few Kind Words for Uncle Tom." See, too, similar conclusions in Ismar Schorsch's classic essay, "On the Political Judgment of the Jew."

33. Kristol, "A Few Kind Words for Uncle Tom," 95. He may have been indebted to Myrdal, who used the terms "protest" and "accommodationist" to describe African American political behavior. See Myrdal, *An American Dilemma*, 720–56.

34. Kristol, "A Few Kind Words for Uncle Tom," 96. The emphasis is mine.

35. This binary has had remarkable staying power. See Roth, *The Plot Against America*, 359, where the young protagonist reflects on his relatives' political choices during the crisis-ridden years of Nazi leadership in the United States: "My father chooses *resistance*, Rabbi Bengelsdorf chooses *collaboration*, and Uncle Monty chooses himself." Emphases are mine.

36. Kristol defined African American culture only in terms of victimhood, comparing it to John-Paul Sartre's definition of Jewishness's essence as "something that can be fully explained in terms of the existence of anti-Semitism." For Kristol, Jewishness had to mean "also something positive and meritorious and gratifying." He queried, "Don't American Negroes have a similar conception of themselves?" Kristol, "A Few Kind Words for Uncle Tom," 98.

37. Arendt, *Eichmann in Jerusalem*, 116.

38. Kristol, "A Few Kind Words for Uncle Tom," 97.

39. See Elazar, "American Political Theory," and Sarna, "Jewish Prayers for the U.S. Government."

40. Dawidowicz, "[Book Review] Nathan Glazer . . . and Daniel Aaron," 192.
41. Abram regularly asked Dawidowicz to "boil down" his writing for speeches and op-ed pieces. Morris B. Abram to Lucy S. Dawidowicz, February 13, 1967, and May 22, 1967, AJC/AJA, box G10, folder 9.
42. On Abram's work as the Johnson administration's US delegate to the UN Commission on Human Rights, see Loeffler, *Rooted Cosmopolitans*, 265–67, 273–75.
43. See, too, Howe, "In This Moment of Grief."
44. Dawidowicz travel diary, April 5, 1968, Dawidowicz private papers.
45. "For Morris B. Abram," May 20, 1968, AJC/AJA, box G10, folder 9.
46. Mishnah Avot, 3:2.
47. Lucy S. Dawidowicz, "For Morris B. Abram," May 20, 1968, AJC/AJA, box G10, folder 9.
48. One year later, when students at Brandeis occupied two of the university's halls, demanding greater minority representation, Dawidowicz sent Abram a supportive letter, to which he responded, "We are trying to resolve the crisis by a mixture of firmness and compassion [but] no one can guarantee that any given course will succeed." He did not succeed and stepped down in 1970 after a tenure of just two years. Lucy S. Dawidowicz to Morris Abram, May 21, 1968, and Morris Abram to Lucy S. Dawidowicz, January 16, 1969, AJC/AJA, box G10, folder 9.
49. Wolfe, "The Me Decade and the Third Great Awakening."
50. Ibid., 279.
51. Schulman, *The Seventies*, 93–99.
52. Kristol, "Christianity, Judaism, and Socialism," 436.
53. Sarna, *American Judaism*, 274. See, too, Lederhendler, *New York Jews*, 117, 121–24.
54. Wertheimer, *A People Divided*, 66–70.
55. Siegel, Strassfeld, and Strassfeld, *The First Jewish Catalog*.
56. Ibid., dedication page. *Daven* is the Yiddish word for "to pray." *Yavneh* was the mythical center of post–Second Temple Judaism, viewed in rabbinic literature as its foundational site.
57. The word "havurah" (fellowship) referred to communal fellowship bonds of religious adepts in the Second Temple period as well as to Jewish mystics in the sixteenth century. Lerner, "The *Havurot*"; the essays in "Part Two: Religious Imagination" in Sleeper and Mintz, *The New Jews*, 153–243; Prell, *Prayer and Community*.
58. Alter, "Revolutionism and the Jews," 47–54.
59. Ibid. See, too, Isidore Silver, "What Flows from Neo-Conservatism."
60. Borowitz, "At the Beginning." *Sh'ma*, literally "Listen!" in Hebrew, directly alludes to a centerpiece of the Jewish liturgy, the assertion of monotheism declaimed before the reading of the Torah.
61. Borowitz, "Have Your Read *Commentary* Lately?" In the same issue, Maurice Friedberg took Borowitz to task for not recognizing that *Commentary* had asked him to write an article on the plight of Soviet Jewry seven years earlier, indicating that the journal's *Jewish* concerns were not recent.
62. *Sh'ma* published the letter as Dawidowicz, "*Sh'ma's* Anti-Responsibility." Dawidowicz shared the letter beforehand with Norman Podhoretz. Lucy S. Dawidowicz to Nor-

man Podhoretz, April 22, 1971, Fund for the Translation of Jewish Literature Archives, *Commentary* Papers, American Jewish Committee. Used with permission of Neal Kozodoy.

63. Dawidowicz, "*Sh'ma*'s Anti-Responsibility."

64. https://yivoencyclopedia.org/article.aspx/Litvak. On regionalism within early modern Polish Jewish culture, see Davis, "The Reception of the Shulhan 'Arukh."

65. Allen Hoffman to Lucy S. Dawidowicz, March 19, 1990, Dawidowicz Papers, box 71, folder 8. See the full letter in the appendix.

66. Ruth Wisse to Lucy S. Dawidowicz, April 22, 1989, Dawidowicz Papers, box 71, folder 8.

67. Echols, *Daring to Be Bad*, and Haywood and Drake, *Third Wave Agenda*. Her intellectual opposition to feminism as an ideology did not preclude Dawidowicz's commitment to women's history. Five folders on Jewish women's history are contained in her archive.

68. Jeane Kirkpatrick's biographer positioned her as a female intellectual who did not need "the institutional brace of a movement," words fitting for Dawidowicz's views of feminism. Collier, *Political Woman*, 77.

69. Brooklyn Bridge Collective, "Jewish Women," reprinted in Staub, *The Jewish 1960s*, 325–27.

70. Lucy S. Dawidowicz to Henia Karmel-Wolfe, November 15, 1970, Dawidowicz Papers, box 77, folder 13.

71. Emphasis is mine. Lucy S. Dawidowicz to Nancy Neiman, September 30, 1974, Dawidowicz Papers, box 66, folder 10. See, too, Lucy S. Dawidowicz to Roswell McClelland, the US representative to the War Refugee Board in Switzerland, January 3, 1975, where she commented that her book did not reflect her rage and anguish "at the Germans for having done what they did, and—though it is sacriligious [*sic*] to mention them together—against the Jewish God for having permitted the murder to have been committed . . . except in a muted and highly controlled form." Dawidowicz Papers, box 76, folder 4.

72. Klagsbrun, "Eulogies." Klagsbrun's homage noted that Dawidowicz did not share her feminist commitments.

73. Milton Himmelfarb, "The Vanishing Jews."

74. Morgan, "The Vanishing American Jew." See, too, Goldscheider, "Demography and American Jewish Survival."

75. Interview with Francine Klagsbrun, October 21, 2009.

76. Lucy S. Dawidowicz to Joel Carmichael, July 28, 1985, Dawidowicz Papers, box 78, folder 9, and Dawidowicz, "Symposium." See, too, Lucy S. Dawidowicz to Edward Alexander, July 4, 1986, Dawidowicz Papers, box 79, folder 4b.

77. Syrkin, "Does Feminism Clash with Jewish National Need?" and Dawidowicz, "Symposium." The symposium also included Elyse M. Goldstein, Daniel J. Elazar, and Emanuel Rackman, as well as Syrkin's summary comments. See Syrkin, "Symposium," where she highlighted the demographic challenge facing the Westernized, acculturated Jewish community.

78. Murray Friedman, *The Neoconservative Revolution*; Kristol, "Christianity, Judaism, and Socialism"; and Kristol, "Why Religion Is Good for the Jews."

79. Dawidowicz was often a guest at the Mirsky family's Sabbath table when she lived on West Eighty-Sixth Street. Interview with Yehuda Mirsky, July 13, 2006. Dawidowicz lovingly eulogized Mirsky at Yeshiva University on April 17, 1983. See Dawidowicz Papers, box 44, folder 7.

80. *Knaidlach* refers to the traditional dumplings made of matzoh meal that are served at the seder meal in Ashkenazic homes.

81. Kessner, "From This Place and Time," 29.

82. Dawidowicz, "On Being a Woman in Shul" (1968), 71.

83. Ibid., 72.

84. Sarna, *American Judaism*, 243–49; Moore, *At Home in America*; and Gurock and Schacter, *A Modern Heretic and a Traditional Community*. Kaplan's daughter Judith was said to have been the first American bat mitzvah.

85. Dawidowicz, "On Being a Woman in Shul" (1968), 73. The essay was reprinted as Dawidowicz, "On Being a Woman in Shul," in *The Jewish Presence: Essays on Identity and History* (1977). See, too, Ozick's reference to the "leftist paganism" of feminist theologians, in Cynthia Ozick to Lucy S. Dawidowicz, December 12, 1983, Dawidowicz private papers.

86. Dawidowicz, "On Being a Woman in Shul" (1968), 74.

87. Lucy S. Dawidowicz to Pearl Ketcher, Yael Katz and David Pearlman, Private Collection.

88. Solomon Birnbaum to Lucy S. Dawidowicz, August 14, 1968, Birnbaum Archives. Norma Rosen disagreed with the piece's substance, warning Lucy that the piece would "scandalize" her "earnest critics." Nonetheless, Rosen admitted that she loved the irreverence toward "the (secular) pieties." Norma Rosen to Lucy S. Dawidowicz, July 29, 1977, Dawidowicz private papers. Many other American Jewish women found Dawidowicz's embrace of traditional sex roles in Jewish religious and communal life insupportable. In 1972, a group of committed Jewish women, most of whom were educated in the Conservative movement, founded Ezrat Nashim, a feminist group that demanded women be treated equally as members of synagogues and prayer quorums (*minyanim*) and as prayer leaders and witnesses of Jewish legal proceedings. See their manifesto, "Jewish Women Call for Change," in Staub, *The Jewish 1960s*, 338–39; the essays in Koltun, *The Jewish Woman*; and those in "Chapter 7: The Jewish Woman," in Porter and Dreier, *Jewish Radicalism*, 245–72. For an Orthodox feminist view, see Greenberg, *On Women and Judaism*.

89. Meyer, "On the Role of the Sexes in Modern Judaism." Michael A. Meyer to Lucy S. Dawidowicz, August 28, 1968, and Lucy S. Dawidowicz to Michael A. Meyer, September 9, 1968, Dawidowicz Papers, box 77, folder 11.

90. Meyer, "On the Role of the Sexes in Modern Judaism," 44.

91. Ibid., 46.

92. Feiner, "The Modern Jewish Woman."

93. Kessner, "From This Place and Time," 29–31. She informed a dinner host in the late 1970s that "Not being very consistent (the mark of Conservative Judaism), I do eat non-kosher meat, but would prefer fish." Lucy S. Dawidowicz to Lacey Baldwin Smith, March 14, 1977, Dawidowicz Papers, box 42, folder 6.

94. "Shaping of Interfaith Relations," lecture to the rabbinic alumni of Yeshiva University, March 18, 1971, Dawidowicz Papers, box 70, folder 3.

95. As noted above, Dawidowicz considered much of the new spirituality of the 1970s "inauthentic." Dawidowicz, "The Relevance of an Education in the Sholem Aleichem Schools: Some Personal Remarks."

96. Voegelin, an Austrian Christian who fled Nazi Europe in 1938 and immigrated to the United States, explained modern political messianism and nihilism as the reemergence of subterranean religious forces and symbols that had been rejected by radical Enlightenment thinkers. Hoeveler, *Watch on the Right*, and Lilla, *The Shipwrecked Mind*, 25–42. Haym Maccoby, "The Greatness of Gershom Scholem," *Commentary*, September 1983, 37–46, and Haym Maccoby, "Christianity's Break with Judaism," *Commentary*, August 1984, 38–42.

97. Kristol, "Christianity, Judaism, and Socialism." It is notable that Kristol conceded the point that socialism's emphasis on community distinguished it from capitalism's stress on individualism, a "crucial" weakness of the liberal, capitalist society of the modern era. Ibid., 437.

98. Dawidowicz Papers, boxes 10–11, 23–28.

99. See her correspondence with archivists and historians on the topic. Lucy S. Dawidowicz to Shirley Tanzer, May 22, 1977, Dawidowicz Papers, box 16, folder 7; Lucy S. Dawidowicz to Samuel Rezneck, June 8, 1978, Dawidowicz Papers, box 16, folder 7.

100. The drafts can be found in Dawidowicz Papers, box 23, folder 11. See, too, Dawidowicz, "The Business of American Jews."

101. Dawidowicz, "The Business of American Jews," 239.

102. Her notes also illuminated scandals, such as that of Abram Jesse Dittenhoefer, a lawyer who was implicated in the Whiskey Ring, which siphoned off taxes on alcohol into the coffers of the Republican Party. See the recent work of Davis, *Jews and Booze*, and Kobrin, "Destructive Creators."

103. On the emergence of new forms of radical history writing in the late 1960s that emphasized the politically and socially disenfranchised, see Tilly, "The Old New Social History," and Wiener, "Radical Historians," 399–434.

104. Dawidowicz, "The Business of American Jews," 252.

105. Podhoretz, *Making It*.

106. Hoeveler, *Watch on the Right*, 81–111, and Gertrude Himmelfarb, *The De-Moralization of Society*, 170–87.

107. "Capitalism, Socialism, and Democracy," 29.

108. Michael Walzer quipped, "'Ineluctability' is a nice word. I wonder if the editors of *Commentary* have themselves been converted to historical determinism." Ibid., 70.

109. Bloch, "The Emergence of Neoconservatism in the United States," 287, 290, 313–16, 327.

110. She remarked to more than one friend when she was close to death that at least she did not have to finish "the damn book." Interview with Neal Kozodoy, July 19, 2006, and with Tom Wallace, July 12, 2011.

111. In 1974 Dawidowicz wrote to a colleague that after completing what she hoped would be a definitive essay on Holocaust historiography (which became *The Holocaust and*

the Historians) she planned to "retire from the subject and turn to something more cheerful." Lucy S. Dawidowicz to Lawrence V. Berman, November 6, 1974, Dawidowicz Papers, box 77, folder 14.

112. Dawidowicz, "A Century of Jewish History, 1881–1981," later published as Dawidowicz, *On Equal Terms*; and Dawidowicz, "[Book Review] Getting and Spending: *Jews and Money*."

113. Hollinger, "Rich, Powerful, and Smart"; Kuznets, *Jewish Economics*; and Kobrin, *Chosen Capital*.

12. WARSAW AND VILNA ON HER MIND

1. Shandler, *While America Watches*; Mintz, *Popular Culture*; and Lipstadt, *Holocaust*.
2. Lucy S. Dawidowicz to Alfred Kazin, January 22, 1978, Manuscript box (Kazin). A.L.S., T.L.S., card to Alfred Kazin. Folder 1, Alfred Kazin Papers, Henry W. and Albert A. Berg Collection of English and American Literature, New York Public Library, Astor Lenox and Tilden Foundations. See, too, Lucy S. Dawidowicz to Roswell McClelland, May 22, 1979, Dawidowicz Papers, box 76, folder 5, and to Gerald Fleming, June 27, 1984, box 78, folder 4, about her fatigue with the Holocaust as a subject of research.
3. This need became acute after Szymon's death on June 1, 1979. Dawidowicz expressed appreciation to Alvin Rosenfeld for inviting her to Indiana University because "Szymon is no longer here to take care of me." Lucy S. Dawidowicz to Alvin Rosenfeld, June 25, 1979, Dawidowicz Papers, box 76, folder 5, and Lucy S. Dawidowicz to Ruth Wisse, June 25, 1979, requesting an invitation to speak at McGill University, box 77, folder 16.
4. Dawidowicz's expertise was sought after by social policy institutes, book and magazine editors, and other scholars seeking letters of reference, including Peter Steinfels, an associate for the humanities at the Institute of Society, Ethics, and the Life Sciences, and the sociologist Robert Jay Lifton, best known for *The Nazi Doctors: Medical Killing and the Psychology of Genocide*, among others. Peter Steinfels to Lucy S. Dawidowicz, Dawidowicz Papers, March 12 and March 26, 1976, April 21, 1976, Dawidowicz Papers, box 68, folder, 4; Robert Jay Lifton to Lucy S. Dawidowicz, June 1, 1977, September 23, 1981, November 24, 1981; and Lucy S. Dawidowicz to Robert Jay Lifton, November 2, 1981, Dawidowicz Papers, box 69, folder 6.
5. Elie Wiesel chaired the thirty-four-member commission, which included Holocaust survivors, lay and religious leaders of all faiths, scholars, and members of Congress. Some have argued that Carter created the commission to curry favor with the official Jewish community, which had been alienated by his foreign policy and arms deals. Linenthal, *Preserving Memory*, 18–23, 52. See the note regarding the phone call from Ellen Goldstein, assistant director of Carter's Domestic Policy Staff, July 26, 1978, Dawidowicz Papers, box 46, folder 10.
6. Lucy S. Dawidowicz's Statement for the President's Commission on the Holocaust, February 15, 1979, Dawidowicz Papers, box 45, folder 10. See, too, Dawidowicz, "The Holocaust Was Unique." Several years later, she would participate in a symposium

sponsored by *Midstream* magazine comparing the Holocaust with the Armenian genocide. She, with Yehuda Bauer, Helen Fein, Nora Levin, and Elie Wiesel, responded to Papazian, "A Unique Uniqueness?" Dawidowicz rejected Papazian's analogy. See, too, Gavriel D. Rosenfeld, "The Politics of Uniqueness."

7. Lucy S. Dawidowicz's Statement for the President's Commission on the Holocaust, February 15, 1979, Dawidowicz Papers, box 45, folder 10.

8. A copy of Gerson Cohen's letter can be found in Dawidowicz Papers, box 46, folder 4.

9. A copy of Bookbinder's letter to Wiesel, April 26, 1979, can be found in Dawidowicz Papers, box 46, folder 4. See, too, a copy of Bookbinder's letter to Benjamin Meed, a survivor of the Warsaw Ghetto, in which he insisted that "All agree: *the Holocaust is a unique piece of Jewish and human history, though its significance extends to all peoples,*" voicing concern that the American Jewish community not think that the "universalists" have triumphed over the "particularists." Emphasis in the original. Hyman Bookbinder to Benjamin Meed, May 22, 1979, Dawidowicz Papers, box 46, folder 4. The final report's language showed the tensions and contortions of the negotiations: "The universality of the Holocaust lies in its uniqueness: the Event is essentially Jewish, yet its interpretation is universal." Linenthal, *Preserving Memory*, 36.

10. Lucy S. Dawidowicz to Irving Greenberg, September 6, 1979, Dawidowicz Papers, box 46, folder 3. The commission defined the non-Jewish victims as victims of *Nazism*, not of the Holocaust, which allowed for their inclusion in the memorial without diminishing the Jewish particularism of the Holocaust. Email with Michael Berenbaum, January 21, 2019.

11. Elie Wiesel to Lucy S. Dawidowicz, October 26, 1979, Dawidowicz Papers, box 79, folder 4. Wiesel did not attend the ceremony marking the unveiling of the museum's cornerstone in October 1988. Miller, "A Washington Memorial."

12. Linenthal, *Preserving Memory*, 41. The museum that was a product of the order and of the congressional bill establishing the United States Holocaust Memorial Council struggled with the representation of the distinctiveness of Jewish suffering while making the Holocaust comprehensible to an American audience.

13. Lucy S. Dawidowicz to Judith Miller, December 29, 1989, Dawidowicz private papers.

14. Allan Greenberg to Lucy S. Dawidowicz, May 16, 1990, and Lucy S. Dawidowicz to Allan Greenberg, May 28, 1990, Dawidowicz Papers, box 64, folder 7.

15. Linenthal, *Preserving Memory*, 53.

16. Ibid., 38–42.

17. On the contested memory in the regions first occupied by the Soviets and then attacked by the Nazis, see Barkan, Cole, and Struve, *Shared History—Divided Memory*.

18. Ozick, "Carter and the Jews," 15.

19. Dawidowicz, "Boy Meets Girl in the Warsaw Ghetto," reprinted in Staub, *The Jewish 1960s*, 53–57.

20. Shandler, *While America Watches*, 42–56, 180–81.

21. Dawidowicz, "Boy Meets Girl in the Warsaw Ghetto," in Staub, *The Jewish 1960s*, 55–56.

22. Stingo is the name of the southern gentile character in William Styron's 1979 award-winning book, *Sophie's Choice*. When the novel was adapted for film in 1982, Meryl Streep played Sophie, winning the Academy Award for Best Actress. Polish film critics found both the book and the film wanting, their harsh, negative portrayals of Poles as equivalent to Nazis characteristic of American ignorance of Eastern Europe and of Poland's tragic fate during the German occupation. Biskupski, "Poland and the Poles," 30–31.

23. She dedicated *The Golden Tradition* to "Zelig and Riva Kalmanovich, Two of Six Million"; *The War Against the Jews* to "Toba (Tobtshe) Dawidowicz, Warsaw 1924–Warsaw Ghetto 1943 and Zarek Dawidowicz, Warsaw 1927–Treblinka 1942 (?) Two of Six Million"; *A Holocaust Reader* to the "memory of the six million," with a citation from Kalmanovich's diary; *The Jewish Presence* to "Szymon," her refugee husband; *The Holocaust and the Historians* to the "memory of the murdered Jewish historians (Dubnow, Bałaban, Schipper, and Ringelblum)"; and *From That Place and Time*, to the "memory of the murdered Jews of Vilna," with the Hebrew phrase "*eleh ezkerah*" (these I will remember) from the liturgical poem to commemorate Jewish martyrdom.

24. Myers, "Jews Without Memory," and Foley, "Fact, Fiction, Fascism," 356.

25. Sundquist, *Strangers in the Land*, 443–44, inclusive of footnote.

26. Alvin H. Rosenfeld, "The Holocaust According to William Styron," 44.

27. Alvin Rosenfeld to Lucy S. Dawidowicz, June 19, 1979, and Dawidowicz to Rosenfeld, June 25, 1979, Dawidowicz Papers, box 76, folder 5.

28. Housden, *Hans Frank*, and Friedländer, *The Years of Extermination*, 35–40.

29. Rosenfeld later deepened his critique of Styron's characterization of Nathan Landau, interpreting him as a sadistic Svengali, reviving the "wildest of antisemitic fantasies of the Jew as sexual predator." Alvin H. Rosenfeld, *Imagining Hitler*, 51.

30. Alvin Rosenfeld to Lucy S. Dawidowicz, June 19, 1979, Dawidowicz Papers, box 76, folder 5.

31. Rittner and Roth, *Memory Offended*; Huener, *Auschwitz, Poland, and the Politics of Commemoration*; and Zubrzycki, *The Crosses of Auschwitz*.

32. Today it is much more common for scholars—and increasingly the public—to focus on the mass destruction waged by the Wehrmacht and the Einsatzgruppen on occupied Polish lands from the spring of 1941 forward, but it was not the case in Dawidowicz's day. Desbois, *The Holocaust by Bullets*; Snyder, "Holocaust"; Snyder, *Bloodlands*; and Himka, "The Reception of the Holocaust in Postcommunist Ukraine."

33. In June 1978, Dawidowicz wrote to Harvey Shapiro, editor in chief of the *New York Times Book Review*, asking if she could review Rubenstein's book. Lucy S. Dawidowicz to Harvey Shapiro, June 8, 1978, and Harvey Shapiro to Lucy S. Dawidowicz, June 26, 1978, Dawidowicz private papers. After reading Styron's "wickedly obtuse" introduction, she decided not to review the book. Lucy S. Dawidowicz to William A. Clebsch, February 1, 1979, Dawidowicz Papers, box 77, folder 16.

34. Styron, "Introduction."

35. Ibid., xiii.

36. Ibid., xiv. Rubenstein patted Styron's back again by giving *Sophie's Choice* a glowing review in the *Michigan Quarterly Review* in 1981. Sundquist, *Strangers in the Land*, 629n17.

37. In an unpublished interview transcript for *Reconstructionist* magazine, Dawidowicz expressed her disregard for fictional representations of the Holocaust, though she grudgingly acknowledged that a rare gifted poet, like a Paul Celan or Irving Feldman, could express the Jewish perspective on the events. She added, "if one wants to transmit the horror of what the Germans did, the model is Richard Strauss's opera, *Salome* ... [which] is about utter evil, corruption, and ugliness. ... It serves as an archetype of what one might call Holocaust art." Dawidowicz allowed that Elie Wiesel's *Night* was a great book, but one she increasingly regarded as a memoir tempered by the art of fiction: "It's worked over." Dawidowicz private papers. See, too, Lucy S. Dawidowicz to John Felstiner—a translator of Celan's *Todesfuge*—April 20, 1984, John Felstiner personal papers. I am grateful to John Felstiner for sharing this letter with me. See, too, John Felstiner to Dawidowicz, April 30, 1984, Dawidowicz Papers, box 78, folder 7.

38. Dawidowicz, "Babi Yar's Legacy," reprinted as Dawidowicz, "The True History of Babi Yar." For the article's research notes and drafts, see Dawidowicz Papers, box 45, folders 1–6 and box 64, folder 5.

39. Dawidowicz, *The Holocaust and the Historians*, 68–87.

40. Irving Howe to Lucy S. Dawidowicz, April 21, 1978, Dawidowicz Papers, box 77, folder 15.

41. Her archives include clippings from the extensive reviews, Dawidowicz Papers, box 59 and box 74, folder 3.

42. The *Historikerstreit* was sparked by Ernest Nolte's 1986 article in the *Frankfurter Allgemeine Zeitung*, "The Past That Will Not Go Away." A new generation of historians, many of whom were influenced by New Left politics and post-structuralist theories, rejected the thesis that the Holocaust was a singular historical event and break with Germany's past. Rather, they claimed that the Holocaust was continuous with Germany's reactionary culture and given added force by interwar German society's fear of communism. The new historians' source base looked "below" to *Alltagsgeschichte*, the everyday life of "ordinary" Germans, playing down the role of antisemitism among the German elite. Friedländer, "A Conflict of Memories?"; Rabinbach, "Editor's Introduction to Special Issue on the *Historikerstreit*"; the articles by Martin Broszat, Friedländer, Jürgen Habermas, and Andrei S. Markovits; and Kansteiner, "From Exception to Exemplum." Dawidowicz reacted to the *Historikerstreit* in Dawidowicz, "Observations: Perversions of the Holocaust."

43. These forms came into existence immediately after the Bolshevik revolution and continued well into the end of the Soviet period. See Veidlinger, *The Moscow State Yiddish Theater*; Estraikh, *In Harness*; Murav, *Music from a Speeding Train*; Shneer, *Yiddish and the Creation of Soviet Jewish Culture*; and Shternshis, *Soviet and Kosher*.

44. Dawidowicz, *The Holocaust and the Historians*, 70.

45. Ibid., 79. Dawidowicz's views about Soviet erasure of Jewish suffering at Babi Yar are confirmed in Gitelman, "Politics and the Historiography of the Holocaust"; Bartov, *Erased*; and Himka, "The Reception of the Holocaust."

46. Lucy S. Dawidowicz to Alexander M. Nekrich, November 4, 1977, Dawidowicz Papers, box 77, folder 15.

47. Dawidowicz, *The Holocaust and the Historians*, 80. See, too, Dawidowicz, *The War Against the Jews*, 148.

48. Dawidowicz relied on Philip Friedman's work for her views of Ukrainian collaboration. Philip Friedman, *Roads to Extinction*, and Dawidowicz, "[Book Review] Holocaust Historian," 18.

49. Dawidowicz, "Babi Yar's Legacy," 49.

50. Himka, "Ukrainian Collaboration."

51. Susan Jacoby to Lucy S. Dawidowicz, undated, but after 1972 and before the publication of Dawidowicz's piece on Babi Yar in the *Times*, Dawidowicz Papers, box 45, folder 6, and Jacoby, *Moscow Conversations*.

52. Dawidowicz, "Babi Yar's Legacy," 50.

53. After Dawidowicz appeared on Richard Heffner's *The Open Mind* in November 1982 to discuss her book, he received angry letters from Ukrainian viewers. See Dawidowicz Papers, box 42, folder 1. The pushback continues today. See Bartov, "Introduction to the Ukrainian Translation of *Erased*," 122n1, on the debate in the journal *Ukraina Moderna* that ensued after his book's publication.

54. Lev E. Dobriansky, letter to the editor, *New York Times*, December 13, 1981. See, too, the letter to the editor by Vitaly Korotych, editor of *Vsesvit*, of February 14, 1982, emphasizing the murder of non-Jews.

55. In 2008, Karel Berkhoff, who affirmed that the massacre at Babi Yar was the largest single Nazi shooting of Jews, took Dawidowicz to task for her attitude toward the Ukrainian population and her disregard for "the courageous (and well-documented) condemnation of antisemitism that the Ukrainian writer Ivan Dziuba delivered during the ceremony" commemorating the massacre's twenty-fifth anniversary. Nonetheless, he concluded that "postwar sources indicate that Ukrainian policemen were indeed involved in the Babi Yar massacre"; every record of Pronicheva's testimony confirmed that the Ukrainian auxiliary police "readied the Jews for their murder by stripping them." Berkhoff, "Dina Pronicheva's Story," 303. See, too, Finder and Prusin, "Collaboration in Eastern Galicia."

56. Beckerman, *When They Come for Us, We'll Be Gone*, and Korey, "A Monument Over Babi Yar?" See, too, the correspondence between Solomon Birnbaum and Dawidowicz over his son Jacob's activism on behalf of Soviet Jewry. Lucy S. Dawidowicz to Solomon Birnbaum, April 5, 1970, and November 28, 1971, and Solomon Birnbaum to Szymon and Lucy S. Dawidowicz, June 28, 1970, Birnbaum Archives.

57. At the same time, Ehrenburg and Grossman used their reporting to give voice to the specific Jewish suffering they witnessed. Zavadivker, "Preserving 'Events That Are Vanishing Like Smoke.'"

58. Arendt, "[Book Review] *The Black Book* and *Hitler's Professors*."

59. Rubenstein, "The Black Book." For a near-complete version, see Ehrenburg and Grossman, *The Complete Black Book of Russian Jewry*. Rubenstein would later write a biography of Ehrenburg—*Tangled Loyalties: The Life and Times of Ilya Ehrenburg*—and edit a full version of *The Black Book*. Rubenstein and Altman, *The Unknown Black Book*.

60. Dawidowicz, *The Holocaust and the Historians*, 81.

61. Dawidowicz, "Letters from Readers," *Commentary*, January 1983, 5–8.

62. On the shifts in Soviet historiography that critiqued the "totalitarian" school's political science–informed perspective on the USSR as a hermetically sealed authoritarian system with no room for human agency "from below," see Hellbeck, *Revolution on My Mind*; Fitzpatrick, "Revisionism in Soviet History"; and Krylova, "Soviet Modernity." I am grateful to Andrew Sloin for pointing me in the direction of these interpretations.

63. Joshua Rubenstein, "Letter to the Editor," *Commentary*, January 1983, 10. See, too, Murav, *Music from a Speeding Train*, chap. 3, "Fighting the Great Patriotic War."

64. Zoë Waxman, "[Book Review] *The Unknown Black Book*," 136.

65. It continues to be so. See Zimmerman, *Contested Memories*; Polonsky, "Poles, Jews, and the Problems of Divided Memory"; Cherry and Orla-Bukowska, *Rethinking Poles and Jews*; and Grudzińska-Gross and Nawrocki, *Poland and Polin*.

66. For short overviews of two seminal conferences in the early 1980s treating Polish-Jewish relations, see Hirszowicz, "A Conference on Polish-Jewish Relations," and Polonsky, "Oxford Conference on Polish Jewish Relations."

67. Harold B. Segel to Lucy S. Dawidowicz, June 18, 1981, Dawidowicz Papers, box 77, folder 16.

68. Ibid.

69. Lucy S. Dawidowicz to Harold B. Segel, June 21, 1981, and Harold B. Segel to Lucy S. Dawidowicz, June 24, 1981, Dawidowicz Papers, box 77, folder 16. A positive, if qualified, Polish review of *The War Against the Jews* appeared as Tomaszewski, "Review of Lucy S. Dawidowicz, *The War Against the Jews, 1933–1945*."

70. Dawidowicz did not read Polish, so her analysis depended upon translations and bibliographic suggestions given to her by Polish Jewish colleagues and friends, including Dina Abramowicz, Lucjan Dobroszycki, a Łódź-born YIVO survivor historian, Mark Nowogrodzki, Isaiah Trunk, and her husband, Szymon. Dawidowicz, *The Holocaust and the Historians*, 165.

71. Dawidowicz, *The Holocaust and the Historians*, 124. In the wake of the Six-Day War and motivated by Soviet directives and internecine Polish Communist Party struggles, Gomułka accused Polish Jews of being a Zionist Fifth Column. Roughly thirteen thousand Polish Jews left the country, passportless and with one-way tickets. Dawidowicz referred to the events as the "anti-Semitic" campaign so as not to accept the pretext that the remaining community of Polish Jews, who were thoroughly secular, Polanized, and largely identified with the regime, were Zionists. Stola, *Kampania Antysyjonistyczna w Polsce 1967–1968*; and Eisler, "Antisemitism, Emigration."

72. Typescript for lecture, "Shaping of Interfaith Relations," March 18, 1971, Dawidowicz Papers, box 70, folder 3. On Polish romantic messianism and the image of Poland as the Christ of Nations, see Mickiewicz, *The Books and the Pilgrimage of the Polish Nation*, and Brock, "Polish Nationalism."

73. Dawidowicz, *The Holocaust and the Historians*, 108.

74. Ibid., 107.

75. Ibid., 119.

76. Władysław Bartoszewski, *Ten jest z ojczyzny mojej: Polacy z pomocą Żydom 1939–1945* (Krakow: Znak, 1969), and in English as Bartoszewski, *Righteous among the Gentiles: How the Poles Helped the Jews* (London: Earlscourt, 1969).

77. Dawidowicz, *The Holocaust and the Historians*, 117.

78. Ibid., 93.

79. Ibid., 100–101. For a newer treatment of Mark, see Nalewajko-Kulikov, "Sylwetki." See, too, Shmeruk, "A briv in redaktsiye" [Letter to the Editor], where Shmeruk related his and Israel Halperin's meeting with Mark in 1956 in Paris on the occasion of the unveiling of the Holocaust memorial. One evening Mark broke down in tears, begging Halperin to help him atone for his sin of publishing tendentious accounts in the Stalinist period of the Communist role in the Warsaw Ghetto Uprising. Halperin suggested that Mark microfilm as many documents as possible on Polish Jewish history for Yad Vashem and the Israeli historical community, which had no access to Polish materials. From 1956 to 1967, Mark sent millions of microfilmed documents to Israel. I am grateful to Samuel Kassow for telling me about this letter and to Gabriel Finder for calling my attention to Mark's posthumously published work, *Megiles oyshvits*, in which he attempted to rectify his earlier historiography.

80. Dawidowicz, "The Epic of the Warsaw Ghetto," and Dawidowicz, "[Book Review] A Doomed Struggle." Her review of Reuben Ainsztein's book specifically targeted his dependence upon Mark's writing, uncritical use of Soviet sources, and debt to Raul Hilberg's views on historical Jewish passivity, which resulted in "old-fashioned Jewish apologetics." Ainsztein responded with a letter to the editor, claiming that Dawidowicz's review was a smear of Jewish historians writing "under the most difficult circumstances" who "did their beset to record the history of Jewish martyrdom and heroism in Eastern Europe." Reuben Ainsztein, "To the Editor," *Times Literary Supplement*, July 18, 1975, 4. See, too, letters from July 15 and August 1, 1975. Eric Sundquist noted that Ainsztein had enlarged a gunfight between prisoners and the SS—which was put down— to "an attempt at armed revolt inside of the cremetoria." Cited in Sundquist, "The Historian's Anvil, the Novelist's Crucible," 262.

81. Finder, "The Warsaw Ghetto Uprising in the Courtroom." I am grateful to Dr. Finder for sharing this unpublished paper with me.

82. Zuckerman was able to make his way to Palestine after the war and became a founder of the Ghetto Fighters Kibbutz (*Kibuz Loḥamei Hageta'ot*). Zuckerman, *A Surplus of Memory*, became an important chronicler of the resistance during the Holocaust. See, too, Itamar Levin, "'It's difficult to understand what he himself saw': Notes on Yitzhak Antek Zuckerman's Description of the Warsaw Ghetto Uprising," *Moreshet* 10 (2013): 81–103, and Havi Dreifuss's response, "Zuckerman: A Witness and Resource, A Leader and A Man," *Moreshet* 10 (2013): 104–27.

83. Libe S. Davidovitsh to Yitskhok Tsukerman, September 29, 1972, "Special" section, Archive of the Ghetto Fighters' House in memory of Yitzhak Katznelson, folder 803. See, too, Polonsky, "Heroes, Hucksters, and Storytellers."

84. Yitskhok Tsuckerman to Libe S. Davidovitsh, December 31, 1972, "Special" section, Archive of the Ghetto Fighters' House in memory of Yitzhak Katznelson, file 803. Led by Pinkus Kartin (Andrzej Schmidt) and Joseph Lewartowski, the Anti-Fascist Bloc, founded by Communists, was the first to organize efforts to resist the Nazis in German-occupied Poland. Dreifuss, "The Leadership of the Jewish Combat Organization," 26.

85. Dawidowicz, *A Holocaust Reader*, 333n3, 362n21. Libe S. Davidovitsh to Yitskhok Tsukerman, "Special" section, Archive of the Ghetto Fighters' House in memory of Yitzhak Katznelson, file 803, and in Dawidowicz private papers.

86. Hirszowicz, "A Conference on Polish-Jewish Relations," 67–68.

87. Polonsky, "Oxford Conference on Polish Jewish Relations." Three more international conferences would be held in the 1980s. Blejwas, "The National Polish American-Jewish American Council," 263.

88. Polonsky, "Oxford Conference on Polish Jewish Relations," 54. Gutman had been an activist in the Warsaw Ghetto Uprising and became one of the most important survivor historians of Polish Jewry. His output was prodigious. See, among many other works, Gutman, *The Jews of Warsaw, 1939–1943*, and Gutman and Krakowski, *Unequal Victims*.

89. The interview first appeared in the Wrocław-based monthly *Odra* (1976). The text "exploded like an SOS flare" on the public landscape of postwar Poland. Ash, "Introduction," x. On Krall, see https://jwa.org/encyclopedia/article/krall-hanna. Edelman had written about his own experiences shortly after the uprising. Edelman, *Getto Walczy*, translated as *The Ghetto Fights*.

90. Natalia Aleksiun, "'What Matters Most Is Life Itself.'" See, too, a view of Edelman as the icon of the Warsaw Ghetto Uprising in Shore, "The Jewish Hero History Forgot."

91. Epigraph to Krall, *Shielding the Flame*, 37.

92. Ash, "Introduction," xi.

93. Liebman, *Claude Lanzmann's Shoah*. Recently, other films, some coming from non-Jewish Polish directors, such as *Ida* (2013), *Scandal in Ivansk* (2016), and *Aftermath* (2017), have also proven controversial.

94. Biskupski, "Poland and the Poles." The film set off a torrent of protests among American Poles once reviews from its first screening in France appeared. Blejwas, "The National Polish American-Jewish American Council," 264–67.

95. She considered the film "self-indulgent," suggesting that Lanzmann believed that he had "invented the Shoah," which she communicated to Cynthia Ozick. Cynthia Ozick to Lucy S. Dawidowicz, August 27, 1985, Dawidowicz private papers.

96. Lucy S. Dawidowicz to Edward Alexander, July 4, 1986, Dawidowicz Papers, box 79, folder 4b.

97. Antony Polonsky posed the question this way: "How powerful was antisemitism in interwar Poland and to what degree did the Soviet occupation inflame it?" Polonsky, "Poles, Jews, and the Problems of Divided Memory," 136.

98. Brumberg, "[Book Review] *The Last Jews of Poland* and *Shielding the Flame*"; Davies, "The Survivor's Voice"; Brumberg and Davies, "Poles and Jews." See, too, Wandycz, Switalski, and Brumberg, "Poland and the Jews."

99. On the nineteenth-century insurrections, see Brock, "Polish Nationalism," and Walicki, *The Enlightenment and the Birth of Modern Nationhood*.

100. Brumberg, "[Book Review] *The Last Jews of Poland* and *Shielding the Flame*." The 1985 interview with Edelman was translated and published in English as "You Have to Be on the Side of the Weak: A Conversation with Marek Edelman."

101. Norman Davies, "The Deep Stains of Dictatorship," *New York Review of Books*, May 9, 2013.
102. Davies, "The Survivor's Voice."
103. Ibid.
104. Brumberg and Davies, "Poles and Jews."
105. Ibid.
106. Ibid.
107. Dawidowicz, "The Curious Case of Marek Edelman." It was reprinted as "Poles, Jews, and History" in Dawidowicz, *What Is the Use of Jewish History?* 134–44. See, too, Dawidowicz Papers, box 44, folders 1–5. In folder 3, Dawidowicz's notes on two of Davies's book included this list: (a) equivalence of Polish anti-Semitism and Jewish anti-Polonism; (b) Snide attacks on Jews; (c) Denial of anti-Semitism; (d) Stupid mistakes and caricatures, and (e) Jew-Communist stereotype.
108. Davies had been a visiting professor at Stanford in the 1985–86 academic year and believed himself to be the front-runner for a tenured position in the History Department. He was not offered the position and filed a suit on April 30, 1986, against the university for three million dollars and a subsequent suit in March 1987 for nine million dollars. Stanford won in March 1988. See the *Stanford Daily*, January 1986–April 1988, January 8, 1990, and January 13, 2005; and the *New York Times*, March 13, 1987. See, too, Wiener, "When Historians Judge Their Own." Peter Stansky, who had been chair of Stanford's History Department when Davies was a visiting professor but had moved on to the dean's office during the departmental vote, recalled that Dawidowicz had nothing to do with the Davies case. Interview with Peter Stansky, April 21, 2017. The faculty files are restricted for seventy-five years and could not be consulted. It is not unreasonable to imagine that friends of Dawidowicz in the Stanford History Department may have been influenced by her views on prewar and wartime Polish antisemitism when they evaluated those periods in Davies, *God's Playground*.
109. Norman Davies to Brenda Brown, March 23, 1987, Dawidowicz Papers, box 44, folder 5.
110. Letters to *Commentary* challenging Dawidowicz's perspective came from Leonard Shatzkin, Norman Davies, Maciej Kozlowski, Charles Chotkowski, Steven H. Kon, Christopher DeRosa, Henry D. Fetter, Gaston L. Schmir, Henry Regensteiner, and Irène Lasota. "Letters from Readers," *Commentary*, August 1987, 2–12. Brenda Brown, *Commentary's* associate editor, wrote to Dawidowicz that the volume of letters did not augur "well for Polish Jewish relations." Brenda Brown to Lucy S. Dawidowicz, April 10, 1987, Dawidowicz Papers, box 44, folder 5.
111. Davies, *God's Playground*, 264, and Dawidowicz, "Letters from Readers," *Commentary*, August 1987, 11.
112. Dawidowicz, "Letters from Readers," *Commentary*, August 1987, 11.
113. Lucy S. Dawidowicz to Edward Alexander, August 30, 1987, Dawidowicz Papers, box 79, folder 4b.
114. Dawidowicz, "Letters from Readers," *Commentary*, August 1987, 12.
115. Gelles, "Lucy Dawidowicz, PW Interviews," 264. Since 1989, unfettered by the communist substratum, Polish-Jewish studies has grown exponentially. But the field

is now subject to other political and historiographic pressures. The accusations and recriminations about Polish culpability in the murder of the Jews on Polish soil during the German occupation from 1939 to 1945 were reopened with the publication of Gross, *Neighbors*; with the imposition of martial law in Poland after the emergence of the Solidarity movement; and more recently, with the opening of *Polin*: Museum of the History of Polish Jews. In 2017–18, the "Holocaust Law"—forbidding the use of the term "Polish concentration camps" in Polish public discourse—promulgated by the Law and Justice Party, stirred the simmering pot of Polish-Jewish relations. See Polonsky, *"My Brother's Keeper?"*; Brumberg, "Murder Most Foul" and the letters that followed the review's publication; Polonsky and Michlic, *The Neighbors Respond*; Bikont, *The Crime and the Silence*; Grudzińska-Gross and Nawrocki, *Poland and Polin*; and Applebaum, "The Stupidity and Unenforceability of Poland's Speech Law."

13. RAPPROCHEMENT WITH REPUBLICANISM

1. Arthur J. Goldberg to Lucy S. Dawidowicz, September 8, 1981, Dawidowicz Papers, box 68, folder 6.

2. Lithuanian-born Hillel Kook immigrated to Palestine in 1924, where he attended both religious and secular schools. In 1931, Kook helped found the Irgun, a militant offshoot of the Haganah. Traveling in Poland in the interwar years, he met Ze'ev Jabotinsky, the founder of Revisionist Zionism, and, at the movement's behest, became its representative in the United States, where he adopted the alias "Peter Bergson."

3. Lucy S. Dawidowicz to Seymour Finger, November 15, 1981, Dawidowicz Papers, box 68, folder 6. She later told Robert King that after her articles were published "Goldberg is no longer talking to me." Robert King, unpublished eulogy for Lucy S. Dawidowicz. I am grateful to Dr. King for sharing this piece with me. Yehuda Bauer, author of several pioneering books on the topic of rescue, also declined the invitation to serve on the commission. Bauer, *My Brother's Keeper*, and Bauer, *American Jewry and the Holocaust*.

4. Dawidowicz, "American Jews and the Holocaust"; Dawidowicz, "Indicting American Jews"; and "Could the United States have Rescued the European Jews from Hitler?," reprinted as "Could America Have Rescued Europe's Jews?"

5. Wieseltier expressed "delight" when Dawidowicz agreed to review Wyman's book in 1984. However, after reading her first draft, he criticized its "tone," a comment that offended her. They continued to discuss the article, but when Dawidowicz refused to submit a "heavily re-edited piece," Wieseltier killed the review. Martin Peretz, the *New Republic*'s publisher, supported Wieseltier's rejection. Leon Wieseltier to Lucy S. Dawidowicz, November 4, 1984; Dawidowicz's notes on Wieseltier's edits, April 25, 1985; notes from a phone meeting on April 29, 1985; Dawidowicz to Wieseltier, June 20, 1985; and Martin Peretz to Lucy S. Dawidowicz, July 16, 1985, Dawidowicz Papers, box 48, folder 1. One of the many sticking points of Dawidowicz's interpretation was her view of the futility of the Allied bombing of Auschwitz to save Jewish lives. Wieseltier, a child of Holocaust survivors, explained to Dawidowicz that his mother had said that the Jews longed for air raids as proof that the Allies were fighting on

their behalf. On the efficacy of bombing Auschwitz, see Neufeld and Berenbaum, *The Bombing of Auschwitz*, 5; they, in summarizing all of the literature, concluded that the window "for Allied forces to have done anything to prevent the murder of more Jews was small and came very late in the game, six months in the summer and fall of 1944." By then, five million Jews had already been murdered. They also concluded that "Auschwitz II-Birkenau could definitely have been bombed by the same U.S. heavy bomber forces that were bombing I. G. Farben-Monwitz," but refrained from a definitive statement that it would have saved Jewish lives. Neufeld and Berenbaum, *The Bombing of Auschwitz*, 10.

6. Dawidowicz, "American Jews and the Holocaust," 48.

7. Baumel, *The "Bergson Boys."* Bergson's Committee for the Jewish Army sponsored the pageant "We Will Never Die" to publicize the murder of European Jewry. Written by Revisionist Zionist playwright Ben Hecht, it was first staged on March 9, 1943, at Madison Square Garden and sold a record forty thousand tickets for its two performances. The pageant was not supported by the mainstream Jewish communal organizations. Ibid., 114.

8. Syrkin, "What American Jews Did During the Holocaust."

9. Marie Syrkin to Lucy S. Dawidowicz, January 27, 1981, Dawidowicz Papers, box 67, folder 14. See, too, Marie Syrkin to Lucy S. Dawidowicz, April 23, 1982, Dawidowicz Papers, box 68, folder 12, and Marie Syrkin to Lucy S. Dawidowicz, June 15, 1982, Dawidowicz Papers, box 68, folder 1.

10. Dawidowicz, "[Book Review] Ben Hecht's 'Perfidy,' " 262. In 1946, Kastner was tried by the one of the Zionist Congress's first honor courts that could not reach a judgment. In 1957, he was assassinated on the streets of Tel Aviv. See Bilsky, "Judging Evil in the Trial of Kastner," and Jockusch and Finder, *Jewish Honor Courts*, for the view of other contemporaries who viewed members of the *Judenräte* as collaborators, 52n17.

11. Dawidowicz, "[Book Review] Ben Hecht's 'Perfidy,' " 263.

12. Dawidowicz, "American Jews and the Holocaust," 102.

13. Dawidowicz, "Could the United States Have Rescued the European Jews from Hitler?"

14. Dawidowicz, "American Jews and the Holocaust," 114, and Erbelding, *Rescue Board*.

15. Dawidowicz, "American Jews and the Holocaust," 109.

16. Howe used much of his letter to defend Leon Trotsky's acknowledgment of Jewish suffering in the late 1930s and to publicize the reportage in the socialist weekly *Labor Action*. Years later, however, he accused himself of neglect, if not indifference, to the plight of European Jewry. He told Marie Syrkin, "Memory points a finger: 'You were slow, you were dull in responding to the Holocaust.' I plead guilty." Cited in Kessner, *Marie Syrkin*, 408.

17. "Letters from Readers," "American Jews and the Holocaust," *Commentary*, September 1983, 4–24. The Yiddish press was equally vociferous in its condemnation of Dawidowicz's defense of American Jewish leadership. S. L. Shnayderman, a Polish-Jewish journalist, wrote an eight-article series in the *Forverts* in May and June 1982, expressing bitterness at Dawidowicz's kid-glove treatment of Roosevelt, the American Jewish establishment, and American Jews themselves.

18. Lucy S. Dawidowicz, "Response to Letters," *Commentary*, September 1983, 24–28.

19. Lipstadt, "The Failure to Rescue," and Lipstadt, *Playing the Blame Game*, 26. When assessing the interpretations of American Jewish behavior during the Holocaust, Gulie Arad concluded that "the historiography of the Holocaust is permeated with moralism." Arad, "Rereading an Unsettling Past," 189. In 1985, Edward S. Shapiro affirmed Dawidowicz's critique of Wyman's book, writing that it "furnished an opportunity for radicals . . . to flay the United States for its bigotry and indifference to suffering." Shapiro, "[Book Review] *The Abandonment of the Jews*," 325, and Shapiro, "Historians and the Holocaust," 6.

20. Lipstadt, *Playing the Blame Game*, 29–30. Michael Berenbaum affirmed the usefulness of the "myth" as a goad for his generation's activism. Interview with Michael Berenbaum, August 3, 2017.

21. Lipstadt, *Playing the Blame Game*, 27.

22. Breitman and Lichtman, *FDR and the Jews*. Anita Shapira wrote to Dawidowicz after reading her critique of Wyman: "I understand the points [you] made. What I don't understand is your display of passion. Moralizing in History is not the worst possible crime. Whitewashing is worse, to my taste. He may have wished to expect too much from a government that did not have any binding commitment. His historical reasoning may be faulty, but why did you use a mortar instead of a shooting-gun, or, better still, a knife? Love you, as always, Anita." Anita Shapira to Lucy S. Dawidowicz, December 27, 1985, Dawidowicz private papers.

23. Farrell, "The New Face of Israel."

24. Over the years, the PLO—with the Popular Front for the Liberation of Palestine and other groups—had made Lebanon its military redoubt and base for raids on Israeli civilian targets, winning the sympathies of some Palestinian refugees while exacerbating tensions with Lebanese Maronite Christians.

25. Markham, "The War That Won't Go Away," 48.

26. "Israel Says Use of Cluster Bomb in Lebanon Was Result of Mistake," 6.

27. Bar-On, *In Pursuit of Peace*. It was in this context that Dawidowicz had signed the *New York Times* ad in 1978 criticizing the "continuing expansion of settlements" and Israel's "apparent insistence" on "indefinite occupation of the entire West Bank." Charlton, "37 Jews in U.S. Applaud Israelis."

28. The incursion's immediate trigger was the assassination attempt against Shlomo Argov, an Israeli diplomat, on June 3, 1982, in London.

29. Scores of books examining the change in the perception of Israel's use or misuse of power emerged after the war, including Oz, *In the Land of Israel*; Ezrahi, *Rubber Bullets*; and Biale, *Power and Powerlessness in Jewish History*.

30. Allen Hoffman to Lucy S. Dawidowicz, June 7, 1982, Dawidowicz private papers.

31. The war took Israel's highest-ranking officer, Major General Yekutiel Adam, in its earliest days, and 130 soldiers in total. Mandel, "Israel in 1982," 10.

32. Arthur Goren to Lucy S. Dawidowicz, June 14, 1982, Dawidowicz private papers. See, too, Arthur A. Cohen's remarks to Dawidowicz, written from Israel during the war, expressing revulsion at the term *tahor haneshek* (purity of arms), a term used by the IDF to distinguish its army's "morality" from others. Arthur A. Cohen to Lucy S. Dawidowicz, July 7, 1982, Dawidowicz private papers.

33. Schiff and Ya'ari, *Israel's Lebanon War*, 151–80.

34. See, for example, "American Friends of 'Peace Now': A Call to Peace," *New York Times*, July 4, 1982; "The People of Lebanon: Innocent Victims of a Senseless War," *New York Times*, July 11, 1982; "Must Beirut Be Destroyed?" *New York Times*, July 25, 1982; "Freedom for Lebanon or Chaos?" *New York Times*, August 2, 1982; "The AFL-CIO Is Not Neutral: We Support Israel," *New York Times*, August 15, 1982.

35. Schiff and Ya'ari concluded that there was no reliable figure for the dead; the Kahan Commission accepted the Israeli intelligence estimate of between seven hundred and eight hundred souls. Rashid Khalidi gives the number of thirteen hundred. Schiff and Ya'ari, *Israel's Lebanon War*, 282.

36. Mandel, "Israel in 1982"; Gruen, "The United States and Israel"; and Rosenfield, "U.S. Public Opinion Polls and the Lebanon War." Recent historiography on the war has emphasized the role of Alexander Haig, Reagan's secretary of state, for giving the Phalangists a "thumbs up" to rid Beirut of Palestinians, with Israeli cooperation. Khalidi, *Under Siege*, and Khalidi, "The United States Was Responsible." https://www.thenation.com/article/the-united-states-was-responsible-for-the-1982-massacre-of-palestinians-in-beirut/

37. Rabinovich, *The War for Lebanon*, 139.

38. *New York Times*, July 24, 1982, B5. In 1983, *Response: A Contemporary Jewish Review*, founded by "New Jews" of the late 1960s, devoted an entire issue to the war in Lebanon. They, and other American peace activists, justified their criticism by pointing to Israeli domestic outcry against the Begin government. "The Fifth War: Israel in Lebanon."

39. Schiff and Ya'ari, *Israel's Lebanon War*, 280.

40. Podhoretz, "J'Accuse." See, too Gruen, "The United States and Israel," 85.

41. Podhoretz, "J'Accuse," 25.

42. Ibid., 28. Ruth Wisse, ten years later, echoed a similar refrain. Wisse, *If I Am Not For Myself . . .*, 79.

43. Lucy S. Dawidowicz to Norman Podhoretz, August 26, 1982. He matched her affection with his reply on August 30, 1982, Dawidowicz Papers, box 78, folder 3. On August 1, 1981, Dawidowicz signed the display ad, "Freedom for Lebanon or Chaos?" in the *New York Times*, which censured continued PLO activity in Lebanon.

44. Mandel, "Israel in 1982," 22.

45. Cited in Schiff and Ya'ari, *Israel's Lebanon War*, 284.

46. Dawidowicz's archives reveal her self-awareness of her toughness. See, for example, a letter from the 1940s in which she wrote that she and another colleague had "reached an agreement not to discuss politics, since we both get excited in our violent disagreements." Letter home, addressee unknown, November 19, 1946. See, too, her mention of "stiff [verbal] fights" in a letter dated April 20, 1947, Dawidowicz Papers, box 55, folder 3. Anita Shapira, a loyal freind, remarked to Dawidowicz after reading an interview with her that she "especially [enjoyed] the paragraph where you talked about still having very strong emotions about various things and easily flaring up: this is really our Lucy, whom we love." Anita Shapira to Lucy S. Dawidowicz, May 29, 1989, Dawidowicz private papers.

47. Leon Wieseltier to Lucy S. Dawidowicz, October 14, 1983, Dawidowicz private papers.

In this letter, which dealt with the *New Republic*'s rejection of her review of David Wyman's book, Wieseltier reminded Dawidowicz of her signing the 1978 *Times*'s ad supporting Peace Now's opposition to continued settlement building. She penciled "not answered" in red on the letter.

48. Lore G. Segal to Lucy S. Dawidowicz, January 1984, unsent, New York Public Library, Lore G. Segal Papers, box 6, folder 6. Segal later defended Dawidowicz against the writer Anne Roiphe's ad hominem attack in *Tikkun* magazine that claimed that Dawidowicz held that American Jews should not support Desmond Tutu's efforts to end apartheid because of his criticism of Israel during the Lebanon War. Roiphe, "The Politics of Anger," 20, and Lore G. Segal to Anne Roiphe, May 2, 1988, box 6, folder 6, and May 25, 1988, box 7.5, Lore G. Segal Papers.

49. Irving Howe to Lucy S. Dawidowicz, December 31, 1921, Dawidowicz Papers, box 76, folder 7.

50. Lucy S. Dawidowicz to Irving Howe, January 6, 1983, Dawidowicz Papers, box 76, folder 7.

51. Marie Syrkin to Lucy S. Dawidowicz, July 15, 1982, Dawidowicz private papers. See, too, Marie Syrkin to Lucy S. Dawidowicz, October 17, 1982, Dawidowicz private papers.

52. See the program for the memorial service for Marie Syrkin, held on May 16, 1989, at the New York Historical Society, Dawidowicz Papers, box 64, folder 7.

53. Kazin, "Saving My Soul at the Plaza."

54. Jumonville, *Critical Crossings*, 230.

55. Kazin, "Saving My Soul at the Plaza," 40.

56. Alfred Kazin to Tom Wallace, January 2, 1975, a copy of which he forwarded to Dawidowicz, Dawidowicz Papers, box 63, folder 5. See, too, Lucy S. Dawidowicz to Alfred Kazin, June 5, 1974, Manuscript box (Kazin), A.L.S., T.L.S., card to Alfred Kazin, folder 1, Alfred Kazin Papers, Henry W. and Albert A. Berg Collection of English and American Literature, New York Public Library, Astor Lenox and Tilden Foundations.

57. Lucy S. Dawidowicz to Alfred Kazin, January 22, 1978, Manuscript box (Kazin), A.L.S., T.L.S., card to Alfred Kazin. Folder 1, Lucy S. Dawidowicz to Alfred Kazin, February 12, 1977, April 3, 1978, and June 18, 1978. A.L.S., T.L.S., card to Alfred Kazin. Folder 2, Alfred Kazin Papers, Henry W. and Albert A. Berg Collection of English and American Literature, New York Public Library, Astor Lenox and Tilden Foundations.

58. Emphasis in the original. Alfred Kazin to Lucy S. Dawidowicz, January 11, 1977, Dawidowicz private papers.

59. Judith Dunford to Lucy S. Dawidowicz, January 14, 1985, Dawidowicz private papers.

60. Lucy S. Dawidowicz to Judith Dunford, January 17, 1985, Dawidowicz private papers. An interview with Dunford in October 2017 confirmed Dawidowicz's slammed-shut door.

61. Kazin, "They Made It!" 615.

62. Dawidowicz's reputation, coupled with her dissociation from the dovish New York Jewish intellectual community, led to Aaron Asher's request for a blurb for Peters, *From Time Immemorial*. The book defended a Zionism that refused to acknowledge the existence or national claims of the Palestinians. Dawidowicz originally demurred,

because she had no standing in the field, but Asher prevailed, telling her that both Saul Bellow and Elie Wiesel had agreed to write and that "her eminent name *would* help." Emphasis in the original. Aaron Asher to Lucy S. Dawidowicz, January 13, 1984, January 20, 1984, and February 17, 1984, and her replies on January 19 and February 5, 1984, Dawidowicz Papers, box 78, folder 7.

63. Dawidowicz lecture notes for a talk at Cornell University, November 1, 1989, "An Inventory of Anti-Semitism in the World Today," Dawidowicz Papers, box 71, folder 1.

64. "The State of World Jewry Address, 1984."

65. Gershon Cohen, "Introduction to Lucy Dawidowicz, The State of World Jewry Address."

66. Audio tape of lecture, "The State of World Jewry Address, 1984," given at New York's 92nd St. YW-YMHA, 92nd Street Y Archives. For the numbers in the hall, see Lavey Derby to Lucy S. Dawidowicz, December 10, 1984, Dawidowicz private papers.

67. Dawidowicz, "The State of World Jewry Address, 1984." Dawidowicz's talk was subsequently published as Dawidowicz, "Politics, the Jews, and the '84 Election," and Dawidowicz, "The Politics of American Jews," with some slight editorial changes. Dawidowicz's worldview remained marked by her Cold War sensibilities until her death. When *Commentary* published Muller, "Communism, Anti-Semitism and the Jews," she took Neal Kozodoy to task for publicizing the role of Communist Party officials of Jewish origin in the Soviet satellites, fearing that the article could be used by antisemites still enthralled with the myth of Żydokomuna. Interview with Jerry Muller, February 28, 2009. Muller noted that "She was right—the piece is cited by several antisemitic websites in a number of languages. I think that her apologetic criterion, while understandable at one time, is now behind us." In 2009, Muller could not have anticipated the persistence of this myth in contemporary Eastern Europe.

68. Dawidowicz, "The State of World Jewry Address, 1984," 9.

69. Sarna, "The Cult of Synthesis in American Jewish Culture."

70. Dawidowicz, "The State of World Jewry Address, 1984," 17. See, too, Lucy S. Dawidowicz to Alexander Schindler, November 25, 1980, in the Papers of Morris Abram, Collection 514, box 55, folder 9, Rose Library, Emory University.

71. Dawidowicz, "The State of World Jewry Address, 1984," 15. See, too, Carenen, *The Fervent Embrace*, 189–201. Despite her sanguinity about the decline of antisemitism from the Right, Dawidowicz was aware of the resurgence of neo-Nazism and Holocaust denial among sectors of the US population. When, in 1980, the Organization of American Historians (OAH) allowed a Holocaust-denial organization, the Institute for Historical Review, to use its membership list, Dawidowicz wrote a strong letter in condemnation of the OAH's decision to discuss, but not to repudiate, the institute's work. See her letter in the *OAH Newsletter*, "Journal of Historical Review," July 1980, 14–15; Dawidowicz, "Lies About the Holocaust"; and Lipstadt, *Denying the Holocaust*, 203. The OAH's equivocation affirmed her jaundiced view of the "liberal" academy's toleration of antisemitism, even if the denial of the Holocaust came from the Right.

72. Dawidowicz, "The State of World Jewry Address, 1984," 14.

73. Ibid., 25.

74. Ibid., 5–6.

75. Ibid., 28.

76. 92nd Street Y Archives, "The State of World Jewry" folder.

77. Dawidowicz, "Politics, the Jews, and the '84 Election."

78. Don Avery, "Letter to the Editor," *Commentary*, May 1985, 16.

79. Dawidowicz's private papers attest to concern among American Jews about Jackson's rhetorical antisemitism. See David Evanier to Lucy S. Dawidowicz, February 16, 1984, Dawidowicz private papers. In May 1984, Dawidowicz wrote to Marshall Breger, special assistant to the president for public liaison, commenting that "Jesse Jackson's ability to housebreak anti-Semitism without arousing outrage from the Democratic party cohorts gives me the shivers. He's introduced a new and alien element in American politics with his Third World views (including anti-Semitism) and I'm astonished—still naive enough for that—to find that only (or so it seems to me) us neoconservatives are agitated about it." Lucy S. Dawidowicz to Marshall Breger, May 30, 1984, Dawidowicz Papers, box 78, folder 7. See, too, Dawidowicz, "Coddling the Clan."

80. Marie Syrkin, "Letters to the Editor," *Commentary*, May 1985, 10.

81. Dawidowicz, "Response to Letters," 17–18, 20.

82. Ibid., 20.

83. Ibid.

84. Lester, "Historian of the Jews," 40.

85. Hartman, "Introduction," 1–12, and Lipstadt, "The Bitburg Controversy."

86. Bernard Weinraub, "Wiesel Confronts Reagan on Trip; President to Visit Bergen-Belsen; Survivor of Holocaust Urges Him Not to Stop at Nazi Cemetery," *New York Times*, April 20, 1985, and Miller, *One by One, by One*, 229. In April, the American Jewish Congress held an "alternative" wreath-laying ceremony at the Munich graves of two anti-Nazi German student activists. Even staunch defenders of Reagan, such as Jeane Kirkpatrick and Robert Dole, criticized the president's decision. Lipstadt, "The Bitburg Controversy."

87. Decter, "Bitburg: Who Forgot What." See, too, Balint, *Running Commentary*, 212.

88. Dawidowicz, "Germany's Answer to Bitburg." Sidney Hook considered Reagan's decision a "blunder," not a sin, and agreed that Reagan should have gone to Spandau. See Sidney Hook to Walter A. Sheldon, May 28, 1985, a copy of which he sent to Dawidowicz. Dawidowicz private papers. See, too, Lucy S. Dawidowicz to Sidney Hook, June 23, 1985, Sidney Hook Papers, box 10, folder 10, Hoover Institution Archives.

89. Lucy S. Dawidowicz, "The Changing Faces of Anti-Semitism," talk given on January 21, 1985, at the Cleveland Foundation, City Club, 4, Typescript in Dawidowicz Papers, box 71, folder 1. The talk was published as Dawidowicz, "In Berlin Again," and reprinted in Dawidowicz, *What Is the Use of Jewish History?* 38–62.

90. En route to Paris in 1967, she had earlier written that "After a very restless night, I rose early. I keep thinking of returning to a Europe that no longer exists, as if by merely wishing it, I could set time back to the good old days of Nazi Germany before the Kristallnacht, when the course could have been foreseen—for war and persecution, but never with the irrevocableness of the Final Solution." Dawidowicz travel diary, July 30, 1967, Dawidowicz private papers.

91. Dawidowicz travel diary, October 26, 1985, Dawidowicz private papers.

92. Ibid, October 27, 1985.

93. Dawidowicz, "Germany's Answer to Bitburg."

94. Dawidowicz, "In Berlin Again," 33.

95. Dawidowicz, "Germany's Answer to Bitburg."

96. Dawidowicz, *From That Place and Time.* See, too, Sinkoff, "*Yidishkayt* and the Making of Lucy S. Dawidowicz."

97. Dawidowicz, *From That Place and Time,* xiv, and Dawidowicz, "History as Autobiography."

98. Dawidowicz was acutely aware of the unreliability of memory, writing that "Subjectivity looms large in the process of transforming the original experience into a memory trace. Our emotions, intentions, and motivations determine the degree of consciousness and attentiveness that we give to any event, experienced or observed, and shape the remembrance of that event. The varying levels of consciousness which different people apply to the same phenomena may well account for the disparate accounts by eyewitnesses of the same events." See her research files on "Memory," Dawidowicz Papers, box 55, folder 6.

99. Dawidowicz, *From That Place and Time,* 289. See, too, Gabriel Weinreich's assessment of his father's compartmentalization of his personal grief and public restraint. Gabriel Weinreich, "Remembering Dr. Max Weinreich," *YIVO bleter: naye serye* 3, ed. David Fishman and Avrum Nowersztern, 1997.

100. Werner Dannhauser to Lucy S. Dawidowicz, February 20, 1990, Dawidowicz Papers, box 71, folder 8; Cynthia Ozick to Lucy S. Dawidowicz, April 8, 1989; Francine Klagsbrun to Lucy S. Dawidowicz, Dawidowicz Papers, all in box 71 folder 8; Norma Rosen to Lucy S. Dawidowicz, May 7, 1989, Dawidowicz Papers, box 71, folder 9.

101. Dawidowicz, "From Past to Past."

102. Reprinted as Dawidowicz, "History as Autobiography," 30.

103. Historians have long recognized that the wall between objective historical research and subjective concerns about the past is hardly impenetrable. Novick, *That Noble Dream,* 22–46. Postmodernism directly challenged historians' belief in "objectivity," setting the profession into a bit of a tailspin after the publication of White, *Metahistory.* See Appleby, Hunt, and Jacob, *Telling the Truth About History,* among many others, who rallied to defend the fundamental distinction between literary and historical narrative and to insist upon the relevance of modern historiography despite the recognition that objectivity was an aspiration, not an immutable truth.

104. Katz, "[Book Review] *The Holocaust and the Historians,*" 211–13. See, too, the correspondence between them from December 1981 until July 1982, Dawidowicz Papers, box 76, folder 7, Dawidowicz private papers, and Katz, "The Accumulation of Thought."

105. Yerushalmi, *Zakhor;* Funkenstein, "Collective Memory and Historical Consciousness"; Rosman, *How Jewish Is Jewish History?;* and Myers, *The Stakes of History.*

106. Langmuir, "Majority History and Post-Biblical Jews," and Langmuir, "Tradition, History, and Prejudice." See, too, Lucy S. Dawidowicz to Alfred Kazin, September 14, 1977, A.L.S., T.L.S., card to Alfred Kazin, folder 1, Alfred Kazin Papers, Henry W.

and Albert A. Berg Collection of English and American Literature, New York Public Library, Astor Lenox and Tilden Foundations.

107. That historian was Jacob Shatzky, who in 1938 wrote an introduction to the reissue of Nathan of Hanover's *Yeven Metsulah*, a Hebrew chronicle of the Cossack rebellion of 1648–49. Shatski, "Historish-kritisher araynfir tsum 'Yeven Metsulah' fun R. Natan Neta Hanover"; Fridman, "Yankev shatskis ort in der mizrekh ayropayisher yidisher geshikhte-shraybung"; and Robert Moses Shapiro, "Jacob Shatzky, Historian of Warsaw Jewry," 207–8.

108. Lucy S. Dawidowicz to Gavin Langmuir, October 16, 1968, Dawidowicz Papers, box 77, folder 11. Langmuir agreed with her about how "immensely difficult" it is to write history "without some interest in the group" and that "it is better to love than to have only a disengaged neutrality about men." Gavin Langmuir to Lucy S. Dawidowicz, December 5, 1968, Dawidowicz private papers.

109. Meyer, *Ideas of Jewish History*.

110. Lucy S. Dawidowicz to Michael A. Meyer, April 26, 1978, Dawidowicz Papers, box 71, folder 6. Dawidowicz judaized Marc Bloch's question in Bloch, *The Historian's Craft*, 3.

111. Arendt and Scholem, "'Eichmann in Jerusalem,'" and Scholem, "Aykhman," later published as "On Eichmann."

112. Michael A. Meyer to Lucy S. Dawidowicz, May 12, 1978, Dawidowicz Papers, box 71, folder 6.

113. Dawidowicz, *What Is the Use of Jewish History?* 19.

114. Ibid. History could be seen as a "binding national force," she wrote in Dawidowicz, "[Book Review] Zakhor," 116. In the mid-1980s, lecturing about antisemitism to an audience in Cleveland, Dawidowicz prefaced her formal remarks with a recognition of the power of the subjective, telling her audience that "For most of us, personal experience is the most persuasive of all teachers" and announcing that she was going to speak "in a confessional mode," since "this way I can personalize and dramatize how, in my own lifetime, anti-Semitism has drastically changed its face." Lucy S. Dawidowicz, "The Changing Faces of Anti-Semitism," Cleveland Foundation, City Club, January 21, 1985, Dawidowicz Papers, box 73, folder 9.

115. Lucy S. Dawidowicz to Ruth Wisse, June 25, 1979, Dawidowicz Papers, box 77, folder 16.

116. Dawidowicz, "[Book Review] Zakhor," 115.

117. Dawidowicz, "[Book Review] Hertzberg's Complaint," 49.

118. Writing to Sidney Hook in 1985, she noted her memoir's working title: "A Personal Account of the End of Ashkenazic Jewry." Lucy S. Dawidowicz to Sidney Hook, June 23, 1985, Hoover Institution on War, Revolution, and Peace, Sidney Hook Papers, box 10, folder 10, Stanford University, Stanford, CA.

119. The Fund for the Translation of Jewish Literature provided subventions for the publication of works by Peretz, Glatshtayn, and An-sky, among others, as well as the translation of Jacob Katz's autobiography, *With My Own Eyes: The Autobiography of an Historian* (Hanover, NH: University Press of New England, 1995) and the translation of Augusto Segre's *Memories of Jewish Life: From Italy to Jerusalem, 1918–1960*, trans. Steve Siporin (Lincoln: University of Nebraska Press, 2008).

120. Lucy S. Dawidowicz to Bernard Rapoport, August 3, 1986, Dawidowicz Papers, box 71, folder 8.
121. In the summer of 1990, she translated eight columns for "Looking Backward," a retrospective section from the Yiddish *Forverts*, Dawidowicz Papers, box 62, folders 4 and 5.
122. In many ways, *From That Place and Time* is a sober *yizker bukh* (memorial book), honoring the conception of secular *yidishkayt* that defined the ethos of much of the modern East European Jewish intelligentsia. On the phenomenon of the *yizker bukh*, the more than five hundred spontaneous, collective compilations commemorating the East European towns with majority Jewish populations destroyed during World War II, see Kugelmass and Boyarin, *From A Ruined Garden*.
123. Howe and Greenberg, *Voices from the Yiddish*, copyright page.
124. Dawidowicz introduced the 1970 poetry reading at Stern College and was, undoubtedly, its prime mover. Mann, "Distinguished Speakers Vivify Yiddish Poetry," and Dawidowicz papers, box 70, folder 7.
125. Lucy S. Dawidowicz to William B. Goodman, November 4, 1974, Dawidowicz Papers, box 77, folder 14.
126. Ibid.
127. In his response, Howe dryly noted Dawidowicz's reliance on the YIVO's transliteration rules, commenting, "what makes YIVO transliteration sacred?" Irving Howe to Lucy S. Dawidowicz, November 13, 1974, Dawidowicz Papers, box 77, folder 14.
128. Irving Howe to Lucy S. Dawidowicz, November 28, 1974, Dawidowicz Papers, box 77, folder 14.
129. Ibid. Howe's definition then appeared in his book. See Howe, *World of Our Fathers*, 16, footnote.
130. Irving Howe to Lucy S. Dawidowicz, November 28, 1974, Dawidowicz Papers, box 77, folder 14.
131. Lucy S. Dawidowicz to Irving Howe, December 6, 1974, Dawidowicz Papers, box 77, folder 14.
132. Ibid.
133. Irving Howe to Lucy S. Dawidowicz, November 28, 1974, Dawidowicz Papers, box 77, folder 14.
134. Lucy S. Dawidowicz to Irving Howe, December 6, 1974, Dawidowicz Papers, box 77, folder 14.
135. Dawidowicz, "The Rise and Fall," 42–45. Weinreich's book was originally published as Maks Vaynraykh, *Geshikhte fun der yidisher shprakh: bagrifn, faktn, metodn*. It was published in English translation as Weinreich, *History of the Yiddish Language* (1980), but this edition was incomplete. It has recently been reissued in full. Weinreich, *History of the Yiddish Language* (2008).
136. Dawidowicz, "The Rise and Fall," 44. See, too, Weinreich, "*Yidishkayt* and Yiddish."
137. Lucy S. Dawidowicz to Solomon A. Birnbaum, February 29, 1980, thanking him for sending his book, Solomon Birnbaum, *Yiddish: A Survey and a Grammar*, Birnbaum Archives. They spoke in August 1980, and Birnbaum followed up their phone conversation to affirm his opinion that the best definition of "ייִדישקייט [the Yiddish original is in the letter] is the sum total of the ideas and practice of traditional Judaism (i.e.,

the Jewish religion). The problem of a translation is, of course, insoluble. 'Jewishness' might mean anything. Occasionally, where it is not of importance, one might use the unsatisfactory 'Judaism.' " Solomon A. Birnbaum to Lucy S. Dawidowicz, August 17, 1980. See, too, his postcard penned on September 7, 1980, and her (undated) response, informing him that she had used his definition in a recent article. Birnbaum Archives.

138. Dawidowicz, "The Rise and Fall," 44.

139. Ibid., 45. Two decades earlier, in her review of the first volume of the *Great Dictionary of the Yiddish Language*, Dawidowicz had already noted that Yiddish retained its currency more effectively in religious than in secular Jewish schools, commenting that "the reason may be—though I am surely simplifying—that among the Hasidim Yiddish still fulfills a real function in the transplanted but living culture. For they believe a Jew must speak Yiddish; otherwise he speaks 'goyish,' that is, any non-Jewish language. They have no need to ideologize Yiddish, for it is part of an organic whole, where the whole person and the whole Jew are identical. But this is scarcely true of most secularists, among whom Yiddish has shrunk from an ideology into a cult or, even worse, a sentimentality." Dawidowicz, "Yiddish," 380. Yofe and Mark, *Groyser verterbukh fun der yidisher shprakh.*

140. Jeffrey Shandler has argued that while Yiddish decisively lost its vernacularity after the Holocaust, it retained its symbolic power. Entering a "postvernacular phase" in postwar America, it became a site for modern Jewish cultural creativity, much of which was emphatically transgressive and unapologetically secular. Shandler, *Adventures in Yiddishland.*

141. Joseph Mlotek, "Letter to the Editor," *Commentary*, February 1981, 6, 10; Kenneth Libo, "Letter to the Editor," where he accused Dawidowicz of "linguistic matricide," *Commentary*, February 1981, 10, 14, and copies in Dawidowicz Papers, box 63, folder 10.

142. Dawidowicz's response to "Letters to the Editor," *Commentary*, February 1981, 14.

143. Edel, "The Making of an Historian."

144. *Zakhor* (Heb. "Remember!").

145. Cynthia Ozick to Lucy S. Dawidowicz, April 8, 1989, Dawidowicz Papers, box 71, folder 8.

EPILOGUE

1. Lucy Schildkret to Evelyn Konoff, November 9, undated year, but likely 1935, Dawidowicz private papers.

2. Dawidowicz travel diary, July 30, 1967, Dawidowicz private papers.

3. See Lucy S. Dawidowicz to Zarek and Senia Dawidowicz, June 10, 1979, Dawidowicz private papers. Excerpts of the letter are reproduced in the appendix.

4. Interview with Ruth Wisse, March 27, 2008.

5. Interview with Norman Podhoretz, September 21, 2009.

6. Klagsbrun, "Eulogies."

7. Dawidowicz, *What Is the Use of Jewish History?* Kozodoy received many effusive letters from Dawidowicz's friends thanking him for issuing the collection and for capturing her principled and forceful personality in his introduction.

8. Dawidowicz, *The War Against the Jews*, xxi.

9. Already, two years earlier, in his review of *The Holocaust and the Historians*, Geoff Eley criticized Dawidowicz's interpretation as "crass particularism." Asking, "How much weight *is* the war against the Jews to be given—in the discussion of Nazism, in the treatment of the Second World War, and in the presentation of 20th-century European history?" Eley wrote that for Dawidowicz "it deserves a primary and even exclusive claim on our priorities, but few would accept such an absolute and prescriptive judgment." Charging that she had no interest in the suffering of non-Jews, Eley wrote that "surely we can acknowledge the centrality of anti-semitism to Nazi ideology, the Jews' leading place in the intended hierarchy of victims, and the irrevocable destruction of East European Ashkenazy [*sic*] culture, without abandoning the effort to see the anti-Jewish programme as an integral part of a larger racist design." Eley, "[Book Review] Holocaust History."

10. Dawidowicz, "The Holocaust and the Textbooks."

11. George Mosse to Lucy S. Dawidowicz, April 7, 1975, Dawidowicz Papers, box 63, folder 8. See Mosse, *The Crisis of German Ideology*.

12. Bauer, *Rethinking the Holocaust*, 42, 48.

13. Bergen, *War and Genocide*, x. See, too, 4–7.

14. Dawidowicz, *The War Against the Jews*, 23. For a reexamination of the fraught question of Lutheran anti-Judaism and its relationship to modern German culture, see Kaufmann, *Luther's Jews.*

15. Friedländer, *Nazi Germany and the Jews: The Years of Persecution*, 83.

16. Ibid., 87.

17. Ibid., 95.

18. Dawidowicz, *The War Against the Jews*, 47.

19. Friedländer, *The Years of Extermination*, 133–34.

20. Dawidowicz, *The War Against the Jews*, 15, and Friedländer, *Nazi Germany and the Jews: The Years of Persecution*, 97–98.

21. Friedländer, *The Years of Extermination*, 133. See, too, Bauer, *Rethinking the Holocaust*, 5.

22. Dawidowicz, *The War Against the Jews*, 124.

23. Friedländer, *Nazi Germany and the Jews: The Years of Persecution*, 4. He sought to distance himself from "reductive interpretations with their sole emphasis on the role (and responsibility) of the supreme leader." Ibid., 3.

24. See, too, Bergen, *War and Genocide*, 29–40.

25. Friedländer, *Nazi Germany and the Jews: The Years of Persecution*, 3.

26. Bauer, *Rethinking the Holocaust*, 42–43.

27. Confino, *A World Without Jews*, 4. The emphasis is mine. See, too, Steigmann-Gall, *The Holy Reich*, and Heschel, *The Aryan Jesus*.

28. Dawidowicz, "The Holocaust Was Unique in Intent, Scope, and Effect." For a brief overview of the contrasting positions on uniqueness and universality in interpretations of the Holocaust, see Berenbaum, "The Uniqueness and Universality of the Holocaust."

29. Dawidowicz, *The War Against the Jews*, 27. Reviewing *The Holocaust and the Historians* in the *New York Times*, John Leonard remarked, "Without quite saying so

out loud, Mrs. Dawidowicz suggests that killing Jews mattered more to Hitler than lebensraum, revanchism, delusions of Aryan superiority, anti-liberalism and anti-internationalism, the military-industrial complex, the cult of youth and worship of nature, the whole madness of blood, soil and steel. Of course, the Nazis murdered gypsies, homosexuals, Soviet prisoners of war and the Polish elite, but 'as a means to practical ends,' whereas 'the destruction of Jewish communal existence' was an 'ultimate goal.'" Leonard, "[Book Review] *The Holocaust and the Historians.*"

30. For a critique of this position, see Schorsch, "The Holocaust and Jewish Survival." Ron Rosenbaum noted that Milton Himmelfarb's essay "No Hitler, No Holocaust" argued that the distancing from Hitler's agency among Jews came out of an embarrassment—or fear—of being singled out for such murderous hatred. See both Milton Himmelfarb, "No Hitler, No Holocaust" and Rosenbaum, *Explaining Hitler*, 391–94. Post-Holocaust theologians, too, have grappled with the religious and philosophical question of the Holocaust's "uniqueness." Braiterman, *(God) After Auschwitz*.

31. Eley, "[Book Review] Holocaust History."

32. Bauer, *Rethinking the Holocaust*, 14, 20, 27–28, 39, 50, 53, 56, 73–74, 265–67. Note that Dawidowicz relied on Karl Jaspers, who, remarking upon the unprecedented nature of Nazism, considered the organized slaughter of the Jews as "fundamentally different from all crimes that had existed in the past." Dawidowicz, *The War Against the Jews*, xv. See, too, the discussion of the word "unprecedented" and of the meaning of "intention" in Lang, *Act and Idea*, 8–9, 22–29.

33. He wrote that "absolute uniqueness thus leads to its opposite, total trivialization: if the Holocaust is a onetime, inexplicable occurrence, then it is a waste of time to deal with it." Bauer, *Rethinking the Holocaust*, 14. The position that the Holocaust is a *mysterium tremendum* is Elie Wiesel's. See Berenbaum, *The Vision of the Void*.

34. Bauer, *Rethinking the Holocaust*, 28.

35. Friedländer, *Nazi Germany and the Jews: The Years of Persecution*, xix.

36. Friedländer, "A Conflict of Memories?" 12.

37. Goldenhersh, "Historian Decrys Nazi Annihilation of the Jews."

38. See an analysis of its earliest articulation, Adler and Paterson, "Red Fascism." The *Historikerstreit* revived the analogy between Hitler and Stalin, focusing on the view of the two regimes' respective criminality. Articles in the *Frankfurter Allgemeine Zeitung* interpreted Hitler's 1941 abrogation of the treaty of nonaggression with the Soviet Union as preemptive. This argument, bolstered by the work of Ernest Nolte, Klaus Hildebrand, and Michael Stürmer, made the Soviets into "perpetrators" like the Nazis. Friedländer, "A Conflict of Memories?" 13–15. Likewise, Andreas Hillgruber examined the experience of German soldiers fighting in the East against the Soviets in the latter part of the war, comparing the brutality of the Red Army to the Wehrmacht. Hillgruber, *Zweierlei Untergang*.

39. Snyder, *Bloodlands*. Snyder, *Black Earth*, expands his conception of the murderous intentions of Hitler's regime to include the destruction of the natural world.

40. Bartov, "Review of Timothy Snyder, *Bloodlands.*" See, too, Rosenbaum, "Hitler, Continued."

41. Bartov, "Review of Timothy Snyder, *Bloodlands*," 428.

42. Goldhagen, *Hitler's Willing Executioners*. Dan Michman noted that Goldhagen's argument that German antisemitism was *the* originative factor in the Final Solution was quite close to Dawidowicz's. Interestingly, Goldhagen mentioned *The War Against the Jews* only once in his copious footnotes. Michman, *Holocaust Historiography*, 50, and Goldhagen, *Hitler's Willing Executioners*, 9, 479n33.

43. The *Sonderweg* school of modern German historiography argued that German history has its own social and political mentalities, which distinguished it from the path of modernization of other West European countries and ensured its development toward Nazism in the twentieth century.

44. Goldhagen, *Hitler's Willing Executioners*, 86.

45. Ibid., 128.

46. Bauer, *Rethinking the Holocaust*, 93–94. On the book's reception in Germany, see Diner, "Negative Symbiose," 9.

47. Aschheim, "Archtypes and the German-Jewish Dialogue," 240. See the many references here: https://goldhagen.com/the-goldhagen-debate. The "Goldhagen Affair" of the 1980s clearly echoed the "Arendt Affair" of the 1960s.

48. Aschheim, "Archtypes and the German-Jewish Dialogue," 244–47, and Bauer, *The Death of the Shtetl*, 155. Note Bauer's own mea culpa regarding his earlier attacks on Goldhagen's work. Bauer, *Rethinking the Holocaust*, 111.

49. Even Raul Hilberg, who did not hide his animosity toward Dawidowicz, reassessed certain historiographic issues at the end of his life, including, most notably, the centrality of Hitler's antisemitism as the motor force of the destruction of the Jews, the untenable situation of the *Judenräte*, and the impossibility of significant Jewish resistance to the Nazis, which had dogged him since the publication of *The Destruction of the European Jews*. In Hilberg, *Perpetrators Victims Bystanders*, he expressed views that were, paradoxically, consonant with Dawidowicz's.

50. Dawidowicz, "[Book Review] Ben Hecht's 'Perfidy,'" 262.

51. The emphasis is mine. Dawidowicz, *The Holocaust and the Historians*, 137–38. On the ways in which American Jews understood historical agency during the Holocaust versus the views of postwar German Jewish survivors, see Baader, "The Shoah, the Sacred, and Jewish Victim Identity."

52. Temporal distance encouraged a kind of "sacralization of the victims." See Baader, "The Shoah, the Sacred, and Jewish Victim Identity," 266–69.

53. Dawidowicz, *The War Against the Jews*, xxxx.

54. Ibid.

55. Dawidowicz, "To the Editor," July 15, 1975, *Times Literary Supplement*, 840.

56. See the citations in chapter 12, footnote 43.

57. Shternshis, *When Sonia Met Boris*.

58. At roughly the same time that Dawidowicz reassessed the role of Judaism in Jewish life, many Soviet Jews, coming to the same conclusion, created an underground movement anchored in Jewish spirituality. See Ro'i, *The Struggle for Soviet Jewish Emigration, 1948–1967*, and Gitelman and Ro'i, *Evolution, Repression, and Revival*.

59. In a talk she gave in 1989, Dawidowicz stated that Louis Farrakhan's most uninhibited

antisemitism was "no different from Polish peasants." "An Inventory of Anti-Semitism in the World Today," Dawidowicz Papers, box 71, folder 1.

60. Lucy S. Dawidowicz, October 1958, "Negro-Jewish Tensions," AJC/digital.

61. See Feingold, "*Bildung*: Was It Good for the Jews?" for a personal reflection on the multilayered nature of "German Jewry" and a view of *Bildung* as a concept linked to "urban/urbane cosmopolitan 'high' culture which developed among post-Emancipation Central European Jewry," not as a German-Jewish national product. East European Jews and their descendants also aspired to be *gebildet*. See, too, Mendelsohn, *On Modern Jewish Politics*, 37–38; and Ribak, *Gentile New York*, 75.

62. For an exposition of these conflicts in towns such as Kiryas Joel in Rockland County, New York, see Stolzenberg, "Tale of Two Villages."

APPENDIX

1. https://yivoencyclopedia.org/article.aspx/Schwarzbart_Ignacy.

2. מכס/*mekhes* (customs), סבלנות/*savlones* (patience), and בסדר/*beseyder* (okay) are all Hebrew-component words of Yiddish. Friedberg transliterated סבלנות and בסדר according to Hebrew, not Yiddish, rules.

3. *Amerika* was the State Department's Russian-language journal.

4. Dawidowicz, "Max Weinreich." Dawidowicz corresponded with President Shazar in the fall of 1965 when she was working on *The Golden Tradition*, requesting that she be able to include excerpts from *Shtern fartog: zikhrones-dertseylungen* (Buenos Aires: Tsentral-farband fun poylishe yidn in argentine, 1952), a book that he had written about Jewish self-defense in Stolpce in 1905. See Israel State Archives, Zalman Shazar papers, box 113, folder 55. Shazar granted her permission. Dawidowicz, *The Golden Tradition* (Holt, Rinehart and Winston), 383–88.

5. Dawidowicz, "Can Anti-Semitism Be Measured?"

6. Rabinowitz, "The Radicalized Professor: A Portrait."

7. https://yivoencyclopedia.org/article.aspx/Zuckerman_Yitshak.

8. Libe S. Davidovitsh to Yitskhok Tsukerman, September 29, 1972, "Special" section, Archive of the Ghetto Fighters' House in memory of Yitzhak Katznelson, file 803.

9. Yitskhok Tsukerman to Libe S. Davidovitsh, December 31, 1974, "Special" section, Archive of the Ghetto Fighters' House in memory of Yitzhak Katznelson, file 803. See chapter 8, footnote 64.

10. Tadeusz Bór-Komorowski (1895–1966) was a commander during the Warsaw Uprising of August 1944, in which Poles—including Jewish Poles—attempted to throw off the German occupation without succumbing to Soviet control. It was unsuccessful.

11. Dr. Adolf Berman (1906–78) was a Jewish Communist and member of the Warsaw Ghetto underground, also serving as general secretary to the Council to Aid Jews.

12. Mordechai Tenenbaum (1916–43) was a member of the ŻOB who fell during a short-lived uprising in the Bialystok ghetto.

13. Mordechai Anielewicz (1919–43) was an activist in the Jewish underground and a

leader of the Warsaw Ghetto Uprising. He perished when the bunker under a house on Miła Street was discovered by the Germans.

14. Eliyahu Gutkowski, a member of the Zionist organization *Po'alei Tsiyon*, was an activist in the underground archival group Oyneg shabes, which recorded daily life in the ghetto. He likely perished during the destruction of the ghetto by the Germans.

15. Zivia Lubetkin, with Zuckerman, escaped from the Warsaw Ghetto before the uprising. They later married.

16. Lehmann-Haupt, "A Key to the 'Final Solution.'"

17. Lamentations is traditionally read on the eve of the fast day of T'isha B'av to commemorate the destruction of the ancient temples in Jerusalem. Ketcher here implicitly invokes how *The War Against the Jews* was continuous with *Khurbn forshung*.

18. Howe had given a speech on Jewish identity at the American Jewish Committee earlier that year.

19. In handwriting, she penned, "telephoned 8/26/76."

20. Howe, *World of Our Fathers*.

21. Kazin, *A Walker in the City*.

22. Berenbaum, "The Uniqueness and Universality of the Holocaust," 85.

23. Dawidowicz, "On Being a Woman in Shul" (1968).

24. Though he hoped to title his anthology *The American Jewess*, it was published as Marcus, *The American Jewish Woman: A Documentary History*. Professor Gary Zola, Marcus's executor, commented in an email exchange with me on January 3, 2019, that he recalled Marcus telling him that the publisher would not allow the word in the book's title, "but he was adamantine. He gave in only because he wanted that excellent work published. He went to the grave convinced they were all wrong."

25. https://chomsky.info/19801011/

26. Serge Thion (1942–2017) was a French sociologist who specialized in Cambodia. He worked at the French National Center for Scientific Research but was dismissed from his position due to his Holocaust denial activities.

27. Syrkin wrote in hand, "Excuse my typing."

28. This is the English translation for the Hebrew word *she'arith*, "those who survived"—of biblical origin—but it refers in this context to Holocaust survivors.

29. The "revisionists" referred to here are the Holocaust deniers affiliated with the Institute for Historical Review. See note 71 to chapter 13.

30. Katz, "[Book Review] *The Holocaust and the Historians*."

31. Lipstadt, *Denying the Holcaust*, and Lipstadt, *History on Trial*.

32. Rudolph Binion (1927–2011) taught modern European history at Brandeis University and was the author of *Frau Lou: Nietzsche's Wayward Disciple; Hitler Among the Germans;* and *After Christianity*.

33. Timothy Mason (1940–90) was a Marxist historian of Nazism whose books included *Social Policy in the Third Reich: The Working Class and the "National Community"* (1977) and *Nazism, Fascism and the Working Class* (1995).

34. Arthur Butz, an associate professor of electrical engineering at Northwestern University, is best known for his denial of the Holocaust, which he outlined in *The Hoax of the Twentieth Century*.

35. Paul Rassinier (1906–67) was a major figure in postwar French culture and Holocaust denial. A pacifist and political activist, Rassinier is often viewed as "the father of Holocaust denial."

36. Dawidowicz, "In Berlin Again."

37. On the Freyland Lige (Jewish Territorialists), see https://yivoencyclopedia.org/article.aspx/Frayland-lige.

38. Leyzer Ran (1912–95) bequeathed his collection to Harvard University. See Leyzer Ran, *Yerushalayim de-Lita: ilustrirt un dokumentirt; groyser albom mit bilder un derklerungen in fir shprakhn: Yidish, hebreish, english, un rusish: provizorisher inhalt* (New York: Vilner albom komitet, 1968).

39. See Abramowicz, *Profiles of a Lost World*, 245, 348n1.

40. Shtaynberg, *Gedanken in tsuzamenklang*, ed. Sholem Lurya.

41. Derrel McKinley "Bud" Harrelson (b. 1944) played shortstop for several Major League baseball teams, including the New York Mets. He took part in both of the Mets' World Series championships, in 1969 as a player and in 1986 as a coach.

42. Cleon Joseph Jones (b. 1942) played left field for the New York Mets and is famous for catching the final out in the 1969 World Series championship against the Baltimore Orioles.

43. Tommie Lee Agee (1942–2001) played center field for the New York Mets and was celebrated for making two game-changing catches in game three of the 1969 World Series.

44. Jesse Russell Orosco (b. 1957) was a relief pitcher for the New York Mets and played in their winning 1986 championship.

45. Hannibal, Missouri, is the hometown of Mark Twain.

46. Born in Imperial Russia to an illustrious rabbinic family, Joseph Ber Soloveitchik (1903–93) was one of the most important Orthodox rabbis in the United States, serving as the head of the Rabbi Isaac Elchanan Theological Seminary at Yeshiva University. His paternal grandfather was Rabbi Chaim Soloveitchik (1853–1918), known as Reb Chaim Brisker, the Brisker Rav.

47. The Talmud.

48. Born in Belarus, Avraham Yeshaya Karelitz (1878–1953), a Talmudic giant, was known by the name of his most important work, *Chazon Ish*.

49. Edwin Donald "Duke" Snider (1926–2011) played center field on the Brooklyn and Los Angeles Dodgers for most of his career, but also spent 1963 with the New York Mets.

50. Willie Howard Mays Jr. (b. 1931), nicknamed "The Say Hey Kid," played center field for over twenty-two years with the New York/San Francisco Giants, yet ended his career with the New York Mets.

BIBLIOGRAPHY

PRIMARY SOURCES

Archives

Morris B. Abram Papers, Stuart A. Rose Manuscript, Archives, and Rare Book Library, Emory University, MS 514

American Jewish Committee Archives, New York

American Jewish Committee Archives, YIVO Institute, RG 347.17.10, Gen-10

American Jewish Committee Collection, American Jewish Archives, Cincinnati, MS-780

American Jewish Committee Online Digital Archives, www.ajcarchives.org

Aspirantur Papers, YIVO Archives, RG 1.3

Salo W. Baron Papers, Department of Special Collections and University Archives, Stanford Libraries, M0580

Nathan and Solomon Birnbaum Archives, Toronto, Canada

Georges Borchardt Inc., Author Correspondence files, Columbia Rare Book and Manuscript Library, MS 0135

Lucy S. Dawidowicz Papers, American Jewish Historical Society, New York, P-675

Displaced Persons Papers, YIVO Archives, RG 294.2

John Felstiner, Personal Papers

Philip Friedman Papers, YIVO Archives, RG 1258

Fund for the Translation of Jewish Literature Archives, *Commentary* Papers, American Jewish Committee. Used with permission of Neal Kozodoy.

John Hersey Papers, Yale Collection of American Literature, Beinecke Rare Book and Manuscript Library, Uncat ZA MS 235

Raul Hilberg Papers, Silver Special Collection Library, University of Vermont, RG 074-005

Sidney Hook Papers, Hoover Institution Library & Archives, Stanford University

Hunter College Libraries, Archives & Special Collections, Hunter College of the City University of New York, New York City

Jewish Publication Society Papers, Special Collections Research Center, Temple University Libraries, SCRC 38

Joint Distribution Committee Archives, Jerusalem

Joint Distribution Committee Archives, New York, New York Collection

Joint Distribution Committee Digital Archives, www.jdc.org

Israel Kaplan Papers, Manuscript and Archives Division, Israel National Library, Jerusalem, Arc 4* 1795

Alfred Kazin Papers, Henry W. and Albert A. Berg Collection of English and American Literature, New York Public Library, Astor Lenox and Tilden Foundations

Carole Kessner, Personal Papers

Moshe Kligsberg Papers, YIVO Archives, RG 719

Leibush Lehrer Papers, YIVO Archives, RG 507

Jacob Rader Marcus Papers, American Jewish Archives, Cincinnati, MS 210

James Marshall Papers, American Jewish Archives, Cincinnati, MS 157

George L. Mosse Papers, Leo Baeck Institute, New York, AR 25137/MF 671

New York Public Library, Public Education Sound Recordings, Astor Lenox and Tilden Foundations

92nd Street Y Archives, New York

Mark Nowogrodzki, Personal Papers

David Pearlman and Yael Katz, Personal Papers

Koppel Pinson Papers, YIVO Archives, RG 462

Seymour J. Pomrenze Papers, American Jewish Historical Society, P-933

Gershom G. Scholem Papers, Manuscript and Archives Division, Israel National Library, Jerusalem, ARC 4* 1599 01 559

Leo W. Schwarz Papers, YIVO Archives, RG 294.1

Lore G. Segal Papers, Manuscripts and Archives Division, New York Public Library, Astor Lenox and Tilden Foundations, MssCol 18766

Zalman Shazar Papers, Israel State Archives, 113/55.

Sholem Aleichem Folk Institute, Camp Boiberik Archives, YIVO Archives, RG 659.1

Stern College–Curriculum Committee Papers, Yeshiva University Archives, YU 2007.012

Marie Syrkin Papers, American Jewish Archives, Cincinnati, MS 615

Elias Tcherikower Papers, YIVO Archives, RG 81

Isaiah Trunk Papers, YIVO Archives, RG 483

Max Weinreich Papers, YIVO Archives, RG 584

Yad Vashem Archives, Collection Josef Rosensaft Bergen-Belsen DP Camp Archives, O.70/17

YIVO Administration, YIVO Archives, RG 1.1

YIVO Administrative Records, Series: Files Relating to Restitution of YIVO Property, RG 100

Yitzhak Zuckerman Papers, "Special" section, Archive of the Ghetto Fighters' House in Memory of Yitzhak Katznelson

Interviews and Email Correspondences

Adam Bellow

Michael Berenbaum

Georges Borchardt

Naomi Cohen

Ted Comet
Anne Davidson
David Evanier
Irving Feldman
Nathan Glazer
Judith Goldstein
Arthur (Aryeh) Goren
Larry Grossman
Rose Grundstein
Gertrude Himmelfarb
Allen Hoffman
Paula Hyman
Johanna Kaplan
Barry M. Katz
Carole Kessner
Robert King
Francine Klagsbrun
Arthur Kurzweil
Chava Lapin
Seth Lipsky
Michael A. Meyer
Yehuda Mirsky
Chana Mlotek
Deborah Dash Moore
Jerry Muller
Samuel Norich
Mark Nowogrodzki
Cynthia Ozick
Norman Podhoretz
Dorothy Rabinowitz
Eleanor (Schildkret) Sapakoff
Laurie Sapakoff (Cohen)
Ismar Schorsch
Robert Seltzer
Alan Septimus
Anita Shapira
Elizabeth Klein Shapiro
Allan Silver
David Singer
Peter Stansky
Tom Wallace
Ruth Wisse
Carole Zabar

Printed Materials

Abramowicz, Hirsz. *Profiles of a Lost World: Memoirs of East European Jewish Life Before World War II*. Ed. Dina Abramowicz and Jeffrey Shandler. Trans. Eva Zeitlin Dobkin. Detroit: Wayne State University Press, 1999.

Alter, Robert. "The Education of Alfred Kazin." *Commentary*, June 1978, 44–51.

———. "Holocaust." [Book Review] *The War Against the Jews, 1933–1945*. *Commentary*, June 1975, 72–73.

———. "Revolutionism and the Jews: 2, Appropriating the Religious Tradition." *Commentary*, February 1971, 47–54.

American Jewish Year Book. 1947–92.

An-Sky, S. A. *1915 Diary of S. An-Sky: A Russian Jewish Writer at the Eastern Front*. Trans. Polly Zavadivker. Bloomington: Indiana University Press, 2016.

Arendt, Hannah. "[Book Review] *The Black Book: The Nazi Crime Against the Jewish People* and *Hitler's Professors: The Part of Scholarship in Germany's Crimes Against the Jewish People*." *Commentary*, January 1946, 291–95.

———. *Eichmann in Jerusalem: A Report on the Banality of Evil*. New York: Viking, 1963.

Arendt, Hannah, and Gershom Scholem. "'Eichmann in Jerusalem': An Exchange of Letters Between Gershom Scholem and Hannah Arendt." *Encounter* 22, no. 1 (1964): 51–56.

Auerbach, Rachela. *Pisma z Getta Warszawskiego* [Writings from the Warsaw Ghetto]. Ed. Karolina Szymaniak. Trans. Anna Ciałowicz and Karolina Szymaniak. Warsaw: Żydowski Instytut Historyczny, 2016.

Babel, Isaac. *1920 Diary*. Ed. and trans. Carol J. Avins. New Haven, CT: Yale University Press, 2002.

Baldwin, James. "Negroes Are Anti-Semitic Because They're Anti-White." *New York Times Magazine*, April 9, 1967, 27, 135–39.

Baldwin, James, Nathan Glazer, Sidney Hook, and Gunnar Myrdal. "Liberalism and the Negro: A Round-Table Discussion." *Commentary*, March 1964, 25–42.

Baron, Jeannette M. "Hannah Arendt: Personal Reflections." *Response: A Contemporary Jewish Review* 12, no. 3 (1980): 58–63.

Baron, Salo W. "Opening Remarks." *Jewish Social Studies* 12, no. 1 (1950): 13–16.

———. "Personal Notes: Hannah Arendt." *Jewish Social Studies* 38, no. 2 (1976): 187–89.

———. "Reflections on the Future of the Jews of Europe." *Contemporary Jewish Record* 3, no. 4 (July–August 1940), 355–69.

———. "The Spiritual Reconstruction of European Jewry." *Commentary*, December 1945, 4–12.

Bell, Daniel. "Columbia and the Left." In *Confrontation*, ed. Daniel Bell and Irving Kristol, 67–107. New York: Basic, 1968.

———. "The Intelligentsia in America." In *Tomorrow's American*, ed. Samuel Sandmel. New York: Oxford University Press, 1977.

———. "The Return of the Sacred: The Argument About the Future of Religion." *Bulletin of the American Academy of Arts and Sciences* 31, no. 6 (1978): 29–55.

———. "Sensibility in the 60's." *Commentary*, June 1971, 63–73.

Bell, Daniel, and Irving Kristol. *Confrontation: The Student Rebellion and the Universities.* New York: Basic, 1968.

Birnbaum, Nathan. "From Freethinker to Believer." In *The Golden Tradition: Jewish Life and Thought in Eastern Europe,* ed. Lucy S. Dawidowicz, 213–22. New York: Holt, Rinehart and Winston, 1967.

———. *Fun an apikoyres gevorn a maymin.* Warsaw: Yeshurun, 1927.

———. *Vom Freigeist zum Gläubigen: Ein Vortrag.* Zürich: Arzenu, 1919.

Birstein, Ann. *What I Saw at the Fair: An Autobiography.* New York: Welcome Rain Publishers, 2003.

Borowitz, Eugene B. "At the Beginning." *Sh'ma: A Journal of Jewish Responsibility* 1, no. 2 (1970): 5–7.

———. "Have Your Read *Commentary* Lately?" *Sh'ma: A Journal of Jewish Responsibility* 1, no. 11 (1971): 81–82.

Brightman, Carol, ed. *Between Friends: The Correspondence of Hannah Arendt and Mary McCarthy, 1949–1975.* New York: Harcourt Brace, 1995.

Brodnitz, Friedrich S. "Memories of the Reichsvertreterung—A Personal Report." *Leo Baeck Institute Year Book* 31, no. 1 (1986): 267–77.

Brooklyn Bridge Collective. "Jewish Women: Life Force of a Culture?" *Brooklyn Bridge* 1, no. 1 (1971).

Brumberg, Abraham. "Murder Most Foul (Review, *Neighbors: The Destruction of the Jewish Community in Jedwabne,* by Jan Gross)." *Times Literary Supplement,* March 2, 2001, 8–9.

———. "[Book Review] *The Last Jews of Poland,* by Malgorzata Niezabitowska, and *Shielding the Flame: An Intimate Conversation with Marek Edelman, the Last Surviving Leader of the Warsaw Ghetto Uprising,* by Hanna Krall." *New York Times Book Review,* October 19, 1986, 402–3.

Brumberg, Abraham, and Norman Davies. "Poles and Jews: An Exchange." *New York Review of Books,* April 9, 1987, 41–44.

"Capitalism, Socialism, and Democracy: A Symposium." *Commentary,* April 1978, 29–71.

Charlton, Linda. "37 Jews in U.S. Applaud Israelis Who Urged Flexibility on Peace." *New York Times,* April 21, 1978, A1, A6.

Czerniaków, Adam. *The Warsaw Diary of Adam Czerniakow: Prelude to Doom.* Ed. Raul Hilberg, Stanisław Staron, and Josef Kermisz. Trans. Staron and the staff of Yad Vashem. New York: Stein and Day, 1979.

Danzig, David. "The Meaning of Negro Strategy." *Commentary,* February 1964, 41–46.

Dawidowicz, Lucy S. "American Jews and the Holocaust." *New York Times Magazine,* April 18, 1982, 47–48, 101–2, 107, 109–12, 114.

———. "'Anti-Semitism' and the Rosenberg Case: The Latest Communist Propaganda Trap." *Commentary,* July 1952, 41–45.

———. "The Arab-Israel War of 1967: American Public Opinion." *American Jewish Year Book* 69 (1968): 198–229.

———. "Babi Yar's Legacy." *New York Times Magazine,* September 27, 1981, 48–50, 54, 59–60, 63, 65, and 67.

———. "Belsen Remembered." *Commentary,* March 1966, 82–85.

Dawidowicz, Lucy S. "[Book Review] Ben Hecht's 'Perfidy.' " *Commentary*, March 1962, 260–64.

———. "[Book Review] *A Cup of Tears: A Diary of the Warsaw Ghetto.*" *New York Newsday, Books*, March 19, 1989, 19 and 24.

———. "[Book Review] Getting and Spending: *Jews and Money: The Myths and Reality*, by Gerald Krefetz." *Commentary*, April 1983, 68–70.

———. "[Book Review] *Israel: A Blessing and a Curse*, by Hedley V. Cooke." *Commentary*, July 1961, 82–84.

———. "[Book Review] Nathan Glazer, *The Social Basis of American Communism*, and Daniel Aaron, *Writers on the Left: Episodes in American Literary Communism.*" *American Jewish Historical Quarterly* 53, no. 2 (1963): 192–97.

———. "[Book Review] *Zakhor: Jewish History and Jewish Memory.*" *American Jewish History* 73, no. 1 (1983): 112–16.

———. "Boy Meets Girl in the Warsaw Ghetto." *Midstream*, Summer 1960, 109–12.

———. "The Business of American Jews (Notes on a Work in Progress)." In *What Is the Use of Jewish History?* 237–53. Ed. Neal Kozodoy. New York: Schocken, 1992.

———. "Can Anti-Semitism Be Measured?" *Commentary*, July 1970, 36–43.

———. "A Century of Jewish History, 1881–1981: The View from America." *American Jewish Year Book* 83 (1982): 3–98.

———. "Church and State." *American Jewish Year Book* 66 (1965): 208–29.

———. "Church and State." *American Jewish Year Book* 67 (1966): 128–50.

———. "Civil Rights and Intergroup Tensions." *American Jewish Year Book* 66 (1965): 155–93.

———. "Coddling the Clan Got Democrats Nowhere, Too." *Wall Street Journal*, July 12, 1984, 36.

———. "The Communists and the Rosenberg Case." *New Leader*, September 8, 1952, 15.

———. "Could America Have Rescued Europe's Jews?" In *What Is the Use of Jewish History?* 157–78. Ed. Neal Kozodoy. New York: Schocken, 1992.

———. "[Book Review] Could the United States Have Rescued the European Jews from Hitler? *The Abandonment of the Jews: America and the Holocaust, 1941–1945*, by David S. Wyman." *This World*, no. 12 (Fall 1985): 15–30.

———. "The Crime of Being a Jew." *Reconstructionist* 18, no. 18 (1953): 8–12.

———. "The Curious Case of Marek Edelman." *Commentary*, March 1987, 66–69.

———. "[Book Review] *A Doomed Struggle: Jewish Resistance in Nazi-Occupied Europe*, by Reuben Ainsztein." *Times Literary Supplement*, June 20, 1975, 694–95.

———. "The Epic of the Warsaw Ghetto." *Menorah Journal* 38, no. 1 (1950): 88–103.

———. "False Friends and Dangerous Defenders." *Reconstructionist* 19, no. 6 (1953): 9–15.

———. "From Past to Past: Jewish East Europe to Jewish East Side." *Conservative Judaism* 22, no. 2 (1968): 19–27.

———. *From That Place and Time: A Memoir, 1938–1947.* New York: Norton, 1989.

———. "Germany's Answer to Bitburg." *Wall Street Journal*, December 6, 1985, 30.

———. *The Golden Tradition: Jewish Life and Thought in Eastern Europe.* New York: Holt, Rinehart and Winston, 1967.

———. *The Golden Tradition: Jewish Life and Thought in Eastern Europe.* Boston: Beacon, 1967.

———. *The Golden Tradition: Jewish Life and Thought in Eastern Europe.* 1967. Reprint, Northvale, NJ: Jacob Aronson, 1989.

———. "[Book Review] Hertzberg's Complaint: *The Jews in America: Four Centuries of an Uneasy Encounter*, by Arthur Hertzberg." *Commentary*, February 1990, 49–52.

———. "History as Autobiography: Telling a Life." In *What Is the Use of Jewish History?* 20–37. Ed. Neal Kozodoy. New York: Schocken, 1992.

———. "[Book Review] Holocaust Historian: *Roads to Extinction: Essays on the Holocaust*, by Philip Friedman, . *New York Times Book Review*, January 11, 1981, 8, 18.

———. *The Holocaust and the Historians.* Cambridge, MA: Harvard University Press, 1981.

———. *A Holocaust Reader.* New York: Behrman, 1976.

———. "The Holocaust and the Textbooks." *Social Studies Review* 30, no. 4 (Spring 1990): 10–11.

———. "The Holocaust Was Unique in Intent, Scope, and Effect." *Center Magazine*, July–August 1981, 56–64.

———. "How They Teach the Holocaust." *Commentary*, December 1990, 25–32.

———. "In Berlin Again." *Commentary*, August 1986, 32–41.

———. "Indicting American Jews." *Commentary*, June 1983, 36–44.

———. "Intergroup Relations and Tensions in the U.S." *American Jewish Year Book* 68 (1967): 63–96.

———. *The Jewish Presence: Essays on Identity and History.* New York: Holt, Rinehart and Winston, 1977.

———. "The Jewishness of the Jewish Labor Movement." In *A Bicentennial Festschrift for Jacob Rader Marcus*, ed. Bertram Wallace Korn, 121–30. New York: KTAV, 1976.

———. "Lies About the Holocaust." *Commentary*, December 1980, 31–37.

———. "Louis Marshall and the *Jewish Daily Forward*: An Episode in Wartime Censorship, 1917–1918." In *For Max Weinreich on His Seventieth Birthday: Studies in Jewish Languages, Literature, and Society*, ed. Lucy S. Dawidowicz et al., 31–43. London: Mouton, 1964.

———. "Louis Marshall's Yiddish Newspaper, *The Jewish World*: A Study in Contrasts." MA thesis, Columbia University, 1961.

———. "Louis Marshall's Yiddish Newspaper: *The Jewish World*: A Study in Contrasts." *Jewish Social Studies* 25, no. 2 (1963): 102–32.

———. "Max Weinreich (1894–1969): The Scholarship of Yiddish." *American Jewish Year Book* 70 (1969): 59–68.

———. "Middle-Class Judaism: A Case Study." *Commentary*, June 1960, 492–503.

———. "Observations: Explaining American Jews." *Commentary*, December 1968, 85–92.

———. "Observations: Perversions of the Holocaust." *Commentary*, October 1989, 56–60.

———. "On Being a Woman in Shul." *Commentary*, July 1968, 71–74.

———. "On Being a Woman in Shul." In *The Jewish Presence: Essays on Identity and History*, 46–57. New York: Holt, Rinehart and Winston, 1977.

———. *On Equal Terms: Jews in America, 1881–1981.* New York: Holt, Rinehart and Winston, 1982.

Dawidowicz, Lucy S. "The Politics of American Jews." In *What Is the Use of Jewish History?* 254–68. Ed. Neal Kozodoy. New York: Schocken, 1992.

———. "Politics, the Jews, and the '84 Election." *Commentary*, February 1985, 25–30.

———. "The Relevance of an Education in the Sholem Aleichem Schools." In *Our First Fifty Years: The Sholem Aleichem Folk Institute (A Historical Survey)*, ed. Saul Goodman, 117–23. New York: Sholem Aleichem Folk Institute, 1972.

———. "[Book Review] *Fragments of Isabella: Memoir of Auschwitz*, by Isabella Leitner, and *The Warsaw Diary of Adam Czerniakow: Prelude to Doom*, ed. Raul Hilberg, Stanislaw Staron, and Josef Kermisz." *New York Times Book Review*, February 25, 1979, 20–21.

———. "Review of Nora Levin, *The Holocaust: The Destruction of European Jewry, 1933–1945.*" *Jewish Social Studies* 32, no. 2 (April 1970): 176–77.

———. "Review of Raul Hilberg, *The Destruction of the European Jews.*" *Washington Times Magazine*, August 19, 1985, 4M–5M.

———. "The Rise and Fall of Yiddish." *Commentary*, November 1980, 42–45.

———. "The Rosenberg Case: 'Hate-America' Weapon." *New Leader*, December 22, 1952, 13.

———. "Sh'ma's Anti-Responsibility." *Sh'ma*, May 28, 1971, 117–18.

———. "The State of World Jewry Address, 1984." Lecture, 92nd Street Y, New York, 1984.

———. "Symposium: Does Judaism Need Feminism?" *Midstream*, April 1986, 39–40.

———. "Toward a History of the Holocaust." *Commentary*, April 1969, 51–56.

———. "Trojan Horse Returns." *New Leader*, March 9, 1953, 12–14.

———. "The True History of Babi Yar." In *What Is the Use of Jewish History?* 101–19. Ed. Neal Kozodoy. New York: Schocken, 1992.

———. "[Book Review] Two of Stalin's Victims: *Henryk Ehrlich un Viktor Alter.*" *Commentary*, January 1951, 614–16.

———. "The United States, Israel, and the Middle East." *American Jewish Year Book* 63 (1962): 272–85.

———. "The United States and the State of Israel." *American Jewish Year Book* 55 (1954): 109–14.

———. "Visualizing the Warsaw Ghetto: Nazi Images of the Jews Refiltered by the BBC. A Critical Review of the BBC Film, 'The Warsaw Ghetto.'" *Shoah: A Review of Holocaust Studies and Commemorations* 1, no. 1 (1978): 5–6, 17.

———. *The War Against the Jews, 1933–1945.* 1st ed. New York: Holt, Rinehart and Winston, 1975.

———. *The War Against the Jews, 1933–1945.* 10th anniversary ed. New York: Bantam, 1986.

———. *What Is the Use of Jewish History?* Ed. Neal Kozodoy. New York: Schocken, 1992.

———. "Yiddish: Past, Present, and Perfect." *Commentary*, May 1962, 375–85.

Dawidowicz, Lucy S., and Leon J. Goldstein. *Politics in a Pluralist Democracy: Studies in Voting in the 1960 Election.* New York: Institute of Human Relations Press, 1963.

Decter, Midge. "Bitburg: Who Forgot What." *Commentary*, August 1985, 21–27.

———. "The Negro and the New York Schools." *Commentary*, September 1964, 25–34.

Deutscher, Isaac. *The Non-Jewish Jew and Other Essays.* London: Oxford University Press, 1968.

Dorman, Joseph, ed. *Arguing the World: The New York Intellectuals in Their Own Words.* New York: Free Press, 2000.

Dubnov-Erlich, Sophie. *The Life and Work of S. M. Dubnow: Diaspora Nationalism and Jewish History.* Trans. Judith Vowles. Ed. Jeffrey Shandler. Bloomington: Indiana University Press, 1991.

Dubnow, Simon. "A bukh vegen problemen in der idisher geshikhte: Dubnow's Review of Salo W. Baron, *A Social and Religious History of the Jews.*" *Di tsukunft* 42 (December 1937): 765–68.

———, ed. *Pinkas hamedinah.* 1925; reprint, Jerusalem, 1968–69.

———. "The Survival of the Jewish People: The Secret of Survival and the Law of Survival." In *Nationalism and History: Essays on Old and New Judaism*, 325–35. Ed. Koppel S. Pinson. New York: Atheneum, 1970.

Dworzecki, Meir. "The Day-to-Day Stand of the Jews." In *Jewish Resistance during the Holocaust: Proceedings of the Conference on Manifestations of Jewish Resistance, Jerusalem, April 7–11, 1968*, 152–81, 186–90 (reply), 427–29 (debate). Jerusalem: Yad Vashem, 1971.

Edelman, Marek. *Getto Walczy: Udział Bundu w Obronie Getta Warszawskiego.* Warsaw: Nakładem C.K. "Bundu," 1945.

———. *The Ghetto Fights.* New York: American Representative of the General Jewish Workers' Union of Poland, May 1946.

Ehrenburg, Ilya, and Vasily Grossman. *The Complete Black Book of Russian Jewry.* Ed. and trans. David Patterson. New Brunswick, NJ: Transaction, 2002.

Eley, Geoff. "[Book Review] Holocaust History: *The Holocaust and the Historians*, by Lucy S. Dawidowicz." *London Review of Books*, March 3, 1983, 6–9.

Evanier, David. *Red Love.* New York: C. Scribner, 1991.

Feigenbaum, M. J. "Life in a Bunker." In *The Root and the Bough: The Epic of an Enduring People*, ed. Leo W. Schwarz, 142–54. New York: Holt, Rinehart, 1949.

Feldman, Irving. *The Pripet Marshes and Other Poems.* New York: Viking, 1965.

"The Fifth War: Israel in Lebanon." *Response: A Contemporary Jewish Review* 16, no. 1 (1983).

Fridman, Filip. "Yankev Shatskis ort in der mizrekh ayropayisher yidisher geshikhte-shraybung." In *Shatski-bukh: opshatsungen vegn d"r yankev shatski*, ed. J. Lipschutz, 11–27. Buenos Aires: YIVO, 1958.

Friedman, Murray. "The White Liberal's Retreat." *Atlantic Monthly*, January 1963, 42–46.

Friedman, Philip. "The Fate of the Jewish Book During the Nazi Era." *Jewish Book Annual* 15 (1957–58): 2–13.

———. "Research and Literature on the Recent Jewish Tragedy." *Jewish Social Studies* 12, no. 1 (1950): 17–26.

———. *Roads to Extinction: Essays on the Holocaust.* New York: Conference on Jewish Social Studies and Jewish Publication Society of America, 1980.

Gershman, Carl. "The Andrew Young Affair." *Commentary*, November 1979, 25–33.

Glatstein, Jacob. *The Glatstein Chronicles.* Ed. Ruth Wisse. Trans. Maier Deshell and Norbert Guterman. New Haven, CT: Yale University Press, 2010.

Glazer, Nathan. "Blacks, Jews & The Intellectuals." *Commentary*, April 1969, 33–39.

———. *The Social Basis of American Communism.* New York: Harcourt, Brace, 1961.

Glazer, Nathan, and Daniel Patrick Moynihan. *Beyond the Melting Pot: The Negroes, Puerto Ricans, Jews, Italians, and Irish of New York City*. Cambridge, MA: MIT Press, 1963.

Goldenhersh, Lucy. "Historian Decrys Nazi Annihilation of the Jews." *Stanford Daily News*, February 4, 1981, 3.

Goldstein, Bernard. *Finf yor in varshever geto*. New York: Undzer tsayt, 1947.

———. *The Stars Bear Witness*. Trans. and ed. Leonard Shatzkin. New York: Viking, 1949.

Goodman, Saul, ed. *Our First Fifty Years: The Sholem Aleichem Folk Institute (A Historical Survey)*. New York: Sholem Aleichem Folk Institute, 1972.

Gornick, Vivian. *The Men in My Life*. Boston: MIT Press, 2008.

Grafton, Anthony. "The Public Intellectual and the Private Sphere: Arendt and Eichmann at the Dinner Table." In *Worlds Made by Words: Scholarship and Community in the Modern West*, 271–87. Cambridge, MA: Harvard University Press, 2009.

Green, Nancy, ed. *Jewish Workers in the Modern Diaspora*. Berkeley: University of California Press, 1998.

Greenberg, Blu. *On Women and Judaism: A View from Tradition*. Philadelphia: Jewish Publication Society of America, 1981.

Gruber, Ruth. *Ahead of Time: My Early Years as a Foreign Correspondent*. New York: Wynwood Press, 1991.

Grubsztein, Meir. *Jewish Resistance During the Holocaust: Proceedings of the Conference on Manifestations of Jewish Resistance, Jerusalem, April 7–11, 1968*. Trans. Esther Varda Bar-on, Moshe M. Kohn, Yehezkel Cohen, and Cecil Hyman. Jerusalem: Yad Vashem, 1971.

Halperin, Israel, ed. *Pinkas va'ad arba' arazot*. Ed. Yisra'el Bartal. 2nd ed. Jerusalem, 1989–90.

Hentoff, Nat. "Blacks and Jews: An Interview with Julius Lester." In *Evergreen Review, 1967–1973*, ed. Barney Rosset, 322–29. New York: Four Walls Eight Windows, 1998.

Herberg, Will. "From Marxism to Judaism: Jewish Belief as a Dynamic of Social Action." *Commentary*, January 1947, 25–32.

———. *Protestant, Catholic, Jew: An Essay in American Religious Sociology*. Garden City, NY: Doubleday, 1955.

Hersey, John. "Life's Reports, Home to Warsaw." *Life Magazine*, April 9, 1945, 16–20.

———. "The Novel of Contemporary History." *Atlantic Monthly*, November 1949, 80, 82, 84.

———. "Prisoner 339, Klooga." *Life Magazine*, October 30, 1944, 72–83.

———. *To Invent a Memory: John Hersey's The Wall*. Maurice A. Still Prize Lecture. Baltimore: Baltimore Hebrew University, 1990.

———. *The Wall*. New York: Knopf, 1950.

Heschel, Abraham Joshua. *The Earth Is the Lord's: The Inner World of the Jew in East Europe*. New York: Henry Schuman, 1950.

Hilberg, Raul. *The Destruction of the European Jews*. Chicago: Quadrangle, 1961.

———. *Perpetrators Victims Bystanders: The Jewish Catastrophe 1933–1945*. New York: Aaron Asher, HarperCollins, 1992.

————. *The Politics of Memory: The Journey of a Holocaust Historian.* Chicago: Ivan R. Dee, 1996.

Himmelfarb, Gertrude. *The De-Moralization of Society: From Victorian Virtues to Modern Values.* London: IEA Health and Welfare Unit, 1995.

————. *The New History and the Old.* Cambridge, MA: Harvard University Press, 1987.

Himmelfarb, Milton. "Carter and the Jews." *Commentary,* August 1976, 45–48.

————. "How High a Wall?" *Commentary,* July 1966, 23–29.

————. "Is American Jewry in Crisis?" *Commentary,* March 1969, 33–42.

————. "Negroes, Jews and Muzhiks." In *The Ghetto and Beyond: Essays on Jewish Life in America,* ed. Peter I. Rose, 409–18. New York: Random House, 1969.

————. "No Hitler, No Holocaust." *Commentary,* March 1984, 37–43.

————. "Paganism, Religion & Modernity." *Commentary,* November 1968, 89–95.

————. "This Aquarian Age." *Commentary,* April 1970, 38–41.

————. "The Vanishing Jews." *Commentary,* September 1963, 249–51.

Hook, Sidney. *Heresy, Yes—Conspiracy, No!* American Committee for Cultural Freedom, 1953.

Howe, Irving. *Decline of the New.* New York: Harcourt, Brace, 1970.

————. "In This Moment of Grief." *Dissent,* May–June 1968, 197.

————. *A Margin of Hope: An Intellectual Autobiography.* New York: Harcourt Brace Jovanovich, 1982.

————. "The New York Intellectuals: A Chronicle and a Critique." *Commentary,* October 1968, 29–51.

————. "Review of *The Golden Tradition.*" *Book Week,* February 12, 1967, 3, 15.

————. "Review of *The War Against the Jews, 1933–1945.*" *New York Times Book Review,* April 20, 1975, 1–2.

————. *Steady Work: Essay in the Politics of Democratic Radicalism, 1953–1966.* New York: Harcourt, Brace, 1966.

Howe, Irving, and Eliezer Greenberg, eds. *Voices from the Yiddish: Essays, Memoirs, Diaries.* Ann Arbor: University of Michigan Press, 1972.

Humphrey, Grace. *Poland, the Unexplored.* Indianapolis: Bobbs-Merrill, 1931.

Isaac, Rael Jean. *Breira: Counsel for Judaism.* New York: Americans for a Safe Israel, 1977.

"Israel Says Use of Cluster Bomb in Lebanon Was Result of Mistake." *New York Times,* April 21, 1978, 6.

Karmel-Wolfe, Henia. *The Baders of Jacob Street.* New York: HarperCollins, 1970.

Katz, Shlomo, ed. *Negro and Jew: An Encounter in America.* New York: Macmillan, 1967.

————, ed. "Negro-Jewish Relations in America: A Symposium." *Midstream* 12, no. 10 (1966): 1–91.

Kazin, Alfred. *New York Jew.* New York: Knopf, 1978.

————. "Saving My Soul at the Plaza." *New York Review of Books,* March 31, 1983, 38–42.

————. *Starting Out in the Thirties.* Boston: Little, Brown, 1965.

————. "They Made It! From the Notebooks of a New Yorker." *Dissent,* Fall 1987, 612–17.

————. "The United States Was Responsible for the 1982 Massacre of Palestinians in Beirut." *The Nation,* September 14, 2017. https://www.thenation.com/article/the-united-states-was-responsible-for-the-1982-massacre-of-palestinians-in-beirut/

Kazin, Alfred. *A Walker in the City*. New York: Harcourt, Brace, 1951.

Klagsbrun, Francine. "Eulogies." *Moment*, April 1991, 14, 16.

Koltun, Elizabeth, ed. *The Jewish Woman: New Perspectives*. New York: Schocken, 1976.

Konvitz, Milton R. "YIVO Comes to Morningside: America Gains a New Institute of Learning." *Commentary*, January 1947, 48–54.

Kristol, Irving. "Christianity, Judaism, and Socialism." In *Neoconservatism: The Autobiography of an Idea*, 429–41. New York: Free Press, 1995.

———. "Elegy for a Lost World: [Book Review] *The Earth Is the Lord's*, by Abraham J. Heschel." *Commentary*, May 1950, 490–91.

———. "A Few Kind Words for Uncle Tom." *Harper's Magazine*, February 1965, 95–99.

———. "A Foolish Americanism—Utopianism," *New York Times Magazine*, November 14, 1971, 31–42.

———. *The Neoconservative Persuasion: Selected Essays, 1942–2009*. Ed. Gertrude Himmelfarb. New York: Basic, 2011.

———. *Reflections of a Neoconservative: Looking Back, Looking Ahead*. New York: Basic, 1983.

———. "Why Religion Is Good for the Jews." *Commentary*, August 1994, 19–21.

Kurzweil, Arthur. "The *Jewish Book News* Interview with Lucy Dawidowicz." *Jewish Book News*, April 1989, 7–11.

Laqueur, Walter. "Revolutionism and the Jews: 1, New York and Jerusalem." *Commentary*, February 1971, 38–46.

Lehrer, Leibush. "Camp Boiberik: The Growth of an Idea." Paper presented, in part, to the adult audience at Camp Boiberik, New York, on Tisha B'Ov, 1959.

Lehrer, Leibush. "The Jewish Secular School." *Jewish Social Service Quarterly* (1936): 308–17.

———. "The Objectives of Camp Boiberik." In *Our First Fifty Years: The Sholem Aleichem Folk Institute (A Historical Survey)*, ed. Saul Goodman, 57–73. New York: Sholem Aleichem Folk Institute, 1972.

———. *Reactions of Second Generation American Jews to Problems of Jewish Living: A Study of Former Campers and Staff Members of Camp Boiberik*. Camp Boiberik, New York, 1961.

Lehrer, Leybush. *Azoy zenen yidn* [So Are the Jews]. New York: Matones, 1959.

———. *Simbol un tokh* [Symbol and Substance]. Trans. Lucy S. Dawidowicz. Introduction by Arn Tseytlin. New York: [o. fg.], 1965.

———. "Yidishkayt—vos darf men ton?" *Yidishe shriftn* 1, no. 1 (1941): 42–52.

Leviant, Curt. "The Spirit of Zion." Review of *The Golden Tradition*. *New York Times Book Review*, November 26, 1967, 288.

"Liberalism and the Jews: A Symposium." *Commentary*, January 1980, 15–82.

Mark, Bernard. *Megiles oyshvits*. Tel Aviv: Yisroyel-bukh, 1977.

M.[endelsohn], S.[hlomo]. "Di yidishe geto in varshe." *YIVO bleter* 16, no. 2 (1940): 200–201.

Meyer, Michael A. "On the Role of the Sexes in Modern Judaism." *Variant* 1, no. 1 (1961): 43–47.

Mickiewicz, Adam. *The Books and the Pilgrimage of the Polish Nation*. Trans. James Ridgway. London: T. Brettell, 1833.

Moynihan, Daniel P. "The President and the Negro: The Moment Lost." *Commentary*, February 1967, 31–45.

———. "[Book Review] *Politics in a Pluralist Democracy: Studies of Voting in the 1960 Election*, by Lucy S. Dawidowicz and Leon J. Goldstein." *Commentary*, October 1964, 87–89.

———. "The United States in Opposition." *Commentary*, March 1975, 31–44.

Myrdal, Gunnar. *An American Dilemma: The Negro Problem and American Democracy.* New York: Harper and Brothers, 1944.

Neusner, Jacob. "Religion." *American Jewish Year Book* 63 (1962): 49–60.

Noy, Melech. *Khurbn un oyfstand fun di yidn in varshe: eydes-bleter un azkores.* 3rd ed. Trans. D. B. Malkin. Tel Aviv: Ahdut, 1948.

Ozick, Cynthia. "America: Toward Yavneh." *Judaism* 19 (Summer 1970): 264–82.

———. "Carter and the Jews: An American Political Dilemma." *New Leader*, June 30, 1980: 3–23.

Peretz, Martin. "The American Left and Israel." *Commentary*, November 1967, 27–34.

Podhoretz, Norman. *Ex-Friends: Falling Out with Allen Ginsberg, Lionel and Diana Trilling, Lillian Hellman, Hannah Arendt, and Norman Mailer.* New York: Free Press, 1999.

———. "Hannah Arendt on Eichmann: A Study in the Perversity of Brilliance." *Commentary*, September 1963, 201–8.

———. "J'Accuse." *Commentary*, September 1982, 21–31.

———. *Making It.* New York: Random House, 1967.

———. "My Negro Problem—and Ours." *Commentary*, February 1963, 93–101.

———. "'My Negro Problem—and Ours' at 50." *Commentary*, May 2013, 11–17.

Pogrebin, Letty Cottin. "Anti-Semitism in the Women's Movement." *Ms.*, June 1982, 45–46, 48–49, 62, 65–66, 69–72.

Pomrenze, Seymour [Sholem Pomerants]. "'Operation Offenbach': Saving Jewish Cultural Treasures in Germany." *YIVO bleter* 29, no. 2 (1947): 282–85.

Porter, Jack Nusan, and Peter Dreier, eds. *Jewish Radicalism: A Selected Anthology.* New York: Grove, 1973.

Poste, Leslie I. "Books Go Home from the Wars." *Library Journal*, December 1, 1948, 1699–704.

Proceedings of Breira's First Annual Membership Conference. New York: Breira, 1977.

Rabinowitz, Dorothy. "The Radicalized Professor: A Portrait." *Commentary*, July 1970, 62–64.

Rakovsky, Puah. *My Life as a Radical Jewish Woman: Memoirs of a Zionist Feminist in Poland.* Trans. Barbara Harshav and Paula E. Hyman. Bloomington: Indiana University Press, 2002.

Reuben, William A. "The Rosenberg Conviction: Is This the Dreyfus Case of Cold War America?" *National Guardian*, April 25, 1951, 1, 4.

———. "Truth About the Rosenbergs' Case." *Jewish Life*, November 1951, 4–7.

———. "What Was the Rosenbergs' Crime?" *Jewish Life*, December 1951, 21–23.

Reznikoff, Charles, ed. *Louis Marshall: Champion of Liberty.* Vol. 1. Philadelphia: Jewish Publication Society of America, 1957.

Roiphe, Anne. "The Politics of Anger." *Tikkun* 1, no. 2 (1986): 18–22.

Rosenberg, Bernard, and Ernest Goldstein, eds. *Creators and Disturbers: Reminiscences by Jewish Intellectuals of New York.* New York: Columbia University Press, 1982.

Rosenfield, Geraldine. "U.S. Public Opinion Polls and the Lebanon War." *American Jewish Year Book* 84 (1983): 105–16.

Roth, Philip. *The Plot Against America*. New York: Vintage, 2004.

Schachner, Nathan. "Church, State and Education." *American Jewish Year Book* 49 (1947–48): 1–48.

Schwarz, Leo W. *A Golden Treasury of Jewish Literature*. New York: Farrar & Rinehart, 1937.

———, ed. *The Jewish Caravan: Great Stories of Twenty-Five Centuries*. New York: Farrar & Rinehart, 1935.

———. *Memoirs of My People: Through a Thousand Years*. Philadelphia: Jewish Publication Society of America, 1943.

———. *The Root and the Bough: The Epic of an Enduring People*. New York: Rinehart, 1949.

Shapira, Avraham, ed. *The Seventh Day: Soldiers' Talk About the Six-Day War*. London: Deutsch, 1970.

———, ed. *Si'ah Lohamim: Pirkei hakshavah vehitbonenut*. Tel Aviv: Behoza'at kevzat haverim ze'irim mehatenu'at hakibuzit, 1968.

Shatski, Yankev. "Historish-kritisher araynfir tsum 'Yeven Metsulah' fun R. Natan Neta Hanover." In *Gezeres takh*, 9–159. Vilna: YIVO Institute, Historical Section, 1938.

Shattan, Joseph. "Why Breira?" *Commentary*, April 1977, 60–66.

S[hildkret], L[ibe]. "Anti-natsi literatur." *YIVO bleter*, May–June 1941, 276.

———. "Der oyslay fun yidishe un hebreyishe bikher in di shtotishe bibliotekn." *YIVO bleter*, March–April 1941, 178–80.

———. "'Hashofar': a kapitl geshikhte fun der yidisher prese in england." *YIVO bleter*, March–April 1940, 217–24.

———. "[Book Review] Maks Vaynraykh, *Der veg tsu undzer yugnt: yesodes, metodn, problemen fun yidisher yugnt-forshung*." *Shrift*, May 1937, 18–19.

———. "Der siyem fun der aspirantur un pro-aspirantur." *Yedies fun yidishe visnshaftlekhn institut* 85–86, no. 5–6 (1939): 1–4.

———. "Yidn in poyln." *Shrift*, February 1940, 9–12.

———. "Ir vet zey nit aroystraybn," *Shrift*, June–July 1937, 3.

Siegel, Richard, Michael Strassfeld, and Sharon Strassfeld, eds. *The First Jewish Catalog: A Do-It-Yourself Kit*. Philadelphia: Jewish Publication Society of America, 1976.

Simon, Kate. *Bronx Primitive: Portraits in a Childhood*. New York: Viking, 1983.

———. *A Wider World: Portraits in Adolescence*. New York: Harper & Row, 1987.

Sleeper, James A., and Alan L. Mintz, eds. *The New Jews*. New York: Vintage, 1971.

Styron, William. "Introduction." In *The Cunning of History: The Holocaust and the American Future*, Richard L. Rubenstein, vii–xiv. New York: HarperCollins, 1978.

———. *Sophie's Choice*. New York: Vintage, 1979; reprint, 1992.

Syrkin, Marie. "Does Feminism Clash with Jewish National Need?" *Midstream*, June–July 1985, 8–12.

———. "[Book Review] Nazi Fury: *The War Against the Jews, 1933–1945*, by Lucy S. Dawidowicz." *New Republic*, May 17, 1975, 26–27.

———. *The State of the Jews*. Washington, DC: New Republic, 1980.

———. "Symposium: Does Judaism Need Feminism?" *Midstream*, April 1986, 42–43.

———. "What American Jews Did During the Holocaust." *Midstream*, October 1982, 6–12.

Trilling, Diana. "Arguing the World: The Reminiscences of Diana Trilling." Interview by Joseph Dorman. Oral History Research Office, Columbia University, 2000.

Trunk, Isaiah. "The Historian of the Holocaust at YIVO." In *Creators and Disturbers: Reminiscences by Jewish Intellectuals of New York*, ed. Bernard Rosenberg and Ernest Goldstein, 61–74. New York: Columbia University Press, 1982.

Vaynraykh, Maks. *Der veg tsu undzer yugnt: yesodes, metodn, problemen fun yidisher yugnt-forshung*. Vilna: YIVO, 1935.

———. "Di untershte shure fun ershtn yor aspirantur." *YIVO bleter* 10, no. 1–2 (1936): 99–102.

———. *Geshikhte fun der yidisher shprakh: bagrifn, faktn, metodn*. New York: YIVO, 1973.

———. "Undzer aspirantur un ire perspektivn." *YIVO bleter* 12, no. 4–5 (1937): 559–64.

———, ed. *YIVO bibliografye: a reshime fun di bikher, zhurnaln, broshurn, artiklen, retsenzies, vos der yidisher visnshaftlekher institut hot publikirt in di yorn 1925–1941*. New York: YIVO, 1943.

Weinreich, Max. *Geschichte der Jiddischen Sprachforschung*. Ed. Jerold Frakes. Atlanta: Scholars Press, 1993.

———. *History of the Yiddish Language*. Trans. Shlomo Noble and Joshua Fishman. Chicago: University of Chicago Press, 1980.

———. *History of the Yiddish Language*. Ed. Paul Glasser. Trans. Shlomo Noble and Joshua A. Fishman. New Haven, CT: Yale University Press, 2008.

———. *Hitler's Professors: The Part of Scholarship in Germany's Crimes Against the Jewish People*. New York: Yiddish Scientific Institute—YIVO, 1946.

———. "Internal Bilingualism in Ashkenaz." In *Voices from the Yiddish: Essays, Memoirs, Diaries*, ed. Irving Howe and Eliezer Greenberg, 279–88. Ann Arbor: University of Michigan Press, 1972.

———. "The Reality of Jewishness Versus the Ghetto Myth: The Sociolinguistic Roots of Yiddish." In *To Honour Roman Jakobson: Essays on the Occasion of His Seventieth Birthday*. The Hague: Mouton, 1967.

———. "Yidishkayt and Yiddish: On the Impact of Religion on Language in Ashkenazic Jewry." In *Mordecai M. Kaplan Jubilee Volume on the Occasion of His Seventieth Birthday (English Section)*, 481–514. Jewish Theological Seminary of America, 1953.

Wolfe, Tom. "The Me Decade and the Third Great Awakening." In *The Purple Decades: A Reader*, 265–93. New York: Farrar, Straus and Giroux, 1982.

"You Have to Be on the Side of the Weak: A Conversation with Marek Edelman." *Across Frontiers* 3, no. 3 (1987): 3–7, 30–33.

Zuckerman, Yitzchak. *A Surplus of Memory: Chronicle of the Warsaw Ghetto Uprising*. Trans. and ed. Barbara Harshav. Berkeley: University of California Press, 1993.

SECONDARY SOURCES

Aaron, Daniel. "Some Reflections on Communism and the Jewish Writer." *Salmagundi* 1, no. 1 (1965): 23–36.

Abbott, David W., Louis H. Gold, and Edward T. Rogowsky. *Police, Politics, and Race: The New York City Referendum on Civilian Review*. New York: American Jewish Committee and the Joint Center for Urban Studies of the Massachusetts Institute of Technology and Harvard University, 1969.

Abrams, Nathan. *Norman Podhoretz and Commentary Magazine: The Rise and Fall of the Neocons*. New York: Continuum, 2010.

Adler, Eliyana. "Dawidowicz, Lucy S." In *Jewish Women in America: An Historical Encyclopedia*, ed. Paula E. Hyman and Deborah Dash Moore, 317–19. New York: Routledge, 1997.

Adler, Les K., and Thomas G. Paterson. "Red Fascism: The Merger of Nazi Germany and Soviet Russia in the American Image of Totalitarianism, 1930's-1950's." *American Historical Review* 75, no. 4 (1970): 1046–64.

Adorno, Theodor W., et al. *The Authoritarian Personality*. New York: Harper, 1950.

Aleksiun, Natalia. "The Central Jewish Historical Commission in Poland, 1944–47." *Polin: Making Holocaust Memory* 20 (2008): 74–97.

———. *Conscious History: Polish Jewish Historians Before the Holocaust*. Oxford: Littman Library of Jewish Civilization, 2019.

———. "Philip Friedman and the Emergence of Holocaust Scholarship: A Reappraisal." *Simon Dubnow Institute Yearbook* 11 (2012): 333–46.

———. "Studenci z pałkami: rozruchy antyżydowskie na Uniwersytecie Stefana Batorego w Wilnie." In *Pogroms in Interwar Poland*, ed., Kamil Kijek, Artur Markowski, and Konrad Zieliński. Warsaw: Instytut Historii PAN, forthcoming.

———. "'What Matters Most Is Life Itself': Europe in the Eyes of Marek Edelman." In *Europe in the Eyes of Survivors of the Holocaust*, ed. Zeev Mankowitz, David Weinberg, and Sharon Kangisser Cohen, 91–126. Jerusalem: Yad Vashem, 2014.

Alexander, Edward. "Irving Howe and the Holocaust: Dilemmas of a Radical Jewish Intellectual." *American Jewish History* 88, no. 1 (2000): 95–113.

Almog, Shmuel. "Productivization, Proletarianization, and 'Hebrew Labor.'" In *Transformation in Modern Jewish History: Essays Presented in Honor of Shmuel Ettinger*, ed. Shmuel Almog, Israel Bartal, Michael Graetz, Arthur Herzberg, Otto Dov Kulka, Menahem Stern, Isadore Twersky, and Zvi Yekutiel, 41–70. Jerusalem: Zalman Shazar Center for Jewish History, 1987.

Alroey, Gur. *Zionism Without Zion: The Jewish Territorial Organization and Its Conflict with the Zionist Organization*. Detroit: Wayne State University Press, 2016.

Amit, Gish. "'The Largest Jewish Library in the World': The Books of Holocaust Victims and Their Redistribution Following World War II." *Dapim* 27, no. 2 (2013): 107–28.

Antler, Joyce. *Radical Jewish Feminism: Voices from the Women's Liberation Movement*. New York: New York University Press, 2018.

Applebaum, Anne. "The Stupidity and Unenforceability of Poland's Speech Law." *Washington Post*, February 2, 2018.

Appleby, Joyce, Lynn Hunt, and Margaret Jacob. *Telling the Truth About History*. New York: Norton, 1994.

Arad, Gulie Ne'eman. "Rereading an Unsettling Past: American Jews During the Nazi Era." In *Thinking About the Holocaust: After Half a Century*, ed. Alvin H. Rosenfeld, 182–209. Bloomington: Indiana University Press, 1997.

Aschheim, Steven E. "Archtypes and the German-Jewish Dialogue: Reflections Occasioned by the Goldhagen Affair." *German History* 15, no. 2 (1997): 240–50.

———. *Brothers and Strangers: The East European Jew in German and German Jewish Consciousness, 1800–1923.* Madison: University of Wisconsin Press, 1982.

———, ed. *Hannah Arendt in Jerusalem.* Berkeley: University of California Press, 2001.

Ash, Timothy Garton. "Introduction." In *Shielding the Flame: An Intimate Conversation with Dr. Marek Edelman, the Last Surviving Leader of the Warsaw Ghetto Uprising,* by Hanna Krall. Trans. Joanna Stasinska and Lawrence Weschler. New York: Henry Holt, 1986.

Atlas, James. *Bellow.* New York: Random House, 2000.

Auerbach, Ephraim, Isaac Charlish, and Moses Starkman, eds. *Leksikon fun der nayer yidisher literatur.* 8 vols. New York: Alveltlekhn yidishn kultur-kongres, 1956–81.

Baader, Benjamin M. "The Shoah, the Sacred, and Jewish Victim Identity in Postwar Germany and North America: The Scar Without the Wound and the Wound That Did Not Close." In *History, Memory, and Jewish Identity,* ed. Naftali Cohn, Lorenzo DiTomasso, and Ira Robinson, 257–93. Boston: Academic Studies Press of Boston, 2015.

Bacon, Gershon C. *The Politics of Tradition: Agudat Yisrael in Poland, 1916–1939.* Jerusalem: Magnes Press, 1996.

———. "Polish Jews and the Minorities Treaties Obligations, 1925: The View from Geneva (Documents from the League of Nations Archives)." *Gal-Ed* 18 (2002): 145–76.

Balin, Carole. *"To Reveal Our Hearts": Russian-Jewish Women Writers in Imperial Russia.* Cincinnati: Hebrew Union College Press, 2001.

Balint, Benjamin. *Running Commentary: The Contentious Magazine That Transformed the Jewish Left into the Neoconservative Right.* New York: Public Affairs, 2010.

Barkan, Elazar, Elizabeth A. Cole, and Kai Struve, eds. *Shared History—Divided Memory: Jews and Others in Soviet-Occupied Poland, 1939–1941.* Berlin: Simon-Dubnow-Institut für Jüdische Geschichte und Kultur, 2007.

Baron, Lawrence. "The Holocaust and American Public Memory, 1945–1960." *Holocaust and Genocide Studies* 17, no. 1 (2003): 62–88.

Bar-On, Mordecai. *In Pursuit of Peace: A History of the Israeli Peace Movement.* Washington, DC: United States of Peace Press, 1996.

Baron, Salo W. "Ghetto and Emancipation: Shall We Revise the Traditional View?" *Menorah Journal,* June 1928, 515–26.

———. *The Jewish Community: Its History and Structure to the American Revolution.* Westport, CT: Greenwood, 1942.

———. *A Social and Religious History of the Jews.* New York: Columbia University Press, 1937.

Bartal, Israel. *Galut Ba'arez: Yishuv erez-yisra'el beterem ziyonut, kovez maso umekhkarim.* Jerusalem: Zionist Library, 1994.

———. "The Image of Germany and German Jewry in East European Jewish Society During the Nineteenth Century." In *Danzig: Between East and West,* ed. Isadore Twersky, 1–17. Cambridge, MA: Harvard University Press, 1985.

Bartal, Israel. "The *Pinkas* of the Council of the Four Lands." In *The Jews in Old Poland, 1000–1795,* ed. Antony Polonsky, Jakub Basista, and Andrzej Link-Lenczowski, 110–18. London: I. B. Tauris, 1993.

Bartov, Omer. *Erased: Vanishing Traces of Jewish Galicia in Present-Day Ukraine.* Princeton, NJ: Princeton University Press, 2007.

———. *Germany's War and the Holocaust: Disputed Histories.* Ithaca, NY: Cornell University Press, 2003.

———. "Introduction to the Ukrainian Translation of *Erased.*" *Ab Imperio,* no. 1 (2010): 120–26.

———. "Review of Timothy Snyder, *Bloodlands: Europe Between Hitler and Stalin.*" *Slavic Review* 70, no. 2 (2011): 424–28.

Bauer, Yehuda. *American Jewry and the Holocaust: The American Jewish Joint Distribution Committee, 1939–1945.* Detroit: Wayne State University Press, 1981.

———. *The Death of the Shtetl.* New Haven, CT: Yale University Press, 2009.

———. *My Brother's Keeper: A History of the American Jewish Joint Distribution Committee, 1929–1939.* Philadelphia: Jewish Publication Society of America, 1974.

———. *Rethinking the Holocaust.* New Haven, CT: Yale University Press, 2001.

Baumel, Judith Tydor. *The "Bergson Boys" and the Origins of Contemporary Zionist Militancy.* Syracuse, NY: Syracuse University Press, 2005.

Beckerman, Gal. *When They Come for Us, We'll Be Gone: The Epic Struggle to Save Soviet Jewry.* New York: Mariner Books, Houghton Mifflin Harcourt, 2010.

Bender, Thomas. *Intellect and Public Life: Essays on the Social History of Academic Intellectuals in the United States.* Baltimore: Johns Hopkins University Press, 1993.

Benhabib, Seyla, and Raluca Eddon. "From Antisemitism to 'the Right to Have Rights': The Jewish Roots of Hannah Arendt's Cosmopolitanism." In *Antisemitism and Philosemitism in the Twentieth and Twenty-First Centuries,* ed. Phyllis Lassner and Lara Turbowitz, 63–80. Newark: University of Delaware Press, 2008.

Benton, Maya. *Roman Vishniac Rediscovered.* New York: International Center for Photography and DelMonico Books-Prestel, 2015.

Berenbaum, Michael. "The Uniqueness and Universality of the Holocaust." *American Journal of Theology and Philosophy* 2, no. 3 (1981): 85–96.

———. *The Vision of the Void: Theological Reflections on the Works of Elie Wiesel.* Middletown, CT: Wesleyan University Press, 1979.

Bergen, Doris L. *War and Genocide: A Concise History of the Holocaust.* New York: Rowman & Littlefield, 2003.

Berger, Alan L., and Naomi Berger, eds. *Second Generation Voices: Reflections by Children of Holocaust Survivors and Perpetrators.* Syracuse, NY: Syracuse University Press, 2001.

Berkhoff, Karel C. "Dina Pronicheva's Story of Surviving the Babi Yar Massacre: German, Jewish, Soviet, Russian, and Ukrainian Records." In *The Shoah in Ukraine: History, Testimony, Memorialization,* ed. Ray Brandon and Wendy Lower, 291–318. Bloomington: Indiana University Press, in association with the United States Holocaust Memorial Museum, 2008.

Biale, David. *Power and Powerlessness in Jewish History.* New York: Schocken, 1986.

Bikont, Anna. *The Crime and the Silence: Confronting the Massacre of Jews in Wartime Jedwabne*. New York: Farrar, Straus and Giroux, 2015.

Bildstein, Gerald. "A Note on the Function of 'The Law of the Land is the Law.'" *Jewish Journal of Sociology* 15 (1973): 213–19.

Bilsky, Leora. "Judging Evil in the Trial of Kastner." *Law and History Review* 19, no. 1 (2001): 117–60.

Birnbaum, Pierre. "Between Social and Political Assimilation: Remarks on the History of Jews in France." In *Paths of Emancipation: Jews, States, and Citizenship*, ed. Pierre Birnbaum and Ira Katznelson, 94–127. Princeton, NJ: Princeton University Press, 1995.

Birnbaum, Pierre, and Ira Katznelson, eds. *Paths of Emancipation: Jews, States, and Citizenship*. Princeton, NJ: Princeton University Press, 1995.

Birnbaum, Solomon A. *Yiddish: A Survey and a Grammar*. Toronto: University of Toronto Press, 1979.

Biskupski, Mieczysław. "Poland and the Poles in the Cinematic Portrayal of the Holocaust." In *Rethinking Poles and Jews: Troubled Past, Brighter Future*, ed. Robert Cherry and Annamaria Orla-Bukowska, 27–43. New York: Rowman & Littlefield, 2007.

Blejwas, Stanislaus A. "The National Polish American-Jewish American Council: A Short History." *Polin* 19 (2007): 257–85.

Bloch, Avital Hadassah. "The Emergence of Neoconservatism in the United States, 1960–1972." PhD diss., Columbia University, 1990.

Bloch, Marc. *The Historian's Craft*. New York: Vintage, 1953.

Blower, Brooke Lindy. *Becoming Americans in Paris: Transatlantic Politics and Culture Between the World Wars*. New York: Oxford University Press, 2011.

Borstelmann, Thomas. *The 1970s: A New Global History from Civil Rights to Economic Inequality*. Princeton, NJ: Princeton University Press, 2012.

Braiterman, Zachary. *(God) After Auschwitz: Tradition and Change in Post-Holocaust Jewish Thought*. Princeton, NJ: Princeton University Press, 1998.

Breitman, Richard, and Allan J. Lichtman. *FDR and the Jews*. Cambridge, MA: Belknap Press, 2013.

Brenner, Michael. *After the Holocaust: Rebuilding Jewish Lives in Postwar Germany*. Princeton, NJ: Princeton University Press, 1997.

———. *Prophets of the Past: Interpreters of Jewish History*. Trans. Steven Rendall. Princeton, NJ: Princeton University Press, 2010.

Brick, Howard, and Christopher Phelps. *Radicals in America: The U.S. Left since the Second World War*. Cambridge: Cambridge University Press, 2015.

Bridenbaugh, Carl. "The Great Mutation." *American Historical Review* 68, no. 2 (1963): 315–31.

Brinkley, Alan. "1968 and the Unraveling of America." In *1968: The World Transformed*, ed. Carole Fink, Philipp Gassert, and Detlef Junker, 219–36. Washington, DC: German Historical Institute and Cambridge University Press, 1998.

———. *Voices of Protest: Huey Long, Father Coughlin, and the Great Depression*. New York: Vintage, 1982.

Brock, Peter. "Polish Nationalism." In *Nationalism in Eastern Europe*, ed. Peter Sugar and Ivo Lederer, 310–72. Seattle: University of Washington Press, 1969.

Brodkin, Karen. *How Jews Became White Folks and What That Says About Race in America*. New Brunswick, NJ: Rutgers University Press, 1998.

Bruch, Mia Sara. "The Fatherhood of God and the Brotherhood of Man: American Jews and American Religious Pluralism, 1939–1960." PhD diss., Stanford University, 2006.

Bruford, W. H. *The German Tradition of Self-Cultivation: "Bildung" from Humboldt to Thomas Mann*. Cambridge: Cambridge University Press, 1975.

Buhle, Paul. "Jews and American Communism: The Cultural Question." *Radical History Review* 3 (Spring 1980): 9–33.

Carenen, Caitlin. *The Fervent Embrace: Liberal Protestants, Evangelicals, and Israel*. New York: New York University Press, 2012.

Carlebach, Elisheva. *The Pursuit of Heresy: Rabbi Moses Hagiz and the Sabbatian Controversies*. New York: Columbia University Press, 1990.

Chazan, Robert. *European Jewry and the First Crusade*. Berkeley: University of California Press, 1987.

Cherry, Robert. "Middle Minority Theories: Their Implications for Black-Jewish Relations." *Journal of Ethnic Studies* 17 (Spring 1990): 117–38.

Cherry, Robert, and Annamaria Orla-Bukowska, eds. *Rethinking Poles and Jews: Troubled Past, Brighter Future*. New York: Rowman & Littlefield, 2007.

Clark, Kenneth B. "Candor About Negro-Jewish Relations." *Commentary*, February 1946, 8–14.

Cohen, Boaz. "Rachel Auerbach, Yad Vashem, and Israeli Holocaust Memory." *Polin* 20 (2008): 197–220.

Cohen, Naomi W. *Not Free to Desist: The American Jewish Committee, 1906–1966*. Philadelphia: Jewish Publication Society of America, 1972.

Cohen, Richard I. "Breaking the Code: Hannah Arendt's *Eichmann in Jerusalem* and the Public Polemic—Myth, Memory and Historical Imagination." *Michael* 13 (1993): 29–85.

———. "A Generation's Response to *Eichmann in Jerusalem*." In *Hannah Arendt in Jerusalem*, ed. Steven Aschheim, 253–77. Berkeley: University of California Press, 2001.

———. "Jews and the State: The Historical Context." In *Studies in Contemporary Jewry*, vol. 19: *Dangerous Alliances and the Perils of Privilege*, ed. Ezra Mendelsohn, 3–16. New York: Oxford University Press, 2003.

Cohen Grossman, Grace. "Scholar as Political Activist: Salo W. Baron and the Founding of Jewish Cultural Reconstruction." In *For Every Thing a Season: Proceedings of the Symposium on Jewish Ritual Art*, ed. Joseph Gutmann, 146–57. Cleveland: Cleveland State University, 2002.

Cole, Diane. "Lucy Dawidowicz—A Profile." *Present Tense* 11, no. 1 (1983): 22–25.

Collier, Peter. *Political Woman: The Big Little Life of Jeane Kirkpatrick*. New York: Encounter, 2012.

Collini, Stefani. "'Every Fruit-Juice Drinker, Nudist, Sandal-Wearer': Intellectuals as Other People." In *The Public Intellectual*, ed. Helen Small, 203–23. Cambridge: Oxford University Press, 2002.

Confino, Alon. *A World Without Jews: The Nazi Imagination from Persecution to Genocide*. New Haven, CT: Yale University Press, 2014.

Cook, Richard M. *Alfred Kazin: A Biography*. New Haven, CT: Yale University Press, 2007.

Cooney, Terry A. "New York Intellectuals and the Question of Jewish Identity." *American Jewish History* 80, no. 3 (1991): 344–60.

———. *The Rise of the New York Intellectuals: Partisan Review and Its Circle*. Madison: University of Wisconsin Press, 1986.

Davies, Norman. *God's Playground: A History of Poland*. New York: Columbia University Press, 1982.

———. "The Survivor's Voice (Review, *Shielding the Flame: Conversations with Dr. Marek Edelman, the Last Surviving Leader of the Warsaw Ghetto Uprising*)." *New York Review of Books*, November 20, 1986, 21–23.

Davis, Joseph. "The Reception of the Shulhan 'Arukh and the Formation of Ashkenazic Jewish Identity." *AJS Review* 26, no. 2 (2002): 251–76.

Davis, Marni. *Jews and Booze: Becoming American in the Age of Prohibition*. New York: New York University Press, 2012.

Dawidowicz, Lucy S., Alexander Erlich, Rachel Erlich, and Joshua A. Fishman, eds. *For Max Weinreich on His Seventieth Birthday: Studies in Jewish Languages, Literature, and Society*. London: Mouton, 1964.

Dekel-Chen, Jonathan, David Gaunt, Natan M. Meir, and Israel Bartal, eds. *Anti-Jewish Violence*. Bloomington: Indiana University Press, 2010.

Desbois, Patrick. *The Holocaust by Bullets: A Priest's Journey to Uncover the Truth Behind the Murder of 1.5 Million Jews*. New York: Palgrave Macmillan, 2008.

Deslippe, Dennis. *Protesting Affirmative Action: The Struggle over Equality after the Civil Rights Revolution*. Baltimore: Johns Hopkins University Press, 2012.

Deutscher, Isaac. *The Non-Jewish Jew and Other Essays*. London: Oxford University Press, 1968.

Diner, Dan. "Hannah Arendt Reconsidered: On the Banal and the Evil in Her Holocaust Narrative." *New German Critique* 71 (Spring–Summer 1997): 177–90.

———. "Negative Symbiose: Deutsche und Juden nach Auschwitz." *Babylon: Beiträge zur jüdischen Gegenwart* 1 (1986): 9–20.

Diner, Hasia R. *The Jews of the United States, 1654–2000*. Berkeley: University of California Press, 2004.

———. *We Remember with Reverence and Love: American Jews and the Myth of Silence after the Holocaust, 1945–1962*. New York: New York University Press, 2009.

Dobroszycki, Lucjan, and Barbara Kirshenblatt-Gimblett. *Image Before My Eyes: A Photographic History of Jewish Life in Poland, 1864–1939*. New York: Schocken, 1977.

Dollinger, Marc. "Exceptionalism Revisited." *American Jewish History* 90, no. 2 (2002): 161–64.

———. *Quest for Inclusion: Jews and Liberalism in Modern America*. Princeton, NJ: Princeton University Press, 2000.

Dorrien, Gary J. *The Neoconservative Mind: Politics, Culture, and the War of Ideology*. Philadelphia: Temple University Press, 1993.

Dreifuss, Havi. "The Leadership of the Jewish Combat Organization during the Warsaw Ghetto Uprising: A Reassessment." *Holocaust and Genocide Studies* 31, no. 1 (2017): 24–60.

Dubin, Lois C. "Yosef Hayim Yerushalmi, the Royal Alliance, and Jewish Political Theory." *Jewish History* 28 (2014): 51–81.

Dubnov, Arie. "From Hilberg to Arendt (and Back Again?): Notes on *The Destruction of the European Jews* and the Banality of Evil." *Tabor* 7 (2016): 54–62.

Dynner, Glenn, and François Guesnet, eds. *Warsaw: The Jewish Metropolis: Essays in Honor of the 75th Birthday of Antony Polonsky.* Leiden and Boston: Brill, 2015.

Echols, Alice. *Daring to Be Bad: Radical Feminism in America, 1967–1975.* Minneapolis: University of Minnesota Press, 1989.

Edel, Leon. "The Making of an Historian." *Partisan Review* 57, no. 2 (1990): 306–8.

Efron, John M. *German Jewry and the Allure of the Sephardic.* Princeton, NJ: Princeton University Press, 2016.

Ehrman, John. "*Commentary*, the *Public Interest*, and the Problem of Jewish Conservatism." *American Jewish History* 87, no. 2–3 (1999): 159–81.

———. *The Eighties: America in the Age of Reagan.* New Haven, CT: Yale University Press, 2005.

———. *The Rise of Neoconservatism: Intellectuals and Foreign Affairs, 1945–1994.* New Haven, CT: Yale University Press, 1995.

Eisenbach, Artur. "Jewish Historiography in Interwar Poland." In *The Jews of Poland between Two World Wars*, ed. Yisrael Gutman, Ezra Mendelsohn, Jehuda Reinharz, and Chone Shmeruk, 453–93. Hanover, NH: University Press of New England, 1989.

Eisler, Jerzy. "Antisemitism, Emigration." In *1968: Forty Years After*, ed. Leszek W. Głuchowski and Antony Polonsky, 37–61. *Polin*, vol. 21. Oxford: Littman Library of Jewish Civilization, 2009.

Elazar, Daniel J. "American Political Theory and the Political Notions of American Jews: Convergences and Contradictions." In *The Ghetto and Beyond: Essays in Jewish Life in America*, ed. Peter I. Rose, 203–27. New York: Random House, 1969.

Ellis, John Tracy. *American Catholicism.* Chicago: University of Chicago Press, 1969.

Engel, David. "Crisis and Lachrymosity: On Salo Baron, Neobaronianism, and the Study of Modern European Jewish History." *Jewish History* 20, no. 3–4 (2006): 243–64.

———. *Historians of the Jews and the Holocaust.* Stanford, CA: Stanford University Press, 2010.

———. "The Holocaust: History and Metahistory in Three Recent Works." *Jewish Quarterly Review* 95, no. 4 (2005): 685–93.

———. *The Holocaust: The Third Reich and the Jews.* London: Longman, Pearson, 2000.

———. "Perceptions of Power—Poland and World Jewry." *Jahrbuch des Simon-Dubnow-Instituts* 1 (2002): 17–28.

Erbelding, Rebecca. *Rescue Board: The Untold Story of America's Efforts to Save the Jews of Europe.* New York: Doubleday, 2018.

Estraikh, Gennady. *In Harness: Yiddish Writers' Romance with Communism.* Syracuse, NY: Syracuse University Press, 2005.

Ettinger, Shmuel. "The Beginnings of the Change in the Attitude of European Society Towards the Jews." *Scripta Hierosolymitana* 7 (1961): 193–219.

———. "The Council of the Four Lands." In *The Jews in Old Poland, 1000–1795*, ed. Antony Polonsky, Jakub Basista, and Andrzej Link-Lenczowski, 93–109. London: I. B. Tauris, 1993.

Ezrahi, Yaron. *Rubber Bullets: Power and Conscience in Modern Israel*. New York: Farrar, Straus and Giroux, 1997.

Farrell, William E. "The New Face of Israel: Hawk on a Mission of Peace." *New York Times Magazine*, July 17, 1977, 47–52.

Feinberg, Melissa. "Die Durchsetzung einer neuen Welt. Politische Prozesse in Osteuropa, 1948–1954." In *Angst im Kalten Krieg*, ed. Bernd Greiner, Christian Th. Müller, and Dierk Walter, 190–219. Hamburg: Hamburger Edition, 2009.

Feiner, Shmuel. *The Jewish Enlightenment*. Trans. Chaya Naor. Philadelphia: University of Pennsylvania, 2004.

———. "The Modern Jewish Woman: Test Case in the Relationship between the Haskalah and Modernity." *Zion* 58, no. 4 (1993): 453–99.

———. "Toward a Historical Definition of the Haskalah." In *New Perspectives on the Haskalah*, ed. Shmuel Feiner and David Sorkin, 184–219. London: Littman Library of Jewish Civilization, 2001.

Feingold, Henry. "*Bildung*: Was It Good for the Jews?" *American Jewish Archives* 40, no. 2 (1988): 243–47.

Feld, Marjorie N. *Nations Divided: American Jews and the Struggle over Apartheid*. New York: Palgrave Macmillan, 2014.

Fermaglich, Kirsten. *American Dreams and Nazi Nightmares: Early Holocaust Consciousness and Liberal America, 1957–1965*. Waltham, MA: Brandeis University Press and University Press of New England, 2006.

Finder, Gabriel N. "The Warsaw Ghetto Uprising in the Courtroom." Paper presented at the annual conference of the Association for Jewish Studies, San Diego, 2016.

Finder, Gabriel N., and Alexander V. Prusin. "Collaboration in Eastern Galicia: The Ukrainian Police and the Holocaust." *East European Jewish Affairs* 34, no. 2 (2014): 95–118.

Fishman, David E. *The Book Smugglers: Partisans, Poets, and the Race to Save Jewish Treasures from the Nazis*. Lebanon, NH: ForeEdge, 2017.

———. *Embers Plucked from the Fire: The Rescue of Jewish Cultural Treasures in Vilna*. New York: YIVO Institute for Jewish Research, 1996.

———. "From Yiddishism to American Judaism: The Impact of American Yiddish Schools on Their Students." In *Imagining the American Jewish Community*, ed. Jack Wertheimer, 271–86. Waltham, MA: Brandeis University Press, 2007.

———. *The Rise of Modern Yiddish Culture*. Pittsburgh: University of Pittsburgh Press, 2005.

———. *Russia's First Modern Jews: The Jews of Shklov*. New York: New York University Press, 1995.

Fitzpatrick, Sheila. "Revisionism in Soviet History." *History and Theory* 46, no. 4 (2007): 77–91.

Flamm, Michael W. "'Law and Order' at Large: The New York Civilian Review Board Referendum of 1966 and the Crisis of Liberalism." *Historian* 64, no. 3–4 (2002): 643–65.

Foley, Barbara. "Fact, Fiction, Fascism: Testimony and Mimesis in Holocaust Narrative." *Comparative Literature* 34, no. 4 (1982): 330–60.

Frankel, Jonathan. *Prophecy and Politics: Socialism, Nationalism, and the Russian Jews, 1862–1917.* Cambridge: Cambridge University Press, 1981.

Freidenreich, Fradle Pomerantz. *Passionate Pioneers: The Story of Yiddish Secular Education in North America, 1910–1960.* New York: Holmes & Meier, 2010.

Friedberg, Maurice. *A Decade of Euphoria: Western Literature in Post-Stalin Russia, 1954–64.* Bloomington: Indiana University Press, 1977.

———. *Literary Translation in Russia: A Cultural History.* University Park: Pennsylvania State University, 1997.

———. *Russian Classics in Soviet Jackets.* New York: Columbia University Press, 1962.

Friedländer, Saul. "A Conflict of Memories? The New German Debates About the 'Final Solution.'" *Leo Baeck Memorial Lecture* 31 (1987): 3–24.

———. *Nazi Germany and the Jews: The Years of Persecution, 1933–1939.* New York: HarperCollins, 1997.

———. *The Years of Extermination: Nazi Germany and the Jews, 1939–1945.* New York: HarperCollins, 2007.

Friedman, Murray. *The Neoconservative Revolution: Jewish Intellectuals and the Shaping of Public Policy.* Cambridge: Cambridge University Press, 2005.

———. *What Went Wrong? The Creation and Collapse of the Black-Jewish Alliance.* New York: Free Press, 1995.

Friesel, Ofra. "Equating Zionism with Racism: The 1965 Precedent." *American Jewish History* 97, no. 3 (2013): 283–313.

Funkenstein, Amos. "Collective Memory and Historical Consciousness." In *Perceptions of Jewish History*, 3–21. Berkeley: University of California Press, 1993.

———. *Perceptions of Jewish History.* Berkeley: University of California Press, 1993.

Galchinsky, Michael. *The Origin of the Modern Jewish Woman Writer: Romance and Reform in Victorian England.* Detroit: Wayne State University Press, 1996.

Gallas, Elisabeth. *"Das Leichenhaus der Bücher": Kulturrestitution und jüdisches Geschichts-denken nach 1945.* Göttingen: Vandenhoeck & Ruprecht, 2013.

———. "Preserving East European Jewish Culture—Lucy Dawidowicz and the Salvage of Books After the Holocaust." *Jahrbuch Des Simon-Dubnow Instituts/Simon Dubnow Institute Yearbook* 11 (2012): 73–89.

Gans, Herbert. "The Origin of a Jewish Community in the Suburbs." In *American Jews: A Reader*, ed. Marshall Sklare, 153–71. New York: Behrman, 1983.

Garrett, Leah. *Young Lions: How Jewish Authors Reinvented the American War Novel.* Evanston, IL: Northwestern University Press, 2015.

Gelles, Walter. "Lucy Dawidowicz, PW Interviews." *Publishers Weekly*, May 12, 1989, 264–65.

Gerstle, Gary. "The Protean Character of American Liberalism." *American Historical Review* 99, no. 4 (1994): 1043–73.

Gitelman, Zvi. "Politics and the Historiography of the Holocaust in the Soviet Union." In *Bitter Legacy: Confronting the Holocaust in the USSR*, 14–42. Bloomington: Indiana University Press, 1997.

Gitelman, Zvi, and Yaacov Ro'i, ed. *Evolution, Repression, and Revival: The Soviet Jewish Experience.* Lanham: Rowman & Littlefield, 2007.

Glenn, Susan A. *Daughters of the Shtetl: Life and Labor in the Immigrant Generation.* Ithaca, NY: Cornell University Press, 1990.

———. "The Vogue of Jewish Self-Hatred in Post-World War II America." *Jewish Social Studies* (New Series) 12, no. 3 (2006): 95–136.

Goffman, Ethan. *Imagining Each Other: Blacks and Jews in Contemporary American Literature.* Albany: State University of New York Press, 2000.

Goldhagen, Daniel Jonah. *Hitler's Willing Executioners: Ordinary Germans and the Holocaust.* New York: Knopf, 1996.

Goldman, Karla. "The Public Lives of Cincinnati's Jewish Women." In *Women and American Judaism*, ed. Pamela S. Nadell and Jonathan D. Sarna, 107–23. Hanover, NH: Brandeis University Press, 2001.

Goldscheider, Calvin. "Demography and American Jewish Survival." In *Zero Population Growth—For Whom? Differential Fertility and Minority Group Survival*, ed. Milton Himmelfarb and Victor Baras, 119–47. Westport, CT: Greenwood, 1975.

Goldstein, Eric L. *The Price of Whiteness: Jews, Race, and American Identity.* Princeton, NJ: Princeton University Press, 2006.

Gordon, Adi, and Udi Greenberg. "*The City of Man*, European Émigrés, and the Genesis of Postwar Conservative Thought." *Religions* 3 (2012): 681–98.

Gordon, Albert Isaac. *Jews in Suburbia.* Boston: Beacon, 1959.

Gorelick, Sherry. *City College and the Jewish Poor: Education in New York, 1880–1924.* New Brunswick, NJ: Rutgers University Press, 1981.

Goren, Arthur A. "A 'Golden Decade' for American Jews: 1945–1955." In *Studies in Contemporary Jewry*, vol. 8: *A New Jewry? America Since the Second World War*, ed. Peter Y. Medding, 3–20. New York: Oxford University Press, 1992.

———. *New York Jews and the Quest for Community: The Kehillah Experiment, 1908–1922.* New York: Columbia University Press, 1970.

———. "Orthodox Politics, Republican and Jewish: Jacob Saphirstein and the *Morgen Zhurnal*." *Proceedings of the Eighth World Congress of Jewish Studies* (1984): 63–71.

Gornick, Vivian. *The Men in My Life.* Boston: MIT Press, 2008.

Green, Nancy, ed. *Jewish Workers in the Modern Diaspora.* Berkeley: University of California, 1998.

Greenberg, Cheryl Lynn. *Troubling the Waters: Black-Jewish Relations in the American Century.* Princeton, NJ: Princeton University Press, 2006.

Greenfield, Jeanette. *The Return of Cultural Treasures.* Cambridge: Cambridge University Press, 2007.

Grinberg, Ronnie Avital. "Jewish Intellectuals, Masculinity, and the Making of Modern American Conservatism, 1930–1980." PhD diss., Northwestern University, 2010.

Gross, Jan T. *Fear: Anti-Semitism in Poland after Auschwitz.* Princeton, NJ: Princeton University Press, 2006.

———. *Neighbors: The Destruction of the Jewish Community in Jedwabne, Poland.* Princeton, NJ: Princeton University Press, 2001.

Grossmann, Atina. *Germans, Jews, and Allies: Close Encounters in Occupied Germany*. Princeton, NJ: Princeton University Press, 2007.

Grudzińska-Gross, Irena, and Iwa Nawrocki, eds. *Poland and Polin: New Interpretations in Polish-Jewish Studies*. New York: Peter Lang, 2016.

Gruen, George E. "The United States and Israel: Impact of the Lebanon War." *American Jewish Year Book* 84 (1983): 73–103.

Gruenewald, Max. "The Beginning of the 'Reichsvertreterung.'" *Leo Baeck Institute Year Book* 1, no. 1 (1956): 57–68.

Grupińska, Anka, Jan Jagielski, and Paweł Szapiro. *Warsaw Ghetto = Getto Warszawskie*. Warszawa: Wydawn. Parma-Press, 2002.

Gurock, Jeffrey S., and Jacob J. Schacter. *A Modern Heretic and a Traditional Community: Mordecai M. Kaplan, Orthodoxy, and American Judaism*. New York: Columbia University Press, 1997.

Gutman, Israel. *The Jews of Warsaw, 1939–1943: Ghetto, Underground, Revolt*. Bloomington: Indiana University Press, 1982.

Gutman, Israel, and Shmuel Krakowski. *Unequal Victims: Poles and Jews during World War II*. New York: Holocaust Library, 1986.

Hacohen, Malachi Haim. "'The Strange Fact That the State of Israel Exists': The Cold War Liberals between Cosmopolitanism and Nationalism." *Jewish Social Studies: History, Culture, Society* 15, no. 2 (2009): 37–81.

Hamerow, Theodore S. *Reflections on History and Historians*. Madison: University of Wisconsin Press, 1987.

Hamerow, Theodore S., Gertrude Himmelfarb, Lawrence W. Levine, Joan Wallach Scott, and John E. Toews. "AHR Forum: The Old History and the New." *AHR* 94 (June 1989).

Hartman, Geoffrey H. "Introduction." In *Bitburg in Moral and Political Perspective*, ed. Geoffrey H. Hartman, 1–12. Bloomington: Indiana University Press, 1986.

Haynes, Stephen R. "Holocaust Education at American Colleges and Universities: A Report on the Current Situation." *Holocaust and Genocide Studies* 12, no. 2 (1998): 282–306.

Haywood, Leslie, and Jennifer Drake, eds. *Third Wave Agenda: Being Feminist, Doing Feminism*. Minneapolis: University of Minnesota Press, 1977.

Heilbrunn, Jacob. *They Knew They Were Right: The Rise of the Neocons*. New York: Doubleday, 2008.

Hellbeck, Jochen. *Revolution on My Mind: Writing a Diary under Stalin*. Cambridge, MA: Harvard University Press, 2006.

Heller, Celia S. *On the Edge of Destruction: Jews of Poland between the Two World Wars*. New York: Columbia University Press, 1977.

Herman, Dana. "*Hashavat Avedah*: A History of Jewish Cultural Reconstruction, Inc." PhD diss., McGill University, Montreal, 2008.

Herzog, Jonathan P. *The Spiritual-Industrial Complex: America's Religious Battle against Communism in the Early Cold War*. New York: Oxford University Press, 2011.

Heschel, Susannah. *The Aryan Jesus: Christian Theologians and the Bible in Nazi Germany*. Princeton, NJ: Princeton University Press, 2008.

Higham, John. *Strangers in the Land: Patterns of American Nativism, 1850–1925.* New Brunswick, NJ: Rutgers University Press, 1958.

Hillgruber, Andreas. *Zweierlei Untergang: Die Zerschlagung des Deutschen Reiches und das Ende des Europäischen Judentums.* Berlin: Corso bei Siedler, 1986.

Himka, John-Paul. "The Reception of the Holocaust in Postcommunist Ukraine." In *Bringing the Dark Past to Light: The Reception of the Holocaust in Postcommunist Europe,* ed. John-Paul Himka and Joanna Beata Michlic, 626–61. Lincoln: University of Nebraska Press, 2013.

———. "Ukrainian Collaboration in the Extermination of the Jews during the Second World War: Sorting Out the Long-Term and Conjunctural Factors." In *Studies in Contemporary Jewry,* vol. 13: *The Fate of the European Jews, 1939–1945, Continuity or Contingency?* ed. Jonathan Frankel, 170–89. New York: Oxford University Press, 1997.

Hirszowicz, Łukasz. "A Conference on Polish-Jewish Relations." *Soviet Jewish Affairs* 13, no. 2 (1986): 67–70.

Hitchcock, William I. *The Bitter Road to Freedom: A New History of the Liberation of Europe.* New York: Free Press, 2008.

Hoeveler, J. David, Jr. *Watch on the Right: Conservative Intellectuals in the Reagan Era.* Madison: University of Wisconsin Press, 1991.

Hoffman, Matthew. "From Czernowitz to Paris: The International Yiddish Culture Congress of 1937." In *Czernowitz at 100: The First Yiddish Language Conference in Historical Perspective,* ed. Kalman Weiser and Joshua A. Fogel, 151–64. Lanham, MD: Rowman & Littlefield.

———. "From *Pintele Yid* to *Racenjude*: Chaim Zhitlovsky and Racial Conceptions of Jewishness." *Jewish History* 19 (2005): 65–78.

Hofstadter, Richard. *Anti-Intellectualism in American Life.* New York: Knopf, 1963.

Hollinger, David A. "Christianity and Its American Fate: Where History Interrogates Secularization Theory." In *The Worlds of American Intellectual History,* ed. Joel Isaac, James T. Kloppenberg, Michael O'Brien, and Jennifer Ratner-Rosenhagen, 280–303. New York: Oxford University Press, 2017.

———. "Ethnic Diversity, Cosmopolitanism and the Emergence of the American Liberal Imagination." *American Quarterly* 27, no. 2 (1975): 133–51.

——— "Rich, Powerful, and Smart: Jewish Overrepresentation Should Be Explained Instead of Avoided or Mystified." *Jewish Quarterly Review* 94, no. 4 (2004): 595–602.

———. *Science, Jews, and Secular Culture: Studies in Mid-Twentieth Century American Intellectual History.* Princeton, NJ: Princeton University Press, 1996.

Housden, Martyn. *Hans Frank: Lebensraum and the Holocaust.* New York: Palgrave Macmillan, 2003.

Howe, Irving. *World of Our Fathers: The Journey of the East European Jews to America and the Life They Found and Made.* With the assistance of Kenneth Libo. New York: Harcourt Brace Jovanovich, 1976.

Hudnut-Beumler, James. *Looking for God in the Suburbs: The Religion of the American Dream and Its Critics, 1945–1965.* New Brunswick, NJ: Rutgers University Press, 1994.

Huener, Jonathan. *Auschwitz, Poland, and the Politics of Commemoration, 1945–1979.* Athens: Ohio University Press, 2003.

Hundert, Gershon David. *Jews in Poland-Lithuania in the Eighteenth Century: A Genealogy of Modernity*. Berkeley: University of California Press, 2004.

——. "Some Basic Characteristics of Jewish Life in Poland." *Polin* 1, no. 1 (1986): 28–34.

Huppatz, Kate. "Reworking Bourdieu's 'Capital': Feminine and Female Capitals in the Field of Paid Caring Work." *Sociology* 43, no. 1 (2009): 45–66.

Hyman, Paula E. "We Are All Post-Jewish Historians Now: What American Jewish History Brings to the Table." *American Jewish History* 95, no. 1 (2009): 53–60.

Intrator, Miriam. *Books Across Borders: UNESCO and the Politics of Postwar Cultural Reconstruction, 1945–1951*. New York: Palgrave Macmillan, 2019.

Isenberg, Sheila. *A Hero of Our Own: The Story of Varian Fry*. New York: Random House, 2001.

Jackson, Kenneth T. *Crabgrass Frontier: The Suburbanization of the United States*. New York: Oxford University Press, 1985.

Jacobs, Jack. *The Frankfurt School, Jewish Lives, and Antisemitism*. New York: Cambridge University Press, 2015.

Jacobson, Matthew Frye. *Roots Too: White Ethnic Revival in Post-Civil Rights America*. Cambridge, MA: Harvard University Press, 2006.

——. *Whiteness of a Different Color: European Immigrants and the Alchemy of Race*. Cambridge, MA: Harvard University Press, 1999.

Jacoby, Susan. *Moscow Conversations*. New York: Coward, McCann & Geoghegan, 1972.

Janowsky, Oscar. *The Jews and Minority Rights (1898–1919)*. New York: AMS, 1966.

Jockusch, Laura. "Chroniclers of Catastrophe: History Writing as a Jewish Response to Persecution Before and After the Holocaust." In *Holocaust Historiography in Context: Emergence, Challenges, Polemics, and Achievements*, ed. David Bankier and Dan Michman, 135–66. Jerusalem: Yad Vashem, 2008.

——. *Collect and Record! Jewish Holocaust Documentation in Early Postwar Europe*. New York: Oxford University Press, 2012.

——. "*Khurbn Forshung*: Jewish Historical Commissions in Europe, 1943–1949." *Simon Dubnow Institute Yearbook* 6 (2007): 441–73.

Jockusch, Laura, and Gabriel N. Finder, eds. *Jewish Honor Courts: Revenge, Retribution, and Reconciliation in Europe and Israel after the Holocaust*. Detroit: Wayne State University Press, 2015.

Jumonville, Neil. *Critical Crossings: The New York Intellectuals in Postwar America*. Berkeley: University of California Press, 1991.

Kadosh, Sara, and Eric Nooter. "The American Jewish Joint Distribution Committee and Bergen-Belsen." In *Jewish Displaced Persons in Camp Bergen-Belsen 1945–1950: The Unique Photo Album of Zippy Orlin*, ed. Erik Somers and René Kok, 110–21. Seattle: University of Washington Press in association with Netherlands Institute for War Documentation, 1997.

Kahn, Ava F., and Adam D. Mendelsohn, eds. *Transnational Traditions: New Perspectives on American Jewish History*. Detroit: Wayne State University Press, 2014.

Kansteiner, Wulf. "From Exception to Exemplum: The New Approach to Nazism and the 'Final Solution.'" *History and Theory* 33, no. 2 (1994): 145–71.

Kaplan, Alice. *Dreaming in French: The Paris Years of Jacqueline Bouvier Kennedy, Susan Sontag, and Angela Davis*. Chicago: University of Chicago Press, 2012.

Kaplan, Edward K. *Spiritual Radical: Abraham Joshua Heschel in America, 1940–1972*. New Haven, CT: Yale University Press, 2007.

Karlip, Joshua M. "At the Crossroads between War and Genocide: A Reassessment of Jewish Ideology in 1940." *Jewish Social Studies* (New Series) 11, no. 2 (2005): 170–201.

———. *The Tragedy of a Generation: The Rise and Fall of Jewish Nationalism in Eastern Europe*. Cambridge, MA: Harvard University Press, 2013.

Kassow, Samuel D. *Who Will Write Our History? Emanuel Ringelblum, the Warsaw Ghetto, and the Oyneg Shabes Archive*. Bloomington: Indiana University Press, 2007.

Katriel, Tamar. *Dialogic Moments: From Soul Talks to Talk Radio in Israeli Culture*. Detroit: Wayne State University Press, 2004.

Katz, Barry M. "The Accumulation of Thought: Transformations of the Refugee Scholar in America (Review Essay)." *Journal of Modern History* 63, no. 4 (1991): 740–52.

———. "[Book Review] *The Holocaust and the Historians*, by Lucy S. Dawidowicz." *New German Critique* 26 (Spring–Summer 1982): 211–13.

Katznelson, Ira. "Between Separation and Disappearance: Jews on the Margins of American Liberalism." In *Paths of Emancipation: Jews, States, and Citizenship*, ed. Pierre Birnbaum and Ira Katznelson, 157–205. Princeton, NJ: Princeton University Press, 1995.

Kaufman, Jonathan. "Blacks and Jews: The Struggle in the Cities." In *Struggles in the Promised Land: Toward a History of Black-Jewish Relations in the United States*, ed. Jack Salzman and Cornel West, 107–21. New York: Oxford University Press, 1997.

———. *Broken Alliance: The Turbulent Times between Blacks and Jews in America*. New York: Charles Scribner's Sons, 1988.

Kaufmann, Thomas. *Luther's Jews: A Journey into Anti-Semitism*. Trans. Lesley Sharpe and Jeremy Noakes. New York: Oxford University Press, 2017.

Kershaw, Ian. *The Nazi Dictatorship: Problems and Perspectives of Interpretation*. New York: E. Arnold, 1989.

Kessner, Carole S., ed. "From This Place and Time: An Interview with Lucy Dawidowicz." *Reconstructionist* 55, no. 3 (1990): 28–31.

———. *Marie Syrkin: Values Beyond the Self*. Hanover, NH: Brandeis University Press and University Press of New England, 2008.

———. *The "Other" New York Jewish Intellectuals*. New York: New York University Press, 1994.

Khalidi, Rashid. *Under Siege: P.L.O. Decisionmaking During the 1982 War*. New York: Columbia University Press, 1986.

Kimmage, Michael. *The Conservative Turn: Lionel Trilling, Whittaker Chambers, and the Lessons of Anti-Communism*. Harvard University Press, 2009.

Kirshenblatt-Gimblett, Barbara. "Imagining Europe: The Popular Arts of American Jewish Ethnography." In *Divergent Centers: Shaping Jewish Cultures in Israel and America*, ed. Deborah Dash Moore and Ilan Troen, 155–91. New Haven, CT: Yale University Press, 2001.

———. "Introduction." In *Awakening Lives: Autobiographies of Jewish Youth in Poland before the Holocaust*, ed. Barbara Kirshenblatt-Gimblett, Marcus Moseley, Michael Stanislawski, and Jeffrey Shandler. New Haven, CT: Yale University Press, 2002.

Kirshenblatt-Gimblett, Barbara, ed. *Writing a Modern Jewish History: Essays in Honor of Salo W. Baron*. New Haven, CT: Yale University Press, 2006.

Klapper, Melissa. *Ballots, Babies, and Banners of Peace: American Jewish Women's Pre–World War II Activism*. New York: New York University Press, 2012.

———. "'A Long and Broad Education': Jewish Girls and the Problem of Education in America, 1860–1920." *Journal of American Ethnic History* 22, no. 1 (2002): 3–31.

Klatch, Rebecca E. *Women of the New Right*. Philadelphia: Temple University Press, 1987.

Klier, John D., and Shlomo Lambroza, eds. *Pogroms: Anti-Jewish Violence in Modern Russian History*. Cambridge: Cambridge University Press, 1992.

Kobrin, Rebecca A. "American Jewish Philanthropy, Polish Jewry and the Crisis of 1929." In *1929: Mapping the Jewish World*, ed. Hasia Diner and Gennady Estraikh, 73–93. New York: New York University Press, 2013.

———, ed. *Chosen Capital: The Jewish Encounter with American Capitalism*. New Brunswick, NJ: Rutgers University Press, 2012.

———. "Destructive Creators: Sender Jarmulowsky and Financial Failure in the Annals of American Jewish History." *American Jewish History* 97, no. 2 (2013): 105–37.

———. *Jewish Bialystok and Its Diaspora*. Bloomington: Indiana University Press, 2010.

Königseder, Angelika, and Juliane Wetzel. "DP Camps 1945–1950: The British Section." In *Belsen in History and Memory*, ed. Jo Reilly, David Cesarani, Tony Kushner, and Colin Richmond, 42–55. London: Frank Cass, 1997.

———. *Waiting for Hope: Jewish Displaced Persons in Post-World War II Germany*. Evanston, IL: Northwestern University Press, 2001.

Korey, William. "A Monument Over Babi Yar?" In *The Holocaust in the Soviet Union: Studies and Sources on the Destruction of the Jews in the Nazi-Occupied Territories of the USSR, 1941–1945*, ed. Lucjan Dobroszycki and Jeffrey S. Gurock, 61–74. Armonk, NY: M. E. Sharpe, 1993.

Korman, Gerd. "The Holocaust in American Historical Writing." *Societas: A Review of Social History* 2 (Summer 1972): 250–70.

Krah, Markus. *American Jewry and the Re-Invention of the East European Jewish Past*. Oldenbourg: De Gruyter, 2018.

———. "Role Models or Foils for American Jews? The Eternal Light, Displaced Persons, and the Construction of Jewishness in Mid-Twentieth-Century America." *American Jewish History* 96, no. 4 (2010): 265–86.

Krall, Hanna. *Shielding the Flame: An Intimate Conversation with Dr. Marek Edelman, the Last Surviving Leader of the Warsaw Ghetto Uprising*. Trans. Joanna Stasinska and Lawrence Weschler. New York: Henry Holt, 1986.

Krylova, Anna. "Soviet Modernity: Stephen Kotkin and the Bolshevik Predicament." *Contemporary European History* 23, no. 2 (2014): 167–92.

Kugelmass, Jack, and Jonathan Boyarin, eds. *From a Ruined Garden: The Memorial Books of Polish Jewry*. Bloomington: Indiana University Press, 1998.

Kurtz, Michael J. *America and the Return of Nazi Contraband: The Recovery of Europe's Cultural Treasures*. Cambridge: Cambridge University Press, 2006.

Kuznets, Simon. *Jewish Economics: Development and Migration in American and Beyond*. Ed. Stephanie Lo and E. Glen Weyl. New Brunswick, NJ: Transaction, 2012.

Kuznitz, Cecile E. "An-Sky's Legacy: The Vilna Historic-Ethnographic Society and the Shaping of Modern Jewish Culture." In *The Worlds of S. An-Sky*, ed. Gabriella Safran and Steven J. Zipperstein, 320–45. Stanford, CA: Stanford University Press, 2006.

———. "On the Jewish Street: Yiddish Culture and the Urban Landscape in Interwar Vilna." In *Yiddish Language and Culture: Then and Now*, ed. Leonard J. Greenspoon, 65–92. Omaha: NE, Creighton University Press, 1998.

———. *YIVO and the Making of Modern Jewish Culture: Scholarship for the Yiddish Nation*. New York: Cambridge University Press, 2014.

Lang, Berel. *Act and Idea in the Nazi Genocide*. Syracuse, NY: Syracuse University Press, 2003.

Langmuir, Gavin I. *History, Religion, and Antisemitism*. Berkeley: University of California Press, 1990.

———. "Majority History and Post-Biblical Jews." *Journal of the History of Ideas* 27, no. 3 (1966): 343–64.

———. *Toward a Definition of Antisemitism*. Berkeley: University of California Press, 1990.

———. "Tradition, History, and Prejudice." *Jewish Social Studies* 30, no. 3 (1968): 157–68.

Lavsky, Hagit. "British Jewry and the Jews in Post-Holocaust Germany: The Jewish Relief Unit, 1945–1950." *Journal of Holocaust Education* 4, no. 1 (1995): 29–40.

Lederhendler, Eli. *New York Jews and the Decline of Urban Ethnicity, 1950–1970*. Syracuse, NY: Syracuse University Press, 2001.

———. *The Road to Modern Jewish Politics: Political Tradition and Political Reconstruction in the Jewish Community of Tsarist Russia*. New York: Oxford University Press, 1989.

Leff, Lisa Moses. *The Archive Thief: The Man Who Salvaged French Jewish History in the Wake of the Holocaust*. New York: Oxford University Press, 2015.

Lehmann-Haupt, Christopher. "A Key to the 'Final Solution.'" Review of Lucy S. Dawidowicz, *The War Against the Jews*." *New York Times*, June 12, 1975, 35.

Leonard, John. "[Book Review] *The Holocaust and the Historians*, by Lucy S. Dawidowicz." *New York Times*, September 3, 1981.

Lerner, Stephen C. "The *Havurot*: An Experiment in Jewish Communal Living." In *Jewish Radicalism*, ed. Jack Nusan Porter and Peter Dreier, 149–67. New York: Grove, 1973.

Lester, Eleanor. "Historian of the Jews: A Life in Progress." *Jewish Week*, June 9, 1989, 2, 40.

Lester, Julius. *Lovesong: Becoming a Jew*. New York: Henry Holt, 1988.

Levavi, Ya'akov. *Hahityashvut hayehudit bebirobig'an*. Jerusalem: Hahevrah hahistorit hayis-re'elit, 1965.

Levin, Dov. "The Jews of Vilna under Soviet Rule, 19 September–28 October 1939." *Polin* 9 (1996): 107–37.

Levin, Nora. *The Holocaust: The Destruction of European Jewry, 1933–1945*. New York: T. Y. Crowell, 1978.

Levinson, Julian. *Exiles on Main Street: Jewish American Writers and American Literary Culture*. Bloomington: Indiana University Press, 2008.

Levitt, Laura. "Impossible Assimilations, American Liberalism, and Jewish Difference: Revisiting Jewish Secularism." *American Quarterly* 59, no. 3 (2007): 807–32.

Lewis, David Levering. "Parallels and Divergences: Assimilationist Strategies of Afro-American and Jewish Elites from 1910 to the Early 1930s." *Journal of American History* 71, no. 3 (1984): 543–64.

Liberles, Robert. *Salo Wittmayer Baron: Architect of Jewish History*. New York: New York University Press, 1995.

Liebman, Arthur. "The Ties That Bind: Jewish Support for the Left in the United States." In *Essential Papers on Jews and the Left*, ed. Ezra Mendelsohn, 322–57. New York: New York University Press, 1997.

Liebman, Stuart. *Claude Lanzmann's Shoah: Key Essays*. Oxford: Oxford University Press, 2007.

Lifshits, Y., ed. *Shatski-bukh: Opshatsungen vegn yankev shatski un shatskis zikhroynes, briv, referatn un eseyen*. New York and Buenos Aires: YIVO, 1958.

Lifton, Robert Jay. *The Nazi Doctors: Medical Killing and the Psychology of Genocide*. New York: Basic, 1986.

Lilla, Mark. *The Shipwrecked Mind: On Political Reaction*. New York: New York Review Books, 2016.

Linden, Diana L. "An Introduction to the Visual and Material Culture of New York City Jews, 1920–2010." In *City of Promises: A History of the Jews of New York*, by Annie Polland and Daniel Soyer, 2:223–54. New York: New York University Press, 2012.

Linenthal, Edward T. *Preserving Memory: The Struggle to Create America's Holocaust Museum*. New York: Penguin, 1995.

Lipstadt, Deborah E. "The Bitburg Controversy." *American Jewish Year Book* 87 (1986): 21–37.

———. *Denying the Holocaust: The Growing Assault on Truth and Memory*. New York: Free Press, 1993.

———. "The Failure to Rescue and Contemporary American Jewish Historiography of the Holocaust: Judging from a Distance." In *The Bombing of Auschwitz: Should the Allies Have Attempted It?* ed. Michael J Neufeld and Michael Berenbaum, 227–36. New York: St. Martin's, 2000.

———. *History On Trial: My Day in Court with David Irving*. New York: Ecco, 2005.

———. *Holocaust: An American Understanding*. New Brunswick, NJ: Rutgers University Press, 2016.

———. *Playing the Blame Game: American Jews Look Back at the Holocaust*. Ann Arbor: Regents of the University of Michigan, Jean & Samuel Frankel Center for Judaic Studies, 2011.

Liskofsky, Sidney. "U.N. Resolution on Zionism." *American Jewish Year Book* 77 (1977): 97–126.

Litvak, Olga. *Haskalah: The Romantic Movement in Judaism*. New Brunswick, NJ: Rutgers University Press, 2012.

Loeffler, James. *Rooted Cosmopolitans: Jews and Human Rights in the Twentieth Century*. New Haven, CT: Yale University Press, 2018.

Mack, Phyllis. "Religion, Feminism, and the Problem of Agency: Reflections on Eighteenth-Century Quakerism." *Signs* 29, no. 1 (2003): 149–77.

MacLean, Nancy. *Freedom Is Not Enough: The Opening of the American Workplace*. New York and Cambridge, MA: Russell Sage Foundation and Harvard University Press, 2006.

Malia, Martin. "What Is the Russian Intelligentsia?" *Daedalus* 89, no. 3 (1960): 441–58.

Mandel, Ralph. "Israel in 1982: The War in Lebanon." *American Jewish Year Book* 84 (1983): 3–72.

Mankowitz, Zeev W. *Life Between Memory and Hope: The Survivors of the Holocaust in Occupied Germany*. Cambridge: Cambridge University Press, 2002.

Mann, Rochelle. "Distinguished Speakers Vivify Yiddish Poetry." *Observer*, May 29, 1970, 8.

Marcus, Jacob Rader. *The American Jewish Woman: A Documentary History*. New York: Ktav, 1981.

Markham, James M. "The War That Won't Go Away." *New York Times Magazine*, October 9, 1977, 33, 45, 48, 52.

Markowitz, Ruth Jacknow. *My Daughter, The Teacher: Jewish Teachers in the New York City Schools*. New Brunswick, NJ: Rutgers University Press, 1993.

Marrus, Michael R. *The Holocaust in History*. New York: New American Library, 1987.

Martin, Sean. *Jewish Life in Cracow, 1918–1939*. London: Vallentine Mitchell, 2004.

Martin, Terry. *The Affirmative Action Empire: Nations and Nationalism in the Soviet Union, 1923–1939*. Ithaca, NY: Cornell University Press, 2001.

Mazower, Mark. *No Enchanted Palace: The End of Empire and the Ideological Origins of the United Nations*. Princeton, NJ: Princeton University Press, 2009.

McAlister, Melani. "One Black Allah: The Middle East in the Cultural Politics of African American Liberation, 1955–1970." *American Quarterly* 51, no. 3 (1999): 622–56.

Mendelsohn, Ezra. "Interwar Poland: Good for the Jews or Bad for the Jews?" In *The Jews in Poland*, ed. Chimen Abramsky, Maciej Jachimczyk, and Antony Polonsky, 130–39. Oxford: Basil Blackwell, 1986.

———. *The Jews of East Central Europe between the World Wars*. Bloomington: Indiana University Press, 1983.

———. *On Modern Jewish Politics*. Oxford: Oxford University Press, 1993.

Mendes-Flohr, Paul. "The Berlin Jew as Cosmopolitan." In *Berlin Metropolis: Jews and the New Culture, 1890–1918*, ed. Emily Bilski, 14–31. Berkeley: University of California Press, 1999.

Mendes-Flohr, Paul, and Jehuda Reinharz. *The Jew in the Modern World: A Documentary History*. 3rd ed. Oxford: Oxford University Press, 2010.

Meyer, Michael A., ed. *Ideas of Jewish History*. New York: Behrman, 1974.

Michels, Tony. *A Fire in Their Hearts: Yiddish Socialists in New York*. Cambridge, MA: Harvard University Press, 2005.

———. "Socialism with a Jewish Face: The Origins of the Yiddish-Speaking Communist Movement in the United States, 1907–1923." In *Yiddish and the Left: Papers of the Third Mendel Friedman International Conference on Yiddish*, ed. Gennady Estraikh and Mikhail Krutikov, 24–55. Oxford: Legenda, 2001.

———. "Socialism and the Writing of American Jewish History: *World of Our Fathers* Revisited." *American Jewish History* 88, no. 4 (2000): 521–46.

Michman, Dan. *Holocaust Historiography: A Jewish Perspective*. London: Vallentine Mitchell, 2003.

———. "Jewish Leadership in Extremis." In *The Historiography of the Holocaust*, ed. Dan Stone, 319–40. Basingstoke, UK: Palgrave Macmillan, 2004.

Miller, Judith. *One by One, by One: Facing the Holocaust*. New York: Simon and Schuster, 1990.

———. "A Washington Memorial Has Been Tangled in Bitter Disputes Over What It Should Be." *New York Times Magazine*, April 22, 1990, 35, 42, 47–48.

Mintz, Alan. *"Banished from Their Father's Table": Loss of Faith and Hebrew Autobiography*. Bloomington: Indiana University Press, 1989.

———. *Popular Culture and the Shaping of Holocaust Memory in America*. Seattle: University of Washington Press, 2001.

Miron, Guy. "Autobiography as a Source for Writing Social History—German Jews in Palestine/Israel as a Case Study." *Tel Aviver Jahrbuch für Deutsche Geschichte* 29 (2000): 251–81.

Moore, Deborah Dash, ed. *At Home in America: Second Generation New York Jews*. New York: Columbia University Press, 1981.

———, ed. *East European Jews in Two Worlds: Studies from the YIVO Annual*. Evanston, IL: Northwestern University Press, 1990.

———. "From David to Goliath: American Representations of Jews Around the Six-Day War." In *The Six-Day War and World Jewry*, ed. Eli Lederhendler, 69–80. Baltimore: University Press of Maryland, 2000.

———. *GI Jews: How World War II Changed a Generation*. Cambridge, MA: Belknap Press of Harvard University, 2004.

———. "Reconsidering the Rosenbergs: Symbol and Substance in Second Generation American Jewish Consciousness." *Journal of American Ethnic History* 8, no. 1 (1988): 20–37.

Morgan, Thomas B. "The Vanishing American Jew." *Look*, May 5, 1964, 42–46.

Moseley, Marcus. *Being for Myself Alone: Origins of Jewish Autobiography*. Stanford, CA: Stanford University Press, 2006.

Mosse, George L. *The Crisis of German Ideology: Intellectual Origins of the Third Reich*. New York: Grosset & Dunlap, 1964.

Muller, Jerry Z. "Communism, Anti-Semitism and the Jews." *Commentary*, August 1988, 28–39.

Murav, Harriet. *Music from a Speeding Train: Jewish Literature in Post-Revolution Russia*. Stanford, CA: Stanford University Press, 2011.

Murch, Donna Jean. *Living for the City: Migration, Education, and the Rise of the Black Panther Party in Oakland, California*. Chapel Hill: University of North Carolina Press, 2010.

Myers, David G. "Jews Without Memory: 'Sophie's Choice' and the Ideology of Anti-Liberal Judaism." *American Literary History* 13, no. 3 (2001): 499–529.

Myers, David N. *Re-Inventing the Jewish Past: European Jewish Intellectuals and the Zionist Return to History*. New York: Oxford University Press, 1995.

———. *The Stakes of History: On the Use and Abuse of Jewish History for Life*. New Haven, CT: Yale University Press, 2018.

Nalewajko-Kulikov, Joanna. "Sylwetki: Trzy Kolory: Szary. Szkic do Portretu Bernarda Marka." *Zagłada Żydów. Studia i Materiały* 4 (2008): 263–84.

Nathans, Benjamin. "On Russian-Jewish Historiography." In *Historiography of Imperial Russia: The Profession and Writing of History in a Multinational State*, ed. Thomas Sanders, 397–432. Armonk, NY: M. E. Sharpe, 1999.

Neal, Larry. "The Black Arts Movement." In *A Turbulent Voyage: Readings in African American Studies*, ed. Floyd W. Hayes III, 236–46. San Diego: Collegiate, 2000.

Neufeld, Michael J., and Michael Berenbaum, eds. *The Bombing of Auschwitz: Should the Allies Have Attempted It?* New York: St. Martin's Press, 2000.

Newman, Roberta. "Home Movies and the Alte Heym (Old Home): American Jewish Travel Films in Eastern Europe in the 1920s and 1930s." *Jewish Folklore and Ethnology Review* 15, no. 1 (1993): 1–9.

Norich, Anita. *Discovering Exile: Yiddish and Jewish American Culture during the Holocaust*. Stanford, CA: Stanford University Press, 2007.

Norwood, Stephen H. "Marauding Youth and the Christian Front: Antisemitic Violence in Boston and New York during World War II." *American Jewish History* 91, no. 2 (2003): 233–67.

Novick, Peter. *The Holocaust in American Life*. Boston: Houghton Mifflin, 1999.

Novick, Robert. *That Noble Dream: The "Objectivity Question" and the American Historical Profession*. Cambridge: Cambridge University Press, 1988.

Olson, Jess. *Nathan Birnbaum and Jewish Modernity: Architect of Zionism, Yiddishism, and Orthodoxy*. Stanford, CA: Stanford University Press, 2013.

O'Neill, William L. *Coming Apart: An Informal History of America in the 1960s*. Chicago: Quadrangle, 1971.

Oppenheimer, Daniel. *Exit Right: The People Who Left the Left and Reshaped the American Century*. New York: Simon & Schuster, 2016.

Orleck, Annaliese. *Common Sense and a Little Fire: Women and Working-Class Politics in the United States, 1900–1965*. Chapel Hill: University of North Carolina Press, 1995.

Papazian, Pierre. "A Unique Uniqueness?" *Midstream*, April 1984, 14–18.

Parush, Iris. *Reading Jewish Women: Marginality and Modernization in Nineteenth-Century Eastern European Jewish Society*. Trans. Saadya Sternberg. Brandeis Series on Jewish Women. Tauber Institute for the Study of European Jewry series. Hanover, NH: Brandeis University Press, 2004.

Patt, Avinoam J. *Finding Home and Homeland: Jewish Youth and Zionism in the Aftermath of the Holocaust*. Detroit: Wayne State University Press, 2009.

Pedersen, Susan. *The Guardians: The League of Nations and the Crisis of Empire*. Oxford: Oxford University Press, 2015.

Peters, Joan. *From Time Immemorial: The Origins of the Arab-Jewish Conflict over Palestine*. New York: Harper & Row, 1984.

Pianko, Noam. *Jewish Peoplehood: An American Innovation*. New Brunswick, NJ: Rutgers University Press, 2015.

Podair, Jerald. *The Strike That Changed New York: Blacks, Whites, and the Ocean Hill-Brownsville Crisis*. New Haven, CT: Yale University Press, 2002.

Polonsky, Antony. "Heroes, Hucksters, and Storytellers: A New History of the Jewish Military Union (ŻZW) in the Warsaw Ghetto (Review of *Bohaterowie, Hochsztaplerzy, Opisywacze: Wokół Żydowskiego Związku Wojskowego* by Dariusz Libionka and Laurence Weinbaum)." *Yad Vashem Studies* 41, no. 2 (2013): 243–53.

Polonsky, Antony, ed. *"My Brother's Keeper?" Recent Polish Debates on the Holocaust*. Oxford: Routledge, 1990.

———. "Oxford Conference on Polish Jewish Relations." *Soviet Jewish Affairs* 14, no. 3 (1984): 51–56.

———. "Poles, Jews and the Problems of Divided Memory." *Ab Imperio* 2 (2004): 123–44.

Polonsky, Antony, and Joanna B. Michlic, eds. *The Neighbors Respond: The Controversy over the Jedwabne Massacre in Poland*. Princeton, NJ: Princeton University Press, 2004.

Polukhina, Valentina. "He Landed Among Us Like a Missile: An Interview with Susan Sontag." In *Brodsky through the Eyes of His Contemporaries, Vol. 2 (1996–2008)*, ed. Valentina Polukhina, 324–32. Boston: Academic Studies Press, 2008.

Porter, Brian. *When Nationalism Began to Hate: Imagining Modern Politics in Nineteenth-Century Poland*. New York: Oxford University Press, 2000.

Porter-Szűcs, Brian. *Poland in the Modern World: Beyond Martyrdom*. West Sussex, UK: Wiley Blackwell, 2014.

Prashad, Vijay. *The Darker Nations: A People's History of the Third World*. New York: New Press, 2007.

Prell, Riv-Ellen. *Prayer and Community: The Havurah in American Judaism*. Detroit: Wayne State University Press, 1989.

———, ed. *Women Remaking American Judaism*. Detroit: Wayne State University Press, 2007.

Rabinbach, Anson. "Editor's Introduction to Special Issue on the *Historikerstreit*." *New German Critique* 44 (Spring–Summer 1988): 3–4.

———. "Eichmann in New York: The New York Intellectuals and the Hannah Arendt Controversy." *October* 108, no. 3 (Spring 2004): 97–111.

Rabinovich, Itamar. *The War for Lebanon, 1970–1985*. Ithaca, NY: Cornell University Press, 1985.

Rabinovitch, Simon. *Jewish Rights, National Rights: Nationalism and Autonomy in Late Imperial and Revolutionary Russia*. Stanford, CA: Stanford University Press, 2014.

———, ed. *Jews and Diaspora Nationalism: Writings on Jewish Peoplehood in Europe and the United States*. Waltham, MA: Brandeis University Press, 2012.

Rabinowitz, Dan. *The Lost Library: The Legacy of Vilna's Strashun Library in the Aftermath of the Holocaust*. Waltham, MA: Brandeis University Press, an imprint of the University Press of New England, 2019.

Raeff, Marc. *Origins of the Russian Intelligentsia: The Eighteenth-Century Nobility*. New York: Harcourt, Brace & World, 1966.

Raider, Mark A. "The Aristocrat and the Democrat: Louis Marshall, Stephen S. Wise and the Challenge of American Jewish Leadership." *American Jewish History* 94, no. 1–2 (2008): 91–113.

———. "Introduction, Special Issue on Louis Marshall." *American Jewish History* 94, no. 1–2 (2008): ix–xiii.

———. "'Irresponsible, Undisciplined Opposition': Ben Halpern on the Bergson Group and Jewish Terrorism in Pre-State Palestine." *American Jewish History* 92, no. 3 (2004): 313–60.

Raisin, Jacob. *The Haskalah Movement in Russia*. Philadelphia: Jewish Publication Society of America, 1913.

Reed, Victoria. "Ardelia Hall: From Museum of Fine Arts to Monuments Woman." *International Journal of Cultural Property* 21, no. 1 (2014): 79–93.

Ribak, Gil. *Gentile New York: The Images of Non-Jews among Jewish Immigrants*. New Brunswick, NJ: Rutgers University Press, 2012.

———. "'They Are Slitting the Throats of Jewish Children': The 1906 New York School Riots and Contending Images of Gentiles." *American Jewish History* 94, no. 3 (2008): 175–96.

Rischin, Moses. *The Promised City: New York's Jews, 1870–1914*. Cambridge, MA: Harvard University Press, 1962.

Rittner, Carol, and John K. Roth. *Memory Offended: The Auschwitz Convent Controversy*. New York: Praeger, 1991.

Roemer, Nils H. *Jewish Scholarship and Culture in Nineteenth-Century Germany: Between History and Faith*. Madison: University of Wisconsin Press, 2005.

Ro'i, Yaacov. *The Struggle for Soviet Jewish Emigration, 1948–1967*. Cambridge, MA: Cambridge University Press, 1991.

Rosenbaum, Ron. *Explaining Hitler: The Search for the Origins of His Evil*. New York: Random House, 1990.

———. "Hitler, Continued: Afterword from the Updated Edition of 'Explaining Hitler: The Search for the Origins of Evil.'" *Los Angeles Review of Books*, July 10, 2014. https://lareviewofbooks.org/article/hitler-continued-afterword-updated-edition-explaining-hitler-search-origins-evil/#!

Rosenfeld, Alvin H. "The Holocaust According to William Styron." *Midstream*, December 1979, 43–49.

———. "The Holocaust as Entertainment." *Midstream*, October 1979, 55–58.

———. *Imagining Hitler*. Bloomington: Indiana University Press, 1985.

Rosenfeld, Gavriel D. "The Politics of Uniqueness: Reflections on the Recent Polemical Turn in Holocaust and Genocide Scholarship." *Holocaust and Genocide Studies* 13, no. 1 (1999): 28–61.

Roskies, David G. "Maks Vaynraykh: oyf di shpurn fun a lebedikn over." *YIVO bleter* 3, new series (1997): 308–18.

Roskies, David, and Diane K. Roskies. *The Shtetl Book*. New York: KTAV, 1975.

Rosman, Moshe. *Founder of Hasidism: A Quest for the Historical Ba'al Shem Tov*. Berkeley: University of California Press, 1996.

———. *How Jewish Is Jewish History?* Oxford: Littman Library of Jewish Civilization, 2007.

———. "Jewish History Across Borders." In *Rethinking European Jewish History*, ed. Jeremy Cohen and Moshe Rosman, 15–29. Oxford: Littman Library of Jewish Civilization, 2009.

Rosset, Barney, ed. *Evergreen Review Reader, 1967–1973*. New York: Four Walls Eight Windows, 1998.

Roth, Nina. "The Neoconservative Backlash against Feminism in the 1970s and 1980s: The Case of *Commentary*." In *Consumption and American Culture*, ed. David E. Nye and Carl Pedersen, 83–98. Amsterdam: VU University Press, 1991.

Rubenstein, Joshua. "The Black Book." *Commentary*, September 1982, 58–60.

———. *Tangled Loyalties: The Life and Times of Ilya Ehrenburg*. New York: Basic, 1996.

Rubenstein, Joshua, and Ilya Altman, eds. *The Unknown Black Book: The Holocaust in German-Occupied Soviet Territories*. Trans. Christopher Morris and Joshua Rubenstein. Bloomington: Indiana University Press, 2008.

Rudnicki, Szymon. "Anti-Jewish Legislation in Interwar Poland." In *Antisemitism and Its Opponents in Modern Poland*, ed. Robert Blobaum, 148–70. Ithaca, NY: Cornell University Press, 2005.

———. "Ritual Slaughter as a Political Issue." *Polin: A Journal of Polish-Jewish Studies* 7 (1992): 147–60.

Rustow, Marina. *Heresy and the Politics of Community: The Jews of the Fatimid Caliphate*. Ithaca, NY: Cornell University Press, 2008.

Sanders, David. *John Hersey*. New York: Twayne, 1967.

———. *John Hersey Revisited*. Boston: Twayne, 1990.

Sanua, Marianne Rachel. *Let Us Prove Strong: The American Jewish Committee, 1945–2006*. Waltham, MA: Brandeis University Press and University Press of New England, 2007.

Sarna, Jonathan. "American Jewish Political Conservatism in Historical Perspective." *American Jewish History* 87, no. 2–3 (1999): 113–22.

———. *American Judaism*. New Haven, CT: Yale University Press, 2004.

———. "The Cult of Synthesis in American Jewish Culture." *Jewish Social Studies* (New Series) 5, no. 1–2 (1998–99): 52–79.

———. "Jewish Prayers for the U.S. Government: A Study in the Liturgy of Politics and the Politics of Liturgy." In *Moral Problems in American Life: New Perspectives on Cultural History*, ed. Karen Halttunen and Lewis Perry, 201–21. Ithaca, NY: Cornell University Press, 1998.

Schidorsky, Dov. "Hannah Arendt's Dedication to Salvaging Jewish Culture." *Leo Baeck Institute Yearbook* (2014): 1–15.

Schiff, Ze'ev, and Ehud Ya'ari. *Israel's Lebanon War*. Ed. and trans. Ina Friedman. New York: Simon and Schuster, 1984.

Scholem, Gershom. "Aykhman." *Ammot* 1, no. 1 (August–September 1962): 10–11. Reprinted as "On Eichmann," in *On Jews and Judaism in Crisis: Selected Essays*, ed. Werner J. Dannhauser, 298–300. New York: Schocken, 1976.

———. *Sabbatai Sevi: The Mystical Messiah, 1626–1676*. Trans. R. J. Werblowsky. Princeton, NJ: Princeton University Press, 1973.

Schorsch, Ismar. *From Text to Context: The Turn to History in Modern Judaism*. Hanover, NH: University Press of New England, 1994.

———. "The Holocaust and Jewish Survival." *Midstream*, January 1981, 38–42.

———. "The Myth of Sephardic Supremacy." In *From Text to Context: The Turn to History in Modern Judaism*, 71–92. Hanover, NH: University Press of New England, 1994.

———. "On the Political Judgment of the Jew." In *From Text to Context: The Turn to History in Modern Judaism*, 118–32. Hanover, NH: University Press of New England, 1994.

Schulman, Bruce J. *The Seventies: The Great Shift in American Culture, Society, and Politics*. New York: Free Press, 2001.

Schultz, Kevin M. *Tri-Faith America: How Catholics and Jews Held Postwar America to Its Protestant Promise*. Oxford: Oxford University Press, 2011.

Schwartz, Shuly Rubin. *The Rabbi's Wife: The Rebbetzin in American Jewish Life*. New York: New York University Press, 2006.

Schwarz, Jan. *Survivors and Exiles: Yiddish Culture after the Holocaust*. Detroit: Wayne State University Press, 2015.

Seidman, Naomi. *A Marriage Made in Heaven: The Sexual Politics of Hebrew and Yiddish*. Berkeley: University of California Press, 1997.

Seltzer, Robert M. "Affirmation of the Diaspora: America and Palestine in Dubnow's Thought." In *A Bicentennial Festschrift for Jacob Rader Marcus*, ed. Bertram Wallace Korn, 529–38. New York: KTAV, 1976.

———. "[Book Review] *A Missionary for History: Essays in Honor of Simon Dubnov*." In *Studies in Contemporary Jewry*, vol. 19: *Dangerous Alliances and the Perils of Privilege*, ed. Ezra Mendelsohn, 299–300. New York: Oxford University Press, 2003.

———. "Simon Dubnow and the Nationalist Interpretation of Jewish History." In *The Jews of North America*, ed. Moses Rischin, 144–52. Detroit: Wayne State University Press, 1987.

Shandler, Jeffrey. *Adventures in Yiddishland: Postvernacular Language and Culture*. Berkeley: University of California Press, 2006.

———. "Heschel and Yiddish: A Struggle with Signification." *Journal of Jewish Thought and Philosophy* 2 (1999): 245–99.

———. "Introduction." In *Awakening Lives: Autobiographies of Jewish Youth in Poland before the Holocaust*, ed. Barbara Kirshenblatt-Gimblett, Marcus Moseley, Michael Stanislawski, and Jeffrey Shandler. New Haven, CT: Yale University Press, 2002.

———. *Shtetl: A Vernacular Intellectual History*. New Brunswick, NJ: Rutgers University Press, 2014.

———. "'The Time of Vishniac': Photographs of Prewar East European Jewry in Postwar Contexts." *Polin* 16 (2003): 313–33.

———. *While America Watches: Televising the Holocaust*. New York: Oxford University Press, 1999.

Shandler, Jeffrey, and Elihu Katz. "Broadcasting American Judaism: The Radio and Television Department of JTS." In *Tradition Renewed: A History of JTS*, ed. Jack Wertheimer, 2:363–401. New York: Jewish Theological Seminary of America, 1997.

Shapiro, Edward S. "[Book Review] *The Abandonment of the Jews: America and the Holocaust, 1941–1945*, by David S. Wyman." *American Jewish History* 74, no. 3 (1985): 325–28.

———. "Historians and the Holocaust: The Role of American Jewry." *Congress Monthly*, May–June 1986, 5–8.

Shapiro, Robert Moses. "Jacob Shatzky, Historian of Warsaw Jewry." *Polin* 3 (1998): 200–213.

Shavit, Sarit, and Dan Michman. "Hannah Arendt and Leni Yahil: A Friendship That Failed the Test." *Yad Vashem Studies* 37, no. 2 (2009): 19–39.

Shilo, Bilha. "'Funem Folk, Farn Folk, Mitn Folk': Historiyah shel asufei YIVO le'aḥar milḥemet ha'olam hasheniyah." MA thesis, Hebrew University, Jerusalem, 2016.

———. "'*Funem Folk, Farn Folk, Mitn Folk*': The Restitution of YIVO's Collections from Offenbach to New York." *Moreshet*, December 2016, 268–303.

Shils, Edward. "The Virtue of Civil Society." *Government and Opposition* 26, no. 1 (1991): 3–20.

Shklar, Judith N. "Hannah Arendt as Pariah." In *Political Thought and Political Thinkers*, by Judith N. Shklar, 363–75. Ed. Stanley Hoffmann. Chicago: University of Chicago Press, 1998.

Shmeruk, Chone. "A briv in redaktsiye" [Letter to the Editor]. *Di goldene keyt* 140 (1995): 214–16.

Shneer, David. *Yiddish and the Creation of Soviet Jewish Culture, 1918–1930*. Cambridge: Cambridge University Press, 2004.

Shore, Marci. "Children of the Revolution: Communism, Zionism, and the Berman Brothers." *Jewish Social Studies* (New Series) 10, no. 3 (2004): 23–86.

———. "The Jewish Hero History Forgot." *New York Times*, April 18, 2013.

Shtaynberg, Aron. *Gedanken in tsuzamenklang*. Ed. Sholem Lurya. Haifa: University of Haifa Press, 1987.

Shternshis, Anna. *Soviet and Kosher: Jewish Popular Culture in the Soviet Union, 1923–1939*. Bloomington: Indiana University Press, 2006.

———. *When Sonia Met Boris: An Oral History of Jewish Life under Stalin*. New York: Oxford University Press, 2017.

Silk, Mark. "Notes on the Judeo-Christian Tradition in America." *American Quarterly* 36, no. 1 (1984): 65–85.

Silver, Isidore. "What Flows from Neo-Conservatism." *The Nation*, July 9, 1977, 44–51.

Silver, Matthew M. *Louis Marshall and the Rise of Jewish Ethnicity in America: A Biography*. Syracuse, NY: Syracuse University Press, 2013.

Singer, David. "Remembering Milton Himmelfarb (1918–2006)." *American Jewish Year Book* 61 (2006): 695–710.

Sinkoff, Nancy. "Fiction's Archive: Authenticity, Ethnography, and Philosemitism in John Hersey's *The Wall*." *Jewish Social Studies* 17, no. 2 (2011): 48–79.

———. "From the Archives: Lucy S. Dawidowicz and the Restitution of Jewish Cultural Property." *American Jewish History* 100, no. 1 (2016): 117–47.

———. "'Learning to Be Free': Socialist and Communist Yiddish Schools in the 1930s." Harvard-Radcliffe College, 1982.

———. *Out of the* Shtetl: *Making Jews Modern in the Polish Borderlands*. Providence, RI: Brown Judaic Studies 336, 2004.

———. "The Polishness of Lucy S. Dawidowicz's Postwar Jewish Cold War." In *The Jewish Feminine Mystique? Jewish Women in Postwar America*, ed. Hasia Diner, Shira Kohn, and Rachel Kranson, 31–47. New Brunswick, NJ: Rutgers University Press, 2010.

———. "*Yidishkayt* and the Making of Lucy S. Dawidowicz." In *From That Place and Time: A Memoir, 1938–1947*, Lucy S. Dawidowicz, xiii–xxxix. New Brunswick, NJ: Rutgers University Press, 2008.

Sklare, Marshall. "Lakeville and Israel: The Six-Day War and Its Aftermath." In *American Jews: A Reader*, ed. Marshall Sklare, 413–59. New York: Behrman, 1983.

Smith, Bonnie G. *The Gender of History: Men, Women, and Historical Practice*. Cambridge, MA: Harvard University Press, 1998.

Snyder, Timothy. *Black Earth: The Holocaust as History, and Warning*. New York: Tim Duggan, 2015.

———. *Bloodlands: Europe between Hitler and Stalin*. New York: Basic, 2010.

———. "Holocaust: The Ignored Reality." *New York Review of Books* 56 (July 16, 2009): 14–16.

Socher, Abraham P. *The Radical Enlightenment of Solomon Maimon: Judaism, Heresy, and Philosophy*. Stanford, CA: Stanford University Press, 2006.

Sorin, Gerald. *The Prophetic Minority: American Jewish Immigrant Radicals, 1880–1920*. Bloomington: Indiana University Press, 1985.

Sorkin, David. *The Transformation of German Jewry, 1780–1840*. New York: Oxford University Press, 1987.

———. "Wilhelm von Humboldt: The Theory and Practice of Self-Formation (*Bildung*), 1791–1810." *Journal of the History of Ideas* 44 (1983): 55–73.

Soyer, Daniel. "Making Peace with Capitalism? Jewish Socialism Enters the Mainstream, 1933–1944." In *Chosen Capital*, ed. Rebecca Kobrin, 215–33. New Brunswick, NJ: Rutgers University Press, 2012.

———. "Soviet Travel and the Making of an American Jewish Communist: Moissaye Olgin's Trip to Russia in 1920–1921." *American Communist History* 4, no. 5 (2005): 1–20.

Stanislawski, Michael. *Autobiographical Jews: Essays in Jewish Self-Fashioning*. Seattle: University of Washington Press, 2004.

———. *For Whom Do I Toil? Judah Leib Gordon and the Crisis of Russian Jewry*. New York: Oxford University Press, 1988.

———. *Tsar Nicholas I and the Jews*. Philadelphia: Jewish Publication Society of America, 1983.

Staub, Michael E., ed. *The Jewish 1960s: An American Sourcebook*. Hanover, NH: University Press of New England, 2004.

———. *Torn at the Roots: The Crisis of Jewish Liberalism in Postwar America*. New York: Columbia University Press, 2002.

Stauber, Roni. "Confronting the Jewish Response during the Holocaust: Yad VaShem, a Commemorative and a Research Institute in the 1950s." *Modern Judaism* 20 (2000): 278–98.

———. "Darko shel Filip Fridman beheker Hashoah." *Gal-Ed* 21 (2008): 77–114.

Steigmann-Gall, Richard. *The Holy Reich: Nazi Conceptions of Christianity, 1919–1945*. New York: Cambridge University Press, 2003.

Steinfels, Peter. *The Neoconservatives: The Men Who Are Changing America's Politics*. New York: Simon and Schuster, 1979.

Stern, Geraldine. *Daughters from Afar: Profiles of Israeli Women.* New York: Bloch, 1958.

Stola, Dariusz. *Kampania Antysyjonistyczna w Polsce 1967–1968.* Warsaw: ISP PAN, 2000.

Stolzenberg, Nomi Maya. "Tale of Two Villages (or Legal Realism Comes to Town)." In *NOMOS XXXIX: Ethnicity and Group Rights,* ed. Ian Shapiro and Will Kymlicka, 289–348. New York: New York University Press, 1997.

Sundquist, Eric J. "The Historian's Anvil, the Novelist's Crucible." In *Literature of the Holocaust,* ed. Alan Rosen, 252–67. Cambridge: Cambridge University Press, 2013.

———. *Strangers in the Land: Blacks, Jews, Post-Holocaust America.* Cambridge, MA: Belknap Press of Harvard University Press, 2005.

Sutcliffe, Adam. "Can a Jew Be a Philosophe? Isaac de Pinto, Voltaire, and Jewish Participation in the European Enlightenment." *Jewish Social Studies* (New Series) 6, no. 3 (2000): 31–51.

Svonkin, Stuart. *Jews Against Prejudice: American Jews and the Fight for Civil Liberties.* New York: Columbia University Press, 1997.

Sznaider, Natan. "Hannah Arendt's Jewish Cosmopolitanism: Between the Universal and the Particular." *European Journal of Social Theory* 10, no. 112 (2007): 112–22.

Szulc, Tad. "A Nazi Hunter Takes on the Russians." *New York,* December 19, 1977, 44–47.

Thompson, Dorothy. "America Demands a Single Loyalty: The Perils of a 'Favorite' Foreign Nation." *Commentary,* January 1950, 210–19.

Tilly, Charles. "The Old New Social History and the New Old Social History." *Review* (Fernand Braudel Center) 7, no. 3 (1984): 363–406.

Tomaszewski, Jerzy. "Review of Lucy S. Dawidowicz, *The War Against the Jews, 1933–1945.*" *Biuletyn Żydowskiego Historycznego w Polsce* 104, no. 4 (Październik-Grudzień 1977): 75–78.

Trilling, Lionel. *Beyond Culture: Essays on Literature and Learning.* New York: Viking, 1965.

Troy, Gil. *Moynihan's Moment: America's Fight against Zionism as Racism.* Oxford: Oxford University Press, 2013.

Trunk, Isaiah. *Judenrat: The Jewish Councils in Eastern Europe under Nazi Occupation.* New York: Macmillan, 1972.

Umansky, Ellen M., and Dianne Ashton, eds. *Four Centuries of Jewish Women's Spirituality: A Sourcebook.* Boston: Beacon, 1992.

Vaïsse, Justin. *Neoconservatism: The Biography of a Movement.* Cambridge, MA: Harvard University Press, 2010.

Veidlinger, Jeffrey. *The Moscow State Yiddish Theater: Jewish Culture on the Soviet Stage.* Bloomington: Indiana University Press, 2000.

Volkov, Shulamit. "The Written Matter and the Spoken Word, on the Gap between Pre-1914 and Nazi Anti-Semitism." In *Unanswered Questions: Nazi Germany and the Genocide of the Jews,* ed. François Furet, 33–55. New York: Schocken, 1989.

Waite, Robert G. "Returning the Jewish Cultural Property: The Handling of Books Looted by the Nazis in the American Zone of Occupation 1945 to 1952." *Libraries and Culture* 37, no. 3 (2002): 213–28.

Wald, Alan M. *The New York Intellectuals: The Rise and Decline of the Anti-Stalinist Left from the 1930s to the 1980s.* Chapel Hill: University of North Carolina Press, 1987.

Wald, Kenneth D. "The Choosing People: Interpreting the Puzzling Politics of American Jewry." *Politics and Religion* 8 (2015): 4–35.

Walicki, Andrzej. *The Enlightenment and the Birth of Modern Nationhood: Polish Political Thought from Noble Republicanism to Tadeusz Kosciuszko.* Notre Dame, IN: University of Notre Dame Press, 1989.

Walzer, Michael. *Just and Unjust Wars: A Moral Argument with Historical Illustrations.* New York: Basic, 1977.

———. "Why Are Jews Liberal? (An Alternative to Norman Podhoretz)." *Dissent*, October 30, 2009.

Walzer, Michael, Menachem Lorberbaum, and Noam J. Zohar, eds. *The Jewish Political Tradition.* New Haven, CT: Yale University Press, 2000.

Wandycz, Piotr S. "Fascism in Poland: 1918–1939." In *Native Fascism in the Successor States, 1914–1945,* ed. Peter F. Sugar, 92–97. Santa Barbara, CA: ABC-Clio, 1971.

Wandycz, Piotr S., John Switalski, and Abraham Brumberg. "Poland and the Jews: An Exchange." *New York Review of Books* 30, no. 13 (August 18, 1983): 51–52.

Wasserstein, Bernard. "Blame the Victim: Hannah Arendt among Nazis, The Historian and Her Sources." *Times Literary Supplement*, October 9, 2009, 13–15.

Waxman, Chaim I. "The Limited Impact of the Six-Day War on America's Jews." In *The Six-Day War and World Jewry,* ed. Eli Lederhendler, 99–115. Baltimore: University Press of Maryland, 2000.

Waxman, Zoë. "[Book Review] *The Unknown Black Book: The Holocaust in German-Occupied Soviet Territories,* ed. Joshua Rubenstein and Ilya Altman, trans. Christopher Morris and Joshua Rubenstein." *Kritika: Explorations in Russian and Eurasian History* 10, no. 1 (2009): 135–38.

Wedgwood, Ruth. "Zionism and Racism, Again: Durban II." *World Affairs* 171, no. 4 (2009): 84–88.

Weinberg, David H. *Between Tradition and Modernity: Haim Zhitlowski, Simon Dubnow, Ahad Ha-Am, and the Shaping of Modern Jewish Identity.* New York: Holmes & Meier, 1996.

Weinberg, Robert. *Stalin's Forgotten Zion: Birobidzhan and the Making of a Soviet Jewish Homeland.* Berkeley: University of California Press, 1998.

Weiner, Melissa F. *Power, Protest, and the Public Schools: Jewish and African American Struggles in New York City.* New Brunswick, NJ: Rutgers University Press, 2010.

Weisbord, Robert G., and Richard Kazarian Jr. *Israel in the Black American Experience.* Westport, CT: Greenwood, 1985.

Weiser, Kalman. "Coming to America: Max Weinreich and the Emergence of YIVO's American Center." In *Choosing Yiddish: New Frontiers of Language and Culture,* ed. Lara Rabinovitch, Shiri Goren, and Hannah S. Pressman, 233–52. Detroit: Wayne State University Press, 2013.

———. "The Jewel in the Yiddish Crown: Who Will Occupy the Chair in Yiddish at Vilnius University?" *Polin: Studies in Polish Jewry* 24 (2012): 223–55.

Weiser, Kalman, and Joshua A. Fogel, eds. *Czernowitz at 100: The First Yiddish Language Conference in Historical Perspective.* Lanham, MD: Lexington, 2010.

Wenger, Beth S. *New York Jews and the Great Depression: Uncertain Promise.* New Haven, CT: Yale University Press, 1996.

Wertheimer, Jack. "From the French Revolution to Neo-conservatism: The Evolution of Modern Jewish Politics." Series 8, Re-Visioning America: Cultural Wars and the Jewish Tradition. Jewish Theological Seminary of America, Department of Community Education, October 19, 1995.

Wertheimer, Jack. *A People Divided: Judaism in Contemporary America.* New York: Basic, 1993.

———. *Unwelcome Strangers: East European Jews in Imperial Germany.* New York: Oxford University Press, 1987.

White, Hayden V. *Metahistory: The Historical Imagination in Nineteenth-Century Europe.* Baltimore: Johns Hopkins University Press, 1973.

Wiener, Jonathan M. "Radical Historians and the Crisis in American History, 1959–1980." *Journal of American History* 76, no. 2 (1989): 399–434.

———. "When Historians Judge Their Own." *The Nation,* November 21, 1987, 584–88.

Wilkerson, Isabel. *The Warmth of Other Suns: The Epic Story of America's Great Migration.* New York: Random House, 2010.

Wisse, Ruth R. "Fairy Tale: Review of *King of the Jews* by Leslie Epstein." *Commentary,* May 1979, 76–78.

———. *If I Am Not For Myself . . . The Liberal Betrayal of the Jews.* New York: Free Press, 1992.

Wolin, Richard. "The Ambivalences of German-Jewish Identity: Hannah Arendt in Jerusalem." *History and Memory* 8, no. 2 (1996): 9–34.

Yadgar, Yaacov. "Tradition." *Hum Stud* 36 (October 9, 2013): 451–70.

———. "Traditionism." *Cogent Social Sciences* (2015): 1–17.

Yahil, Leni. *The Holocaust: The Fate of European Jewry, 1932–1945.* Trans. Ina Friedman and Haya Galai. New York: Oxford University Press, 1990.

Yerushalmi, Yosef Hayim. *The Lisbon Massacre of 1506 and the Royal Image in the Shebet Yehudah.* Cinncinnati: Hebrew Union College Press, 1976.

———. *"Servants of Kings and Not Servants of Servants": Some Aspects of the Political History of the Jews.* Tenenbaum Family Lecture Series in Judaic Studies. Atlanta: Rabbi Donald A. Tam Institute for Jewish Studies, 2005.

———. *Zakhor: Jewish History and Jewish Memory.* Seattle: University of Washington Press, 1982.

Yofe, Yehudah A., and Yudl Mark, eds. *Groyser verterbukh fun der yidisher shprakh.* New York: Committee for the Great Dictionary of the Yiddish Language, 1961.

Young, Jennifer. "The Scorched Melting Pot: The Jewish People's Fraternal Order and the Making of American Jewish Communism." In *A Vanished Ideology: Essays on the Jewish Communist Movement in the English-Speaking World in the Twentieth Century,* ed. Matthew Hoffman and Henry Felix Srebrnik, 47–76. Albany: State University of New York, 2018.

Young-Bruehl, Elisabeth. *Hannah Arendt: For Love of the World.* New Haven, CT: Yale University Press, 1982.

Zavadivker, Polly. "Preserving 'Events That Are Vanishing Like Smoke': *The Black Book* as Community of Survivors and Writers, 1943–1946." *Zutot: Perspectives on Jewish Culture* 11 (2014): 1–12.

Zeitz, Joshua M. *White Ethnic New York: Jews, Catholics, and the Shaping of Postwar Politics.* Chapel Hill: University of North Carolina Press, 2007.

Zenderland, Leila. "Social Science as a 'Weapon of the Weak': Max Weinreich, the Yiddish Scientific Institute, and the Study of Culture, Personality, and Prejudice." *Isis* 104 (2013): 742–72.

Zimmerman, Joshua D. *Contested Memories: Poles and Jews during the Holocaust and Its Aftermath.* New Brunswick, NJ: Rutgers University Press, 2003.

Zubrzycki, Geneviève. *The Crosses of Auschwitz: Nationalism and Religion in Post-Communist Poland.* Chicago: University of Chicago Press, 2006.

INDEX

Page numbers in *italics* indicate photographs and illustrative material.

CPSIA information can be obtained
at www.ICGtesting.com
Printed in the USA
LVHW091455230120
644583LV00008B/195

9 780814 345108